THE CAKE BIBLE

Rose Levy Beranbaum formerly owned the renowned
Cordon Rose Cooking School in New York City. She has instructed
hundreds of students in the art of making cakes and has written more
than fifty cover stories for food magazines, women's magazines and
newspapers, including the *New York Times*. Her MA in food science
and culinary arts is the foundation of her years of experience, which
she enjoys conveying to her students and readers in the clearest,
simplest language.

THE
CAKE
BIBLE

Rose Levy Beranbaum

Edited by Maria D. Guarnaschelli
Photographs by Vincent Lee
Food styling by Rose Levy Beranbaum
Line drawings by Dean Bornstein
Foreword by Maida Heatter

PAPERMAC

First published in Great Britain 1992 by Macmillan London Limited

This edition published 1993 by Papermac
a division of Pan Macmillan Publishers Limited
Cavaye Place London SW10 9PG
and Basingstoke

Associated companies throughout the world

ISBN 0 333 51183 2

1 3 5 7 9 8 6 4 2

A CIP catalogue record for this book is available from
the British Library

Typeset by Wyvern Typesetting Ltd, Bristol
Printed in Hong Kong

Contents

PART III INGREDIENTS AND EQUIPMENT

PART IV SPECIAL SECTION FOR PROFESSIONALS AND PASSIONATE AMATEURS

Foreword

Rose Levy Beranbaum has an amazing ability to learn everything there is to know about a recipe, and then to teach it carefully to her readers. She was born to teach. Her patience is extraordinary. She writes with loving care and attention. She tells you not only 'how' but 'why'. If you ever bake a cake, or if you always bake cakes – professionally or not – this book will become your partner in the kitchen.

Although many of the cakes have names that you will recognise, all through the book you will come across new ways of doing things. I am intrigued by the technique for putting together a butter cake. The dry ingredients are mixed in a bowl, then the butter and the liquids are added (just the reverse of starting by beating or creaming the butter). It is quick and easy – and the results are delicious.

The first cakes I made from this book were simple little butter cakes made in loaf tins. They were Lemon Poppy Seed Pound Cake and White Spice Pound Cake. I simply followed the meticulously complete instructions – and had great fun while doing it. When I served the cakes to two European-trained pastry chefs who are friends of ours, they liked them so much they wanted the recipes.

Then (using the same technique) I made the Chocolate Domingo Cake, about which Rose says, 'The most intense, round, full, chocolate flavour of any. . . .' How could I resist? It is wonderful – and it is quick and easy. It is a round cake that does not have any icing – it doesn't need any.

Making yeast doughs can be one of the most absorbing and gratifying – and addictive – techniques of all baking. When I read the recipe for Rose's Holiday Hallelujah Streusel Brioche I knew it would not be long before I tried it. Actually, I waited only a few minutes. As with the other recipes I made, I felt Rose guiding me every step of the way. And then, 'hallelujah' to be sure. It is as pretty as a picture. It can be made ahead and frozen. As Rose says, 'It is guaranteed to become one of your favourites.'

Many of us have pet peeves in the kitchen; things we would rather not have to do. I have only a few. One procedure I have always disliked is sifting cocoa. I usually have to spend more time cleaning up after it than actually doing it. In this book I read a tip about processing it in the food processor to get the same results as straining. I tried it. It is a pleasure. I'll never do it any other way from now on.

Rose developed a trick for making real old-fashioned whipping cream that has enough fat content when the only kind you can buy has a low fat content. And she lets you in on a secret for making whipped cream that will hold up for six hours without separating, even at room temperature.

It was difficult not to spend all my time making one after another of these cakes. They all cry out, 'Make me'. It is seldom that I really want to make every single recipe from cover to cover in a book. I do in this book.

This is a grand, encyclopedic collection of cakes and everything related to them – crystallised flowers, fondant, thirty-eight different buttercreams, white or dark chocolate roses, lifelike bees made of marzipan, spun sugar, chocolate ribbons, caramel cages, chocolate writing, 22K gold-leaf letters and decorations, enough piped flowers to fill a florist's shop, and still more. Throughout it all I have the feeling that Rose really shines the brightest when she is talking about cakes for special occasions. Show-off cakes. Wedding cakes. Celebration cakes. Cakes to serve a hundred and fifty people. They are splendid, breathtaking, dramatic, exquisite, memorable works of art.

Frankly, I am in awe of Rose's scientific and scholarly mind. She approaches a recipe like a chemist in a laboratory. But mainly, Rose is a wonderful cook and baker – and her book is, to be sure, a bible.

MAIDA HEATTER

Acknowledgements

I must begin by thanking my parents: my mother for passing on the spectre of perseverance (my favourite and most vital attribute), my father for his hands of gold, and both my parents for their example of love of their craft. I cannot think of a more precious gift, except perhaps for another one, that of kindness.

This book could not have been written without the total support and consideration of my husband, Elliott. I also want to thank my stepchildren, Beth and Michael, who offered so much enthusiasm and advice over the years while they and these recipes were growing up.

Much credit goes to my generous and brilliant friend Shirley Corriher, who cares more than anyone else I know what really happens inside a cake and has offered me unending conversation and information to this effect.

There is simply no way to do justice to Maria Guarnaschelli. I feel that I am among the luckiest authors in the world to have her as my editor. Never have I felt more encouraged or better understood. Not only did we share the same vision, we both were always open to possibilities and ready to put aside our own egos for the sake of what was 'best for the book'. I am especially grateful to Maria for offering me total creative freedom and all the time that I needed in which to accomplish my best work. Her brilliantly unswerving wisdom and personal touches made the book come alive.

Vincent Lee is an artist with a camera. Without his exquisite colour photographs, this book would be a mere shadow of what it is. I am thankful for his untiring patience, his infinite inventiveness and his friendship. Working with him has been a special joy.

No one has contributed more to this book than my assistant, David Shamah. When I first started this book, he was still in high school. In the interim he graduated from the Culinary Institute of America. Despite distance, long and early hours in the kitchen, and final exams, hardly a night went by that we did not have long conversations about cake concepts and what is new in the culinary world. David is well acquainted with every theory, every recipe and every word in this book. In fact, it is often hard to separate the ideas that originated from his brilliantly inquiring young mind. He has worked on this book with as much love as if it were his own. I am blessed with his friendship.

I want to express my undying gratitude to all the people who involved themselves with the production of this book, taking a personal interest and making it a part of their lives. It has been a privilege to be part of a team, a network of such extraordinary dedication and creativity.

Chief copy editor: Deborah Weiss
Managing editor: Andrew Ambraziejus
Assistant to the editor: John Guarnaschelli
Production: Harvey Hoffman
My chief proofreader: Heidi Trachtenberg. *Other proofreaders:* Shirley Corriher, Dr Lillian Wager Levy, David Shamah, Madeline Shamah.
Testers: Nancy Blitzer, Marion Bush, Judi Elkins, Ruth Margolies, David Shamah
Chief technical consultant: Shirley Corriher, Research Biochemist of Confident Cooking, Atlanta, Georgia
Technical advisers: ALBERT USTER IMPORTS: Albert Uster and Ben Reed, Claude Burke; CHOCOLATE GALLERY: Joan Mansour; CPC INTERNATIONAL: Sherry McGoldrick; CUISINARTS, INC.: Carl Sontheimer; HAUSER CHOCOLATIER: Rüdi Hauser; LINDT: Rudolph Sprüngli and Arthur Oberholzer; Deanne Miller; SUGAR ASSOCIATION: Jack O'Connell; THOMAS J. LIPTON, INC., KNOX GELATIN: Anna Marie Coccia; TOBLER/SUCHARD: Dr Buser and Marcus Gerber; TUSCAN DAIRIES: Helen Shull; WILTON ENTERPRISES: Zella Junkin; Richard Walker; WOLF RANGE COMPANY: Laxminarasimhan Vasan.

Special thanks to:
Bert Greene for naming this book.
Terron Hecht for her contribution to the artwork.
Bernard and Florence Wager, my chemist uncle who devoted his Saturday mornings to tutor me through high-school chemistry and my aunt who made delicious lunches for afterwards.
Eleanor Lynch and Cecily Brownstone for encouraging me to continue my studies.
Dr Jed H. Irvine, Dr Stephen L. Gumport, and Dr Harold H. Sage for enabling me to finish college.
James Beard and Julia Child, my first teachers, for setting a wonderful example of passion and professionalism.
John Clancy, for his generosity, humour and unforgettable pastry lessons.
Maida Heatter, my sweets guru, whose wonderful writing and recipes showed me just how sensational a dessert could be and who graces this book with her wonderful presence.
Sue Huffman, former food editor of the *Ladies' Home Journal*, who had faith in me.

Linda Foster Gomé, former head of the *Ladies' Home Journal* test kitchen, who took me under her wing and taught me the principles of food styling, recipe testing and development – I know no hands more skilled than hers.

Lydie Marshall for encouraging me to specialise in cakes.

Mimi Sheraton for first telling me about LeNôtre.

Irena Chalmers, my first publisher, for showing me the way to be a food writer.

Barbara Langley and Gus Belverio of Pinehill Farms for their neverending supply of fresh farm eggs.

Paula Perlis for her neverending supply of friendship.

PHOTO CREDITS

Over the years, both Vincent Lee and I have been collecting the many beautiful plates, serving pieces, and linens shown in these photographs. I'd like to express special gratitude to my friends for generously offering me some of their treasures with which to enhance my cakes.

NANCY BLITZER
Georgian sterling-silver plate (Black Forest Cake)
Crown Derby dessert plate (Orange Chocolate Crown)

CHELSEA PASSAGE AT BARNEYS
antique lace cloth (White Lilac Nostalgia Cake)

JUDI ELKINS
glass cake stand (Golden Cage)
lace tablecloth (La Porcelaine)
purple cake plate and vase (White Lilac Nostalgia)

MUMM
Cordon Rosé champagne (Rose Trellis)

Special Categories

RECIPES WITH LOW CHOLESTEROL AND SATURATED FAT

CAKES BETTER MADE AHEAD

CAKES FOR PASSOVER (WITHOUT FLOUR)

QUICK-TO-MIX CAKES THAT ARE GREAT WITHOUT ICING OR ADORNMENT

*Use a double recipe – 2 layers – of Bittersweet Cocoa Almond Génoise (page 232) instead of Moist Chocolate Génoise

Introduction

Friends and students often regard my commitment to the art of confectionery as treasonous since my mother was a dentist. That is not, however, entirely the case – although I was aware of the pitfalls of sweets at a very young age. My father remembers that I confiscated his sweets, stating matter of factly that it would give him 'tavities!'

It was when I wrote my master's dissertation on whether sifting affects the quality of a yellow cake that I discovered my calling. My conclusions were so thorough I received not only an A+ but also an invitation to read my paper to the next class the following year. Feeling proud, after seven years of night school as a food major, I presented my paper to a boyfriend who was a physician.

To my amazement, he actually snickered, saying: 'Is this what you consider a suitable topic for a dissertation?'

It only required a week's interval to recover sufficiently to hazard showing the paper on a first date to Elliott Beranbaum, also a physician whose speciality was radiology of the gastrointestinal tract. By then the paper had taken on the aspect of a test of sorts. I watched as he leafed through the twenty-four pages, gravely nodding his head. Finally, I couldn't resist asking:

'You don't find this topic a little funny?'

'Not at all,' he replied, 'I have encountered the same problem with dry ingredients for my digestion studies and my conclusion is the same as yours: sifting does not uniformly mix dry ingredients – it merely aerates them, helping them absorb the liquid more uniformly. In fact,' he continued, 'I bought a blender to mix the dry ingredients after sifting.' This was so remarkably similar to my solution of beating dry ingredients together in a mixer that with a burst of intuition I thought to myself: 'Ah hah! This is the man I'm going to marry. We have the same approach to life.'

It was never the flavour of desserts alone that beguiled me. It was also my fascination with the variety of textures derived from so few ingredients. When reading through cookbooks I encountered endless variations of cakes and buttercreams and descriptions of how delicious they were. But nowhere was there an explanation of how they compared to each other or a clue as to how they looked and tasted. When faced with three chocolate buttercream recipes – one with yolks, one with whites and one with cream – how could one decide which to make?

It became increasingly apparent to me that there were certain basic formulas from which all these seemingly disparate recipes evolved. I began to long for a book which would demystify and reveal all the basic and classic cakes, buttercreams, icings, fillings and toppings in their simplest form and then show how to combine them to create just about any cake imaginable. While I would have preferred to be mixing a cake batter or shaping a chocolate rose, I finally realised that in order to have the ideal cake book I was going to have to write it!

This book is dedicated to my husband who, among other wonderful qualities, unquestioningly supports my commitment to my profession, and to the many students and readers who want to understand the basics of baking in order to be free to create new and wondrous desserts of their own.

Special Note on the Weights and Measuring System

Three systems have been used throughout this book: volume, avoirdupois and metric. Each of these methods will yield perfect results. Personally, I prefer weighing to measuring because it is much faster and more precise, but measuring is fine if you measure with care. Bear in mind that the measures quoted follow the American system and that the American tablespoon equates to the UK dessertspoon.

Do not expect the mathematics of the metric system to correlate exactly with the avoirdupois system. The grams have been rounded off to the nearest whole number without decimal points (except for the raising agent, which needs to be more precise) whereas the ounces have been rounded off to the nearest quarter ounce.

Note to the British Edition

Cookbooks, particularly baking books, that cross the Atlantic have the well-earned reputation of being troublemakers. Differences in flour have long been suspected of being the culprit. Determined to get to the bottom of this culinary Tower of Babel, Caroline Liddel, my British counterpart, started sending me kilograms of self-raising and plain flour and I started baking.

Much to my alarm, the cakes produced with the British flour were practically unrecognisable from their original models. Could innocent flour really be responsible for such a dramatic difference? The logical way to conquer this problem seemed clear: if I were to retest and redevelop the cakes in this book to work as well as the originals, the only place to do it was clearly in the UK with native equipment and, most importantly, native ingredients.

Kyle Cathie, my brilliant British editor with pioneering spirit and the enthusiasm of Macmillan London, made it a dream come true. She purchased a Kenwood mixer, food processor, 12 dozen eggs and arranged a shopping tour to Sainsbury and a charming airy flat in Earl's Court where I spent fourteen solid days and nights baking cakes.

It was an adventure well worth the effort. After all, who but the British have consecrated a special time of day, and built a veritable institution around the art of eating cakes known world over as 'tea' (certainly a more suitable way to enjoy these rich desserts that never were intended to be consumed as 'pudding' after a filling dinner)? The British have a definite advantage over Americans when it comes to cake baking. To begin with, they weigh instead of measure – a giant step in the right direction. And they use the metric system – far more precise than the avoirdupois system of pounds and ounces which makes it so easy to confuse fluid ounces, which is volume measured in a cup, with solid ounces, which are weighed on a scale.

UK dairy products, critical for fine flavour in cakes, are in general far superior to ours. I delighted in the pure uncooked flavour of double cream and the wondrous clotted cream, which is divine simply spread on cake in place of buttercream. And I was grateful for the butterfat content listed on all containers, making it possible to rebalance my recipes.

Then there is the glorious golden syrup, the ever-present castor sugar (perfect granulation for cake baking); marzipan with superb flavour and texture and all manner and forms of nuts. Carrots have such a marvellous flavour that my carrot cake has never been better. No one ever told me that the UK was a baker's utopia.

But paradise had one serious flaw – the cake flour. Bleached cake flour is indispensable for butter cakes (see page 537). British cake flour is called self-raising sponge flour because the leavening or baking powder is already in it. When a cake uses an acid ingredient such as sour cream, it needs to be tempered with bicarbonate of soda. But when the flour already contains the maximum amount of baking powder, adding bicarbonate of soda is impossible as the combined leavening would be too high and the cake would collapse. Also, large wedding butter cakes will collapse unless the baking powder is decreased.

Fortunately, plain flour is just

fine for all the whisked sponge cakes and oil cakes in this book. Three solutions presented themselves for the butter cakes:

Main solution: In almost all instances (except with the large butter wedding cakes) it was possible *to create a blend of self-raising and plain flour* in order to lower the overall leavening but still have the benefit of the cake flour. This necessitated other changes, such as replacing all yolk cakes with whole eggs and decreasing butter to strengthen the cakes' structure. With sour cream cakes, extra sugar was needed for aeration despite cutting back on butter.

Solution II: *To age the self-raising sponge flour*, because after a year the baking powder begins to deactivate (not very practical, but for people with wine cellars . . . !)

Solution III: *To import American 'Softasilk' cake flour*, which is the ideal flour for cake baking. A trip to Milford-on-Sea, to the dynamic and charming importer Paul Vegoda, dubbed Mr America for all the American products he has introduced to the UK, means that in the very near future the UK will have at its fingertips the finest cake flour in the world and a true baker's paradise.

I am honoured by the opportunity to share my treasured recipes and research with bakers of the UK. And I am particularly grateful to my friends in the UK and at Macmillan for standing behind this book in such a way that when you are tasting a cake in your home, it essentially will be the same flavour and texture as the one in mine.

It is my sincerest wish that my recipes give you a lifetime of pleasure.

TIPS FOR THE UK TO ENSURE SUCCESS

- weighing most ingredients is faster and more accurate than measuring
- Imperial and American fluid ounces are the same. (Note, however, as a point of interest – though not useful for the recipes in this book – that the Imperial pint is 20 fluid ounces whereas the American pint is 16 fluid ounces)
- for baking powder and bicarbonate of soda use measuring teaspoons not flatware, which are not standard
- use the flour specified in the recipe
- use unsalted butter, preferably from France
- use size 2 eggs
- when sugar is called for castor sugar is the preferable degree of granulation
- *fromage frais* is not interchangeable with *crème fraîche*
- pay close attention to tin sizes
- when using convector ovens – to get 350°F I had to use 165°C not 180°C. Read manufacturers' directions carefully and gauge from baking time

PART I
CAKES

Simply Delicious Foolproof Cakes

Few pleasures are greater than turning out a perfect cake. And perfect cakes can be achieved by any cook who is careful and who is willing to follow recipe directions. Cake-making is an exact process; the ingredients and their relation to each other are balanced like a chemical formula; in fact, during the baking, a chemical process takes place transforming the raw ingredients into a delicious new entity. . . . However inspired, no written definition of the word 'cake' could approximate the glories of sweetened dough, baked, filled, iced and made ravishing with edible decorations. Such creations can bring happiness to both our childhood and mature years, for few, if any, people are immune to their charm, and memories of them will lighten the dark corners of life.*

This chapter contains my favourite foolproof renditions of most basic cakes, including cheesecakes, breakfast cakes, vegetable cakes and even a brioche cake (which is really a bread). Not only are Amendola and Lundberg absolutely correct in stating that working from a well-balanced recipe will yield perfect cakes, I know that they also agree about how fascinating it is to have a peek behind the scenes and understand what goes into the creation of a cake formula and how one type of cake differs from another. It is fascinating, and also puts you in control. If something goes wrong, for example, it is possible to figure out the problem and correct it. If you want to alter a component, you must understand what it consists of and how it contributes to the cake. I have organised this chapter so that you can start baking with as little interference and as much basic guidance as possible. Separate from each recipe are pointers that highlight key factors and also, for those who are interested, a little about the science of each cake and how it compares to others.

I am beginning with pound cake because it is from this basic formula that all other sponge or butter cakes evolve. For a fuller understanding of cake formulation, ingredients and baking, there is an in-depth section called Understanding Cakes at the back of the book (page 535).

*Joseph Amendola and Donald E. Lundberg, *Understanding Baking* (Boston: CBI Publishing Company, 1970), p. 98.

Baking and Storing Cakes

CAKE TINS

Rapid heat penetration gives superior cake texture, so ideally cake tins are manufactured from highly conductive metals such as aluminium, that have a dull, heat-absorbing finish. Stainless steel tins with their shiny, heat-reflective finish, are poor heat conductors and should not be used for baking cakes. (They make pretty planters if you already happen to have them.) Black metal is also a poor choice because it absorbs heat too quickly and overbrowns the crust.

What is best for the inside of a cake is not, unfortunately, best for the outside. The sides of the cake, touching the hot metal, bake and set faster than the centre, which continues to rise resulting in a peaked surface. The solution is to slow down the baking at the sides while promoting rapid and even penetration at the bottom of the tin. Magi-Cake Strips (pages 516 and 523) are made of aluminised fabric which, when moistened and wrapped around a tin, keep the sides cooler. This slows down the baking at the perimeter so that it rises at the same rate as the centre and results in a level top.

The size of the tin in relation to the amount of batter also influences how the cake bakes. Ideally, the tin should be the same height as the cake will be at its highest point during baking. Tins should be filled no less than one-half full. If the tin is too big, the sides shield the batter and slow down the baking. The resulting cake will be drier with a paler surface. If the tin is too small, the batter will run over the sides and the cake will collapse from inadequate support.

PREPARING THE TINS:

I like to use a round of parchment to line the bottom to ensure that the bottom crust releases completely. While this is not essential for yellow or white cakes, chocolate cakes are notorious for sticking, so lining the tin is important insurance.

A tin for a cake that will rise must never be greased without flouring because a slippery surface will prevent the cake from adhering and rising to its full volume.

For a smooth, tightly sealed crust, use a non-stick vegetable spray. Alternatively, solid vegetable fat is preferable to butter and can be applied with a piece of clingfilm. Butter, unless it is clarified, will leave gaps where the flour will not adhere but the cake unfailingly will. After greasing the tin, add some flour, tilt the tin and rotate it, tapping the sides to spread the flour evenly. Invert the tin and tap lightly. Return the excess flour to the bin. If desired, wrap the tin with Magi-Cake Strips.

BAKING THE CAKE

Most cakes (with the exception of very low sheet cakes, which bake in the lower third of the oven), should be baked as close to the centre of the oven as possible, with room for air circulation between the tins. I find 350°F/180°C/gas mark 4 the ideal temperature for baking most cakes. Lower than this, the texture will be coarse for layer cakes and lacking volume for sponge-type cakes. Higher than 375°F/190°C/gas mark 5, layer-cake tops will peak and whisked sponge cakes will overbrown.

When a cake is at the end of its baking period, the walls surrounding the air bubbles rupture, releasing their leavening gases and causing the cell walls to shrink very slightly. There is a visible lowering in the tin at this point – a clue to doneness.

To test for doneness, insert a wire cake tester or toothpick as close to the centre as possible. It should come out clean, with no crumbs clinging to it. Cakes should also spring back when pressed lightly in the centre. Layer cakes under 25.5 centimetres/10 inches should not start shrinking from the sides of the tin before being removed from the oven or they will be slightly dry.

Cakes that require more than 40 minutes' baking time usually need to be covered loosely with lightly greased foil after 40 minutes to prevent overbrowning.

HIGH ALTITUDE

Problems with cake baking usually begin at over 3,000 feet. Lower air pressure causes water to boil at a lower temperature so that more evaporation takes place during baking and cakes may be dry. If too much evaporation takes place, there will not be adequate moisture to fully gelatinise the starch and set the structure. Structure is further weakened by the tendency for cakes to rise too much at decreased air pressure and subsequently collapse.

Decreasing the sugar to make more liquid available for gelatinising the starch is one of the standard approaches to this problem. Since my butter-cake formulas have less sugar than most (equal weights of sugar and flour) and are more velvety than those made by the creaming method (where one creams the butter and sugar before adding the other ingredients), they will be less affected by high altitude. Also, decreasing the sugar would adversely affect the flavour balance, so I recommend slightly decreasing the raising agent and slightly increasing the liquid. The next possibility would be to increase the number of eggs to add more structure.

At elevations above 3,500 feet, increasing the oven temperature by 25°F/10°C/1 gas mark will help to set the structure faster. For a butter cake which uses very little baking powder and a high level of butter, such as a pound cake, it may help to strengthen the cake's structure by decreasing the butter. As each cake formula varies, guidelines can be given but experimentation is the only sure way.

Whisked sponge cakes are affected by high altitude in a way similar to butter cakes. In a whisked sponge cake that does not contain baking powder, it is advisable to decrease the sugar. This will speed coagulation of the egg proteins which stabilise or set the cake and interfere less with gelatinisation of the starch. Alternatively, slightly more flour can be added to strengthen the structure and, over 3,500 feet the temperature can be increased to 375°F/190°C/gas mark 5.

TURNING OUT THE CAKE

Génoise and *biscuit* must be turned out of their tins as soon as they are baked to prevent steam from softening the cake and collapsing it. Whisked sponge cakes that are usually baked in ungreased two-piece tube tins – such as chiffon and angel food – need to cool upside down in the tin to prevent collapsing.

Small butter cakes can be turned out immediately, but butter cakes larger than 23 centimetres/9 inches risk breaking if turned out too soon. To be on the safe side, it's fine to wait 10 to 20 minutes before turning the cakes out on to lightly greased racks. Always run a small metal spatula around the sides first to be sure they are completely dislodged. Be careful to press the spatula against the sides of the tin, not the sides of the cake.

It is usually best to reinvert turned-out cakes so that the top side is up. This prevents splitting if the top is rounded, and the firm top crust helps to maintain maximum volume.

Allow cakes to cool fully before storing or icing or residual heat will make them soggy and melt the icing.

STORING THE CAKE

Refrigerated or frozen cakes must be stored airtight to prevent drying out or absorbing odours. Wrap them first in clingfilm, then in heavy-duty foil.

To freeze an iced cake, place it uncovered in the freezer just until the icing is very firm and it should not be damaged by wrapping. Wrap first in clingfilm, then in heavy-duty foil, trying to eliminate as much air space as possible without pressing on decorations. Place the cake in the centre of the foil and bring the two long sides together so that the edges meet. Fold the edges over several times until close to the cake. Proceed in the same way for the short ends. Delicate decorations can be protected further by placing the wrapped cake in a rigid box.

TO DEFROST CAKE

For uniced cake, remove from the freezer and thaw without unwrapping. If desired, freshen the thawed cake by placing it in a 350°F/180°C/gas mark 4 oven for 5 minutes or in a microwave oven on low power for a few seconds.

To thaw iced cake, unwrap it and place it in the refrigerator overnight. It is best to keep the cake in a large airtight container such as a cake carrier or glass dome (page 527) to avoid absorbing any odours. Iced cakes should be defrosted gradually to prevent moisture condensation or beading.

Sponge or Butter Cakes

The pound cake, according to *Larousse Gastronomique*, originated in England and was the first 'butter cake'. France adopted it, calling it *quatre-quarts* because traditionally it was prepared using one-quarter flour, one-quarter butter, one-quarter eggs and one-quarter sugar.

The pound cake is often thought of as the 'mother' cake from which all other sponge or butter cakes (usually referred to as layer cakes) evolved. The butter cake contains 6 to 12 per cent solid butter (not including the liquid and milk solids in the butter) or other fat, 18 to 36 per cent liquid (usually milk or water), 27 per cent flour or a combination of flour and cocoa, 27 to 40 per cent sugar, 5 to 10 per cent egg, a small amount of salt and flavouring, and a raising agent such as baking powder and/or bicarbonate of soda.

The butter cake derives its light texture from the air bubbles produced by creaming the sugar and fat and by the raising agent – which enlarges these bubbles during baking. In the traditional method, the butter and sugar are creamed before adding the other ingredients. The method I have chosen for my butter cakes is faster, easier, and virtually eliminates any possibility of toughening the cake by overbeating. Creaming still takes place but in a different way: all the dry ingredients are first combined with the butter and a minimum amount of liquid, which coats the flour before adding the remaining liquid ingredients.

The butter cake is flavourful yet not too sweet, soft and light in texture, and moist enough to stand on its own or to accommodate a variety of icings and toppings. It is one of the world's great cakes.

Note: All butter cake recipes can be doubled if you have extra tins. Be sure to place them in the oven so air can circulate freely around the sides of all the tins. If you lack room, pour the batter into the tins and refrigerate them until the first set of cake layers has baked. (Do not refrigerate batter in a bowl as it will lose rising power if not transferred to tins soon after mixing.)

HIGHLIGHTS FOR SUCCESSFUL BUTTER CAKES

For fuller details, see the suggested page number.

- Have all ingredients near room temperature (65° to 75°F/18° to 24°C, page 542).
- Use the flour specified.
- Use a combination of sifted self-raising sponge flour and sifted plain flour where called for (page 493).
- Use castor sugar for finest texture (page 500).

- Use unsalted butter (pages 490 and 539).
- Measure or weigh ingredients carefully (page 505). Use measuring spoons for bicarbonate of soda, not flatware spoons which are not standard.
- If using a hand-held mixer, beat at high speed.
- Use the correct tin size (page 515).
- For very even layers and maximum height use Magi-Cake Strips (pages 516 and 522).
- Check for accurate oven temperature (page 514).
- Use correct baking time; do not overbake (page 5).
- Wrap cake layers well or ice them when cool (page 6).

Perfect Pound Cake

Serves 8

This cake not only has a silky-smooth dissolving texture but also the incomparable moist, buttery flavour of a home-baked cake. It is very similar to Victoria sandwich cake. Its excellent keeping qualities make it ideal for slicing ahead and taking on picnics.

TINS: One 20 × 10 × 6-centimetre/ 8 × 4 × 2½-inch/4 cup (1 litre) loaf tin – most attractive size – or any 6-cup loaf (1½ litre) or fluted tube tin, greased and floured. If using a loaf tin, grease it, line the bottom with parchment or greaseproof paper, and then grease again and flour.

FINISHED HEIGHT: In a 4-cup (1 litre) loaf: 5.5 centimetres/ 2¼ inches at the sides and 9 centimetres/3½ inches in the middle. In a 6-cup (1½ litre) loaf: 4.5 centimetres/1¾ inches at the sides and 6 centimetres/2½ inches in the middle. In a 6-cup fluted tube: 5.5 centimetres/2¼ inches in the middle.

STORE: Airtight: 3 days room temperature, 1 week refrigerated, 2 months frozen. Texture is most evenly moist when prepared at least 8 hours before serving.

COMPLEMENTARY ADORNMENT: A simple dusting of icing sugar.

SERVE: Room temperature.

POINTERS FOR SUCCESS: See pages xx and 8. Be sure to use a wooden toothpick to test for doneness. The cake will spring back when pressed lightly in the centre even before it is done. If the cake is underbaked, it will have tough, gummy spots instead of a fine, tender crumb.

INGREDIENTS	WEIGHT		MEASURE
room temperature	*grams*	*pounds/ounces*	*volume*
milk	45 grams	1½ ounces	3 tablespoons
3 eggs, size 2	150 grams	5¼ ounces (weighed without shells)	scant 5 fluid ounces
pure vanilla extract	6 grams		1½ teaspoons
sifted self-raising sponge flour	100 grams	3½ ounces	1 cup + 2 tablespoons
plain flour	50 grams	1¾ ounces	⅓ cup (dip and sweep method)
castor sugar	150 grams	5¼ ounces	¾ cup
salt	—	—	¼ teaspoon
unsalted butter (must be softened)	150 grams	5¼ ounces	10½ tablespoons

Preheat the oven to 350°F/180°C/gas mark 4.

In a medium bowl lightly combine the milk, eggs and vanilla.

In a large mixing bowl combine the dry ingredients and mix on low speed for 30 seconds to blend. Add the butter and half the egg mixture. Mix on low speed until the dry ingredients are moistened. Increase to medium speed (high speed if using a hand mixer) and beat for 1 minute to aerate and develop the cake's structure.

Scrape down the sides. Gradually add the remaining egg mixture in two batches, beating for 20 seconds after each addition to incorporate the ingredients and strengthen the structure. Scrape down the sides.

Scrape the batter into the prepared tin and smooth the surface with a spatula. The batter will be almost 1 centimetre/½ inch from the top of the loaf tin. (If your tin is slightly smaller, use any excess batter for cupcakes.) Bake for 55 to 65 minutes (35 to 45 minutes in a fluted tube tin) or until a wooden toothpick inserted in the centre comes out clean. Cover loosely with buttered foil after 30 minutes to prevent overbrowning. *The cake should start to shrink from the sides of the tin only after removal from the oven.*

To get an attractive split down the middle of the crust, wait until the natural split is about to develop (about 20 minutes) and then with a lightly greased sharp knife or single-edged razor blade make a shallow mark about 15 centimetres/6 inches long down the middle of the cake. This must be done quickly so that the oven door does not remain open very long or the cake will fall. When the cake splits, it will open along the mark. Let the cake cool in the tin on a rack for 10 minutes and invert it on to a greased wire rack. If baked in a loaf tin, to keep the bottom from splitting, reinvert so that the top is up and cool completely before wrapping airtight.

UNDERSTANDING

In creating this recipe I started out with the classic pound cake proportions: equal weights of flour, sugar, eggs and butter and no baking powder. But I soon discovered that the traditional balance of ingredients benefits from the addition of a small amount of milk, which adds marvellous moisture and also strengthens the cake's structure by gelatinising the flour and joining the gluten-forming proteins.

Over forty trials have led me to believe that there is no way to get this melting texture in a pound cake that is larger so it is best to keep the cake small. If you happen to prefer a denser, chewier cake, however, replace the castor sugar with equal weight icing sugar. (The smooth grains of the icing sugar do not trap air the way the sharp-edged grains of granulated or castor sugar do. The cornflour added to icing sugar to prevent lumping also increases the chewy quality of the cake.)

VARIATIONS

DELUXE DOUBLE-VANILLA POUND CAKE:

Tiny black grains from the vanilla pod offer a round, full flavour and a barely perceptible crunch. Using a vanilla pod along with vanilla extract is a technique that can be applied to any cake or custard sauce. The vanilla pod imparts a deeper, sweeter, more aromatic flavour, but not in a sugary sense. By contrast increasing the extract would add a hint of bitterness.
To make Deluxe Double-Vanilla Pound Cake: You will need 1 vanilla pod (½ pod if it is Tahitian, exceptionally aromatic and delicious). With a small, sharp knife split it in half lengthwise. Place it in a small saucepan with the 3 tablespoons of milk and scald the milk (small bubbles will start to form around edges). Cover immediately, remove from the heat, and allow to cool to room temperature. Remove the vanilla pod and scrape the black grains from its centre into the milk. (Vanilla pods may be saved for future use, see page 504.) Add the vanilla-infused milk to the vanilla extract and eggs and proceed as usual with the recipe.

Note: This cake is very attractive made in individual portions. A 6-cake Bundt-lette tin (page 517) is the perfect size. This recipe will make 6 individual cakelettes, which require about 20 minutes to bake.

LEMON POPPY SEED POUND CAKE:

This is perhaps my favourite way to eat pound cake! The fresh light flavour of lemon blends beautifully with the buttery flavour of pound cake. The lemon syrup tenderises, adds tartness and helps to keep the cake fresh for a few days longer than usual. Poppy seeds add a delightful crunch. Lemon blossoms and lemon leaves make a lovely and appropriate garnish.

To make Lemon Poppy Seed Pound Cake:
You will need
6 grams (1 tablespoon) loosely packed grated lemon zest
28 grams (1 ounce/3 tablespoons) poppy seeds
75 grams (2¾ ounces/¼ cup + 2 tablespoons) sugar
63 grams (2 ounces/¼ cup) freshly squeezed lemon juice

Add the lemon zest and poppy seeds to the dry ingredients and proceed as above. Shortly before the cake is done, prepare the Lemon Syrup: In a small pan over medium heat, stir the sugar and lemon juice until dissolved. As soon as the cake comes out of the oven, place the pan on a rack, prick the cake all over with a wire tester and brush it with half the syrup. Cool in the tin for 10 minutes. Loosen the sides with a spatula and invert on to a greased wire rack. Prick the bottom of the cake with the wire tester, brush it with some syrup, and reinvert on to a greased wire rack. Brush the sides with the remaining syrup and allow to cool before wrapping airtight. Store for 24 hours before eating to give the syrup a chance to distribute evenly. The syrup will keep the cake fresh a few days longer than a cake without syrup.

Chocolate Bread

Serves 8

The individual slices of this cake resemble pieces of dark bread, so it is a delightful surprise to discover instead a moist, exceptionally full-flavoured chocolate pound cake! This is, in fact, a chocolate cake quite unlike any other butter cake and deserves a category of its own. This is perfect to take to the beach because it requires no icing.

TINS: One 20 × 10 × 6-centimetre/ 8 × 4 × 2½-inch/4 cup (1 litre) loaf tin – most attractive size – or any 6-cup (1½ litre) loaf or fluted tube tin, greased and floured. If using a loaf tin, grease it, line the bottom with parchment or greaseproof paper, and then grease again and flour.

FINISHED HEIGHT: In a 4-cup (1 litre) loaf: 6 centimetres/ 2½ inches at the sides, and 9 centimetres/3 inches in the middle. In a 6-cup (1½ litre) loaf: 4.5 centimetres/1¾ inches at the sides, and 6 centimetres/2½ inches in the middle.

STORE: Airtight: 3 days room temperature, 1 week refrigerated, 2 months frozen. Texture is most evenly moist when prepared at least 8 hours ahead of serving.

COMPLEMENTARY ADORNMENT: A simple dusting of icing sugar.

SERVE: Room temperature.

POINTERS FOR SUCCESS: See pages xx and 8. Be sure to use a wooden toothpick to test for doneness. The cake will spring back when pressed lightly in the centre even before it is done. If the cake is underbaked, it will have tough, gummy spots instead of a fine, tender crumb.

INGREDIENTS	WEIGHT		MEASURE
room temperature	*grams*	*pounds/ounces*	*volume*
unsweetened cocoa (preferably Dutch-processed)	21 grams	3/4 ounce	3 tablespoons + 1½ teaspoons
boiling water	44 grams	1½ ounces	3 tablespoons
pure vanilla extract	6 grams	—	1½ teaspoons
3 eggs, size 2	150 grams (weighed without shells)	5¼ ounces	scant 5 fluid ounces
sifted self-raising sponge flour	100 grams	3½ ounces	1 cup + 2 tablespoons
sifted plain flour	25 grams	1 ounce	3 tablespoons
castor sugar	175 grams	6 ounces	3/4 cup + 2 tablespoons
salt	—	—	1/4 teaspoon
unsalted butter (must be softened)	150 grams	5¼ ounces	10½ tablespoons

Preheat the oven to 350°F/180°C/gas mark 4.

In a medium mixing bowl whisk together the cocoa and water until smooth. Allow to cool to room temperature and lightly whisk in the vanilla and eggs.

In a large mixing bowl combine the remaining dry ingredients and mix on low speed for 30 seconds to blend. Add half the chocolate mixture and the butter. Mix on low speed until the dry ingredients are moistened. Increase to medium speed (high speed if using a hand mixer) and beat for 1 minute to aerate and develop the cake's structure. Scrape down the sides. Gradually add the remaining chocolate mixture in two batches, beating for 20 seconds after each addition to incorporate the ingredients and strengthen the structure. Scrape down the sides.

Scrape the batter into the prepared tin and smooth the surface with a spatula. The batter will be almost 1 centimetre/½ inch from the top of the tin. (If your tin is slightly smaller, use any excess batter for cupcakes.) Bake for 50 to 60 minutes (40 to 50 minutes in fluted tube tin) or until a wooden toothpick inserted in the centre comes out clean. Tent loosely with buttered foil after 25 minutes to prevent overbrowning. *The cake should start to shrink from the sides of the tin only after removal from the oven.*

To get an attractive split down the middle of the crust, wait until the natural split is about to develop (about 20 minutes) and then with a lightly greased sharp knife or single-edged razor blade make a shallow mark 15 centimetres/ 6 inches long down the middle of the cake. This must be done quickly so that the oven door does not remain open very long or the cake will fall. When the cake splits, it will open along the mark.

Let the cake cool in the tin on a rack for 10 minutes. Loosen the sides with a small metal spatula and invert on to a greased wire rack. If baked in a loaf tin, to keep the bottom from splitting, reinvert so that the top is up and cool completely before wrapping airtight.

UNDERSTANDING
This is a variation on the basic formula for Perfect Pound Cake. Some of the flour is replaced by cocoa and the sugar increased slightly to balance the bitterness. The result is a dense, velvety cake.

Note: For extra moistness and a subtle coffee accent, brush the cake with syrup. *To make syrup:* In a small pan, stir together 2 fluid ounces water and 2 tablespoons sugar. Bring to a full rolling boil. Cover and remove from heat. When cool, add 1 tablespoon Kahlúa (coffee liqueur).

When the cake is baked, brush half the syrup on to the top. Cool the cake for 10 minutes and invert it on to a lightly greased rack. Brush the bottom and sides with the remaining syrup. Reinvert on to a rack, top side up, to finish cooling. The coffee flavour stays in the background, accentuating the chocolate.

White Spice Pound Cake

Serves 10

This variation on basic pound cake eliminates some of the cholesterol by using egg whites instead of egg yolks. The cake, however, seems just as rich because of the fragrant addition of cinnamon, cloves and cocoa. The inspiration for this special blend is a gift from my wonderful friend Nancy Blitzer. When making her spice cake, she also replaces the usual vanilla with brandy – an interesting subtlety that I have adopted for mine as well.

This cake is exceptionally moist and velvety with a positively addictive flavour. It is great to have on hand in the freezer for unexpected company.

TINS: One 6-cup (1½ litre) loaf tin or fluted tube tin, greased and floured. If using a loaf tin, grease it, line the bottom with parchment or greaseproof paper, and then grease again and flour.

FINISHED HEIGHT: In a loaf tin: 5 centimetres/2 inches at the sides and 6 centimetres/2½ inches in the middle. In a 6-cup (1½ litre) fluted tube: 10 centimetres/4 inches in the middle.

STORE: Airtight: 3 days room temperature, 1 week refrigerated, 2 months frozen.

COMPLEMENTARY ADORNMENT: A simple dusting of icing sugar.

SERVE: Room temperature.

POINTERS FOR SUCCESS: See pages xx and 8.

Preheat the oven to 350°F/180°C/gas mark 4.

In a medium bowl lightly combine the milk, egg whites and brandy.

In a large mixing bowl combine the dry ingredients and mix on low speed for 30 seconds to blend. Add the butter and half the egg mixture. Mix on low speed until the dry ingredients are moistened. Increase to medium speed (high speed if using a hand mixer) and beat for 1 minute to aerate and develop the cake's structure. Scrape down the sides. Gradually add the remaining egg mixture in two batches, beating for 20 seconds after each addition to incorporate the ingredients and strengthen the structure. Scrape down the sides.

INGREDIENTS	WEIGHT		MEASURE
room temperature	*grams*	*pounds/ounces*	*volume*
milk	60 grams	2 ounces	2 fluid ounces
4 egg whites, size 2	120 grams	4¼ ounces	4 fluid ounces
brandy	8 grams	—	2 teaspoons
sifted self-raising sponge flour	130 grams	4¾ ounces	1½ cups
sifted plain flour	70 grams	2¼ ounces	½ cup + 1 tablespoon
castor sugar	200 grams	7 ounces	1 cup
salt	3.5 grams	—	½ teaspoon
cinnamon	—	—	½ teaspoon
cloves	—	—	½ teaspoon
unsweetened cocoa	—	—	1½ teaspoons
unsalted butter (must be softened)	190 grams	6¾ ounces	13½ tablespoons

Scrape the batter into the prepared tin and smooth the surface with a spatula. The batter will almost fill the tin. Bake for 45 to 55 minutes (40 to 50 minutes in a fluted tube tin) or until a wire cake tester inserted in the centre comes out clean and the cake springs back when pressed lightly in the centre. *The cake should start to shrink from the sides of the tin only after removal from the oven.*

To get an attractive split down the middle of the crust when using a loaf tin, wait until the natural split is about to develop (about 20 minutes) and then with a lightly greased sharp knife or single-edged razor blade make a shallow mark 15 centimetres/6 inches long down the middle of the cake. This must be done quickly so that the oven door does not remain open very long or the cake will fall. When the cake splits, it will open along the mark.

Let the cake cool in the tin on a rack for 10 minutes and invert on to a greased wire rack. If baked in a loaf tin, to keep the bottom from splitting, reinvert so that the top is up and cool completely before wrapping airtight.

UNDERSTANDING
Aside from the flavouring and the substitution of egg whites for whole eggs, the formula for this cake is identical to the one for Perfect Pound Cake but is one-third larger. In this version it is still possible to have a melting, tender quality despite the larger size because there are no yolks to toughen it.

Chocolate Cherry Almond Pound Cake

Serves 10

The uniquely flavourful base for this moist cake is the creation of one of my favourite of all pastry chefs: Peter Roggensinger. His grandmother made it for him when he was a child in Switzerland. He normally uses an apricot and a lemon glaze, which is wonderful, but as I adore the flavours of chocolate, almond and cherry, I am offering this cherry version.

TINS: One 23 × 13 × 7.5-centimetre/9 × 5 × 3-inch/8-cup loaf tin, greased, bottom lined with parchment or greaseproof paper, then greased again and floured.

FINISHED HEIGHT OF CAKE: 6 centimetres/2½ inches.

STORE: Airtight: 3 days at room temperature, 5 days refrigerated, 3 months frozen.

SERVE: Room temperature.

POINTERS FOR SUCCESS: See pages xx and 8. To get nice tiny chunks of chocolate, use a sharp knife. To keep nuts from becoming oily while grinding, use the fine shredding disc of the food processor and then the metal blades.

INGREDIENTS	WEIGHT		MEASURE
room temperature	*grams*	*pounds/ounces*	*volume*
maraschino cherries in syrup	–	–	1 cup, drained
hazelnuts with skins	113 grams	4 ounces	¾ cup
cornflour	7.5 grams	¼ ounce	1 tablespoon
chocolate (preferably extra–bittersweet or bittersweet)	128 grams	4½ ounces	1½ (3-ounce) bars
sifted plain flour	100 grams	3½ ounces	¾ cup + 1 tablespoon
2 eggs, size 2	100 grams (weighed without shells)	3½ ounces	3 fluid ounces
2 egg whites, size 2	60 grams	2 ounces	2 fluid ounces
pure vanilla extract	–	–	¾ teaspoon
softened unsalted butter	113 grams	4 ounces	8 tablespoons
marzipan	85 grams	3 ounces	5 tablespoons
castor sugar	160 grams	5½ ounces	¾ cup
hot water	60 grams	2 ounces	¼ liquid cup
cream of tartar	–	–	⅜ teaspoon
cherry jam, melted and sieved	77 grams	2¾ ounces	¼ cup

Preheat oven to 350°F/180°C/gas mark 4.

Place the cherries in a single layer in the bottom of the prepared tin. Toast the hazelnuts for 10 to 15 minutes or until the skins split and the nuts are lightly brown. Cool completely, grind finely and mix with the cornflour. Place in a medium bowl.

Using a sharp knife, chop the chocolate into coarse little pieces and add to the nuts. Mix in the flour and set aside.

Divide the eggs between 2 bowls, placing 3 egg whites in a

large bowl and 1 whole egg plus 1 yolk in a smaller bowl. Add the vanilla to egg yolks and mix lightly to blend.

In a mixing bowl, at medium speed, cream butter, marzipan and all but 53 grams/1¾ ounces/¼ cup sugar until fluffy. Gradually beat in the egg yolk mixture until incorporated. Add the flour mixture and beat just until mixed into the batter. Beat in the hot water and set aside. On low speed, beat the egg whites until foamy. Add the cream of tartar, raise speed to medium, and beat until soft peaks form when the beater is raised. Gradually add the remaining sugar. Raise the speed to high and beat until stiff peaks form when the beater is raised slowly. With a large rubber spatula, stir about one-quarter of the egg whites into the batter until blended. Gently but rapidly fold in the remaining whites. Scrape the batter into the prepared tin.

Bake for one hour and check for doneness. The cake tests done when a small sharp knife inserted in the centre comes out clean.

Let the cake cool in the tin on a rack for 10 minutes. Loosen the sides with a small metal spatula and invert on to a serving plate or greased rack. Remove parchment and brush with heated cherry jam. Cool completely before wrapping airtight.

Note: To make the apricot version, use a 6-cup (1½-litre) loaf tin to bake the cake; omit the cherries and replace the cherry jam with sieved apricot jam. After spreading the glaze on the cake, allow it to set for about 10 minutes. Stir together 28 grams/ 1 ounce/¼ cup icing sugar and 2 teaspoons lemon juice and spread on top of the apricot glaze.

UNDERSTANDING
This cake contains about half the butter of other pound cakes. Less butter is required to tenderise it because nuts replace some of the flour, affording less structure. Because baking powder is not needed to tenderise the cake, the egg whites, beaten into a meringue, are used instead for extra volume. Hot water is added to the batter to make it less stiff and easier to fold in the egg whites.

Golden Butter Cream Cake

Serves 8

If you love butter, this will be your favourite cake. There is, quite simply, no cake with more mellow, buttery flavour or golden colour. It needs no buttercream but marries well with one if you should choose to ice it. The high proportion of butter makes it seem dense at first bite, but this cake instantly dissolves in the mouth, leaving behind a heavenly flavour and the illusion of lightness.

TINS: One 23 × 5-centimetre/ 9 × 2-inch cake or quiche tin or 23-centimetre/9-inch springform tin, greased, bottom lined with parchment or greaseproof paper, and then greased again and floured.

FINISHED HEIGHT: 3.5 centimetres/1³⁄₈ inches; 2.75 centimetres/1¹⁄₈ inches in quiche tin.

STORE: Airtight: 3 days room temperature, 1 week refrigerated, 2 months frozen. Moisture distributes most evenly the day after baking.

COMPLEMENTARY ADORNMENTS: A simple dusting of icing sugar. Royal Honey Buttercream (page 271). Perfect Whipped Cream (page 294), clotted cream and fresh strawberries.

SERVE: Room temperature.

POINTERS FOR SUCCESS: See pages xx and 8.

Preheat the oven to 350°F/180°C/gas mark 4.

In a medium bowl lightly combine the yolks, 2 tablespoons cream and vanilla.

In a large mixing bowl combine the dry ingredients and mix on low speed for 30 seconds to blend. Add the butter and remaining 6 tablespoons cream. Mix on low speed until the dry ingredients are moistened. Increase to medium speed (high speed if using a hand mixer) and beat for 1¹⁄₂ minutes to aerate and develop the cake's structure. Scrape down the sides. Gradually add the egg mixture in three batches, beating for 20 seconds after each addition to incorporate the ingredients and strengthen the structure. Scrape down the sides.

Scrape the batter into the prepared tin and smooth the surface

INGREDIENTS	WEIGHT		MEASURE
room temperature	*grams*	*pounds/ounces*	*volume*
3 egg yolks, size 2	56 grams	2 ounces	scant 2 fluid ounces
double cream	116 grams	4 ounces	4 fluid ounces
pure vanilla extract	3 grams	—	3/4 teaspoon
sifted cake flour*	150 grams	5 1/4 ounces	1 1/2 cups
castor sugar	150 grams	5 1/4 ounces	3/4 cup
baking powder	6 grams	—	1 1/4 teaspoons
salt	—	—	1/4 teaspoon
unsalted butter (must be softened)	140 grams	5 ounces	10 tablespoons

*Cake flour *without* raising agent must be used for this cake (see page 493).

with a spatula. Bake for 25 to 35 minutes or until a wire cake tester inserted in the centre comes out clean and the cake springs back when pressed lightly in the centre. *The cake should be just starting to shrink from the sides of the tin.* It will shrink quite a bit while cooling.

Let the cake cool in the tin on a rack for 10 minutes. It will have a level top. Loosen the sides with a small metal spatula and invert on to a greased wire rack. For an attractive top crust, reinvert so that the top is up and cool completely before wrapping airtight.

UNDERSTANDING

This cake is a cross between Perfect Pound Cake and Yellow Butter Cake, with the incomparable, flowery flavour of cream replacing the milk. The butter content is about the same as in Perfect Pound Cake when one takes into account the butterfat in the cream. Compared to Perfect Pound Cake, Rich Butter Cream Cake has egg yolks instead of whole eggs, to add colour and fineness of crumb. It also has baking powder for a more tender, lighter texture.

This cake is used to make Rose Trellis (page 239).

Sour Cream Butter Cake

Serves 8 to 10

This moist, tender yellow cake has a light, soft crumb. The sour cream imparts a mellow undertone which blends perfectly with the buttery flavour. This is one of my favourite cakes to make in summer, and I serve it with *crème fraîche* and fresh berries, peaches or nectarines.

TINS: One 23-centimetre/9-inch springform tin, greased, bottom lined with parchment or greaseproof paper, and then greased again and floured.

FINISHED HEIGHT: 4.5 centimetres/1¾ inches.

STORE: Airtight: 2 days room temperature, 5 days refrigerated, 2 months frozen. Moisture distributes evenly and any pastiness disappears the day after baking.

COMPLEMENTARY ADORNMENTS: A simple dusting of icing sugar. *One recipe:* Apricot Buttercream (page 270). Sour Cream Ganache (page 318). *Crème fraîche* (page 299) topped with fresh peaches.

SERVE: Room temperature.

POINTERS FOR SUCCESS: See pages xx and 8.

Preheat the oven to 350°F/180°C/gas mark 4.

In a medium bowl lightly combine the yolks, 2 tablespoons of the sour cream and the vanilla.

In a large mixing bowl combine the dry ingredients and mix on low speed for 30 seconds to blend. Add the butter and the remaining sour cream. Mix on low speed until the dry ingredients are moistened. Increase to medium speed (high speed if using a hand mixer) and beat for 1½ minutes to aerate and develop the cake's structure. Scrape down the sides. Gradually add the egg mixture in three batches, beating for 20 seconds after each addition to incorporate the ingredients and strengthen the structure. Scrape down the sides. Scrape the batter into the prepared tin and smooth the surface with a spatula.

Bake for 40 to 50 minutes or until a wire cake tester inserted in the centre comes out clean and the cake springs back when pressed lightly in the centre. *The cake should start to shrink from the sides of the tin only after removal from the oven.*

INGREDIENTS	WEIGHT		MEASURE
room temperature	*grams*	*pounds/ounces*	*volume*
4 egg yolks, size 2	74 grams	2½ ounces	2 full fluid ounces
sour cream	160 grams	5½ ounces	⅔ cup
pure vanilla extract	6 grams	—	1½ teaspoons
sifted self-raising sponge flour	150 grams	5¼ ounces	1⅔ cups
sifted plain flour	100 grams	3½ ounces	¾ cup
castor sugar	250 grams	8¾ ounces	1¼ cups
bicarbonate of soda	2.5 grams	—	½ teaspoon
salt	3.5 grams	—	½ teaspoon
unsalted butter (must be softened)	170 grams	6 ounces	12 tablespoons

Let the cake cool in the tin on a rack for 10 minutes. It will have a level top. Loosen the sides with a small metal spatula and remove the sides of the tin. Invert on to a lightly greased cake rack and cool completely before wrapping airtight. If you wish to remove the tin bottom, slide a cardboard round at least 23 centimetres/9 inches in diameter between the parchment and metal bottom when the cake is completely cool.

UNDERSTANDING
The ratio of ingredients is similar to Rich Butter Cream Cake except for a decrease in butter which makes the cake lighter and more suitable with fillings and toppings. Bicarbonate of soda is used to temper the acidity of the sour cream. The combined leavening is higher in this cake to compensate for the lower amount of butter. (Both butter and raising agents tenderise cake. Butter, however, produces a denser texture while raising agents create a lighter texture.)

Golden Almond Cake

Serves 8 to 10

This butter cake has the lovely flavour of almond. It also has a soft and dissolving texture, with a beautiful golden crust. The cake takes no time at all to make. When the mood strikes I can assemble and mix the batter in the time it takes to preheat the oven (using the microwave to soften the butter). I bake it for 45 minutes and, ignoring the safety precaution of cooling the cake in the tin for 10 minutes before turning it out, turn it out on to a rack, place it in the freezer for 10 minutes and then cut a piece to eat. Still slightly warm, it is at its most tender.

TINS: One 23 × 5-centimetre/ 9 × 2-inch cake tin or 23 centimetre/ 9-inch springform tin, greased, bottom lined with parchment or greaseproof paper, and then greased again and floured.

POINTERS FOR SUCCESS: See pages xx and 8.

FINISHED HEIGHT: 4 centimetres/ 1½ inches at the sides and 4.5 centimetres/1¾ inches in the middle.

STORE: Airtight: 2 days room temperature, 5 days refrigerated, 2 months frozen.

COMPLEMENTARY ADORNMENTS: A simple dusting of icing sugar. Raspberries, peaches and chocolate all have a natural affinity with almonds. *One recipe:* Raspberry Buttercream (page 270 or 281). Sour Cream Ganache (page 318). *Crème fraîche* (page 299) topped with fresh peaches or raspberries.

SERVE: Room temperature.

Preheat the oven to 350°F/180°C/gas mark 4.

In a medium bowl lightly combine the eggs, one-quarter of the sour cream, and the almond and vanilla extracts.

In a large mixing bowl combine the dry ingredients and mix on low speed for 30 seconds to blend. Add the butter and remaining sour cream. Mix on low speed until the dry ingredients are moistened. Increase to medium speed (high speed if using a hand mixer) and beat for 1½ minutes to aerate and develop the cake's structure. Scrape down the sides. Gradually add the egg mixture in three batches, beating for 20 seconds after each addition to incorporate the

INGREDIENTS	WEIGHT		MEASURE
room temperature	*grams*	*pounds/ounces*	*volume*
2 eggs, size 2	100 grams (weighed without shells)	3½ ounces	3 fluid ounces
sour cream	160 grams	5½ ounces	⅔ cup
almond extract	4 grams	—	1 teaspoon
pure vanilla extract	—	—	¼ teaspoon
sifted self-raising sponge flour	150 grams	5¼ ounces	1⅔ cups
sifted plain flour	65 grams	2¼ ounces	½ cup
unblanched sliced almonds, toasted and finely ground	35 grams	1¼ ounces	⅓ cup (ground)
castor sugar	250 grams	8¾ ounces	1¼ cup
bicarbonate of soda	2.5 grams	—	½ teaspoon
salt	3.5 grams	—	½ teaspoon
unsalted butted (must be softened)	140 grams	5 ounces	10 tablespoons

ingredients and strengthen the structure. Scrape down the sides.

Scrape the batter into the prepared tin and smooth the surface with a spatula. Bake for 40 to 50 minutes or until a wire cake tester inserted in the centre comes out clean and the cake springs back when pressed lightly in the centre. *The cake should start to shrink from the sides of the tin only after removal from the oven.*

Let the cake cool in the tin on a rack for 10 minutes. Loosen the sides with a small metal spatula and turn out the cake or remove the sides of the springform tin. Allow to cool completely before wrapping airtight.

UNDERSTANDING
The formula for this cake is the same as that for Sour Cream Butter Cake except that 35 grams/ 1¼ ounces/⅓ cup flour is replaced by the same quantity of finely ground almonds. The almonds add flavour and bulk but do not contribute structure so whole eggs are needed. The small amount of vanilla is added to enhance the almond flavour.

Yellow Butter Cake

Serves 12

If I had to choose among all my cakes, this one would win first place because it is delicious by itself yet versatile enough to accommodate a wide range of buttercreams. The cake combines the soft texture of white cake with the buttery flavour of yellow cake. Using all yolks instead of whole eggs produces a rich yellow colour, fine texture and delicious flavour.

TINS: Two 23 × 4-centimetre/ 9 × 1½-inch cake tins, greased, bottoms lined with parchment or greaseproof paper, and then greased again and floured.

FINISHED HEIGHT: Each layer is 3 centimetres/1¼ inches.

STORE: Airtight: 2 days room temperature, 5 days refrigerated, 2 months frozen. Texture is most perfectly moist the same day as baking.

COMPLEMENTARY ADORNMENTS: A simple dusting of icing sugar. *One recipe:* Any buttercream, glaze or fondant.

SERVE: Room temperature.

POINTERS FOR SUCCESS: See pages xx and 8.

Preheat the oven to 350°F/180°C/gas mark 4.

In a medium bowl lightly combine the yolks, one quarter of the milk and the vanilla.

In a large mixing bowl combine the dry ingredients and mix on low speed for 30 seconds to blend. Add the butter and remaining milk. Mix on low speed until the dry ingredients are moistened. Increase to medium speed (high speed if using a hand mixer) and beat for 1½ minutes to aerate and develop the cake's structure. Scrape down the sides. Gradually add the egg mixture in three batches, beating for 20 seconds after each addition to incorporate the ingredients and strengthen the structure. Scrape down the sides.

Scrape the batter into the prepared tins and smooth the surface with a spatula. The tins will be about half full. Bake for 25 to 35 minutes or until a tester inserted near the centre comes out clean and

INGREDIENTS	WEIGHT		MEASURE
room temperature	*grams*	*pounds/ounces*	*volume*
6 egg yolks, size 2	112 grams	4 ounces	3.5 fluid ounces
milk	242 grams	8½ ounces	8 fluid ounces
pure vanilla extract	9 grams	—	2¼ teaspoons
sifted self-raising sponge flour	300 grams	10½ ounces	3⅓ cups
castor sugar	300 grams	10½ ounces	1½ cups
baking powder	19.5 grams	—	1 tablespoon + 1 teaspoon
salt	5 grams	—	¾ teaspoon
unsalted butter (must be softened)	170 grams	6 ounces	12 tablespoons

the cake springs back when pressed lightly in the centre. *The cakes should start to shrink from the sides of the tins only after removal from the oven.*

Let the cakes cool in the tins on racks for 10 minutes. Loosen the sides with a small metal spatula and invert on to greased wire racks. To prevent splitting, reinvert so that the tops are up and cool completely before wrapping airtight.

UNDERSTANDING
Compared to Perfect Pound Cake, this cake has more than double the raising agent, because of the added baking powder, less than half the butter, and no egg whites. The decrease in butter is responsible for the lighter and softer texture. The added baking powder further lightens the cake and also makes it more tender.

VARIATION

MAPLE BUTTER CAKE:

This cake has a deep golden colour and a real New England flavour. It is superb iced with Neoclassic Maple Buttercream (page 269) and encrusted with toasted walnuts, coarsely chopped (page 373).

To make this cake, simply replace the sugar with an equal weight of maple sugar (or 400 grams/14 ounces/2 cups). Decrease the vanilla to ¾ teaspoon and add 1 teaspoon of maple flavouring.

Note: Maple sugar is available in speciality stores. It is expensive, but the resulting cake, iced with Maple Buttercream, is uniquely delicious.

Buttermilk Cake

Serves 8

Buttermilk imparts a slightly tangy and rich flavour to butter cake, although it is actually lower in cholesterol than whole milk. This cake is delicious with softly whipped *crème fraîche* and ripe peaches. I also like to bring it plain to picnics and serve it with windfalls of fresh wild berries.

TINS: One 23 × 5-centimetre/ 9 × 2-inch cake tin or 23-centimetre/ 9-inch springform tin, greased, bottom lined with parchment or greaseproof paper, and then greased again and floured.

FINISHED HEIGHT: 4 centimetres/ 1½ inches at the sides and 5 centimetres/2 inches in the middle.

STORE: Airtight: 3 days room temperature, 5 days refrigerated, 2 months frozen. Texture is most perfectly moist the same day as baking.

COMPLEMENTARY ADORNMENTS: A simple dusting of icing sugar. *One recipe:* Lemon Buttercream (page 270). *Crème fraîche* (page 299) topped with peach slices.

SERVE: Room temperature.

POINTERS FOR SUCCESS: See pages xx and 8.

Preheat the oven to 350°F/180°C/gas mark 4.

In a medium bowl lightly combine the yolks, one quarter of the buttermilk and the vanilla.

In a large mixing bowl combine the dry ingredients and mix on low speed for 30 seconds to blend. Add the butter and remaining buttermilk. Mix on low speed until the dry ingredients are moistened. Increase to medium speed (high speed if using a hand mixer) and beat for 1½ minutes to aerate and develop the cake's structure. Scrape down the sides. Gradually add the egg mixture in three batches, beating for 20 seconds after each addition to incorporate the ingredients and strengthen the structure. Scrape down the sides.

Scrape the batter into the prepared tin and smooth the surface with a spatula. The tin will be about half full. Bake for 30 to 40 minutes or until a tester inserted near the centre comes out clean and the cake springs back when pressed

INGREDIENTS	WEIGHT		MEASURE
room temperature	grams	pounds/ounces	volume
4 egg yolks, size 2	74 grams	2½ ounces	2 full fluid ounces
buttermilk	160 grams	5½ ounces	5 fluid ounces
pure vanilla extract	6 grams	—	1½ teaspoons
sifted cake flour*	200 grams	7 ounces	2 cups
castor sugar	200 grams	7 ounces	1 cup
baking powder	15 grams	—	1 tablespoon
salt	3.5 grams	—	½ teaspoon
unsalted butter (must be softened)	113 grams	4 ounces	8 tablespoons

*Cake flour *without* raising agent must be used for this cake (see page 493).

lightly in the centre. *The cake should start to shrink from the sides of the tin only after removal from the oven.*

Let the cake cool in the tin on a rack for 10 minutes. Loosen the sides with a small metal spatula and invert on to a greased wire rack. To prevent splitting, reinvert so that the top is up and cool completely before wrapping airtight.

UNDERSTANDING
This cake is similar to Yellow Butter Cake, except that buttermilk replaces the whole milk. Although buttermilk has a tangy taste and most recipes using buttermilk call for bicarbonate of soda to temper it, it is not necessary to use bicarbonate of soda. Actually, when buttermilk is added to a batter, it does not lower the pH (make it more acid). Instead, the buttermilk acts as a buffer, neutralising any extremes of acid or base already in the batter. Using baking powder instead of bicarbonate of soda allows the subtle, delicious tanginess of the buttermilk to come through and results in a cake with a much finer texture.

Chestnut Sand Cake

Serves 12

Chestnut flour gives this cake its lovely hue and fine, moist texture. In combination with bread flour, it produces a tender layer cake with unusual, subtle chestnut flavour and a suggestion of spiciness. I fill and ice this cake with Chestnut Buttercream (page 269, 281 or 405) and call it Le Marron, which in French means 'chestnut'.

TINS: Two 23 × 4-centimetre/ 9 × 1½-inch cake tins greased, bottoms lined with parchment or greaseproof paper, and then greased again and floured.

FINISHED HEIGHT: Each layer is 2.75 centimetres/1⅛ inches.

STORE: Airtight: 2 days room temperature, 5 days refrigerated, 2 months frozen. Moisture distributes most evenly the day after baking.

COMPLEMENTARY ADORNMENTS: A simple dusting of icing sugar. *One recipe:* Chestnut Buttercream or any dark chocolate icing or glaze such as ganache (page 312) or Chocolate Cream Glaze (page 314).

SERVE: Room temperature.

POINTERS FOR SUCCESS: See pages xx and 8.

Preheat the oven to 350°F/180°C/gas mark 4.
    In a medium bowl lightly combine the eggs, one-quarter of the milk and the vanilla.

In a large mixing bowl combine the dry ingredients and mix on low speed for 30 seconds to blend. Add the butter and remaining milk. Mix on low speed until the dry ingredients are moistened. Increase to medium speed (high speed if using a hand mixer) and beat for 1½ minutes to aerate and develop the cake's structure. Scrape down the sides. Gradually add the egg mixture in three batches, beating for 20 seconds after each addition to incorporate the ingredients and strengthen the structure. Scrape down the sides.

Scrape the batter into the prepared tins and smooth the surface with a spatula. The tins will be about half full. Bake for 25 to

INGREDIENTS	WEIGHT		MEASURE
room temperature	*grams*	*pounds/ounces*	*volume*
3 eggs, size 2	150 grams (weighed without shells)	5¼ ounces	scant 5 fluid ounces
milk	242 grams	8½ ounces	8 fluid ounces
pure vanilla extract	9 grams	—	2¼ teaspoons
sifted strong white flour	190 grams	6¾ ounces	1⅔ cups
sifted chestnut flour	110 grams	3¾ ounces	1 cup
castor sugar	300 grams	10½ ounces	1½ cups
baking powder	14.5 grams	—	1 tablespoon
salt	3.5 grams	—	½ teaspoon
unsalted butter (must be softened)	170 grams	6 ounces	12 tablespoons

35 minutes or until a tester inserted near the centre comes out clean and the cake springs back when pressed lightly in the centre. *The cakes should start to shrink from the sides of the tins only after removal from the oven.*

Let the cakes cool in the tins on racks for 10 minutes. Loosen the sides with a small metal spatula and invert on to greased wire racks. To prevent splitting, reinvert so that the tops are up and cool completely before wrapping airtight.

UNDERSTANDING
Chestnut flour can be difficult to find in the United Kingdom – but if you can get hold of some, it is delicious (see page 484). It contains mainly starch and has no gluten to support a cake's structure – so I added sufficient strong white flour to provide the necessary gluten. This cake also contains whole eggs instead of yolks and less baking powder than Yellow Butter Cake to further strengthen its structure.

Golden Grand Marnier Cake

Serves 12

The divine flavours of orange, Grand Marnier, chocolate and almond – supported by a mellow sour cream butter cake base – combine to produce a sensational cake. The orange flower water enhances the flavour. The Grand Marnier syrup makes the cake soft and moist (though not at all wet) and helps to preserve it so well that I used to ship this cake to the University of Michigan for my daughter Beth's birthday. I once added a little extra Grand Marnier and sent it airmail to a friend in France!

TINS: One 9-cup (2¹/₈-litre) fluted tube tin, greased and floured.

FINISHED HEIGHT: Depends on design of tin.

INGREDIENTS	WEIGHT		MEASURE
room temperature	*grams*	*pounds/ounces*	*volume*
chocolate mini-chips or bittersweet chocolate chopped into ¹/₄-inch/5 millimetre pieces	85 grams	3 ounces	¹/₂ cup
Grand Marnier	–	–	¹/₄ teaspoon
plain flour	–	–	1¹/₂ teaspoons
3 eggs, size 2	150 grams (weighed without shells)	5¹/₄ ounces	scant 5 fluid ounces
sour cream	242 grams	8¹/₂ ounces	1 cup
orange flower water or pure vanilla extract	8 grams 6 grams	2 teaspoons 1¹/₂ teaspoons	2 teaspoons 1¹/₂ teaspoons
sifted self-raising sponge flour	225 grams	8 ounces	2¹/₂ cups
sifted plain flour	90 grams	3 ounces	³/₄ cup

STORE: Airtight, 3 days room temperature, 7 days refrigerated, 2 months frozen. Moisture distributes most evenly one day after baking.

COMPLEMENTARY ADORNMENTS: A light dusting of icing sugar. Half recipe Chocolate Cream Glaze (page 314).

SERVE: Room temperature.

POINTERS FOR SUCCESS: See pages xx and 8.

Preheat the oven to 350°F/180°C/gas mark 4.

In a small bowl toss the chocolate chips and Grand Marnier until the chips are moistened and shiny. Add the 1½ teaspoons flour and toss until evenly coated.

In a medium bowl lightly combine the eggs, one-quarter of the sour cream, and orange flower water or vanilla.

In a large mixing bowl combine the dry ingredients and orange zest and mix on low speed for 30 seconds to blend. Add the butter

INGREDIENTS	WEIGHT		MEASURE
room temperature	*grams*	*pounds/ounces*	*volume*
unblanched sliced almonds, toasted and finely ground	60 grams	2 ounces	½ cup + 1 tablespoon (ground)
castor sugar	225 grams	8 ounces	1 cup + 2 tablespoons
bicarbonate of soda	5 grams	–	1 teaspoon
salt	5 grams	–	¾ teaspoon
grated orange zest	12 grams	–	2 tablespoons
unsalted butter (must be softened)	200 grams	7 ounces	14 tablespoons
GRAND MARNIER SYRUP			
castor sugar	100 grams	3½ ounces	½ cup
orange juice, freshly squeezed	60 grams	2 ounces	2 fluid ounces
Grand Marnier	80 grams	2¾ ounces	2½ fluid ounces

and remaining sour cream. Mix on low speed until the dry ingredients are moistened. Increase to medium speed (high speed if using a hand mixer) and beat for 1½ minutes to aerate and develop the cake's structure. Scrape down the sides. Gradually add the egg mixture in three batches, beating for 20 seconds after each addition to incorporate the ingredients and strengthen the structure. Scrape down the sides. Stir in the chocolate chips.

Scrape the batter into the prepared tin and smooth the surface with a spatula. Bake for 55 to 65 minutes or until a wire cake tester inserted in the centre comes out clean and the cake springs back when pressed lightly in the centre. *The cake should start to shrink from the sides of the tin only after removal from the oven.*

Shortly before the cake is done, prepare the syrup: Heat the sugar, orange juice and Grand Marnier until the sugar is dissolved. Do not boil. As soon as the cake comes out of the oven, place the tin on a rack, prick the top all over with a wire tester, and brush on half the syrup. Cool in the tin on the rack for 10 minutes, then invert on to a serving plate or cardboard round. Brush with the remaining syrup and cool completely before glazing with chocolate or wrapping airtight.

UNDERSTANDING

This cake is similar to Buttermilk Cake with the less tangy sour cream replacing the buttermilk. A more significant difference, however, is that 50 grams/ 1¾ ounces/½ cup flour is replaced by ground almonds and that 100 grams/3½ ounces/½ cup sugar, dissolved in orange juice and Grand Marnier, is added to the cake after baking.

To compensate for the missing 100 grams/3½ ounces/½ cup of sugar during baking, there is a greater quantity of raising agent to aerate and tenderise the texture. I like to add tiny chocolate chips to the batter because dark chocolate blends so beautifully with the orange flavour. This cake can support the chips because of both the decrease in sugar and the acid provided by the sour cream. An old baker's trick to suspend ingredients in a batter is to make the batter more acid. The acid coagulates the egg faster, in effect setting the cake's structure before the heavier particles can fall to the bottom. A decrease in sugar also enables the egg to coagulate faster and the starch in the flour to gelatinise better, also strengthening the structure. Another trick is coating the chips with flour, giving them a rougher surface with which to cling to the batter.

Note: This cake is very attractive made in individual portions. A 6-cake Bundt-lette tin (page 517) is the perfect size. This recipe will make 9 individual cakelettes, so you will need either to make only two-thirds of the recipe or to bake the cakelettes in two batches. Be sure to fill any unused sections of the tin with water to promote even baking. The cakelettes require 30 to 40 minutes' baking time.

White Velvet Butter Cake

Serves 12

This is the softest and most delicate of all butter cakes. The butter and vanilla give the cake an off-white colour but also contribute delicious flavour. This versatile cake blends well with just about any buttercream except for chocolate – which tends to overwhelm the delicate flavour.

TINS: Two 23 × 4–centimetre/ 9 × 1½-inch cake tins, greased, bottoms lined with parchment or greaseproof paper, and then greased again and floured.

FINISHED HEIGHT: Each layer is 2.75 centimetres/1⅛ inches.

STORE: Airtight: 2 days room temperature, 5 days refrigerated, 2 months frozen. Texture is most perfectly moist the same day as baking.

COMPLEMENTARY ADORNMENTS: A simple dusting of icing sugar. Any non–chocolate buttercream, glaze or fondant.

SERVE: Room temperature.

POINTERS FOR SUCCESS: See pages xx and 8.

Preheat the oven to 350°F/180°C/gas mark 4.

In a medium bowl lightly combine the egg whites, one-quarter of the milk and the vanilla.

In a large mixing bowl combine the dry ingredients and mix on low speed for 30 seconds to blend. Add the butter and remaining milk. Mix on low speed until the dry ingredients are moistened. Increase to medium speed (high speed if using a hand mixer) and beat for 1½ minutes to aerate and develop the cake's structure. Scrape down the sides. Gradually add the egg mixture in three batches, beating for 20 seconds after each addition to incorporate the ingredients and strengthen the structure. Scrape down the sides.

Scrape the batter into the prepared tins and smooth the surface with a spatula. The tins will be about half full. Bake for 25 to 35 minutes or until a tester inserted near the centre comes out clean and the cake springs back when pressed lightly in the centre. *The cakes should start to shrink from the sides of*

INGREDIENTS	WEIGHT		MEASURE
room temperature	grams	pounds/ounces	volume
4½ egg whites, size 2	135 grams	4¾ ounces	4 full fluid ounces
milk	242 grams	8½ ounces	8 fluid ounces
pure vanilla extract	9 grams	—	2¼ teaspoons
sifted self-raising sponge flour	300 grams	10½ ounces	3⅓ cups
castor sugar	300 grams	10½ ounces	1½ cups
salt	5 grams	—	¾ teaspoon
unsalted butter (must be softened)	170 grams	6 ounces	12 tablespoons

the tins only after removal from the oven.

Let the cakes cool in the tins on racks for 10 minutes. Loosen the sides with a small metal spatula and invert on to greased wire racks. To prevent splitting, reinvert so that the tops are up and cool completely before wrapping airtight.

UNDERSTANDING
This cake is identical to Yellow Butter Cake except that every 2 egg yolks are replaced by 1½ whites. Egg whites produce a softer cake than yolks or whole eggs.

This cake is used to make White Lilac Nostalgia (page 190).

Golden Luxury Butter Cake

Serves 12

No one would ever guess that white chocolate is one of the ingredients in this cake. The addition of *real* white chocolate (the kind which contains cocoa butter) to a cake adds a velvety texture, deepens the yellow colour and heightens the 'melt-in-the-mouth' quality. This is because cocoa butter is very firm at room temperature but melts faster than butter at body temperature. Cocoa butter is also a splendid emulsifier and is responsible for the extra smoothness of the batter and the velvety grain of the baked cake. The slight acidity of the cocoa butter, together with the milk solids in the chocolate, perfumes the cake with an almost lemony edge. Accentuate this flavour with a lemon buttercream.

TINS: Two 23 × 4-centimetre/ 9 × 1½-inch cake tins, greased, bottoms lined with parchment or greaseproof paper, and then greased again and floured.

FINISHED HEIGHT: Each layer is 3 centimetres/1¼ inches.

STORE: Airtight: 2 days room temperature, 5 days refrigerated, 2 months frozen. Texture is most perfectly moist the same day as baking.

Preheat the oven to 350°F/180°C/gas mark 4.

In a double boiler melt the chocolate over hot (not simmering) water, stirring frequently. Remove from the water.

COMPLEMENTARY ADORNMENTS: A simple dusting of icing sugar. *One recipe:* Lemon Buttercream (page 270 or 284). White Chocolate Buttercream or Glaze (page 285 or 287).

In a medium bowl lightly combine the yolks, one-quarter of the milk and the vanilla.

In a large mixing bowl combine the dry ingredients and mix on low speed for 30 seconds to blend. Add the butter and remaining milk. Mix on low speed until the dry ingredients are moistened. Increase to medium speed (high speed if using a hand mixer) and beat for

SERVE: Room temperature.

POINTERS FOR SUCCESS: See pages xx and 8 and Melting White Chocolate (page 288).

INGREDIENTS	WEIGHT		MEASURE
room temperature	*grams*	*pounds/ounces*	*volume*
white chocolate	170 grams	6 ounces	–
6 egg yolks, size 2	112 grams	4 ounces	3.5 fluid ounces
milk	242 grams	8½ ounces	8 fluid ounces
pure vanilla extract	6 grams	–	1½ teaspoons
sifted self-raising sponge flour	300 grams	10½ ounces	3⅓ cups
castor sugar	240 grams	8½ ounces	1 cup + 3 tablespoons
salt	5 grams	–	¾ teaspoon
unsalted butter (must be softened)	128 grams	4½ ounces	9 tablespoons

1½ minutes to aerate and develop the cake's structure. Scrape down the sides. Gradually add the egg mixture in three batches, beating for 20 seconds after each addition to incorporate the ingredients and strengthen the structure. Scrape down the sides. Add the melted chocolate and beat to incorporate.

Scrape the batter into the prepared tins and smooth the surface with a spatula. The tins will be a little more than half full. Bake for 25 to 35 minutes or until a tester inserted near the centre comes out clean and the cake springs back when pressed lightly in the centre. *The cakes should start to shrink from the sides of the tins only after removal from the oven.*

Let the cakes cool in the tins on racks for 10 minutes. Loosen the sides with a small metal spatula and invert on to greased wire racks. To prevent splitting, reinvert so that the tops are up and cool completely before wrapping airtight.

UNDERSTANDING
The formula for this cake is, beneath the surface, practically identical to Yellow Butter Cake. The added fat from the cocoa butter is balanced by removing the equivalent butter from the basic recipe. The added sugar in the chocolate has also been subtracted. The milk solids are the only extra.

White Chocolate
Whisper Cake

Serves 12

White chocolate offers the double advantage of velvety, melt-in-the-mouth texture and, because of white cake's gentle flavour, a definite whisper of cocoa butter. This special flavour blends well with a lemon buttercream or, of course, a white chocolate buttercream or glaze.

TINS: Two 23 × 4–centimetre/ 9 × 1½-inch cake tins, greased, bottoms lined with parchment or greaseproof paper, and then greased again and floured.

FINISHED HEIGHT: Each layer is 3 centimetres/1¼ inches (4.5 centimetres/1¾ inches when baked in oval tins).

STORE: Airtight: 2 days room temperature, 5 days refrigerated, 2 months frozen. Texture is most perfectly moist the same day as baking.

COMPLEMENTARY ADORNMENTS: A simple dusting of icing sugar. *One recipe:* Lemon Buttercream (page 270 or 284). White Chocolate Buttercream or Glaze (page 285 or 287).

SERVE: Room temperature.

POINTERS FOR SUCCESS: See pages xx and 8.

Preheat the oven to 350°F/180°C/gas mark 4.

In a double boiler melt the chocolate over hot (not simmering) water, stirring frequently. Remove from the water.

In a medium bowl lightly combine the egg whites, one-quarter of the milk and the vanilla.

In a large mixing bowl combine the dry ingredients and mix on low speed for 30 seconds to blend. Add the butter and remaining milk. Mix on low speed until the dry ingredients are moistened. Increase to medium speed (high speed if using a hand mixer) and beat for 1½ minutes to aerate and develop the cake's structure. Scrape down the sides. Gradually add the egg mixture in three batches, beating for 20 seconds after each addition to incorporate the ingredients and strengthen the structure. Scrape down the sides. Add the melted chocolate and beat to incorporate.

Scrape the batter into the prepared tins and smooth the surface with a spatula. The tins will

INGREDIENTS	WEIGHT		MEASURE
room temperature	*grams*	*pounds/ounces*	*volume*
white chocolate	170 grams	6 ounces	
4½ egg whites, size 2	135 grams	4¾ ounces	4 full fluid ounces
milk	242 grams	8½ ounces	8 fluid ounces
pure vanilla extract	6 grams	–	1½ teaspoons
sifted self-raising sponge flour	300 grams	10½ ounces	3⅓ cups
castor sugar	240 grams	8½ ounces	1 cup + 3 tablespoons
salt	7 grams	–	¾ teaspoon
unsalted butter (must be softened)	128 grams	4½ ounces	9 tablespoons

be about half full. Bake for 25 to 35 minutes or until a tester inserted near the centre comes out clean and the cake springs back when pressed lightly in the centre. *The cakes should start to shrink from the sides of the tins only after removal from the oven.*

Let the cakes cool in the tins on racks for 10 minutes. Loosen the sides with a small metal spatula and invert on to greased wire racks. To prevent splitting, reinvert so that the tops are up and cool completely before wrapping airtight.

UNDERSTANDING
Real white chocolate is made up of one-third cocoa butter, one-third sugar, one-third milk solids, and a tiny amount of vanilla and lecithin, a natural emulsifier found in soya beans. In this cake a small amount of white chocolate is added and comparable amounts of fat (butter) and sugar are subtracted. The result, compared to White Velvet Butter Cake, is a more velvety crumb and fuller flavour. Because of the extra milk solids and the lecithin, the cake is also higher, lighter and more golden in colour.

The cocoa butter, which is firmer than butter yet melts in the mouth, makes this cake easy to cut.

This cake is used to make Blueberry Swan Lake (page 186).

Checkerboard Cake

Serves 12

A delightful *trompe-l'œil* of yellow and chocolate checkerboard with the same exquisite texture and well-balanced flavour of Yellow Butter Cake (page 28). A great party cake, especially for children.

TINS: A set of three 23 × 2.5-centimetre/9 × 1-inch checkerboard cake tins, greased, bottoms lined with parchment or greaseproof paper, and then greased again and floured.

FINISHED HEIGHT: Each layer is 2.75 centimetres/1⅛ inches.

STORE: Airtight: 2 days room temperature, 5 days refrigerated, 2 months frozen. Texture is most perfectly moist the same day as baking.

COMPLEMENTARY
ADORNMENTS: *One recipe:* Any dark chocolate icing or glaze such as Chocolate Cream Glaze (page 314) or Classic Buttercream (page 268).

SERVE: Room temperature.

POINTERS FOR SUCCESS: See pages xx and 8.

Preheat the oven to 350°F/180°C/gas mark 4.

In a double boiler melt the chocolate over hot (not simmering) water, stirring frequently. Remove from the water.

In a medium bowl lightly combine the eggs, one-quarter of the milk and the vanilla.

In a large mixing bowl combine the dry ingredients and mix on low speed for 30 seconds to blend. Add the butter and remaining milk. Mix on low speed until the dry ingredients are moistened. Increase to medium speed (high speed if using a hand mixer) and beat for 1½ minutes to aerate and develop the cake's structure. Scrape down the sides. Gradually add the egg mixture in three batches, beating for 20 seconds after each addition to incorporate the ingredients and strengthen the structure. Scrape down the sides.

Divide the batter approximately in half (793 grams/1¾ pounds in one bowl, 680 grams/1½ pounds in another bowl). Stir the melted chocolate into the smaller batch of batter until uniform in colour. Fill

INGREDIENTS	WEIGHT		MEASURE
room temperature	*grams*	*pounds/ounces*	*volume*
extra bittersweet or semisweet chocolate	85 grams	3 ounces	
4 large eggs	200 grams (weighed without shells)	7 ounces	6 full fluid ounces
milk	320 grams	11¼ ounces	10½ fluid ounces
pure vanilla extract	12 grams	—	1 tablespoon
sifted self-raising sponge flour	400 grams	14 ounces	4½ cups
castor sugar	400 grams	14 ounces	2 cups
salt	7 grams	—	1 teaspoon
unsalted butter (must be softened)	227 grams	8 ounces	1 cup

two large icing bags fitted with large round tubes 2 centimetres/ ¾ inch in diameter with the two batters.*

Place the divider rings in one of the prepared tins and pipe batter into each section, alternating batter colours. The batter should fill the tin about half full. Using a small metal spatula or the back of a spoon, smooth any seams or divisions in the batter. Now carefully lift out the divider and rinse it off. When piping batter for the second layer, alternate the colours, i.e. if you started with yellow for the outside ring, start

with chocolate. Pipe batter for the third layer exactly like the first.

Bake for 25 minutes or until a tester inserted near the centre comes out clean and the cakes spring back when pressed lightly in the centres. *The cakes should start to shrink from the sides of the tins only after removal from the oven.*

Let the cakes cool in the tins on racks for 10 minutes. Loosen the sides with a small metal spatula and invert on to greased wire racks. To prevent splitting, reinvert so that the tops are up and cool completely before wrapping airtight.

When stacking the layers, use a

*You may also use glass measuring jugs to pour the batter into the tins, but icing bags are faster and easier to use.

very thin coating of yellow or chocolate icing to adhere the layers without disturbing the checkerboard effect.

UNDERSTANDING
Whole eggs provide the structure to accommodate the melted chocolate, which is stirred into half the batter at the very end of mixing. The batter is thick enough to pipe through an icing bag, making filling the special sections of these tins quick and easy.

I use melted chocolate instead of cocoa because it is convenient to add to the batter and also because its less intense chocolate flavour blends better with the more subtle yellow cake.

Perfect Chocolate
Butter Cake

Serves 12

This cake has a full chocolate flavour and exceptionally soft, fine texture for a chocolate butter cake. Dutch-processed cocoa makes the neutralising effect of bicarbonate of soda unnecessary, eliminating the slightly bitter edge often associated with bicarbonate of soda chocolate cakes. Ross Horowitz, after photographing this cake for the American *Chocolatier* magazine, came up with a marvellous description: 'When you bite into this cake,' he rhapsodised, 'it seems light; then it becomes fudgy and chocolaty; then, just when you begin to think you have something, it simply vanishes so you want to take another bite!' My mother was more succinct: 'It tastes just like a chocolate bar but softer.' (And that was my goal.)

TINS: Two 23 × 4–centimetre/ 9 × 1½-inch cake tins, greased, bottoms lined with parchment or greaseproof paper, and then greased again and floured.

FINISHED HEIGHT: Each layer is about 2.75 centimetres/1⅛ inches.

STORE: Airtight: 2 days room temperature, 5 days refrigerated, 2 months frozen. Texture is most perfectly moist the same day as baking.

COMPLEMENTARY ADORNMENTS: A simple dusting of icing sugar. *One recipe:* Any buttercream except for lemon. Any glaze or fondant.

SERVE: Room temperature.

POINTERS FOR SUCCESS: See pages xx and 8.

INGREDIENTS	WEIGHT		MEASURE
room temperature	*grams*	*pounds/ounces*	*volume*
unsweetened cocoa (preferably Dutch-processed)	63 grams	2¼ ounces	½ cup + 3 tablespoons (lightly spooned into cup)
boiling water	236 grams	8¼ ounces	8 fluid ounces
3 eggs, size 2	150 grams (weighed without shells)	5¼ ounces	scant 5 fluid ounces
pure vanilla extract	9 grams	—	2¼ teaspoons
sifted self-raising sponge flour	235 grams	8¼ ounces	2⅔ cups
castor sugar	300 grams	10½ ounces	1½ cups
salt	5 grams	—	¾ teaspoon
unsalted butter (must be softened)	170 grams*	6 ounces	12 tablespoons

* If a very fudgy, shallower cake is desired, increase the butter to 227 grams/8 ounces/1 cup.

Preheat the oven to 350°F/180°C/gas mark 4.

In a medium bowl whisk together the cocoa and boiling water until smooth. Cool to room temperature.

In another bowl lightly combine the eggs, one-quarter of the cocoa mixture and the vanilla.

In a large mixing bowl combine the remaining dry ingredients and mix on low speed for 30 seconds to blend. Add the butter and remaining cocoa mixture. Mix on low speed until the dry ingredients are moistened. Increase to medium speed (high speed if using a hand mixer) and beat for 1½ minutes to aerate and develop the cake's structure. Scrape down the sides. Gradually add the egg mixture in three batches, beating for 20 seconds after each addition to incorporate the ingredients and strengthen the structure. Scrape down the sides.

Scrape the batter into the prepared tins and smooth the surface with a spatula. The tins will be about half full. Bake for 25 to 35 minutes or until a tester inserted near the centre comes out clean and the cake springs back when pressed lightly in the centre. *The cakes should start to shrink from the sides of the tins only after removal from the oven.*

Let the cakes cool in the tins on racks for 10 minutes. Loosen the sides with a small metal spatula and invert on to greased wire racks. To prevent splitting, reinvert so that the tops are up and cool completely before wrapping airtight.

UNDERSTANDING

The formula for this cake is similar to Yellow Butter Cake with just a few minor concessions to the special nature of chocolate. Some of the flour is replaced with equal weight of cocoa. (Cocoa gives a fuller chocolate flavour than bitter chocolate in a cake. See page 486.) The butter is increased because cocoa creates a stronger and drier structure. Water replaces the milk because, in a chocolate layer cake, milk protein brings out the bitterness in chocolate and ties up flavour – whereas water allows for quick release of full chocolate flavour. Whole eggs are used instead of yolks for practicality, because the flavour improvement offered by yolks alone is not as noticeable in a chocolate cake as it is in a yellow cake.

This cake is used to make La Porcelaine (page 230).

Perfect Chocolate Torte

Serves 8

To my taste, there is no more appealing presentation than an elegant torte glazed with a shiny coating of dark or white chocolate. (Especially if one suspects that there is more chocolate within!)

This richly chocolate butter cake is 4.5 centimetres/1¾ inches high – just right for a torte. It is easy to serve and, with a single long-stemmed rose on top, elegant enough for a black-tie dinner party.

TINS: One 23 × 5-centimetre/ 9 × 2-inch cake tin or 23-centimetre/ 9-inch springform tin, greased, bottom lined with parchment or greaseproof paper, and then greased again and floured.

FINISHED HEIGHT: 4.5 centimetres/1¾ inches.

STORE: Airtight: 2 days room temperature, 5 days refrigerated, 2 months frozen. Texture is most perfectly moist the same day as baking.

COMPLEMENTARY ADORNMENTS: A simple dusting of icing sugar. *One recipe:* Any chocolate glaze (white chocolate is especially attractive) or fondant.

SERVE: Room temperature.

POINTERS FOR SUCCESS: See pages xx and 8. Magi-Cake Strips (pages 516 and 522) give the best shape for glazing.

Preheat the oven to 350°F/180°C/gas mark 4.

In a medium bowl whisk together the cocoa and boiling water until smooth. Cool to room temperature.

In another bowl lightly combine the eggs, one-quarter of the cocoa mixture and the vanilla.

In a large mixing bowl combine the remaining dry ingredients and mix on low speed for 30 seconds to blend. Add the butter and remaining cocoa mixture. Mix on low speed until the dry ingredients are moistened. Increase to medium speed (high speed if using a hand mixer) and beat for 1½ minutes to aerate and develop the cake's structure. Scrape down the sides. Gradually add the egg mixture in three batches, beating for 20 seconds after each addition to incorporate the ingredients and

INGREDIENTS	WEIGHT		MEASURE
room temperature	*grams*	*pounds/ounces*	*volume*
unsweetened cocoa (preferably Dutch-processed)	42 grams	1½ ounces	¼ cup + 3 tablespoons
boiling water	156 grams	5½ ounces	5 fluid ounces
2 eggs, size 2	100 grams (weighed without shells)	3½ ounces	3 fluid ounces
pure vanilla extract	3 grams	—	¾ teaspoon
sifted self-raising sponge flour	156 grams	5½ ounces	1¾ cups
castor sugar	200 grams	7 ounces	1 cup
salt	3.5 grams	—	½ teaspoon
unsalted butter (must be softened)	113 grams*	4 ounces	8 tablespoons

*If a very fudgy, shallower cake is desired, increase the butter to 142 grams/5 ounces/10 tablespoons.

strengthen the structure. Scrape down the sides.

Scrape the batter into the prepared tin and smooth the surface with a spatula. The tin will be about half full. Bake for 30 to 40 minutes or until a tester inserted near the centre comes out clean and the cake springs back when pressed lightly in the centre. *The cake should start to shrink from the sides of the tin only after removal from the oven.*

Let the cake cool in the tin on a rack for 10 minutes. Loosen the sides with a small metal spatula, invert on to a greased wire rack, and cool completely before wrapping airtight.

UNDERSTANDING

The formula for this cake is almost identical to the preceding one with the exception that only two-thirds the amount of batter is prepared.

This cake is used to make Bittersweet Royale Torte (page 229).

Chocolate Domingo Cake

Serves 10 to 12

This is quite simply the tenor of chocolate butter cakes. It has the most intense, round, full chocolate flavour notes of any I have experienced, mainly due to the almost double amount of butter it contains. In effect, I have taken the butter usually used in the buttercream and put it in the cake, making it unnecessary and almost undesirable to ice the cake. This cake literally melts in the mouth. The extra butter in this cake also makes it slightly fudgy and easy to slice without crumbs.

In the ancient tradition of creating a fabulous recipe for a favourite opera star, this cake is named for mine: Placido Domingo, in gratitude for the pleasure of his incomparable performances.

TIN: One 23 × 5-centimetre/
9 × 2-inch cake tin or a
23-centimetre/9-inch springform
tin, greased, bottom lined with
parchment or greaseproof paper,
and then greased again and floured.

FINISHED HEIGHT: 4 centimetres/
1½ inches (the top of the cake
will be rounded when done and
will become perfectly flat on
cooling).

SERVE: Room temperature.

POINTERS FOR SUCCESS: See
pages xx and 8. This cake is divine
eaten hot from the oven.

STORE: Airtight: 2 days room
temperature, 5 days refrigerated,
2 months frozen. Texture is most
perfectly moist the same day as
baking.

Preheat the oven to
350°F/180°C/gas mark 4.

In a medium bowl whisk
together the cocoa, sour cream,
eggs and vanilla until smooth.

COMPLEMENTARY
ADORNMENTS: A dusting of icing
sugar and a red chocolate rose
(page 450) or real red rose. Or the
special Chocolate Fossil technique
(page 445).

In a large mixing bowl combine
all the remaining dry ingredients
and mix on low speed for
30 seconds to blend. Add the butter
and half the cocoa mixture. Mix on
low speed until the dry ingredients

INGREDIENTS	WEIGHT		MEASURE
room temperature	grams	pounds/ounces	volume
unsweetened cocoa (preferably Dutch-processed) or ½ cup nonalkalised cocoa	42 grams	1½ ounces	¼ cup + 3 tablespoons
sour cream	160 grams	5½ ounces	⅔ cup
2 eggs, size 2	100 grams (weighed without shells)	3½ ounces	3 fluid ounces
pure vanilla extract	6 grams	—	1½ teaspoons
sifted cake flour*	156 grams	5½ ounces	1½ cups + 1 tablespoon
castor sugar	200 grams	7 ounces	1 cup
bicarbonate of soda	1.5 grams	—	¼ teaspoon
salt	3.5 grams	—	½ teaspoon
unsalted butter (must be softened)	200 grams	7 ounces	14 tablespoons

*Cake flour *without* raising agent must be used for this cake (see page 493).

are moistened. Increase to medium speed (high speed if using a hand mixer) and beat for 1½ minutes to aerate and develop the cake's structure. Scrape down the sides. Gradually add the remaining cocoa mixture in two batches, beating for 20 seconds after each addition to incorporate the ingredients and strengthen the structure. Scrape down the sides.

Scrape the batter into the prepared tin and smooth the surface with a spatula. The tin will be about half full. Bake for 30 to 40 minutes or until a tester inserted near the centre comes out clean and the cake springs back when pressed lightly in the centre. *The cake should start to shrink from the sides of the tin only after removal from the oven.*

Let the cake cool in the tin on a rack for 10 minutes. Loosen the sides with a small metal spatula and invert on to a greased wire rack. Reinvert so that the top is up and cool completely before wrapping airtight.

UNDERSTANDING

This formula is similar to Perfect Chocolate Torte, but sour cream replaces the water to add a lovely, mellow flavour to the chocolate. Although the protein in sour cream normally acts as a flavour inhibitor in chocolate cakes, the close to double amount of butter (this includes the butterfat in the sour cream) corrects this tendency because it is a superb releaser of other flavours. Butter tenderises cake, so I decreased the raising agent to equal half the raising power of the Perfect Chocolate Torte (page 50).

Note: This cake was created at the insistence of my incomparable assistant, David Shamah. He loves the quality that sour cream gives to yellow cake and felt certain it would do something equally wonderful for chocolate unlike milk or buttermilk. He was right; sour cream, it seems, is an exception, and this has become his favourite chocolate cake.

Chocolate Fudge Cake

Serves 12

The molasses in the brown sugar gives this cake a distinctive and pleasantly bitter edge. The texture is soft and light yet moist with good chocolate flavour impact and a lingering bittersweet aftertaste. The particular bittersweet chocolate flavour of this cake goes splendidly with Milk Chocolate Buttercream (page 291).

TINS: Two 23 × 4-centimetre/ 9 × 1½-inch cake tins, greased, bottoms lined with parchment or greaseproof paper, and then greased and floured.

FINISHED HEIGHT: Each layer is 2.75 centimetres/1⅛ inches.

STORE: Airtight: 2 days room temperature, 5 days refrigerated, 2 months frozen. Texture is most perfectly moist same day as baking.

INGREDIENTS	WEIGHT		MEASURE
room temperature	*grams*	*pounds/ounces*	*volume*
unsweetened cocoa (preferably Dutch-processed) *or* 1 cup nonalkalised cocoa	85 grams	3 ounces	¾ cup + 3 tablespoons (lightly spooned into a cup)
boiling water	354 grams	12½ ounces	12 fluid ounces
3 eggs, size 2	150 grams (weighed without shells)	5¼ ounces	scant 5 fluid ounces
pure vanilla extract	6 grams	—	1½ teaspoons
sifted self-raising sponge flour	300 grams	10½ ounces	3⅓ cups
light brown sugar	434 grams	15¼ ounces	2 cups (firmly packed)
bicarbonate of soda	7 grams	—	1¼ teaspoons
salt	5 grams	—	¾ teaspoon
unsalted butter (must be softened)	227 grams	8 ounces	1 cup

COMPLEMENTARY ADORNMENTS: A simple dusting of icing sugar. *One recipe:* Milk Chocolate Buttercream (page 291). Ganache Icing (page 309).

SERVE: Room temperature.

POINTERS FOR SUCCESS: See pages xx and 8.

Preheat the oven to 350°F/180°C/gas mark 4.
    In a medium bowl whisk together the cocoa and boiling water until smooth. Cool to room temperature.
    In another bowl lightly combine the eggs, one-quarter of the cocoa mixture, and the vanilla.
    In a large mixing bowl combine the remaining dry ingredients and mix on low speed for 30 seconds. Add the butter and remaining cocoa mixture. Mix on low speed until the dry ingredients are moistened. Increase to medium speed (high speed if using a hand

mixer) and beat for 1½ minutes to aerate and develop the cake's structure. Scrape down the sides. Gradually add the egg mixture in three batches, beating for 20 seconds after each addition to incorporate the ingredients and strengthen the structure. Scrape down the sides.

Scrape the batter into the prepared tins and smooth the surface with a spatula. The tins will be about half full. Bake for 20 to 30 minutes or until a tester inserted near the centre comes out clean and the cake springs back when pressed lightly in the centre. *The cakes should start to shrink from the sides of the tins only after removal from the oven.*

Let the cakes cool in the tins on racks for 10 minutes. Loosen the sides with a small metal spatula and invert on to greased wire racks. To prevent splitting, reinvert so that tops are up and cool completely before wrapping airtight.

UNDERSTANDING
The formula for this cake is similar to Perfect Chocolate Butter Cake. The most significant differences are brown sugar instead of castor and extra liquid (from the water and the molasses in the brown sugar) replacing one of the eggs. Bicarbonate of soda is used to neutralise some of the molasses' acidity. Less vanilla is necessary because the brown sugar contributes so much flavour. This cake has less structure (egg) and more liquid, therefore it is moister, softer and more tender.

This cake is used to make Chocolate Spike (page 228).

Triple Layer Devil's Food Cake

Serves 18

This is a moist, fine-textured, intensely chocolate cake, with a flavour strongly reminiscent of the beloved deeply cocoa cake of childhood.

TINS: Three 23 × 4–centimetre/ 9 × 1½–inch cake tins, greased, bottoms lined with parchment or greaseproof paper, then greased again and floured.

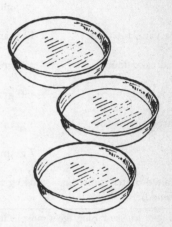

FINISHED HEIGHT: Each layer about 2.75 centimetres/1⅛ inches.

STORE: Airtight: 2 days room temperature, 5 days refrigerated, 2 months frozen. Texture is most perfectly moist the same day as baking.

COMPLEMENTARY ADORNMENTS: *One recipe:* Milk Chocolate Buttercream (page 291) or Classic Coffee Buttercream (page 268).

SERVE: Room temperature.

POINTERS FOR SUCCESS: See pages xx and 8.

Preheat the oven to 350°F/180°C/gas mark 4.

In a medium bowl whisk together cocoa and boiling water until smooth and cool to room temperature.

In a second medium bowl lightly combine eggs, about one-quarter of the cocoa mixture, and the vanilla.

In a large mixing bowl combine the remaining dry ingredients and mix on low speed for 30 seconds. Add butter and the remaining cocoa mixture. Mix on low speed until the dry ingredients are moistened. Increase to medium speed (high speed if using hand mixer) and beat for 1½ minutes to aerate and develop the cake's structure. Scrape down the sides.

INGREDIENTS	WEIGHT		MEASURE
room temperature	*grams*	*pounds/ounces*	*volume*
unsweetened cocoa (nonalkalised)	82 grams	3 ounces	1 cup (lightly spooned into cup)
boiling water	354 grams	12½ ounces	12 fluid ounces
4 eggs, size 2	200 grams (weighed without shells)	7 ounces	6 full fluid ounces
pure vanilla extract	12 grams	—	1 tablespoon
sifted cake flour*	350 grams	12¼ ounces	3½ cups
castor sugar	450 grams	15¼ ounces	2¼ cups
bicarbonate of soda	5 grams	—	1 teaspoon
salt	7 grams	—	1 teaspoon
unsalted butter (must be softened)	340 grams	12 ounces	1½ cups

*Cake flour *without* raising agent must be used for this cake (see page 493).

Gradually add the egg mixture to the batter in three batches, beating for 20 seconds after each addition to incorporate the ingredients and strengthen the cake's structure. Scrape down the sides.

Scrape the batter into prepared tins and smooth the surface with a spatula. The tins will be about half full. Bake for 20 to 30 minutes or until a tester inserted near the centre comes out clean and the cake springs back when pressed lightly in the centre. *The cakes should start to shrink from the sides of the tins only after removal from the oven.* Let the cakes cool in the tins on racks for

10 minutes. Loosen the sides with a small metal spatula and invert on to greased wire racks. To prevent splitting, reinvert so that the tops are up and cool completely before wrapping airtight.

UNDERSTANDING
This cake is essentially the same formula as Perfect Chocolate Butter Cake, one and a half times the quantity. The difference is the use of nonalkalised cocoa and bicarbonate of soda to neutralise its acidity. The texture is quite similar, due to having maintained the acid balance. It is perhaps a shade less

moist due to a slight decrease in cocoa butter contained in the nonalkalised cocoa. The flavour, however, packs a strong, less subtle chocolate punch.

Down-Home Chocolate Mayonnaise Cake

Serves 10

This recipe was given to me by Pauline Howard, of Wardsboro, Vermont, when I was a very young bride who didn't know how to cook or bake. It was invented by the wife of a Hellmann's mayonnaise salesman who was trying to help her husband. It's a homely-looking cake with a glossy dark-brown crust that dips in the centre. Coarse yet tender and utterly moist, it's the kind of cake that your mother may have made for you if you were a child in the fifties. Like my mother, yours probably misplaced the recipe, and you have longed for its strangely satisfying, unique flavour ever since. There are a few people, I am sure, who will be as overjoyed as I that I found the original recipe, written on a 4-cent postcard, over twenty-five years later. This book would not be complete without it – my first chocolate cake recipe!

TINS: Two 20 × 4-centimetre/ 8 × 1½-inch cake tins, greased, bottoms lined with parchment or greaseproof paper, then greased again and floured.

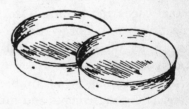

FINISHED HEIGHT: Each layer is 3 centimetres/1¼ inches (2.75 centimetres/ 1⅛ inches in centre).

STORE: Airtight: 3 days room temperature, 5 days refrigerated, 2 months frozen.

COMPLEMENTARY ADORNMENTS: A simple dusting of icing sugar. *One recipe:* Any buttercream except for lemon.

SERVE: Room temperature.

INGREDIENTS	WEIGHT		MEASURE
room temperature	*grams*	*pounds/ounces*	*volume*
unsweetened cocoa (nonalkalised)	28 grams	1 ounce	⅓ cup (lightly spooned into cup)
boiling water	236 grams	8¼ ounces	8 fluid ounces
pure vanilla extract	4 grams	—	1 teaspoon
mayonnaise	160 grams	5½ ounces	¾ cup
sifted cake flour★	200 grams	7 ounces	2 cups
castor sugar	200 grams	7 ounces	1 cup
bicarbonate of soda	10 grams	—	2 teaspoons
salt	—	—	½ teaspoon

★Cake flour *without* raising agent must be used for this cake (see page 493).

POINTERS FOR SUCCESS: See pages xx and 8.

Preheat the oven to 350°F/180°C/gas mark 4.

In a medium bowl whisk together cocoa and boiling water until smooth and cool to room temperature. Whisk in the vanilla and mayonnaise.

In a large mixing bowl combine the remaining ingredients and mix on low speed for 30 seconds to blend. Add the chocolate mixture. Mix on low speed until the dry ingredients are moistened. Increase to medium (high speed if using a hand mixer) and beat for 1 minute to aerate and develop the cake's structure. Scrape the batter into prepared tins (it will be very liquid) and fill the tins only about one-third full.

Bake for 20 to 25 minutes or until a tester inserted near the centre comes out clean and the cake springs back when pressed lightly in the centre. *The cakes should start to shrink from the sides of the tins only after removal from the oven.* Allow the cakes to cool in the tins on racks for 10 minutes. Loosen the sides with a small metal spatula and invert on to greased wire racks. Cool completely before wrapping airtight.

UNDERSTANDING
No one will ever divine the mystery ingredient, but

mayonnaise is simply an emulsification of egg yolk and oil with a tiny bit of vinegar. The large amounts of oil (in the mayonnaise) and bicarbonate of soda account for the tenderness of this cake. The extra bicarbonate of soda also creates the slightly dipped centre and the coarse, dark, reddish crumb with a deliciously bitter edge.

Fruit, Vegetable and Bread Cakes

The cakes in this section are all (with the exception of brioche) variations of basic sponge or butter cake, with fruit or vegetable purées supplying most of the liquid. Banana Cake, one of my personal favourites, is the most similar in texture to butter cake. The other cakes are denser, moister and chewier and for the most part speedy to make. Because of their moistness and complexity of flavours and textures, they require no icing and have a longer shelf-life than most other cakes. These qualities also make them suitable for present-giving. To offer as a more lavish gift, wrap and present the cake in the tin in which it was baked. (Be sure to spray the tin with non-stick vegetable spray before returning the cake to the tin.)

Note: Recipes can be doubled if you have extra tins.

Plum Cake

Serves 10 to 12

Fruitcake is one of the most personal cakes. Either you love it or hate it; prefer all fruit to a more cake-like type; prefer the cake saturated with spirits or the spirits in the background.

Robert Farrar Capon stated his case with eloquent and zany humour in a Christmas article called 'Fruitcakes: Solid Evidence of Christmas', written some years ago for *The New York Times*. He begins with the question 'Whatever happened to the cake in these concoctions?' and proceeds with the following possible explanation as to its disappearance:

'Since the public would be unwilling to purchase fruitcakes of a size large enough to contain all of these ingredients [the usual assortment of dried fruits and nuts] – and since making them smaller [the fruitcakes] would raise the probability that a given fruit or nut might not find its way into a given cake – the purveyors of fruitcakes found themselves forced to choose between the two basic components of their product. The cake, of course, lost, giving rise to the now omnipresent and unavoidable holiday gift: the fruit brick. In recent studies by the physics departments of major universities, the atomic weight of this remarkable confection has been calculated to be just below that of uranium.

'This extreme density, it was discovered, is due to the method by which modern fruitcakes are made. After the manufacturers abandoned the use of agglutinating agents such as flour and eggs, they developed a special bonding technique by which the fruits and nuts were compacted by a hydraulic press. This special piece of "bakery" equipment, seventy times more powerful than the ram that reduces used cars to crumpled blocks, creates in the "cake" an internal pressure so great that the fruits and nuts adhere to each other by their own molecular attraction.'

My fruited offering to posterity is an answer to Capon's opening question 'Whatever happened to the cake . . . ?' It's back. In fact, it is the sort of fruitcake that has more batter than fruit and is so moist it can almost be described as a pudding. Black treacle provides the slightly bitter edge to temper the sweetness of the glacéed fruit. The rum flavour comes through as aromatic but subdued. It took years to perfect this recipe because each version had to ripen for three months before tasting, and many months would pass between tasting and subsequent rebaking. A taste of this triumphant final fruitcake calls up images of dark Victorian houses filled with secret corners and haunting old memories.

The texture and flavour of this cake are at their best when baked in small tins, which also makes serving the small, rich portions easier. Decorative baking moulds such as the Turk's head provide attractive shapes for gift-giving.

As a special note I must add that my friend Blair Brown offered her six-month-old daughter, Julia, a taste of this cake and she wanted more. (We call her Julia child.) It was the first cake she'd ever eaten and, I would say, a dramatic initiation into the world of sweets!

INGREDIENTS	WEIGHT		MEASURE
room temperature	*grams*	*pounds/ounces*	*volume*
small mixed candied fruit	64 grams	2¼ ounces	½ cup
candied citron	35 grams	1¼ ounces	2 tablespoons
dried currants	35 grams	1¼ ounces	¼ cup
broken pecans	28 grams	1 ounce	¼ cup
dark rum	110 grams	3¾ ounces	4 fluid ounces
unsifted plain flour	65 grams	2¼ ounces	¼ cup + 2 tablespoons (dip and sweep method)
cinnamon	—	—	¼ teaspoon
bicarbonate of soda	—	—	⅛ teaspoon
salt	3.5 grams	—	¼ teaspoon
unsalted butter (must be softened)	113 grams	4 ounces	8 tablespoons
dark brown sugar	60 grams	2 ounces	¼ cup (firmly packed)
1 egg, size 2	50 grams (weighed without shell)	1¾ ounces	3 tablespoons
unsulphured black treacle	80 grams	2¾ ounces	2 fluid ounces
milk	30 grams	1 ounce	2 tablespoons

TINS: One 1-litre/1¾-pint/3½ to 4-cup baking mould or a 15 × 5-centimetre/6 × 2-inch cake tin, greased and floured. My favourite mould is a ¾-litre/1¼-pint/3-cup Turk's head (page 517). If using the Turk's head, fill it only three-quarters full and bake the remaining batter in small greased and floured muffin tins.

FINISHED HEIGHT: Baked in a ¾-litre/1¼-pint/3-cup Turk's head mould: 6 centimetres/2½ inches.

STORE: Keep at cool room temperature for 3 months without opening the container. This will allow the rum to mellow. If you plan to store it longer, unwrap the cake and sprinkle it with an additional tablespoon of rum or else the aromatic edge of the rum will dull and the cake will become dry. Repeat this procedure every 3 months. Fruitcakes have been known to keep for years. (I usually eat the little ones baked in the muffin tins as soon as they're baked – still warm from the oven!)

COMPLEMENTARY ADORNMENTS: If baked in a decorative mould, the cake is beautiful unadorned or with a simple wreath of holly. Baked in a plain cake tin, the cake can be covered with rolled fondant and decorated. The contrast of the pristine white fondant against the almost black colour of the fruitcake is breathtaking.

SERVE: Room temperature, cut into thin slivers with a serrated knife.

POINTERS FOR SUCCESS: See pages xx and 8.

Preheat the oven to 325°F/160°C/gas mark 3.

At least 24 hours ahead, mince the candied fruit and citron (a food processor sprayed lightly with non-stick vegetable spray works beautifully for this sticky task) and soak them with the currants and nuts in half the rum. Cover tightly and store at room temperature.

In a small bowl whisk the flour, cinnamon, bicarbonate of soda and salt to combine. In a large mixing bowl cream the butter and sugar until light and fluffy. Beat in the egg and then the flour mixture in three batches, alternating with the treacle and milk. Add the candied fruit mixture with the soaking rum and beat until blended. The batter will be slightly curdled because of the small amount of flour but this will not affect the cake's texture.

Scrape the batter into the prepared mould or tin and bake for 40 to 45 minutes or until the cake springs back when lightly touched and just begins to shrink from the sides of the tin and a tester comes out clean.

Let the cake cool in the tin for 10 minutes and then sprinkle with 2 tablespoons rum. Place a piece of clingfilm large enough to wrap the cake on the worktop. Moisten a piece of cheesecloth also large enough to wrap the cake with

1 tablespoon rum. Place the cheesecloth on the clingfilm, turn out the cake on to it, and sprinkle the top with the remaining 1 tablespoon rum. Drape the top and sides of the hot cake with the cheesecloth and clingfilm, pressing closely to the cake.

Let the cake cool to room temperature before covering tightly with heavy-duty foil. Place the cake in an airtight container such as a small tin or heavy-duty plastic container. If using a tin, run a piece of masking tape around the rim to create a better seal.

VARIATIONS

FRUIT CUPCAKES:

For some mystical reason, these little gems require no mellowing. They are delicious warm from the oven and remain moist for up to 6 weeks! Fill 8 greased and floured muffin tins three-quarters full and bake for 20 minutes or until a cake tester inserted in the centre comes out clean. Sprinkle each with 1 teaspoon rum, turn them out of the tins after 5 minutes and store airtight at room temperature. For a more decorative shape, use a Bundt-style muffin tin (see page 517 and Maid of Scandinavia, page 531). The batter makes 11 little cakes.

DUNDEE CAKE:

Halfway through baking, scatter blanched split almonds over the top of the cake.

For those who prefer a sweeter cake without the bitter edge: Replace 2 tablespoons of the black treacle with Lyle's golden syrup. The cake will not be such a dark brown.

Cordon Rose Banana Cake

Serves 8

This moist, light, exquisitely tender cake with the rich taste of banana is accented by the lively tang of sour cream and lemon. The 2-inch/ 5-centimetre layer is perfect as a European-style torte. Uniced, it makes a great picnic cake. Because chocolate and banana are such a perfect combination, Sour Cream Ganache (page 318) is sublime with this cake. For a more subtle combination, pick up the lemon accent instead and ice with Lemon Buttercream (page 270 or 284).

TINS: One 23 × 5-centimetre/ 9 × 2-inch cake tin or 23-centimetre 9-inch springform tin, greased, bottom lined with parchment or greaseproof paper, and then greased again and floured.

FINISHED HEIGHT: 5 centimetres/ 2 inches to within 2.5 centimetres/ 1 inch of the side; 4 centimetres/ 1½ inches at the side.

STORE: Airtight: 2 days room temperature, 5 days refrigerated, 2 months frozen.

COMPLEMENTARY ADORNMENTS: A simple dusting of icing sugar. *One recipe:* Sour Cream Ganache (page 318). *A half recipe:* Lemon Buttercream (page 270 or 284) or Passion Buttercream (page 271) and chopped macadamia nuts.

SERVE: Room temperature.

POINTERS FOR SUCCESS: See pages xx and 8.

Preheat the oven to 350°F/180°C/gas mark 4.

In a food processor process the banana and sour cream until smooth. Add the eggs, lemon zest and vanilla and process briefly just to blend.

In a large mixing bowl combine the dry ingredients and mix on low speed for 30 seconds to blend. Add the butter and half the banana mixture. Mix on low speed until the dry ingredients are moistened. Increase to medium speed (high speed if using a hand mixer) and beat for 1½ minutes to aerate and strengthen the cake's structure. Scrape down the sides. Gradually add the remaining banana mixture in two batches, beating for 20 seconds after each addition to incorporate the ingredients and develop the structure. Scrape down the sides.

Scrape the batter into the prepared tin and smooth the surface with a spatula. Bake for 30 to 40 minutes or until a wire cake tester inserted in the centre comes out clean and the cake springs back when pressed lightly in the centre. *The cake should start to shrink from the sides of the tin only after removal from the oven.*

Let the cake cool in the tin on a rack for 10 minutes. Loosen the sides with a small metal spatula and turn out the cake or remove the sides of the springform tin. Allow the cake to cool completely before wrapping airtight.

UNDERSTANDING

This banana cake is based on a basic sponge or butter cake (page 536). Banana, which is about 75

INGREDIENTS	WEIGHT		MEASURE
room temperature	*grams*	*pounds/ounces*	*volume*
2 large ripe bananas	227 grams	8 ounces	1 cup
sour cream	30 grams	1 ounce	2 tablespoons
2 eggs, size 2	100 grams	3.5 ounces (weighed without shells)	3 fluid ounces
grated lemon zest	4 grams	—	2 teaspoons
pure vanilla extract	6 grams	—	1½ teaspoons
sifted self-raising sponge flour	200 grams	7 ounces	2¼ cups
castor sugar	170 grams	6 ounces	¾ cup + 2 tablespoons
bicarbonate of soda	2.5 grams	—	½ teaspoon
salt	3.5 grams	—	½ teaspoon
unsalted butter (must be softened)	142 grams	5 ounces	10 tablespoons

per cent water, supplies the liquid. Because it also adds sweetness, the sugar is reduced by 15 per cent. The reduction of sugar and the addition of fibre from the banana toughen the cake so an extra ounce of butter is added to compensate for this. Bicarbonate of soda is used to temper the acidity of the banana and the sour cream. The fibre makes it possible to add extra sour cream without weakening the structure.

Pumpkin–Walnut Ring

Serves 6 to 8

This firm, moist cake, fragrant with spices, is perfect for holiday entertaining. Easy to prepare, it freezes beautifully and the flavour and texture actually benefit from preparation a day or two ahead. The subtlety of walnut oil echoes and complements the walnuts in the cake; pumpkin adds the illusion of richness. Actually, it is hard to believe that this delicious cake has low cholesterol (64.5 mg per serving). To make it cholesterol-free, substitute 3 large egg whites (3 fluid ounces) for the 2 whole eggs.

TINS: One 6–cup (1½ litre) baby Bundt tin (page 517), fluted tube tin or loaf tin, greased and floured.

FINISHED HEIGHT: Baked in a 6-cup (1½ litre) Bundt: 7.5 centimetres/3 inches high in the middle.

STORE: When completely cool, wrap well in clingfilm and foil and store at room temperature overnight. Keeps 5 days refrigerated or 3 months frozen. Flavours blend best when prepared 1 day ahead.

COMPLEMENTARY ADORNMENTS: *One recipe:* Chocolate Walnut Drizzle Glaze (page 289). Clotted cream.

SERVE: Room temperature.

POINTERS FOR SUCCESS: See pages xx and 8. Do not double this recipe to bake in a larger tin as the side crust gets too brown.

Preheat the oven to 350°F/180°C/gas mark 4.

In a small bowl combine the flour, bicarbonate of soda, spices and walnuts and whisk to blend.

In a large mixing bowl, beat the eggs, sugar and oils for 2 to 3 minutes or until very smooth. Add the pumpkin and beat just until smooth. Add the flour mixture and beat until completely moistened.

Scrape the batter into the prepared tin and bake for 30 to 35 minutes or until a cake tester inserted in the thickest part of the cake comes out clean. Cool in the tin on a rack for 10 minutes and then turn out the cake on to the rack.

INGREDIENTS	WEIGHT		MEASURE
room temperature	*grams*	*pounds/ounces*	*volume*
sifted plain flour	125 grams	4½ ounces	1 cup
bicarbonate of soda	5 grams	—	1 teaspoon
cinnamon	—	—	1 teaspoon
nutmeg	—	—	½ teaspoon
ground cloves	—	—	¼ teaspoon
salt	—	—	¼ teaspoon
coarsely chopped toasted walnuts	57 grams	2 ounces	½ cup
2 eggs, size 2	100 grams (weighed without shells)	3½ ounces	3 fluid ounces
light brown sugar	163 grams	5¾ ounces	¾ cup (firmly packed)
safflower oil	80 grams	2¾ ounces	3 fluid ounces
walnut oil	28 grams	1 ounce	2 tablespoons
fresh *or* tinned unsweetened pumpkin purée	238 grams	8¼ ounces	1 cup

UNDERSTANDING
Compared to a butter cake, the addition of nuts and the fibre from the pumpkin are compensated for by using less flour. Oil replaces the butter (a little less is used because oil is 100 per cent fat, whereas butter is only 81 per cent fat). The liquid is provided by the pumpkin, which is 90 per cent water. Bicarbonate of soda is used to temper the acidity of the pumpkin and the molasses in the brown sugar, and 60 grams/2 ounces/ ¼ cup extra sugar is added to balance the pumpkin and spice flavours.

Courgette Cupcakes

Makes 14 to 16 cupcakes

These cupcakes are miniature versions of courgette bread, which, to my mind, has always seemed more like a cake than a bread. Perhaps it was dubbed 'bread' because it is traditionally baked in a loaf tin. The cupcakes are less sweet than most cakes in this book and far less sweet than commercial muffins.

These healthy, easy-to-make gems are delicious treats to pack in lunch boxes or to serve for breakfast. The optional raisins make the cupcakes even moister and more nutritious. To make them cholesterol free, substitute 3 large egg whites (3 fluid ounces) for the 2 whole eggs.

Although courgette 'breads' are usually made with white sugar, I prefer the richer colour and flavour of brown sugar.

TINS: Greased and floured muffin tins.

STORE: Airtight: 3 days room temperature, 5 days refrigerated, or 3 months frozen. The flavour is even more delicious the day after baking.

SERVE: Room temperature.

POINTERS FOR SUCCESS: See pages xx and 8. Use a food processor with the shredding disc or the largest holes on a hand grater to grate the courgettes. To promote even baking, add a few tablespoons of water to any unfilled muffin tins.

Preheat the oven to 350°F/180°C/gas mark 4.

In a small bowl combine the flour, bicarbonate of soda, spices and walnuts and whisk to blend.

In a mixing bowl beat the eggs, sugar and oil for 2 to 3 minutes or until very smooth. Add the courgettes and beat just until smooth. Add the dry ingredients and optional raisins and beat until completely moistened.

Scrape the batter into the prepared muffin tins, filling each cup three-quarters full, and bake for 20 to 25 minutes or until a cake tester inserted in the centre comes out clean. Cool in the tin on a rack for 5 minutes. Turn out on to the rack. Cool and wrap airtight.

UNDERSTANDING

This formula is almost identical to Pumpkin–Walnut cake. Since pumpkin supplies a little more

INGREDIENTS	WEIGHT		MEASURE
room temperature	*grams*	*pounds/ounces*	*volume*
sifted plain flour	220 grams	7¾ ounces	1¾ cups
bicarbonate of soda	6.25 grams	—	1¼ teaspoons
cinnamon	—	—	1 teaspoon
ground ginger	—	—	½ teaspoon
ground cloves	—	—	¼ teaspoon
salt	—	—	¼ teaspoon
coarsely chopped toasted walnuts (page 373)	75 grams	2½ ounces	⅔ cup
2 eggs, size 2	100 grams (weighed without shells)	3½ ounces	3 fluid ounces
light brown sugar	163 grams	5¾ ounces	¾ cup (firmly packed)
safflower oil	107 grams	3¾ ounces	½ cup
grated courgettes	227 grams	8 ounces	2 cups (firmly packed)
optional: raisins	72 grams	2½ ounces	½ cup

structure than courgettes, extra flour is added to compensate.

If using all whites instead of whole eggs, the cakes will be slightly more chewy.

Note: If you prefer a paler version with a more delicate flavour, replace the brown sugar with 150 grams/5¼ ounces/¾ cup castor sugar, reduce the bicarbonate of soda to ½ teaspoon, and add ½ teaspoon baking powder.

Golden Wheat Carrot Ring

Serves 10 to 12

This cake, inspired by Jean Hewitt's Carrot Cake,* is moist without being heavy. It is wheat coloured with flecks of golden carrot throughout, and has a fresh, wheaty, delicious flavour with the sweet perfume of honey coming through only as a wonderful lingering aftertaste. Of course, it is lovely with White Chocolate Cream Cheese Buttercream, but I'd just as soon eat this cake *au naturel*. I'm sure it is an illusion, but eating this cake makes me feel pure and healthy!

TINS: One 6–cup (1½–litre) savarin ring mould, well-buttered. (No flour necessary. The butter gives a lovely flavour to the outside of the cake.)

FINISHED HEIGHT:
5.5 centimetres/2¼ inches.

STORE: When completely cool, wrap well in clingfilm and foil and store at room temperature overnight. Keeps 5 days refrigerated or 3 months frozen.

COMPLEMENTARY
ADORNMENTS: A light dusting of icing sugar and cinnamon. *One recipe:* White Chocolate Cream Cheese Buttercream (page 274).

SERVE: Room temperature.

POINTERS FOR SUCCESS: See pages xx and 8.

Preheat the oven to 350°F/180°C/gas mark 4.

In a small bowl combine the carrots and lemon juice.

In a large mixing bowl combine the dry ingredients and mix for 30 seconds to blend. Add the eggs, butter, honey and the carrot mixture. Mix on low speed until the dry ingredients are moistened. Increase to medium speed (high speed if using a hand mixer) and beat for 30 seconds or until well mixed.

Scrape the batter into the prepared mould and bake for 30 minutes or until the cake springs back when lightly pressed in the centre and a tester comes out clean.

*Jean Hewitt, *The New York Times Natural Foods Cookbook* (NewYork: Quadrangle Books, 1971).

INGREDIENTS	WEIGHT		MEASURE
room temperature	*grams*	*pounds/ounces*	*volume*
finely shredded carrots	200 grams	7 ounces	2 cups
lemon juice, freshly squeezed	62 grams	2 ounces	2 fluid ounces
sifted wholewheat flour	125 grams	4½ ounces	1 cup
sifted plain flour	100 grams	3½ ounces	1 cup + 2 tablespoons
salt	3.5 grams	—	½ teaspoon
bicarbonate of soda	3.75 grams	—	¾ teaspoon
cinnamon	—	—	1 teaspoon
2 eggs, size 2	100 grams (weighed without shells)	3½ ounces	3 fluid ounces
unsalted butter, melted	142 grams	5 ounces	10 tablespoons
honey	250 grams	8¾ ounces	6 fluid ounces

Let the cake cool for 10 minutes in the tin on a rack. Turn it out on to a lightly greased rack and cool completely.

UNDERSTANDING

Compared to basic sponge or butter cake (page 536), the 250 grams/8¾ ounces/¾ cup of honey replaces the sweetness of 200 grams/7 ounces/1 cup of sugar, and the carrots, which are 88 per cent water, provide the liquid. To compensate for the extra water provided by the honey and carrots, 25 grams/1 ounce/¼ cup flour has been added. Because more flour and water tend to toughen and strengthen a cake's structure, an extra 28 grams/1 ounce/2 tablespoons of butter and extra raising agent have been added. To temper the acidity of the honey and lemon juice, part of the raising agent is bicarbonate of soda. The butter is melted to increase its tenderising capability. The extra raising also helps to lighten the texture.

Gingerbread

Serves 10 to 12

Kyle Cathie, my clever and discerning British editor, informed me in no uncertain terms that this book would be incomplete without beloved gingerbread. Now that I have tasted it, I quite agree. It is a moist, spicy cake with an intriguing blend of flavours. I can't believe I lived so long without it!

TIN: One 20 × 4-centimetre/ 8 × 1½-inch square cake tin, greased, bottom lined with parchment or greaseproof paper, then greased and floured.

FINISHED HEIGHT: About 5 centimetres/2 inches.

STORE: Airtight: 24 hours before eating, 2 days room temperature, 5 days refrigerated, 2 months frozen. Flavours mature if allowed to sit for at least 24 hours after baking.

Preheat oven to 325°F/160°C/gas mark 3.

In a small, heavy saucepan, on medium low heat, stir together the butter, golden syrup, sugar and marmalade until melted and uniform. Set aside until just barely warm, then whisk in the eggs and milk. In a large bowl, whisk together all the remaining dry ingredients. Add the liquid mixture to the dry ingredients, stirring with a large spoon or rubber spatula just until batter is smooth.

Pour the batter into the prepared tin. Bake for 50–60 minutes or until a tester inserted near the centre comes out clean and the cake springs back when pressed lightly in the centre. *The cake should start to shrink from the sides of the pan only after removal from the oven.*

Let the cake cool in the tin on a rack for 10 minutes. Loosen the sides with a small metal spatula and invert on a greased wire rack. To prevent splitting, reinvert so that the top is up. For extra moistness, cover the cake with clingfilm while still hot. For extra moistness and lilting edge, brush the cake with syrup. *To make syrup:* In a small pan, stir together 2 tablespoons lemon juice, 2 tablespoons (28 grams/1 ounce) softened, unsalted butter and 3 tablespoons sugar. Heat, stirring, until the butter is melted and the sugar dissolved.

INGREDIENTS	WEIGHT		MEASURE
room temperature	*grams*	*pounds/ounces*	*volume*
unsalted butter	115 grams	4 ounces	½ cup
golden syrup	230 grams	8 ounces	10 fluid ounces
dark brown sugar	60 grams	2 ounces	—
marmalade	40 grams	1½ ounces	1 heaped tablespoon
2 eggs, size 2	100 grams (weighed without shells)	3½ ounces	3 fluid ounces
milk	150 grams	5¼ ounces	5 fluid ounces
self-raising sponge flour	115 grams	4 ounces	1 cup (lightly spooned)
sifted wholemeal flour	115 grams	4 ounces	1 cup − 1 tablespoon
salt	—	—	a pinch
powdered ginger	—	—	1 teaspoon
cinnamon	—	—	1 teaspoon
bicarbonate of soda	—	—	½ teaspoon

When the cake is baked, brush half the syrup on to the top. Cool the cake for 10 minutes and invert it on to a lightly greased rack. Brush the bottom with the remaining syrup. Reinvert on to a rack, top side up, to finish cooling. Cover with a piece of clingfilm directly after brushing with syrup to retain the moisture.

La Brioche Cake

Serves 14 to 16 (iced)

A fine bread such as brioche makes a glorious base for a cake. It offers a satiny-soft, resilient texture, yeasty flavour, and the advantage of very little sugar (only enough to feed the yeast). This means that the cake can be refreshingly saturated with syrup without becoming cloyingly sweet.

My favourite buttercream for this cake is Praline Silk Meringue Buttercream or Crème Ivoire Praliné. Both blend beautifully with the faint edge of treacle and burnt sugar in the dark rum syrup.

Although this brioche takes two days to make, the total working time only adds up to about 15 minutes!

TINS: One 20 × 5-centimetre/ 8 × 2-inch cake tin or 20-centimetre/8-inch springform tin, buttered.

FINISHED HEIGHT: 4 centimetres/ 1½ inches.

STORE: Syrup: 1 month refrigerated in an airtight container. *Brioche:* Wrapped airtight, 2 days room temperature and 3 months frozen. It is best not to refrigerate brioche as it hardens.

COMPLEMENTARY ADORNMENTS: *Half recipe:* Praline Silk Meringue Buttercream (page 279) or *one recipe* Crème Ivoire Praliné (page 289) and toasted chopped hazelnuts (page 495).

SERVE: Room temperature or lightly chilled.

POINTERS FOR SUCCESS: Use bread flour. *Do not* use easy-blend yeast. Be sure the yeast is active. Do not allow rising dough to be in an area over 80° to 85°F/27° to 30°C. Do not allow the dough to rise more than the recommended amounts or it will weaken the structure. Do not deflate the dough before chilling or the butter will leak out. If this should happen inadvertently, chill the dough for 1 hour and knead the butter back into the dough.

DAY BEFORE MAKE THE SPONGE

When using yeast always begin by proving it to make sure it is alive. If using fresh yeast, smell it to be sure it doesn't have a sour odour. To prove the yeast, use warm water (hot water would kill it). In a small bowl combine the water (ideally a tepid 100°F/38°C if using fresh yeast; a little warmer,

INGREDIENTS	WEIGHT		MEASURE
room temperature	*grams*	*pounds/ounces*	*volume*
water	37 grams	1¼ ounces	2½ tablespoons
sugar	25 grams	1 ounce	2 tablespoons
fresh yeast*/or	14 grams	½ ounce	2 packed teaspoons
dried yeast (*not* easy-blend)	4.5 grams	–	1½ teaspoons
unsifted strong white flour	227 grams	8 ounces	about 1⅔ cups (dip and sweep method)
1 egg, size 2 2 eggs, size 2, cold	170 grams (weighed in the shells)	6 ounces	–
salt	3.5 grams	–	½ teaspoon
unsalted butter	142 grams†	5 ounces†	10 tablespoons
syrup:	510 grams	18 ounces	1¾ cups
castor sugar	150 grams	5¼ ounces	¾ cup
water	295 grams	10½ ounces	10 fluid ounces
dark rum	82 grams	3 ounces	6 tablespoons

* Fresh yeast causes dough to rise faster.
† 113 to 170 grams/4 to 6 ounces/8 to 12 tablespoons of butter may be used. The lesser amount offers a lighter texture, the higher amount a richer flavour. (Brioche Mousseline is made with equal weight of butter and flour, but it must be prepared by hand. Madeleine Kamman tells me that in France the dough for this brioche is mixed using only the fingertips so as not to develop much gluten. This keeps the butter from oozing out during baking.)

110°F/43°C, if using dry), ½ teaspoon sugar, and the yeast. If using fresh yeast, crumble it slightly while adding. Set aside in a draught-free spot for 10 to 20 minutes. By this time, the mixture should be full of bubbles. If not, the yeast is too old to be useful.

Place 50 grams/1¾ ounces/⅓ cup of the flour and 1 egg in a food processor (preferably with the dough blade) and process for a few seconds until mixed. Add the yeast mixture and stir with a rubber scraper until smooth. Sprinkle the remaining flour over the mixture but do not mix it in. Cover and let it stand for 1½ to 2 hours.

KNEADING THE DOUGH
Add the remaining sugar, the salt and remaining 2 cold eggs and process for 1½ minutes or until the dough is smooth, shiny and cleans the bowl. Let it rest for 5 minutes with the feed tube open. Add the butter in two batches and process for 20 seconds after each addition or until incorporated. (The butter must be soft so as not to overtax the motor of the processor. If the processor should stall, let it rest for 5 minutes.)★

FIRST RISE
Scrape the dough into a lightly buttered bowl. It will be very soft and elastic. Sprinkle lightly with flour to prevent a crust from forming. Cover the bowl tightly with clingfilm and let rise in a warm place (80°F/27°C but not above or the yeast will develop a sour taste) until double in bulk, about 2 hours. Refrigerate for at least 30 minutes to 1 hour. Deflate the dough by gently stirring it and refrigerate for another hour.

REDISTRIBUTING THE YEAST
Turn the dough on to a lightly floured surface and gently press it into a rectangle. Fold the dough into thirds (as in folding a business letter) and again press it out into a rectangle, lightly flouring the surface as needed to prevent stickiness. Fold it again into thirds and dust it lightly with flour on all sides. Wrap it loosely but securely in clingfilm and then foil and refrigerate it for 6 hours or up to 2 days to allow the dough to ripen and harden.

Gently deflate the dough by kneading lightly with floured hands, and press it into the prepared tin.

Cover the dough loosely with buttered clingfilm and let it rise in a warm, preferably humid, area away from draughts for 1½ to 3 hours or until it has almost tripled in bulk. It will reach the top of a 5-centimetre/2-inch-high cake tin.

Place a baking sheet in the oven and preheat to 425°F/220°C/gas mark 7. (The hot baking sheet will boost the 'oven spring' – the sudden expansion of the dough during the first few minutes of baking.)

Place the cake tin on the hot baking sheet and bake for 5 minutes. Lower the temperature to 375°F/190°C/gas mark 5 and bake for 20 minutes or until a skewer comes out clean. Turn out the brioche and cool on a rack. When

★To prepare brioche dough in a heavy-duty mixer such as the KitchenAid, use the flat beater and, when the dough starts to climb up the beater, change to the dough hook. Beat for about 5 minutes on medium speed or until the dough is smooth, shiny, very elastic and begins to clean the bowl. Beat in the butter by the tablespoon until incorporated.

ready to complete the cake, trim the top, bottom and sides with a serrated knife so that the brioche measures 18 × 4 to 4.5 centimetres/ 7 × 1½ to 1¾ inches (about 450 grams/1 pound in weight).

Place in a 23-centimetre/9-inch tin and pour the syrup on top. Let stand for 10 minutes or until the syrup is absorbed, turning the cake over to help absorption.

TO MAKE SYRUP
In a small saucepan with a tight-fitting lid combine the sugar and water and bring to a rolling boil, stirring constantly. Cover immediately, remove from the heat and cool completely. Transfer to a liquid measuring jug and stir in the rum. If the syrup has evaporated slightly, add enough water to equal 510 grams/18 ounces/1¾ cups syrup.

UNDERSTANDING
Unlike a cake, which is primarily a starch structure, bread depends on protein in the form of gluten to create its framework. The higher the protein content of the flour, the stronger the structure will be and the finer the grain of the bread (directly the opposite of cake). This dough is exceptionally wet. Just enough extra flour is added to handle it for shaping, resulting in a very light, soft brioche.

I do not use easy-blend yeast because the flavour development and texture are superior with slower rising. During extended periods of rising, the yeast produces a desirable acidic quality, and it is for this reason that dough is refrigerated overnight before baking. A brilliant technique, discovered by Shirley Corriher, to simulate this acidity when time does not allow to let the dough rest overnight is to add ½ teaspoon cider vinegar or mild-flavoured fruit vinegar for every 212 grams/ 7.5 ounces/1½ cups of flour. Add it to the flour and salt before blending. Do not add any more vinegar or it will weaken the gluten.

Paula Wolfert (in her superb articles on brioche in *The Pleasures of Cooking*, which greatly influenced the development of this recipe) recommends melting and browning one-fifth (2 tablespoons) of the butter for extra-rich flavour. Be sure to let the butter cool before adding it along with the rest of the butter. I add the browned particles as well.

Paula's sponge method and technique for redistributing the yeast result in the lightest, finest-grained brioche possible. The dough actually surges upwards, practically leaping from the tin, when baked!

Brioche made in a food processor is a speedy and simple operation. If you wish to double this recipe, it is safer to use the heavy-duty mixer method because a larger amount of dough might overheat some food processors, causing them to stall. (I have successfully made a double batch in a heavy-duty mixer by melting the butter and allowing it to cool to barely tepid before adding it with the motor running.)

This cake is used to make Praline Brioche (page 195).

VARIATION

STRAWBERRY SAVARIN:

A Savarin is actually a brioche dough baked in the shape of a ring. Use a well-buttered 6-cup (1½-litre) ring mould. Baking time is the same as for brioche baked in a cake tin. For the syrup, replace the dark rum with 2 tablespoons of freshly squeezed lemon juice, 56 grams/2 ounces/¼ cup kirsch and 1 tablespoon finely grated lemon zest.

For an attractive and delicious accompaniment, fill the centre of the ring with 2–3 punnets of strawberries, washed and hulled, and brush savarin and berries with 75 grams/2½ ounces/¼ cup redcurrant jelly, heated and strained. Garnish with rosettes of lightly sweetened Perfect Whipped Cream (page 294) and Crystallised Violets (page 375).

Custard Cakes

The two basic cakes in this section, Cheesecake and Chocolate Mousse or Truffle Cake, contain no flour, rise little, and are cooked in water baths to keep them creamy. They are actually custard fillings in the shape of cakes – rich, delicious and lush in texture.

These cakes are probably the two most beloved and timeless of American cakes, so I have included all my favourite permutations. A bonus: these cakes are quick and easy to make.

Note: Recipes can be doubled if you have extra tins. Dental floss, held taut, works beautifully to cut a custard cake. Pull it out sideways after each cut.

CHEESECAKES

I am passionate on the subject of cheesecake. While many ethnic groups have versions of cheesecake, my favourite is my own culture's claim to fame: New York Jewish. It is one of the things displaced New Yorkers seem to miss most. (Why else would menus as far away as California boast 'New York Cheesecake'?) It is a thoroughly creamy cheesecake, smooth and dense yet easy to eat because of the refreshing tartness of lemon and sour cream.

Cheesecake could really be classified more as a custard than as a cake. When this realisation first hit me I decided to treat cheesecake as a custard and bake it in a water bath. To my delight, the result was perfectly creamy from stem to stern (without the usual dry outer edge).

It has been reported to me that this cheesecake converts people who think they don't like cheesecake and that it spoils those who are already devotees. A friend told me that after making this cake for every major family event during the past three years, one of her nephews turned down the cheesecake at a renowned restaurant stating: 'I don't eat cheesecake out!' This same friend, Shirley Corriher, once featured this cake on her local radio programme. The station informed her several weeks later that the programme brought in more letters requesting the recipe than did any other in the history of the station. The gem of the collection was from the Atlanta Federal Penitentiary which read (and you have to supply the southern drawl): 'We simply must have the recipe for that Cordon Rose Cheesecake!'

Cordon Rose Cream Cheesecake

Serves 8 to 12

TINS: One 20 × 6-centimetre/
8 × 2½-inch or higher springform
tin, greased and bottom lined with
greased parchment or greaseproof
paper; outside of the tin wrapped
with a double layer of heavy-duty
foil to prevent seepage.
One 25.5-centimetre/10-inch cake
tin or roasting tin to serve as a
water bath.

FINISHED HEIGHT: 6 centimetres/
2½ inches.

STORE: 1 week refrigerated. Do
not freeze because the texture will
become less smooth.

COMPLEMENTARY
ADORNMENTS: 225 grams/
7¾ ounces/¾ cup Lemon Curd
(page 389). *One recipe:* White
Chocolate Cream Cheese
Buttercream (page 274). Cherry
Topping (page 393 or 395).
Blueberry Topping (page 399 or
400). Cran-Raspberry Glaze (page
379).

POINTERS FOR SUCCESS:
Wrapping the tin with foil keeps it
watertight. Grease the sides of the
tin so the surface will not crack
when the cake starts to shrink on
cooling. Chill thoroughly before
unmoulding.
The water bath tin must not be
higher than the springform tin or it
will slow down baking.

Preheat the oven to
350°F/180°C/gas mark 4.
In a large mixing bowl beat the
cream cheese and sugar until very
smooth (about 3 minutes),
preferably with a whisk beater.
Beat in the cornflour if desired.
Add the eggs, one at a time,
beating after each addition until
smooth and scraping down the
sides. Add the lemon juice, vanilla
and salt and beat until
incorporated. Beat in the sour
cream just until blended.
Pour the batter into the prepared
tin. Set the tin in the larger tin and
surround it with 2.5 centimetres/
1 inch of very hot water. Bake for
45 minutes. Turn off the oven
without opening the door and let

INGREDIENTS	WEIGHT		MEASURE
room temperature	*grams*	*pounds/ounces*	*volume*
cream cheese*	454 grams	1 pound	2 (227-gram/ 8-ounce) packets
castor sugar	200 grams	7 ounces	1 cup
optional: cornflour†	8 grams	—	1 tablespoon
3 eggs, size 2	150 grams (weighed without shells)	5¼ ounces	scant 5 fluid ounces
freshly squeezed lemon juice	47 grams	1½ ounces	3 tablespoons
pure vanilla extract	6 grams	—	1½ teaspoons
salt	—	—	¼ teaspoon
sour cream	726 grams	1 pound 9½ ounces	3 cups

* Don't be tempted to use the more expensive 'natural' cream cheese. Philadelphia brand, available even in Japan, offers the best and most consistent flavour for this cake.
† If cornflour is omitted, a small amount of liquid will seep out after turning out the cake. If the cake has a sponge base, this is no problem. Otherwise, liquid can be absorbed with a paper towel, I prefer not using the cornflour as the cake is a shade more creamy. Also, it makes it suitable to serve as a Passover dessert.

the cake cool for 1 hour. Remove to a rack and cool to room temperature (about 1 hour). Cover with clingfilm and refrigerate overnight.

To turn out the cake: Have ready a serving plate and a flat plate at least 20 centimetres/8 inches in diameter, covered with clingfilm. Place the tin on a heated burner and move it around for 15 seconds. Wipe the sides of the tin with a hot, damp tea-towel.

Run a thin metal spatula around the sides of the cake and release the sides of the springform tin. Place the clingfilm-wrapped plate on top and invert. Remove the bottom of the tin and the parchment. Reinvert on to the serving plate and use a small metal spatula to smooth the sides. Refrigerate until shortly before serving.

Notes: A 20 × 7.5-centimetre/ 8 × 3-inch solid cake tin can be used instead of a springform. To turn out the cake, run a thin spatula around the sides, place the tin on a heated burner for 10 to 20 seconds, moving the tin back and forth, and then invert. If the cake does not release, return to the hot burner for a few more seconds.

For a richer, denser cheesecake that completely holds its moisture without cornflour, replace the 3 whole eggs with 6 egg yolks.

PROCESSOR METHOD
A food processor also works well to mix this batter. Process the cream cheese and sugar for 30 seconds or until smooth. Add the cornflour if desired and pulse to blend. Add the eggs, one at a time, with the motor running. Add the lemon juice, vanilla, salt and sour cream and pulse to combine.

BOTTOMS FOR CHEESECAKE

AU NATUREL:

This cheesecake is firm enough to be turned out and served without a base if desired.

BISCUIT ROULADE:

A very elegant presentation is to 'sandwich' the cheesecake between soft layers of whisked sponge cake. Almond Biscuit blends particularly well with the lemon and cheese flavours. Bake Almond Biscuit (page 160) and cut it into two 20-centimetre/8-inch rounds. Use one round to line the bottom of the parchment-lined springform tin before pouring in the batter. After baking the cheesecake, top it with the second round. Chill and turn out as usual. Sprinkle with icing

sugar if desired. Cake scraps can be cut into shapes to decorate the sides.

BISCUIT À LA CUILLÈRE:

Homemade or packaged sponge fingers can be used to line the bottom and sides of the cake tin. Use a 23 × 7.5-centimetre/ 9 × 3-inch tin and butter to grease the sides of the tin; this holds the sponge fingers in position. After baking for 25 minutes, cover the top of the cheesecake loosely with foil to prevent overbrowning. Before turning out, wipe the outside of the tin with a hot, wet tea-towel.

BISCUIT-CRUMB CRUST:

Chocolate biscuits blend well with cherry topping. Ginger, graham and lemon-nut cookies go well with fruit-flavoured fillings or toppings. As crumb crusts become soggy if placed in the tin before baking, I prefer to pat the crumbs on to the cake after baking and turning out. You will need about 75 grams/1¾ ounces/¾ cup if you wish to do the bottom as well as the sides. Use the same technique as for applying chopped nuts (page 373).

FILLINGS AND RECIPE VARIATIONS
There are so many possible ways to flavour a cheesecake that entire books have been devoted to the

subject. Herewith are some of my personal favourites.

WHITE CHOCOLATE CHEESECAKE:

Fine-quality white chocolate, such as Tobler Narcisse (which contains cocoa butter), adds a luscious flavour to the cream-cheese base. The cake is mildly reminiscent of white chocolate and slightly tangy. It is not cloyingly sweet because the amount of sugar contained in the white chocolate is removed from the amount of sugar in the batter. The texture of this cake is slightly firmer because of the cocoa butter but is still creamy with a special melt-in-the-mouth quality.

To make White Chocolate Cheesecake: Reduce the sugar to 50 grams/1¾ ounces/¼ cup and the lemon juice to 2 tablespoons. Melt 255 grams/9 ounces white chocolate and cool. Blend into the batter after the sour cream is incorporated.

BANANA CHEESECAKE:

Anyone who has ever eaten bananas and sour cream and loved it will know before even tasting this cake just how mellow and delicious it's going to be. The bananas seem to have some preserving quality as well because this cake stays fresh tasting for at least 12 days! Bananas and sour cream have about the same moisture content so all you do is replace one-third of the sour cream with mashed banana (see below). Blueberry Topping (page 399 or 400) is a perfect complement.

To make Banana Cheesecake: Replace 242 grams/8½ ounces/1 cup sour cream with 227 grams/8 ounces/1 cup mashed banana. (You will need two very ripe bananas.) To keep the banana from discolouring, stir the 3 tablespoons of lemon juice into the mashed banana. Blend into the batter after the sour cream is incorporated.

FRUIT SWIRL CHEESECAKE:

Tart, assertive fruit purées such as apricot, raspberry and strawberry are splendid additions to a cheesecake base.

To make Fruit Swirl Cheesecake: Add 5 fluid ounces/260 grams/9¼ ounces lightly sweetened fruit purée (page 384, 385 or 386) in the following way: Pour one-third of the cheesecake batter into the prepared tin. Drizzle half the purée over it. Add another third of the batter and repeat with the remaining purée. Top with the remaining batter. Using a small spatula or knife, cut through the batter and swirl to marble the purée throughout the filling (including the top).

Tip: Do not use peach purée as it curdles the filling.

Note: If you like apricots, please try the apricot version. My assistant and collaborator, David Shamah, did not like cheesecake before he tried this cake. Now it is one of his favourite cakes in this book, and he insisted that I sing its praises. (I don't disagree!)

Chocolate Oblivion Truffle Torte

Serves 16

This cake is my favourite way to eat chocolate. It is easy to make and contains only three essential ingredients: the very best chocolate,* for a full, rich flavour and smooth, creamy texture; unsalted butter to soften the chocolate and release the flavour; and eggs to lighten it. The result is like the creamiest truffle wedded to the purest chocolate mousse. It is chocolate at its most intense flavour and perfect consistency. I prefer to serve this cake at room temperature because, when served chilled, the texture metamorphoses into dense fudge. But as my friend Susan Wyler says: 'Who on earth is going to complain about that?'

TINS: One 20-centimetre/8-inch springform tin at least 6 centimetres/2½ inches high, buttered and bottom lined with buttered parchment or greaseproof paper; outside of tin wrapped with a double layer of heavy-duty foil to prevent seepage.
One 25.5-centimetre/10-inch cake tin or roasting tin to serve as a water bath.

FINISHED HEIGHT: 4 centimetres/ 1½ inches.

STORE: 2 weeks refrigerated. Do not freeze because freezing changes the texture.

COMPLEMENTARY ADORNMENTS: A chocolate band or encasement of chocolate rose leaves (page 447 or 444) filled with Brandied Burgundy Cherries (page 397) or ruffles of whipped cream (either piped shortly before serving or stabilised, pages 295 to 296), served with Raspberry Sauce (page 386). Ice with: *One recipe:* White Chocolate Buttercream (page 284 or 287), White Ganache (page 320),

*Two of my favourites are Lindt Courante (page 485) and Tobler extra bittersweet. If using Courante chocolate, add ⅓ cup/66 grams/2¼ ounces sugar to the eggs while beating. If using the extra bittersweet, add 3 tablespoons/37 grams/1½ ounces sugar. Lindt and Tobler bittersweet are also excellent.

INGREDIENTS	WEIGHT		MEASURE
room temperature	*grams*	*pounds/ounces*	*volume*
bittersweet chocolate	454 grams	1 pound	5⅓ (3–ounce) bars
unsalted butter	227 grams	8 ounces	1 cup
6 large eggs	300 grams (weighed without shells)	10.5 ounces	1¼ scant liquid cups

or Chocolate Cream Glaze (page 314) or top with Jewel Glaze (page 378). Serve with whipped cream and Raspberry Sauce (page 386) or *crème anglaise* flavoured with any liqueur of your choice (pages 323 to 329).

SERVE: Room temperature. Cut into narrow wedges with a thin sharp knife that has been dipped in hot water.

POINTERS FOR SUCCESS: For a moist airy texture, be sure to add beaten eggs to chocolate mixture and not the chocolate to the eggs. Wrapping the tin with foil keeps it watertight. Chill thoroughly before turning out. Use the plastic-wrapped plate when turning out to protect the surface of cake if you're not planning to use a topping.

Preheat the oven to 425°F/220°C/gas mark 7.

In a large metal bowl set over a pan of hot, not simmering, water (the bottom of the bowl should not touch the water) combine the chocolate and butter and let stand, stirring occasionally, until smooth and melted. (The mixture can be melted in the microwave on high power, stirring every 15 seconds. Remove when there are still a few lumps of chocolate and stir until fully melted.)

In a large bowl set over a pan of simmering water heat the eggs, stirring constantly to prevent curdling, until just warm to the touch. Remove from the heat and beat, using the whisk beater, until tripled in volume and soft peaks form when the beater is raised, about 5 minutes. (To ensure maximum volume if using a hand mixer, beat the eggs over simmering water until they are hot to the touch, about 5 minutes. Remove from the heat and beat until cool.)

Using a large wire whisk or rubber spatula, fold half the eggs into the chocolate mixture until almost incorporated. Fold in the remaining eggs until just blended and no streaks remain. Finish by using a rubber spatula to ensure that the heavier mixture at the bottom is incorporated. Scrape into the prepared tin and smooth with the spatula. Set the tin in the larger tin and surround it with 2.5 centimetres/1 inch very hot water. Bake for 5 minutes. Cover loosely with a piece of buttered foil and bake for 10 minutes. (The cake will look soft, but this is as it should be.)

Let the cake cool on a rack for 45 minutes. Cover with clingfilm and refrigerate until very firm, about 3 hours.

TO TURN OUT
Have ready a serving plate and a flat plate at least 20 centimetres/ 8 inches in diameter, covered with clingfilm. Wipe the sides of the tin with a hot, damp towel.

Run a thin metal spatula around the sides of the cake and release the sides of the springform tin. Place the clingfilm-wrapped plate on top and invert. Wipe the bottom of the tin with a hot, damp towel. Remove the bottom of the tin and the parchment. Reinvert on to the serving plate.

Tip: If you have an oven with a pilot light, it can save you a lot of time. The night before baking, place the chocolate and butter in the oven along with the eggs *still in their shells* in another mixing bowl. (Eggs should weigh about 340 grams/12 ounces.) The next morning, the chocolate and butter

will be fully melted and the eggs the perfect temperature. Stir the chocolate and butter until smooth and be sure to remove it and the eggs from the oven before preheating oven!

Note: A 20 × 5-centimetre/ 8 × 2-inch solid cake tin can be used instead of a springform – or a 20 × 7.5 centimetre/8 × 3-inch tin if adding other ingredients from the variation section (page 89). Once in San Francisco I made this cake for my newly married brother and his wife using a straight-sided Calphalon saucepan because they had no cake tins. The handle worked well to turn out the cake! To turn it out, run a thin spatula around the sides, place the tin on a heated burner for 10 to 20 seconds, moving it back and forth, and then invert. If the cake does not release, return it to the hot burner for a few more seconds.

A triple recipe of this cake is used to make the Art Deco Cake (page 236).

UNDERSTANDING
Just as for cheesecake, baking the Oblivion in a water bath keeps the texture creamy throughout. When this cake is served at room temperature, you get a rush of chocolate from the moment it enters your mouth. The full flavour of chocolate can best be appreciated only in a softened state. (A chocolate bar, for example, has to

start melting in the mouth before the flavour comes through.) The butter and eggs do not distract. Instead they contribute structure and the desired creamy texture.

VARIATIONS

These variations are so special that over the years I have given each its own special name.

MINI-MOUSSE TORTE:

A darling size, just right for 6 to 8 servings.
To make Mini-Mousse Torte: Use half the recipe in a 15 × 5-centimetre/6 × 2-inch tin. Bake for the same amount of time.

CHOCOLATE INDULGENCE:

Smooth praline paste (page 497), commercially made with hazelnuts and 50 per cent sugar, stays in the background but does wonders to intensify the chocolate flavour. It is important to use a chocolate that is not too sweet as the praline paste adds about 78 grams/2¾ ounces of sugar.
To make Chocolate Indulgence: Use Lindt Courante or Tobler extra bittersweet chocolate. Add 156 grams/5½ ounces/½ cup praline paste to the chocolate before melting. (If using Courante, add 1 tablespoon sugar to the eggs while beating.)

CHOCOLATE DEPENDENCE:

Liqueur heightens the flavour of chocolate. Stir 2 tablespoons of your favourite into the melted chocolate mixture and serve with *crème anglaise* flavoured with the same liqueur. A few of my favourites are Grand Marnier, Cointreau, Mandarine Napoléon, poire William, Cognac, bourbon and Pistasha (pistachio liqueur).

CHOCOLATE FLAME:

Raspberry Purée (page 386) blends magnificently with the chocolate, brightening the flavour and deepening the colour. Add ruby Raspberry Jewel Glaze (page 378) and serve with *crème anglaise* flavoured with Chambord (black raspberry liqueur).
To make Chocolate Flame: Stir 169 grams/6 ounces/⅔ cup slightly sweetened Raspberry Sauce (page 386) or 163 grams/5½ ounces/¾ cup sieved Cordon Rose Raspberry Conserve (page 380) into the melted chocolate mixture and add 50 grams/1¾ ounces/¼ cup sugar when beating the eggs. You may also use 163 grams/5½ ounces/¾ cup commercial seedless raspberry jam, but, to cut the sweetness, use extra bittersweet chocolate for the cake.

CHOCOLATE TORTURE:

My friend Paula Perlis, an enchanting resourceress, once creatively mispronounced Chocolat Teuscher (TOYsher), a renowned Swiss chocolate boutique. I saved this best name of all for the best version of this cake, which incorporates both coffee and hot fudge. It is divine accompanied by Brandied Burgundy Cherries (page 397) and creamy Vanilla Ice Cream (page 329) – a deluxe hot fudge sundae cake. If desired, warm the cherries and flambé them by heating a little cognac in a ladle over the flame and tipping it slightly to ignite or using a long match.
To make Chocolate Torture: Make Hot Fudge (recipe follows). For the batter, Tobler extra bittersweet chocolate is preferable. Add 2 tablespoons instant espresso powder to the melted chocolate mixture. Before beating the eggs, warm the Hot Fudge until just pourable. Scrape half the batter into the prepared tin. Pour on half the Hot Fudge and top with the remaining batter. Pour on the remaining Hot Fudge and bake.

Hot Fudge

Makes about ⅔ cup

This sticky, intense hot fudge is as fabulous over Vanilla Ice Cream (page 329) as it is in Chocolate Torture (page 89). The chocolate contributes the irresistible edge of burnt sugar; the cocoa offers a deep chocolate flavour and rich, dark colour.

STORE: 1 month refrigerated.

INGREDIENTS	WEIGHT		MEASURE
room temperature	*grams*	*pounds/ounces*	*volume*
chocolate, preferably Tobler extra bittersweet or bittersweet	43 grams	1½ ounces	½ (3-ounce) bar
unsweetened cocoa	12 grams	½ ounce	2 tablespoons
water	80 grams	2¾ ounces	2¾ fluid ounces
unsalted butter	43 grams	1½ ounces	3 tablespoons
castor sugar	66 grams	2¼ ounces	⅓ cup
corn syrup	41 grams	1½ ounces	2 tablespoons
pinch of salt	—	—	—
pure vanilla extract	—	—	½ teaspoon

In a small heavy saucepan (ideally with a non-stick lining) melt the chocolate and cocoa with the water, stirring constantly. Add the butter, sugar, corn syrup and salt. Simmer, stirring until the sugar has completely melted. Stop stirring and cook at a moderate boil for 5 to 10 minutes or until the mixture thickens and reduces to just under 5¼ fluid ounces (grease a heatproof glass jug before measuring). Swirl the mixture in the pan occasionally but do not stir.

Cool slightly and add the vanilla. Keep warm or reheat in a water bath or microwave, stirring gently.

Note: The microwave is great for making hot fudge because the chocolate does not come into contact with direct heat so there is less risk of scorching. Use a 1½-litre/2-pint/4-cup heatproof glass measure or bowl as the fudge will bubble while reducing.

Breakfast Cakes

I never have time on weekdays for more than a hurried cup of coffee for breakfast, so indulging in pancakes or waffles at weekends is a special treat.

A pancake or waffle is similar to a butter cake except it has about half the flour and no sugar. A cake baked without sugar is usually rubbery and tough, but a pancake, if not overmixed, manages to be even more tender than a butter cake. This contradiction is because of the low amount of flour and because, during the mixing stage, almost no gluten is activated. The structure relies on the intense heat of frying to set the outside and support the incredibly soft, light interior. Also, unlike cakes, pancakes are eaten hot while still at their most tender. The absence of sugar makes it possible to add lots of maple syrup!

A pancake or waffle batter is much more forgiving than a regular cake batter. The size of the eggs or the type of flour is far less important. Plain flour works almost as well as self-raising sponge flour (although the latter makes more tender pancakes), and it really isn't necessary to sift.

I am presenting these recipes in the usual precise way for consistency of style, but weekends are the time to relax and it's great to know that you can have your cake and eat it too!

Often, I mix all the dry ingredients and remove the eggs and butter from the refrigerator the night before. Raised Waffles are ideal for slow risers as most of the batter must be prepared the night before.

I don't mind waking up a little early at weekends at our country house in Hope, New Jersey, just to be able to have the pleasure of an old-fashioned breakfast. I always accompany my pancakes or waffles with corncob-smoked bacon or sausage, fried crisp and sprinkled with freshly ground pepper and thyme from my garden. In the autumn I can't resist adding apple rings, fried in a little butter with chopped walnuts and a drizzle of maple syrup.

Leftover pancakes and waffles freeze beautifully for future carefree yet indulgent weekend breakfasts.

Two marvellous old-fashioned cakes, Sour Cream Coffee Cake (page 93) and Pineapple Upside-Down Cake (page 96), are terrific for brunch.

This chapter also includes crêpes, the world's most delicate pancakes, and buckwheat blini, the ultimate vehicle for caviar, both eminently suitable for special brunches.

You will also find two of my favourite breakfast treats – Holiday Halielujah Streusel Brioche (page 98) and Sticky Buns (page 103) – glorious yeast breads, perfect for pampering weekend guests.

Sour Cream Coffee Cake

Serves 8 to 10

This is the most delicious streusel coffee cake I have ever tasted and is one of my favourite cakes. The combination of ingredients was inspired by a recipe my old friend Elaine Marie Kohut once entered in a contest. (She won first prize: a set of silverware.) The buttery flavour has the mellow undertone of sour cream. The combination of cake, optional melting layer of thin apple or peach slices, and crunchy sprinkling of cinnamon-scented nuts is close to perfection. The apple adds a moist tartness, the peach mellowness.

TINS: One 23-centimetre/9-inch springform tin, greased, bottom lined with parchment or greaseproof paper, and then greased again and floured. Magi-Cake Strips (pages 516 and 522) are especially useful for this cake because the side crust tends to brown more than with other cakes due to the use of all yolks and the long baking period.

FINISHED HEIGHT: 5 centimetres/ 2 inches.

STORE: Airtight: 2 days room temperature, 5 days refrigerated, 2 months frozen. Moisture distributes most evenly the day after baking.

SERVE: Room temperature.

POINTERS FOR SUCCESS: See pages xx and 8.

Optional: 1 Granny Smith apple, peeled, cored, sliced 5 mm/¼ inch thick (1 heaped cup of slices), and sprinkled with 2 teaspoons fresh lemon juice. *Or* 1 heaped cup drained tinned or frozen peaches, thawed on paper towels and sliced 5 mm/¼ inch thick while still partially frozen.

INGREDIENTS	WEIGHT		MEASURE
room temperature	*grams*	*pounds/ounces*	*volume*
STREUSEL TOPPING AND FILLING			
light brown sugar	72 grams	2½ ounces	⅓ cup (firmly packed)
granulated sugar	26 grams	1 ounce	2 tablespoons
walnuts or pecans	113 grams	4 ounces	1 cup
cinnamon	—	—	1½ teaspoons
sifted plain flour	65 grams	2¼ ounces	½ cup
unsalted butter (must be softened)	57 grams	2 ounces	4 tablespoons
pure vanilla extract	—	—	½ teaspoon
BATTER			
4 egg yolks, size 2	74 grams	2½ ounces	2 full fluid ounces
sour cream	160 grams	5½ ounces	⅔ cup
pure vanilla extract	6 grams	—	1½ teaspoons
sifted self-raising sponge flour	150 grams	5¼ ounces	1½ cups
sifted plain flour	100 grams	3½ ounces	1 cup
castor sugar	250 grams	8¾ ounces	1¼ cups
bicarbonate of soda	2.5 grams	—	½ teaspoon
salt	—	—	¼ teaspoon
unsalted butter	170 grams	6 ounces	12 tablespoons

Preheat the oven to
350°F/180°C/gas mark 4.

TO MAKE STREUSEL TOPPING AND FILLING

In a food processor fitted with the metal blade, pulse the sugars, nuts and cinnamon until the nuts are coarsely chopped. Reserve 84 grams/3 ounces/¾ cup to use as a filling. To the remainder add the flour, butter and vanilla and pulse briefly to form a coarse, crumbly mixture for the topping.

TO MAKE BATTER

In a medium bowl lightly combine the yolks, 2 tablespoons of the sour cream, and the vanilla.

In a large mixing bowl combine the dry ingredients and mix on low speed for 30 seconds to blend. Add the butter and remaining sour cream. Mix on low speed until the dry ingredients are moistened. Increase to medium speed (high speed if using a hand mixer) and beat for 1½ minutes to aerate and develop the cake's structure. Scrape down the sides. Gradually add the egg mixture in three batches, beating for 20 seconds after each addition to incorporate the ingredients and strengthen the structure. Scrape down the sides.

Reserve about one-third of the batter and scrape the remainder into the prepared tin. Smooth the surface, preferably with a small angled spatula. Sprinkle with the streusel filling and top with the apple or peach slices if desired. Drop the reserved batter in large blobs over the fruit and spread evenly with the spatula. Sprinkle with the streusel topping and bake for 55 to 65 minutes or until a wire cake tester inserted in the centre comes out clean and the cake springs back when pressed lightly in the centre. (Move aside a small patch of the streusel before testing.) *The cake should start to shrink from the sides of the pan only after removal from the oven.* Cover loosely with buttered foil after 45 minutes to prevent overbrowning.

Let the cake cool in the tin on a rack for 10 minutes. The cake will have a level top. Loosen the sides with a small metal spatula and remove the sides of the springform tin. Cool completely before wrapping airtight. If you wish to remove the bottom of the tin, slide a cardboard round at least 23 centimetres/9 inches in diameter between the parchment and the bottom when the cake is completely cool.

Pineapple Upside-Down Cake

Serves 8 to 10

This is a true American classic, traditionally baked in a cast-iron skillet. When inverted, the pineapple slices lining the pan encase the cake, moistening its buttery, soft crumb with delicious caramelised juices. The sour cream batter provides the perfect flavour balance for any fruit. Try an apple, pear, plum, peach, apricot or even banana variation.

TIN: One 25.5-centimetre/10-inch cast-iron skillet (measured at bottom; top measures 28 centimetres/11 inches).

FINISHED HEIGHT: 4 centimetres/ 1½ inches.

STORE: Airtight: 1 day room temperature, 3 days refrigerated, 2 months frozen.

SERVE: Warm or room temperature.

POINTERS FOR SUCCESS: See pages xx and 8.

Preheat oven to 350°F/180°C/gas mark 4.

Position a shelf in the lower third of the oven.

TO MAKE FRUIT TOPPING

Drain the pineapple slices and cherries and place them on paper towels to absorb excess moisture. You will need 8 whole pineapple slices and 8 whole cherries. Halve 6 of the remaining slices and the remaining cherries.

In the skillet, melt the butter over medium heat. Stir in the brown sugar until moistened and remove from the heat.

Place 1 whole pineapple slice in the centre of the pan and 7 whole slices surrounding it. Place the half slices side by side against the sides of the pan, the two cut edges down, touching the brown sugar. Place the whole cherries in the centre of the whole pineapple slices; the halved cherries in the centre of the half slices. Tuck the pecans into any gaps between the fruit.

TO MAKE CAKE BATTER

In a medium bowl, lightly combine the yolks, about one-quarter of the sour cream, and the vanilla.

In a large mixing bowl, combine the dry ingredients and mix on low speed for 30 seconds to blend. Add the butter and the remaining sour cream. Mix on low speed until the

INGREDIENTS	WEIGHT		MEASURE
room temperature	*grams*	*pounds/ounces*	*volume*
FRUIT TOPPING			
14 pineapple slices, fresh or tinned – packed in unsweetened pineapple juice	—	—	1½ (20-ounce) cans
14 sweet cherries, stoned	—	—	—
unsalted butter	57 grams	2 ounces	4 tablespoons
light brown sugar	108 grams	3¾ ounces	½ cup (firmly packed)
pecan halves	28 grams	1 ounce	¼ cup
CAKE BATTER			
3 egg yolks, size 2	56 grams	2 ounces	2 scant fluid ounces
sour cream	121 grams	4¼ ounces	½ cup
pure vanilla extract	4 grams	—	1 teaspoon
sifted self-raising sponge flour	150 grams	5¼ ounces	1½ cups
sifted plain flour	100 grams	3½ ounces	1 cup
castor sugar	250 grams	8¾ ounces	1¼ cups
bicarbonate of soda	—	—	¼ teaspoon
salt	—	—	¼ teaspoon
unsalted butter (must be softened)	128 grams	4½ ounces	9 tablespoons

dry ingredients are moistened. Increase to medium (high speed if using hand mixer) and beat for 1½ minutes to aerate and develop the cake's structure. Scrape down the sides.

Gradually add the egg mixture to the batter in three batches, beating for 20 seconds after each addition to incorporate the ingredients and strengthen the structure. Scrape down the sides. Scrape the batter into the fruit-lined skillet, smoothing it evenly with a spatula. Bake for 45 to 55 minutes or until golden brown and the wire cake tester inserted in the centre comes out clean and the cake springs back when pressed lightly in the centre. Run a small metal spatula around the sides and invert at once on to a serving plate. Leave the skillet in place for 1 or 2 minutes before lifting it. If any fruit has stuck to the skillet, simply use a small spatula to place it back on the cake.

UNDERSTANDING
A cast-iron skillet is ideal for preparing this cake not only because the butter and brown sugar for the topping can be heated directly in it on top of the stove, but because it helps the brown-sugar topping to caramelise while baking. If you prefer to use a 25.5-centimetre/10-inch springform tin, it is advisable to wrap the outside in heavy-duty foil to prevent leakage. Preheat an aluminium baking sheet and place the springform directly on it to help caramelise the sugar.

Holiday Hallelujah Streusel Brioche

Serves 12

There is simply nothing more soul-satisfying with which to start the day than this cinnamon-imbued brioche. Everyone adores its springy crumb and the delectable yeasty buttery flavour.

Streusel brioche is easy to make. And since it freezes well, it can be baked several weeks ahead and frozen. Thawed overnight at room temperature and warmed briefly before serving, it tastes as fresh as if it had just come out of the oven.

I created this recipe for *Family Circle*'s December 1987 holiday baking issue. The name I gave it expresses my unbridled enthusiasm for it. It is guaranteed to become part of your heirloom repertoire.

TINS: One large brioche mould (23 centimetres/9 inches at the widest point by 7.5 centimetres/ 3 inches high) or a 20 × 5-centimetre/8 × 2-inch cake tin or springform tin, well buttered.

STORE: Airtight: 2 days refrigerated, 3 months frozen. To reheat, wrap loosely in foil and bake for 10 minutes at 350°F/180°C/gas mark 4.

COMPLEMENTARY ADORNMENTS: Buttery enough to serve plain, the Streusel Brioche is also delicious with softened, unsweetened butter. Serve with a cup of steaming hot coffee or a glass of milk.

POINTERS FOR SUCCESS: Use bread flour. *Do not* use easy-blend yeast. Be sure the yeast is active. Do not allow rising dough to be in an area over 80° to 85°F/27–30°C. Do not allow the dough to rise more than recommended amounts or it will weaken the structure. Do not deflate the dough before chilling or the butter will leak out. If this should happen inadvertently, chill the dough for 1 hour and knead the butter back into the dough.

DAY BEFORE MAKE THE SPONGE

When using yeast always begin by proving it to make sure it is alive.

If using fresh yeast, smell it to be sure it doesn't have a sour odour. To prove the yeast, use warm water (hot water would kill it). In a small bowl combine the water (ideally a tepid 100°F/38°C if using fresh yeast; a little warmer, 110°F/43°C, if using dry), 1/2 teaspoon of the sugar and the yeast. If using fresh yeast, crumble it slightly while adding. Set aside in a draught-free spot for 10 to 20 minutes. By this time, the mixture should be full of bubbles. If not, the yeast is too old to be useful.

Place 40 grams/1 1/2 ounces/1/3 cup of the flour and 1 egg in a food processor (preferably with the dough blade) and process for a few seconds until mixed. Add the yeast mixture and stir with a rubber scraper until smooth. Sprinkle the remaining flour over the mixture but do not mix it in. Cover and let stand for 1 1/2 to 2 hours.

KNEADING THE DOUGH

Add the remaining sugar, salt and remaining 2 cold eggs and process for 1 1/2 minutes or until the dough is smooth, shiny and cleans the bowl. Let it rest for 5 minutes with the feed tube open. Add the butter in two batches and process for 20 seconds after each addition or until incorporated. (The butter

INGREDIENTS	WEIGHT		MEASURE
room temperature	*grams*	*pounds/ounces*	*volume*
BRIOCHE DOUGH			
water	38 grams	1¼ ounces	2½ tablespoons
castor sugar	40 grams	1¼ ounces	3 tablespoons
fresh yeast* *or*	11 grams	½ ounce	2 packed teaspoons
dried yeast (*not* easy-blend)	4.5 grams	—	1½ teaspoons
unsifted strong white flour	227 grams	8 ounces	about 1⅔ cups (dip and sweep method)
1 egg, size 2	170 grams	6 ounces	—
2 eggs, size 2, cold	(weighed in the shells)		—
salt	3.5 grams	—	½ teaspoon
unsalted butter (must be very soft)	142 grams†	5 ounces†	10 tablespoons
STREUSEL FILLING			
sultanas	72 grams	2½ ounces	½ cup
white rum	28 grams	1 ounce	2 tablespoons
boiling water	60 grams	2 ounces	¼ cup
brown sugar	56 grams	2 ounces	¼ cup (firmly packed)
granulated sugar	13 grams	½ ounce	1 tablespoon
cinnamon	—	—	2 teaspoons

* Fresh yeast causes dough to rise faster.
† 113 to 170 grams/4 to 6 ounces/8 to 12 tablespoons of butter may be used. The lesser amount offers a lighter texture, the higher amount a richer flavour.

INGREDIENTS	WEIGHT		MEASURE
room temperature	grams	pounds/ounces	volume
pecans, finely chopped	56 grams	2 ounces	½ cup
unsalted butter, melted	28 grams	1 ounce	2 tablespoons
milk	—	—	about 2 tablespoons
EGG GLAZE			
1 large egg yolk lightly beaten with 1½ teaspoons double cream	—	—	—
Optional: APRICOT GLAZE			
melted, strained apricot jam	75 grams	2½ ounces	¼ cup

must be soft so as not to overtax the motor of the processor. If the processor should stall, let it rest for 5 minutes.)★

FIRST RISE
Scrape the dough into a lightly buttered bowl. It will be very soft and elastic. Sprinkle lightly with flour to prevent a crust from forming. Cover the bowl tightly with clingfilm and let rise in a warm place (80°F/27°C but not above or the yeast will develop a sour taste) until double in bulk, about 2 hours. Refrigerate for at least 30 minutes to 1 hour. Deflate the dough by gently stirring it and refrigerate for another hour.

REDISTRIBUTING THE YEAST
Turn the dough on to a lightly floured surface and gently press it into a rectangle. Fold the dough into thirds (as in folding a business letter) and again press it out into a rectangle, lightly flouring the surface as needed to prevent stickiness. Fold it again into thirds and dust it lightly with flour on all sides. Wrap it loosely but securely

★To prepare brioche dough in a heavy-duty mixer such as the KitchenAid, use a flat beater and, when the dough starts to climb up the beater, change to the dough hook. Beat for about 5 minutes on medium speed or until the dough is smooth, shiny, very elastic and begins to clean the bowl. Beat in the butter by the tablespoon until incorporated.

in clingfilm and then foil and refrigerate it for 6 hours or up to 2 days to allow the dough to ripen and harden.

TO MAKE STREUSEL FILLING

In a small heatproof bowl place the sultanas and white rum. Add the boiling water, cover and let stand for at least 1 hour. When ready to fill the dough, drain the sultanas. Use your fingers or a fork to blend all the ingredients except the butter and milk.

The dough will have expanded. Gently deflate it by kneading lightly with floured hands. Roll it out on a heavily floured surface into a 46 × 20-centimetre/ 18 × 8-inch rectangle. Brush with the melted butter, sprinkle with the streusel and sultanas, and roll up from a short end, brushing off the excess flour as you go.

Use a sharp knife or string to cut the roll into four pieces if using a large brioche mould, eight pieces if using a cake tin. Stand the slices cut ends up and down, wedging them into the tin and brushing between them with the milk so they will adhere well during baking.

Let rise for 1 to 2 hours (fresh yeast rises faster) or until the dough comes to the top of the tin and is very light.

Place a foil-lined baking sheet in the oven and preheat to 425°F/220°C/gas mark 7. (The hot baking sheet will boost the 'oven spring' of the brioche; the foil will catch any bubbling caramelised sugar.)

Brush the brioche with the egg glaze, being careful not to drip any on the side of the tin or it will impede rising (although little can stop this energetic dough).

Place the brioche on the hot baking sheet and bake for 5 minutes. Lower the heat to 375°F/190°C/gas mark 5 and bake for 20 to 25 minutes or until a wooden skewer inserted in the centre comes out clean. Cover loosely with foil after 10 to 15 minutes or when the crust starts to darken.

Turn out on to a wire rack and reinvert to cool top side up. For a glistening surface, brush with Apricot Glaze.

UNDERSTANDING
See page 79.

Sticky Buns

Serves 12

The same dough used to make Streusel Brioche makes the most glorious
sticky buns imaginable. They are everything you'd want a sticky bun to
be: gooey with buttery caramel and crunchy pecan topping; airy, soft,
moist, buttery, yeasty dough beneath coiled around a spiral filling of
rum-plumped raisins, brown sugar and cinnamon. Make this recipe one
day ahead and reheat to serve warm at breakfast.

TIN: One 20 × 5-centimetre/
8 × 2-inch square tin, lightly
greased.

Day ahead, prepare the Brioche
Dough. The Sticky Bun Topping
and Filling can also be prepared the
day ahead.

STORE: Airtight: 2 days room
temperature, 3 months frozen.

COMPLEMENTARY
ADORNMENTS: The textural
variation and moisture from the
caramel makes any addition to the
Sticky Buns unnecessary.
However, they cry out for a cup of
hot coffee or a glass of cold milk.

SERVE: Preferably warm.

POINTERS FOR SUCCESS: Use
bread flour. *Do not* use easy-blend
yeast. Be sure the yeast is active.
Do not allow rising dough to be in
an area over 80° to 85°F/27–30°C.
Do not allow the dough to rise
more than the recommended
amounts or it will weaken the

structure. Do not deflate the dough
before chilling or the butter will
leak out. If this should happen
inadvertently, chill the dough for
1 hour and knead the butter back
into it.

TO MAKE THE STICKY BUN FILLING

In a small heatproof bowl place the
raisins and rum. Add the boiling
water, cover and let stand for at
least 1 hour. When ready to fill the
dough, drain the raisins, reserving
the soaking liquid.

In another bowl combine the
sugars and cinnamon.

TO MAKE THE STICKY BUN TOPPING

In a small bowl stir together the
butter and sugar until well mixed.
Spread evenly in the prepared tin

INGREDIENTS	WEIGHT		MEASURE
room temperature	*grams*	*pounds/ounces*	*volume*
1 recipe Holiday Hallelujah Streusel Brioche dough (page 98)	—	—	—
STICKY BUN FILLING			
raisins	72 grams	2½ ounces	½ cup
dark rum	28 grams	1 ounce	2 tablespoons
boiling water	60 grams	2 ounces	¼ cup
light brown sugar	56 grams	2 ounces	¼ cup (firmly packed)
granulated sugar	13 grams	½ ounce	1 tablespoon
cinnamon	—	—	2 teaspoons
unsalted butter, melted	28 grams	1 ounce	2 tablespoons
STICKY BUN TOPPING			
unsalted butter, softened	56 grams	2 ounces	¼ cup
light brown sugar	112 grams	4 ounces	½ cup (firmly packed)
pecan halves	56 grams	2 ounces	½ cup
STICKY BUN GLAZE			
reserved raisin-soaking liquid	—	—	—
unsalted butter	14 grams	½ ounce	1 tablespoon

with a small spatula or rubber scraper. Top with the pecan halves top sides down.

FILLING THE DOUGH

Roll out the dough on a well-floured surface into a 36 × 30-centimetre/14 × 12-inch rectangle. Brush with the 2 tablespoons of melted butter and sprinkle with the sugar mixture and raisins. Roll up from a short end, brushing off the excess flour as you go. The dough will have that lively, silky, 'soft as a baby's bottom' feel.

Using a very sharp knife, cut the roll into four pieces and then cut each piece into thirds. Place each piece cut side down in the prepared tin, pressing the tops so that the sides touch. Cover with well-buttered clingfilm and let rise until the dough reaches the top of the tin (about 1 hour if using fresh yeast, up to 2 hours if using dry).

TO MAKE THE STICKY BUN GLAZE

In a small saucepan over high heat or in a 1-litre/1-pint/2-cup heatproof measuring jug in a microwave on high power reduce the raisin-soaking syrup to 1 table-spoon. Add the butter and stir until melted. The glaze should be lukewarm when used. Set a foil-lined baking sheet on the lowest shelf and preheat the oven to 425°F/220°C/gas mark 7. (The hot baking sheet will boost the 'oven spring' of the brioche; the foil will catch any bubbling caramelised syrup.)

Brush the buns with the glaze. Place the tin on the hot baking sheet and bake for 10 minutes. Lower the heat to 375°F/190°C/gas mark 5 and bake for 15 minutes or until a skewer inserted in the centre comes out clean. If becoming too brown, cover loosely with foil after 5 or 10 minutes.

Let the buns cool in the tin for 3 minutes before turning them out on to a serving plate or foil-lined counter. Sticky buns may be eaten at once or reheated in a 350°F/180°C/gas mark 4 oven for 10 minutes, loosely wrapped in foil.

Notes: The butter and raisin syrup glaze keeps the tops of the buns soft. My friend Shirley Corriher swears by the plumping-raisins method. She says she hates finding a hard, dried-up raisin in an otherwise soft dough.

Paula Wolfert (in her superb articles on brioche in *The Pleasures of Cooking*, which greatly influenced the development of this recipe) recommends melting and browning about one-fifth of the butter (2 tablespoons) for an extra-rich, delicious flavour. Be sure to let the butter cool before adding it along with the rest of the butter. Add the browned particles as well.

Brioche made in a food processor is a speedy and simple operation. If you wish to double this recipe, it is safer to use the heavy-duty mixer method as a larger amount of dough might overheat some food processors, causing them to stall. (I have successfully made a double batch in a heavy-duty mixer by melting the butter and allowing it to cool to barely tepid before adding it, with motor running.)

Blueberry Buttermilk Pancakes

Serves 4 to 6

Buttermilk makes the most delicious pancakes, especially if no bicarbonate of soda is used to dull the slightly tangy flavour. Beaten egg whites contribute to the raising. In fact, these are the lightest pancakes I have ever tasted.

Blueberry buttermilk pancakes are my favourite version, and the secret for having plump, juicy, evenly distributed berries is to add them fresh or still frozen to the pancakes after they're on the griddle.

STORE: 3 days refrigerated, 2 months frozen. Best served fresh.

COMPLEMENTARY ADORNMENTS: Warm maple syrup, crisp corncob-smoked bacon, sausages, or sprinkle with fried sage or thyme. No extra butter is necessary as there's plenty in the pancakes!

SERVE: Hot on warmed plates.

POINTERS FOR SUCCESS: Do not overmix batter. If using frozen blueberries, be sure they remain frozen when added to the batter.

To coat griddle with a thin film of butter, run a frozen piece of butter lightly across it.

Preheat a griddle or frying pan.

In a large bowl whisk the flour and salt until blended.

In a small bowl beat the yolks and buttermilk to blend slightly.

In a mixing bowl beat the egg whites until foamy. Add the cream of tartar and beat until stiff peaks form when the beater is raised slowly.

Add the yolk mixture to the flour mixture and mix lightly with

INGREDIENTS	WEIGHT		MEASURE
room temperature	*grams*	*pounds/ounces*	*volume*
unsifted self-raising sponge flour *or*	227 grams	8 ounces	1¾ cups (dip and sweep method)
plain flour and baking powder	227 grams	8 ounces	1⅔ cups (dip and sweep method)
baking powder (with plain flour only)	19.5 grams	—	4 teaspoons
salt	3.5 grams	—	½ teaspoon
4 eggs, size 2, separated			
yolks	68 grams	2½ ounces	2 full fluid ounces
whites	120 grams	4¼ ounces	4 fluid ounces
buttermilk	484 grams	17 ounces	16 fluid ounces
cream of tartar	—	—	½ teaspoon
unsalted butter, melted and cooled	57 grams	2 ounces	4 tablespoons
blueberries, fresh or frozen and unthawed	227 grams	8 ounces	2 cups

a fork until the flour is moistened. Stir in the butter. The batter should be lumpy as overmixing will produce tough pancakes. Add the whites and fold in with a slotted skimmer or rubber spatula.

The griddle or frying pan should be hot enough to sizzle a drop of water. Lightly butter it and pour on the batter in 10-centimetre/ 4-inch rounds. Quickly drop 6 berries on to each pancake. Test for doneness by lifting a corner of each pancake with a metal spatula. When golden brown, turn over and cook for 30 seconds on the other side.

Remove the pancakes to warm plates and keep warm in a low oven while cooking the remaining batter.

Makes about 22 pancakes.

UNDERSTANDING

Self-raising sponge flour makes a more tender pancake because it contains less gluten-forming protein than does plain.

VARIATION

BUTTERMILK PUFFS:

Frying the batter in a Danish Ebleskiver pan, which has 8 round recesses, produces pancake puffs with a delightfully airy and moist texture. You will need 1½ tablespoons clarified butter for brushing on the preheated pan before frying. Fill each recess half full with batter. Use a small metal spatula to turn the puffs. Blueberries tend to stick slightly, making it necessary to wash the pan between batches, so, if you add them, use only 2 per puff and push them in slightly so they are covered with batter. The batter makes 54 puffs.

Blueberry Buckwheat Pancakes

Serves 4 to 6

These pancakes have a light, tender texture with the earthy flavour of buckwheat.

STORE: 3 days refrigerated, 2 months frozen. Best served fresh.

COMPLEMENTARY ADORNMENTS: Warm maple syrup, crisp corncob-smoked bacon, sausages, or sprinkle with fried sage or thyme. No extra butter is necessary as there's plenty in the pancakes!

SERVE: Hot on warmed plates.

POINTERS FOR SUCCESS: Do not overmix batter. If using frozen blueberries, be sure they remain frozen when added to the batter. To coat griddle with a thin film of butter, run a frozen piece of butter lightly across it.

Preheat a griddle or frying pan.

In a large bowl, whisk the flours, bicarbonate of soda and salt until blended.

In a small bowl, beat the yolks, milk and sour cream to blend slightly.

In a mixing bowl, beat the egg whites until foamy. Add the cream of tartar and beat until stiff peaks form when the beater is raised slowly.

Add the yolk mixture to the flour mixture and mix lightly with a fork until the flour is moistened.

INGREDIENTS	WEIGHT		MEASURE
room temperature	*grams*	*pounds/ounces*	*volume*
unsifted buckwheat flour	188 grams	6¾ ounces	1½ cups
plain flour	36 grams	1¼ ounces	¼ cup (lightly spooned)
bicarbonate of soda	5 grams	—	1 teaspoon
salt	3.5 grams	—	½ teaspoon
4 eggs, size 2, separated			
yolks	68 grams	2½ ounces	2 full fluid ounces
whites	120 grams	4¼ ounces	4 fluid ounces
milk	242 grams	8½ ounces	8 fluid ounces
sour cream	242 grams	8½ ounces	1 cup
cream of tartar	—	—	½ teaspoon
unsalted butter, melted and cooled	57 grams	2 ounces	4 tablespoons
blueberries, fresh or frozen and unthawed	227 grams	8 ounces	2 cups

Stir in the butter. The batter should be lumpy because overmixing will produce tough pancakes. Add the whites and fold in with a slotted skimmer or rubber spatula.

The griddle or frying pan should be hot enough to sizzle a drop of water. Lightly butter it and pour on batter in 10-centimetre/4-inch rounds. Quickly drop 6 berries on to each pancake.

Test for doneness by lifting a corner of each pancake with a metal spatula. When golden brown, turn over and cook for 30 seconds on the other side.

Remove the pancakes to warm plates and keep warm in a low oven while cooking the remaining batter. Makes about 22 pancakes.

UNDERSTANDING
Self-raising sponge flour makes a more tender pancake because it contains less gluten-forming protein than does plain.

Bicarbonate of soda is used to temper the acidity of the sour cream. The sour cream is thinned with milk to produce a lighter, more tender texture.

Buttermilk Waffles

Serves 6 to 8

The ingredients for this waffle batter are exactly the same as for the buttermilk pancake batter except for the butter. Because of the different cooking technique, the waffle batter is able to incorporate four times the amount of butter without becoming too tender and falling apart (as would a cake). Also, the egg whites are not beaten separately because the heavy pressure of the waffle-iron lid would defeat the purpose.

I like to use an 18-centimetre/7-inch diameter, heart-shaped waffle iron to make five waffle hearts at a time. With a non-stick coating no extra butter is necessary. Electric waffle irons are the easiest to use because both top and bottom heat evenly.

STORE: 2 months frozen. Reheat in a toaster. Best served fresh.

COMPLEMENTARY ADORNMENTS: Warm maple syrup, and crisp corncob-smoked bacon, sausage, or sprinkle with fried sage or thyme. (Please, no more butter!)

SERVE: Hot on warmed plates.

POINTERS FOR SUCCESS: Do not overmix the batter. Use a sizzling hot waffle iron.

Preheat a waffle iron. (For crispy waffles, be sure to preheat both sides until very hot before adding the batter.)

In a large bowl whisk the flour and salt until blended.

In a small bowl beat the eggs and buttermilk until well mixed. Add

INGREDIENTS	WEIGHT		MEASURE
room temperature	*grams*	*pounds/ounces*	*volume*
unsifted self-raising sponge flour *or*	227 grams	8 ounces	1¾ cups (lightly spooned)
plain flour and baking powder	227 grams	8 ounces	1⅔ cups (dip and sweep method)
baking powder (with plain flour only)	19.5 grams	—	4 teaspoons
salt	3.5 grams	—	½ teaspoon
4 eggs, size 2	200 grams (weighed without shells)	7 ounces	6 full fluid ounces
buttermilk	484 grams	17 ounces	16 fluid ounces
unsalted butter, melted and cooled	227 grams	8 ounces	16 tablespoons

to the flour mixture and mix lightly with a fork until the flour is moistened. Stir in the butter. The batter should be lumpy as overmixing will produce tough waffles.

The waffle iron should be hot enough to sizzle a drop of water. Pour the batter on to the centre of the waffle iron, using a light hand because the batter will spread when the lid is lowered. If using an 18-centimetre/7-inch heart-shaped iron, use a scant 4 fluid ounces batter and a spoon or small metal spatula to spread it around the outer edges. Lower the lid and cook until the bottom is golden brown. Flip the waffle iron over and briefly cook the other side until just golden brown. (If using an electric waffle iron, follow the manufacturer's directions.)

Keep the waffles warm and crisp by placing them in a single layer on racks in a warm oven with the door slightly ajar to allow any moisture to escape. Makes about twelve 18-centimetre/7-inch heart-shaped waffles or about six 23-centimetre/9-inch square waffles.

UNDERSTANDING
Self-raising sponge flour makes a more tender waffle because it contains less gluten-forming protein than does plain.

Marion Cunningham's Raised Waffles

Serves 6 to 8

When I visited my cousin Joan in Berkeley, California, we went to breakfast at a charming spot, the Bridge Creek Restaurant, where I enjoyed the most ethereal waffles I had ever experienced. When my feet touched ground again, I discovered Marion Cunningham sitting nearby and learned that she was part owner and chief menu consultant. To my delight she not only promised to send me the recipe but also allowed me to offer it in this book.

STORE: The batter keeps well for several days refrigerated or frozen for up to 2 months. To use frozen batter, thaw in the refrigerator overnight.

COMPLEMENTARY ADORNMENTS: Warm maple syrup, and crisp corncob-smoked bacon, sausage, or sprinkle with fried sage or thyme.

SERVE: Hot on warmed plates.

POINTERS FOR SUCCESS: Do not overheat the yeast. Use a large bowl as the batter will rise to three times its original volume. Use a sizzling hot waffle iron. Do not use easy-blend yeast.

NIGHT BEFORE
In a large mixing bowl (at least 3.5 litres/6 pints in capacity) combine the warm water (100°F/138°C if using fresh yeast,

110°F/43°C if using dry yeast), sugar and yeast. Stir and let stand for 10 to 20 minutes to prove. If the yeast is active, it will produce many bubbles.

Add the milk, butter, salt and flour and beat until smooth and blended. (Marion likes to use a hand-rotary beater to get rid of the lumps.) Cover the bowl with clingfilm and let stand overnight at room temperature. (The batter will triple in volume and then collapse.)

INGREDIENTS	WEIGHT		MEASURE
room temperature	*grams*	*pounds/ounces*	*volume*
warm water	120 grams	4¼ ounces	4 fluid ounces
castor sugar	4 grams	—	1 teaspoon
fresh yeast *or*	21 grams	¾ ounce	1 packed tablespoon
dried yeast	7 grams	¼ ounce	2¼ teaspoons
warm milk	484 grams	17 ounces	16 fluid ounces
unsalted butter, melted	113 grams	4 ounces	8 tablespoons
salt	5 grams	—	¾ teaspoon
unsifted plain flour	284 grams	10 ounces	1¾ cups (dip and sweep method)
2 eggs, size 2	100 grams (weighed without shells)	3½ ounces	3 fluid ounces
bicarbonate of soda	—	—	¼ teaspoon

MORNING

Preheat the waffle iron until it is hot enough to sizzle a drop of water. (For crispy waffles, be sure to preheat both sides until very hot before adding the batter.)

Beat in the eggs. Add the bicarbonate of soda and stir until well mixed. The batter will be very thin.

Pour the batter on to the centre of the waffle iron, using a light hand because the batter will spread when the lid is lowered. If using an 18-centimetre/7-inch heart-shaped iron, use a scant 2½ fluid ounces of batter. Tilt the waffle iron to spread the batter around the edges. Lower the lid and cook until the bottom is golden brown. Flip the waffle iron over and briefly cook the other side until just golden brown. (If using an electric waffle iron, follow the manufacturer's directions.)

Keep the waffles warm and crisp by placing them in a single layer on racks in a warm oven with the door slightly ajar to allow any moisture to escape. Makes about eight 23-centimetre/9-inch-square waffles or about sixteen 18-centimetre/7-inch heart-shaped waffles.

UNDERSTANDING
The formula for these waffles is quite similar to Buttermilk Waffles except that they have half the eggs and butter. This is part of the reason for their lightness, but the real secret is that they are leavened with yeast. The tiny amount of bicarbonate of soda does not add leavening – instead it rounds out the slightly acidic flavour produced by the yeast. The yeast also contributes a richness and depth of flavour.

Best Buckwheat Blini La Tulipe

Serves 8 to 10

A good recipe for buckwheat blini is very hard to find. The combination of assertive buckwheat flavour and light tender texture is elusive.

I fell in love with these blini at a New York Women's Culinary Alliance caviar tasting given several years ago by Sara Moulton, the group's founder. She was then *chef tournant* at La Tulipe, one of my favourite Greenwich Village restaurants, and was honour-bound not to divulge the recipe.

It was almost as this book went to press that it suddenly occurred to me to ask Sally Darr, chef–owner of La Tulipe, if I could include her blini recipe. She said yes. I lived in fear for one week that she might change her mind. These blini are that wonderful.

STORE: Blini are best fresh but can be refrigerated 3 days and reheated, covered, in a 300°F/150°C/gas mark 2 oven for 10 to 15 minutes or for a few seconds in a microwave oven, uncovered.

COMPLEMENTARY
ADORNMENTS: Sour cream or *crème fraîche* (page 299) and caviar.

Or thin slivers of smoked salmon and sprigs of fresh dill.

POINTERS FOR SUCCESS: Stone-ground buckwheat flour produces the best texture.

The batter requires 3½ hours rising time, so you must start it at least 4 hours before serving the blini.

INGREDIENTS	WEIGHT		MEASURE
room temperature	*grams*	*pounds/ounces*	*volume*
fresh yeast★ *or*	11 grams	½ ounce	2 packed teaspoons
dried yeast (*not* easy-blend)	4 grams	—	1½ teaspoons
warm milk	605 grams	1 pound 5¼ ounces	2½ cups
castor sugar	15 grams	½ ounce	1 tablespoon + ½ teaspoon
stone-ground buckwheat flour	57 grams	2 ounces	½ cup (lightly spooned into cup)
unsifted plain flour	284 grams	10 ounces	1¾ cups (dip and sweep method)
3 egg yolks, size 2	56 grams	2 ounces	3½ tablespoons
1 egg white, size 2	30 grams	1 ounce	2 tablespoons
salt	—	—	½ teaspoon
double cream	232 grams	8 ounces	1 cup
clarified butter★	25 grams	1 ounce	2 tablespoons

★ If you do not have clarified butter on hand, you will need to clarify 43 grams/1½ ounces/3 tablespoons unsalted butter. In a heavy saucepan melt the butter over medium heat, partially covered to prevent splattering. When it looks clear, cook, uncovered, watching carefully until the solids drop and begin to brown. Pour immediately through a fine strainer or a strainer lined with cheesecloth.

I suggest starting the batter the day before.

DAY BEFORE
When using yeast always begin by proving it to make sure it is alive. To prove the yeast, use warm liquid (hot liquid would kill it). In a small bowl combine 121 grams/ 4¼ ounces/½ cup warm milk (ideally a tepid 100°F/38°C, if using fresh yeast; a little warmer,

110°F/43°C, if using dried yeast), ½ teaspoon of the sugar, and the yeast. If using fresh yeast, crumble it slightly while adding. Set aside in a draught-free spot for 10 to 20 minutes. By this time, the mixture should be full of bubbles. If not, the yeast is too old to be useful.

Transfer the mixture to a large bowl (at least 2-litre/4-pint/10-cup capacity) and stir in the buckwheat flour and 363 grams/12¾ ounces/

1½ cups warm milk. Cover and allow to stand in a warm place for 2 hours.

Stir in the plain flour and the remaining 121 grams/4¼ ounces/½ cup milk until smooth. Add the egg yolks, remaining sugar, and the salt. Mix well, cover and allow to stand in a warm place for 1 hour. (The recipe may be prepared to this point 1 day ahead.) Refrigerate overnight. The batter will be thick and have bubbles all over the surface.

Whip the cream until soft peaks form when the beater is raised and fold into the batter.

Beat the egg white until soft peaks form when the beater is raised and fold into the batter. You will have about 8 cups (2 litres) of batter.

SERVING DAY
Preheat the oven to 300°F/150°C/gas mark 2.

Pour 6-centimetre/2½-inch rounds of batter (2 scant tablespoons) on to a hot griddle, lightly greased with the clarified butter between each batch. Cook until puffed and golden: about 1½ minutes. Turn and cook the other side for 30 seconds or until lightly brown. Place in the oven for 10 minutes to finish cooking the inside of the blini. Makes 70 blini.

Swedish Pancakes

(Plättar)

Serves 8 to 10

My assistant, David Shamah, a graduate of the Culinary Institute of America, raved about these pancakes, which he learned from chef–instructor John Jensen. The original recipe used part single cream and milk, but here I have converted it to double cream and milk (maintaining the same percentage of butterfat).

Swedish pancakes are a cross between American pancakes and crêpes. Sprinkled with icing sugar and topped with lingonberries, they are traditionally eaten with the fingers as a lovely brunch dish or as an unusual dessert for an informal dinner.

INGREDIENTS	WEIGHT		MEASURE
room temperature	*grams*	*pounds/ounces*	*volume*
4 eggs, size 2	200 grams (weighed without shells)	7 ounces	6 fluid ounces
double cream	116 grams	4 ounces	½ cup
plain flour	145 grams	5 ounces	1 cup − 2 tablespoons (measured by dip and sweep method)
milk	363 grams	12¾ ounces	12 fluid ounces
unsalted butter, melted	43 grams	1½ ounces	3 tablespoons
salt	−	−	½ teaspoon
grated lemon zest	−	−	½ teaspoon
clarified butter*	25 grams	1 ounce	2 tablespoons

* If you do not have clarified butter on hand, you will need to clarify 43 grams/1½ ounces/3 tablespoons unsalted butter. In a heavy saucepan melt the butter over medium heat, partially covered to prevent splattering. When it looks clear, cook, uncovered, watching carefully until the solids drop and begin to brown. Pour immediately through a fine strainer or a strainer lined with cheesecloth.

STORE: 3 days refrigerated. Reheat, loosely covered, in a 300°F/150°C/gas mark 2 oven for 10 to 15 minutes or for a few seconds in a microwave oven, uncovered. Best served fresh.

COMPLEMENTARY ADORNMENTS: Icing sugar and lingonberries in syrup (available at speciality food stores).

In a large bowl beat the eggs and cream. Add the flour and beat until smooth. Beat in the remaining ingredients. The batter is quite thin.

Pour 6-centimetre/2½-inch rounds of batter (1 tablespoon) on to a hot griddle, lightly greased with clarified butter between each batch. Cook over medium–high heat for 1½ minutes or until golden brown. Turn and cook the other side for 30 seconds or until lightly brown. The pancakes will be 3 millimetres/⅛ inch thick.

Remove the pancakes to warm plates and keep warm in a low oven while cooking the remaining batter. Makes 4 dozen pancakes.

Chantilly Crêpes

Serves 6 to 8

These are the lightest, laciest, tenderest crêpes imaginable. I discovered the idea of using cornflour instead of the usual flour when I did a freelance project at CPC International (Corn Products) many years ago. In addition to producing tenderer crêpes, you can also cook the crêpes immediately after mixing the batter, unlike the hour-long wait when using flour.

I discovered that using half the recommended amount of cornflour produces crêpes that are as delicate as handkerchiefs.

TIN: One 15-centimetre/6-inch crêpe pan.

STORE: 2 days refrigerated, 3 months frozen.

INGREDIENTS	WEIGHT		MEASURE
room temperature	*grams*	*pounds/ounces*	*volume*
3 eggs, size 2	150 grams (weighed without shells)	5¼ ounces	scant ⅔ cup
milk	242 grams	8½ ounces	1 cup
pure vanilla extract	4 grams	—	1 teaspoon
unsalted butter, melted	43 grams	1½ ounces	3 tablespoons
Grand Marnier	15 grams	½ ounce	1 tablespoon
cornflour*	90 grams	3 ounces	¾ cup
salt	—	—	⅛ teaspoon
castor sugar	12 grams	½ ounce	1 tablespoon
clarified butter†	12 grams	½ ounce	1 tablespoon

* You can use up to 120 grams/4¼ ounces/1 cup cornflour if you prefer a thicker crêpe with more bite.
† If you do not have clarified butter on hand, you will need to clarify 43 grams/1½ ounces/3 tablespoons unsalted butter. In a heavy saucepan melt the butter over medium heat, partially covered to prevent splattering. When it looks clear, cook, uncovered, watching carefully until the solids drop and begin to brown. Pour immediately through a fine strainer or a strainer lined with cheesecloth.

The easiest and fastest way to mix the batter is in a blender. Place the ingredients in the order given in a blender and blend at high speed for 10 seconds.

Heat the crêpe pan on medium-high heat until hot enough to sizzle a drop of water. Brush lightly with clarified butter and pour a scant 2 tablespoons batter into the centre. Immediately tilt the pan to the left and then down and around to the right so that the batter moves in an anti-clockwise direction, covering the entire pan.

Cook until the top starts to dull and the edges begin to brown, about 15 to 20 seconds. I like to use a small metal spatula to lift the upper edge and check to see if the crêpe is golden brown. Then, grasping the edge of the crêpe with my fingers, I flip it over and cook it for 10 seconds, or just until lightly browned. Invert the pan over the worktop and the crêpe will release.

It is fine to place one crêpe on top of another if serving the same day. If refrigerating or freezing the crêpes, however, separate them with pieces of greaseproof paper or they may stick to each other. Makes 21 to 24 crêpes (the larger amount if using 120 grams/4¼ ounces/1 cup cornflour).

Crêpes Suzette

Serves 6 to 8

This is one of the world's most glorious and dramatic desserts. There was a time, when I first discovered Crêpes Suzette in a class with James Beard, that everyone I loved had to experience them. I made them for my parents when they invited me for dinner; for my mentor Cecily Brownstone and her sister when I graduated from college; for a sophisticated Parisian girlfriend who picked up her plate and licked it (prompting me to do the same); for a cellist who broke our date and never knew what he missed (I never forgave him). Then for years I stopped making them only to rediscover them with renewed interest. My favourite sauce version was inspired by Julia Child and Simone Beck in *Mastering the Art of French Cooking*. Although it is traditional to rub sugar cubes on the orange rind to absorb the oils, I candy the rind instead and use it to garnish the crêpes. It is delicious to eat.

TO CANDY THE ORANGE RIND

Use a stripper (page 525) or vegetable peeler to peel one of the oranges. Be sure to remove only the orange portion and not the bitter white pith beneath. If using the vegetable peeler, cut the strips with a knife to make them narrower (about 5 millimetres/ ¼ inch wide).

Place the strips in a saucepan of boiling water and simmer for 15 minutes. Drain and rinse under cold water.

In a small saucepan combine the sugar, water and corn syrup and bring to a boil, stirring constantly. Stop stirring, add the orange strips, and cover tightly. Simmer on low heat for 15 minutes without stirring or uncovering. Cool covered.

TO MAKE THE ORANGE BUTTER SAUCE

Remove the rind of the second orange with a zester or vegetable peeler and chop into fine zest.

Squeeze both oranges and strain the juice. You should have 5¼ fluid ounces/165 grams/ 5¾ ounces. Add the lemon juice.

In a mixing bowl, with a whisk beater cream the butter and sugar for 1 minute or until very soft. Very gradually beat in the juice, chopped zest and the 3 tablespoons of Grand Marnier. (Makes 495 grams/17¼ ounces/2¾ cups orange butter sauce.) Set aside at room temperature for 1 day, refrigerate for up to 5 days or freeze for up to 3 months.

INGREDIENTS	WEIGHT		MEASURE
room temperature	*grams*	*pounds/ounces*	*volume*
1 recipe Chantilly Crêpes (page 118)			
FOR CANDYING THE RIND			
1 large orange			
castor sugar	67 grams	2¼ ounces	⅓ cup
water	79 grams	2¾ ounces	2½ fluid ounces
corn syrup	—	—	1 teaspoon
ORANGE BUTTER SAUCE			
1 large orange	—	—	—
lemon juice, freshly squeezed	—	—	1½ teaspoons
unsalted butter	227 grams	8 ounces	1 cup
castor sugar	50 grams	1¾ ounces	¼ cup
Grand Marnier	46 grams	1½ ounces	3 tablespoons
FOR FLAMBÉING			
icing sugar	38 grams	1¼ ounces	3 tablespoons
Grand Marnier *or* Curaçao	80 grams	2¾ ounces	2½ fluid ounces
brandy	74 grams	2½ ounces	2½ fluid ounces

To Serve: Lay a crêpe with its most attractive side down and spread it lightly with the orange butter. Fold in half and spread with more orange butter. Fold into triangles by folding in half or thirds. (To fold in thirds, the centre of the flat edge will become the point of the triangle. Fold each side down so that they meet in the centre, spread with a little more orange butter and fold in half.) Use a total of 1 tablespoon orange butter for each crêpe. Place the remaining orange butter in a large crêpe or sauté pan and heat until melted and bubbling. Place the crêpes and candied orange rind in the pan. Heat for 1½ minutes, spooning the orange butter over the crêpes. Remove from the heat and sprinkle with the icing sugar.

Place the liqueur in a large ladle or saucepan with a long handle. Heat until very hot and starting to flame. If necessary, tilt the ladle slightly so that the gas-burner flame will ignite it or use a very long match. Pour over the crêpes and allow to flame until it goes out.

Serve the crêpes garnished with the orange rind.

Note: The butter-spread, folded crêpes and remaining orange butter can be frozen for 3 months. Reheat covered in a 350°F/180°C/gas mark 4 oven for 20 to 30 minutes or until bubbling hot.

Lemon Crêpes Suzette

Serves 6 to 8

Lovers of lemon may prefer this lilting butter sauce to the traditional orange one. White rum accentuates the refreshing lemon flavour. Fresh blueberries are a colourful addition.

In a mixing bowl with a whisk beater, cream the butter and sugar for 1 minute or until very soft. Very gradually beat in the lemon zest and juice. (Makes 500 grams/ 17½ ounces/2¼ cups lemon butter sauce.) Set aside at room temperature for 1 day, refrigerate for up to 5 days, or freeze for up to 3 months.

To Serve: Lay a crêpe with its most attractive side down and spread it lightly with the lemon butter. Fold in half and spread with more lemon butter. Fold into triangles by folding in half or thirds. (To fold in thirds, the centre of the flat edge will become the point of the triangle. Fold each side down so that they meet in the centre, spread with a little more lemon butter and fold in half.) Use a total of 1 tablespoon lemon butter for each crêpe. Place the remaining lemon butter in a large crêpe or sauté pan and heat until melted and bubbling. Place the crêpes and optional blueberries in the pan. Heat for 1½ minutes, spooning the

INGREDIENTS	WEIGHT		MEASURE
room temperature	*grams*	*pounds/ounces*	*volume*
1 recipe Chantilly Crêpes (page 118)			
LEMON BUTTER SAUCE			
unsalted butter	170 grams	6 ounces	¾ cup
castor sugar	200 grams	7 ounces	1 cup
grated lemon zest	4 grams	—	2 teaspoons
lemon juice, freshly squeezed	125 grams	4¼ ounces	4 fluid ounces
optional: fresh blueberries	114 grams	4 ounces	1 cup
FOR FLAMBÉING			
icing sugar	38 grams	1¼ ounces	3 tablespoons
white rum	56 grams	2 ounces	4 fluid ounces

lemon butter over the crêpes. Remove from the heat and sprinkle with the icing sugar.

Place the rum in a large ladle or saucepan with a long handle. Heat until very hot and starting to flame. If necessary, tilt the ladle slightly so that the gas-burner flame will ignite it or use a very long match. Pour over the crêpes and allow to flame until it goes out.

Note: The butter-spread, folded crêpes and remaining lemon butter can be frozen for 3 months.

Lemon Cream Illusion
Crêpes

Serves 6 to 8

These individual little lemon souffléed crêpes are absolutely divine. They were inspired by the invention of Lemon Cream Illusion. This lemon curd and Italian meringue mixture is layered into each crêpe. During baking, it puffs up slightly to form an airy but creamy filling. This elegant presentation, unbelievably, can be assembled 1 day ahead and briefly baked just before serving.

TINS: One large sheet cake or Swiss-roll tin, lightly buttered.

Lay a crêpe with its most attractive side down on a work surface and spread one half with 2 tablespoons Lemon Cream Illusion. Fold, spread 1 tablespoon of cream on half, and fold again.

Place the crêpes in the prepared tin. If not baking the same day, cover with clingfilm and refrigerate.

When ready to bake, preheat the oven to 350°F/180°C/gas mark 4.

To Serve: Bake for 10 minutes or until slightly puffed. (Bake for 15 minutes if the crêpes were refrigerated.) Sprinkle with icing sugar, if desired.

INGREDIENTS

1 recipe Lemon Cream Illusion *without* gelatin (page 308)

1 recipe Chantilly Crêpes (page 118)

Chocolate Velour Crêpes
with Orange–Apricot Sauce

Serves 6

The flavour combination of velvety bittersweet chocolate and tangy, golden honeyed apricot is a marriage made in heaven. A scoop of Vanilla Ice Cream (page 329), slowly melting in the hot apricot sauce, is not entirely unwelcome.

INGREDIENTS	WEIGHT		MEASURE
room temperature	*grams*	*pounds/ounces*	*volume*
BATTER			
1 egg, size 2	50 grams (weighed without shell)	1¾ ounces	3 tablespoons + ½ teaspoon
1 egg yolk, size 2	19 grams	½ ounce	1 tablespoon + ½ teaspoon
milk	160 grams	5½ ounces	⅔ cup
pure vanilla extract	3 grams	–	¾ teaspoon
unsalted butter, melted	35 grams	1¼ ounces	2½ tablespoons
cognac	9 grams	–	2 teaspoons
cornflour	40 grams	1½ ounces	⅓ cup
unsweetened Dutch-processed cocoa *or* ¼ cup nonalkalised cocoa	18 grams	¾ ounce	3 tablespoons
castor sugar	38 grams	1¼ ounces	3 tablespoons
salt	–	–	pinch
clarified butter*	12 grams	½ ounce	1 tablespoon

* If you do not have clarified butter on hand, you will need to clarify 25 grams/1 ounce/2 tablespoons unsalted butter. In a heavy saucepan melt the butter over medium heat, partially covered to prevent splattering. When the butter looks clear, cook, uncovered, watching carefully until the solids drop and begin to brown. Pour immediately through a fine strainer or a strainer lined with cheesecloth.

INGREDIENTS	WEIGHT		MEASURE
room temperature	*grams*	*pounds/ounces*	*volume*
ORANGE–APRICOT SAUCE			
grated orange zest	4 grams	—	2 teaspoons
orange juice, freshly squeezed	121 grams	4¼ ounces	4 fluid ounces
unsalted butter	28 grams	1 ounce	2 tablespoons
apricot lekvar *or* jam	—	—	½ cup
FOR FLAMBÉING			
icing sugar	13 grams	½ ounce	2 tablespoons
Barack Palinka or apricot brandy	56 grams	2 ounces	2 fluid ounces

TIN: One 15 × 10-centimetre/ 6 × 4-inch crêpe pan.

STORE: 2 days refrigerated, 3 months frozen.

TO MAKE BATTER

The easiest and fastest way to mix the batter is in a blender. Place the ingredients in the order given into a blender and blend at high speed for 10 seconds.

Heat the crêpe pan on medium heat until hot enough to sizzle a drop of water. Brush lightly with clarified butter and pour a scant 2 tablespoons batter (1 tablespoon if using a 10-centimetre/4-inch pan) in the centre. Immediately tilt the pan to the left and then down and around to the right so that the batter moves in an anti-clockwise direction, covering the entire pan.

Cook until the top starts to dull and the edges begin to brown, about 15 to 20 seconds. I like to use a small metal spatula to lift the upper edge and check to see if the crêpe is golden brown. Then, grasping the edge of the crêpe with my fingers, I flip it over and cook for 10 seconds, or just until lightly browned. Do not use too high a heat as chocolate crêpes are more prone to burning. Invert the pan over the worktop and the crêpe will release.

It is fine to place 1 crêpe on top of another if serving the same day. If refrigerating or freezing the crêpes, however, separate them with pieces of wax paper or they may stick to each other. Makes fourteen 15-centimetre/6-inch crêpes or twenty-four 10-centimetre/4-inch crêpes.

TO MAKE ORANGE–APRICOT SAUCE
In a bowl stir together the orange zest, juice, butter and jam until smooth.

To Serve: Lay a crêpe with its most attractive side down and spread very lightly with the orange–apricot butter. Fold in half and spread with more butter. Fold into triangles by folding in half or thirds. (To fold in thirds, the centre of the flat edge will become the point of the triangle. Fold each side down so that they meet in the centre, spread with a little more orange–apricot butter and fold in half.) Use ½ tablespoon orange–apricot butter for each crêpe.

Place the remaining orange–apricot butter in a large, attractive crêpe or sauté pan and heat until melted and bubbling. Place the crêpes in the pan. Heat for 1½ minutes, spooning the orange–apricot sauce over the crêpes. Remove from the heat and sprinkle with the icing sugar.

Place the liqueur in a large ladle or saucepan with a long handle. Heat until very hot and starting to flame. If necessary tilt the ladle slightly so that the gas-burner flame will ignite it or use a very long match. Pour over the crêpes and allow to flame until it goes out.

Note: The butter-spread, folded crêpes and remaining orange–apricot butter can be frozen for 3 months.

Génoise and Other Whisked Sponge Cakes

Whisked sponge cakes depend on a large amount of beaten egg for their light, airy texture. These are the cakes to consider if you are trying to cut cholesterol, as most do not use butter and the angel food cake uses no egg yolks, making it cholesterol free.

Some of these cakes, such as chiffon cake, are moist enough to be eaten without a soaking syrup and therefore maintain their springy, lighter-than-air quality. The texture and flavours are so delightful that these cakes are usually eaten without icing.

Other whisked sponge cakes, such as classic *génoise* and Biscuit de Savoie, would seem dry and even rubbery without a soaking syrup and rather plain without whipped cream or buttercream. Liqueur-flavoured syrup transforms the resilient quality of *génoise* or *biscuit* into a delightfully tender and soft crumb.

Génoise is a European whisked sponge cake which differs from American whisked sponge in that it contains butter to tenderise partially and flavour it, and much less sugar. Even when syrup has been added to *génoise*, it is still less sweet than sponge cake, though a lot more moist. With a judicious amount of syrup, *génoise* is moist without being wet. Europeans, however, tend to favour a greater amount of syrup than do Americans. This is a question of personal preference.

Biscuit de Savoie is also a European whisked sponge-type cake which, like American sponge, contains no butter or oil but a lot more egg, making it lighter, drier and tougher until well soaked with syrup. Because it contains no added fat, it is lighter and can absorb more syrup than a *génoise* without losing its delicate texture. This makes it an especially refreshing cake.

For a detailed explanation of sponge-type cakes and a chart comparing the percentage of components in all cakes, see pages 535 and 536.

HIGHLIGHTS FOR SUCCESSFUL GÉNOISE, BISCUIT AND SPONGE CAKES

Note: It is best not to double most recipes in this chapter as standard mixing bowls are too small to accommodate their volume.

For fuller details see the suggested page number.
- Use plain flour that does not contain a raising agent (page 493). (Do not use self-raising sponge flour.)
- Use castor sugar for finest texture (page 500).
- Measure or weigh ingredients carefully (page 505).

- Heat eggs (or allow to warm) to temperature indicated in recipe.
- If a recipe indicates heating the egg–sugar mixture and you are using a hand–held mixer, beat the mixture over hot water until thickened. Then remove and continue beating until cool.
- When beating egg whites, use cream of tartar or beat just until stiff peaks form when the beater is raised slowly.
- Work quickly once the eggs are beaten so that they do not deflate.

- Fold flour gently but *thoroughly* into the batter.
- Bake immediately after mixing.
- Use the correct tin size (page 515).
- For very even layers and maximum height use Magi-Cake Strips (pages 516 and 522).
- Check for accurate oven temperature (page 514).
- Use correct baking time; do not underbake (page 5).
- Wrap cake layers well or glaze and ice them when cool (page 6).

Génoise Classique

Serves 8

A *génoise* that is gossamer and perfectly moistened and perfumed with syrup is pure poetry. The flavour and texture come to life only with the right amount of syrup. Too little will make the cake seem dry and tasteless; too much causes it to become heavy and sodden. I find the perfect amount of syrup to be 3 to 4 tablespoons for every egg used in the batter. If the cake is several days old and on the dry side, I add the extra tablespoon.

This *génoise* is the best I have ever experienced. It is very light yet perfectly fine-grained. The *beurre noisette* makes it seem rich without having to add so much butter that the texture loses its airy quality.

Since this recipe first appeared in print in 1981, I have received more calls about it from readers than for any other recipe. Many say that for the first time in their lives they have succeeded in making a perfect *génoise*.

INGREDIENTS	WEIGHT		MEASURE
room temperature	*grams*	*pounds/ounces*	*volume*
clarified *beurre noisette*★	37 grams	1¼ ounces	3 tablespoons
pure vanilla extract	4 grams	—	1 teaspoon
4 eggs, size 2	200 grams (weighed without shells)	7 ounces	6 full fluid ounces
castor sugar	100 grams	3½ ounces	½ cup
sifted plain flour	50 grams	1¾ ounces	¼ cup + 2 tablespoons
cornflour, lightly spooned	50 grams	1¾ ounces	½ cup − 1 tablespoon
SYRUP			
castor sugar	56 grams	2 ounces	¼ cup + 1½ teaspoons
water	118 grams	4 ounces	4 fluid ounces
liqueur of your choice	28 grams	1 ounce	2 tablespoons

★ If you do not have clarified butter on hand, you will need to clarify 57 grams/2 ounces/4 tablespoons unsalted butter. In a heavy saucespan melt the butter over medium heat, partially covered to prevent splattering. When the butter looks clear, cook uncovered, watching carefully until the solids drop and begin to brown. Pour immediately through a fine strainer or a strainer lined with cheesecloth.

TINS: One 23 × 5-centimetre/ 9 × 2-inch tin or 23-centimetre/ 9-inch springform tin or 23 × 5-centimetre/9 × 2-inch heart-shaped tin or 20 × 5-centimetre/8 × 2-inch square tin, greased, bottom lined with parchment, and then greased again and floured.

FINISHED HEIGHT: After trimming bottom and top crusts: 4 centimetres/1½ inches.

STORE: Syrup: 1 month refrigerated in an airtight container. *Génoise:* Without syrup, 2 days room temperature, 5 days refrigerated, 2 months frozen. After adding the syrup the flavours ripen and the moisture is more evenly distributed 1 day later. The completed cake can be refrigerated up to 5 days and frozen up to 2 months.

COMPLEMENTARY ADORNMENTS: *One recipe:* Any buttercream, whipped cream, glaze, or fondant.

SERVE: Room temperature or lightly chilled.

POINTERS FOR SUCCESS: See pages xx and 128. A large balloon whisk or a slotted skimmer is ideal for folding in the flour with the least amount of air loss. If using the whisk, periodically shake out the batter which collects on the inside.

Preheat the oven to 350°F/180°C/gas mark 4.

Warm the *beurre noisette* until almost hot (110°–120°F/43°–49°C). Add the vanilla and keep warm.

In a large mixing bowl set over a pan of simmering water heat the eggs and sugar until just lukewarm, stirring constantly to prevent curdling. (The eggs may also be heated by placing them *still in their shells* in a large mixing bowl in an oven with a pilot light for 3 hours or up to overnight. The weight of the unshelled eggs should be 228 grams/8 ounces.) Using the whisk beater, beat the mixture on high speed for 5 minutes or until

tripled in volume. (A hand beater may be used but it will be necessary to beat for at least 10 minutes.)

While the eggs are beating, sift together the flour and cornflour.

Remove 1 scant cup of the egg mixture and thoroughly whisk it into the *beurre noisette*.

Sift half the flour mixture over the remaining egg mixture and fold it in gently but rapidly with a large balloon whisk, slotted skimmer or rubber spatula until almost all the flour has disappeared. Repeat with the remaining flour mixture until the flour has disappeared completely. Fold in the butter mixture until just incorporated.

Pour immediately into the prepared tin (it will be about two-thirds full) and bake for 25 to 35 minutes or until the cake is golden brown and starts to shrink slightly from the sides of the tin. (No need for a cake tester. Once the sides shrink the cake is done.) Avoid opening the oven door before the minimum time or the cake could fall. Test towards the end of baking by opening the door slightly and, if at a quick glance it does not appear done, close the door at once and check again in 5 minutes.

Loosen the sides of the cake with a small metal spatula and turn it out at once on to a lightly greased rack. Reinvert to cool. Trim the bottom and top crust when ready to complete the cake and sprinkle the syrup evenly on both sides (page 409).★

TO MAKE SYRUP

In a small saucepan with a tight-fitting lid bring the sugar and water to a rolling boil, stirring constantly. Cover immediately, remove from the heat and allow to cool completely. Transfer to a liquid-measuring jug and stir in the liqueur. If the syrup has evaporated slightly, add enough water to equal ¾ cup (200 grams/7 ounces) syrup.

UNDERSTANDING

It is fascinating to compare *génoise* to basic butter cake. For the same size cake, the *génoise* uses double the egg, half the sugar, flour/cornflour and butter, and no chemical raising agent or added liquid. This explains why the *génoise* is 'lighter than air'! With the addition of syrup, however, the sugar level is almost as high as in the butter cake.

I once spent an entire week playing with *génoise* variations, proportions and techniques. I discovered by accidentally burning the butter that brown butter (*beurre noisette*) transforms the flavour of a *génoise*, adding richness and dimension. (This was published in the American *Cook's* magazine, May/June 1981.) Butter is warmed before folding into the batter so that it stays liquid and does not weigh down the batter.

Replacing some of the flour with cornflour tightens the grain and holds the moisture supplied by the eggs and sugar. Although using part plain flour produces the best texture, other flours (with the exception of self-raising sponge flour) will work, even flours that are all starch such as potato flour (although the higher the starch content, the lower the *génoise*). I have demonstrated this cake throughout Europe and even in Japan with 'native' flours and always with success.

VARIATION

GÉNOISE RICHE:

For a more buttery *génoise* that is denser and moister, use 71 grams/2½ ounces/⅓ cup *beurre noisette*. This *génoise* will require only half the syrup for moisture and flavour so it will be richer but less sweet!

This cake is used to make A Taste of Heaven (page 188), Star-Spangled Rhapsody (page 193) and Chocolate Chip Charlotte (page 204).

★After being sprinkled with syrup, *génoise* becomes fragile and more prone to splitting when moved. Use a cardboard round or a removable cake-tin bottom for support.

Chestnut Génoise

Serves 8

Chestnut flour (see page 484) has almost the same starch content as cornflour, so it occurred to me one day to try substituting it for the cornflour portion of a *génoise*. The result was exciting: the incredible lightness of *génoise* remained, augmented by the mild spiciness of chestnut. This particular *génoise* tastes exquisite with rum syrup and filled and topped with Chestnut Mousse Cream. I call the finished cake La Châtaigne (page 216), a lovely French word for 'chestnut'. This cake makes an elegant and unusual dessert for a special occasion.

TINS: Two 23 × 4-centimetre/ 9 × 1½-inch tins, greased, bottoms lined with parchment, and then greased again and floured.

FINISHED HEIGHT: After trimming the bottom and top crusts each layer is 2.5 centimetres/1 inch.

STORE: Syrup: 1 month refrigerated in airtight container. *Génoise:* Without syrup, 2 days at room temperature, 5 days refrigerated, 2 months frozen. After adding the syrup the flavours ripen and the moisture is more evenly distributed 1 day later. The completed cake can be refrigerated up to 5 days and frozen up to 2 months.

COMPLEMENTARY ADORNMENTS: Chestnut Mousse Cream (page 303).

SERVE: Lightly chilled.

POINTERS FOR SUCCESS: See pages xx and 128. A large balloon whisk or a slotted skimmer is ideal for folding in the flour with the least amount of air loss. If using the whisk, periodically shake out the batter which collects on the inside.

INGREDIENTS	WEIGHT		MEASURE
room temperature	*grams*	*pounds/ounces*	*volume*
clarified *beurre noisette**	50 grams	1¾ ounces	¼ cup
pure vanilla extract	6 grams	—	1½ teaspoons
6 eggs, size 2	300 grams (weighed without shells)	10½ ounces	10 scant fluid ounces
castor sugar	150 grams	5¼ ounces	¾ cup
plain flour	75 grams	2.63 ounces†	½ cup (dip and sweep method)
sifted chestnut flour	75 grams	2.63 ounces†	⅔ cup
RUM SYRUP			
castor sugar	88 grams	3 ounces	¼ cup + 3 tablespoons
water	177 grams	6 ounces	6 fluid ounces
dark rum	40 grams	1½ ounces	3 tablespoons

*If you do not have clarified *beurre noisette* on hand, you will need to clarify 78 grams/2¾ ounces/ 5½ tablespoons unsalted butter. In a heavy saucepan melt the butter over medium heat, partially covered to prevent splattering. When the butter looks clear, cook uncovered, watching carefully until the solids drop and begin to brown. When they become deep brown, pour immediately through a fine strainer or a strainer lined with cheesecloth.
†If you don't have an electronic scale, don't worry about getting the ounces for the cake flour and chestnut flour exact as long as their combined total is 5¼ ounces.

Preheat the oven to 350°F/180°C/gas mark 4.

Warm the *beurre noisette* until almost hot (110°–120°F/43°–49°C). Add the vanilla and keep warm.

In a large mixing bowl set over a pan of simmering water heat the eggs and sugar until just lukewarm, stirring constantly to prevent curdling. (The eggs may also be heated by placing them *still in their shells* in a large mixing bowl in an oven with a pilot light for 3 hours or up to overnight. The weight of the unshelled eggs should be 342 grams/12 ounces.) Using the whisk beater, beat the mixture on high speed for 5 minutes or until tripled in volume. (A hand beater may be used but it will be necessary to beat for at least 10 minutes.)

While the eggs are beating, sift together the flours.

Remove 1 scant cup of the egg mixture and thoroughly whisk it into the *beurre noisette*.

Sift half the flour mixture over the remaining egg mixture and fold it in gently but rapidly with a large balloon whisk, slotted skimmer or rubber spatula until almost all the flour has disappeared. Repeat with the remaining flour mixture until the flour has disappeared completely. Fold in the butter mixture until just incorporated.

Pour immediately into the prepared tins (they will be almost two-thirds full) and bake for 25 to 30 minutes or until the cakes are golden brown and start to shrink slightly from the sides of the tins. (No need for a cake tester. Once the sides shrink the cakes are done.) Avoid opening the oven door before the minimum time or the cakes could fall. Test towards the end of baking by opening the door slightly and, if at a quick glance they do not appear done, close the door at once and check again in 5 minutes.

Loosen the sides of the cakes with a small metal spatula and turn them out at once on to lightly greased racks. Reinvert to cool. Trim the bottom and top crusts when ready to complete the cakes and sprinkle the syrup evenly on all sides (page 409).★

TO MAKE SYRUP
In a small saucepan with a tight-fitting lid bring the sugar and water to a rolling boil, stirring constantly. Cover immediately, remove from the heat and allow to cool completely. Transfer to a liquid measuring jug and stir in the rum. If the syrup has evaporated slightly, add enough water to equal 1 cup + 2 tablespoons (300 grams/ 10½ ounces) syrup.

This cake is used to make Chestnut Chocolate Embrace (page 216).

★After being sprinkled with syrup, *génoise* becomes fragile and more prone to splitting when moved. Use a cardboard round or a removable cake-tin bottom for support.

Golden Génoise

Serves 12

This unique *génoise* has the most velvety, tender texture and rich golden colour of any cake in this book. The batter, by the way, also makes the loveliest of *madeleines* (shell-shaped biscuits).

Golden Génoise is so moist no syrup is necessary, but a sprinkling of liqueur is a fine enhancement. The fine, dense texture of this cake can support any buttercream, from classic to mousseline. This is a superb party cake – a real favourite.

TINS: One 23 × 5-centimetre/ 9 × 2-inch heart-shaped tin or a 23-centimetre/9-inch springform tin, greased, bottom lined with parchment, and then greased again and floured. Or a 9-cup (2⅛-litre) Kugelhopf tin (page 517), greased and floured.

FINISHED HEIGHT: 5 centimetres/ 2 inches including crust. Kugelhopf is 7.5 centimetres/3 inches.

STORE: 2 days room temperature, 5 days refrigerated, 2 months frozen.

COMPLEMENTARY ADORNMENTS: The texture of this cake is firm enough to support any non-chocolate buttercream (chocolate would overwhelm the flavour) but interesting enough to stand up beautifully under just a light sprinkling of icing sugar. Suggested buttercreams: *One recipe:* Any fruit-flavoured buttercream such as Apricot Buttercream (page 270 or 281) or Orange Blossom Buttercream (page 271) or Praline Buttercream (page 268 or 279).

SERVE: Room temperature.

POINTERS FOR SUCCESS: See pages xx and 128. A large balloon whisk or a slotted skimmer is ideal for folding in the flour with the least amount of air loss. If using the whisk, periodically shake out the batter which collects on the inside.

Preheat the oven to 350°F/180°C/gas mark 4.

Warm the *beurre noisette* until almost hot (110°–120°F/43°–49°C). Add the vanilla and keep warm.

In a large mixing bowl set over a pan of simmering water heat the yolks and sugar until almost hot to

INGREDIENTS	WEIGHT		MEASURE
room temperature	*grams*	*pounds/ounces*	*volume*
clarified *beurre noisette*★	85 grams	3 ounces	3.5 fluid ounces (a scant ½ cup)
pure vanilla extract	4 grams	—	1 teaspoon
12 egg yolks, size 2	223 grams	7¾ ounces	7 fluid ounces
castor sugar	175 grams	6 ounces	¾ cup + 2 tablespoons
sifted plain flour	100 grams	3½ ounces	1 cup − 3 tablespoons
unsifted cornflour	24 grams	¾ ounce	3 tablespoons
water	60 grams	2 ounces	2 fluid ounces

★ If you do not have clarified *beurre noisette* on hand, you will need to clarify 128 grams/4½ ounces/ 9 tablespoons unsalted butter. In a heavy saucepan melt the butter over medium heat, partially covered to prevent splattering. When the butter looks clear, cook uncovered, watching carefully until the solids drop and begin to brown. When they become deep brown, pour immediately through a fine strainer or a strainer lined with cheesecloth.

the touch, stirring constantly to prevent curdling. Using a whisk beater, beat the mixture on high speed for 5 minutes or until tripled in volume. (A hand beater may be used but it will be necessary to beat for at least 10 minutes.)

While the eggs are beating, sift together the flour and cornflour. Decrease the speed and beat in the water. Sift half the flour mixture over the egg mixture and fold it in gently but rapidly with a large balloon whisk, slotted skimmer or rubber spatula until almost all the flour has disappeared. Repeat with the remaining flour mixture until the flour has disappeared

completely. Fold in the *beurre noisette* in two batches until just incorporated.

Pour immediately into the prepared tin (no more than three-quarters full) and bake for 30 to 40 minutes or until the cake is golden brown and springs back when pressed lightly in the centre.

(In the Kugelhopf tin the cake should start to shrink slightly from the sides. In the heart-shaped tin it will rise about 1 centimetre/½ inch above the top during baking and will start to sink slightly when done. No need for a cake tester. Once the sides shrink the cake is done.) Avoid opening the oven door before the minimum time or the cake could fall. Test towards the end of baking by opening the door slightly and, if at a quick glance it does not appear done, close the door at once and check again in 5 minutes.

Turn the cake out at once on to a lightly greased rack. Reinvert to cool. If sprinkling with liqueur, trim the top and bottom crusts to prevent pastiness. The cake may be split horizontally to make two layers. I love the texture of this cake so much I prefer one uninterrupted layer with icing on the top.

UNDERSTANDING
In contrast to classic *génoise*, this recipe uses all yolks instead of whole eggs, more butter and less flour. A small amount of water is added because the yolks alone make such a thick batter.

This cake is used to make Golden Cage (page 196).

White Génoise

Serves 10 to 12

This is another unusual *génoise* with less cholesterol than the classic formula. It is a cross between an angel food cake and a *génoise*: less airy than the angel food but buttery and more tender. Syrup makes the cake's texture pasty, so for flavour orange zest is added to the batter instead. For a delightful orange blossom flavour, replace 1 tablespoon of the water with orange flower water. Any fruit-flavoured buttercream, especially orange, is a fine complement.

TINS: Two 23 × 4–centimetre/ 9 × 1½-inch tins, greased, bottoms lined with parchment, and then greased again and floured.

FINISHED HEIGHT: After trimming the bottom and top crusts each layer is 3 centimetres/1¼ inches.

STORE: 1 day room temperature, 3 days refrigerated, 2 months frozen.

INGREDIENTS	WEIGHT		MEASURE
room temperature	*grams*	*pounds/ounces*	*volume*
clarified *beurre noisette*★	80 grams	2¾ ounces	3 full fluid ounces (6.5 tablespoons)
pure vanilla extract	6 grams	—	1½ teaspoons
grated orange zest	12 grams	½ ounce	2 tablespoons
plain flour	170 grams	6 ounces	1⅓ cups (lightly spooned into cup)
cornflour	85 grams	3 ounces	¾ cup − 2 teaspoons (lightly spooned into cup)
9 egg whites, size 2	270 grams	9½ ounces	9 fluid ounces
castor sugar	255 grams	9 ounces	1¼ cups
water	177 grams	6¼ ounces	6 fluid ounces
optional: Cointreau	122 grams	4¼ ounces	½ cup

★ If you do not have clarified *beurre noisette* on hand, you will need to clarify 128 grams/4½ ounces/ 9 tablespoons unsalted butter. In a heavy saucepan melt the butter over medium heat, partially covered to prevent splattering. When the butter looks clear, cook uncovered, watching carefully until the solids drop and begin to brown. When they become deep brown, pour immediately through a fine strainer or a strainer lined with cheesecloth.

COMPLEMENTARY ADORNMENTS: *One recipe:* Orange, Lemon, or Raspberry Buttercream (pages 270 to 271). Any flavoured whipped cream, especially Chocolate Chip (page 298). Rolled Fondant (page 354).

SERVE: Room temperature.

POINTERS FOR SUCCESS: See pages xx and 128. A large balloon whisk or slotted skimmer is ideal for folding in the flour with the least amount of air loss. If using the whisk, periodically shake out the batter that collects on the inside.

Preheat the oven to 350°F/180°C/gas mark 4.
    Warm the *beurre noisette* until almost hot (110°–120°F/43°–49°C). Add the vanilla and orange zest and keep warm.
    Sift together the flour and cornflour.

In a large mixing bowl beat the egg whites until soft peaks form when the beater is raised. Gradually beat in the sugar, beating just until stiff peaks form when the beater is raised slowly. Gradually beat in the water until incorporated. Remove 1 scant cup of the mixture and thoroughly whisk it into the butter.

Sift half the flour mixture over the remaining egg mixture and fold it in gently but rapidly with a large balloon whisk, slotted skimmer or rubber spatula until the flour has disappeared. Repeat with the remaining flour mixture. Fold in the butter mixture until just incorporated.

Pour immediately into the prepared tins and bake for 20 to 25 minutes or until the cake is golden brown and a tester inserted in the centre comes out clean. Avoid opening the oven door before the minimum time or the cakes could fall. Test towards the end of baking by opening the door slightly and, if at a quick glance they do not appear done, close the door at once and check again in 5 minutes.

Turn out the cakes at once on to lightly greased racks. Reinvert to cool.

Trim the bottom and top crusts when ready to complete the cake. For extra moistness and flavour, sprinkle evenly on all sides with Cointreau (page 409).

UNDERSTANDING

The proportions of this cake are similar to classic *génoise* (equal weight sugar and flour/cornflour: one-quarter their combined weight in butter, before it has been clarified) but the yolks are replaced by water. The water enables the whites to stretch and expand in the oven resulting in a fine-textured, tender cake.

This cake is used to make White Lily Cake (page 234).

Génoise au Chocolat

Serves 8

This *génoise* variation is as light and airy as a classic *génoise* but with the magic seduction of rich chocolate flavour! A syrup maintains a moist, tender quality. Be sure to flavour the syrup with a complementary liqueur. Coffee, hazelnut, raspberry and orange are all delicious with chocolate. An airy icing (flavoured to correspond with the syrup) such as a Fruit Cloud Cream (page 306) or Fruit Mousseline (page 284) adds just the right touch.

This elegant cake is light enough to serve at the end of an elaborate dinner party. Conveniently, it benefits from advance preparation.

TINS: One 23 × 5-centimetre/ 9 × 2-inch tin, 23-centimetre/ 9-inch springform tin, or a 23 × 5-centimetre/9 × 2-inch heart-shaped tin, greased, bottom lined with parchment or greaseproof paper, and then greased again and floured.

FINISHED HEIGHT: After trimming the bottom and top crusts: 4 centimetres/1½ inches.

STORE: Syrup: 1 month refrigerated in airtight container. *Génoise:* Without syrup, 2 days at room temperature, 5 days refrigerated, 2 months frozen. After adding the syrup the flavours ripen and the moisture is more evenly distributed 1 day later. The completed cake can be refrigerated up to 5 days and frozen up to 2 months.

COMPLEMENTARY ADORNMENTS: *One recipe:* Any glaze, fondant, buttercream, or whipped cream – especially coffee, praline, chestnut, orange, apricot and raspberry.

SERVE: Room temperature or lightly chilled.

POINTERS FOR SUCCESS: See pages xx and 128. The cocoa mixture must be thoroughly mixed into the batter to keep from dropping to the bottom. The cake must start shrinking from the sides of the tin before removal from the oven or it will fall slightly on cooling.

INGREDIENTS	WEIGHT		MEASURE
room temperature	*grams*	*pounds/ounces*	*volume*
clarified *beurre noisette**	37 grams	1¼ ounces	3 tablespoons
unsweetened cocoa (preferably Dutch processed) *or* ¼ cup + 2 tablespoons nonalkalised cocoa	28 grams	1 ounce	⅓ cup (lightly spooned into cup)
boiling water	60 grams	2 ounces	2 fluid ounces
pure vanilla extract	4 grams	—	1 teaspoon
5 eggs, size 2	250 grams (weighed without shells)	8¾ ounces	8 fluid ounces
castor sugar	100 grams	3½ ounces	½ cup
sifted plain flour	75 grams	2½ ounces	½ cup (dip and sweep method)
SYRUP			
castor sugar	56 grams	2 ounces	¼ cup + 1½ teaspoons
water	118 grams	4 ounces	4 fluid ounces
liqueur of your choice	28 grams	1 ounce	2 tablespoons

*If you do not have clarified *beurre noisette* on hand, you will need to clarify 57 grams/2 ounces/ 4 tablespoons unsalted butter. In a heavy saucepan melt the butter over medium heat, partially covered to prevent splattering. When the butter looks clear, cook uncovered, watching carefully until the solids drop and begin to brown. When they become deep brown, pour immediately through a fine strainer or a strainer lined with cheesecloth.

Preheat the oven to 350°F/180°C/gas mark 4.

Warm the *beurre noisette* until almost hot (110°–120°F/43°–49°C) and keep warm.

In a small bowl whisk together the cocoa and boiling water until the cocoa is completely dissolved. Stir in the vanilla and set aside, leaving the whisk in the bowl, and cover with clingfilm.

In a large mixing bowl set over a pan of simmering water heat the eggs and sugar until just lukewarm, stirring constantly to prevent curdling. (The eggs may also be heated by placing them *still in their shells* in a large bowl in an oven with a pilot light for at least 3 hours. The weight of the unshelled eggs should be 285 grams/ 10 ounces.) Using the whisk beater, beat the mixture on high speed for 5 minutes or until tripled in volume. (A hand beater may be used but it will be necessary to beat for at least 10 minutes.)

Remove 2 cups of the egg mixture and whisk it into the cocoa mixture until smooth.

Sift the flour over the remaining egg mixture and fold it in gently but rapidly with a slotted skimmer or large rubber spatula until the flour has disappeared. Fold in the cocoa mixture until almost incorporated. Fold in the *beurre noisette* in two batches with a large whisk or rubber spatula until just incorporated.*

Pour immediately into the prepared tin (it will be about three-quarters full) and bake for 30 to 35 minutes or until the cake starts to shrink from the sides of the tin. (No need for a cake tester. Once the sides shrink the cake is done.) Avoid opening the oven door before the minimum time or the cake could fall. Test towards the end of baking by opening the oven door slightly and, if at a quick glance it does not appear done,

close the door at once and check again in 5 minutes.

Loosen the sides of the cake with a small metal spatula and turn it out at once on to a lightly greased rack. Reinvert to cool. The firm upper crust prevents falling. Trim the bottom and top crusts when ready to complete the cake and sprinkle the syrup evenly on both sides (page 409).†

TO MAKE SYRUP

In a small saucepan with a tight-fitting lid bring the sugar and water to a rolling boil, stirring constantly. Cover immediately, remove from the heat and allow to cool completely. Transfer to a liquid measuring jug and stir in the liqueur. If the syrup has evaporated slightly, add enough water to equal ¾ cup (200 grams/7 ounces) syrup.

UNDERSTANDING

I have never before liked chocolate *génoise* as much as classic *génoise* because I feel a mere shadow of chocolate is not enough to justify the loss of delicate texture. The problem is that cocoa is very difficult to incorporate into an egg mixture as it tends to lump and drop to the bottom. Also, it does not release its full flavour unless it has been dissolved in water before being added to the batter

*Using your fingers is actually the best way to feel for lumps of flour. Dissolve them by pressing them between thumb and forefinger.
†After being sprinkled with syrup, *génoise* becomes fragile and more prone to splitting when moved. Use a cardboard round or a removable cake-tin bottom for support.

(page 541). Although water is not conventionally used in *génoise*, to solve these problems I combined the cocoa with just enough water to dissolve it and softened the resulting 'cream' by whisking in 2 cups (½ litre) of the beaten egg–sugar mixture before folding it into the remainder. An extra egg has been added to make up for deflating some of the batter with the cocoa. For further lightness, the cornflour has been eliminated. The cocoa–flour mixture is equal in weight to the cornflour/flour mixture of classic *génoise*.

This cake is used to make Strawberry Maria (page 210).

VARIATION

NUT-FLAVOURED CHOCOLATE GÉNOISE:

This interesting variation substitutes nut oil for the butter, giving it nut flavour without affecting the lovely, light texture of the *génoise*. It also lowers the cholesterol content. The nut motif can be enhanced by using Frangelico as the liqueur in the syrup. *To make Nut-Flavoured Chocolate Génoise:* Substitute 40 grams/1½ ounces/ 3 tablespoons walnut or hazelnut oil for the butter. There is no need to warm the oil as it remains liquid at room temperature and does not harden when added to the batter.

Notes: The ideal amount of syrup to use for the finished *génoise* is equal in volume to the flour.

The upper crust of a chocolate *génoise* is usually easy to remove in one piece. It has a wonderful texture and very chocolaty flavour so I usually spread it with a layer of lightly sweetened whipped cream, roll and slice it, and serve the slices as petits fours.

Moist Chocolate Génoise

Serves 10 to 12

This cake has the light texture of a *génoise* but is more velvety and moist. An equivalent amount of chocolate is used instead of cocoa, but a special technique is employed to intensify the flavour. Before being added to the batter, the chocolate is cooked with water which releases its flavour (page 541). This enables you to have a *génoise* the flavour of your favourite bittersweet chocolate bar!

TINS: Two 23 × 5-centimetre/ 9 × 2-inch cake tins or 23-centimetre/9-inch springform tins, greased, bottoms lined with parchment, and then greased again and floured.

FINISHED HEIGHT: After trimming the bottom and top crusts each layer is 3 centimetres/ 1¼ inches.

STORE: Syrup: 1 month refrigerated in an airtight container.

Génoise without syrup: 2 days room temperature, 5 days refrigerated, 2 months frozen. After adding the syrup the flavours ripen and the moisture is more evenly distributed 1 day later. The completed cake can be refrigerated up to 5 days and frozen up to 2 months.

COMPLEMENTARY ADORNMENTS: A light sprinkling of liqueur. Any ganache (pages 309 to 313). This cake is not too sweet so it is perfect as a base for some of the sweeter decorative toppings such as Chocolate Praline Sheets (page 446). It also makes an excellent base for the Swiss Black Forest Cake (page 218).

SERVE: Room temperature or lightly chilled.

POINTERS FOR SUCCESS: See pages xx and 128.

INGREDIENTS	WEIGHT		MEASURE
room temperature	*grams*	*pounds/ounces*	*volume*
bittersweet chocolate	227 grams	8 ounces	—
boiling water	236 grams	8¼ ounces	8 fluid ounces
8 eggs, size 2	400 grams (weighed without shells)	14 ounces	12 fluid ounces
castor sugar	200 grams	7 ounces	1 cup
sifted plain flour	150 grams	5¼ ounces	1 cup + 3 tablespoons
SYRUP			
castor sugar	88 grams	3 ounces	¼ cup + 3 tablespoons
water	182 grams	6 ounces	6 fluid ounces
liqueur of your choice	40 grams	1½ ounces	3 tablespoons

Preheat the oven to 350°F/180°C/gas mark 4.

In a heavy saucepan bring the chocolate and water to a boil over low heat, stirring constantly. Simmer, stirring, for 5 minutes or until the chocolate thickens to a blancmange-like consistency. (It will fall from the spoon and pool slightly before disappearing.) Cool completely.

In a large mixing bowl, beat the eggs and sugar with the whisk beater on high speed for 5 minutes or until tripled in volume. (A hand beater may be used but it will be necessary to beat for at least 10 minutes.)

Sift half the flour over the egg mixture and fold it in gently but rapidly with a slotted skimmer or large rubber spatula until some of the flour has disappeared. Repeat with the remaining flour until all the flour has disappeared. Fold in the chocolate mixture until incorporated.

Pour immediately into the prepared tins (they will be about two-thirds full) and bake for 30 to 35 minutes or until a tester inserted in the centres enters as easily as it does when inserted closer to the sides. The cakes rise to the tops of the tins during baking and will lower slightly when done, pulling slightly away from the sides. Avoid opening the oven door before the minimum time or the cakes could fall.

Loosen the sides of the cakes with a small metal spatula and turn them out at once on to lightly greased racks. Reinvert to cool. The firm upper crusts prevent falling. Trim the bottom and top crusts when ready to complete the cake and sprinkle syrup evenly on all sides.★

TO MAKE SYRUP
In a small saucepan with a tight-fitting lid bring the sugar and water to a rolling boil, stirring constantly. Cover immediately, remove from the heat and allow to cool completely. Transfer to a liquid measuring cup and stir in the liqueur. If the syrup has evaporated slightly, add enough water to equal 1 cup plus 2 tablespoons (300 grams/10½ ounces) syrup.

UNDERSTANDING
The ratio of ingredients in this cake is similar to Génoise au Chocolat. The Moist Chocolate Génoise has the same amount of sugar and flour as the same size Génoise au Chocolat (the 113 grams/4 ounces of sugar provided by the bittersweet chocolate are exactly equal to the 113 grams/4 ounces of sugar provided by the syrup used for two layers of the Génoise au Chocolat). Moist Chocolate Génoise, however, contains a little less egg, more than double the water, and, instead of butter, 71 grams/2½ ounces of cocoa butter contained by the chocolate. All of these variables are responsible for making this cake's texture more moist and dense than classic Génoise au Chocolat. Because this cake is not as light and airy, two layers are necessary for sufficient height. Since the chocolate contains vanilla, no extra vanilla is added.

This cake is used to make Swiss Black Forest Cake (page 218) and Triple Chocolate Cake (page 232).

★After being sprinkled with syrup, a *génoise* becomes fragile and more prone to splitting when moved. Use a cardboard round or removable bottom of a cake tin to support it.

Queen Mother's Cake

Serves 8

The perfect cake for the cocoa lover, this recipe was inspired by Maida Heatter's glorious Queen Mother's Cake, which has become a classic. It is so chocolaty and moist without being sweet that I like to serve it without even a sprinkling of icing sugar. But if you insist on gilding the lily, the ideal way to do it is with lightly sweetened whipped cream (page 294) on the side.

It is not necessary to grease and flour the sides of the cake tin (making it a totally flourless cake, ideal for Passover, but omit the cream of tartar) because it is easy to dislodge the cake using a small metal spatula.

TIN: One 21-centimetre/8¼-inch springform tin ungreased, bottom lined with parchment or greaseproof paper, sides wrapped with Magi-Cake Strips (pages 516 and 522). With this cake it is particularly wise to use Magi-Cake Strips to prevent the sides from overbrowning during the long baking time.

FINISHED HEIGHT: 4 centimetres/1½ inches at the sides, 3 centimetres/1¼ inches in the centre.

STORE: 3 days room temperature, 5 days refrigerated, 2 months frozen.

COMPLEMENTARY ADORNMENTS: A light dusting of icing sugar. Perfect Whipped Cream (page 294).

SERVE: Room temperature or very lightly chilled.

POINTERS FOR SUCCESS: See pages xx and 128.

Preheat the oven to 350°F/180°C/gas mark 4.

In a small bowl stir together the cocoa and boiling water until the cocoa is dissolved and the mixture is the consistency of smooth buttercream. Stir in the vanilla and cool.

In a mixing bowl beat the butter and 200 grams/7 ounces/1 cup sugar for 3 minutes or until light and fluffy. Add the egg yolks and beat until incorporated, scraping down the sides. Add the cocoa mixture and almonds and beat until blended, scraping down the sides.

In a large mixing bowl beat the egg whites and salt until foamy.

INGREDIENTS	WEIGHT		MEASURE
room temperature	*grams*	*pounds/ounces*	*volume*
unsweetened cocoa (preferably Dutch-processed)	50 grams	1¾ ounces	½ cup + 1 tablespoon (lightly spooned into cup)
boiling water	100 grams	3½ ounces	3.5 fluid ounces
pure vanilla extract	4 grams	—	1 teaspoon
unsalted butter (must be softened)	227 grams	8 ounces	16 tablespoons
castor sugar	227 grams	8 ounces	1 cup + 2 tablespoons
6 eggs, size 2, separated			
yolks	112 grams	4 ounces	3.5 fluid ounces
whites	180 grams	6¼ ounces	6 fluid ounces
unblanched sliced almonds, toasted and finely ground	170 grams	6 ounces	scant 1⅔ cups (ground)
salt	—	—	⅛ teaspoon
cream of tartar	—	—	¾ teaspoon

Add the cream of tartar and beat until soft peaks form when the beater is raised. Gradually beat in the remaining sugar, beating until stiff peaks form when the beater is raised slowly. Stir one-quarter of the whites into the chocolate mixture to lighten it. Then gently fold in the remaining whites with a large rubber spatula.

Pour into the prepared tin (it will be about half full) and bake for 70 minutes. After 30 minutes, cover the top loosely with foil to prevent overbrowning. Cool the cake in the tin for 45 minutes. Run a small metal spatula around the sides of the cake and remove the sides of the tin. Invert on to a lightly greased rack and reinvert to cool. The cake sinks very slightly in the centre which adds interest to its shape!

UNDERSTANDING
The formula for Chocolate Nut Génoise is almost identical to Maida Heatter's Queen Mother's

Cake,★ with the chocolate replaced by cocoa, which contains less cocoa butter and no sugar. Therefore the sugar has been increased and butter replaces the cocoa butter. A small amount of water releases and intensifies the flavour of the cocoa. The result is a cake with assertive flavour but lighter texture than the original, particularly because butter is softer at room temperature and cocoa butter is firm. Cream of tartar is used to stabilise the egg whites as the chocolate mixture is quite heavy and tends to break them down.

Fudgy Génoise Jeffrey

Serves 8

This unusual *génoise* is delicate yet moist and fudgy with a crisp meringue-like crust. It was offered to me by a brilliant young doctor who turned his scientific talents to creating a cake which uses less than half the flour of ordinary chocolate *génoise* and no butter. Dr Elterman prefers to use Lindt Excellence chocolate to make this cake. (I have no complaint!)

TINS: Two 23 × 4-centimetre/ 9 × 1½-inch tins, greased, bottoms lined with parchment or greaseproof paper, and then greased again and floured.

STORE: 2 days room temperature, 5 days refrigerated. Freezing is not recommended as the texture becomes heavy after thawing and the flavour alters.

FINISHED HEIGHT: After trimming the bottom and top crusts, each layer is almost 2.5 centimetres/1 inch.

COMPLEMENTARY ADORNMENTS: Cake can be served plain in small wedges or with a dollop of Perfect Whipped Cream (page 294) or Light Whipped Ganache (page 310) spooned on top.

SERVE: Room temperature.

★Maida Heatter, *Maida Heatter's Book of Great Desserts* (New York: Alfred A. Knopf, 1974).

INGREDIENTS	WEIGHT		MEASURE
room temperature	*grams*	*pounds/ounces*	*volume*
bittersweet chocolate	284 grams	10 ounces	—
8 eggs, size 2, separated			
yolks	150 grams	5¼ ounces	4.5 fluid ounces
whites	240 grams	8½ ounces	8 fluid ounces
castor sugar	250 grams	8¾ ounces	1¼ cups
cream of tartar	3 grams	—	1 teaspoon
sifted plain flour	65 grams	2¼ ounces	½ cup

POINTERS FOR SUCCESS: See pages xx and 128.

Preheat the oven to 350°F/180°C/gas mark 4.

In a double boiler set over hot (not simmering) water, on low heat, melt the chocolate.

In a large mixing bowl set over a pan of simmering water heat the yolks and 50 grams/1¾ ounces/ ¼ cup sugar until almost hot to the touch, stirring constantly to prevent curdling. Using the whisk beater, beat the mixture on high speed for 5 minutes or until tripled in volume. (A hand beater may be used but it will be necessary to beat for at least 10 minutes.) Add the chocolate and immediately beat until incorporated.

In another large mixing bowl beat the egg whites until foamy, add the cream of tartar and beat until soft peaks form when the beater is raised. Gradually beat in the remaining sugar, beating until stiff peaks form when the beater is raised slowly.

Stir one-quarter of the whites into the chocolate batter to lighten it. Sift one-third of the flour over the batter and fold it in with a large rubber spatula gently but rapidly until partially blended. Add one-third of the remaining whites and fold until partially blended. Repeat twice more, starting with the flour and ending with the egg whites. After the final batch of flour, make sure all of it has disappeared before adding the whites.

Pour immediately into the prepared tins and bake for 35 minutes.

Loosen the sides with a small metal spatula and turn out the cakes at once on to lightly greased racks. Reinvert to cool.

UNDERSTANDING

Apart from the unusually small quantity of flour, this cake is similar in formula to Moist Chocolate Génoise. The chocolate, however, is not cooked in water (which would release more flavour). Instead, an extra ounce is used to intensify flavour. Also, more sugar is added to produce a chocolaty flavour without a bittersweet edge. As in Moist Chocolate Génoise, the only fat here comes from the cocoa butter in the chocolate.

Chocolate Cloud Roll

Serves 4

This is more a flourless soufflé than a cake. It is so light and delicate (both in texture and flavour) it has to be baked in a Swiss-roll tin or it will fall. I have discovered since including it in my first cookbook (*Romantic and Classic Cakes*) that severely cutting back the sugar not only intensifies the chocolate flavour but also improves the texture and helps to prevent cracking when the cake is rolled! Attractive as a cake roll, it also may be cut into squares, rounds or ovals and used as a layer cake.

Optional nuts add a subtle texture and flavour. Omit the nuts for an uninterrupted silken-smooth texture. Filled with whipped cream and fresh berries, this cake is the perfect light summer dessert for chocolate lovers.

TIN: One 30 × 20-centimetre/ 12 × 8-inch Swiss-roll tin, greased, bottom lined with a non-stick liner or foil (extending slightly over the sides), and then greased again and floured. (For Passover, it's fine to omit the flour as the cake will release almost as smoothly without it. Also omit the cream of tartar.)

FINISHED HEIGHT: 1 centimetre/ ½ inch before rolling.

STORE: 3 days room temperature, 5 days refrigerated, 2 months frozen.

COMPLEMENTARY FILLINGS: *One recipe:* Perfect Whipped Cream or Raspberry Jam Cream (page 294 or

INGREDIENTS	WEIGHT		MEASURE
room temperature	*grams*	*pounds/ounces*	*volume*
castor sugar	40 grams	1½ ounces	3 tablespoons
3 eggs, size 2, separated			
yolks	56 grams	2 ounces	1¾ fluid ounces
whites	90 grams	3 ounces	3 fluid ounces
bittersweet chocolate, melted	57 grams	2 ounces	—
optional: unblanched sliced almonds, toasted and finely ground	20 grams	¾ ounce	3 tablespoons (finely ground)
cream of tartar	—	—	⅜ teaspoon
unsweetened cocoa	3 grams	⅛ ounce	½ tablespoon

305). Mocha Whipped Cream (page 295). Light Whipped Ganache (page 310).

SERVE: Lightly chilled. If used as a roll, cut on the diagonal to form oval slices.

POINTERS FOR SUCCESS: See pages xx and 128. A large balloon whisk or slotted skimmer is ideal for folding in the egg whites with the least amount of air loss. If using the whisk, periodically shake out the batter which collects inside.

Position a shelf in the lower third of the oven.

Preheat the oven to 350°F/180°C/gas mark 4.

In a mixing bowl beat 2 table-spoons sugar and the egg yolks for 5 minutes or until light and fluffy. Add the chocolate, and almonds if desired, and beat until incorporated, scraping down the sides.

In a large mixing bowl beat the egg whites until foamy, add the cream of tartar, and beat until soft peaks form when the beater is raised. Gradually beat in the remaining sugar, beating until stiff peaks form when the beater is raised slowly.

With a large balloon whisk, slotted skimmer, or rubber spatula fold one-quarter of the whites into the chocolate mixture to lighten it. Then gently fold in the remaining egg whites.

Pour into the prepared tin,

spreading evenly with a spatula, and bake for 16 minutes. The cake will have puffed and lost its shine and will spring back when lightly pressed with a finger.

Wet a clean tea-towel and wring it out well. Remove the cake from oven and leave it in the tin. Dust with the cocoa and cover immediately with the damp tea-towel. (Use a dry tea-towel if planning to cut the cake into shapes.) Allow the cake to cool. Remove the tea-towel and, lifting by a long edge of the liner or foil overhang, gently slide the cake from the tin on to a flat surface. To use as a roll, spread at once with 1 cup filling and roll up, using the liner or foil for support and gently peeling it away as you go. To use as layers, double the recipe and bake in two tins. Use a 19-centimetre/7½-inch cardboard round to cut two rounds or a 23-centimetre/9-inch cardboard oval to cut out two ovals.

UNDERSTANDING
A larger amount of sugar causes chocolate rolls to crack because it absorbs some of the batter's moisture, making the cake more brittle.

This cake is used to make Chocolate Pine Cone (page 225) and Cordon Rose Chocolate Christmas Log (page 227).

Cocoa Soufflé Roll

Serves 4

This chocolate roll is airy yet exceptionally moist and intensely chocolate. The high moisture makes it virtually incapable of cracking! It is perfect with any whipped cream filling.

TINS: One 30 × 20-centimetre/ 12 × 8-inch Swiss-roll tin, greased, bottom lined with a non-stick liner or foil (extending slightly over the sides), and then greased again and floured. (For Passover, it's fine to omit the flour because the cake will release almost as smoothly without it. Also omit the cream of tartar.)

FINISHED HEIGHT: 1 centimetre/ ½ inch before rolling.

STORE: 3 days room temperature,

INGREDIENTS	WEIGHT		MEASURE
room temperature	*grams*	*pounds/ounces*	*volume*
unsweetened cocoa (preferably Dutch-processed *or* 3¹/₂ tablespoons nonalkalised cocoa	20 grams	1¹/₄ ounces	3 tablespoons + ¹/₂ teaspoon (lightly spooned into cup)
boiling water	30 grams	1 ounce	2 tablespoons
pure vanilla extract	2 grams	—	¹/₂ tablespoon
unsalted butter (must be softened)	15 grams	¹/₂ ounce	1 tablespoon
castor sugar	65 grams	2¹/₄ ounces	¹/₃ cup
3 eggs, size 2, separated			
yolks	56 grams	2 ounces	1³/₄ fluid ounces
whites	90 grams	3¹/₄ ounces	3 fluid ounces
optional: unblanched sliced almonds, toasted and finely ground	20 grams	³/₄ ounce	3 tablespoons (finely ground)
cream of tartar	—	—	³/₈ teaspoon

5 days refrigerated, 2 months frozen.

COMPLEMENTARY ADORNMENTS: *One recipe:* Perfect Whipped Cream (page 294) or Raspberry Jam Cream (page 305). Mocha Whipped Cream (page 295). Light Whipped Ganache (page 310).

SERVE: Lightly chilled. If used as a roll, cut on the diagonal to form oval slices.

POINTERS FOR SUCCESS: See pages xx and 128. A large balloon whisk or slotted skimmer is ideal for folding in the egg whites with the least amount of air loss. If using the whisk, periodically shake out the batter which collects inside.

Position a shelf in the lower third of the oven.

Preheat the oven to 350°F/180°C/ gas mark 4.

In a small bowl stir together all but 1 tablespoon of the cocoa and the boiling water until the cocoa is completely dissolved. Stir in the vanilla and butter and cool.

In a mixing bowl beat 2 tablespoons sugar and the egg yolks for 5 minutes or until light and fluffy. Add the chocolate mixture and almonds if desired and beat until incorporated, scraping down the sides.

In a large bowl beat the egg whites until foamy, add the cream of tartar, and beat until soft peaks form when the beater is raised. Gradually beat in the remaining sugar, beating until stiff peaks form when the beater is raised slowly. With large balloon whisk, slotted skimmer, or rubber spatula fold one-quarter of the whites into the chocolate mixture to lighten it. Then gently fold in the remaining egg whites.

Pour into the prepared tin, spreading evenly with a spatula, and bake for 18 minutes. The cake will have puffed and lost its shine and will spring back when lightly pressed with a finger.

Wet a clean tea-towel and wring it out well. Remove the cake from oven and leave it in the tin. Dust with the remaining 1 tablespoon cocoa and cover immediately with the damp tea-towel. (Use a dry tea-towel if planning to cut the cake into shapes.) Allow the cake to cool. Remove the towel and, lifting by a long edge of the liner or foil overhang, gently slide the cake from the tin on to a flat surface. To use as a roll, spread at once with about 245 grams/8½ ounces/2 cups filling and roll up, using the liner or foil for support and gently peeling it away as you go. To use as layers, cut in half for two rectangles or use a 14-centimetre/5½-inch cardboard round to cut out two rounds.

UNDERSTANDING

Cocoa replaces the cocoa solids previously provided by the chocolate. In the same way butter compensates for the cocoa butter and extra sugar for the sugar originally contained in the bittersweet chocolate. Water is used to dissolve the cocoa, releasing fuller chocolate flavour and providing moisture.

This cake is used to make The Enchanted Forest (page 224).

Biscuit Roulade

Serves 8

When moistened with syrup, Biscuit Roulade is one of the most tender and ethereal of cakes. It is similar to a Swiss roll but without baking powder. A sheet of *biscuit* has many possibilities. It can be filled with whipped cream and loosely rolled. It can be spread with jam, tightly rolled, and sliced to line a mould (as for Scarlet Empress, page 201). It can be cut with scissors into rounds to serve as a base and top for cheesecake or even cut with a biscuit cutter to decorate the sides of a cheesecake.

If this roulade is used with moist fillings such as whipped cream, Bavarian cream or cheesecake, a syrup would make the cake too wet. With a less moist filling, such as Lemon Curd, I sprinkle the cake roll with about 4 teaspoons of syrup for each whole egg used in the batter.

TINS: Two 30 × 20-centimetre/ 12 × 8-inch Swiss-roll tins, greased, bottoms lined with a non-stick liner or parchment, and then greased again and floured. (Liner extends slightly over the sides.)

FINISHED SIZE: Two 29 × 19 × 1 centimetres/ 11½ × 7½ × ½ inch. When the cake is rolled or assembled, it compresses to 7.5 millimetres/ ⅜ inch high.

STORE: 1 month refrigerated in an airtight container. *Biscuit:* 3 days room temperature, 5 days refrigerated, 2 months frozen.

COMPLEMENTARY FILLINGS: *One recipe:* Perfect Whipped Cream (page 294) or Raspberry Jam Cream (page 305). Lemon Curd Cream (page 306). Bavarian Cream if making Charlotte (page 331).

SERVE: Lightly chilled. If used as a roll, cut on the diagonal to form oval slices.

POINTERS FOR SUCCESS: See pages xx and 128. A large balloon whisk or slotted skimmer is ideal for folding in the flour with the least amount of air loss. If using the whisk, periodically shake out the batter which collects on the inside.

INGREDIENTS	WEIGHT		MEASURE
room temperature	*grams*	*pounds/ounces*	*volume*
sifted plain flour	35 grams	1¼ ounces	¼ cup + 1½ teaspoons
unsifted cornflour	23 grams	¾ ounce	3 tablespoons
4 eggs, size 2	227 grams (weighed in the shell)	8 ounces	—
1 egg yolk, size 2	18 grams	½ ounce	3½ teaspoons
castor sugar	113 grams	4 ounces	½ cups + 1 tablespoon
pure vanilla extract	3 grams	—	¾ teaspoon
cream of tartar	—	—	¼ teaspoon
SYRUP (*optional*)			
castor sugar	28 grams	1 ounce	2 tablespoons + a pinch
water	59 grams	2 ounces	2 fluid ounces
liqueur of your choice	14 grams	½ ounce	1 tablespoon

Position a shelf in the lower third of the oven.

Preheat the oven to 450°F/230°C/gas mark 8.

In a small bowl whisk together the flour and cornflour.

Separate 2 of the eggs, placing the yolks in one large mixing bowl and the whites in another. To the yolks, add the additional yolk, the 2 remaining eggs, and 100 grams/3½ ounces/½ cup sugar. Beat on high speed for 5 minutes or until thick, fluffy and tripled in volume.

Beat in the vanilla.

Sift half the flour mixture over the egg mixture and fold it in gently but rapidly with a large balloon whisk, slotted skimmer or rubber spatula until the flour has disappeared. Repeat with the remaining flour mixture.

Beat the egg whites until foamy, add the cream of tartar, and beat until soft peaks form when the beater is raised. Beat in the remaining sugar and beat until stiff peaks form when the beater is raised slowly. Fold the whites into the batter and pour into the prepared tins, using an angled metal spatula to level it.

Bake for 7 minutes or until golden brown, a cake tester comes out clean, and the cake is springy to the touch.

Loosen the edges with a small metal spatula or sharp knife and, lifting by a long edge of the liner or parchment overhang, gently slide the cake from the tins on to a flat surface. To use the *biscuit* for a round cake base or cut-outs, allow to cool flat, covered with a clean tea-towel. To use it for a roll, sprinkle lightly with icing sugar and roll it up while still hot. If using a liner, tightly roll up the *biscuit* with the liner. (This keeps the *biscuit* especially moist.) If using parchment, flip the *biscuit* on to a clean tea-towel, carefully remove the parchment, and roll it up tightly, tea-towel and all. Cool on a rack. When ready to fill, unroll the *biscuit*. (If a liner was used, first detach the cake from the liner and then replace it on the liner.) If using the syrup, sprinkle it on the cake before spreading it with about 122 grams/4¼ ounces/1 cup of filling for each cake.

TO MAKE SYRUP

In a small saucepan with a tight-fitting lid bring the sugar and water to a rolling boil, stirring constantly. Cover immediately, remove from the heat and cool.

Transfer to a liquid measuring jug and stir in the liqueur. If the syrup has evaporated slightly, add enough water to equal 2½ fluid ounces syrup.

UNDERSTANDING

This *biscuit* is even lighter than a *génoise* because it contains no butter and because some of the whites are beaten separately and folded into the batter.

When baking the *biscuit* as a thin sheet, less structural support is necessary, so the flour/cornflour mixture can be reduced to about half of what is used for classic *génoise* (instead of equal weight flour mixture and sugar, the Biscuit Roulade uses only half the weight in flour mixture). A high oven temperature, however, is necessary to set the cake's structure before it can fall. And an extra yolk is added to increase flexibility for rolling the sheet if desired.

This cake is used to make: Ethereal Pear Charlotte (page 199), Scarlet Empress (page 201) and Barquettes Chez L'Ami Louis (page 213).

VARIATIONS

GINGER BISCUIT:

1 tablespoon ginger juice added to the yolk mixture cuts the sweetness and adds a unique, subtle flavour. (To make ginger juice, grate fresh ginger on a fine grater and press with your fingers to squeeze out as much juice as possible.)

COMPLEMENTARY FILLING:

Perfect Whipped Cream (page 294) and poached pears.

CHOCOLATE BISCUIT:

Ideal for use as a chocolate version of the Scarlet Empress (page 201) because it is firmer than the Cloud Roll. It also has an excellent texture to use as ice-cream roll. Replace the cornflour with equal weight or ¼ cup cocoa. Dissolve the cocoa in 3 tablespoons boiling water and cool. Stir in the vanilla and add to the beaten yolk mixture, beating a few seconds or until incorporated. If not using the syrup, increase the sugar to 145 grams/5 ounces/ ⅔ cup plus 1 tablespoon.

COMPLEMENTARY FILLINGS:

Perfect Whipped Cream (page 294), Light Whipped Ganache (page 310), Bavarian Cream (pages 331–3), especially orange or raspberry.

ALMOND BISCUIT:

My favourite of all *biscuits* – moist, tender and flavourful because there are more almonds than flour.

In place of the flour/cornflour mixture,

use 35 grams/1¼ ounces/⅓ cup blanched, toasted and finely ground almonds and 21 grams/¾ ounce/2 tablespoons unsifted plain flour.

COMPLEMENTARY FILLINGS:

Perfect Whipped Cream (page 294), Raspberry Jam Cream (page 294) or any Cloud Cream. This is wonderful as a bottom for cheesecake.

GREEN TEA BISCUIT:

The moss-green tea of the Japanese tea ceremony adds a lovely colour and exquisitely haunting flavour to the delicacy of *biscuit*. Filled with Green Tea Mousse Cream (page 302), it is an unforgettable dessert. It must be served the day it is baked or the elusive flavour is lost. To make this *biscuit*, replace 1 tablespoon of the cornflour with equal measure or weight of powdered green tea (available in stores where Japanese and Oriental products are sold).

COMPLEMENTARY FILLINGS:

Perfect Whipped Cream (page 294) or Green Tea Mousse Cream (page 302).

Biscuit de Savoie

Serves 12 to 14 (3 round layers)

This lovely cake bears the name of the Savoie region in the French Alps, where it is said to have originated. Biscuit de Savoie makes an excellent layer cake and, after dousing with syrup, is exceptionally light, soft and moist without ever becoming soggy. It can be used interchangeably with a *génoise* and is an especially refreshing alternative for summertime cakes.

For a tender texture, it is essential to moisten the baked Biscuit de Savoie with at least 2 fluid ounces syrup (page 409) for every egg used in the batter. Another rule of thumb is to use syrup equal in weight to the baked and trimmed *biscuit*. This will transform the *biscuit* from dry and rubbery to moist and dissolving!

I tip my *toque* to my friends and colleagues Bruce Healy and Paul Bugat (*Mastering the Art of French Pastry*) for their superb method of folding the whites together with the flour mixture. This achieves the highest, lightest possible result!

TINS: Three 23 × 4–centimetre/ 9 × 1½–inch cake tins, bottoms greased and lined with parchment or greaseproof paper. Do *not* grease or flour sides.

FINISHED HEIGHT: After trimming the bottom and top crusts, each layer is 2.5 centimetres/1 inch.

STORE: Syrup: 1 month refrigerated in an airtight container. *Biscuit*: Without syrup, 2 days room temperature, 5 days refrigerated, 2 months frozen. After sprinkling with the syrup the flavours ripen and the moisture is more evenly distributed 1 day later. The completed cake can be refrigerated up to 5 days or frozen up to 2 months.

COMPLEMENTARY ADORNMENTS: *One recipe:* Any buttercream, whipped cream, or glaze.

SERVE: Room temperature or lightly chilled.

INGREDIENTS	WEIGHT		MEASURE
room temperature	*grams*	*pounds/ounces*	*volume*
8 eggs, size 2, separated			
yolks	150 grams	5¼ ounces	4½ fluid ounces
whites	240 grams	8½ ounces	8 fluid ounces
castor sugar	200 grams	7 ounces	1 cup
pure vanilla extract	10 grams	—	2½ teaspoons
warm water	15 grams	½ ounce	1 tablespoon
sifted plain flour	115 grams	4 ounces	1 cup − 1 tablespoon
cornflour	66 grams	2¼ ounces	½ cup + 1 tablespoon (lightly spooned into cup)
crream of tartar	3 grams	—	1 teaspoon
SYRUP			
castor sugar	175 grams	6 ounces	¾ cup + 2 tablespoons
water	355 grams	12½ ounces	12 fluid ounces
liqueur of your choice	90 grams	3 ounces	3 fluid ounces

POINTERS FOR SUCCESS: See pages xx and 128. A large balloon whisk or slotted skimmer is ideal for folding in the flour with the least amount of air loss. If using the whisk, periodically shake out the batter which collects inside.

Preheat the oven to 325°F/160°C/gas mark 3.

In a large mixing bowl beat the yolks and 132 grams/4½ ounces/ ⅔ cup sugar on high speed for 5 minutes or until the mixture is very thick and ribbons when dropped from the beater. Lower the speed and beat in the vanilla and water. Increase to high speed and beat for 30 seconds or until it thickens again.

Stir together the flour and cornflour. Sift over the yolk mixture without mixing in and set aside.

In another large mixing bowl beat the whites until foamy, add the cream of tartar and beat until soft peaks form when the beater is raised. Gradually beat in the remaining sugar, beating until stiff peaks form when the beater is raised slowly. Add one-third of the whites to the yolk mixture and with a large balloon whisk, skimmer or rubber spatula fold until incorporated. Gently fold in the remaining whites.

Pour into the prepared tins. (They will be almost half full.) Bake for 25 minutes or until a cake tester inserted in the centre comes out clean. Loosen the sides with a small metal spatula and turn out the cakes at once on to lightly greased racks and reinvert to cool. The firm upper crust prevents falling and results in a light texture.

Trim the crust when ready to complete the cake and sprinkle the syrup evenly on all sides (page 409).*

TO MAKE SYRUP

In a small saucepan with a tight-fitting lid bring the sugar and water to a rolling boil, stirring constantly. Cover immediately, remove from the heat and cool. Transfer to a liquid measuring jug and stir in the liqueur. If the syrup has evaporated slightly, add enough water to equal 2 cups (590 grams/ 21 ounces).

UNDERSTANDING

When *biscuit* is baked as a round layer cake, it requires much more structure than a low sheet cake, so proportionally more flour/cornflour mixture is used and all the whites are beaten separately.

The absence of butter is what makes Biscuit de Savoie lighter than a *génoise*. Since butter has a tenderising effect, its absence will make the *biscuit* rubbery unless it is adequately moistened with a syrup.

Since the *biscuit* can be saturated with syrup without becoming soggy, there is no danger of dryness, so the cake can be made as light and high-rising as possible. By not greasing and flouring the sides of the tins, the batter can rise better, attaining maximum height.

This cake is used to make Queen Bee cake (page 211).

*After syruping a *biscuit* layer becomes fragile and more prone to splitting when moved. Use a cardboard round or removable bottom of a cake tin to support it.

Oval Biscuit

This is the same recipe as the preceding one, but it yields about two-thirds of the amount. It makes two oval layers that are perfect in cakes such as Baked Hawaii (page 191).

TINS: Two 23.5 × 16.5-centimetre/ 9¼ × 6⅝-inch oval tins (page 517) bottoms greased and lined with parchment or greaseproof paper. Do not grease or flour sides.

FINISHED HEIGHT: After trimming the bottom and top crusts, each layer is 4.5 centimetres/1¾ inches.

Beat 50 grams (1¾ ounces/¼ cup) sugar instead of 66 grams/

2¼ ounces/⅓ cup with the whites and beat the remainder with the yolk mixture. Proceed as for the full-size recipe (page 162).

INGREDIENTS	WEIGHT		MEASURE
room temperature	_grams_	_pounds/ounces_	_volume_
6 eggs, size 2, separated			
yolks	112 grams	4 ounces	3½ fluid ounces
whites	180 grams	6¼ ounces	6 fluid ounces
castor sugar	132 grams	4½ ounces	⅔ cup
pure vanilla extract	7 grams	—	1¾ teaspoons
warm water	10 grams	—	2 teaspoons
plain flour	75 grams	2½ ounces	½ cup (dip and sweep method)
cornflour	45 grams	1½ ounces	⅓ cup + 2 teaspoons (lightly spooned into cup)
cream of tartar	—	—	¾ teaspoon

Divide the batter between two oval cake tins and bake for 25 minutes or until the cakes test done. Loosen the sides with a small metal spatula; turn them out at once on to lightly greased racks and reinvert to cool.

Biscuit à la Cuillère

Makes about 2 dozen ladyfingers and a 20-centimetre/8-inch circular cake base or about 3½ dozen fingers

The name *cuillère*, the French word for 'spoon', was given to these traditional sponge fingers because they were originally shaped with a spoon. Using a pastry bag, however, results in a more uniform shape and much greater speed.

This *biscuit* is so light that it stales quickly. It is best to eat it the day it is baked. For less fresh *biscuit*, sprinkle lightly with liqueur.

Sponge fingers have the perfect, ethereal but firm texture to encase and support a Bavarian cream filling such as Orange Chocolate Crown (page 206).

TINS: Two large baking sheets, lined with non-stick liner, parchment, or foil and outlined with piping guides (parallel lines 7.5 centimetres/3 inches apart and 20 to 23-centimetre/8 to 9-inch circle, page 517). A large pastry bag fitted with a 2-centimetre/ ¾-inch diameter pastry tube.

FINISHED SIZE: Ladyfingers: 3 strips, each 30 centimetres/ 12 inches long, or 2 strips, each 46 centimetres/18 inches long. Cake base: 18 to 20 centimetres/ 7 to 8 inches (for a 20 or 23-centimetre/8 or 9-inch charlotte).

STORE: Use same day or freeze 1 month.

COMPLEMENTARY ADORNMENTS: Sponge finger-lined moulds can be filled with *one recipe:* Bavarian Cream (pages 331 to 337), Fruit Cloud Cream (page 306), or Lemon Cream Illusion (page 308).

SERVE: Room temperature if served plain, lightly chilled if used in a Charlotte (page 206).

POINTERS FOR SUCCESS: See pages xx and 128. Egg whites must

INGREDIENTS	WEIGHT		MEASURE
room temperature	*grams*	*pounds/ounces*	*volume*
6 eggs, size 2, separated			
yolks	112 grams	4 ounces	3½ ounces
whites	180 grams	6¼ ounces	6 fluid ounces
castor sugar	150 grams	5¼ ounces	¾ cup
pure vanilla extract	10 grams	—	2½ teaspoons
warm water	15 grams	½ ounce	1 tablespoon
sifted plain flour	150 grams	5¼ ounces	1 cup + 3 tablespoons
cream of tartar	—	—	¾ teaspoon
icing sugar for dusting	—	—	about 1 cup

be beaten stiffly enough for the batter to hold its shape and form attractive designs. If the proper amount of cream of tartar is used it is virtually impossible to overbeat the whites. A slotted skimmer is ideal for folding in the flour with the least amount of air loss.

Preheat the oven to 400°F/200°C/gas mark 6.

In a large mixing bowl beat the yolks and 100 grams/3½ ounces/ ½ cup sugar on high speed for 5 minutes or until the mixture is very thick and ribbons when dropped from the beater. Lower the speed and beat in the vanilla and water. Increase to high speed and beat for 30 seconds or until thick again. Sift the flour over the yolk mixture without mixing in and set aside.

In another large mixing bowl beat the whites until foamy, add the cream of tartar and beat until soft peaks form when the beater is raised. Gradually beat in the remaining sugar, beating until very stiff peaks form when the beater is raised slowly. Add one-third of the whites to the yolk mixture and with a skimmer or rubber spatula fold until all the flour is incorporated. Gently fold in the remaining whites.

Working quickly so that the batter does not lose volume, scoop 4 cups (1 litre) into the pastry bag and pipe out the disc for the base (page 429). A 20-centimetre/8-inch charlotte requires about 17 sponge fingers to go around the sides, an 18-centimetre/7-inch base to fit inside the fingers, and a 20-centimetre/8-inch top if desired. A 23-centimetre/9-inch charlotte requires about 19 sponge fingers to go around the sides, a 20-centimetre/8-inch base to fit inside the fingers, and a 23-centimetre/9-inch top if desired. (To make a decorative top you will need to make another half batch of batter.)

Scoop the remaining batter into the pastry bag and pipe out 7.5 × 4-centimetre/3 × 1½-inch side-by-side 'fingers'. Be sure to hold the pastry tube high enough above the surface of the sheet so that the batter can fall freely from the tube and not get flattened by the edge of the tube (page 429). There should be a 5-millimetre/¼-inch space between the 'fingers' as they spread sideways as they are piped. (After baking, the sponge fingers will be attached to one another in continuous strips. Each finger will be about 4 centimetres/1½ inches wide.) Sift the icing sugar completely over the fingers. After a few seconds the batter will dissolve and absorb some of the sugar. For a pearled effect, sprinkle with a second coat. Bake for 8 to 10 minutes or until light golden brown and springy to the touch. Remove the sheets to racks and cool slightly. To prevent cracking, remove from the sheets while still warm with a long, thin spatula or pancake turner. For discs, invert on to a rack covered with a paper towel, peel off the liner and reinvert on to a second rack. Cool on racks and then wrap airtight.

UNDERSTANDING

This *biscuit* recipe has the same weight flour and sugar and double the egg as Génoise Classique but no butter. Biscuit à la Cuillère has more flour than Biscuit de Savoie in order to hold its shape when piped. (It is also baked at a higher temperature to set the shape faster.)

To achieve a lighter texture no cornflour is used and all the egg whites are beaten separately and *very stiffly*.

Nancy Blitzer's
Classic Sponge Cake

Serves 10

My friend Nancy has been baking for family and friends for over forty years. This perfect sponge cake is her creation and is so pure and simple it needs no adornment. Nancy serves it plain with tea or sometimes even lightly toasted for breakfast. This cake contains no sodium and only about 226 mg cholesterol per serving.

TIN: One ungreased two-piece 25.5-centimetre/10-inch tube tin.

FINISHED HEIGHT: 8 centimetres/3⅛ inches high overall, 7 centimetres/2¾ inches at the sides.

STORE: 3 days room temperature, 5 days refrigerated, 2 months frozen.

COMPLEMENTARY ADORNMENTS: A light sprinkling of icing sugar. Or decorate the base and centre with fresh flowers.

SERVE: Room temperature or lightly chilled.

POINTERS FOR SUCCESS: See pages xx and 128. A slotted skimmer is ideal for folding in the flour with the least amount of air loss.

Preheat the oven to 350°F/180°C/gas mark 4.

In a small bowl combine the water, vanilla and lemon zest.

Remove 1 tablespoon of the sugar and reserve it to beat with the whites.

In another small bowl whisk together the flour and 3 table-spoons of the sugar.

In a large mixing bowl beat the yolks and the remaining sugar on high speed for 5 minutes or until the mixture is very thick and ribbons when dropped from the beater. Lower the speed and gradually add the water mixture. Increase to high speed and beat for 30 seconds. Sift the flour mixture over the yolk mixture without mixing in and set aside.

Beat the whites until foamy, add

INGREDIENTS	WEIGHT		MEASURE
room temperature	*grams*	*pounds/ounces*	*volume*
water	30 grams	1 ounce	2 tablespoons
pure vanilla extract	—	—	½ teaspoon
grated lemon zest	—	—	1½ teaspoons
castor sugar	200 grams	7 ounces	1 cup
sifted self-raising sponge flour	135 grams	4¾ ounces	1½ cups
6 eggs, size 2, separated			
yolks	112 grams	4 ounces	3½ fluid ounces
whites	180 grams	6¼ ounces	6 fluid ounces
cream of tartar	—	—	¾ teaspoon

the cream of tartar, and beat until soft peaks form when the beater is raised. Beat in the reserved tablespoon of sugar and beat until very stiff peaks form when the beater is raised slowly. Add one-third of the whites to the yolk mixture and with a large skimmer or rubber spatula fold until incorporated. Gently fold in the remaining whites in two batches.

Pour into the tin. (It will be a little more than half full.) Bake for 30 to 35 minutes or until golden brown and a cake tester comes out clean when inserted in the centre. Invert the tin, placing the tube opening over the neck of a soda or wine bottle to suspend it well above the worktop, and cool the cake completely in the tin (this takes about 1 hour).

Loosen the sides with a long metal spatula and remove the centre core of the tin. (To keep the sides attractive, press the spatula against the sides of the tin and avoid any up-and-down motion.) Dislodge the bottom and centre core with a metal spatula or thin, sharp knife. (A wire cake tester works well around the core.) Invert on to a greased wire rack and reinvert on to a serving plate. Wrap airtight.

UNDERSTANDING

This sponge cake contains the same basic ingredients as Biscuit de Savoie except that the *biscuit* has half the weight of sugar to eggs and this sponge has almost as much sugar as eggs. The high quantity of sugar produces a sponge cake so moist and tender that no syrup or icing is necessary. Some of the sugar is added to the flour to separate the grains and help keep it from clumping when folded into the batter.

The addition of lemon zest tempers the sweetness. Baking at 350°F/180°C/gas mark 4 rather than 325°F/160°C/gas mark 3 ensures a tenderer and moister cake (page 543).

Bert Greene's Special Sponge Cake

Serves 8

I am so pleased to be able to present this extraordinary recipe, offered by one of my dearest friends and most esteemed colleagues. Bert has come up with some truly original and inventive tricks to create one of the moistest and tenderest sponge cakes I've ever tasted.

As a special touch, some of the sugar is sprinkled on top of the raw batter to produce a delightfully crunchy crust. This cake is perfect for the person with a really sweet tooth, although extra lemon zest helps temper the sweetness and makes salt unnecessary. As an added bonus, it has only 161 mg cholesterol per serving.

TIN: One ungreased 25.5-centimetre/10-inch two-piece tube tin, preheated for at least 5 minutes.

FINISHED HEIGHT: 7.5 centimetres/3 inches.

STORE: 3 days room temperature, 5 days refrigerated, 2 months frozen.

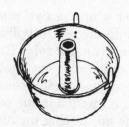

COMPLEMENTARY ADORNMENTS: Decorate base and centre with fresh flowers.

INGREDIENTS	WEIGHT		MEASURE
room temperature	*grams*	*pounds/ounces*	*volume*
orange juice	30 grams	1 ounce	2 tablespoons
grated lemon zest	4 grams	—	2 teaspoons
pure vanilla extract	6 grams	—	½ teaspoon
castor sugar	288 grams	10 ounces	1 cup + 7 tablespoons
sifted self-raising sponge flour	100 grams	3½ ounces	1 cup + 2 tablespoons
5 eggs, size 2, separated, + 3 additional whites			
yolks	93 grams	3¼ ounces	full 6 fluid ounces
whites	240 grams	8½ ounces	8 fluid ounces
cream of tartar	3 grams	—	1 teaspoon

SERVE: Room temperature or lightly chilled.

POINTERS FOR SUCCESS: See pages xx and 128. Castor sugar is important to attain maximum volume and for sprinkling on top of the cake. Heating the yolks also improves volume. A slotted skimmer is ideal for folding in the flour with the least amount of air loss.

Preheat the oven to 350°F/180°C/gas mark 4.

In a small bowl combine the orange juice, lemon zest and vanilla.

Remove 2 tablespoons of the sugar and reserve them to beat with the whites. Remove another 2 tablespoons of the sugar and reserve them to sprinkle on top of the raw batter.

Remove 3 more tablespoons of the sugar and whisk them together with the flour.

Rinse a large mixing bowl with hot water and wrap the sides with a hot tea-towel. (If using a hand mixer, place the bowl in a sink partially filled with hot water.)

Beat the yolks, gradually adding the remaining sugar, on high speed for 5 minutes or until the mixture is very thick and ribbons when dropped from the beater. Lower the speed and gradually add the orange juice mixture. Increase to high speed and beat for 30 seconds. Sift the flour mixture over the yolk mixture without mixing in and set aside.

Beat the whites until foamy, add the cream of tartar, and continue to beat until soft peaks form when the beater is raised. Gradually beat in the 2 tablespoons of reserved sugar, beating until very stiff peaks form when the beater is raised slowly. Add one-third of the whites to the yolk mixture and with a large skimmer or rubber spatula fold until incorporated. Gently fold in the remaining whites in two batches.

Pour the batter into the hot tin. (It will be a little more than half full.) Sprinkle the top evenly with the remaining 2 tablespoons sugar. Bake for 35 to 40 minutes or until golden brown and a cake tester comes out clean when inserted in the centre. Invert the tin, placing the tube opening over the neck of a soda or wine bottle to suspend it well above the worktop, and cool the cake completely in the tin (this takes about 1 hour).

Loosen the sides with a long metal spatula and remove the centre core of the tin from the sides. (To keep the sides attractive, press the spatula against the sides of the tin and avoid any up-and-down motion.) Dislodge the bottom and centre core with a spatula or thin, sharp knife. (A wire cake tester works well around the core.) Invert on to a greased wire rack and reinvert on to a serving plate. Wrap airtight.

UNDERSTANDING

One of the secrets of this cake's exceptional moistness and tenderness is using 35 grams/ 1¼ ounces/6 tablespoons less flour than classic sponge cake for a very high proportion of sugar (100 grams/3½ ounces/almost ½ cup more). For additional volume, Bert applies heat while beating the yolks and uses 3, sometimes even 4, extra egg whites to compensate for structure usually provided by a higher quantity of flour. To ensure that the cake will not collapse during baking, he preheats the empty tin so that the batter starts to expand and set immediately.

Note: Bert eliminates the cream of tartar and uses a copper bowl to whisk the egg whites by hand. This results in extra-high volume for those of you who have the strength (not to mention the will) to do it.

Chiffon Cakes

When Harry Baker, a Los Angeles insurance salesman who baked for private Hollywood parties, invented the chiffon cake, it was the first major new type of cake since the angel food cake, invented about one hundred years before it. He kept the recipe a secret for twenty years and finally, deciding to share it with the world, approached Betty Crocker, owned by General Mills. They purchased the recipe in 1947 and billed it as 'glamorous as an angel food cake but easier to make'.

The chiffon cake combines the moist richness of a butter cake with the lightness of a sponge cake. Because oil, which remains liquid at room temperature, is used instead of butter, the texture is much softer than a layer cake. Even refrigerated, the oil in the cake remains soft (unlike butter). Oil also tenderises and provides moisture, making the chiffon cake much more tender than a *biscuit*. Safflower oil is my preference (except for the chocolate chiffon, which is much more delicious with walnut oil) because it contains no silicates (which inhibit foaming).

A chiffon cake has many virtues. It is easy to make, keeps exceptionally well and slices easily even when frozen. It has about half the fat of a butter or sponge cake and less cholesterol and saturated fat than any other cake except for angel food. But, unlike angel food, it does not have the disadvantage of excessive sweetness. On top of all these wonderful qualities, it also provides a use for your extra-egg-white collection.

Chiffon cakes are best baked at 325°F/160°C/gas mark 3 because the tops crack more at higher temperatures.

I don't like to ice chiffon cakes because that defeats the lightness and the low cholesterol advantage. (The icings of my preference all have either butter or cream.)

Any of the following chiffon recipes can be halved and baked in a 23-centimetre/9-inch tube tin for a 7.5-centimetre/3-inch-high cake that serves 6 to 8. Bake for only 35 minutes or until the cake tests done.

HIGHLIGHTS FOR SUCCESSFUL CHIFFON AND ANGEL FOOD CAKES

For fuller details see the suggested page number.

- Use self-raising sponge flour (see page 493).
- Use castor sugar for finest texture and maximum volume (page 498).
- Measure or weigh ingredients carefully (page 505).
- Do not use oil that contains silicates – it will be listed on the label (page 497).
- Egg whites must be free of even a trace of yolk and the bowl must be spotless.

- When beating egg whites, use cream of tartar or be careful to beat just until stiff peaks form when the beater is raised slowly.
- Fold flour gently but *thoroughly* into the batter.
- Use the correct tin size (page 515).
- Bake immediately after mixing.

- Check for accurate oven temperature (page 514).
- Use correct baking time; do not underbake (page 5).
- Cool cakes upside down, well elevated from the worktop, in a draught-free area (page 545).
- Wrap cakes well when cool (page 6).

Orange Glow Chiffon Cake

Serves 14

Moist, billowy, light as a feather and perfumed with fresh orange juice and zest, this is an incomparably refreshing cake. If you live in a part of the world where oranges grow, you could not ask for a more appropriate and aromatic adornment than orange blossoms, but fresh daisies also convey the light-hearted spirit of this lovely cake. A serving contains only 129 mg of cholesterol.

TIN: One ungreased 25.5-centimetre/10-inch two-piece tube tin.

STORE: 3 days room temperature, 10 days refrigerated, 2 months frozen.

COMPLEMENTARY ADORNMENTS: A light sprinkling of icing sugar and/or decorate the base and centre with orange blossoms or fresh daisies. Candied Orange Zest (page 392) scattered on top also makes an attractive and flavourful addition.

FINISHED HEIGHT: 11.5 centimetres/4½ inches high in the middle.

SERVE: Room temperature or lightly chilled. Cut with a serrated knife.

INGREDIENTS	WEIGHT		MEASURE
room temperature	*grams*	*pounds/ounces*	*volume*
sifted self-raising sponge flour	225 grams	8 ounces	2½ cups
castor sugar	300 grams	10½ ounces	1½ cups
salt	3.5 grams	—	½ teaspoon
safflower oil	108 grams	3¾ ounces	4 fluid ounces
7 eggs, size 2, separated, + 3 additional whites			
yolks	130 grams	4½ ounces	4 fluid ounces
whites	300 grams	10½ ounces	10 fluid ounces
orange juice, freshly squeezed	182 grams	6¼ ounces	6 fluid ounces
grated orange zest	12 grams	—	2 tablespoons
pure vanilla extract	4 grams	—	1 teaspoon
cream of tartar	4 grams	—	1¼ teaspoons

POINTERS FOR SUCCESS: See pages xx and 173. An angel food cake folder, large balloon whisk, or slotted skimmer is ideal for folding in the flour with the least amount of air loss. If using the whisk, periodically shake out the batter which collects inside.

Preheat the oven to 325°F/160°C/gas mark 3.

In a large mixing bowl combine the flour, all but 2 tablespoons of the sugar, and the salt and beat for 1 minute to mix. Make a well in the centre. Add the oil, egg yolks, orange juice, orange zest and vanilla and beat for 1 minute or until smooth.

In another large mixing bowl beat the egg whites until frothy, add the cream of tartar, and beat until soft peaks form when the beater is raised. Beat in the remaining sugar and beat until stiff peaks form when the beater is raised slowly. Gently fold the egg whites into the batter with a large balloon wire whisk, slotted skimmer or angel food cake folder until just blended.

Pour into the tube tin (the batter

will come to 2.5 centimetres/1 inch from the top) and bake for 55 minutes or until a cake tester inserted in the centre comes out clean and the cake springs back when lightly pressed in the centre. Invert the tin, placing the tube opening over the neck of a soda or wine bottle to suspend it well above the worktop, and cool the cake completely in the tin (this takes about 1½ hours).

Loosen the sides with a long metal spatula and remove the centre core of the tin. Dislodge the bottom and centre core with a metal spatula or thin, sharp knife. (A wire cake tester works well around the core. To keep the sides attractive, press the spatula against the sides of the tin and avoid any up-and-down motion.) Invert on to a greased wire rack and reinvert on to a serving plate. Wrap airtight.

Lemon Glow Chiffon Cake

Serves 14

This cake offers the lilting flavour of lemon, balanced by the moist, light texture found only in a chiffon cake. A serving contains only 129 mg cholesterol.

TINS: One ungreased 25.5-centimetre/10-inch two-piece tube tin.

FINISHED HEIGHT:
11.5 centimetres/4½ inches high in the middle.

STORE: 3 days room temperature, 10 days refrigerated, 2 months frozen.

COMPLEMENTARY ADORNMENTS: A light sprinkling of icing sugar and/or decorate the base and centre with lemon blossoms or fresh daisies.

SERVE: Room temperature or lightly chilled. Cut with a serrated knife.

POINTERS FOR SUCCESS: See pages xx and 173. An angel food

INGREDIENTS	WEIGHT		MEASURE
room temperature	*grams*	*pounds/ounces*	*volume*
sifted self-rising sponge flour	225 grams	8 ounces	2½ cups
castor sugar	300 grams	10½ ounces	1½ cups
salt	3.5 grams	—	½ teaspoon
safflower oil	108 grams	3¾ ounces	4 fluid ounces
7 eggs, size 2, separated, + 3 additional whites			
yolks	130 grams	4½ ounces	4 fluid ounces
whites	300 grams	10½ ounces	10 fluid ounces
water	156 grams	5½ ounces	5¼ fluid ounces
lemon juice, freshly squeezed	30 grams	1 ounce	2 tablespoons
grated lemon zest	6 grams	—	1 tablespoon
pure vanilla extract	4 grams	—	1 teaspoon
cream of tartar	4 grams	—	1¼ teaspoons

cake folder, large balloon whisk, or slotted skimmer is ideal for folding in the flour with the least amount of air loss. If using the whisk, periodically shake out the batter which collects inside.

Preheat the oven to 325°F/160°C/gas mark 3.

In a large mixing bowl combine the flour, all but 2 tablespoons of the sugar, and the salt and beat for 1 minute to mix. Make a well in the centre. Add the oil, egg yolks, water, lemon juice, lemon zest and vanilla and beat for 1 minute or until smooth.

In another large mixing bowl beat the egg whites until frothy, add the cream of tartar, and beat until soft peaks form when the beater is raised. Beat in the 2 tablespoons sugar and beat until stiff peaks form when the beater is raised slowly. Gently fold the egg whites into the batter with a large balloon wire whisk, slotted skimmer or angel food cake folder until just blended.

Pour into the tube tin (the batter will come to 2.5 centimetres/1 inch from the top) and bake for 55 minutes or until a cake tester inserted in the centre comes out clean and the cake springs back when lightly pressed in the centre. Invert the tin, placing the tube opening over the neck of a soda or wine bottle to suspend it well above the worktop, and cool the cake completely in the tin (this takes about 1½ hours).

Loosen the sides with a long metal spatula and remove the centre core of the tin. Dislodge the bottom and centre core with a metal spatula or thin, sharp knife. (A wire cake tester works well around the core. To keep the sides attractive, press the spatula against the sides of the tin and avoid any up-and-down motion.) Invert on to a greased wire rack and reinvert on to a serving plate. Wrap airtight.

Guilt-Free Chocolate Chiffon Cake

Serves 14

It is a rare thing indeed that so intensely chocolate a cake can boast a minuscule cholesterol content. It happened behind my back.

I never liked chocolate chiffon cakes because the oil did not seem to enhance the flavour of chocolate the way butter does and because the lower part of the cake always seemed heavy and gummy. But my mother so loudly sang the praises of its possibilities ('It has delicate chocolate flavour and heavenly texture even eaten directly from the freezer') that I decided to give it one last try. I took advantage of the synergistic effect of chocolate and walnut by replacing some of the vegetable oil with walnut oil. Cocoa offered richness, and extra whites and 1 less yolk perfected the texture so beautifully that I now use a total of 10 whites for the orange and lemon chiffon cakes as well. A serving of this cake contains only 110.6 mg cholesterol.

INGREDIENTS	WEIGHT		MEASURE
room temperature	*grams*	*pounds/ounces*	*volume*
unsweetened cocoa (preferably Dutch-processed) *or* ½ cup + 2 tablespoons nonalkalised cocoa	50 grams	1¾ ounces	½ cup + 1 tablespoon (lightly spooned into cup)
boiling water	177 grams	6¼ ounces	6 fluid ounces
sifted self-raising sponge flour	175 grams	6 ounces	2 cups
castor sugar	350 ounces	12¼ ounces	1¾ cups
salt	3.5 grams	—	½ teaspoon
walnut oil	80.5 grams	2¾ ounces	3 fluid ounces
safflower oil	27 grams	1 ounce	2 tablespoons
6 eggs, size 2, separated + 4 additional whites			
yolks	113 grams	4 ounces	3½ fluid ounces
whites	300 grams	10½ ounces	10 fluid ounces
pure vanilla extract	8 grams	—	2 teaspoons
cream of tartar	4 grams	—	1¼ teaspoons

TIN: One ungreased 25.5-centimetre/10-inch two-piece tube tin.

FINISHED HEIGHT: 10 centimetres/ 4 inches high in the middle.

STORE: 3 days room temperature, 10 days refrigerated, 2 months frozen.

COMPLEMENTARY ADORNMENTS: A light sprinkling of icing sugar or cocoa. Or decorate the base and centre with fresh flowers such as freesia.

SERVE: Room temperature or lightly chilled. Cut with a serrated knife.

POINTERS FOR SUCCESS: See pages xx and 173. An angel food cake folder, large balloon whisk, or slotted skimmer is ideal for folding in the flour with the least amount of air loss. If using the whisk, periodically shake out the batter which collects on the inside.

Preheat the oven to 325°F/160°C/gas mark 3.

In a medium bowl combine the cocoa and boiling water and whisk until smooth. Cool.

In a large mixing bowl combine the flour, all but 2 tablespoons of the sugar, and the salt and beat for 1 minute to mix. Make a well in the centre. Add the oils, egg yolks, chocolate mixture and vanilla and beat for 1 minute or until smooth.

In another large mixing bowl beat the egg whites until frothy, add the cream of tartar, and beat until soft peaks form when the beater is raised. Beat in the remaining 2 tablespoons of sugar and beat until stiff peaks form when the beater is raised slowly. Fold 1 heaped cup of egg whites into the chocolate mixture with a large balloon wire whisk, slotted skimmer or angel food cake folder. Gently fold in the remaining egg whites until just blended.

Pour into the tube tin (the batter will come to 4.5 centimetres/ 1¾ inches from the top) and bake for 60 minutes or until a cake tester inserted in the centre comes out clean and the cake springs back when lightly pressed in the centre. Invert the tin, placing the tube opening over the neck of a soda or wine bottle to suspend it well above the worktop, and cool the cake completely in the tin (this takes about 1½ hours).

Loosen the sides with a long metal spatula and remove the centre core of the pan. Dislodge the bottom and centre core with a metal spatula or thin, sharp knife. (A wire cake tester works well around the core. To keep the sides attractive, press the spatula against the sides of the tin and avoid any up-and-down motion.) Invert on to a greased wire rack and reinvert on to a serving plate. Wrap airtight.

Chocolate Lover's Angel Food Cake

Serves 14

This cake has many special qualities, not least of which is that it is the only cake I deem worth eating that has not even a smidgen of 'devil' cholesterol!* It is lovely on its own, with fresh strawberries or raspberries, or for dipping into chocolate fondue.

Angel food cake is one of the sweetest cakes because it has virtually no fat to tenderise it and relies on an extra-high proportion of sugar for this purpose. I find white angel food overpoweringly sweet but cocoa does wonders to temper the sweetness in this version.

Interestingly, everyone who has tasted this cake, when questioned individually about the sweetness level, has said: 'I don't usually like sweet things, but this cake is so moist, light and wonderful, I don't find it too sweet at all.' My doorman went one step further: all smiles, eyes glowing, and seemingly at a loss for words, he expressed himself most eloquently by kissing my hand. Coincidentally, his name is Angelo!

TIN: One ungreased 25.5-centimetre/10-inch two-piece tube tin.

FINISHED HEIGHT: 10 centimetres/ 4 inches high in the middle.

STORE: 3 days room temperature, 10 days refrigerated. Freezing toughens the texture.

COMPLEMENTARY ADORNMENTS: A light sprinkling of cocoa. Lacy drizzles of Chocolate Lattice (page 447). Or fresh flowers.

SERVE: Room temperature or lightly chilled. Lovely with ice cream and/or chocolate sauce. Or, to keep totally free of cholesterol, Tofutti and/or Raspberry Sauce (page 386). Cut with a serrated knife.

POINTERS FOR SUCCESS: See pages xx and 173. An angel food cake folder, large balloon whisk, or slotted skimmer is ideal for folding in the flour with the least amount

*The cocoa contains 7 grams or less of saturated fat.

INGREDIENTS	WEIGHT		MEASURE
room temperature	*grams*	*pounds/ounces*	*volume*
unsweetened cocoa (preferably Dutch-processed)	28 grams	1 ounce	¼ cup + 1 tablespoon (lightly spooned into cup)
boiling water	60 grams	2 ounces	2 fluid ounces
pure vanilla extract	8 grams	—	2 teaspoons
castor sugar	350 grams	12¼ ounces	1¾ cups
sifted self-raising sponge flour	100 grams	3½ ounces	1 cup + 2 tablespoons
salt	1.7 grams	—	¼ teaspoon
16 egg whites, size 2	480 grams	17 ounces	16 fluid ounces
cream of tartar	6 grams	—	2 teaspoons

of air loss. If using the whisk, periodically shake out the batter which collects on the inside.

Preheat the oven to 350°F/180°C/gas mark 4.

In a medium bowl combine the cocoa and boiling water and whisk until smooth. Whisk in the vanilla.

In another medium bowl combine 150 grams/5¼ ounces/¾ cup sugar, the flour and salt and whisk to blend.

In a large mixing bowl beat the egg whites until frothy, add the cream of tartar, and beat until soft peaks form when the beater is raised. Gradually beat in the remaining sugar, beating until very stiff peaks form when the beater is raised slowly. Remove 1 heaped cup of egg whites and place it on to the cocoa mixture.

Dust the flour mixture over the remaining whites, one-quarter at a time, and fold in quickly but gently. It is not necessary to incorporate every speck until the last addition. The ideal implement was designed in England especially for this type of cake (page 516), but a large balloon wire whisk or slotted skimmer also works well.

Whisk together the egg white and cocoa mixture and fold into the batter until uniform. Pour into the tube tin (the batter will come to 2 centimetres/¾ inch from the top), run a small metal spatula or knife through the batter to prevent air pockets, and bake for 40 minutes or until a cake tester inserted in the centre comes out clean and the cake springs back when lightly pressed. (The centre will rise above the tin while baking and sink slightly when done. The surface will have deep cracks like a soufflé.)

Invert the tin, placing the tube opening over the neck of a soda or wine bottle to suspend it well above the worktop, and cool the cake completely in the tin (this takes about 1½ hours).

Loosen the sides with a long metal spatula and remove the centre core of the tin. Dislodge the bottom and centre core with a metal spatula or thin, sharp knife. (A wire cake tester works well around the core. To keep the sides attractive, press the spatula against the sides of the tin and avoid any up-and-down motion.) Invert on to a serving plate. Wrap airtight.

UNDERSTANDING
In contrast to Chocolate Chiffon Cake, an equal volume of egg whites replaces the whole eggs, and the oil is eliminated. This produces a stronger structure so the flour can be cut back by 75 grams/ 2½ ounces/¾ cup, yielding a lighter texture. The sugar remains the same because it is needed to tenderise what would otherwise be a rubbery cake. This means that the sugar in relation to the other ingredients is higher than for the chiffon cake so the angel food cake is somewhat sweeter. Part of the sugar is beaten into the whites to add stability and the remainder is mixed with the flour to separate the grains, which helps it to incorporate evenly into the resulting meringue.

A small amount of cocoa tempers the excessive sweetness so often objectionable in an angel food. As in the Génoise au Chocolat, I have used my new technique of adding water (not traditionally called for in this type of cake) to the cocoa. The water adds moisture, tenderises the cake and dissolves the cocoa, thereby both facilitating its incorporation and intensifying the flavour. Also, a slightly higher baking temperature is used compared to chiffon cake to produce a lighter, tenderer and moister cake.

Showcase Cakes

The cakes in this chapter illustrate how to achieve glorious creations from the basic recipes in the rest of the book. They are perfect for important occasions like weddings, anniversaries, birthdays, graduations, promotions, holidays and dinner parties. Some have appeared already in magazines, others only at private gatherings. Each cake has its own story, and – for inspiration and amusement – I am including two of the most dramatic in this chapter.

To invoke romance and poetry, some of my cakes bear European titles but most are as American as I am. The European classics have undergone contemporary culinary evolution. They contain less sugar, are lighter in texture and have more pronounced flavours.

For the sake of practicality and purity of flavour, I limit the number of components in each cake to three or four. Although narrow layers filled with many varying creams sound exciting and scrumptious, the taste tends to confuse the palate and diminish eating pleasure – the way mixing together too many colours in a painting results in loss of individual identity.

Cakes made for special occasions must dazzle the eye. But no matter how carried away I get with decorating, my chief concerns are always flavour and texture. If a cake isn't going to taste absolutely delicious, there is no point in making it!

Once you have learned some of the techniques in this book, the special cakes in this chapter will be showcases for all your baking and decorating skills. Believe it or not, the cakes are easy to assemble. The components can be made in steps and, as much as possible, I have suggested timing and plans for preparation at the beginning of each cake. The recipes for the individual components (given in other chapters) also contain tips for advance preparation and storage.

Of course recipe components can be used interchangeably and the cakes decorated in any number of ways, including the simple icing techniques on page 410. But for special occasions, here are some examples to inspire you to ever greater flights of fantasy.

Tips for Showcase Cakes

EXTRA BUTTERCREAM
The buttercream recipes in this chapter are generous to ensure that there will be enough to complete the cake. Any leftover buttercream can be frozen for future use. In fact, when I have collected several different varieties, I make cupcakes using the Yellow Butter Cake (page 28) or Perfect Chocolate Butter Cake (page 47). A half-recipe of either makes 9 cupcakes. Add 1/4 teaspoon baking powder for half a recipe of yellow cake, 1/4 teaspoon of baking powder for half a recipe of chocolate cake. Fill paper-lined or greased and floured muffin tins two-thirds full and bake for 20 to 25 minutes or until the cupcakes test done. I ice the cupcakes with thawed, rebeaten buttercream. Arranged on a serving plate, they are most attractive, often displaying a rainbow of colours.

STORING A COMPLETED CAKE
Cakes and buttercreams are prone to absorbing other flavours so, if cakes are iced far ahead, precautions must be taken. A small cake can be stored in an airtight plastic cake carrier or glass cake dome (page 527). A large tiered cake can be placed in a heavy cardboard box and taped shut.

FREEZING A COMPLETED CAKE
If you are planning to freeze an iced cake, place it uncovered in the freezer just until the icing is very firm and it will not be damaged by wrapping. Wrap the cake first in clingfilm, then in heavy-duty foil, trying to eliminate as much air as possible without pressing on the decorations. Place the cake in the centre of the foil and bring the two long sides together so that the edges meet. Fold the edges over several times until close to the cake. Proceed in the same way for the short ends. Delicate decorations can be protected further by placing the wrapped cake in a rigid box.

Be sure to defrost the cake overnight in the refrigerator and then allow it to come to room temperature before serving. Gradual defrosting prevents water droplets from forming on the icing. When you remove the cake from the freezer, take off the wrapping while the icing is still frozen solid – before refrigerating the cake in an airtight container.

STORING LEFTOVER CAKE

Begin by offering any leftover cake to guests who drop in unexpectedly; it's rare to receive a refusal. Most cakes are still delicious the day after if wrapped airtight in clingfilm and foil, even without refrigeration. I sometimes cut individual pieces of leftover cake, wrap them tightly in clingfilm and foil, and freeze them for future desserts or afternoon tea.

Caveat: Butter cake must be eaten at room temperature to appreciate fully the flavours and soft, tender texture. Cakes cold from the refrigerator have muted flavours and much firmer textures.

Blueberry Swan Lake

Serves 12

The fanciful image of this cake reflects the flavour within: soft-as-swan's-down white butter cake, silky lemon buttercream, and a shimmering lake of dark blueberry topping.

This cake is lovely to serve any time of year and satisfying yet light enough as the finale for a grand dinner.

TIMING: The cake can be assembled 1 day ahead and refrigerated except for the blueberry topping and swans, which should be placed on the cake no more than 2 hours before serving. The iced cake (without the swans or blueberry topping) can be frozen for 2 months.

SERVE: If the cake has been refrigerated, allow it to come to room temperature before serving (at least 2 hours). Cut into wedges radiating from the centre.

SPECIAL EQUIPMENT NEEDED

- Plastic swans can be used in place of piped meringue swans. They are available at party supply stores and can be painted with a thin coating of Royal Icing (page 340).
- Two 23.5 × 17-centimetre/ 9¼ × 6⅝-inch oval tins (page 517)
- Oval platter or board, flat portion at least 25.5 × 18 centi-metres/10 × 7 inches
- Pastry bag and 4-millimetre star tube with 5-millimetre-deep cuts

CAKE COMPONENTS

- 2 meringue swans (pages 434 and 435) and 58 grams/2 ounces/ ¼ cup Super-Stabilised Whipped Cream (page 295)
- 1 recipe White Chocolate Whisper Cake (page 42), baked in two 23.5 × 17-centimetre/ 9¼ × 6⅝-inch oval cake tins (page 517)
- 1 recipe Neoclassic or Classic Lemon Buttercream (page 270)
- 1 recipe Winter Blueberry Topping (page 400)

METHOD FOR ASSEMBLING CAKE

1. Ice directly on a serving plate, using strips of greaseproof paper slid under the sides. Or make a cardboard base, using one of the cake tins as a template.
2. Spread a little buttercream on the base so that the cake will stick to it.
3. Fill and ice the layers with a 5-millimetre/¼-inch-thick layer of buttercream. Use a small metal spatula to create vertical lines to represent waves on the sides.
4. With the remaining buttercream pipe a border of sideways shells (page 461 – reverse shell technique without altering direction), using a 4-millimetre star tube with 5-millimetre-deep cuts. Chill for 30 minutes.
5. Up to 2 hours before serving, carefully, so as not to damage the border, spoon room-temperature Winter Blueberry Topping smoothly over the cake.
6. Complete the swans by piping the whipped cream and securing the heads and necks and set on the cake.

A Taste of Heaven

Serves 8 to 10

This is my personal translation of the classic Swiss Zuger Kirschtorte. In Swiss German the word *Zuger* sounds like the word *Zucker*, which means 'sugar'. Actually, *Zuger* refers to something that comes from the town of Zug, renowned for its kirsch (cherry liqueur).*

In Switzerland this cake ranks as the favourite non-chocolate cake. Truly, it is a miracle of textures – a small taste of heaven. My version consists of a *génoise* heart drenched in kirsch syrup, cloaked in pale pink buttercream, and embraced by a pair of crisp, heart-shaped *dacquoise*. Due to the nature of the components, this is one of the sweeter cakes in this book. It is, however, less sweet than the Swiss version because I have decreased the sugar in the syrup and opted for *dacquoise* rather than the sweeter meringue normally used.

Traditionally, Zuger Kirschtorte is round, but I think the heart shape emphasises the romance of this exquisite dessert. And it provides the perfect centrepiece for a Valentine's Day celebration or engagement party.

TIMING: The cake can be assembled 2 days ahead and refrigerated. It can be frozen for 2 months.

SERVE: Lightly chilled or room temperature. (Buttercream should be warm enough to be creamy.) Cut with a serrated knife into wedges radiating from the centre.

SPECIAL EQUIPMENT NEEDED
- 23 × 5-centimetre/9 × 2-inch heart-shaped tin. (The cake can also be made in a 23 × 5-centimetre/9 × 2-inch cake tin or a 23-centimetre/9-inch springform tin.)

CAKE COMPONENTS
- 1 recipe Génoise Classique (page 129), baked in a 23 × 5-centimetre/9 × 2-inch heart-shaped tin (page 517) and top and bottom crusts removed
- 1 recipe syrup flavoured with kirsch (page 132)
- 1 recipe Dacquoise (page 349), piped in two heart-shaped discs slightly smaller than the outline of the tin to allow for spreading during baking (page 432)
- 1 recipe Neoclassic or Classic Buttercream (page 266 or 264), flavoured with 5¼ fluid ounces kirsch and tinted pale pink with 6 drops of red food colour
- 85 grams/3 ounces/1 cup sliced

*The best kirsch I have ever tasted is Etter Kirsch, manufactured in the town of Zug in Switzerland. If you visit Switzerland, be sure to bring back a bottle.

blanched almonds, toasted at 350°F/180°C/gas mark 4 for a few minutes until lightly browned

METHOD FOR ASSEMBLING CAKE

1. Use the heart-shaped tin to trace a heart-shaped cardboard base.
2. Sprinkle each side of the cake with 3 tablespoons syrup.
3. Spread a few small dabs of buttercream on the cardboard base and place one *dacquoise* disc flat side down on it.
4. Spread a thin layer of buttercream on the *dacquoise* and top with the *génoise* layer. Spread another thin layer of buttercream on the *génoise* and top with the second *dacquoise* flat side up.
5. Use the remaining buttercream to ice the top and sides.
6. Gently press the toasted almond slices on the sides, supporting the cake on the palm of one hand and tilting it slightly towards the other hand, cupped to hold the nuts.
7. Refrigerate for up to 1 hour before serving.

White Lilac Nostalgia

Serves 10 to 12

One of my earliest memories is of the smell of lilacs, and sunshine glinting through their leaves as my pushchair was pushed to and fro to encourage the ever resisted afternoon nap. Individual lilac blossoms are exquisite. Crystallised with lavender sugar and embedded in white chocolate buttercream, they make magnificent cake decorations. The pale pink of Raspberry Mousseline Buttercream against the pale yellow cake provides a harmony of colour and flavour.

TIMING: The cake can be assembled 1 day ahead. It can be frozen without the lilacs for 2 months.

SERVE: Room temperature. Cut with a thin, sharp knife.

CAKE COMPONENTS

- 1 recipe White Velvet Butter Cake (page 38), layers split in half horizontally
- ½ recipe Raspberry Mousseline (page 284), tinted with 3 drops of red food colour
- 1 recipe Crème Ivoire Deluxe (page 285)
- Crystallised Lilacs (page 375)

METHOD FOR ASSEMBLING CAKE

1. Spread a little mousseline on a 23-centimetre/9-inch cardboard round so the cake layers adhere.
2. Stack the cake layers on top of each other, sandwiching each with 143 grams/5 ounces/¾ cup mousseline (⅓ of the mousseline in between each layer).
3. Chill the cake for 10 minutes.
4. Ice with Crème Ivoire Deluxe.
5. Decorate the sides and top with the crystallised lilacs. If necessary, make a tiny hole in the icing with a skewer before inserting a lilac. The cake can be held at cool room temperature until the following day.

Baked Hawaii

Serves 10 to 12

Many years ago, on my first trip to France, I was invited by Stella Standard to eat at the legendary Left Bank bistro Chez Allard. It was renowned for its *canard aux navets* ('duck with turnips'), but it was a dessert, in all its perfect simplicity, which most intrigued me: ripe fresh pineapple, bathed in a fine-quality kirsch. That was all. And it was divine.

The combination of pineapple and kirsch experienced those twenty years ago is what inspired this special version of Baked Alaska. Every component contains either kirsch or pineapple and sometimes both. The kirsch keeps the ice cream and *biscuit* from freezing too hard, while fresh pineapple juice keeps the Italian meringue from being too sweet.

This is a real showstopper dessert. Although the meringue must be piped and browned just before serving, it's quick and easy to do, and guests enjoy the anticipation of watching the final preparations.

TIMING: The cake should be assembled 1 to 2 days ahead. The meringue must be applied and baked for 5 minutes in a very hot oven just before serving.

SERVE: Starting at the bottom, cut thin slices – making the first slice thicker as it will contain less of the ice cream – with a thin, sharp knife dipped in hot water. If the ice cream is very firm, allow the cut pieces to sit for 10 minutes or until it starts to soften slightly before serving.

STORE: Leftovers will stay delicious for at least 2 days if wrapped airtight and kept frozen.

SPECIAL EQUIPMENT NEEDED
- Two 23.5 × 17-centimetre/ 9¼ × 6⅝-inch oval tins (page 517)
- Ice-cream freezer
- Pastry bag and a large 1½-centimetre star tube

CAKE COMPONENTS
- 1 recipe Fresh Preserved Pineapple in syrup (page 402). Be sure to save the pineapple juice while cutting pineapple for the meringue. The preserved pineapple is used in the ice cream, the syrup for brushing on the cake.
- 900 grams/1 lb 5 ounces/4 cups Pineapple Ice Cream (pages 331 and 402), slightly softened
- 1 recipe Oval Biscuit (page 164)

- 2 tablespoons melted and strained apricot jam
- 8 fluid ounces Pineapple Kirsch Syrup: Stir together 6 fluid ounces reserved pineapple poaching syrup (page 402) and 2 fluid ounces kirsch
- 1½ recipes Light Italian Meringue (page 344), replacing the water with fresh pineapple juice

METHOD FOR ASSEMBLING CAKE

1. Cut one *biscuit* oval in half horizontally for the top and bottom of the cake.
2. Cut out the centre of the second oval, leaving a 2-centimetre/³⁄₄-inch ring. Reserve the centre for another use.★
3. Sprinkle 3 tablespoons syrup on each side of the two ovals and brush 2 tablespoons on each side of the ring.
4. Use an oval cake tin to make an oval cardboard base. Wrap the base in foil.

5. Place one *biscuit* oval on the base and carefully stack the ring on top, brushing the ring and the outside perimeter of the base with the apricot jam to make them adhere. (Support the ring with a flat baking sheet when lifting.)
6. Spoon softened ice cream into the centre of the ring, mounding it.
7. Top with the second oval.
8. Wrap with clingfilm, then with foil, and freeze for at least 24 hours.
9. Just before serving, place a rack in the upper third of the oven and preheat the oven to 500°F/260°C/gas mark 10. Spread the cake with the Italian Meringue to seal it. Pipe connecting stars of meringue with a large 3-millimetre star tube.
10. Bake the cake for 3 to 5 minutes or until the meringue begins to brown. Watch carefully to prevent burning.

★I freeze this centre oval until I am ready to use it. Then I sprinkle it with its weight in Pineapple Kirsch Syrup, ice it with Pineapple Buttercream, and adorn it with grated coconut.

Star-Spangled Rhapsody

Serves 14 to 16

Raspberry-scented buttercream encases a complexity of textures from soft moist *génoise* to crisp meringue. Fresh raspberries and blueberries interrupt the crunchy layers with bursts of juicy tartness.

This pretty and delectable cake works with other fruit themes as well (see Note). I designed the raspberry red, white and blueberry theme for a 100th anniversary of the Statue of Liberty party. When I use blueberries alone, my husband calls the cake 'Rhapsody in Blueberries'.

TIMING: The cake should be assembled 1 to 3 days ahead and refrigerated. The berries should not be placed on top until the day of serving. The completed cake freezes well without the fruit topping for 3 months.

SERVE: Lightly chilled or room temperature. (Buttercream should be warm enough to be creamy.) Cut with a serrated knife.

SPECIAL EQUIPMENT NEEDED
- Pastry bag and 1.5-millimetre round tube and 4-millimetre star tube with 5-millimetre-deep cuts.

CAKE COMPONENTS
- 1 recipe Crisp French Meringue (page 342), piped in two 21.5-centimetre/8½-inch spiral discs
- 1 recipe Génoise Classique (page 129), top and bottom crusts removed and sliced in half horizontally
- 1 recipe syrup flavoured with *crème de myrtilles* (blueberry liqueur), framboise (eau-de-vie of raspberries), or amaretto (page 132)
- 1 recipe Mousseline Buttercream (page 282) flavoured with framboise eau-de-vie (which is clear in colour)
- 77 grams/2¾ ounces/⅓ cup double cream softly whipped with ¼ teaspoon pure vanilla extract (page 504)
- 215 grams/7½ ounces/1 cup Fresh Blueberry Topping (use large blueberries) (page 399) and 225 grams/8 ounces/2 cups small raspberries

METHOD FOR ASSEMBLING CAKE
1. Trim the meringue discs to the same diameter or slightly smaller than the *génoise*. Use a small serrated knife and support the discs on a cardboard round or removable cake-tin bottom, allowing the part to be trimmed to extend slightly over the edge.

2. Sprinkle each side of the *génoise* with 3 tablespoons syrup.

3. Spread a little mousseline on the 23-centimetre/9-inch cardboard round and attach a meringue disc, flat side down. Spread with a thin layer (about 3 millimetres/⅛ inch) of mousseline and top with a layer of *génoise*.

4. Spread the whipped cream on the *génoise* and top with 54 grams/1¾ ounces/¼ cup each Fresh Blueberry Topping and raspberries, saving the most attractive berries for garnish.

5. Top with the second *génoise* layer. Spread the curved top side of the second meringue disc with another thin layer of mousseline and place on top of the *génoise* layer.

6. Ice the sides and top with some of the remaining mousseline.

7. Pipe mousseline decorations with a 1.5-millimetre round tube for the string work (page 466) and a 4-millimetre star tip with 5-millimetre-deep cuts for the shell border (page 461). Refrigerate until firm.

8. Top with the remaining Fresh Blueberry Topping and raspberries in a decorative pattern. Use the 4-millimetre star tip to pipe stars (page 459).

Note: Other fruit possibilities: Fresh or Winter Cherry Topping (page 393 or 395), fresh strawberries, or a 300-gram/ 11-ounce tin of mandarin orange slices, drained and marinated overnight in 2 tablespoons Mandarine Napoléon liqueur. Use liqueurs for the syrup and buttercream to complement the fruit (kirsch for the cherries, Grand Marnier for the strawberries, and Mandarine Napoléon for the oranges). Mandarine Napoléon is especially pretty because it gives the mousseline a pale apricot hue.

Praline Brioche Cake

Serves 14 to 16

The first time I encountered brioche as a cake was at LeNôtre's school in Plaisir, France. It was my favourite of all the cakes we made during that intensive week of classes.

The original version of this cake was in my first book, *Romantic and Classic Cakes*. I have since made my praline buttercream much less sweet and sometimes vary the recipe by using white chocolate praline buttercream in its place.

The cake is a study in contrasts – gossamer-soft brioche saturated with a refreshingly light rum syrup and encased by a rich, light, smooth praline buttercream. The nutty richness makes it especially suitable for cool weather occasions.

TIMING: The cake can be assembled 1 to 4 days ahead and refrigerated. The completed cake can be frozen for 3 months.

SERVE: Lightly chilled or room temperature. (Buttercream should be warm enough to be creamy.)

SPECIAL EQUIPMENT NEEDED
- 5-centimetre/2-inch high expandable flan ring and a 20-centimetre/8-inch cardboard round. Or a 20-centimetre/8-inch loose-bottom or springform tin fitted with cardboard rounds until the correct depth is obtained
- Pastry bag and 4-millimetre star tube with 5-millimetre-deep cuts

CAKE COMPONENTS
- 1 recipe La Brioche Cake (page 76), trimmed to 18 × 4 to 4.5 centimetres/7 × 1½ to 1¾ inches
- 1 recipe Rum Syrup (page 135)
- ½ recipe Praline Silk Meringue Buttercream (page 279) or 1 recipe Crème Ivoire Praliné (page 289)
- 57 grams/2 ounces/½ cup skinned and toasted hazelnuts (page 495). Reserve 24 whole nuts for the garnish and coarsely chop the remainder.

METHOD FOR ASSEMBLING CAKE
1. Place the brioche cake in a large tin and pour the syrup over it. Allow it to sit for 10 minutes or until the syrup is absorbed. Turn the brioche occasionally or use a bulb baster to help it absorb as much syrup as possible.
2. Spread the cardboard round with a very thin layer of

buttercream and place it in the bottom of the ring. If using a bottomless ring, set it on a baking sheet for support.

3. Using a small metal spatula, spread a thin layer of buttercream inside the ring.

4. Slide the brioche into the ring and top with some buttercream. Use a long metal spatula to create a smooth top, allowing the blade to rest on the sides of the ring to create a very even surface.

5. Refrigerate for at least 30 minutes.

6. *To turn out the cake:* Very briefly heat the sides of the ring or tin with a hairdryer on the hot setting or a hot, wet towel (page 411).

7. Place the cake on top of a firm object slightly smaller in diameter than the bottom, such as a canister. Pull the ring firmly down, away from the cake.

8. Gently press the chopped nuts on the sides, supporting the cake on the palm of one hand and tilting it slightly towards the other hand, cupped to hold the nuts.

9. Use the reserved whole hazelnuts to form a border, alternating with buttercream piped from a 4-millimetre star tube with 5-millimetre-deep cuts to resemble hazelnuts.

10. Refrigerate for up to 30 minutes before serving.

Golden Cage

(Zauber Torte)

Serves 12 to 16

The German name of this cake was inspired by Mozart's joyful opera *Die Zauberflöte* (*The Magic Flute*).

Beneath a shimmering golden caramel cage lies still more gold: buttery, dense golden *génoise* frosted with tart Apricot Silk Meringue Buttercream and sprinkled with Caramel Gold Dust. I serve this dessert for very special occasions (fiftieth birthday parties, golden wedding anniversaries). For extra golden glitter, present it with a sparkler and serve it with Sauternes or an Eiswein (the most glorious of dessert wines).

TIMING: The cake can be assembled 1 day ahead and refrigerated or frozen for 2 months. The caramel cage, however, should not be refrigerated or frozen. Remove the iced cake from the refrigerator at least 2 hours before serving and place the cage on top.

SERVE: Room temperature. Light the candles or sparkler. Remove the cage before cutting. Break the cage into pieces and use for garnish.

SPECIAL EQUIPMENT NEEDED
- one 9-cup (2⅛-litre) Kugelhopf tin (page 517)

CAKE COMPONENTS
- 1 recipe Golden Génoise (page 136), baked in the 9-cup (2⅛-litre) Kugelhopf pan
- 2 tablespoons Barack Palinka (apricot eau-de-vie) or apricot brandy
- ½ recipe Apricot Silk Meringue Buttercream (page 281)
- Gold Dust and Caramel Cage (page 361)

OPTIONAL DECOR
- Crystallised Violets (page 375)
- A sparkler or long, thin, dripless candles

METHOD FOR ASSEMBLING CAKE
1. Ice directly on a serving plate, using strips of greaseproof paper slid under the sides. Or make a cardboard base, using the inverted cake tin as a guide.
2. Split the *génoise* in half horizontally with a serrated knife. Sprinkle each cut side with 1 tablespoon Barack Palinka.
3. Sandwich the layers together with 66 grams/2⅓ ounces/ ⅓ cup buttercream. Remove any loose crust and spread the remaining buttercream over the outside of the cake. If not serving the same day, refrigerate.
4. Using a small strainer, sift the Gold Dust over the buttercream, tilting the cake to get an even coating. Place the cake on a large flat platter or serving plate and cover it with the Caramel Cage. (If the cage should accidentally break, use the broken pieces as decoration immediately on the icing.)
5. Attach the crystallised violets, if desired, with tiny dabs of caramel. (Leftover caramel from the cage can be re-melted in a microwave on high power or in a small heavy saucepan over medium heat.)
6. If desired, insert candles through the cage so that they radiate from the centre. If using a sparkler, insert it at an angle away from the cake so that sparks do not fall on the cake.

Charlottes

A charlotte is made by lining a mould with gossamer *biscuit* or *génoise* (whisked sponge cakes) in varying geometrical shapes, and then filling the mould with an airy Bavarian or whipped cream. When surrounded by slices of multilayered sponge cake and jam it is called charlotte royale. When surrounded by sponge fingers, it is known as a charlotte russe. The charlotte is so popular in France it is constantly reappearing in new guises and names. In America the charlotte has appeared and disappeared over the years, usually under the prosaic name 'icebox cake', probably in deference to the advance preparation and prolonged refrigeration necessary before unmoulding and serving it.

When I think of an icebox cake, I picture an easy-to-prepare cake that uses packaged sponge fingers. These are not a bad product, but, when you make your own sponge fingers or cake sheets, icebox cake is transformed into a charlotte and becomes one of my favourite desserts. Both from a visual and gustatory standpoint, one can ask for no more elegant finale to a dinner party.

Note: A charlotte must be prepared at least 4 hours in advance but can be refrigerated for up to 3 days with no loss of texture or flavour. The cake-lined mould must be prepared in advance. In fact, it can be frozen for 3 months, making it a simple matter to complete the dessert well in advance of a party.

Ethereal Pear Charlotte

Serves 8 to 10

This dessert, inspired by LeNôtre, one of the world's great *pâtissiers*, is perhaps my favourite of all charlottes. The flavour is pure pear and the texture is incomparably creamy and billowy.

TIMING: The charlotte must be assembled 4 hours to 3 days ahead. It can also be frozen for 3 weeks. The mould must be lined with the *biscuit* before preparing the filling.

SERVE: Chilled. For an elegant effect, pour raspberry sauce on to the centre of each serving plate and tilt to coat evenly. Top with a slice of the charlotte.

SPECIAL EQUIPMENT NEEDED
- 23-centimetre/9-inch springform or loose bottom tin or a flan ring at least 6 centimetres/2½ inches high
- Two 30 × 20-centimetre/ 12 × 8-inch Swiss-roll tins

CAKE COMPONENTS
- 1 recipe Biscuit Roulade for the sides of the mould and base (page 157)
- 82 grams/2¾ ounces/ 6 tablespoons Cordon Rose Raspberry Conserve (page 380) or seedless raspberry jam
- 1 recipe Poached Pears (page 401)
- 1 recipe Pear Bavarian Cream (page 334)

- 80 grams/3 ounces/¼ cup Apple Jewel Glaze (page 378), thinned with poire William. Or Shiny Apple Jewel Glaze (page 379) if preparing the charlotte more than 1 day ahead.
- *Optional:* 1 recipe Raspberry Sauce (page 386) to echo the filling and contrast with the pale green colour

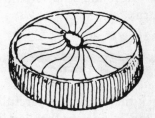

METHOD FOR ASSEMBLING CHARLOTTE
Lining the mould:
1. Bake the *biscuits*. Allow them to cool flat. Cut a 20-centimetre/8-inch disc from one *biscuit* patching if necessary.
2. To cut the other *biscuit*, use a pizza wheel or a sharp knife and a ruler to score where the

cuts should be and then use sharp shears to do the actual cutting. Trim the edges so that the *biscuit* measures exactly 25.5 × 19 centimetres/ 10 × about 7½ inches. Now cut the *biscuit* lengthwise into four equal rectangles 6 centimetres/2½ inches wide by about 19 centimetres/ 7½ inches long.

3. Spread three of the rectangles with a smooth layer of the raspberry conserve or jam. If the jam is too thick to spread easily, thin it with 1½ teaspoons Chambord (black raspberry liqueur) or warm water. If using commercial jam, heat and strain it and use warm.

4. Stack the rectangles carefully on top of one another, ending with the one that has no jam. The flat side of a long metal ruler, pressed against the side, helps to even the layers.

5. You now have a four-layer rectangle, exactly 6 centimetres/2½ inches wide, about 19 centimetres/7½ inches long and 5 centimetres/2 inches

high. (The only important measure is the width because when sliced and positioned in the tin, it will determine the height of the striped border.)

6. Wrap the rectangle in greaseproof paper and put it in a large heavy-duty plastic freezer bag. Place it on a baking sheet to maintain its shape and freeze until firm.

7. Use a small serrated knife to cut the rectangle into 9-millimetre/⅜-inch slices. If necessary, trim each slice so that it is exactly 6 centimetres/2½ inches high when the stripes are up and down.

8. If moulding the charlotte in a springform tin, remove the inner disc and place the outer ring directly on a serving plate. If using a loose-bottom tin, leave the inner disc in place but line it with a parchment round if planning to remove it before serving.

9. Lightly oil the inside of the ring. Place the striped slices around the ring so that the stripes are straight up and down. Brush one side of each slice with a light coating of conserve before placing the next slice firmly against it.

10. Trim the *biscuit* base if necessary and fit it snugly into the bottom of the lined ring. Re-cover tightly with the clingfilm.

11. Poach the pears, reserving the liquid for the filling.

12. Prepare the Pear Bavarian Cream and scoop it into the prepared mould. Level with a small angled spatula. Cover tightly and refrigerate for at least 30 minutes.

13. Use a thin, sharp knife to cut the poached pears lengthwise into thin slices. Place a fan of overlapping slices on top of the filling with the pointed ends at the centre. To form a centre pear-shaped decoration, place two small pear slices (slightly overlapping) and a small piece of stem at the top.

14. If serving the same day, brush the pears with a thin film of Apple Jewel Glaze. For a thicker glaze that keeps the pears moist and fresh for several days, brush with Shiny Apple Jewel Glaze instead. Allow the charlotte to set for 4 hours to 3 days before unmoulding.

To unmould: For a springform, release the sides of the tin and lift away. For a loose-bottom tin, place on top of a sturdy canister smaller than the tin's bottom and press firmly downwards. The tin's sides will slip down to the worktop and the charlotte can be lifted off the canister because it is supported by the tin's base. Use a heavy-duty spatula turner to slide between the parchment and pan base and place the charlotte on a serving plate.

Scarlet Empress

Serves 6 to 8

Spiral slices of jam-filled tender Biscuit Roulade form a dome to encase a smooth Vanilla Bavarian Cream. This is a light, intensely flavourful cake with a dramatic design. It is especially delicious and attractive served with a tart raspberry sauce.

TIMING: The charlotte must be assembled 8 hours to 3 days ahead. It can also be frozen for 3 weeks. The mould must be lined with the Swiss-roll slices before preparing the filling.

SERVE: Chilled. For an elegant effect, pour raspberry sauce on to the centre of each serving plate and tilt it to coat evenly. Top with a slice of the charlotte.

SPECIAL EQUIPMENT NEEDED
- 1½-litre/2½-pint/6-cup round-bottom bowl
- Two 30 × 20-centimetre/ 12 × 8-inch Swiss-roll tins

CAKE COMPONENTS
- 109 grams/3½ ounces/½ cup Cordon Rose Raspberry Conserve (page 380) or seedless raspberry jam
- 1 recipe Biscuit Roulade (page 157) for jam-filled roll and base
- 1 recipe Vanilla Bavarian Cream (page 331)
- *Optional:*
  Shiny Apricot Glaze (page 203) for a transparent golden film which keeps the cake fresh and adds a pleasant tartness
  1 recipe Raspberry Sauce (page 386)

METHOD FOR ASSEMBLING CHARLOTTE
Lining the mould:
1. Lightly oil the bowl and line it as smoothly as possible with a sheet of clingfilm, leaving a small overhang. Measure the diameter of the bowl. You will need a round *biscuit* base that just fits inside.

2. As soon as the *biscuits* have finished baking, use the lining to slip them out of the tins on to the worktop. Immediately, while still hot, roll one biscuit as indicated in the recipe and allow it to cool. Cut the *biscuit* base mentioned in step 1 from the second *biscuit*.

3. While still hot, roll the remaining *biscuit* as indicated in the recipe and allow it to cool.

4. When the cut strip has cooled, cut it with scissors into a circle for the base. Wrap in clingfilm and set aside.

5. The Swiss-roll slices used to line this charlotte must be tightly rolled for the most attractive appearance. To accomplish this, unroll the cooled *biscuit*, leaving it on the non-stick liner or tea-towel, and spread the crust side with a very thin layer of raspberry conserve or jam. If the jam is too thick to spread easily, thin it with 2 teaspoons Chambord (black raspberry liqueur) or warm water.

6. Roll up the *biscuit* tightly about one-third of the way and turn it so that the unrolled portion is facing you. Fold over the lining or tea-towel to cover the

rolled section and a little of the flat section. With the edge of a straight-sided baking sheet held at an angle on top of the towel just at the point where the rolled section ends, press firmly against the roll and tug the bottom of the tea-towel towards you to compress the roll. Lift away the tea-towel overlap, roll up another third of the way, and repeat the process. Repeat once more, again angling the baking sheet at the base of the roll. The completed roll will be 5 centimetres/2 inches in diameter.

7. Wrap snugly with clingfilm and then foil, and freeze until firm enough to slice.

8. With a small serrated knife, cut the roll into 5-millimetre/ 1/4-inch slices.

9. To line the bowl, place one slice in the centre and place other slices around it as tightly as possible to avoid gaps. It is usually necessary to cut the slices in half or smaller to fit the last row (Figs. 1 and 2).

10. Cover the lined bowl tightly to keep it from drying out until the filling is ready.

11. Make the Vanilla Bavarian Cream, spoon it into the mould, and place the round *biscuit* base in place. Cover tightly and refrigerate until set (at least 8 hours).

To unmould: Invert on to a serving plate and lift away the bowl, tugging gently on the clingfilm to release it. To prevent drying out, glaze with Shiny Apricot Glaze or simply leave the clingfilm in place until shortly before serving time.

TO MAKE SHINY APRICOT GLAZE

Sprinkle 1 teaspoon gelatin over 4 fluid ounces water and allow to sit for at least 3 minutes. Heat until the gelatin is dissolved. Heat 75 grams/2³/₄ ounces/¹/₄ cup apricot preserves and strain it. Stir in the gelatin mixture and allow to thicken slightly. Or stir briefly over ice water until syrupy before brushing on to the cake.

A TOUCH OF CHOCOLATE

Chocolate Chip Charlotte

Serves 6 to 8

The dramatically complex shape of this charlotte is deceptively simple –
merely cut and overlap rectangular strips of *génoise*. The easy-to-make
Chocolate Chip Whipped Cream filling is light, crunchy and utterly
delectable.

TIMING: *Génoise* should be baked
1 day ahead to be firm enough for
cutting. The charlotte must be
assembled 2 hours to 3 days ahead.
It can also be frozen for 3 weeks.
The cream filling is prepared just
before lining the mould with the
cake so that some of the whipped
cream can be used to attach the
cake strips.

SERVE: Chilled. For an elegant
effect, pour Ganache Sauce on to
the centre of each serving plate and
tilt it to coat evenly. Top with a
slice of the charlotte. If the ganache
is too thick to pour, warm it gently
in a double boiler. For extra
flavour, add 1 tablespoon cognac or
amaretto.

SPECIAL EQUIPMENT
NEEDED
- 1½-litre/2½-pint/6-cup round
  bottom bowl

- 20 × 5-centimetre/8 × 2-inch
  square metal tin
- Pastry bag and 11-millimetre-
  long teardrop-shape tube

CAKE COMPONENTS
- 1 recipe Génoise Classique
  (page 129), baked in a
  20 × 5-centimetre/8 × 2-inch
  square metal tin
- 85 grams/3 ounces/½ cup
  Ganache Icing (page 312), made
  with 56.75 grams/2 ounces
  bittersweet chocolate and
  58 grams/2 ounces/¼ cup double
  cream
- ½ the syrup recipe on page 130,
  made with Cognac or
  amaretto
- 1 recipe Chocolate Chip
  Whipped Cream (page 298)
- *Optional:*
  275 grams/9½ ounces/1 cup
  Ganache Sauce is a nice textural
  contrast to the soft cake and

creamy filling. Simply make extra ganache when preparing it for icing the *génoise*.

METHOD FOR ASSEMBLING CHARLOTTE

Lining the mould:

1. Use a soft tape measure to measure the inside of the bowl, measuring from the centre to the edge and making sure that the tape follows the curve of the bowl. It should measure about 14 centimetres/5½ inches. Using a long serrated knife, remove the top crust of the *génoise* and trim it so that it is perfectly square. Cut off one edge so that one side measures exactly 15 centimetres/6 inches (one inch more than the curve of the bowl for a safety margin).

2. Prepare the Ganache Icing and spread 2 tablespoons of the hot ganache on the top of the cake. Chill the cake for 15 minutes to set the ganache. Set aside the remaining ganache at room temperature.

3. Invert the cake, ganache side down, on to lightly greased foil and cut it into 15-centimetre × 5-millimetre/6 × ¼-inch strips with a thin, sharp knife, wiping the blade between each slice. Cut one end of the uniced side of each strip on the diagonal so that it comes to a point (Fig. 1). This will prevent too much cake from building up in the centre.

Keep the slices covered with clingfilm to prevent drying.

4. Prepare the Chocolate Chip Whipped Cream and set aside while lining the mould.

5. Lightly oil the glass bowl and line it smoothly with buttered clingfilm, buttered side up, allowing a slight overhang. Starting at the bottom centre of the bowl, place a strip of *génoise* from the centre to the edge of the bowl, placing the pointed end at the centre, the plain edge facing right, and the iced edge facing left (Fig. 2).

6. Brush the strip with the syrup and a thin coating of the plain whipped cream reserved from the filling recipe. Place a second strip beside it in the same manner, slightly overlapping the first strip at the rim. Brush it

with the syrup and whipped cream. Continue working clockwise, from right to left, always having the iced edge facing left so that it will show on the outside and create a striped motif when the charlotte is unmoulded. When you come to the last strip, tuck the side under the first strip.

7. Trim the excess *génoise* flush with the edge of the bowl with sharp scissors (Fig. 3). Cover tightly with clingfilm while preparing the filling.

8. Fill the lined mould with the Chocolate Chip Whipped Cream and chill until set (at least 2 hours).

9. Unmould on to a serving plate, tugging gently on the clingfilm overhang to release the cake. Use the remaining ganache to pipe a fluted design on top to cover any imperfections.

A TOUCH OF CHOCOLATE

Orange Chocolate Crown

Serves 8 to 10

A crown of sponge fingers encases layers of Orange Bavarian Cream and Light Whipped Ganache. The contrasting flavours and textures are so pleasing that, even if time does not allow to make your own sponge fingers, the charlotte is still delicious with the packet variety, freshened with a light sprinkling of Grand Marnier. The fingers can also be cut for the base and tapered to form a daisy top.

TIMING: The charlotte must be assembled 4 hours to 3 days ahead. It may also be frozen for 3 weeks. The mould must be lined with the *biscuit* or sponge fingers before preparing the filling.

SERVE: Remove from the refrigerator 1 hour before serving. For an elegant effect, pour the *crème anglaise* on to the centre of each serving plate and tilt it to coat evenly. Top with a slice of the charlotte and garnish with the orange zest.

SPECIAL EQUIPMENT NEEDED
- Pastry bag and large tube (2 centimetre/³⁄₄-inch diameter) for piping sponge fingers and discs
- 23 × 5 or 7.5-centimetre/9 × 2 or 3-inch loose-bottom tin, springform tin, or flan ring

CAKE COMPONENTS
- 1 recipe Biscuit à la Cuillère (page 165), piped to make 2 dozen sponge fingers (you will need at least 19) and a 21.5-centimetre/8¹⁄₂-inch base (page 429)
- ¹⁄₂ recipe Biscuit à la Cuillère, piped to make a 23-centimetre/ 9-inch daisy top (page 430)
- If using packet sponge fingers for the sides, base and top, buy two packets (48 fingers)
- 1 recipe Orange Bavarian (page 333)
- ¹⁄₄ recipe Light Whipped Ganache (page 310)
- *Optional:*
  Orange Zest (page 392), a pretty garnish that adds a real sparkle of orange flavour and delightful chewy candied texture
  1 recipe Grand Marnier Crème Anglaise (page 323); fragrant with vanilla and a hint of orange, it ties together all the harmonious elements of this cake
  Brown and orange grosgrain or satin ribbons, to hint at the chocolate and orange flavours within

GUIDELINES FOR PIPING THE SPONGE FINGERS, BASE AND DAISY TOP
A non-stick liner, parchment or foil can be used to line the tins for piping the Biscuit à la Cuillère batter. If using parchment, lines can be drawn directly on it with pen or pencil. The parchment is turned over before piping so that the lines show through but the ink or pencil marks don't come into direct contact with the batter. Lines for foil can be marked with a skewer. A non-stick liner, however, is my favourite surface because the baked *biscuit* slides off it without hesitation. I use a bright felt-tip marker to make lines on a brown paper bag and cover it with the non-stick liner. It is also possible to grease and flour the tin and create lines in the surface of the flour. For piping sponge

fingers, make parallel lines 7.5 centimetres/3 inches apart. For discs, use a round cake tin to mark circles (20 centimetres/8 inches for the base, 23 centimetres/9 inches for the top).

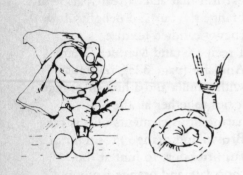

Piping Method Tips: *Biscuit* batter flows fairly easily so it is unnecessary to squeeze the pastry bag. If the piped designs do not hold their shape, it means that the egg whites were not beaten stiffly enough. To stop the flow of batter, tilt the tube up just before you think it will be necessary. Work steadily so that the batter can be baked soon after preparing it. This will enable it to retain as much air and lightness as possible.

PIPED SPONGE FINGERS:

Pipe the sponge fingers leaving 5-millimetre/¼-inch space in between because the batter will spread sideways while piping the next finger. (After baking, the sponge fingers will be attached to each other in continuous strips. Each finger will be about 4 centimetres/1½ inches wide.)

Start piping just inside the top line and stop shortly before reaching the bottom line, moving the tip slightly forward and up to control the batter flow.

PIPED SPIRAL BASE:

To pipe a spiral base, hold the pastry bag in a vertical (straight up-and-down) position, with the tube at least 4 centimetres/1½ inches above the tin. To achieve full height and a rounded shape, the batter must be allowed to fall from the tube and not be pressed against the tin. Start in the centre, moving the tip by turning the entire arm in smooth circles. To prevent gaps, allow the spirals of batter to fall against the sides – almost on top of – previous spirals. The weight of the batter will cause them to fall exactly in place.

PIPED DAISY TOP:

Making this fancy design to top the charlotte involves piping a tear-drop shape or shell design without ridges, radiating from the outline to centre. See piped shell borders (page 461). Finish the centre with a round dot. *Pearled Sugar Effect:* After piping the fingers and daisy top, use a strainer and spoon to sift icing sugar over them. After a few seconds, the batter will dissolve and absorb some of the sugar. For a pearled effect, sprinkle with a second coat.

Preheat the oven to 400°F/200°C/gas mark 6.

BAKING BISCUIT:

Bake for 8 to 10 minutes or until light golden brown and springy to the touch. Remove the tins to racks and cool slightly. To prevent cracking, remove from the tins while still warm with a long, thin spatula or pancake turner. For discs, invert on to a rack covered with a paper towel, peel off the backing, and reinvert on to a second rack. Finish cooling on racks and then wrap airtight.

METHOD FOR ASSEMBLING CHARLOTTE

Lining the tin:

1. If moulding the charlotte in a springform tin, you may remove the inner disc and place the outer ring directly on a serving plate. If using a loose-bottom tin, leave the inner disc in place but line with a parchment round if planning to remove the disc before serving. Lightly oil the inside of the ring.

2. If the sponge fingers have not been freshly baked, sprinkle them with a little Grand Marnier. Use the sponge-finger strips to line the inside of the ring.

3. Place the *biscuit* base in the bottom, trimming it if necessary for a snug fit.

4. Prepare the Orange Bavarian and scoop it into the lined mould. Level with a small angled spatula.

5. Add the Light Whipped Ganache and spread smoothly.

6. If not using the daisy top, garnish with the optional orange zest.

7. If using the daisy top, trim the tops of the sponge fingers, encircling the mould so that they are flush with the filling and cover with the daisy top, sprinkled with Grand Marnier.

A TOUCH OF CHOCOLATE

Strawberry Maria

Serves 12

The idea for this cake comes from one of my favourite things to do to a strawberry before eating it: dip it in bittersweet chocolate and then inject it with Grand Marnier. This special creation exploits the same irresistible flavour combination and was designed with love and reverence for my editor, Maria Guarnaschelli.

TIMING: The torte should be assembled 4 hours to 1 day ahead.

SERVE: Lightly chilled or room temperature. Break the chocolate lattice band and use the pieces for garnish.

SPECIAL EQUIPMENT NEEDED
- Parchment for cone to pipe the chocolate
- Pastry bag and large 1½-centimetre star tube

CAKE COMPONENTS
- 1 recipe Génoise au Chocolat (page 141), top and bottom crust removed and split horizontally
- 1 recipe syrup flavoured with Grand Marnier (page 132)
- 1 recipe Strawberry Cloud Cream (page 307)
- *Optional:*
  1 Chocolate Lattice Band (page 447), 75 centimetres/29 inches long and 7.5 centimetres/3 inches high

Small strawberries dipped in quick-tempered chocolate (page 439)

METHOD FOR ASSEMBLING CAKE
1. Spread a little Strawberry Cloud Cream on a 23-centimetre/ 9-inch cardboard round to attach the cake.
2. Sprinkle each side of the cake layers with 3 tablespoons syrup.
3. Sandwich the cake layers with 215 grams/7½ ounces/1½ cups Strawberry Cloud Cream.
4. Spread 71 grams/2½ ounces/ ½ cup Strawberry Cloud Cream evenly on the top and the same amount around the sides.
5. Use a large 3-millimetre star tube and the remaining cream to pipe rows of shells on top of the cake. Start from a middle edge and reverse the direction of the shells for each row.
6. Pipe the Chocolate Lattice Band and when it just begins to dull, wrap it around the cake, peeling

back one end slightly to overlap the ends.

7. Refrigerate for 10 minutes or until the chocolate is firm enough to allow easy removal of the greaseproof paper.

8. Refrigerate the cake for 30 minutes to 3 hours before serving time.

9. Garnish if desired with the chocolate-dipped strawberries.

A TOUCH OF CHOCOLATE

Queen Bee

Serves 14 to 16

The quintessential show-off cake. It was inspired by a Swiss confectionery bar containing honey and chocolate. Honey has been incorporated into almost every component but kept in the background as a subtle flavour that never becomes cloyingly sweet.

As optional garnish, marzipan honey bees can be placed on the 'hive' and suspended on angel-hair pasta to give the illusion of bees hovering over the cake.

TIMING: The cake should be assembled 1 to 5 days ahead and refrigerated. The completed cake (without the bees) can be frozen for 3 months.

SERVE: Lightly chilled or at room temperature. (Buttercream should be warm enough to be creamy.) Score the chocolate disc with a knife that has been dipped in hot water and dried to facilitate cutting.

SPECIAL EQUIPMENT NEEDED
• A plastic squeeze dispenser is

helpful for filling the hive openings with honey

CAKE COMPONENTS
• I recipe Biscuit de Savoie (page 161), bottom and top crusts removed
• 1 recipe Rum Nectar: When making the syrup for the *biscuit* (page 163), use dark rum as the liqueur and add 1 teaspoon freshly squeezed lemon juice and 1 teaspoon honey
• 1 recipe Royal Honey Buttercream (page 271)
• A 23-centimetre/9-inch chocolate

disc made with 84 grams/
3 ounces quick-tempered
chocolate and 2.5-centimetre/
1-inch random holes cut in it
(pages 439 and 445)
- 1 recipe Nougatine Honey
Crunch (page 367)
- 2 tablespoons clear honey in a
plastic squeeze dispenser
- *Optional:*
Marzipan Bees (page 421)
A few strands of dried uncooked
capellini (angel-hair pasta)

METHODS FOR ASSEMBLING CAKE

1. Spread a little buttercream on a
23-centimetre/9-inch cardboard
round to attach the cake.
2. Sprinkle each side of the cake
layers with 2½ fluid ounces
Rum Nectar.
3. Sandwich the cake layers with
100 grams/3½ ounces/½ cup
buttercream spread 3
millimetres/⅛ inch thick
between each layer, ending
with a layer of buttercream.
4. Use a sturdy broad spatula to
lift the chocolate disc and place
it on top of the buttercream.
5. Refrigerate for 10 minutes or
until the buttercream firms
enough to hold the chocolate
securely in place.
6. Spread the sides with the
remaining buttercream.
7. Gently press the Nougatine
Honey Crunch on the sides,
supporting the cake on the
palm of one hand and tilting it
slightly towards the other
hand, cupped to hold the
nougatine.
8. Using a plastic dispenser bottle
or small teaspoon, fill the cut-
outs in the chocolate with little
pools of honey. For a casual
look, allow some honey to drip
randomly on to the chocolate
or brush some on the surface in
irregular patterns.
9. Refrigerate if preparing 1 day
ahead. Remove from the
refrigerator at least 30 minutes
before serving.
10. Garnish with the optional
marzipan bees. To suspend the
bees on pasta strands, use a
heated metal cake tester to bore
a small hole in the chocolate
disc for inserting the pasta (for
maximum support) or insert
the pasta into the honey pools.
Place a few bees near the honey
pools so that they appear to be
drinking the honey.

A TOUCH OF CHOCOLATE

Barquettes Chez l'Ami Louis

Serves 12

These multilayered little jewels are a treat of textures and flavours and are an adaptation of those served at my favourite Parisian two-star bistro, Chez l'Ami Louis. (I am grateful to my dear friend Heidi Trachtenberg for directing me there to taste and 'figure out what's in it'.) The barquette is a boat-shaped crunch of nougatine filled with soft, rum-saturated *biscuit*, topped with buttercream, and then glazed with bittersweet ganache.

Admittedly time-consuming to prepare, this recipe can be made well in advance – even frozen – and requires considerably less time and money than flying to Paris! Another advantage is that this version is a lot less sweet than the original French creation.

TIMING: All the components of these barquettes can be made several days ahead – even the nougatine if the weather is not humid. Barquettes may be assembled 1 day ahead and refrigerated or assembled 1 week ahead and frozen. (To prevent droplets of moisture and stickiness, defrost uncovered in the refrigerator for at least 6 hours before removing to room temperature.)

SERVE: Room temperature. Barquettes are most gracefully eaten by hand.

Caveat: Moulding the nougatine barquettes requires advanced pastry skills.

SPECIAL EQUIPMENT NEEDED
- Lightly oiled barquette form, 10 x 4.25 centimetres/$3^7/8 \times 1^5/8$ inches (to use as a mould)
- Pastry bag and 1-millimetre star tube (for optional piped decoration)

CAKE COMPONENTS
- 1 recipe Biscuit Roulade (page 157), cooled flat without rolling
- 1 recipe Nougatine (page 366)

- Scant 2 fluid ounces *Rum Syrup*: In a small saucepan with a tight-fitting lid, stir together 2 table-spoons water and 1 tablespoon sugar over high heat, until a full rolling boil is reached. Cover immediately, turn off the heat, and allow to cool. Pour into an 8 fluid ounce glass measure and add 1 tablespoon dark rum. If the syrup has evaporated, add enough water to equal a scant 2 fluid ounces (65 grams/ 2¼ ounces) syrup.

- ¾ cup *Neoclassic Buttercream*: The following recipe will yield 200 grams/7 ounces/1 cup, but the recipe requires only three-quarters of that. Freeze the extra to use for cupcakes. In a bowl beat 2 large egg yolks with an electric mixer until light in colour. In a small saucepan (preferably with a non-stick lining) combine 50 grams/ 1¾ ounces/¼ cup sugar and 3 tablespoons corn syrup and cook over high heat, stirring constantly, until the sugar dissolves and the syrup comes to a rolling boil. (The entire surface will be covered by large bubbles.) Immediately transfer the syrup to a glass bowl to stop the cooking. Beat the hot syrup into the yolks, avoiding pouring it on the beaters. When cool, beat in 5 ounces (10 tablespoons) softened unsalted butter until smooth and creamy.

- about 175 grams/6 ounces/⅔ cup *Dark Ganache Icing*: Stir 58 grams/2 ounces/¼ cup double cream into 112 grams/4 ounces melted bittersweet chocolate until smooth. Use at once while still soft, or reheat gently in a double boiler or for a few seconds in a microwave. (If planning to pipe the optional shell border, double the recipe and allow the remainder to cool until firm enough to pipe.)

- *Optional:* A small amount of whipped cream and Crystallised Lilacs or Violets (page 375).

METHOD FOR ASSEMBLING CAKE
Preheat the oven to 300°F/150°C/gas mark 2 for warming the nougatine.

1. To cut ovals of nougatine for the barquettes, make a foil template by pressing foil into the barquette mould, then flattening it and cutting out the shape.

2. After the nougatine is cool enough to handle, cut it into four equal parts and roll one of them into an 18 × 11.5-centimetre/7 × 4½-inch rectangle 3 millimetres/⅛ inch thick. Keep the other three pieces warm in the oven with the door ajar. If the nougatine has cooled and hardened, warm it again until soft enough to mark easily.

3. Using a pizza cutter and the template as a guide, mark oval shapes on the nougatine rectangle. When cool enough to handle, cut out the ovals with scissors. Each rectangle will make three barquette ovals.

4. Press one oval into the barquette mould. The nougatine must still be warm enough to remain flexible. If necessary, return it briefly to a heat source until just flexible (not too long or it will lose its shape).

5. When cool, remove the hardened nougatine barquette from the mould and make more in the same manner. The barquettes keep for several weeks if stored airtight at room temperature away from direct sunlight, heat and humidity.

6. Cut out ovals of *biscuit* with scissors, using the barquette mould as a guide.

7. Sprinkle ½ teaspoon rum syrup on each side of each *biscuit* oval and fit it into a nougatine shell.

8. With a small metal spatula spread 1 tablespoon buttercream in the centre of each barquette, mounding it slightly in the centre to create a ridge at the top. Freeze for 5 minutes to firm the buttercream.

9. Using the same size spatula, spread a thin coat of ganache over the buttercream, also mounding it slightly in the centre. To form an attractive centre crest, hold the barquette in one hand and with the other hand hold the spatula against the side, angled slightly inward. Start at one end and bring the spatula smoothly to the other end. Repeat on reverse side.

10. Pipe a trimming of tiny ganache shells along the ridge and sides if desired. Or garnish with Crystallised Lilacs or Violets. (Use ice to chill your hand so the chocolate will stay firm enough to pipe.)

VERY CHOCOLATE

Chestnut Chocolate Embrace

(La Châtaigne)

Serves 12

This fabulous cake is perfect for the holiday season, when fresh chestnuts abound. Although spicy and almost earthy in flavour, it is delicate enough to serve after a bountiful Thanksgiving or Christmas dinner. Chestnut Whipped Cream is a Swiss creation and so delicious it inspired my invention of the Chestnut Génoise to go with it. The band dramatically encases the cake while tying in the lovely combination of chocolate and chestnut.

TIMING: The cake can be assembled 1 day ahead and refrigerated.

SERVE: Lightly chilled or at room temperature. Break the chocolate band into pieces and use it for garnish.

SPECIAL EQUIPMENT NEEDED
• Pastry bag and large 3.5-millimetre star tube

CAKE COMPONENTS
• 1 recipe Chestnut Génoise (page 133), top and bottom crusts removed
• 1 recipe Chestnut Mousse Cream (page 303)
• 1 recipe Rum Syrup (page 135)
• 1 Chocolate Band (page 447)
• *Marrons glacés* (candied chestnuts), brushed with chocolate

METHOD FOR ASSEMBLING CAKE
1. The cake can be iced directly on a serving plate, using strips of greaseproof paper slid under the sides. Or use a 23-centimetre/ 9-inch cardboard round as a base.
2. Spread a little Chestnut Mousse Cream on the plate or cardboard round to attach the cake.
3. Sprinkle each side of the cake layers with 4½ tablespoons syrup.
4. Place the cake layers on the base and sandwich them with 330 grams/11½ ounces/2 cups Chestnut Mousse Cream.
5. Reserve 165 grams/5¾ ounces/ 1 cup Chestnut Mousse Cream

for piping the garnish and ice the cake with the remainder.

6. Make the Chocolate Band: The circumference of the cake is about 74 centimetres/29 inches so cut a piece of greaseproof paper 79 centimetres/31 inches long. Fold the greaseproof paper so that it is at least 2.5 centimetres/1 inch higher than the finished height of the cake (about 7 centimetres/2¾ inches). If planning to scallop the band, add an extra inch or two. Temper 112 to 224 grams/4 to 8 ounces dark chocolate, preferably *couverture*, using the classic or quick-temper methods on pages 438 and 439. (If you don't temper the chocolate when melting it or if room temperature is too warm, the band may not be firm enough to wrap around the cake. 112 grams/4 ounces of chocolate will be enough for a band 9.5 centimetres/3¾ inches high. 224 grams/8 ounces will make a band 13 centimetres/5 inches high.) Using an angled spatula, spread the chocolate evenly on the greaseproof-paper strip, making it a little longer than the desired length. Lift the strip by the ends and transfer to clean section of the worktop for the chocolate to set.

7. When the chocolate is firm but still malleable, use a small sharp knife to cut a straight line or a free-form scallop along one side. Attach the strip scallop side up around the cake. Gently pull away the ends of the greaseproof paper and use a bit of melted chocolate to attach the overlapping ends. If the chocolate sticks to the paper, let it set longer or refrigerate for a few minutes until firm enough to release cleanly. The cut edge will break away easily on slight pressure.

8. Decorate the top of the cake with swirls of Chestnut Mousse Cream piped with a large 3.5-millimetre star tube.

9. Garnish with the *marrons glacés*.

VERY CHOCOLATE

Swiss Black Forest Cake

(Schwarzwalder Kirschtorte)

Serves 10 to 12

My version of this classic was inspired by Confiserie Tschirren in Berne, Switzerland. They brought the recipe from Germany after World War II; and it has since become the national cake of Switzerland.

The Swiss rendition is far lighter and more delicate than the original German one, which also includes buttercream. A lofty layer of whipped cream studded with liqueur-soaked cherries is sandwiched between two thin, light layers of liqueur-moistened chocolate *génoise*. The chocolate flakes on top dissolve like snowflakes on the tongue.

In Switzerland, the Black Forest Cake is served in all *confiseries* and *konditorei* for afternoon tea, but the cake is elegant enough for fancy dinner parties as well.

TIMING: The cake should be assembled 4 to 12 hours ahead.

SERVE: Chilled.

SPECIAL EQUIPMENT
- 22 × 6-centimetre/8⅝ × 2⅜-inch French flan ring (page 516). Or a 23-centimetre/9-inch springform or loose-bottom tin fitted with cardboard rounds until a depth of 6 centimetres/2½ inches is achieved. Moulding the cake this way makes it perfectly symmetrical. The French flan ring is the ideal size because the 23 centimetre/9-inch cake layer shrinks to just that size after baking. The springform tin also works but the sides of the finished cake will not be quite as even.
- Pastry bag and a large 1½-centimetre star tube

CAKE COMPONENTS
- 2 fluid ounces kirsch or brandy
- 1 recipe Brandied Burgundy Cherries (page 397), well drained and the syrup reserved
- ½ recipe (1 layer) Moist Chocolate Génoise (page 145), top and bottom crusts removed and split in half horizontally to make two 1-centimetre/½-inch layers
- 3 times the quantity of recipe for

Super-Stabilised Whipped Cream
(page 295)
• 40 grams/1½ ounces/½ cup
Chocolate Snowflakes (page 440)

METHOD FOR ASSEMBLING CAKE

1. Place the flan ring on a serving plate or cut out a cardboard round to fit the diameter of the ring. Or use a loose-bottom or springform tin fitted with cardboard rounds to a depth of 6 centimetres/2½ inches.
2. Add the kirsch or brandy to the reserved cherry syrup to make 4 fluid ounces (½ cup). Sprinkle each side of the cake layers with 2 tablespoons syrup.
3. Reserve 12 whole cherries for garnish and cut the remaining cherries in half if they are large.
4. Reserve 18 fluid ounces (2¼ cups) whipped cream for the top of the cake and the rosettes. (This may be refrigerated for up to 6 hours.)
5. Place one cake layer in the bottom of the flan ring and top with the remaining whipped cream.
6. Poke the cherries into the whipped cream, pressing some of the cut sides against the tin.
7. Use a small angled spatula to level the cream and top with the second cake layer.
8. Spread with 8 fluid ounces/ 1 cup of the reserved whipped cream. Use a long metal spatula to create a smooth top, allowing the blade to rest on the sides of the ring to create a very even surface.
9. Cover with foil and refrigerate for at least 4 hours.
10. Wipe the sides of the ring with a warm, damp tea-towel and lift away the ring or remove the sides of the tin.
11. Use the remaining whipped cream to decorate the top with rosettes using a large 1½-centimetre star tube. Top the rosettes with the reserved whole cherries. Spoon the Chocolate Snowflakes in the centre.

VARIATION

Three times the quantity of recipe for White Ganache (page 320) or 1½ times the quantity of recipe for Light Whipped Ganache (page 310) may be used in place of the whipped cream for a more chocolaty effect.

VERY CHOCOLATE

Black Forest
Ice Cream Torte

Serves 12

This summertime version of classic Black Forest Torte was inspired by Kleiner Konditorei in Zürich. It works as a frozen dessert because the liqueur keeps it from freezing too firmly. Chocolate Biscuit Roulade is an excellent base because it remains soft when frozen.

When the chocolate glaze is poured over the frozen ice cream, it sets immediately into an effortlessly even, shiny topping.

TIMING: The cake should be assembled 1 to 5 days ahead.

SPECIAL EQUIPMENT NEEDED
- Two 25.5-centimetre/10-inch round cake tins
- 23 × 7.5-centimetre/9 × 3-inch springform or loose-bottom tin, outside of tin wrapped with a double layer of heavy-duty foil
- *Optional:* pastry bag and large 3-millimetre star tube

CAKE COMPONENTS
- 1 recipe Brandied Burgundy Cherries (page 397)
- 1 recipe Vanilla Ice Cream (page 329), using 2 tablespoons kirsch. Or 1.25 kilograms/2¾ lb/5 cups commercial vanilla ice cream
- 1 recipe Chocolate Biscuit Roulade (page 160), baked in

two 25.5-centimetre/10-inch round tins. When cool, trim with scissors to 23 centimetres/ 9 inches (the exact diameter of the springform tin)
- Chocolate Cream Glaze: Process or chop 84 grams/3 ounces bittersweet chocolate until very fine and place in a small bowl. Scald 77 grams/2¾ ounces/ ⅓ cup double cream and add to the chocolate. Cover and allow to sit for 5 minutes. Add 1 teaspoon cognac and stir gently until the chocolate is fully melted and the mixture smooth. Cool until just tepid. When a small amount of glaze is dropped back on to the surface it should disappear smoothly.
- *Optional:*
174 grams/6 ounces/¾ cup double cream whipped with 2 teaspoons sugar and

½ teaspoon pure vanilla extract
(for rosettes)

METHOD FOR ASSEMBLING CAKE

1. Drain the cherries, reserving 2 fluid ounces syrup. Dry the cherries well on paper towels. Refrigerate 12 whole cherries for the garnish and slice the remaining cherries in half.
2. Remove the ice cream from the freezer and allow to soften slightly until spreadable.
3. While assembling the cake, set the springform tin in a larger tin surrounded by ice to keep the ice cream from melting.
4. Sprinkle each side of the cake layers with 1 tablespoon syrup.
5. Place one cake layer in the bottom of the springform tin and spread with half the ice cream. Top with the cherries, pressing some of the cut sides against the sides of the tin, and top with the remaining ice cream. Arrange the second cake layer on top. Cover with foil and freeze for at least 24 hours.
6. Up to 4 hours ahead glaze the cake. Pour tepid Chocolate Cream Glaze on to the centre of the cake and quickly tilt the tin to coat evenly. The glaze will set almost immediately.
7. Wipe the sides of the springform tin with a hot, damp tea-towel and remove the sides. Refrigerate for 1 hour to soften. Just before serving, pipe rosettes of whipped cream on top if desired and garnish with the reserved whole cherries.

VERY CHOCOLATE

Black Forest
Ice Cream Roll

Serves 6

Black Forest Ice Cream Cake also makes a terrific ice cream roll. The chocolate *biscuit* is the perfect cake to use because it stays flexible enough to roll, even when spread with ice cream. The attractive slices are even more delicious when topped with a hot ganache sauce and brandied cherries.

TIMING: The cake should be assembled 1 to 5 days ahead.

SPECIAL EQUIPMENT NEEDED
- 30 × 20-centimetre/12 × 8-inch Swiss-roll tin
- Optional: pastry bag and large 3-millimetre star tube

CAKE COMPONENTS
- ½ recipe Brandied Burgundy Cherries (page 397)
- ¼ recipe Vanilla Ice Cream (page 329), using ½ tablespoon kirsch. Or 250 grams/9 ounces/1 cup commercial vanilla ice cream
- 1 recipe Chocolate Biscuit Roulade (page 160), baked in a 30 × 20-centimetre/12 × 8-inch Swiss-roll tin. (Roll the cake while still hot.)
- *Optional:*
174 grams/6 ounces/½ cup double cream whipped with

1½ teaspoons sugar and ½ teaspoon pure vanilla extract (for rosettes)
- 40 grams/1½ ounces/½ cup Chocolate Snowflakes (page 440)
- Ganache Sauce: In a food processor grate finely 168 grams/6 ounces bittersweet chocolate. Heat 174 grams/6 ounces/¾ cup double cream to boiling point and add to the chocolate. Process for a few seconds or until smooth.

METHOD FOR ASSEMBLING CAKE ROLL
1. Place a 30 × 20-centimetre/12 × 8-inch Swiss-roll tin in the freezer to chill.
2. Drain ½ cup of the cherries (about 70 grams/5 ounces), reserving the syrup. Dry the cherries well on paper towels. Refrigerate 6 whole cherries for

the garnish and slice the remaining cherries in half.

3. Remove the ice cream from the freezer and allow to soften slightly until spreadable.

4. Unroll the chocolate *biscuit* on to the back of the chilled Swiss-roll tin, leaving the towel underneath the *biscuit*.

5. Brush the cake evenly with 2½ tablespoons brandied cherry syrup.

6. Using an angled spatula, quickly spread the softened ice cream over the cake, leaving 2.5 centimetres/1 inch uncovered along one long side. (Freeze any leftover ice cream.)

7. If the ice cream begins to melt, place the tin in the freezer for 5 to 10 minutes or until firm.

8. Scatter the halved cherries over the ice cream.

9. Starting with the long side that is covered with ice cream, use the towel to roll the cake. Set seam side down, cover lightly with clingfilm, and return to the freezer.

10. When the roll is very firm, wrap airtight in foil and freeze for at least 12 hours before serving.

11. For an attractive presentation, use a large 1½-centimetre star tube to pipe 6 whipped cream rosettes on top of the roll. Place 1 whole cherry in the centre of each. (Sprinkle with Chocolate Snowflakes. This may be done up to 3 hours ahead and the cake returned to the freezer.)

12. Gently heat the Ganache Sauce in a double boiler set over simmering water, stirring constantly, until hot. Or use a microwave on high power, stirring every 3 seconds. Heat the remaining cherries in any remaining syrup until just hot. Top each slice of ice-cream roll with Ganache Sauce and Brandied Cherries or pass them separately.

VERY CHOCOLATE

The Enchanted Forest

(La Fôret Enchantée)

Serves 10

When you cut into this fantasy cake, you will experience three distinctly different chocolates: velvety Light Whipped Ganache, moist flourless Cocoa Soufflé Roll, and the lightest crisp Cocoa Meringue.

The meringue sticks keep their shape below the surface of the cake but turn mousse-like. Above the surface they stay perfectly crunchy.

I recently made this cake in a larger round shape and renamed it for the occasion: Mom's Chocolate Candle 75th Birthday Cake.

TIMING: The cake can be assembled 2 days ahead and refrigerated or frozen for 2 months, but it is best not to place the meringue sticks in the filling more than 1 hour before serving. If you must insert them earlier and they start to soften and tilt, simply push them slightly further into the cake.

SERVE: Room temperature. Cut into wedges radiating from the centre.

SPECIAL EQUIPMENT NEEDED
• Pastry bag and 7-millimetre round tube

CAKE COMPONENTS
• 2 recipes Cocoa Soufflé Roll (page 154)

• 1 recipe Light Whipped Ganache (page 310)
• 1 recipe Cocoa Meringue (page 344), piped in sticks

METHOD FOR ASSEMBLING CAKE

1. Use an inverted oval tin as a template or draw a free-form 25 × 18-centimetre/9¾ × 7-inch oval on cardboard. Use the cardboard oval and a sharp knife to cut two ovals from the Cocoa Soufflé Rolls. Carefully slide a long metal spatula under ovals to dislodge them. Remove all the cake surrounding the ovals.

2. Spread a little ganache on the cardboard oval so that the cake will stick to it. Carefully slide a long broad spatula under one cake oval and transfer it to the cardboard.

3. Spread two-thirds of the ganache (a 1-centimetre/¹/₂-inch layer) over the oval and top with the second oval. Spread the remaining ganache on the top and sides. The cake will be about 4 centimetres/1¹/₂ inches high.

4. Surround the cake with some of the meringue sticks, using random lengths and pressing the flat sides against the ganache.

This can be done 2 days ahead. Refrigerate uncovered.

5. Up to 1 hour before serving, insert the remaining meringue sticks into the cake so that they reach the base. All flat ends should face the same direction. For a pretty effect, dip the tops of the sticks in cocoa or icing sugar. Allow the cake to sit at room temperature for 1 hour.

VERY CHOCOLATE

Chocolate Pine Cone

Serves 14

Small petals of chocolate create the illusion of a pine cone. They are held in place by bittersweet ganache textured with chopped pine nuts. The ganache fills and ices a moist light chocolate cake. Because it contains no flour this cake is marvellous for a Passover seder. The chocolate petals provide a lovely crunch against the soft and creamy textures within the cake. The petals look perky and adorable when the cake is cut, giving the individual pieces great visual distinction.

TIMING: The cake may be assembled 2 days ahead and refrigerated.

SERVE: Room temperature. Cut the cake into narrow curved strips, starting from the pointed end and working towards the back.

CAKE COMPONENTS
• 2 recipes Chocolate Cloud Roll (page 152)
• 1 recipe Dark Chocolate Ganache Icing (page 312), with 70 grams/ 2¹/₂ ounces/²/₃ cup chopped pine nuts added while still warm
• 225 grams/8 ounces Chocolate Pine Cone Petals (page 442)

- 1 tablespoon pine nuts for garnish

METHOD FOR ASSEMBLING CAKE

1. Draw a free-form 29 × 19-centimetre/11½ × 7½-inch oval on a piece of cardboard, tapering one end slightly to resemble a pine cone. Use the oval and a sharp knife to cut two ovals from the Chocolate Cloud Roll. Remove the scraps and stir them into the ganache. Carefully slide a long metal spatula under the ovals to dislodge them.

2. Spread a little ganache on to the cardboard oval so that the cake will stick to it. Carefully slide a long broad spatula under one cake oval and transfer it to the cardboard.

3. Spread half the ganache on the cake and top with the second cake oval. Spread the remaining ganache on the top and sides, mounding it slightly in the centre.

4. Insert the Chocolate Pine Cone Petals, starting at the tapered end and staggering each row. Place the whole pine nuts under some of the petals.

VERY CHOCOLATE

Cordon Rose Chocolate Christmas Log *(Bûche de Noël)*

Serves 6

I made this traditional holiday cake for Christmas dinner in France some years ago in the home of my dear friends the Brossollets. (Something like bringing coals to Newcastle!) It quickly became a family project, with Martin, the youngest, running out to the corner shop to buy parchment for piping the meringue mushrooms and Nadège sneaking her husband's oldest rum for the ganache, saying he would have a fit if he knew it was being used for a cake. The best part, however, was when Max (Papa) contributed his antique toy buglers for the decoration.

My version uses a moist chocolate roll and whipped cream instead of the usual yellow cake roll and chocolate buttercream, which I always found too rich and heavy under the chocolate 'bark'.

TIMING: The cake can be assembled and refrigerated 2 days ahead. The meringue mushrooms should not be set on the log until serving day.

SERVE: Lightly chilled or room temperature. Cut diagonal slices with a thin, sharp knife.

CAKE COMPONENTS
- 1 recipe Chocolate Cloud Roll (page 152)
- ½ recipe Perfect Whipped Cream (page 294)
- ¾ recipe Dark Chocolate Ganache Icing (page 312)

OPTIONAL DECOR
- Meringue Mushrooms (pages 433 and 434)
- Pistachio Màrzipan Ivy Leaves (pages 371 and 417)
- Green Tea Pine Needles (pages 344 and 431)

METHOD FOR
ASSEMBLING CAKE
1. Fill the Chocolate Cloud Roll with the Perfect Whipped Cream. Roll from the long 30-centimetre/12-inch edges.
2. Chill for at least 1 hour.
3. Cut a diagonal slice from one end of the roll and place on top to form a knot.
4. Spread the ganache over the log

and use the tines of a fork to make lines resembling bark. Make a few round swirls with the fork on top of the knot.
5. Decorate with the meringue mushrooms, marzipan leaves, green tea pine needles, and any small appropriate figures such as porcelain elves or trumpeters.
6. Refrigerate until 1 hour before serving.

INTENSELY CHOCOLATE

Chocolate Spike

Serves 10 to 12

This casual, homely cake is quick to make and elegant enough for special occasions as well. Perky little spikes of milk chocolate icing encase bittersweet Chocolate Fudge Cake.

TIMING: The cake can be iced 1 day ahead and does not require refrigeration. It can be frozen for 2 months.

SERVE: Room temperature.

CAKE COMPONENTS
• 1 recipe Chocolate Fudge Cake (page 54)
• 1 recipe Milk Chocolate Buttercream (page 291)

METHOD FOR ASSEMBLING CAKE
1. Ice the cake directly on a serving plate, using strips of greaseproof paper slid under the sides. Or use a 23-centimetre/9-inch cardboard round as a base.
2. Spread a little buttercream on the serving plate or cardboard to attach the cake.
3. Place the cake layers on the plate or cardboard and sandwich and ice with the buttercream.
4. For a decorative wave design on top, use a long serrated knife, moving it from left to right as you pull it forward.
5. For spikes, use a small metal spatula to lift the buttercream away from the sides in peaks (page 413).

INTENSELY CHOCOLATE

Bittersweet Royale Torte

Serves 8 to 10

This elegant torte has the flavour of a fine-quality Swiss chocolate bar but the soft, appealing texture of layer cake. An optional layer of Classic Chocolate Buttercream provides an interesting contrast in colour and texture.

The chocolate roses are hand-modelled, but you can substitute real roses if you like.

TIMING: The cake should be filled, iced, and refrigerated 4 hours to 1 day ahead. The glaze is most shiny when not refrigerated so it is best to glaze and decorate the cake the same day as serving. The cake can stay unrefrigerated for 1 day.

SERVE: Room temperature.

SPECIAL EQUIPMENT NEEDED
- Fresh rose leaves without tears or holes
- Artist's paint brush or small metal spatula

CAKE COMPONENTS
- *Optional:*
½ recipe Neoclassic or Classic Chocolate Buttercream (page 266 or 264)
- 1 recipe Perfect Chocolate Torte (page 50)
- 1 recipe Chocolate Cream Glaze (page 314)
- 20 chocolate rose leaves, each

6 centimetres/2½ inches long, and 9 smaller chocolate rose leaves (page 444 – use about 84 grams/3 ounces of chocolate)
- 4 Red Chocolate Roses (pages 374 and 450), each slightly larger than the next

METHOD FOR ASSEMBLING CAKE
1. If using the optional Classic Chocolate Buttercream, make a 23-centimetre/9-inch cardboard round for the base. If not using the buttercream, trim the cardboard round to 21.5 centimetres/8½ inches or slightly smaller than the diameter of the cake.
2. Spread a little buttercream or ganache on the cardboard round to attach the cake.
3. If using the buttercream, ice the cake and refrigerate it for at least 1 hour or until very firm.
4. Glaze the cake as per instructions in the Chocolate

Cream Glaze recipe. (Use the extra glaze which falls on to the sheet to attach the rose leaves.)

5. Place the cake on a serving plate and attach the large chocolate rose leaves, using little dabs of room temperature Chocolate Cream. Angle each leaf a little to the right, overlapping slightly.

6. Use the back of a wooden spoon to make shallow depressions in the cake for the chocolate roses. Set the roses in place.

7. Insert the small chocolate rose leaves into the glaze, using little mounds of the Chocolate Cream to support them.

INTENSELY CHOCOLATE

La Porcelaine

Serves 10 to 12

Red 'porcelainised' roses against a dark chocolate fondant-covered cake provide stunning visual appeal. This cake is at once elegant and richly, warmly inviting. The theme of long-stemmed chocolate roses was inspired by a cake I designed for *Good Housekeeping* magazine's one hundredth anniversary. The roses smell chocolaty and can even be eaten, but are best saved as mementoes.

This cake is a soft, full chocolate sensation; it is filled with my favourite ganache tinged with a scarlet edge of raspberry, and encased in fudgy chocolate fondant. Make this cake to celebrate the best events of your life.

TIMING: The cake can be assembled 1 day ahead without refrigeration or refrigerated 3 days.

SERVE: Room temperature. Cut with a thin, sharp knife.

Note: If making fondant stems for the roses, allow at least 30 minutes

for them to dry before placing on the cake.

SPECIAL EQUIPMENT NEEDED

- Sheet of heavy-duty plastic, 79 × 15 centimetres/ 31 × 6 inches (can be purchased in hardware shops)

CAKE COMPONENTS

- 1 recipe Raspberry Ganache (page 319)
- 1 recipe Perfect Chocolate Butter Cake (page 47)
- 1 recipe Chocolate Rolled Fondant (page 356)
- 8 Red Porcelain Roses (page 451) and chocolate fondant stems (see below), or fresh roses
- 20 Chocolate Rose Leaves (page 444), using about 84 grams/ 3 ounces of chocolate and reserving the leftover melted chocolate to attach the roses and leaves

METHOD FOR ASSEMBLING CAKE

1. Spread a little ganache on a 23-centimetre/9-inch cardboard round and centre one cake layer on it.
2. Fill and lightly ice the cake layers with the remaining ganache. (Use 260 grams/ 9¼ ounces/1 cup between the layers and the remaining 525 grams/18½ ounces/2 cups to ice the top and sides.) Chill until firm. Use a heavy-duty bread spatula to transfer the cake to a serving plate.
3. Make the fondant disc and band. On a piece of clingfilm, roll a piece of the chocolate fondant (about 235 grams/8¼ ounces/ ¾ cup) into a 3-millimetre/ ⅛-inch-thick disc. Transfer the clingfilm and disc to a baking sheet and cut into a circle slightly larger than the diameter of the cake, using an inverted cake tin or lid as a guide and cutting with a pizza cutter or the tip of a sharp knife. Freeze for 10 minutes or until very firm. Invert on to another piece of clingfilm, peel off the plastic from the bottom, and reinvert on to the cake while still firm enough to handle easily. Smooth the edges to follow the contour of the cake. Allow the fondant to sit for 10 to 20 minutes or until no longer sticky. Use the palm of your hand to smooth it to a soft shine.

For the band, you will need a piece of fondant 72 centimetres/ 28¼ inches long and 10 centimetres/4 inches high. Place the sheet of heavy-duty plastic on a flat surface. Roll the fondant into a long rope and lay it in the middle. Roll the fondant the length of the plastic into a thin band 3 millimetres/ ⅛ inch thick. Using a long plastic ruler and a pizza cutter or sharp knife, even the edges, cutting the bottom edge flush with the bottom of the plastic. Use your finger to smooth the upper edge so that it thins slightly. Use the plastic to lift the fondant and curve it around the sides of the cake. Peel away the plastic, overlap the ends and curve the upper edge gently towards the top of the cake to create a graceful free-form design.

4. Make the fondant rose stems. Roll a few small pieces of fondant into thin 10-centimetre/4–inch ropes. Gently curve a few to use around the base. Place on clingfilm and allow to dry for at least 30 minutes or until stiff enough to transfer to the cake.

5. Sepals. Cut from little scraps of rolled fondant and press gently on to the roses.

6. Place the roses on top of the cake, securing them in place with dabs of melted chocolate.

7. Place the stems at the bases of the roses. Place the leaves on top, also securing with dabs of melted chocolate.

8. Store the cake uncovered or the fondant will absorb moisture from the cake and become sticky.

INTENSELY CHOCOLATE

Triple Chocolate Cake

Serves 14 to 16

This intense chocolate cake resembles an abstract sculpture and consists of three distinct chocolate experiences: crunchy, creamy and velvety soft.

Making it is always an exciting experience because it never looks the same twice. Eating it is even more exciting. It seems to elicit dramatic responses. Over the years, I have received several marriage proposals at first bite and one thoroughly seduced victim suggested renaming it 'The Triple Chocolate Orgasm'. Why not?

TIMING: The cake can be assembled 1 day ahead and refrigerated. The completed cake can be frozen 4 months. Freeze until firm, wrap with clingfilm, and then wrap in heavy-duty foil. Place in a cake container or box to protect it.

SERVE: Room temperature. Cut with a thin, sharp knife. The Chocolate Praline Sheets will shatter – which is part of the special effect.

CAKE COMPONENTS
• 1 recipe Light Whipped Ganache (page 310), preferably made with extra bittersweet chocolate
• 1 recipe Moist Chocolate Génoise (page 145), top and bottom crusts removed
• 1 recipe Syrup (page 132),

flavoured with Frangelico (hazelnut liqueur)
- 1 recipe Chocolate Praline Sheets (pages 363 and 446)
- *Optional:*
  1 teaspoon icing sugar

METHOD FOR ASSEMBLING CAKE

1. Ice the cake directly on a serving plate, using strips of greaseproof paper slid under the sides. Or use a 23-centimetre/9-inch cardboard round as a base. Place a dab of ganache on the base to attach the cake.
2. Sprinkle 2 fluid ounces syrup on each side of the cake layers.
3. Place one layer on the plate or cardboard (support the layer when lifting it with a spare cardboard round). Sandwich the layers with 170 grams/ 6 ounces/1 cup ganache. Reserve 45 grams/1½ ounces/¼ cup ganache to attach the praline sheets and ice the top and sides of the cake with the remainder.
4. Applying the Chocolate Praline Sheets. A warm room (80 to 85°F/27 to 30°C) will make the sheets more flexible. (Any leftover can be remelted, retempered, and cut into decorative shapes.) Begin by laying each sheet on the worktop and peeling off its top layer of paper. Lift up one sheet, using the bottom paper to support it, and press the long side against the cake, curving it gently to mould it against the side. Carefully peel away the greaseproof paper. Place a dab of icing near the edge of the sheet and attach a second sheet, overlapping the first. Continue with the remaining sheets until the cake is completely surrounded. (Only four sheets are needed to encase a 23-centimetre/9-inch cake so there are two extra in case of breakage.) If the room is warm enough, the sheets will begin to curve downwards towards the centre of the cake. Coax them gently into graceful, undulating shapes, allowing their natural inclination to be your guide. If the chocolate remains resolutely rigid, wave a hairdryer (set on warm) briefly and evenly over the sheets. Stop before they appear to have softened and wait a few moments as it is easy to apply too much heat and melt the chocolate. To this day, this process feels slightly scary, slightly risky and delightfully creative! A word of reassurance: whatever happens, however it winds up looking, the sheets are always delicious.
5. A breath of icing sugar contrasts nicely with the dark chocolate. For the finest possible dusting of sugar, place a few spoonfuls in a fine strainer and flick the side with your finger.

White Lily Cake

Serves 8 to 10

This ethereal vision is lovely for a special anniversary or engagement party. The nosegay of lilies on top is contained by an antique handmade lace handkerchief given to me by my grandmother to carry at my wedding.

All the components are white or pale yellow in colour, light in texture and faintly scented with orange.

TIMING: The cake can be assembled 2 days ahead. Refrigeration is unnecessary.

SERVE: Be sure to remove the lily nosegay as the lilies are inedible. The cake should be served at room temperature. Cut with a thin, sharp knife.

SPECIAL EQUIPMENT NEEDED
- Narrow white satin ribbon to encircle cake
- 2 hatpins or pins with visible heads to hold ribbon while piping dots
- Pastry bag and 0.75-millimetre and 4.5-millimetre round tubes
- Small artist's paint brush
- *Optional:*
  Lace handkerchief and nosegay of lilies of the valley

Note: Lilies of the valley have a short season. Your florist can order them from Holland at any time of the year, but they are expensive. As an alternative, you can use pale lavender cymbidiums or pale sweetheart roses.

CAKE COMPONENTS
- 1 recipe White Génoise (page 138), top and bottom crusts removed and layers split in half horizontally
- 4 fluid ounces Cointreau
- ½ recipe Orange Fruit Mousseline (page 284)
- 1 recipe Rolled Fondant with orange flower water (page 354)
- 1 recipe Royal Icing (page 340)

METHOD FOR ASSEMBLING CAKE
1. Sprinkle each side of the cake layers with 1 tablespoon Cointreau.
2. Spread a small amount of mousseline on a 23-centimetre/9-inch cardboard round and place one cake layer on top.
3. Stack the remaining three layers on top of each other, sandwiching each with 145 grams/5 ounces/¾ cup mousseline.

4. With a small serrated knife bevel the top edges of the cake (page 408).

5. Ice the top and sides with the thinnest possible layer of mousseline (just enough to make the fondant adhere).

6. The fondant should be rolled out on a lightly greased surface to 35 centimetres/14 inches in diameter and 5 millimetres/ ¼ inch thick. Rotate the fondant after every two or three rolls to ensure that it is not sticking. If necessary, apply more non-stick spray or regrease the worktop. With your hands palm sides down, lift the rolled fondant on to the cake. Quickly smooth the top with a circular motion, starting from the centre, to eliminate air bubbles. (Bubbles can be pierced with a needle and smoothed out if necessary.) Smooth the fondant against the sides, working from the top down with a semicircular motion. Oil from your hands will give the fondant a lustrous glow. Use a pizza cutter or small sharp knife to trim the fondant at the base of the cake. Transfer the cake to a serving plate and allow the fondant to dry overnight before decorating.

7. To attach a narrow band of satin ribbon around the cake, pin one end to the cake and then wrap the ribbon evenly around the cake's circumference, overlapping the ends and securing both ends with a second pin. Pipe tiny beads of Royal Icing with an 0.75-millimetre round tube along both edges of the ribbon. When the cake has been completely encircled, the pins can be removed. For a pearl border around the base, use a 4.5-millimetre round tube. If points form, flatten and smooth with a damp artist's paint brush.

8. To pipe lilies, see page 469.

9. If desired, fold the handkerchief and insert fresh lilies in the centre. If the cake is to sit for several hours before serving, use a florist's flower sinker containing a moist sponge to keep them fresh.

Art Deco Cake

Serves 50

The clean lines of the Art Deco look do not prepare you for the shock of bittersweet chocolate within this cake. The chocolate looks almost black against the pristine whiteness of the fondant. People actually gasp when the cake is cut and its velvet dark secret core revealed. The calla lilies are easy to make and in keeping with the Art Deco design.

This cake would be lovely for a small wedding or a black-tie affair. I designed it originally for Marcia Germanow, a New Jersey caterer, whose future son-in-law, an architect, had a special appreciation for the Art Deco period. She designed the entire wedding using the Art Deco motif.

Raspberry sauce and whipped cream are the perfect accompaniments for this cake, but it is also absolutely delicious on its own.

TIMING: The cake layers must be chilled for at least 12 hours before covering with rolled fondant and another 12 hours before placing one tier on top of the other. Preparation should begin 4 days before serving to leave plenty of time for decorating. After tiering, the completed cake can be served the same day or refrigerated for an additional 2 days.

SERVE: Room temperature. Remove the top tier and cut into narrow wedges. Use a thin, sharp knife dipped in hot water and wiped clean between cuts. If serving the raspberry sauce and whipped cream, spoon 2 tablespoons of whipped cream next to each slice of cake. Make a small hollow in it with the back of a spoon and pour 1 tablespoon raspberry sauce into it.

SPECIAL EQUIPMENT NEEDED
- 15-centimetre/6-inch springform tin and 25.5-centimetre/10-inch springform tin, both buttered, lined with parchment paper, and wrapped with a double layer of heavy-duty foil
- 2 larger tins to serve as water baths
- Pastry bag and 1.5, 3 and 4.5-millimetre round tubes
- Artist's paint brush

STRUCTURAL SUPPORTS
- 2 cardboard rounds, 15 and 25.5 centimetres/6 and 10 inches
- 36-centimetre/14-inch-round black glass, silver-foil-covered or mirrored serving board
- 5 rigid plastic drinking straws

CAKE COMPONENTS

- 3 times the quantity of recipe for Chocolate Oblivion Truffle Torte (page 86), using 1 kilogram 362 grams/3 pounds chocolate, 681 grams/ 1½ pounds/3 cups unsalted butter, and 18 eggs (use a 20-pint/11.5-litre mixer to beat eggs or beat them in two batches)
- 2 times the quantity of recipe for Classic Rolled Fondant (page 354)
- 1 recipe Royal Icing (page 340)
- Green liquid food colour
- *Optional:* Silver Leaf (page 495) and 1 lightly beaten egg white or silver cord 3 times the recipe for Rasperry Sauce (page 386) 3 times the recipe for Perfect Whipped Cream (page 294)
- 3 Rolled Fondant Calla Lilies (page 420)

METHOD FOR ASSEMBLING CAKE

1. Prepare batter for Chocolate Oblivion Truffle Torte. Use a 20-pint/11.5-litre or larger bowl to melt the chocolate and butter so there will be room to add the eggs. Fill the 15-centimetre/6-inch springform tin 5 centimetres/2 inches deep and scrape the remainder into the 25.5-centimetre/10-inch tin. Bake in a preheated 425°F/220°C/gas mark 7 oven in water baths – 15 minutes for 15 centimetres/6 inches, 20 minutes for 25.5 centimetres/10 inches, covering loosely with foil after 5 minutes. Cool the cakes on a rack for 45 minutes and refrigerate for at least 4 hours.

2. Wipe the outside of the tins with a hot, damp tea-towel. Run a thin metal spatula around the sides of the cakes and release the sides of the springform tins. Turn out the cakes on to the cardboard rounds and refrigerate for at least 12 hours. Use a hot, wet spatula to smooth the surface of the cakes so they are perfectly smooth. Smooth the edges to bevel slightly. Return to the refrigerator.

3. The fondant should be rolled out on a lightly greased surface in two parts: 25.5 centimetres/10 inches in diameter for the smaller cake and 36 centimetres/14 inches for the larger cake (both should be 5 millimetres/¼ inch thick). Start with a 36-centimetre/ 14-inch piece and knead any clean trimmings into remaining fondant. Rotate the fondant after every two or three rolls to ensure that it is not sticking. Apply more non-stick spray or regrease the surface as necessary. With your hands palm sides down, lift the rolled fondant on to the cakes.

Quickly smooth the tops with a circular motion, starting from the centre, to eliminate air bubbles. (Bubbles can be pierced with a needle and smoothed out if necessary.) Smooth the fondant gently against the sides, working from the top down with a semicircular motion. Oil from your hands will give the fondant a lustrous glow. Use a pizza cutter or small sharp knife to trim the fondant at the bases of the cakes. (Save scraps to tint green for decoration.)

4. Using a heavy-duty broad spatula, transfer the larger cake to the mirrored base, placing it off-centre 2.5 centimetres/ 1 inch from the edge. Use a loop of tape to adhere to it. Allow both tiers to dry overnight.

5. Place the bottom of the 15-centimetre/6-inch tin off-centre on the 25.5-centimetre/10-inch tier 2.5 centimetres/1 inch from the edge and mark a circle with a toothpick. Insert a straw into the centre of the outline, straight through the cake, until it reaches the cardboard bottom. Mark the straw at the surface of the cake, remove it, and cut four more of the same length. Insert four straws at even intervals *inside* the marked outline and the final one in the centre.

6. Using a heavy-duty broad spatula, place the smaller tier off-centre on top of the larger tier.

7. Use a toothpick and a ruler or string to mark lines on the cake for placement of the green fondant strips and Royal Icing lines. (You may instead use silver cord and pin it in place, but be sure to remove the cord and all pins before serving.)

8. Using a 1.5-millimetre round tip, pipe lines of Royal Icing to create two large Vs, starting at the edge of the top tier and continuing down the sides.

9. Tint ¼ cup of the fondant scraps green, kneading well to incorporate the colour. Roll them out 3 millimetres/ ⅛-inch thick and cut out two 1-centimetre/½-inch strips, each 36 centimetres/14 inches long. Work carefully when placing the strips on the cake as the fondant will stick to the fondant beneath it, making repositioning difficult.

10. If desired, apply silver leaf, using a bit of lightly beaten egg white brushed on the Royal Icing lines to make it adhere (page 340).

11. Using a 4.5-millimetre tip, pipe a pearl border at the base of the bottom tier. Use a 3-millimetre tip for the base of the 15-centimetre/6-inch top tier. If points form, flatten and

smooth them with a damp artist's paint brush.

12. Attach the calla lilies with dots of Royal Icing.

Rose Trellis

Serves 16 to 20

This cake was designed for my friends Connie and Marcel Desaulniers. Marcel is chef and part-owner of the Trellis Restaurant in Williamsburg, Virginia. Those fortunate enough to have dined there will understand immediately why it inspired this exquisitely detailed cake and why I intertwined our names in its garnish and title.

The inside is also very special: moist layers of Golden Butter Cream Cake are filled with an airy, fresh tasting strawberry buttercream. The intricacy of this cake makes it comparable to a tiered wedding cake but in miniature form. Make it for small family weddings, engagements, anniversaries, or other very special occasions.

TIMING: If the weather is not humid, the lattice panels can be piped months in advance. The cake can be assembled 1 day ahead if stored in a cool room. The lattice should not be refrigerated as humidity could soften it.

SERVE: Room temperature. Remove the panels and set aside. Cut cake with a thin, sharp knife.

SPECIAL EQUIPMENT NEEDED

- 2 pastry bags and 2 1-millimetre round tubes
- Decorative foil or paper to cover the octagonal cardboard bases (page 530)

CAKE COMPONENTS

- 2 recipes Golden Butter Cream Cake (page 22), baked in two 23 × 5-centimetre/9 × 2-inch tins or two 7.5-centimetre/ 3-inch-high springform pans.
  Note: 2 recipes Golden Almond Cake (page 26) could be substituted here.
- ½ recipe Strawberry Silk Meringue Buttercream (page 281), tinted with 3 drops of red food colour
- 1 recipe Rolled Fondant (page 354), flavoured with rose water
- 2 recipes Royal Icing (page 340) for the lattice. Tint 120 grams/4¼ ounces/½ cup

pink, using 1 drop of red food colour.

METHOD FOR ASSEMBLING CAKE

1. Make the lattice panels, piping the rose with the pink icing. Pipe one pink rose without the rest of the panel to use for the top of the cake.
2. Make an octagonal cardboard template to place on top of the cake as a cutting guide. The baked cake will measure 21 centimetres/8¼ inches in diameter, so first cut a circle of that size. (Plain cardboard is easier to cut than corrugated.) Then make eight 8-centimetre/ 3⅛-inch connecting lines. Each line should begin and end at the edge of the circle. Cut exactly on the lines and the template is complete. Make a second cardboard octagon exactly the same to serve as the first base. (The cake will have three bases, each one larger than the one before.)
3. Make another larger cardboard octagon for the second base by placing the already-made template on a piece of cardboard and drawing lines in a 4-centimetre/1½-inch border all around it. Cover with decorative foil.
4. For the third base, make another still larger octagon using the second base and the same method as for the

previous one (again with 4-centimetre/1½-inch border). Use sturdy cardboard and cover it with decorative foil.
5. Spread a small amount of buttercream on the first cardboard base.
6. Place one cake layer on a 23-centimetre/9-inch cardboard round and ice with 200 grams/ 7 ounces/1 cup buttercream.
7. Add a second layer and place the template on top. Cut eight sides on the cake, cutting straight down. Remove the template.
8. Slightly bevel the edges with a serrated knife and lightly ice the top and sides with the thinnest possible layer of remaining buttercream (just enough to make the fondant adhere).
9. The fondant should be rolled out on a lightly greased surface to 38 centimetres/15 inches in diameter and 5 millimetres/ ¼ inch thick. Rotate the fondant after every two or three rolls to ensure that it is not sticking. Apply more non-stick spray or regrease the worktop as necessary. With your hands palm sides down, lift the rolled fondant on to the cake. Quickly smooth the top with a circular motion, starting from the centre, to eliminate air bubbles. (Bubbles can be pierced with a needle and smoothed out if necessary.)

Smooth the fondant against the sides, working from the top down with a semicircular motion. Oil from your hands will give the fondant a lustrous glow. Use a pizza cutter or small sharp knife to trim the fondant at the base of the cake.

10. Using a heavy-duty broad spatula, centre the cake on the second (foil-covered) cardboard base, using a loop of tape to secure it.

11. Use a second loop of tape to secure the cake to the third (foil-covered) cardboard base. Allow the cake to dry for at least 3 hours.

12. Attach the pink rose outline to the top of the cake with a few tiny dots of Royal Icing. Use pink Royal Icing to pipe a free-form stem and leaves.

13. Carefully attach the filigree panels to the sides with white Royal Icing. The tops of the panels should touch the top of the cake. The bottoms should touch the edge of the second base.

14. Using white Royal Icing, pipe tiny loops suspended from the bottom edge of the panels. Do not allow the loops to touch the base to prevent possible breakage when moving the cake if the base is at all flexible.

My Brother's Wedding Cake *or* The Snowstorm of 1983

Valentine's Day 1983 was the scheduled date for my only and beloved brother's San Francisco wedding. It was with great joy that several weeks before I began to prepare a most spectacular wedding cake in my New York kitchen as my present to Michael and Suzy. The cake was a triple-tiered fantasy, large enough to feed 150 guests (page 254). The tiers consisted of layers of soft white butter cake filled with silky buttercream and topped with pistachio marzipan. The icing was a Swiss white chocolate buttercream invented especially for the occasion, and the decorations were a gold lamé ribbon from Paris, gold dragées, white chocolate rose leaves, and a dozen real pink sweetheart roses.

This was a very special cake not only because it was intended for my brother's wedding but also because it was destined to appear in the June 1983 issue of the American *Cook's* magazine and, subsequently, on the cover and inside thousands of recipe booklets. Its arrival in San Francisco, however, was thwarted by fate: the great snowstorm of

February 1983, which locked in the entire north-east coast – along with me and my cake.

Much planning had gone into the projected transportation of this perishable masterpiece. Because photography for the magazine had been scheduled a few weeks before the wedding, the cake needed to be frozen during the interim. An ordinary freezer was not large enough, but my butcher, Ottomanelli, upon learning that the cake was for a family wedding, sympathetically offered a safe corner in his spacious walk-in freezer.

My father, a cabinetmaker, fashioned a special protective crate to protect the cake from falling sides of beef in the freezer and from unknown hazards in the belly of the aeroplane.

My publicist had arranged special red-carpet treatment for me and the cake *en route*, so the airline consented to store the crated cake in the plane's kitchen. Fresh roses were ordered from the florist. In short, everything was perfectly planned. The plans of mice and men . . .

The snow started falling early in the morning the day of the flight. My ninety-eight-year-old grandmother and my aunt Ruth were already on their way to California from their home in Pompano Beach, Florida. My parents had departed from Kennedy hours before. The airline suggested

that I board an earlier flight than the one I had booked because the snow seemed to be coming faster than anticipated. So I picked up the cake from the butcher's shop, optimistically leaving all the baggage for my husband, who was unable to leave work earlier than planned, and set out for Newark Airport.

No seats in tourist class were available on the earlier flight, so, when the airline offered me a first-class seat, I enthusiastically accepted.

Having made sure that The Cake was safely stored in the kitchen below, I sat looking out of the window, watching the snow steadfastly falling, feeling relieved to have a seat on what might be the last flight leaving Newark that day. 'Let's go! Let's go!' I thought, as the snow fell thicker and thicker. Then came the inevitable announcement: 'We are now below minimal clearance . . . but this flight has not been officially cancelled.' A fellow passenger snickered at the word *officially*. The words *below minimal* and *cancelled* were ignored by my brain as I desperately clung to the *not officially cancelled* part. Gradually, the horrible truth hit me with full impact: not only was my brother not to have this much planned and most extraordinary wedding cake, he was not going to have *me* at his wedding either!

When it was officially decided

that the passengers were to disembark, I obtained permission to store my cake in the terminal's refrigerator. I then called my husband to ask him to pick me up – only to hear that the storm had become so severe that the streets in Manhattan were impassable. He suggested that I take the airport bus to the Port Authority bus terminal.

With some indignation I queued for the bus and soon considered myself lucky to have been the last person to get a seat on the last bus. Four hours later I began to think I would have been luckier to have missed that bus and luckier still to get back to the airport! All traffic had stopped. The bus had no toilet and no gas gauge. The driver was forced to open the door for ventilation, admitting exhaust fumes from countless other vehicles. The situation was unbelievable. Would we freeze to death, stranded between Newark and the Lincoln Tunnel? How could this civilised, familiar terrain have become a wilderness over which we had no control? Would people from nearby houses take us in, or would they panic like those in lifeboats fleeing the sinking *Titanic* and bar their doors?

Passengers started to take sides. The majority wanted to attempt a turnaround and go back to the airport. The unrealistic few who kept insisting that they wanted to go to Manhattan were transferred to a bus behind us. Several young male passengers forged into the snow-filled highway to direct traffic and give us space to turn around. Despite my distress, I could not help but notice what a splendid study of human nature this emergency was presenting. Already our small bus had become a mini-community.

With all remaining passengers in full agreement, we set out for the airport, but got stuck in a drift at the foot of a hill four miles from the first terminal. The snow was already several feet deep, and I started to wonder how long it takes to get frostbitten without boots. Luckily, a nearby taxi offered (after much arm-twisting and demands for fare) to take six of us up to the main terminal. The rest would have to walk.

The first terminal (where my cake was stored) was dark and locked for the night, but the second terminal, a quarter of a mile down the road, was filled with people who had already commandeered sleeping areas for themselves and their families. Hordes of people were stretched out on every available chair and all over the floor. Any food in the canteens had long since been consumed. I found a relatively cosy spot on the red-carpeted snail-shaped section of the baggage-unloading area and curled up to sleep. (Here, at last, was my red-carpet treatment!) I slept fitfully all night, awakened occasionally by the surrounding noise and the empty feeling in my stomach from not having eaten since the night before. Remembering that I was going to miss the wedding, I would cry against my better judgement and then go back to sleep. There was nothing else to do.

When dawn broke, we were informed that no planes would be able to take off until one or two days later. I managed to locate a manager and asked if the airline would hold my cake until I could come back by car to reclaim it. He looked at me in a puzzled way and said: 'There is no more cake.' When he smiled, I thought he was teasing me. 'Well, what happened to the cake?' I asked, pretending to go along with the ill-fated joke. 'Oh, we ate the cake,' he said with imperturbable calm. 'You what!' I practically screamed. He then explained, with total confidence that I would see the logic of his decision, that there had been no room in the terminal refrigerators for food from the stranded planes so the crew had removed my cake to make room for those incomparable airline delicacies. Then, evidently assuming (incorrectly) that the cake would spoil unrefrigerated, they ate it to keep it from going to waste. Not even the special crate remained. (Could they have been that hungry?)

Somehow, hours later, I got back to our Manhattan apartment.

The streets were like ski trails, and it didn't seem at all like New York. My husband greeted me at the door and said there was no point crying. I had already reached that conclusion myself, and it didn't help.

I eventually got a full report of the wedding from my mother, which is about as close as I could get to having been there myself. (She always knows what I'm most interested in hearing.) For a wedding cake a few of my brother's friends had chipped in and purchased one of those hulking white baroque numbers, adorned with plastic Grecian columns and insipid cupids. A lot had been left over because, according to my mother, it was very, very sweet.

Months later I presented my brother and new sister-in-law with a framed photo of their intended wedding cake, clipped from *Cook's*, together with an article from *The New York Times* in which the cake had been immortalised by Marion Burros as one of the great mishaps of the snowstorm of 1983. Eating the cake ourselves couldn't have been as unforgettable.

Sequel: Seven months later I baked and iced one layer exactly like the original and dropped it off in San Francisco, *en route* from teaching in Alaska to food-touring Japan. When I saw the first piece of cake enter my brother's mouth, I could finally lay to rest the whole sad episode. But it will be only with the greatest reluctance that I will ever attempt to fly a wedding cake anywhere again.

The St Clement Wedding Cake *or* The Blackout of 1981

The events surrounding this wedding were so extraordinary it made *The New York Times* under the title 'A Heaven Made in Marriage'. Courtney was an artist from Texas marrying a sculptor from New York. The cake she had commissioned was enormous – large enough to feed at least 280 people, although the guest list was only 150, because 'We Texans eat big.' Courtney even presented me with a watercolour of her cake-to-be: chocolate covered with white fondant and adorned with long-stemmed roses on each tier. She was a dream to work with. She knew just what she wanted, but understood that certain compromises would be necessary due to the fact that the 'medium' of the art material was to be nothing short of delicious to eat.

The theme of the wedding, 'a marriage made in heaven', was to be executed in a friend's SoHo loft, decorated to look as though the event were actually taking place in – you guessed – heaven.

In addition to a ten-thousand-dollar budget, Courtney had a very talented and willing assortment of relatives and friends who were generous with their time and created some fantastic effects. Courtney herself, having worked as a set designer, devoted a year to creating eighteen-foot silver-sprayed facsimiles of her two favourite skyscraper tops: the Empire State and the Chrysler buildings. Her brother Tom, an inventor and art restorer for Sotheby's, strung tiny lights to resemble stars. Dry ice created billowing clouds underfoot and a taxidermist preserved the white pigeon wings worn by the angelic blonde ring bearer.

Courtney's friend Evelyn, a Broadway costume designer, created a white pearl-appliquéd silk chiffon dress, with petal-shaped layers inspired by the Chrysler building – and lovingly embroidered Courtney's name in white inside the white waistband. Another friend designed a sapphire wedding ring, again inspired by the Chrysler building's Art Deco peak. Even the groom's ex-wife contributed Texas chilli!

Weeks before the wedding I started sculpting pink marzipan roses. Courtney's brother cast plaster of Paris leaf moulds so I could create realistic marzipan leaves. The stems were to be piped on the cake after the roses were in place, using pale green royal icing.

Having never made a 15-inch chocolate cake before, I started baking a few days earlier than usual. Fortunately. I assumed (logically though incorrectly) that a larger cake would need extra baking powder in proportion to its other ingredients. Five minutes before the 15-inch layers were done I checked them by gently pressing the centres with my fingertip. Not quite.

Five minutes later, just as I opened the oven door, all the lights in the apartment went out and even the refrigerator motor came to an ominous halt. I could not see the cake, but I would feel it. I extended my index finger to where the centre of one of the layers should be. Where minutes before there had been a cake, none was to be found. I carefully lowered my finger another inch and there was the cake. My aim had been impeccable – the centre had sunk to the bottom of the tin.

It means only one thing when a cake falls five minutes before it has finished baking: the structure was not strong enough and the resulting cake will be heavy and somewhat fudgy. (Our son Michael was delighted because he knew he would get to eat the 'failed' layers.) It turned out, after much analysis, research and more baking the following day, that the larger the cake, the *less* baking powder is required.

The coincidence, though, was staggering. The cake had chosen to fall at the exact moment of one of the two major New York City blackouts. Unfortunately, the reporter for the *Times* could not resist temptation. He dramatised the story by writing that my cake had fallen because of the blackout (my oven was gas, not electric) and blithely implied that I had sold a fallen thousand-dollar cake!

Actually, this cake was most instructive. I went on to develop precise formulas and techniques for achieving enormous, showpiece cakes with the same soft, downy texture and exquisite flavour as small cakes. If you use the same kind of cake flour (either Softasilk or Swan's Down) and carefully weigh or measure the other ingredients, you will be very happy with the results. As one little boy I overheard at a wedding put it: 'But wedding cakes aren't suppose to taste this good!'

Bleeding Heart
Wedding Cake

(Designed for Trish Fleming)

Serves 150

When Trish Fleming ordered her wedding cake, she brought me a picture of bleeding hearts and asked if it was possible to design a cake around this theme. It was a delightful challenge and the blossoms and leaves were fun to pipe. I chose Raspberry Buttercream as the filling to echo the pink blossoms on the rolled fondant.*

TIMING: All the components can be prepared ahead. It is fine to bake the cake 3 to 4 days ahead and refrigerate because the fondant will keep it fresh. The fondant must be applied at least 12 hours before tiering the cake.

SERVE: Room temperature. For cutting instructions, see page 618.

SPECIAL EQUIPMENT NEEDED
(see page 514)
- 2 pastry bags, 1-millimetre and 4-millimetre with 5-millimetre-deep cuts star tubes, and 1-millimetre and 2.5-millimetre round tubes

STRUCTURAL SUPPORTS
- 3 cardboard rounds: 15, 23 and 30.5 centimetres/6, 9 and 12 inches

- Cake plate or foil-covered serving board at least 38 centimetres/15 inches in diameter
- Rigid plastic drinking straws

CAKE COMPONENTS
- 1 recipe for 3-Tier Yellow Butter Wedding Cake to Serve 150 (page 553). *Note:* 1 recipe for a 3-Tier Génoise Classique Wedding Cake to Serve 150 (page 568) could be substituted here.
- *Optional:* 3 times the quantity of the recipe for Syrup flavoured with framboise (page 578)
- 1 large scale recipe (1 kilogram 600 grams/3½ pounds/8 cups) for Neoclassic or Classic Buttercream (page 592 or 594). Beat in 253 grams/8¾ ounces/ 1 cup Raspberry Sauce (page 386) and add enough red food

*See Icing, Tiering, and Storing a Wedding Cake (page 614) and covering a cake with Rolled Fondant (page 414).

colour to attain a pale pink colour

- 1 recipe (3 kilograms 402 grams/7$\frac{1}{2}$ pounds) lemon-flavoured Classic Rolled Fondant for a 3-Tier Cake to Serve 150 (page 612)
- 2 times the quantity of recipe for Royal Icing (page 340). Use red food colour to tint the blossoms pink and some green paste food colour for the leaves
- *Optional:* Gold monogram (page 475)

METHOD FOR ASSEMBLING CAKE

1. Level the cake layers and bevel the edges (page 408). Sprinkle with optional syrup for extra moistness.
2. Spread a small amount of buttercream on the three cardboard rounds and place a cake layer on each. Ice the tops with a generous layer of buttercream (about 9 millimetres/$\frac{3}{8}$ inch thick) and add the second layers. There are now three tiers. Spread the top and sides of each tier with the thinnest possible layer of buttercream – just enough to make the fondant adhere.
3. Roll out three-quarters of the fondant 5 millimetres/$\frac{1}{4}$ inch thick and 43 centimetres/ 17 inches in diameter and cover the largest tier. Trim the bottom flush with the base of the cake and knead all the clean

scraps into the remaining fondant.

4. Attach the tier to the serving board with several loops of tape. The fondant should be allowed to harden for at least 12 hours before tiering cake.
5. Cover the other two tiers with the remaining fondant, rolled out 5 millimetres/$\frac{1}{4}$-inch thick (36 centimetres/14 inches in diameter for the 23-centimetre/9-inch tier and 28 centimetres/11 inches in diameter for the 15-centimetre/ 6-inch tier). Allow all three tiers to sit uncovered for at least 12 hours to firm.
6. Centre a 23-centimetre/9-inch cake tin on the 30.5-centimetre/ 12-inch tier and use a toothpick or skewer to mark a circle. Use a 15-centimetre/6-inch cake tin as a guide to mark a circle on the 23-centimetre/9-inch cake. Working *inside* the marked circle on the 30.5-centimetre/ 12-inch tier, insert a straw straight through the cake until it reaches the cardboard bottom. Mark the place on the straw where it reaches the top of the cake. Remove the straw and cut six more of the same length. Insert the six straws at even intervals *inside* the marked circle. Place the final straw in the centre. Repeat the procedure for the 23-centimetre/9-inch tier, using five straws.

7. Using one or two large spatulas, place the 23-centimetre/9-inch tier on top of the 30.5-centimetre/ 12-inch tier. Carefully centre the 15-centimetre/6-inch tier on the 23-centimetre/9-inch tier.

8. Using a 4-millimetre star tip with 5-millimetre-deep cuts and white Royal Icing, pipe a shell border at the base of each tier. Save a small amount of icing to pipe blossom tips and use the rest to make the pink and green icing. Remember that the colour will continue to deepen for several hours as it sits.

9. Pipe bleeding heart stems and leaves and then the blossoms (page 479).

10. Place optional monogram on top of cake.

Chocolate Praline Wedding Cake

(Designed for Chocolatier *magazine)*

Serves 150

The warmth and elegance of chocolate and gold represent a sophisticated break with tradition. Dark chocolate cake blends with luscious praline buttercream and crunchy hazelnuts.*

TIMING: All the components can be prepared ahead. It is best to bake the cake no more than 1 day before assembling it. The completed cake can be kept at room temperature for 1 day before serving or it can be frozen for 2 months. Allow 24 hours to defrost in the refrigerator and at least 4 additional hours at room temperature.

SERVE: Room temperature. For cutting instructions, see page 618.

SPECIAL EQUIPMENT NEEDED
(see page 514)
• 3 pieces of gold lamé ribbon (page 413): 50, 75.5 and 100 centimetres/20, 30 and 40 inches

CAKE COMPONENTS
• 1 recipe 3-Tier Chocolate Butter Wedding Cake to Serve 150 (page 556). *Note:* 1 recipe for a 3-tier Génoise au Chocolat to serve 150 (page 571) could be substituted here.
• *Optional:*
  3 times the quantity of recipe for Syrup flavoured with Frangelico (page 132)
• 1 recipe (13 cups) for Silk Meringue Praline Buttercream for a 3-Tier Cake (page 605)
• 227 grams/8 ounces/1⅔ cups hazelnuts, skinned, toasted and coarsely chopped to equal 2 cups (page 373)
• Bittersweet Chocolate Curls (a 112-gram/4-ounce block of chocolate) (page 441)
• Red Chocolate Rose (pages 374 and 450)
• Marzipan Stem and Leaves (page 417)

STRUCTURAL SUPPORTS
• 3 cardboard rounds: 15, 23 and 30 centimetres/6, 9 and 12 inches
• Cake plate or foil-covered

*See Icing, Tiering and Storing a Wedding Cake (page 614)

serving board at least 38 centimetres/15 inches in diameter (flat part must be at least 30.5 centimetres/12 inches)

- Rigid plastic drinking straws

METHOD FOR ASSEMBLING CAKE

1. Level the cake layers. Sprinkle with optional syrup for extra moistness.
2. Spread a small amount of buttercream on all three cardboard rounds and place a cake layer on each. Ice the tops with 5 millimetres/¼ inch of buttercream and top with the second layers. There are now three tiers. Ice the top and sides of each tier with the remaining buttercream.
3. Apply the chopped nuts to the sides of each tier (page 373).
4. Attach the largest tier to the serving board with several pieces of double-sided tape or loops of tape.
5. Invert a 23-centimetre/9-inch cake tin over the centre of the 30.5-centimetre/12-inch tier and lightly touch the icing to mark a circle. Invert a 15-centimetre/ 6-inch cake tin over the 23-centimetre/9-inch cake and mark a circle on the 23-centimetre/9-inch cake. Working *inside* the marked circle on the 30.5-centimetre/12-inch tier, insert a straw straight through the cake until it reaches the cardboard bottom. Mark the place on the straw where it reaches the top of the cake. Remove the straw and cut six more of the same length. Insert the six straws at even intervals *inside* the marked circle. Place the final straw in the centre. Repeat the procedure for the 23-centimetre/9-inch tier, using five straws.
6. Using one or two large spatulas, place the 23-centimetre/9-inch tier on top of the 30-centimetre/ 12-inch tier. Carefully centre the 15-centimetre/6-inch tier on the 23-centimetre/9-inch tier. Using a spoon, distribute the chocolate curls over the exposed areas of each tier. Do not place chocolate curls on top of the cake.
7. Encircle the cake with the ribbon if desired.
8. Place the chocolate rose, marzipan stem and leaves on top.

Golden Glory
Wedding Cheesecake

(Designed for the Joan Beranbaum/Judge John Stackhouse Wedding)

Serves 150

Creamy cheesecake, marbled with apricot and iced with White Chocolate Cream Cheese Icing. (Where is it written that the bride can't have her favourite cake as a tiered wedding cake?)

This cake was designed for my niece and her bridegroom and was featured in Martha Stewart's fabulous book *Weddings*. The layers do not require a base, but almond *biscuit* is a lovely option.*

TIMING: All the components can be prepared ahead except for the spun sugar, which will last for several hours if the weather is not humid. The cake should be assembled 1 day ahead and refrigerated.

SERVE: Lightly chilled or room temperature. For cutting instructions, see page 618.

SPECIAL EQUIPMENT NEEDED
(See page 514.)
- 3 pieces of gold lamé ribbon (page 413): 51, 76 and 102 centimetres/20, 30 and 40 inches
- Pastry bag and 4-millimetre star tube with 5-millimetre-deep cuts

CAKE COMPONENTS
- 1 recipe 3-tier Wedding Cheesecake to Serve 150 (page 581)
- 1 large-scale recipe Apricot Swirl Filling for Cheesecake (page 584)
- 1 recipe White Chocolate Cream Cheese Icing for a 3-Tier Cake to Serve 150 (page 603)
- *Optional:* 2 recipes Almond Biscuit (page 160), cooled flat
- 310 grams/11 ounces/1 cup Apricot Topaz Jewel Glaze (page 378)
- Fresh wild violets or Crystallised Violets (page 375)
- Spun Sugar (page 364)

STRUCTURAL SUPPORTS
- 3 cardboard rounds: 15, 23 and 30.5 centimetres/6, 9 and 12 inches (preferably the sort that

*See Icing, Tiering and Storing a Wedding Cake (page 614).

have been coated with glassine to waterproof them)

- Cake plate or foil-covered serving board at least 38 centimetres/15 inches in diameter
- Rigid plastic drinking straws

METHOD FOR ASSEMBLING CAKE

1. Spread a thin layer of icing on all three cardboard rounds.
2. If using the optional *biscuit*, cut a 23-centimetre/9-inch and a 15-centimetre/6-inch disc from one sheet and a 30.5-centimetre/12-inch disc from the other. (The baked *biscuit* is 30 × 42.5 centimetres/ 11¾ × 16¾ inches so you will not get a full 30.5-centimetre/ 12-inch circle.) Place a *biscuit* disc on each cardboard round.
3. Turn out the cheesecake layers on to the *biscuit* or cardboard rounds and remove the parchment. There are now three tiers.
4. Ice the top and sides of each tier and chill thoroughly. Reserve any leftover icing at room temperature for piping the borders.
5. Attach the largest tier to the serving board with several pieces of double-sided tape or loops of tape.
6. Invert a 23-centimetre/9-inch cake tin over the centre of the 30.5-centimetre/12-inch tier and lightly touch the icing to

mark a circle. Invert a 15-centimetre/6-inch cake tin over the 23-centimetre/9-inch cake and mark a circle on the 23-centimetre/9-inch cake. Working *inside* the marked circle on the 30.5-centimetre/ 12-inch tier, insert a straw straight through the cake until it reaches the cardboard bottom. Mark the place on the straw where it reaches the top of the cake. Remove the straw and cut six more of the same length. Insert the six straws at even intervals *inside* the marked circle. Place the final straw in the centre. Repeat the procedure for 23-centimetre/ 9-inch tier using five straws.

7. Using one or two large spatulas, place the 23-centimetre/9-inch tier on top of the 30.5-centimetre/ 12-inch tier. Carefully centre the 15-centimetre/6-inch tier on the 23-centimetre/9-inch tier.
8. Encircle the cake with the ribbons if desired.
9. With a small spoon or metal spatula, carefully spread the apricot glaze on each layer.
10. Using a 4-millimetre star tube with 5-millimetre-deep cuts, pipe the remaining icing in a shell border on the edge of each tier. (Chill your hand with ice from time to time to maintain the firm consistency of the icing.)
11. Up to 4 hours ahead, make the

spun sugar and wrap it around the base of the cake. Shortly before presenting the cake, place fresh violets on top and in the sugar strands. (If using crystallised violets, they can be placed as soon as the spun sugar is wrapped around the cake.)

Pistachio and Rose Wedding Cake

(Designed for Michael Levy)

Serves 150

This is the cake that made history – the one that, while *en route* to my brother's San Francisco wedding, was eaten instead by airline employees during a snow layover! I shall always be grateful to Marion Burros and Alex Ward, who immortalised the cake in *The New York Times* and helped to assuage a good deal (but not all) of the pain!

The flavours and textures of this cake are unique. The soft white butter cake is iced with Classic Buttercream. A thin layer of Pistachio Marzipan separates the buttercream from the firmer Crème Ivoire Deluxe (white chocolate buttercream).*

TIMING: All the components can be prepared ahead. It is best to bake the cake no more than 1 day before assembling it. The completed cake can be kept at room temperature for 1 day or it can be frozen for 2 months.

SERVE: Room temperature. For cutting instructions, see pages 413 and 618. Be sure to remove the sweetpeas before serving.

SPECIAL EQUIPMENT NEEDED
(See page 514).
- 3 pieces of gold lamé ribbon (page 413): 51, 76 and 102 centimetres/20, 30 and 40 inches
- Pastry bag and 3.5-millimetre

*See Icing, Tiering and Storing a Wedding Cake (page 614).

star tube with 3-millimetre–deep cuts

STRUCTURAL SUPPORTS

- 3 cardboard rounds: 15, 23 and 30.5 centimetres/6, 9 and 12 inches
- Cake plate or foil-covered serving board at least 38 centimetres/15 inches in diameter (flat part must be at least 30.5 centimetres/12 inches)
- Inflexible plastic drinking straws

CAKE COMPONENTS

- 1 recipe 3-Tier White Butter Wedding Cake to Serve 150 (page 553). *Note:* 1 recipe for a 3-tier Génoise Classique to Serve 150 (page 568) could be substituted here.
- *Optional:* 3 times the quantity of recipe for Syrup flavoured with Pistasha or framboise (page 578)
- 1 large-scale recipe (1 kilogram 600 grams/3½ pounds/8 cups) Neoclassic or Classic Buttercream (pages 592 or 594)
- 1 large-scale recipe (567 grams/ 1¼ pounds) Pistachio Marzipan (page 610)
- 1 large-scale recipe (1 kilogram 660 grams/3 pounds 10 ounces/ 5.25 cups) Crème Ivoire Deluxe (page 599)
- 2 tablespoons (28 grams/1 ounce) gold dragées
- Rose and sweetpea corsage cake top (15 × 7.5 centimetres/

6 × 3 inches) purchased from a florist
- 18 pink sweetheart roses and lavender sweetpeas
- 36 white chocolate rose leaves (page 444)

METHOD FOR ASSEMBLING CAKE

1. Level the cake layers. Sprinkle with optional syrup for extra moistness.
2. Spread a small amount of buttercream on all three cardboard rounds and place a cake layer on each. Ice the tops with 5 millimetres/¼ inch of the buttercream and top with the second layers. There are now three tiers. Ice the top and sides of each tier with the remaining buttercream.
3. Divide the marzipan in half. Roll half between two sheets of clingfilm into a thin circle. Peel the top layer of clingfilm off the marzipan. Using a lightly greased 30.5-centimetre/12-inch cake tin as a guide, cut a circle of marzipan with a sharp knife or pizza cutter. Knead the marzipan scraps into the remaining marzipan. Roll the remaining marzipan between two sheets of clingfilm into a thin circle. Using a 23-centimetre/9-inch cake tin as a guide, cut out a circle. Knead the marzipan scraps together and roll out between two sheets of clingfilm into a thin

circle. Using a 15-centimetre/ 6-inch cake tin as a guide, cut out a circle. It is easiest to apply marzipan if it has been frozen for a few minutes to make it less flexible. Pick up the 30.5-centimetre/12-inch marzipan disc. Invert it (the marzipan will stick to the plastic) and position it over the 30.5-centimetre/12-inch tier. Support it with your palm if necessary and lay it on the cake. It will be difficult to move once it is set down. Invert the 23-centimetre/9-inch and 15-centimetre/6-inch marzipan discs in the same manner.

4. Ice the top and sides of each tier with Crème Ivoire Deluxe.

5. Attach the largest tier to the serving board with strips of double-sided tape or several loops of tape. Allow the icing to set until firm.

6. Centre a 23-centimetre/9-inch cake tin on the 30.5-centimetre/ 12-inch tier and use a toothpick or skewer to mark a circle. Use a 15-centimetre/6-inch cake tin to mark a circle on the 23-centimetre/9-inch cake. Working *inside* the marked circle on the 30.5-centimetre/ 12-inch tier, insert a straw straight through the cake until it reaches the cardboard bottom. Mark the place on the straw where it reaches the top of the cake. Remove the straw and cut six more of the same length. Insert the six straws at even intervals *inside* the marked circle. Place the final straw in the centre. Repeat the procedure for the 23-centimetre/9-inch tier using five straws.

7. Using one or two large spatulas, place the 23-centimetre/9-inch tier on top of the 30.5-centimetre/ 12-inch tier. Carefully centre the 15-centimetre/6-inch tier on the 23-centimetre/9-inch tier.

8. Encircle the cake with the ribbons if desired and place gold dragées in free-form swirls, pressing them lightly into the sides. (A tweezer helps to pick them up.)

9. Using a 3.5-millimetre star tube with 3-millimetre-deep cuts, pipe a shell border of Crème Ivoire Deluxe on the edge of each tier (page 352).

10. Place the corsage on top and the sweetheart roses and chocolate leaves around the tiers up to 4 hours ahead of serving. To keep sweetpeas from wilting, use small flower sinkers (page 530), camouflaged by the chocolate rose leaves, or place on the cake no more than 30 minutes before serving.

Dotted Swiss Dream

(Designed for Bon Appétit magazine)

Three-tier cake serves 150
Four-tier cake* serves 275

When I first designed this wedding cake, I had a vision of pearls on the top tier cascading down the alabaster fondant sides. But perhaps even more than the poetic image of pearls, this cake is reminiscent of the ethereal fabric called dotted Swiss. And many a bride who ordered this cake designed her entire wedding around the theme, from bridesmaids' dresses to tablecloths!

In the years following the cake's first appearance, the outside has remained essentially the same. But instead of a lemon-curd filling, I now use my newest buttercream creation: Lemon Curd Mousseline. Either a white or yellow layer cake blends beautifully with the filling.†

TIMING: All the components can be prepared ahead, in fact, the marzipan roses can be prepared months ahead. (I recommend starting to make them the day the engagement is announced!) It is fine to bake the cake 3 to 4 days ahead as the fondant will keep it fresh even without refrigeration. (The decorated cake may be refrigerated if desired.) Fondant must be applied at least 12 hours before tiering the cake.

SERVE: Room temperature. For cutting instructions, see page 618.

SPECIAL EQUIPMENT NEEDED
(See page 514.)
- Pastry bag and 1.5, 2, 3 and 4.5-millimetre round tubes

STRUCTURAL SUPPORTS
- 3 cardboard rounds: 15, 23 and 30.5 centimetres/6, 9 and 12 inches
- Cake plate or foil-covered serving board at least 38 centimetres/15 inches in diameter
- Inflexible plastic drinking straws

CAKE COMPONENTS
- 1 recipe 3-Tier White or Yellow Wedding Cake to Serve 150 (page 553). *Note:* 1 recipe for a

*See page 259 for four-tier instructions.
†See Icing, Tiering and Storing a Wedding Cake (page 614), covering a cake with Rolled Fondant (page 414), and piping Royal Icing pearls (page 464).

3-tier Génoise Classique to Serve 150 (page 568) could be substituted here.

- *Optional:*
  3 times the quantity of recipe for Syrup flavoured with Barack Palinka, apricot brandy or framboise (page 578)
- 1½ times the quantity of recipe for Fruit Mousseline (page 284), using 1 recipe of Lemon Curd (page 389). With Lemon Curd it will be almost 1 kilogram 585 grams/3 pounds 7½ ounces/ 8 cups.
- 1 recipe (3 kilograms 402 grams/ 7½ pounds) Classic Rolled Fondant for a 3-Tier Cake to Serve 150 (page 612), flavoured with rosewater
- 3 times the quantity of recipe for Royal Icing (page 340)
- 13 pale pink marzipan roses (page 418) or fresh sweetheart roses. You will need 1 recipe of Marzipan for Modelling for the marzipan roses (page 370). Make a large full-blown rose with three rows of petals for the top and smaller roses with two rows of petals for the tiers (page 418).

METHOD FOR ASSEMBLING CAKE

1. Level the cake layers and bevel the edges (page 408). Sprinkle with optional syrup for extra moistness.
2. Spread a small amount of mousseline on all three cardboard rounds and place a cake layer on each. Ice the tops with a generous layer of mousseline (9 millimetres/ ⅜ inch thick) and top with the second layers. There are now three tiers. Ice the top and sides of each tier with the thinnest possible layer of mousseline – just enough to make the fondant adhere.
3. Roll out three-quarters of the fondant (2 kilograms 268 grams/ 5 pounds) 5 millimetres/¼-inch thick and 43 centimetres/ 17 inches diameter and cover the 30.5-centimetre/12-inch tier. Trim the bottom flush with the base of the cake and knead all the clean scraps into remaining fondant.
4. Attach the 30.5-centimetre/ 12-inch tier to the serving board with strips of double-sided tape or several loops of tape. The fondant should be allowed to harden for at least 12 hours before tiering the cake.
5. Cover the remaining tiers with fondant, rolled 5 millimetres/ ¼-inch thick (1 kilogram 587 grams/3½ pounds, 35 centimetres/14 inches in diameter for the 23-centimetre/ 9-inch tier, 907 grams/2 pounds, 28 centimetres/11 inches in diameter for the 15-centimetre/ 6-inch tier). Allow all three tiers to sit uncovered for at least 12 hours to firm.
6. Centre a 23-centimetre/9-inch cake tin on the 30.5-centimetre/

12-inch tier and use a toothpick or skewer to mark a circle. Use a 15-centimetre/6-inch cake tin to mark a circle on the 23-centimetre/9-inch cake. Working *inside* the marked circle on the 30.5-centimetre/12-inch tier, insert a straw straight through the cake until it reaches the cardboard bottom. Mark the place on the straw where it reaches the top of the cake. Remove the straw and cut six more of the same length. Insert the six straws at even intervals *inside* the marked circle. Place the final straw in the centre. Repeat the procedure for the 23-centimetre/9-inch tier using five straws.

7. Using one or two large spatulas, place the 23-centimetre/9-inch tier on top of the 30.5-centimetre/12-inch tier. Carefully centre the 15-centimetre/6-inch tier on the 23-centimetre/9-inch tier.

8. Using a 4.5-millimetre round tube and the Royal Icing, pipe a pearl border at the base of the 30.5-centimetre/12-inch tier (page 464). If points form, flatten and smooth them with a damp artist's paint brush. Make a second row on top of the first if desired, piping the pearls between those on the first row. Use a 3.5-millimetre round tube for the 23-centimetre/9-inch base border and 2-millimetre round tube for the 15-centimetre/6-inch base border. Use a 1.5-millimetre round tube to pipe pearls on the sides of the tiers.

9. Place four roses around the base of the cake, four more on the 30.5-centimetre/12-inch tier, four on the 23-centimetre/9-inch tier, and the full-blown rose on top. Attach them with large dots of Royal Icing.

SPECIAL INSTRUCTIONS FOR A FOUR-TIER CAKE

ADDITIONAL EQUIPMENT NEEDED

- 38-centimetre/15-inch cardboard round
- 46-centimetre/18-inch serving board (instead of the 38-centimetre/15-inch one)
- Lightweight wooden dowels for the bottom tier. (They are needed to support the weight of the three large layers. You will need a heavy-duty clipper or saw to cut them.)

ADDITIONAL CAKE COMPONENTS

- Two 38-centimetre/15-inch cake layers (see chart on page 559)
- *Optional:*
  A total of 6 times the quantity of recipe for Syrup flavoured with Barack Palinka, brandy or framboise (page 578)
- A total of 1 large-scale recipe Lemon Mousseline (page 590),

using 525 grams/1 pound 2¼ ounces/1¾ cups Lemon Curd (page 389). With Lemon Curd, it will be about 2 kilograms 670 grams/5 pounds 13 ounces/ 13 cups

- A total of 5 recipes Rolled Fondant (7 kilograms/ 12.5 pounds) (page 354)
- A total of 6 recipes Royal Icing (page 340)
- A total of 21 marzipan roses (8 for the base, 4 on each tier, and the full-blown rose on top) (pages 370 and 418)

Note: *Rolling Fondant for a 38-centimetre/15-inch Bottom Tier.* Start by rolling 2 kilograms 600 grams/5½ to 6 pounds (about half of the fondant, into a round 51 centimetres/20 inches in diameter and 5 millimetres/¼ inch thick. Cover the 38-centimetre/ 15-inch tier, trim, and knead the clean scraps into the remaining fondant.

When rolling fondant for the 38 and 30.5-centimetre/15 and 12-inch tiers, use a piece of clingfilm to cover the fondant and keep it from drying during the extended time needed to roll the larger diameters.

PART II
COMPLEMENTARY ADORNMENTS FOR ALL CAKES

Buttercream Icings and Fillings

These days it seems that rich buttercreams are suffering in favour of lighter counterparts made with whipped cream or fruit. Some people even prefer their cakes uniced. There are many cakes in this book – such as chiffon cakes, angel food cakes, fruitcakes and my favourite coffee cake, to name just a few – which are more delicious uniced. But there is a time and a place for icings and certain cakes simply cry out for them. One of the most satisfying cakes, Praline Brioche Cake, combines four basic textures: *soft* (La Brioche cake), *moist* (Rum Syrup), *creamy* (Praline Silk Meringue Buttercream), and *crunchy* (chopped hazelnuts).

Special occasion cakes become more festive and memorable with elaborately piped buttercream decorations. When you plan to make a major cake, however, it is important to remember that it is intended to be eaten. Large buttercream swirls and festoons mean large servings of buttercream in proportion to the cake.

My philosophy is that the cake is the main event and should be featured. Buttercream is lovely but should be kept to a minimum. I am not a proponent of seven-layer cakes which contain as much buttercream as cake.

Butter or sponge cakes which are velvety and firmer than whisked sponge cakes lend themselves to buttercream icings, whereas lighter whipped-cream icings are more suitable for *génoise* and *biscuit*. Buttercreams can be used for the lighter cakes too if not applied too thickly.

I think that many people object to buttercreams not because they are too rich but because they are often too sweet. When looking at a buttercream recipe, consider the ratio of butter to sugar and it will tell you more about the flavour than any other factor because if the sugar is too high it will dominate. I find a good balance to be at least double the weight of butter to sugar. Every buttercream recipe in this chapter, except for Crème Ivoire whose major ingredient is white chocolate, has 2.27 times butter to sugar. Crème Ivoire is a wonderful buttercream for wedding cakes because it is pale ivory and very creamy. To temper the sweet richness, I use only about half the thickness I would with another buttercream. And I add contrasting flavours such as Pistachio Marzipan between the outer Crème Ivoire and the inner, less sweet Classic Buttercream.

Consistency is important when working with buttercreams. If a completed buttercream looks curdled and you're not sure whether it needs heating or chilling, take a small amount and try first one method then the other. It's always a question of temperature. To ice a cake, the buttercream should be extremely soft to go on smoothly. Don't be afraid to heat it slightly if it seems too stiff.

I have given weights for the finished base buttercreams to facilitate making optional additions, because the final amounts may vary. If, for example, some of the sugar syrup used for the buttercream remains in the pan and some more spins on to the side of the bowl while mixing, there will be less buttercream at the end.

It may seem that there are a staggering amount of variations, but some buttercream bases blend better with certain additions than do others. These variations were worked out over years of baking and teaching. Although some variations are quite similar, I want to offer them all so that you have the convenience of being able to use whatever is in your larder. BUTTERCREAM THAT APPEARS IN ANOTHER CHAPTER: Easy Chestnut Buttercream (page 405)

Classic Buttercream

Makes 720 grams/1 pound 9.25 ounces/4 cups/950 ml (enough to fill and ice two 23 × 4-centimetre/9 × 1¹/₂-inch layers or three 23 × 2.5-centimetre/9 × 1-inch layers)

This ultimate buttercream is so silky smooth, creamy and buttery, it complements just about any cake.

STORE: 6 hours room temperature, 1 week refrigerated, 8 months frozen.

POINTERS FOR SUCCESS: See Sugar Syrups (page 500). To prevent crystallisation, do not stir after the syrup comes to a boil. To keep the temperature from rising, remove the syrup from the pan as soon as it has reached 238°F/114°C. Don't allow the syrup to fall directly on the beaters as it will spin the syrup around the sides of the bowl. Using a hand–held beater makes this easier.

Have ready a greased ¹/₄-litre/

INGREDIENTS	WEIGHT		MEASURE
room temperature	*grams*	*pounds/ounces*	*volume*
6 egg yolks, size 2	112 grams	4 ounces	3½ fluid ounces
castor sugar	200 grams	7 ounces	1 cup
water	118 grams	4 ounces	½ cup
unsalted butter (must be softened)	454 grams	1 pound	2 cups
optional: liqueur or eau-de-vie of your choice	28 to 56 grams	1 to 2 ounces	2 to 4 tablespoons

½-pint/1-cup heatproof glass measuring jug near the stove.

In a bowl beat the yolks with an electric mixer until light in colour. Meanwhile, combine the sugar and water in a small saucepan (preferably with a non-stick lining) and heat, stirring constantly, until the sugar dissolves and the syrup is boiling. Stop stirring and boil to the soft-ball stage (238°F/114°C). *Immediately transfer the syrup to the glass measure to stop the cooking.*

If using an electric hand-held mixer, beat the syrup into the yolks in a steady stream. Don't allow syrup to fall on the beaters or they will spin it on to the sides of the bowl. If using a stand mixer, pour a small amount of syrup over the yolks with the mixer turned off. Immediately beat at high speed for 5 seconds. Stop the mixer and add a larger amount of syrup. Beat at high speed for 5 seconds. Continue with the remaining syrup. For the last addition, use a rubber scraper to remove the syrup clinging to the glass measure. Continue beating until completely cool.

Gradually beat in the butter and, if desired, any optional flavouring (page 267). Place in an airtight bowl. Bring to room temperature before using. Rebeat if necessary to restore texture.★

★Do not rebeat chilled buttercream until it has reached room temperature or it may curdle.

Neoclassic Buttercream

Makes 800 grams/1¾ pounds/4 cups/950 ml (enough to fill and ice two 23 × 4-centimetre/9 × 1½-inch layers or three 23 × 2.5-centimetre/9 × 1-inch layers)

This is an easier technique than that for Classic Buttercream and yields *identical* results. In fact, since I have come up with this method, I have never gone back to the classic way. I am also pleased to see that other bakers have adapted this technique in their work.

In the neoclassic method, some of the sugar and all of the water is replaced by corn syrup. (Corn syrup, by volume, is about half the sweetness of sugar so 164 grams/5¾ ounces/½ cup is needed to replace the 50 grams/1¾ ounces/¼ cup sugar.) The corn syrup provides just the right amount of water so that, when brought to a *full* boil, the temperature of the syrup is exactly 238°F/114°C. There is no need to use a thermometer. The corn syrup also prevents crystallisation.

STORE: 6 hours room temperature, 1 week refrigerated, 8 months frozen.

POINTERS FOR SUCCESS: The syrup must come to a rolling boil or the buttercream will be too thin.

Don't allow the syrup to fall directly on to the beaters as it will spin the syrup around the sides of the bowl. Using a hand-held beater makes this easier.

INGREDIENTS	WEIGHT		MEASURE
room temperature	*grams*	*pounds/ounces*	*volume*
6 egg yolks, size 2	112 grams	4 ounces	3½ fluid ounces
castor sugar	150 grams	5¼ ounces	¾ cup
corn syrup	164 grams	5¾ ounces	4 fluid ounces
unsalted butter (must be softened)	454 grams	1 pound	2 cups
optional: liqueur or eau-de-vie of your choice	28 to 56 grams	1 to 2 ounces	2 to 4 tablespoons

Have ready a greased ¼-litre/ ½-pint/1-cup heatproof glass measuring jug near the stove.

In a bowl beat the yolks with an electric mixer until light in colour. Meanwhile, combine the sugar and corn syrup in a small saucepan (preferably with a non-stick lining) and heat, stirring constantly, until the sugar dissolves and the syrup comes to a rolling boil. (The entire surface will be covered with large bubbles.) *Immediately transfer the syrup to the glass measure to stop the cooking.*

If using an electric hand-held mixer, beat the syrup into the yolks in a steady stream. Don't allow syrup to fall on the beaters or they will spin it on to the sides of the bowl. If using a stand mixer, pour a small amount of syrup over the yolks with the mixer turned off. Immediately beat at high speed for 5 seconds. Stop the mixer and add a larger amount of syrup. Beat at high speed for 5 seconds. Continue with the remaining syrup. For the last addition, use a rubber scraper to remove the syrup clinging to the glass measure. Continue beating until completely cool.

Gradually beat in the butter and, if desired, any optional flavouring (see below). Place in an airtight bowl. Bring to room temperature before using. Rebeat to restore texture.*

Classic Buttercream Variations

(One Recipe of Classic or Neoclassic Buttercream)

Classic or Neoclassic Buttercream can be used plain or as a base for any number of flavours. One recipe can accommodate as much as 4 fluid ounces liquid without becoming too soft. Spirits can heighten the flavour of a buttercream, but do not add them to buttercreams containing fruit purées as they will become too liquid. Spirits are best kept in the background, so start with 2 tablespoons and add more only to taste.

Fresh fruit purées such as raspberry and strawberry blend beautifully with classic buttercreams and maintain their lovely hues. Apricot purée

*Do not rebeat chilled buttercream until it has reached room temperature or it may curdle.

tends to curdle the buttercream slightly, however, so heated, strained apricot jam or *lekvar* (page 495), cooled to room temperature, is preferable.

The sweetness level of the base buttercream is perfectly balanced so whatever is added must be neither too sweet nor too tart or adjustments to the base need to be made as indicated.

CLASSIC CHOCOLATE:

Classic buttercreams can incorporate about 171 grams/ 6 ounces of melted chocolate without becoming too stiff. This results in a light chocolate colour and flavour which does not overpower yellow or white cake layers.
To make chocolate buttercream: Beat 171 grams/6 ounces melted and cooled chocolate, preferably extra bittersweet or bittersweet, into Classic or Neoclassic Buttercream.

CLASSIC CHOCOLATE CARAMEL CRUNCH:

The flavours of caramel and chocolate blend beautifully and the powdered caramel adds a slightly crunchy texture. Because caramel is sweet it is best to use extra bittersweet chocolate in the base.
To make chocolate caramel crunch buttercream: Beat 47 grams/ 1³/4 ounces/¹/4 cup powdered caramel (page 362) into Classic Chocolate.

CLASSIC COFFEE:

This simple method makes a buttercream with the rich taste of good strong coffee.
To make coffee buttercream: Beat 2 tablespoons instant espresso powder dissolved in 1 teaspoon boiling water into Classic or Neoclassic Buttercream. For a more aromatic flavour, add 2 to 4 tablespoons Kahlúa.

CLASSIC MOCHA ESPRESSO:

Chocolate and coffee always make a lovely combination.
To make mocha espresso buttercream: Beat 2 tablespoons instant espresso powder dissolved in 1 teaspoon boiling water into Classic Chocolate. For more intense coffee flavour, add 2 to 4 tablespoons Kahlúa.

CLASSIC PRALINE:

The best praline paste (page 497), a smooth combination of hazelnuts and caramelised sugar, makes a fabulous addition to any buttercream. Because the paste contains about 50 per cent sugar, it is necessary to remove some of the sugar from the buttercream base.

To make praline buttercream: When making Classic Buttercream, decrease the sugar by 1½ tablespoons. Beat in 77 grams/2¾ ounces/¼ cup praline paste.

CLASSIC CHOCOLATE PRALINE:

Praline intensifies the delicious flavour of chocolate.
To make chocolate praline buttercream: Beat 171 grams/6 ounces melted and cooled bittersweet chocolate into Classic Praline Buttercream. Alternatively, beat 77 grams/2¾ ounces/¼ cup praline paste into Classic Chocolate Buttercream made with extra bittersweet chocolate. (Each method is the same level of sweetness.)

CLASSIC PRALINE CRUNCH:

Praline powder is made of ground hazelnuts and caramel but is not turned into a paste. This gives a crunchy texture to the buttercream.
To make praline crunch buttercream: When making Classic Buttercream, decrease the sugar by 1½ tablespoons. Beat in 45 grams/1½ ounces/⅓ cup praline powder (page 363).

CLASSIC CHOCOLATE PRALINE CRUNCH:

This buttercream is exactly like Classic Chocolate Praline except for the crunchy texture provided by the praline powder.
To make chocolate praline crunch buttercream: Beat 168 grams/6 ounces melted and cooled bittersweet chocolate into Classic Praline Crunch Buttercream. Alternatively, beat 45 grams/1½ ounces/⅓ cup praline powder into Classic Chocolate Buttercream made with extra bittersweet chocolate. (Each method results in the same level of sweetness.)

CLASSIC CHESTNUT:

This buttercream is perfect with Chestnut Sand Cake or with the subtle spicy flavours of Chocolate Fudge Cake.
To make chestnut buttercream: Stir ½ recipe Classic or Neoclassic Buttercream into 1 recipe of lightly sweetened, rum-flavoured Chestnut Purée (page 405). (This will make 600 grams/1 pound 5 ounces/3 full cups buttercream.)

CLASSIC MAPLE:

The essence of pure Vermont maple syrup, this buttercream is excellent with any white or yellow butter cake and is still more delicious encrusted with coarsely chopped walnuts.
To make maple buttercream: When making Neoclassic Buttercream, replace the corn syrup with an equal amount of pure maple syrup. Beat in 2 teaspoons of maple extract to the finished buttercream.

CLASSIC RASPBERRY:

My Raspberry Sauce is so concentrated it scarcely affects the consistency of the buttercream base. This is the purest raspberry flavour of any icing I know.
To make raspberry buttercream: Beat 127 grams/4½ ounces/½ cup lightly sweetened Raspberry Sauce (page 386) into finished buttercream. If not planning to use the same day, add a few drops of red food colour to prevent fading.

CLASSIC STRAWBERRY:

The strawberry flavour is surprisingly fresh and intense. It is also, of course, silky and creamy but has the added interest of tiny strawberry seeds. I find that strawberries frozen without sugar have more flavour than most commercially available fresh strawberries – even at the height of season.
To make strawberry buttercream: Beat 120 grams/4¼ ounces/½ cup unsweetened Strawberry Purée (page 388) into finished buttercream and add a few optional drops of essence of wild strawberry (page 492) for further intensity. If not planning to use the same day, add a few drops of red food colour to prevent fading.

CLASSIC APRICOT:

This buttercream has a tart, honeyed flavour and a very pale golden colour.
To make apricot buttercream: Beat 155 grams/5¼ ounces/½ cup heated, strained and cooled apricot jam or *lekvar* (page 495) into finished buttercream and add a few optional drops of essence of apricot (page 492) for further intensity.

CLASSIC PINEAPPLE:

Home-preserved pineapple is a delicious, slightly tart addition to buttercream.
To make pineapple buttercream: Beat 8 fluid ounces/100 grams/ 3½ ounces puréed pineapple (page 402) into finished buttercream and add 1 to 2 tablespoons kirsch or rum.

CLASSIC LEMON:

To achieve a truly lemon flavour it is necessary to use both fresh lemon juice and lemon extract (actually the pure oil of lemon). Lemon juice alone is not intense enough and the extract alone is too bitter.
To make lemon buttercream: When making Classic Buttercream, replace 2 fluid ounces of the water with freshly squeezed lemon juice. After adding the butter, beat in ¼ teaspoon lemon extract.

CLASSIC ORANGE:

An intense orange flavour is difficult to achieve using orange extract because it is quite bitter. Finely grated orange zest (the orange part of the rind only, as the pith is bitter) and an aromatic French orange essence (page 492), which includes the pulp, do produce an excellent orange flavour, however.

To make orange buttercream: Add 2 teaspoons orange pulp essence and 1 tablespoon grated orange zest.

CLASSIC ORANGE BLOSSOM:

Orange flower water gives this buttercream the perfume of orange blossoms. Be sure to add the essence, which is mainly orange oil. The small amount serves to add the lilting zip associated with fresh orange flavour. This buttercream perfectly complements Orange Glow Chiffon Cake (page 174).

To make orange blossom buttercream: Add 1 teaspoon orange essence dissolved in 2½ fluid ounces orange flower water, 1 tablespoon grated orange zest, and 2 tablespoons Grand Marnier.

CLASSIC PASSION:

This buttercream captures the slightly tart, utterly distinctive taste of fresh passion fruit.

To make passion buttercream: Beat up to 225 grams/8 ounces/¾ cup Passion Curd (page 391) into finished buttercream and add 1 teaspoon of essence of passion fruit (page 492) for further intensity. This buttercream is fabulous with Cordon Rose Banana Cake (page 65).

Royal Honey Buttercream

Makes 600 grams/1 pound 5 ounces/3¾ cups/890 ml (enough to fill and ice two 23 × 4-centimetre/9 × 1½-inch layers or three 23 × 2.5-centimetre/9 × 1-inch layers)

Replacing both the sugar and the corn syrup of Neoclassic Buttercream with honey results in a mellifluous, subtly perfumed buttercream. Mild clover honey, available in supermarkets, produces the best flavour. (I find the more exotic varieties too assertive.) This buttercream is wonderful with any yellow cake but I created it especially for Queen Bee cake (page 211).

INGREDIENTS	WEIGHT		MEASURE
room temperature	*grams*	*pounds/ounces*	*volume*
6 egg yolks, size 2	112 grams	4 ounces	3½ fluid ounces
clover honey	112 grams	4 ounces	2¾ fluid ounces
unsalted butter (must be softened)	454 grams	1 pound	2 cups

STORE: 6 hours room temperature, 1 week refrigerated, 8 months frozen.

POINTERS FOR SUCCESS: The honey must come to a rolling boil or the buttercream will be too thin. Don't allow the honey to fall directly on to the beaters as it will spin the honey around the sides of the bowl.

Have ready a greased heatproof glass measuring jug near the stove. In a bowl beat the yolks with an electric mixer until light in colour. Meanwhile heat the honey in a small saucepan (preferably with a non-stick lining), stirring constantly, until it comes to a rolling boil. *Immediately transfer the honey to the glass measure to stop the cooking.*

If using an electric hand–held mixer, beat the honey into the yolks in a steady stream. Don't allow honey to fall on the beaters or they will spin it on to the sides of the bowl. If using a stand mixer, pour a small amount of honey over the yolks with the mixer turned off. Immediately beat at high speed for 5 seconds. Stop the mixer and add a larger amount of honey. Beat at high speed for 5 seconds. Continue with the remaining honey. For the last addition, use a rubber scraper to remove the honey clinging to the glass measure. Continue beating until completely cool.

Gradually beat in the butter. Place in an airtight bowl. Bring to room temperature before using. Rebeat to restore texture.*

*Do not rebeat chilled buttercream until it has reached room temperature or it may curdle.

Classic Egg White Chocolate Buttercream

Makes 1 kilogram/35 ounces/4¾ cups/1⅛ litres (enough to fill and ice two 23 × 4-centimetre/9 × 1½-inch layers or three 23 × 2.5-centimetre/9 × 1-inch layers)

This special version of chocolate buttercream is the colour of rich milk chocolate and has a more assertive chocolate flavour than the traditional one made with egg yolks. In fact, it is just as smooth and even easier and faster to prepare than Classic or Neoclassic Buttercream because a sugar syrup is not needed.

This buttercream is airy yet, because of the whites' structure, has more body than a buttercream made with all yolks. It is an excellent texture and flavour for both chocolate butter cakes and chocolate *génoise*.

STORE: 3 days room temperature, 2 weeks refrigerated, 6 months frozen.

POINTERS FOR SUCCESS: Have egg whites at room temperature before beating. See Melting Chocolate (page 436).

INGREDIENTS	WEIGHT		MEASURE
room temperature	*grams*	*pounds/ounces*	*volume*
bittersweet chocolate	284 grams	10 ounces	3⅓ (3-ounce) bars
unsalted butter (must be softened)	454 grams	1 pound	2 cups
4 egg whites, size 2	120 grams	4¼ ounces	4 fluid ounces
castor sugar	200 grams	7 ounces	1 cup

Break the chocolate into squares and place in a double boiler over very hot water or low heat. The water must not exceed 160°F/71°C or touch the bottom of the double boiler insert.

Remove the double boiler from the heat and stir frequently until the chocolate begins to melt.

Return to the heat if the water cools, but be careful that it does not get too hot. Stir for

8–10 minutes or until the chocolate is smooth. (Chocolate may be melted in a microwave oven on high power *if stirred every 15 seconds*. Remove before fully melted and stir, using residual heat to complete the melting.)

In a mixing bowl beat the butter until smooth and creamy.

In another mixing bowl beat the egg whites until soft peaks form when the beater is raised. Gradually beat in the sugar until stiff peaks form when the beater is raised slowly. Beat in the butter by the tablespoon. If the mixture looks slightly curdled, increase the speed a little and beat until smooth before continuing to add more butter.

Add the melted and cooled chocolate all at once and beat until smooth and uniform in colour. Place in an airtight bowl. Rebeat to restore texture.*

UNDERSTANDING

While it is necessary to cook egg yolks for a buttercream to prevent bacterial growth, raw egg whites are far less prone to this problem. Because the whites are not thickened by a hot syrup, the resulting buttercream is softer than the Classic or Neoclassic versions and can accommodate 112 grams/ 4 ounces more chocolate without becoming too stiff and unworkable.

White Chocolate
Cream Cheese Buttercream

Makes 765 grams/1 pound 10 ounces/4³/₄ cups/1¹/₈ litres (enough to fill and ice two 23 × 4-centimetre/9 × 1¹/₂-inch layers or three 23 × 2.5-centimetre/ 9 × 1-inch layers)

This ivory buttercream is mellow and creamy. Its luscious, slightly tangy flavour is a perfect complement for yellow cake, carrot cake, and especially cheesecake. It makes a spectacular presentation because it pipes wonderfully and is the identical colour of cheesecake. White chocolate adds firmness of texture, sweetness and an indefinable flavour.

*Do not rebeat chilled buttercream until it has reached room temperature or it may curdle.

STORE: 1 day room temperature, 2 weeks refrigerated, 2 months frozen.

POINTERS FOR SUCCESS: Do not overheat the white chocolate and be sure to stir constantly while melting. Be sure no moisture gets into the melted chocolate (see Melting Chocolate, page 436). Beat constantly while adding the cooled chocolate to prevent lumping. If lumping should occur, it can be remedied by pressing the buttercream through a fine strainer.

The buttercream may separate slightly if room temperature is very warm. This can be corrected by setting the bowl in ice water and whisking the mixture. Buttercream becomes spongy on standing. Rebeat to restore smooth creamy texture. Use ice to chill your hand during piping to maintain firm texture.

INGREDIENTS	WEIGHT		MEASURE
room temperature	*grams*	*pounds/ounces*	*volume*
white chocolate (preferably Tobler Narcisse)	255 grams	9 ounces	3 (3-ounce) bars
cream cheese (must be softened)	340 grams	12 ounces	4 small packages
unsalted butter (must be softened)	170 grams	6 ounces	¾ cup
lemon juice, freshly squeezed	23 grams	—	1½ tablespoons

Break the chocolate into squares and place in the top of a double boiler set over very hot water (no hotter than 160°F/71°C) on low heat. The water must not touch the bottom of the double boiler insert.

Remove the double boiler from the heat and stir until the chocolate begins to melt. Return to the heat if the water cools, but be careful that it does not get too hot. Stir for 10 minutes or until smooth. (The chocolate may be melted in a microwave oven *if stirred every 15 seconds*. Remove before fully melted and stir, using residual heat to complete the melting.) Allow to cool.

In a mixing bowl beat the cream cheese (preferably with a flat beater) until smooth and creamy. Gradually beat in the cooled chocolate until smoothly incorporated. Beat in the butter and lemon juice. Rebeat at room temperature to ensure smoothness before icing.*

Note: My friend Shirley Corriher reports that, when using this icing for a wedding cake in the heat of an Atlanta summer, she tried decreasing the butter to 57 grams/ 2 ounces/¼ cup and it held up quite well.

Silk Meringue Buttercream

Makes 838 grams/2 pounds/4 cups/950 ml (enough to fill and ice two 23 × 4-centimetre/9 × 1½-inch layers or three 23 × 2.5-centimetre/9 × 1-inch layers)

This is the buttercream to have on that proverbial desert island. In fact, it is rather like a floating island buttercream with its combination of *crème anglaise* and Italian meringue!

Although more time-consuming and exacting to prepare than Classic Buttercream, it has the advantage of being equally smooth but more airy, stable, and resistant to warm temperatures. The greater stability makes it a dream for piping decorations. It's great to have a batch of this on hand in the freezer to flavour with any of the additions on page 279.

STORE: 6 hours room temperature, 1 week refrigerated, 8 months frozen. If frozen or refrigerated, be sure to allow the buttercream to come to room temperature before rebeating it or it will break down. Buttercream becomes almost liquid when it has reached room temperature but rebeating will make it as firm as before.

POINTERS FOR SUCCESS: Crème Anglaise: The temperature must reach at least 160°F/71°C and must not exceed 180°F/82°C or it will curdle.

Italian Meringue: For maximum stability, the syrup must reach 248°C/120°C and not exceed 250°F/121°C or the whites will break down. The whites must be

---

*Do not rebeat chilled buttercream until it has reached room temperature or it may curdle.

INGREDIENTS	WEIGHT		MEASURE
room temperature	*grams*	*pounds/ounces*	*volume*
CRÈME ANGLAISE			
castor sugar	100 grams	3½ ounces	½ cup
5 egg yolks, size 2	93 grams	3¼ ounces	3 fluid ounces
milk	121 grams	4¼ ounces	4 fluid ounces
1 large vanilla pod, split lengthwise* or ½ large Tahitian vanilla pod			
ITALIAN MERINGUE			
castor sugar	92 grams	3¼ ounces	⅓ cup + 2 tablespoons
water	30 grams	1 ounce	2 tablespoons
2 egg whites, size 2	60 grams	2 ounces	2 fluid ounces
cream of tartar	—	—	¼ teaspoon
unsalted butter (must be softened)	454 grams	1 pound	2 cups

* A vanilla pod offers the most delicious flavour, but if you wish to avoid the little black specks, replace the pod with 1 teaspoon vanilla essence, added to the cooled *crème anglaise*.

free of any grease or trace of yolk. Do not overbeat.

Finished buttercream: Rebeat when it becomes spongy.

TO MAKE CRÈME ANGLAISE

Have ready a sieve suspended over a bowl, near the stove.

In a medium-size heavy non-corrodible saucepan combine the sugar and yolks.

In a small saucepan bring the milk and vanilla pod to the boil. Add 2 tablespoons of the milk to the yolk mixture, stirring constantly. Gradually add the remaining milk, stirring, and cook over medium-low heat, stirring constantly, until just below boiling point. The mixture will start to steam slightly and an accurate thermometer will register 170°F/77°C. Strain immediately, scraping up any clinging to the bottom of the pan.

Scrape the seeds from the vanilla pod into the custard and cool to room temperature. (To speed cooling, put the bowl in another bowl or sink partially filled with ice water.) Cover and refrigerate for up to 5 days or until ready to complete the buttercream.

TO MAKE ITALIAN MERINGUE

Have ready a heatproof glass measuring jug near the stove.

In a small heavy saucepan (preferably with a non-stick lining) combine 66 grams/2¼ ounces/ ⅓ cup sugar and the 2 tablespoons of water. Heat, stirring constantly, until the sugar dissolves and the mixture is bubbling. Stop stirring and reduce the heat to low. (If using electricity, remove from the heat.)

In a mixing bowl beat the egg whites until foamy. Add the cream of tartar and beat until soft peaks form when the beater is raised. Gradually beat in the remaining sugar until stiff peaks form when the beater is raised slowly.

Increase the heat and boil the syrup until a thermometer registers 248° to 250°F/120° to 121°C (the firm-ball stage). *Immediately transfer the syrup to the glass measure to stop the cooking.*

If using an electric hand-held mixer, beat the syrup into the egg whites in a steady stream. Don't allow syrup to fall on the beaters or they will spin it on to the sides of the bowl. If using a stand mixer, pour a small amount of syrup over the egg whites with the mixer off. Immediately beat at high speed for 5 seconds. Stop the mixer and add a larger amount of syrup. Beat at high speed for 5 seconds. Continue with the remaining syrup. For the last addition, use a rubber scraper to remove the syrup clinging to the glass measure. Lower speed to medium and continue beating until completely cool (about 2 minutes). (The Italian Meringue keeps for 2 days refrigerated. Rebeat briefly before using.)

TO COMPLETE BUTTERCREAM

Place the butter in a large mixing bowl and beat on medium speed for 30 seconds or until creamy. Gradually beat in the *crème anglaise* until smooth. Add the Italian Meringue and beat until just incorporated. If the mixture looks curdled instead of smooth it is too cold. Allow it to sit at room temperature to warm to 70°F/21°C before continuing to beat. Or place the bowl in a hot water bath very briefly until the buttercream touching the bowl just starts to melt. Remove at once and beat until smooth. Beat in optional additions (page 279). Place in an airtight bowl. The buttercream becomes slightly spongy on standing. Rebeat before using.★

UNDERSTANDING

Crème anglaise must be heated to at least 160°F/71°C to adequately thicken the egg yolks. Over 180°F/82°C the yolks will start to curdle and the cream may not be smooth. (Commercial establishments sometimes bring it to the boil and quickly strain it, discarding the curdled part. This is done only to save time and ensure that the temperature is hot enough without bothering with other tests. I do not recommend this method.)

When stirring the hot milk into the yolk mixture, it is best to use a wooden spoon because a whisk will create air bubbles, making it difficult to judge when the mixture is done.

Silk Meringue Buttercream Variations

PRALINE SILK MERINGUE BUTTERCREAM:

The nutty, burnt sugar flavour and smooth texture of fine-quality praline paste (page 497) make this a delicious buttercream. Because praline paste contains at least 50 per cent sugar, it is necessary to use less sugar in the Silk Meringue base.
To make praline buttercream: Use only 50 grams/1¾ ounces/¼ cup sugar instead of 100 grams/3½ ounces/½ cup when making the *crème anglaise*. Beat 154 grams/ 5½ ounces/½ cup praline paste into the buttercream before adding the meringue.
To make chocolate praline buttercream: Add 228 grams/8 ounces melted and cooled extra bittersweet or bittersweet chocolate.

CARAMEL SILK MERINGUE BUTTERCREAM:

This version offers the pure flavour of burnt sugar without any bitter overtones. When making the *crème anglaise*, the sugar is caramelised and dissolved in the milk. Double

*Do not rebeat chilled buttercream until it has reached room temperature or it may curdle.

the milk is needed to compensate for evaporation when added to the hot caramel.

To make caramel buttercream: When making the *crème anglaise,* add the vanilla pod to 242 grams/ 8½ ounces/1 cup milk, bring to the boil, and keep warm. In a heavy pan combine the 100 grams/ 3½ ounces/½ cup sugar with 2 tablespoons water and bring to the boil, stirring constantly. Cook without stirring until deep amber (360°F/182°C). Remove immediately from the heat and slowly pour in the hot milk, reserving the vanilla pod. Return to low heat and cook, stirring, until the caramel is totally dissolved. Proceed as for regular *crème anglaise* by gradually adding the caramel mixture to the yolks, cooking to 170°F/77°C and adding the vanilla seeds.

BURNT ORANGE SILK MERINGUE BUTTERCREAM:

This is an exciting combination of caramel with orange overtones.
To make burnt orange buttercream: Make caramel buttercream and beat in 1 tablespoon thawed orange juice concentrate and 1 tablespoon grated orange zest. (You can make your own concentrate by reducing 4 fluid ounces freshly squeezed orange juice.) If desired, use a tiny dab of orange food colour to tint the buttercream pale orange.

COFFEE CARAMEL SILK MERINGUE BUTTERCREAM:

This subtle combination produces a harmonious melding of flavours.
To make coffee caramel buttercream: Make caramel buttercream and beat in 2½ teaspoons instant espresso powder dissolved in ½ teaspoon very hot water.

ESPRESSO SILK MERINGUE BUTTERCREAM:

Although it is possible to steep ground coffee beans in the *crème anglaise* and then strain it through cheesecloth to give the buttercream a rich coffee flavour, instant espresso is a lot easier to use and also results in a deep rich coffee flavour.
To make espresso buttercream: Dissolve 2 tablespoons instant espresso powder in the hot *crème anglaise.* Beat up to 2 fluid ounces Kahlúa into the finished buttercream.

CHOCOLATE SILK MERINGUE BUTTERCREAM:

Extra bittersweet chocolate adds a *café au lait* hue and thickens the buttercream, making it a dream for decorative piping.
To make chocolate buttercream: Beat 224 grams/8 ounces melted and cooled extra bittersweet or bittersweet chocolate into the finished buttercream.

CHOCOLATE TRUFFLE SILK MERINGUE BUTTERCREAM:

If you happen to have some leftover Light Whipped Ganache, it makes a terrific addition to silk meringue buttercream. The resulting buttercream is more creamy and stable than the airy ganache but lighter than the silk meringue buttercream. It is pale chocolate in colour with a delicate flavour.

To make chocolate truffle buttercream: Beat together equal amounts of silk meringue buttercream base and Light Whipped Ganache (page 310).

CHESTNUT SILK MERINGUE BUTTERCREAM:

The classic combination of chestnut and rum makes a buttercream with spicy, earthy overtones that blends beautifully with chocolate cakes.

To make chestnut buttercream: Use ½ recipe buttercream base and beat in 1 recipe of lightly sweetened Chestnut Purée (page 405) flavoured with rum. (Makes 395 grams/14 ounces/3 full cups.)

APRICOT SILK MERINGUE BUTTERCREAM:

Bright orange, premium-quality dried apricots from California (purchased in health food shops or delicatessens) make an intensely flavoured buttercream. (Fruit purée buttercreams are slightly softer than the other versions but using this base they still pipe exceptionally well.)

To make apricot buttercream: Beat 8 fluid ounces unsweetened apricot purée (page 384) into the finished buttercream. Add 2 teaspoons apricot essence for further intensity if desired (page 492).

RASPBERRY SILK MERINGUE BUTTERCREAM:

Raspberry Conserve or jam gives a better texture to this buttercream than raspberry sauce. This buttercream is slightly less intense in flavour than the classic one and has a lighter texture.

To make raspberry buttercream: Add 109 grams/3½ ounces/½ cup Cordon Rose Raspberry Conserve (page 380) or 155 grams/ 5½ ounces/1 cup commercial seedless raspberry jam plus 1 tablespoon freshly squeezed lemon juice to the finished buttercream. If the conserve or jam is very stiff, heat gently until softened. Add the lemon juice and allow to cool to room temperature before adding to the buttercream. To retain a nice pale pink colour, stir in 6 drops of red food colour.

STRAWBERRY SILK MERINGUE BUTTERCREAM:

Avoid commercial strawberry jams – most are far too sweet to add to buttercream.

To make strawberry buttercream: Add 140 grams/5 ounces/½ cup puréed

Cordon Rose Strawberry Conserve (page 382) to the finished buttercream. To retain a pale pink colour, stir in 6 drops of red food colour. Add a few drops of essence of wild strawberry if desired for further intensity (page 492).

Mousseline Buttercream

Makes 858 grams/1 pound 14 ounces/4½ cups/1 litre 65 ml (enough to fill and ice two 23 × 4-centimetre/9 × 1½-inch layers or three 23 × 2.5-centimetre/ 9 × 1-inch layers)

This buttercream is very light, smooth and incredibly easy to work with. It is soft enough for beautiful shell borders yet strong enough to pipe roses. Liqueur gently perfumes the buttercream, and if it is tinted it also enhances the colour. Mandarine Napoléon, for example, lends the palest aura of apricot.

It is a thrilling buttercream to prepare because it starts out looking thin and lumpy and, about three-quarters of the way through, starts to emulsify and turn into a luxurious cream.

A word of caution: if the butter is too soft or the room too hot, what could have been a satin-smooth cream breaks down into a grainy hopeless puddle. Once the buttercream is made, however, it holds up better than any other.

Be sure to try the fruit variations (page 284). They are all superb and the orange is my favourite of all orange buttercreams. It is excellent with both chocolate and non-chocolate butter cakes and *génoise*.

STORE: 2 days room temperature, 10 days refrigerated, 8 months frozen. Allow to come to room temperature before rebeating or it will break down irretrievably.

POINTERS FOR SUCCESS: Correct butter temperature is crucial. If you suspect that the butter was too warm (or the kitchen is very hot) and the buttercream starts thinning out and curdling, check the temperature. If the mixture does not feel cool, refrigerate until it reaches 65° to 70°F/18° to 21°C or is cool to the touch. If by chance you have used butter straight from the refrigerator and the mixture feels ice-cold, suspend the bowl over a pan of simmering water (don't let the bowl touch the water) and heat very briefly, stirring vigorously when the mixture just starts to melt slightly at the edges. Dip the bottom of the bowl in a larger bowl of ice water for a few seconds to cool it. Remove and beat by hand until smooth.

INGREDIENTS	WEIGHT		MEASURE
room temperature	*grams*	*pounds/ounces*	*volume*
unsalted butter, softened but cool (65°F/18°C)	454 grams	1 pound	2 cups
castor sugar	200 grams	7 ounces	1 cup
water	60 grams	2 ounces	2 fluid ounces
5 egg whites, size 2	150 grams	5¼ ounces	5 fluid ounces
cream of tartar	—	—	½ + ⅛ teaspoon
liqueur such as Mandarine Napoléon, Grand Marnier, or an eau-de-vie	90 grams	3 ounces	3 fluid ounces

In a mixing bowl beat the butter until smooth and creamy and set aside in a cool place.

Have ready a heatproof glass measuring jug near the stove.

In a small heavy saucepan (preferably with a non-stick lining) heat 150 grams/5¼ ounces/¾ cup sugar and the water, stirring constantly, until the sugar dissolves and the mixture is bubbling. Stop stirring and reduce the heat to low. (If using an electric stove remove from the heat.)

In another mixing bowl beat the egg whites until foamy, add the cream of tartar, and beat until soft peaks form when the beater is raised. Gradually beat in the remaining sugar until stiff peaks form when the beater is raised slowly. Increase the heat and boil the syrup until a thermometer registers 248° to 250°F/120° to 121°C (the firm-ball stage). *Immediately transfer the syrup to the glass measure to stop the cooking.*

If using a hand-held mixer beat the syrup into the whites in a steady stream. Don't allow the syrup to fall on the beaters or they will spin it on to the sides of the bowl. If using a stand mixer, pour a small amount of syrup over the whites with the mixer off. Immediately beat at high speed for

5 seconds. Stop the mixer and add a larger amount of syrup. Beat at high speed for 5 seconds. Continue with the remaining syrup. For the last addition, use a rubber scraper to remove the syrup clinging to the glass measure. Lower speed to medium and continue beating for up to 2 minutes or until cool. If not *completely* cool, continue beating on the lowest speed.

Beat in the butter at medium speed 1 tablespoon at a time. At first the mixture will seem thinner but will thicken beautifully by the time all the butter is added. If at any time the mixture looks slightly curdled, increase the speed slightly and beat until smooth before continuing to add more butter.

Lower the speed slightly and drizzle in the liqueur. Place in an airtight bowl. Rebeat lightly from time to time to maintain a silky texture.* Buttercream becomes spongy on standing.

VARIATIONS

CHOCOLATE MOUSSELINE:

Beat in 140 grams/5 ounces of melted and cooled extra bittersweet or bittersweet chocolate.

WHITE CHOCOLATE MOUSSELINE:

Beat in 168 grams/6 ounces melted and cooled white chocolate, preferably Tobler Narcisse.

FRUIT MOUSSELINE:

Add up to 200 grams/7 ounces/3/4 cup lightly sweetened strawberry (page 388–9) or 190 grams/6³/4 ounces/3/4 cup raspberry purée (page 386–7) or 225 grams/scant 8 ounces/3/4 cup orange, passion, lemon or lime curd (pages 389–92).

*Do not rebeat chilled buttercream until it has reached room temperature or it may curdle.

Crème Ivoire Deluxe

(Luxury White Chocolate Buttercream and Glaze)

Makes 820 grams/1 pound 13 ounces/3 cups/710 ml

This glorious buttercream is for the white chocolate lover. The addition of extra cocoa butter, clarified butter and a neutral oil softens the texture and provides a pale ivory colour reminiscent of an antique satin wedding gown. It is excellent as icing for a wedding cake and equally dramatic when used to ice or glaze a one-layer cake such as the Chocolate Oblivion Truffle Cake (page 86). This buttercream pipes with the most exquisite detail. The contrast of the bittersweet chocolate against the white chocolate buttercream is striking.

Crème Ivoire is like the finest bonbon or chocolate truffle. On first bite it seems firm, only to dissolve immediately in the mouth, releasing the buttery and faintly chocolate flavours. Because of its richness, this amount is enough to glaze or lightly frost and decorate a 23 × 7.5-centimetre/ 9 × 3-inch cake.

STORE: Mineral oil (page 497) has an indefinite shelf-life, but safflower oil will become rancid in a matter of weeks. Therefore, if prepared with mineral oil, the buttercream will keep at room temperature 1 month. (The clarified butter shortens the shelf-life at room temperature.) If prepared with other oils, store at room temperature up to 1 week, in the refrigerator up to 3 months or freeze up to 1 year.

POINTERS FOR SUCCESS: When clarifying butter, the solids must begin to brown to ensure that all the water in the butter has evaporated. Be sure that not even a drop of water gets into the melted chocolate. If seeding should occur, try beating with an immersion blender (page 523) or remelt the buttercream, pass through a fine strainer, and chill again, stirring constantly. Be sure to use fine-quality white chocolate which contains cocoa butter. I find Tobler Narcisse to have the best flavour and the least sweetness.

I like to ice the cake first with a thin layer of Classic Buttercream. This offers an interesting textural contrast and gives the Crème Ivoire Deluxe an ideal surface on which to adhere. Otherwise it has a tendency to separate from the cake when serving. (I also use the classic buttercream plain or flavoured as a filling.) Keep piped decorations simple – such as a shell border (page 461).

The heat of your hand makes piping more than a few designs at a time difficult. To counteract this problem, use several parchment bags, placing just a small amount of buttercream in each, and switch bags at first sign of softening. Cooling your hand in ice water also helps.

INGREDIENTS	WEIGHT		MEASURE
room temperature	grams	pounds/ounces	volume
white chocolate (preferably Tobler Narcisse)	680 grams	1½ pounds	8 (3–ounce) bars
cocoa butter, melted*	64 grams	2¼ ounces	2 fluid ounces
clarified unsalted butter†	50 grams	1¾ ounces	2 fluid ounces
flavourless oil such as mineral or safflower	50 grams	1¾ ounces	2 fluid ounces

*Melt cocoa butter in a double boiler, in an oven with the heat of the pilot light, or microwave the same way as chocolate (page 437).
†If you do not have clarified butter on hand, you will need to clarify 78 grams/2¾ ounces/5½ table-spoons unsalted butter. In a heavy saucepan melt the butter over medium heat, partially covered to prevent splattering. When the butter looks clear, cook uncovered, watching carefully until the solids drop and just begin to brown. Pour immediately through a fine strainer or a strainer lined with cheesecloth.

Break the chocolate into squares and place in the top of a double boiler. Add the cocoa butter, clarified butter, and oil and place over very hot water on low heat. The water must not exceed 160°F/71°C or touch the bottom of the double boiler insert.

Remove the double boiler from the heat and stir until the chocolate begins to melt. Return to the heat if the water cools, but be careful that it does not get too hot. Stir for 10 minutes or until smooth. (The chocolate may be melted with the oil and butters in a microwave oven on high power *if stirred every 15 seconds*. Remove before fully melted and stir, using residual heat to complete the melting.)

Because of the milk solids in the white chocolate, the buttercream must be chilled and stirred to prevent seeding (the formation of tiny lumps). Fill a large bowl with ice cubes and water and sprinkle the ice with 1 or 2 tablespoons salt. Fill a second bowl or the sink with very hot water. Set the top of the double boiler directly in the ice water.

TO MAKE A BUTTERCREAM

Stir constantly with a whisk until you just see whisk marks on the surface. Immediately place over a bowl of hot water to take off the chill. This will take only seconds. The bottom of the pan should feel barely cool.

Allow the buttercream to sit for a few minutes, whisking occasionally. If it does not form peaks when the whisk is raised, chill again for a little longer.

TO MAKE A GLAZE

Stir the chocolate with a spoon to avoid air bubbles. Chill only until a small amount dropped from the spoon just mounds before smoothly disappearing into the mixture. For glazing instructions, see page 314.

Crème Ivoire

(White Chocolate Buttercream and Glaze)

Makes 540 grams/1 pound 3 ounces/2 cups/475 ml

The delicious creamy flavour of this buttercream is similar to the preceding recipe but this version is simpler and less expensive to make. It consists of white chocolate softened with a neutral oil to icing or glazing consistency. Its melt-in-the mouth quality comes from the cocoa butter in the white chocolate. (That is the only 'butter' in the buttercream.)

This buttercream is suitable for glazing or icing but is too soft to hold its shape for decorative piping. If you wish to make decorative borders on your cake, prepare the Crème Ivoire Deluxe instead (page 285) or the praline version of this buttercream. A tart filling such as raspberry or lemon buttercream is an ideal contrast to the sweetness of the white chocolate. Because of its richness, 470 grams/1 pound/1¾ cups is enough to glaze or ice a 23 × 7.5-centimetre/9 × 3-inch cake.

STORE: Mineral oil (page 497) has an indefinite shelf-life, but safflower oil will become rancid in a matter of weeks. Therefore, if prepared with mineral oil, the buttercream will keep at room temperature 6 months. If prepared with other oils, store at room temperature 1 week, refrigerate up to 3 months, or freeze up to one year. (The praliné version keeps at room temperature 3 weeks if mineral oil was used instead of safflower oil.)

POINTERS FOR SUCCESS: Be sure that not even a drop of water gets into the melted chocolate. If seeding should occur, try beating with an immersion blender (fitted with a disc blade) or re-melt the buttercream, pass through a fine strainer, and chill again, stirring constantly. If the weather is 80°F/27°C or above, reduce the oil to 6 tablespoons (3 fluid ounces).

INGREDIENTS	WEIGHT		MEASURE
room temperature	grams	pounds/ounces	volume
white chocolate (preferably Tobler Narcisse)	454 grams	1 pound	5⅓ (3-ounce) bars
flavourless oil such as mineral or safflower	87 grams	3 ounces	scant 4 fluid ounces

Break the chocolate into squares and place in the top of a double boiler. Add the oil and place over very hot water on low heat. The water must not exceed 160°F/71°C or touch the bottom of the double boiler insert.

Remove the double boiler from the heat and stir frequently until the chocolate begins to melt. Return to the heat if the water cools, but be careful that it does not get too hot. Stir for 8 to 10 minutes or until smooth. (The chocolate may be melted with the oil in a microwave oven on high power *if stirred every 15 seconds*. Remove before fully melted and stir, using residual heat to complete the melting.)

White chocolate buttercream must be chilled and stirred to prevent seeding (the formation of tiny lumps). Fill a large bowl with ice cubes and water and sprinkle the ice with 1 or 2 tablespoons salt. Fill a second bowl or the sink with very hot water. Set the top of the double boiler directly in the ice water. If making buttercream, whisk constantly until you just see whisk marks on the surface. Immediately place over a bowl of hot water to take off the chill. This will only take seconds. The bottom of the pan should feel barely cool.

Allow the buttercream to sit for a few minutes, stirring occasionally with a whisk. If it does not form peaks when the whisk is raised, chill again for a little longer.

If making a glaze instead of a buttercream, stir the chocolate with a spoon to avoid air bubbles. Chill only until a small amount dropped from the spoon mounds a bit before smoothly disappearing into the mixture. For glazing instructions see page 314.

VARIATION

CRÈME IVOIRE PRALINÉ:

This is the most intense of all praline buttercreams and pipes like a dream. It is imperative to use 100 per cent hazelnut paste *without* sugar. This product must be purchased (page 496) because homemade versions are not smooth enough. To prepare buttercream, whisk 120 grams/4¼ ounces/½ cup pure hazelnut paste into the melted chocolate and oil. (You may use some of the oil which forms on top of the hazelnut paste to make up some of the oil needed for the buttercream.)

Chocolate Walnut Drizzle Glaze

Makes 70 grams/2½ ounces/¼ cup/60 ml

The assertive flavour of walnuts does wonders when used judiciously with chocolate. Using part milk chocolate tempers the slight bitterness of the walnut. The oil softens the chocolate and keeps it dark and shiny.

This glaze is particularly complementary to cakes containing walnuts or walnut oil – such as Pumpkin–Walnut Ring (page 68) or Guilt-Free Chocolate Chiffon Cake (page 178).

STORE: 1 week room temperature, 3 months refrigerated or frozen.

POINTERS FOR SUCCESS: Smell walnut oil to ensure that it is not rancid before adding it to the chocolate.

INGREDIENTS	WEIGHT		MEASURE
room temperature	grams	pounds/ounces	volume
bittersweet chocolate	28 grams	1 ounce	⅓ of a 3-ounce bar
milk chocolate	28 grams	1 ounce	⅓ of a 3-ounce bar
walnut oil	13 grams	½ ounce	1 tablespoon

Break the chocolates into squares and place in the top of a double boiler. Add the oil and place over very hot but not simmering water on low heat. The water must not touch the bottom of the double boiler insert.

Remove the double boiler from the heat and stir until the chocolate begins to melt. Return to the heat if the water cools, but be careful that it does not get too hot. Stir until smooth. (The chocolate may be melted with the oil in a microwave oven *if stirred every 15 seconds*. Remove before fully melted and stir, using residual heat to complete the melting.)

Using a parchment cone (page 454) or cup with a spout, drizzle over the top and sides of the cake. Allow to set for at least 3 hours at room temperature.

Milk Chocolate
Buttercream

Makes 1 kilogram 20 grams/2¼ pounds/3 cups/710 ml (enough to fill and ice two 20 × 4-centimetre/8 × 1½-inch layers or two 23 × 2.5-centimetre/ 9 × 1-inch layers)

This is the quintessential easy-to-make buttercream for the milk chocolate lover. Since melted or softened milk chocolate seems much sweeter than the original bar, I have added half the milk chocolate's weight in bittersweet chocolate to compensate. The result is like eating a slightly softened bar of your favourite milk chocolate! This buttercream is especially good for filling and icing Chocolate Fudge Cake (page 54) or Perfect Chocolate Butter Cake (page 47).

STORE: 3 days room temperature, 3 weeks refrigerated, 6 months frozen.

POINTERS FOR SUCCESS: Be sure that not even a drop of water gets into the melted chocolate.

INGREDIENTS	WEIGHT		MEASURE
room temperature	*grams*	*pounds/ounces*	*volume*
milk chocolate*	454 grams	1 pound	—
dark chocolate, preferably extra bittersweet or bittersweet	227 grams	8 ounces	—
unsalted butter (must be softened)	340 grams	12 ounces	1½ cups

*Lindt offers a smooth texture and caramel undertone.

Break the chocolates into squares and place in the top of a double boiler. Set over hot but not simmering water on low heat. The water must not touch the bottom of the double boiler insert. Remove the double boiler from the heat and stir until the chocolate begins to melt. Return to the heat if the water cools, but be careful that it does not get too hot. Stir until smooth, and cool until no longer warm to the touch. (The chocolate may be melted in a microwave oven *if stirred every 15 seconds*. Remove before fully melted and stir, using residual heat to complete the melting.)

In a bowl beat the butter with an electric mixer at medium speed and beat in the cooled chocolate until uniform in colour.

Cream Icings and Fillings

Double cream is as good a medium as butter for blending flavours, but, because it has a lighter texture and less pronounced flavour, it lets other flavours come through more clearly. Fruit purées lightened with whipped cream have the intense, fresh flavour of the fruit and make heavenly fillings and piped toppings. Chocolate, blended with double cream to become the most divine of all chocolate icings, ganache, can be whipped full of air or left alone to become dense and creamy.

Plain lightly sweetened whipped cream complements any cake because of its soft, cloudlike texture and rich, faintly flowery flavour. It is particularly suited to whisked sponge cakes such as *génoise*, *biscuit*, chiffon and angel food cakes.

When used to fill a cake roll or accompany a slice of cake, whipped cream is loveliest when beaten only until it softly mounds when dropped from a spoon – not until stiff peaks form when the beater is lifted. To avoid overbeating, I usually finish the beating by hand with the detached whisk beater from the machine. When I raise the whisk and small but straight peaks form, the cream is perfect.

When beaten conventionally, double cream at least doubles in volume. The food processor, however, produces a whipped cream that does not increase in volume. Its dense and velvety texture makes it ideal for piping decorative borders.

I like to sweeten whipped cream with 1 tablespoon castor sugar per cup of cream. Icing sugar adds an undesirable, slightly powdery texture because of the cornflour it contains to keep it from lumping. (I use icing sugar only when it is dissolved in liquid and heated to boiling to swell the starch and make its presence undetectable.)

Whipped cream usually must be refrigerated to preserve its texture. So when icing and decorating a cake with whipped cream, select a whisked sponge cake, not a butter cake which would harden if chilled.

The high heat required for UHT treatment destroys some of the butterfat in cream. The combination of UHT and low butterfat content make whipping cream more difficult and causes the finished cream to lack stability, losing 2 or more tablespoons of water per cup of cream if allowed to sit, even in the refrigerator. Consequently UHT cream has many stabilisers added to it to enable it to whip.

Chilling the mixing bowl,

beater, double cream, and even the sugar before beating helps to make the most of what butterfat the cream does contain. Whipped creams flavoured with firm ingredients such as chocolate, cocoa, chestnut, powdered green tea or fruit jams do not require any additional stabiliser. Except for chocolate or chestnut whipped cream, however, they will not hold for prolonged periods at room temperature.

To make plain whipped cream in advance without stabilisers, place the whipped cream in a cheesecloth-lined sieve to allow the liquid to drain off and then refrigerate lightly covered with clingfilm. Or refrigerate the whipped cream and when ready to use whip lightly to reincorporate the liquid.

For icing a cake or making decorations, it is best to use whipped cream as soon as it is made, when its texture is smoothest. Decorated cakes may be kept one or two days in the refrigerator. Place them in an airtight cake carrier or glass dome (page 527) as cream absorbs other odours.

Perfect Whipped Cream

Makes 245 grams/8½ ounces/2 cups (enough to fill a cake roll)

This icing will hold up at room temperature for as long as 6 hours.

INGREDIENTS	WEIGHT		MEASURE
room temperature	*grams*	*pounds/ounces*	*volume*
double cream	232 grams	8 ounces	8 fluid ounces
castor sugar	13 grams	½ ounce	1 tablespoon
pure vanilla extract	—	—	½ teaspoon

POINTERS FOR SUCCESS:
Everything should be well chilled
before beating. Do not overbeat.
Chill the iced cake for at least
1 hour before allowing it to stand
at room temperature.

In a large mixing bowl place all the
ingredients and refrigerate for at
least 15 minutes. (Chill beater
alongside bowl.)

Beat until stiff peaks form when
the beater is raised. (For filling a
cake roll or accompanying a slice of
Chocolate Oblivion Truffle Torte
(page 86), use softly whipped
cream. To make softly whipped
cream, beat only until soft peaks
form or cream mounds softly when
dropped from a spoon.)

Ice and decorate the cake and
chill for at least 1 hour.

VARIATIONS

MOCHA WHIPPED CREAM:

Increase sugar to 2 tablespoons and stir in
1 tablespoon cocoa and 1 teaspoon instant
espresso powder.

COCOA WHIPPED CREAM:

Increase sugar to 32 grams/1¼ ounces/
2½ tablespoons and stir in 2 tablespoons
cocoa. Refrigerate for at least 1 hour to
dissolve the cocoa before beating.

Super-Stabilised
Whipped Cream

Makes 245 grams/8½ ounces/2 cups

Gelatin stiffens whipped cream enough to make it suitable for a deep layer
of filling or for piping roses. The gelatin makes the texture seem fuller
and slightly spongy.

STORE: 2 days refrigerated. Frozen
flowers keep for 1 month.

POINTERS FOR SUCCESS: The
gelatin mixture must not be warm
when added to the cream. The

cream must be cold when beaten.
Do not overbeat. Even a few extra
seconds past stiff peaks and the
consistency will no longer be
velvety smooth.

INGREDIENTS	WEIGHT		MEASURE
room temperature	*grams*	*pounds/ounces*	*volume*
powdered gelatin	—	—	½ to 1 teaspoon*
water	—	—	4 teaspoons
double cream	232 grams	8 ounces	8 fluid ounces
castor sugar	13 grams	½ ounce	1 tablespoon
pure vanilla extract	—	—	½ teaspoon

* Use ½ teaspoon for roses, 1 teaspoon for deep fillings.

Refrigerate the mixing bowl and beater for at least 15 minutes.

In a small heatproof measuring jug place the gelatin and water. Allow to soften for 5 minutes. Set the jug in a pan of simmering water and stir occasionally until the gelatin is dissolved. (This can also be done in a microwave on high power, stirring once or twice.) Remove the jug and cool to room temperature (about 7 minutes). The gelatin must be liquid but not warm when added to the cream.

In the chilled bowl beat the cream and sugar just until traces of the beater marks begin to show distinctly. Add the gelatin mixture in a steady stream, beating constantly. Add the vanilla and beat just until stiff peaks form when the beater is raised. Use at once to pipe the roses (page 471). To keep their shape, freeze the roses before placing them on the cake. Whipped cream can be refrigerated for a few hours before piping rosettes.

Whipped Cream for Piping Borders

Makes 480 grams/1 pound 1 ounce/2 cups

Using a food processor to 'whip' the cream means that it will not be as light and airy as beaten whipped cream because it does not increase in volume. The added density makes this velvety whipped cream pipe like a dream.

STORE: Refrigerated up to 24 hours; cream will not water out.

POINTERS FOR SUCCESS: The cream must be cold when processed. Do not overprocess. Even a few extra seconds past the peaking stage and the consistency will no longer be smooth.

INGREDIENTS	WEIGHT		MEASURE
room temperature	*grams*	*pounds/ounces*	*volume*
double cream	464 grams	1 pound	16 fluid ounces
castor sugar	25 grams	1 ounce	2 tablespoons
pure vanilla extract	—	—	1 teaspoon
	—	—	full ½ teaspoon

Place all the ingredients in the bowl of food processor fitted with the metal blade. Process, checking every few seconds by lifting a small amount of cream with a small metal spatula or spoon. The mixture should look thick and creamy and form a slight peak when lifted. It will not be fluffy. Use at once.

Chocolate Chip Whipped Cream

Makes 720 grams/1 pound 9 ounces/6 cups

This delectable filling has the lightness of whipped cream with the crunchy texture and wonderful flavour of chopped chocolate and almonds. It is the perfect consistency for filling Chocolate Chip Charlotte (page 204).

STORE: 3 days refrigerated.

POINTERS FOR SUCCESS: The gelatin mixture must not be warm when added to the cream. The cream must be cold when beaten. Do not overbeat the cream as whipped cream will continue to stiffen after folding in chocolate and nuts.

Refrigerate the mixing bowl and beater for at least 15 minutes.

In a small heatproof glass measuring jug place the gelatin and water. Allow to soften for 5 minutes. Set the jug in a pan of simmering water and stir occasionally until the gelatin is dissolved. (This can also be done in a microwave on high power,

INGREDIENTS	WEIGHT		MEASURE
room temperature	*grams*	*pounds/ounces*	*volume*
powdered gelatin	6.2 grams	—	2 teaspoons
water	45 grams	1½ ounces	3 tablespoons
double cream	464 grams	1 pound	16 fluid ounces
castor sugar	25 grams	1 ounce	2 tablespoons
pure vanilla extract	4 grams	—	1 teaspoon
finely grated bittersweet chocolate	142 grams	5 ounces	1 cup
finely ground almonds	54 grams	2 ounces	½ cup

stirring once or twice.) Remove the jug and cool to room temperature (about 7 minutes). The gelatin must be liquid but not warm when added to the cream.

In the chilled bowl beat the cream and sugar just until traces of the beater marks begin to show distinctly. Add the gelatin mixture in a steady stream, beating constantly. Add the vanilla and beat just until soft peaks form when the beater is raised. If preparing this filling for Chocolate Chip Charlotte (page 204), remove 1/2 cup/120 ml whipped cream to use for attaching *génoise* strips. Cover with clingfilm and place in the refrigerator. To the remaining whipped cream, add the chocolate and nuts and fold until evenly incorporated. Briefly set aside.

Crème Fraîche Topping

Makes 255 grams/9 ounces/1 cup

This recipe produces a *crème fraîche* reminiscent of the enchanting varieties found in France. I prefer it to any of the available commercial products. The proportion of 1 tablespoon buttermilk to 8 fluid ounces double cream results in a fresh, creamy taste with a gentle tang. I could eat it by the spoonful.

Sweetened with 1 tablespoon sugar and lightly beaten, it's a delightful topping for cheesecake, especially if crowned with fresh peach or banana slices.

INGREDIENTS	WEIGHT		MEASURE
room temperature	*grams*	*pounds/ounces*	*volume*
double cream	232 grams	8 ounces	8 fluid ounces
buttermilk	15 grams	1/2 ounce	1 tablespoon
castor sugar	13 grams	1/2 ounce	1 tablespoon

STORE: 3 weeks refrigerated. *Crème fraîche* will continue to thicken on chilling. When ready to use, add the sugar and whisk lightly until soft mounds form when dropped from the spoon.

Combine the cream and buttermilk in a jar with a tight-fitting lid and place in a warm spot such as the top of the refrigerator or near the stove. Allow to sit undisturbed for 12 to 14 hours or until thickened but still pourable. (UHT cream may take as long as 36 hours.)

Note: *Crème fraîche* is wonderful for finishing sauces not only because of its delicious flavour, but also because it does not curdle like sour cream.

Quick Crème Fraîche

Makes 480 grams/1 pound 1 ounce/3¾ cups

This is an excellent substitute for the preceding recipe when time does not allow waiting for the *crème fraîche* to thicken. The taste is perhaps a bit less tangy.

The yield is perfect for filling 3 crispy rounds of meringue or dacquoise (pages 342 and 349) for a Fresh Berry Meringue Torte. Simply add a handful of fresh berries to each layer and top with a single decorative layer of berries. If you want the torte to stay crispy, assemble it 1 hour before eating. If made several hours ahead, the crisp rounds soften, and the torte becomes so light it seems to levitate.

STORE: 24 hours refrigerated.   Rebeat lightly before using.

INGREDIENTS	WEIGHT		MEASURE
room temperature	*grams*	*pounds/ounces*	*volume*
double cream	348 grams	12 ounces	12 fluid ounces
sour cream	121 grams	4¼ ounces	4 fluid ounces
castor sugar	25 grams	1 ounce	2 tablespoons

In a large mixing bowl place all the ingredients and refrigerate for at least 15 minutes. Beat just until soft peaks form when the beater is raised or until it mounds when dropped from a spoon.

Mascarpone Icing and Filling

Makes 620 grams/1 pound 6 ounces/3 cups

I once saw a sign in Balducci's, a renowned New York food store, announcing: 'Mascarpone Has Arrived from Italy!' My first thought was Marcel Mascarpone? Who is this? When I asked the cheese buyer, he offered me a taste of what turned out to be a creamy, delicious cheese. We both agreed that while similar to *crème fraîche*, it was more flavourful. I decided that I had to find a way to transform this slightly tangy, almost yeasty, utterly luscious cheese into a cake icing.

On the first try, the icing curdled drastically. Disappointed, I kept beating it relentlessly thinking: 'What's the use?' Suddenly it emulsified and gained the perfect consistency for icing or piping. It is especially delicious with fresh strawberries and Golden Butter Cream Cake (page 22).

STORE: 5 days refrigerated, 2 months frozen.

INGREDIENTS	WEIGHT		MEASURE
room temperature	*grams*	*pounds/ounces*	*volume*
mascarpone	454 grams	1 pound	2 cups
castor sugar	33 grams	1¼ ounces	2 tablespoons + 2 teaspoons
double cream	160 grams	5½ ounces	5¼ fluid ounces

In a mixing bowl place the mascarpone and sugar and start beating at medium speed, preferably using a whisk beater. Gradually beat in the cream. The mixture will curdle at first but continue beating and it will become a smooth cream.

Note: Mascarpone varies in flavour. If it is more tangy it will require a bit more sugar.

Green Tea Mousse Cream

Makes 240 grams/8½ ounces/2 cups (enough to fill a cake roll)

The bitter moss green tea of the Japanese tea ceremony lends an exquisite colour and flavour to whipped cream. Used to fill Green Tea Biscuit Roulade (page 160) it creates an extraordinary dessert, especially suitable for a Chinese or Japanese dinner when most Western desserts seem inappropriate. For further drama, make Green Tea Marzipan (page 369) and wrap the individual slices sushi-style by draping each with a thin free-form leaf shape. Oriental vegetable cutters in varying shapes also make dramatic marzipan decorations. Powdered green tea is available in Oriental food shops.

STORE: 8 hours refrigerated.

POINTERS FOR SUCCESS: Make Green Tea Mousse Cream the same day as serving because the flavour diminishes overnight.

INGREDIENTS	WEIGHT		MEASURE
room temperature	*grams*	*pounds/ounces*	*volume*
powdered green tea	—	—	2 teaspoons
castor sugar	16 grams	½ ounce	1 tablespoon + 1 teaspoon
double cream	242 grams	8 ounces	8 fluid ounces

Refrigerate the mixing bowl and beater at least 15 minutes.

In the chilled mixing bowl place the green tea and sugar and gradually whisk in the cream. Beat until cream gently mounds when dropped from a spoon or until small peaks form when the beater is raised. Use at once.

Chestnut Mousse Cream

Makes 800 grams/1³/₄ pounds/5 cups (enough to fill and ice two 23 × 4-centimetre/9 × 1¹/₂-inch cake layers)

Chestnut purée added to whipped cream makes one of my favourite cake fillings and toppings. The texture remains light and airy but the flavour, enhanced with rum, is assertive and earthy. This icing and filling goes beautifully with Chestnut Génoise (page 133) but also blends and contrasts well with any chocolate *génoise* or roll.

STORE: 4 hours room temperature, 24 hours refrigerated.

POINTERS FOR SUCCESS: The type of chestnut purée used will make or break this frosting. Crème de Marrons is cloyingly sweet and should not be used. French chestnut purée (*purée de marrons*), available in specialist food stores (page 484), is softer than homemade but is acceptable. It is best to make your own from fresh or canned chestnuts (page 404) or use 1¹/₄ cups (11.5 ounces/ 327 grams) Clément Fangier's sweetened chestnut purée and omit the icing sugar.

Refrigerate the mixing bowl and beater for at least 15 minutes.

In a food processor fitted with the metal blade process the purée, sugar and rum until smooth.

In the chilled bowl beat the cream until the beater marks just start to appear. Add the chestnut mixture and beat just until stiff peaks form when the beater is raised.

Note: Whipped cream and chestnut purée are two of the components which make up my favourite winter dessert – discovered in Switzerland – Vermicelli. As the third component, *dacquoise*, is also in this book (page 349), I can't resist offering my version.

TO MAKE VERMICELLI
You will need a *dacquoise* disc

INGREDIENTS	WEIGHT		MEASURE
room temperature	*grams*	*pounds/ounces*	*volume*
unsweetened chestnut purée (see below)	264 grams	9¼ ounces	1 cup
icing sugar	75 grams	2½ ounces	⅔ cup (lightly spooned into cup)
dark rum	25 grams	1 ounce	2 tablespoons
double cream	464 grams	1 pound	16 fluid ounces

(page 349), lightly whipped cream (page 294), about 396 grams/ 13¾ ounces/1½ cups sweetened chestnut purée, and optional Chocolate Snowflakes (page 440). (The chocolate flakes are my contribution to this classic dessert.) For the chestnut purée, use the same proportion of unsweetened purée, icing sugar and rum as in the preceding recipe. Do not use tinned purée as it will be too soft. An hour before serving, spoon the whipped cream over the dacquoise. With a potato ricer or food mill fitted with the fine disc press the chestnut purée, allowing it to drop directly on to the whipped cream in vermicelli-like strands. If desired sprinkle with a flurry of chocolate flakes. This dessert can be made in a large 23 to 25.5-centimetre/9 to 10-inch disc or individual 7.5 to 10-centimetre/3 to 4-inch discs. At Confiserie Sprüngli in Zürich, individual portions are served in 7.5-centimetre/3-inch decorative bonbon cups. (I could never pass the Paradeplatz without feeling the pull to go in and consume one.)

Raspberry Jam Cream

Makes 650 grams/1 pound 6 ounces/4½ cups (enough for 2 cake rolls)

Raspberry whipped cream has the fresh tang of the berry with the billowy texture of whipped cream. The natural pectin in the berries acts as a stabiliser for the cream, preventing it from watering out and making it just firm enough for filling cake rolls.

Cordon Rose Raspberry Conserve is more than double the flavour concentration and less than two-thirds the sugar of most jams. If using a commercial seedless raspberry jam in its place, double the amount will be required for equal flavour intensity and the sugar in the recipe should be eliminated.

Raspberry Jam Cream makes a lovely filling for Chocolate Cloud Roll (page 152) or Almond Biscuit Roulade (page 160).

STORE: Filled cake holds for 2 hours at room temperature or 2 days refrigerated.

POINTERS FOR SUCCESS: Cream must be cold when beaten. Do not overbeat.

INGREDIENTS	WEIGHT		MEASURE
room temperature	*grams*	*pounds/ounces*	*volume*
Cordon Rose Raspberry Conserve (page 380)	145 grams	5 ounces	½ cup
Chambord liqueur *or* water	16 grams	—	1 tablespoon
double cream	464 grams	1 pound	16 fluid ounces
castor sugar	26 grams	1 ounce	2 tablespoons

Refrigerate the mixing bowl and beater for at least 15 minutes. In a small bowl place the raspberry conserve or seedless jam and whisk in the Chambord or water to soften it.

In the chilled bowl beat the cream and sugar just until the beater marks begin to show distinctly. Add the conserve and beat just until stiff peaks form when the beater is raised. Use at once.

VARIATIONS

Cordon Rose Strawberry Conserve
(page 382) also makes a delicious Jam
Cream using the same proportions. Purée
the conserve in a food processor before
adding to the cream. (Do not use
commercial strawberry jam; it is much too
sweet.) Strawberry Jam Cream makes an
exquisite filling and topping for Strawberry
Shortcake. Use layers of Golden Butter
Cream Cake (page 22) as the base. Or for a
lighter, more elegant version, try layers of
Génoise Classique (page 129) moistened
with Grand Marnier syrup. (Grand Marnier
and strawberry is a classic and lovely
combination.)

FRUIT CURD CREAM:

Replace the conserve with double the
amount of Lemon, Lime, Passion or
Orange Curd (pages 389 to 392). Omit the
Chambord and use water or a compatible
fruit liqueur.

Fruit Cloud Cream

Makes 700 grams/1½ pounds/5 cups (enough for a 20-centimetre/8-inch charlotte, page 198)

Fruit purées lightened with whipped cream are wonderful charlotte
fillings because of their pure flavour and light texture. A small amount of
gelatin makes the cloud cream just firm enough to unmould and to hold
its form when sliced. This cream is also excellent for icing and decorating
génoise.

STORE: 4 hours to 3 days
refrigerated before unmoulding
filled cake; remove to room
temperature 1 to 2 hours before
serving.

POINTERS FOR SUCCESS: The
cream must be cold when beaten.
The purée should be cool (not
warm or ice cold) when added to
the cream. For velvety smooth
texture, do not overbeat.

Refrigerate the mixing bowl and
beater for at least 15 minutes.

In a small heatproof measuring

jug place the gelatin and one-
quarter cup of the fruit purée and
allow it to sit for 5 minutes. Set the
cup in a pan of simmering water
for a few minutes, stirring
occasionally until the gelatin is
dissolved. (This can also be done in
a few seconds in a microwave on
high power, stirring once or
twice.)

Remove the cup and stir the
gelatin mixture into the remaining
purée. The mixture should now be
cool to the touch (not warm or ice
cold).

In the chilled bowl beat the

INGREDIENTS	WEIGHT		MEASURE
room temperature	*grams*	*pounds/ounces*	*volume*
powdered gelatin	7³/₄ grams	—	2¹/₂ teaspoons
fruit purée, unsweetened and at room temperature	—	—	about 1 cup (see specific variations, below)
double cream	464 grams	1 pound	16 fluid ounces
castor sugar	—	—	7 tablespoons to ²/₃ cup (see specific variations, below)

cream just until it mounds softly when dropped from a spoon. Add the sweetened purée and beat just until stiff peaks form when the beater is raised. Taste and fold in more sugar if you prefer a sweeter flavour. Use as soon as possible.

VARIATIONS

The strawberry and raspberry creams are rose coloured, the apricot pale gold, and the peach pale yellow. All highlight the flavour of the fruit. The peach cream has the most delicate flavour.

STRAWBERRY CLOUD CREAM:

238 grams/8¹/₄ ounces/1 cup unsweetened Strawberry Purée (page 388) mixed with 92 grams/3¹/₄ ounces/7 tablespoons sugar. Serve with optional Grand Marnier Crème Anglaise (page 323).

RASPBERRY CLOUD CREAM:

227 grams/8 ounces/1 cup unsweetened Raspberry Purée (page 386) mixed with 132 grams/4¹/₂ ounces/²/₃ cup sugar. Serve with optional Chambord liqueur or Pistachio Crème Anglaise (page 325).

APRICOT CLOUD CREAM:

270 grams/9¹/₂ ounces/1 cup unsweetened Apricot Purée (page 384) mixed with 100 grams/3¹/₂ ounces/¹/₂ cup sugar. Use only 2 teaspoons gelatin with 1 tablespoon of water when softening in the ¹/₄ cup purée. Serve with optional Barack Palinka (apricot eau-de-vie), apricot brandy, or Pistachio Crème Anglaise (page 325).

PEACH CLOUD CREAM:

510 grams/18 ounces/2¹/₄ cups unsweetened Peach Purée (page 385) mixed with 132 grams/4¹/₂ ounces/²/₃ cup sugar. Use only 12 fluid ounces cream. Serve with optional peach brandy, Pêcher Mignon, or Pistachio Crème Anglaise (page 325).

Note: When serving the charlotte, if desired, use a complementary eau-de-vie or liqueur to flavour *crème anglaise* (page 323) to serve on the side and to flavour the soaking syrup for the *biscuit*. For a lighter touch serve raspberry sauce instead of *crème anglaise*.

Lemon Cream Illusion

Makes 485 grams/1 pound 1 ounce/5 cups (enough for a 20-centimetre/ 8-inch charlotte, page 423)

This tart, intensely lemony cream is not technically a 'cream' at all. Italian meringue replaces the whipped cream and the result is spectacular: lighter texture than Lemon Curd Cream (page 306), more intense lemon flavour, and far fewer calories! It is firm enough to use as a filling for a cake roll but it needs the small amount of gelatin for a moulded dessert such as a charlotte. Raspberry sauce is a perfect complement.

STORE: 4 hours to 3 days refrigerated before unmoulding a filled cake; remove to room temperature 1 to 2 hours before serving.

INGREDIENTS	WEIGHT		MEASURE
room temperature	*grams*	*pounds/ounces*	*volume*
optional: gelatin	–	–	1¼ teaspoons
water	30 grams	1 ounce	2 tablespoons
1 recipe Light Italian Meringue (page 344)	–	–	–
1 recipe Lemon Curd (page 389) prepared with 60 grams/2 ounces/¼ cup sugar			

If using the gelatin: in a small heatproof glass measuring jug place the gelatin and water and allow to sit for 5 minutes. Set the jug in a pan of simmering water for a few minutes, stirring occasionally until the gelatin is dissolved. (This can also be done in a few seconds in a microwave on high power, stirring once or twice.)

Prepare the Light Italian Meringue. When the mixer is on medium speed to cool the meringue, beat in the optional gelatin. When completely cool, add the cold Lemon Curd and beat *just* to incorporate. Taste and fold in more sugar if desired. Use as soon as possible.

Ganache Icing, Filling, Glaze and Sauce

Ganache, a wondrous combination of chocolate and double cream, has many permutations and possibilities. It is said to have originated in Switzerland, where it is used mainly as the base for chocolate truffles. Because of its dark, gleaming colour and rich flavour it is my favourite of all chocolate icings. (Of course, this is dependent on using the finest chocolate!)

Ganache is more chocolaty but less rich and buttery than a buttercream. It is so flavourful, however, that I use only about three-quarters as much ganache icing as buttercream.

The proportion of chocolate to cream can vary widely for a ganache, starting from less than 14 grams/½ ounce of cream per 28 grams/1 ounce of chocolate (for a ganache so fudgy it cannot ice a

cake without separating from the crumb) all the way up to 56 grams/ 2 ounces of cream for every 28 grams/ounce of chocolate (for a light-coloured, airy ganache).

When I use a higher proportion of cream I use a more bitter chocolate because the natural sugar in the cream adds sweetness. In general, I prefer whipped ganache with airy cakes such as *génoise* and denser ganache for chocolate butter cakes.

Any ganache should be smooth and creamy. Overbeating will curdle it and ruin its texture, but it is possible to remelt the mixture in a double boiler or microwave and start again. In the dark ages before food processors, ganache was tricky because the chocolate had to be heated with the cream and sometimes the cocoa butter in the chocolate would separate and come to the surface. In that case, I'd let the mixture cool and stir it back to a smooth emulsion.

The food processor has made this magnificent chocolate icing into the easiest and most foolproof of all icings to prepare! It also ensures the best possible flavour because the chocolate gets heated only enough to melt it. This places me in permanent debt to Carl Sontheimer, who brought the food processor to this country, enormously improved the design, and, in the old days, used to nudge me with occasional phone calls daring me to make the big transition from knife to processor. Actually this was a mental block that took years for the American cooking culture to overcome. As recently as five years ago I remember hearing at least two chocolate celebrities unequivocally state that 'No! Ganache cannot be made in a food processor!' So much for that.

Light Whipped Ganache Filling and Icing

Makes 680 grams/1½ pounds/4 cups (enough to fill and ice two 23 × 4-centimetre/9 × 1½-inch layers)

This ganache has double the weight of cream to chocolate. It is so light and airy it seems to disappear in the mouth. The pale brown colour makes it ideal as a filling rather than an icing, although it pipes well at room temperature. Light ganache is a less conventional filling for Swiss Black Forest Cake (page 218) or any light chocolate cake such as *génoise* and *biscuit*. It also works well as a filling for a charlotte (page 423) and is divine in Triple Chocolate Cake (page 232) encased in sheets of chocolate praline.

STORE: 1 day room temperature, 1 week refrigerated, 3 months frozen.

POINTERS FOR SUCCESS: The temperature of the mixture is critical when beating. If not cold it will not stiffen; if too cold it will not aerate well. Overbeating causes curdling.

INGREDIENTS	WEIGHT		MEASURE
room temperature	*grams*	*pounds/ounces*	*volume*
bittersweet chocolate*	227 grams	8 ounces	2²/₃ (3–ounce) bars
double cream	464 grams	1 pound	16 fluid ounces
pure vanilla extract	—	—	¹/₂ teaspoon

*My favourite sweetness balance is 112 grams/4 ounces semisweet chocolate and 112 grams/4 ounces extra bittersweet. If I am planning a very sweet topping such as Chocolate Praline Sheets (page 363), I use all extra bittersweet.

Break the chocolate into pieces and process in a food processor until very fine. Heat the cream to boiling point and, with motor running, pour it through the feed tube in a steady stream. Process for a few seconds until smooth.

Transfer to a large bowl or electric mixer and refrigerate until cold, stirring once or twice (about 2 hours). You may speed chilling by setting the bowl in an ice water bath and stirring frequently. Do not allow the mixture to get too cold or it will be too stiff to incorporate air.

Add the vanilla and beat the mixture just until very soft peaks form when the beater is raised. It will continue to thicken after a few minutes at room temperature. The safest way not to overbeat is to use an electric mixer until the ganache starts to thicken and then continue with a hand-held whisk.

If the mixture gets overbeaten and grainy, it can be restored by remelting, chilling, and rebeating.

VARIATION

QUICK LIGHT WHIPPED GANACHE:

If you need the whipped ganache sooner and cannot wait for the mixture to chill, the following method gives equal results but involves a little more work.

Refrigerate the mixing bowl and beaters.

Using a double boiler or a microwave on high power (stirring every 10 seconds if a microwave is used), melt the chocolate pieces with 154 grams/5¹/₂ ounces/²/₃ cup cream. Remove from the heat before the chocolate is fully melted and finish melting by stirring constantly. Set aside until no longer warm.

In the chilled bowl beat the cream until traces of beater marks just begin to show distinctly. Add the chocolate mixture and beat just until soft peaks form when the beater is raised.

Dark Chocolate Ganache
Filling, Icing and Sauce

Makes 750–800 grams/1 pound 10 ounces–1³/₄ pounds/2³/₄–3 cups (enough to fill and ice two 20 × 4-centimetre/8 × 1¹/₂-inch layers or two 23 × 2.5-centimetre/ 9 × 1-inch layers)

Classic ganache icing usually has equal weights of chocolate and cream. Since I find this consistency is just a shade too stiff to adhere well to cakes, I have very slightly increased the amount of cream so that the icing is fudgy and thick while still able to cling to the cake. This ganache also makes a superb sauce for a chocolate charlotte, ice cream or poached pears (Poires Belle Hélène).

Because dark ganache is so rich and chocolaty, 800 grams/1³/₄ lb/3 cups is sufficient to fill and ice two 23-centimetre/9-inch round cake layers. The fudgy texture blends best with butter cake, preferably chocolate, as the ganache will overwhelm a more gently flavoured cake. It also happens to blend wonderfully with Chestnut Sand Cake (page 32).

My preference is a dense unbeaten ganache, but, if you would like to try a slightly airier version with the same intensity, use the optional butter (about 1 teaspoon per 28 grams/1 ounce of chocolate) and beat the ganache slightly. The optional Cognac heightens the elegance of the chocolate without imparting any bitterness.

STORE: 3 days room temperature, 2 weeks refrigerated, 6 months frozen. To soften ganache after chilling, allow to warm to room temperature and, if necessary, warm just to soften using a hot water bath or a few seconds in the microwave. Stir gently if you do not wish to aerate.

POINTERS FOR SUCCESS: Your favourite semisweet or bittersweet eating chocolate will result in the best-flavoured ganache. If the chocolate is not smooth-textured in bar form it will not be entirely smooth in the ganache either.

Break the chocolate into pieces and process in a food processor until very fine. Heat the cream to boiling point and, with the motor running, pour it through the feed tube in a steady stream. Process for a few seconds until smooth. Transfer to a bowl and cool completely. Gently stir in the optional butter and/or Cognac. Allow to cool for several hours until of icing consistency. If using butter, whisk for a few

INGREDIENTS	WEIGHT		MEASURE
room temperature	grams	pounds/ounces	volume
bittersweet chocolate	340 grams	12 ounces	4 (3-ounce) bars
double cream	385 grams	13½ ounces	13¼ fluid ounces
optional: unsalted butter, softened	57 grams	2 ounces	¼ cup
Cognac	28 grams	1 ounce	2 tablespoons

seconds to aerate. The colour will lighten.

To use ganache as a sauce, reheat until pourable if made in advance, using a double boiler or a microwave on low power, stirring every 15 seconds.

VARIATION

PRALINE GANACHE:

Add 102 grams/3½ ounces/⅓ cup praline paste (page 497) to the chocolate before processing.

UNDERSTANDING
Students have often asked me why it isn't advisable to add unheated cream to melted chocolate. If the cream is added cold, the chocolate hardens unevenly, forming little specks that melt on the tongue but are not visually attractive. The reason that the cream is brought to boiling point is not only to melt the chocolate but also to give a longer shelf-life to the ganache. In commercial establishments in France, the cream is brought to a full boil three times to destroy any bacteria. This may be because of the temperature to which their cream is pasteurised. It may also be to improve shelf-life in a commercial situation. If using UHT cream, it is unnecessary to bring it to the boil other than to melt the chocolate.

Chocolate Cream Glaze

Makes 480 grams/1 pound 1 ounce/2 full cups (enough to glaze a 23-centimetre/9-inch cake)

There are several ingredients that can be added to chocolate to create a dark, shiny glaze: butter, oil, jam, corn syrup, sugar syrup, even water. But cream seems to bring out the fullest chocolate flavour, so if I have cream on hand a Chocolate Cream Glaze is the only one I use. A tablespoon of Cognac heightens the flavour of the chocolate, but if a fine-quality chocolate is used the Cognac is optional.

A chocolate glaze is an ideal adornment for a cake. It is easy to make and creates a flawless, shiny finish while sealing in freshness.

STORE: 3 days room temperature, 2 weeks refrigerated, 8 months frozen.

POINTERS FOR SUCCESS: Your favourite semisweet or bittersweet eating chocolate will result in the best-flavoured glaze. If the chocolate is not smooth-textured in the bar it will not be entirely smooth in the glaze either.

The butterfat content of cream varies and will affect the glaze. Always check for consistency at a tepid temperature. If it is the correct consistency when tepid, even if it becomes too cool when applied to the cake and lumps, the cake can be placed in a warm oven for a few seconds and the glaze will smoothen. If glaze had been tested when hot and was the right consistency, the extra heat would not help if glaze lumps. On the other hand, if glaze had been the correct consistency when cool, it would never firm adequately on the cake.

To reheat glaze: use a double boiler, stirring gently, or a microwave oven on high power, stirring and folding every 5 seconds.

TO PREPARE CAKE FOR GLAZING

Brush all crumbs from the surface and place on a cardboard round the same size as the cake. Suspend the cake on a rack set on a baking sheet to catch excess glaze.

It is best to have enough glaze to cover the cake with one application as touch-ups don't usually produce as flawless a finish. Excess glaze can be frozen and reheated at a later date.

TO PREPARE GLAZE

Break the chocolate into pieces and process in a food processor until very fine. Remove the chocolate to a small heavy saucepan.

INGREDIENTS	WEIGHT		MEASURE
room temperature	grams	pounds/ounces	volume
bittersweet chocolate	255 grams	9 ounces	3 (3-ounce) bars
double cream	232 grams	8 ounces	8 fluid ounces
optional: Cognac	14 grams	½ ounce	1 tablespoon

Heat the cream to the boiling point and pour three-quarters of it over the chocolate. Cover for 5 minutes to allow the chocolate to melt. Gently stir together until smooth, trying not to create air bubbles. Pass through a fine strainer, stir in the optional Cognac, and allow to cool until just tepid.

CHECK FOR CONSISTENCY

At a tepid temperature a small amount of glaze should mound a bit when dropped from a spoon before smoothly disappearing. If the glaze is too thick and the mound remains on the surface or if the glaze seems curdled, add some of the warm remaining cream by the teaspoon. If the glaze is too thin, gently stir in a small amount of melted chocolate. When the consistency is correct, use at once or store and reheat.

The glaze should be poured on to the centre of the cake, allowing the excess to flow down the sides.

Smooth quickly and evenly with a large metal spatula, moving it lightly back and forth across the top until smooth. If any spots on the sides remain unglazed, use a small metal spatula to lift up some glaze which has fallen on to the baking sheet and apply to the uncovered area.

Lift the rack and tap lightly to settle the glaze. Lift the cake from the rack using a broad spatula and set on a serving plate, or on a clean rack if planning to apply a second coat of glaze.

If you want to cover the cake more thickly and evenly, two coats of glaze can be applied by the following technique. After the first coat is applied, refrigerate the cake for 20 minutes or until the glaze is firm. Apply a second coat of tepid glaze. (You will need 1½ times the glaze for a double coat.)

Allow the cake to set for at least 2 hours at room temperature. Refrigerating the cake will dull the glaze slightly.

Chocolate Butter Glaze

Makes 650 grams/1 pound 7 ounces/2 full cups (enough to glaze one 23-centimetre/9-inch cake)

I use this recipe when I need a dark, shiny chocolate glaze and there is no cream in the house (there's always butter!). It is similar in make-up and flavour to Chocolate Cream Glaze (see Understanding below) but not quite as mellow.

STORE: 3 days room temperature, 2 weeks refrigerated, 6 months frozen.

POINTERS FOR SUCCESS: Your favourite semisweet or bittersweet eating chocolate will result in the best-flavoured glaze. If the chocolate is not smooth-textured in bar form it will not be entirely smooth in the glaze either.

INGREDIENTS	WEIGHT		MEASURE
room temperature	*grams*	*pounds/ounces*	*volume*
bittersweet chocolate, chopped	340 grams	12 ounces	4 (3-ounce) bars
unsalted butter, softened	170 grams	6 ounces	¾ cup
water	118 grams	4 ounces	4 fluid ounces
corn syrup	20 grams	¾ ounce	1 tablespoon
pure vanilla extract	12 grams	½ ounce	1 tablespoon

TO PREPARE CAKE FOR GLAZING

Brush all crumbs from the surface and place on a cardboard round the same size as the cake. Suspend the cake on a rack set on a baking sheet to catch excess glaze.

It is best to have enough glaze to cover the cake with one application as touch-ups don't usually produce as flawless a finish. Excess glaze can be frozen and reheated at a later date.

TO PREPARE GLAZE

Using a double boiler set over hot, not simmering, water on low heat or a microwave on high power (stirring every 10 seconds), melt the chocolate. Remove from the heat before the chocolate is fully melted and stir until melted. Stir in the butter, 1 tablespoon at a time, until blended. If necessary return briefly to the heat but do not allow it to become too hot or the butter will separate.

Heat the water to 120°F/49°C or use hot tap water. Add all at once to the chocolate mixture and stir until smooth. Stir in the corn syrup and vanilla until uniform in colour.

CHECK FOR CONSISTENCY

Allow the glaze to cool, stirring occasionally, until a small amount mounds a bit when dropped from a spoon before smoothly disappearing. The glaze will be cool when the proper consistency is attained but will harden on setting.

Use at once or store and reheat. For a glaze that is perfectly uniform in colour, hold a fine strainer over the cake and pour the glaze through the strainer.

If you want to cover the cake more thickly and evenly, two coats of glaze can be applied by the following technique. Pour the glaze and smooth quickly with a spatula to create a thin, even coating. Refrigerate the cake for 20 minutes or until the glaze is firm. Apply a second coat of tepid glaze.

Allow the cake to set for at least 2 hours at room temperature. Refrigerating the cake will dull the glaze slightly.

UNDERSTANDING

Chocolate Butter Glaze is slightly thinner than Chocolate Cream Glaze (page 314) at a tepid temperature because of the missing milk solids and extra butterfat, but when set it is equally firm because the butter hardens.

Sour Cream Ganache

Makes 740 grams/1 pound 10 ounces/2²/₃ cups (enough to ice one 23 × 5-centimetre/9 × 2-inch cake layer)

Sour cream in place of double cream makes a smooth and lilting icing with excellent piping consistency. This easy-to-make ganache has a unique tanginess which I find delicious with any chocolate layer cake. It is especially good with Cordon Rose Banana Cake (page 65).

STORE: 3 days room temperature, 3 weeks refrigerated, 6 months frozen.

POINTERS FOR SUCCESS: The chocolate must still be warm and the sour cream room temperature when combined or the chocolate will lump.

INGREDIENTS	WEIGHT		MEASURE
room temperature	*grams*	*pounds/ounces*	*volume*
bittersweet chocolate	340 grams	12 ounces	4 (3-ounce) bars
sour cream	400 grams	14 ounces	13¼ fluid ounces

In a double boiler set over hot water or in a microwave on high power, stirring every 10 seconds, melt the chocolate. Remove from the heat and add the sour cream. Stir with a rubber spatula until uniform in colour. If the pan feels warm, transfer to a bowl.

Use at once or store, and when ready to use soften by placing the bowl in a water bath or a microwave for a few seconds, stirring gently.

Raspberry Ganache

*Makes 800 grams/1¾ pounds/3 cups (enough to fill and ice two
20 × 4-centimetre/8 × 1½-inch layers or two 23 × 2.5-centimetre/
9 × 1-inch layers)*

This most unique and glorious of ganache icings is ideal for a special
occasion. Be sure to use imported white chocolate that contains pure
cocoa butter.

The intense purée adds a tangy undertone and lingering taste of
raspberries to the chocolate, creating a subtle reddish brown gleam. A
small amount of white chocolate tames the tartness of the raspberries.

STORE: 1 day room temperature,
10 days refrigerated, 6 months
frozen.

POINTERS FOR SUCCESS: Use
your favourite bittersweet chocolate
and imported white chocolate,
which contains cocoa butter.
Tobler Narcisse is my personal
preference.

INGREDIENTS	WEIGHT		MEASURE
room temperature	*grams*	*pounds/ounces*	*volume*
bittersweet chocolate	340 grams	12 ounces	4 (3-ounce) bars
white chocolate	85 grams	3 ounces	1 (3-ounce) bar
double cream	232 grams	8 ounces	8 fluid ounces
Raspberry Purée, lightly sweetened (page 386)	135 grams	4¾ ounces	4 fluid ounces
optional: Chambord (black raspberry liqueur)	24 grams	—	1½ tablespoons

Break the chocolates into pieces
and process in a food processor
until very fine.

Heat the cream and Raspberry
Purée in a saucepan or microwave
on high power to boiling point.

With the motor running, pour
the cream mixture through the feed
tube in a steady stream. Process for
a few seconds until smooth.

Transfer to a bowl and stir in the optional Chambord. Allow to cool for several hours until the mixture reaches icing consistency.

Tip: Raspberry Ganache makes an excellent glaze but needs to be slightly thinner. Add warm cream or more Chambord by the tablespoon until of glazing consistency (see techniques for Ganache Glaze, page 314). To avoid air bubbles, do not use the food processor.

White Ganache

Makes 315 grams/11 ounces/2 cups (enough to ice one 20 × 7.5-centimetre/ 8 × 3-inch cake layer)

White chocolate is a superb stabiliser for whipped cream. It prevents watering out and enables it to hold its shape for several hours at room temperature. It pipes even from a small tube and also freezes well. If a judicious amount of white chocolate is used, there is no reason for White Ganache to be cloyingly sweet. In fact, the 85 grams/3 ounces white chocolate in this recipe contain only 7 teaspoons sugar, making the ganache just a little sweeter than Perfect Whipped Cream (page 294).

In addition to stabilising and sweetening the cream, the white chocolate also flavours it with vanilla and cocoa butter, lending it a chocolate quality so delicate as not to overwhelm other flavours.

White Ganache can be used in any number of ways. Serve it with fresh berries or fold in a stiffly beaten egg white and have an instant white chocolate mousse to serve with Raspberry (page 386) or Strawberry Sauce (page 388). Use the White Ganache to fill and ice Swiss Black Forest Cake (page 218) or to pipe elaborate festoons on Chocolate Oblivion Truffle Torte (page 86).

STORE: 1 day room temperature, 3 days refrigerated, 2 months frozen.

POINTERS FOR SUCCESS: Use imported white chocolate which contains cocoa butter. Tobler Narcisse is my personal preference. If leaving a decorated cake at room temperature, do not cover it or the ganache will soften.

INGREDIENTS	WEIGHT		MEASURE
room temperature	grams	pounds/ounces	volume
white chocolate, chopped	85 grams	3 ounces	1 (3-ounce) bar
double cream	232 grams	8 ounces	8 fluid ounces

Refrigerate the mixing bowl and beater for at least 15 minutes.

Using a double boiler or microwave on high power (stirring every 10 seconds if using microwave), melt the chocolate with 58 grams/2 ounces/2 fluid ounces cream. Remove from the heat before the chocolate is fully melted and stir until melted. Set aside until no longer warm.

In the chilled bowl beat the cream until traces of beater marks just begin to show distinctly. Add the white chocolate mixture and beat just until stiff peaks form when the beater is raised.

Tip: For a deliciously tart white ganache, great for serving with fresh fruit, replace the double cream with *crème fraîche*.

Custard Cream Fillings and Sauces

Custard creams are the foundation for many desserts. The basic *crème anglaise* (or English custard sauce) consists of egg yolks, sugar, and milk or cream (or a combination of the two) and is a base for Silk Meringue Buttercream (page 276), in accompaniment to charlottes or fresh fruit, an ingredient in Bavarian creams, and the start of the richest, creamiest ice creams.

When making *crème anglaise*, I favour the lighter versions made with all milk to accompany a rich dessert and those with three-quarters cream to serve with fresh fruit. Ice cream has the smoothest texture when *crème anglaise* is made with at least three-quarters cream to one-quarter milk. More than that becomes too rich for my taste.

Three to four egg yolks per 242 grams/8½ ounces/1 cup of cream or milk are ideal to thicken and enrich the sauce. If I am using praline paste, however, which adds more body, I use only two yolks.

I also prefer a rather low amount of sugar, two to three tablespoons per 242 grams/8½ ounces/1 cup of milk or cream. Ice cream requires the higher amount because freezing makes it seem less sweet. In any event, it is a simple matter to stir in more sugar to taste even after making the sauce.

Bavarian cream is a moulded *crème anglaise* with whipped cream added. It relies on gelatin to keep its shape, and, if prepared in a decorative mould, it may be served without cake. Encased by gossamer Biscuit Roulade (page 157) filled with a thin layer of tart jam and served with an intense raspberry sauce, it is (in my book) the most perfect of desserts. I call it the Scarlet Empress (page 201).

It is, of course, possible to flavour Bavarian cream with chocolate or fruit purée, but I find that most of these flavours become overwhelmed and dulled by the Bavarian base. I much prefer flavouring the Bavarian with vanilla and liqueur and making Light Whipped Ganache (page 310) or Fruit Cloud Cream (page 306) instead when I am in the mood for other flavours.

Two noteworthy exceptions are orange and pear Bavarians. For orange Bavarian, the *crème anglaise*'s milk base makes it possible to steep the orange zest, extracting more flavour. For pear Bavarian, using the poaching liquid instead of milk, combined with the Italian meringue, makes it lighter even than a cloud cream.

Liqueur such as kirsch or Grand Marnier is traditionally added to

Bavarian cream not only for its lovely flavour and aroma but also because it effectively masks any gelatin flavour.

Most recipes beat the egg yolks with the sugar until very thick to make an airier Bavarian. But it is my belief that the air completely disappears during the subsequent cooking of the custard. If I want a denser, creamy Bavarian, I rely on whipped cream to lighten it slightly. For a moussier effect I add beaten egg whites and for a billowy, cloudlike Bavarian I use Italian meringue (egg whites stabilised with hot sugar syrup).

I find that the gelatin in Bavarians continues to thicken over a 24-hour period and after that does not get any thicker even when frozen and defrosted. Therefore you can freeze any of the cakes filled with Bavarian cream for at least three weeks without loss of flavour or texture.

Crème Anglaise

Makes 340 grams/12 ounces/1¼ cups

This rich, smooth cream, served cold, is the perfect accompaniment for charlottes filled with Fruit Cloud Cream (page 306) or for seasonal fruit. Use the optional eau-de-vie or liqueur to complement the fruit. One of my favourites is Grand Marnier.

STORE: 5 days refrigerated, 3 months frozen. Sauce thickens slightly overnight in refrigerator.

POINTERS FOR SUCCESS: Don't use whisk to stir if not using accurate thermometer because the foam makes it difficult to see when mixture is getting close to the boiling point. Do not heat above 180°F/82°C or the sauce will begin to curdle. If overheated and *slight* curdling does take place, pour instantly into a blender and blend until smooth before straining.

INGREDIENTS	WEIGHT		MEASURE
room temperature	*grams*	*pounds/ounces*	*volume*
castor sugar	25 grams	1 ounce	2 tablespoons
salt	—	—	pinch
4 egg yolks, size 2	74 grams	2½ ounces	2 fluid ounces
milk	242 grams	8½ ounces	8 fluid ounces
½ vanilla pod* split lengthwise	—	—	—
optional: liqueur *or* eau-de-vie	21 to 35 grams	¾ to 1¼ ounces	2 to 3 tablespoons

*You may substitute 1 teaspoon pure vanilla extract for the vanilla pod, but the pod offers a fuller, more aromatic flavour. If using extract, add it after the sauce is cool. If using a Tahitian pod, use only one-quarter of the pod.

Have a fine strainer ready near the range, suspended over a small mixing bowl.

In a small heavy non-corrodible saucepan stir together the sugar, salt and yolks until well blended, using a wooden spoon.

In another small saucepan (or heatproof glass measure if using a microwave on high power) heat the milk and vanilla pod to the boiling point. Stir a few tablespoons into the yolk mixture; then gradually add the remaining milk and vanilla pod, stirring constantly.

Heat the mixture to just before boiling point (170° to 180°F/77° to 82°C). Steam will begin to appear and the mixture will be slightly thicker than double cream. It will leave a well-defined track when a finger is run across the back of a spoon. Immediately remove from the heat and pour into the strainer, scraping up the thickened cream that settles on the bottom of the pan. Remove the vanilla pod and scrape the seeds into the sauce. Stir until seeds separate. For maximum flavour, return the pod to the sauce until serving time.

Cool in an ice-water bath or the refrigerator. Stir in the optional liqueur.

UNDERSTANDING
Commercial establishments sometimes bring the mixture to the boil and quickly strain it, discarding the curdled part. This is done only to save time and to ensure that the temperature is hot enough without bothering with other tests. (I do not recommend this method.)

Pistachio Crème Anglaise

Makes 365 grams/13 ounces/1 full cup

This sauce is the palest of greens and beautifully perfumed by the pistachio nut. Pistasha liqueur intensifies the flavour and slightly deepens the colour. This contrasts beautifully in colour and flavour with the dark chocolate of Chocolate Oblivion Truffle Torte (page 86). Since I always have difficulty deciding whether I prefer pistachio or raspberry sauce with chocolate, I sometimes drop little pools of raspberry on top of the pistachio (using a squeeze bottle) and intermingle them.

POINTERS FOR SUCCESS: Do not blanch the nuts to remove the skin as they will lose most of their flavour. If too much skin is left, the colour will be slightly brown instead of green. Don't use a whisk to stir if not using an accurate thermometer because the foam makes it difficult to see when the mixture is getting close to boiling.

Do not heat above 180°F/82°C or the sauce will curdle. If overheated and *slight* curdling does take place, pour instantly into a blender and blend until smooth before straining.

Bake nuts in a 350°F/180°C/gas mark 4 oven for 5 to 10 minutes or until the skins separate from the

INGREDIENTS	WEIGHT		MEASURE
room temperature	*grams*	*pounds/ounces*	*volume*
shelled unsalted pistachio nuts	38 grams	1¼ ounces	¼ cup
milk	242 grams	8½ ounces	8 fluid ounces
castor sugar	38 grams	1¼ ounces	3 tablespoons
salt	—	—	pinch
4 egg yolks, size 2	74 grams	2½ ounces	2 fluid ounces
optional: Pistasha (pistachio liqueur)	25 grams	¾ ounce	2 tablespoons

nuts when scratched lightly with a fingernail. Remove as much skin as possible. In a food processor or nut grinder grind the nuts very fine.

In a small saucepan (or heatproof glass measuring jug if using a microwave on high power) place nuts and milk and bring to boiling point. Cover and allow to steep for at least 30 minutes. Strain through cheesecloth, pressing well to remove all milk, and discard the nuts. Return the millk to the saucepan or glass measure.

Have a fine strainer ready near the stove, suspended over a small mixing bowl.

In a small heavy, non-corrodible saucepan stir together the sugar, salt and yolks until well blended, using a wooden spoon.

Heat the milk just to boiling point. Stir a few tablespoons into the yolk mixture; then gradually add the remaining milk, stirring constantly.

Heat the mixture to just below boiling point (170° to 180°F/77° to 82°C). Steam will begin to appear and the mixture will be slightly thicker than double cream. It will leave a well-defined track when a finger is run across the back of a spoon. Immediately remove from the heat and pour into the strainer, scraping up the thickened cream that settles on the bottom of the pan.

Cool in an ice-water bath or the refrigerator. Stir in the optional Pistasha liqueur.

Crème Anglaise Praliné

Makes 340 grams/12 ounces/1¹/₃ full cups

Praline paste made with hazelnuts and caramelised sugar is a flavourful enrichment to *crème anglaise*. The praline paste adds body, so only half the usual number of egg yolks is needed. It also adds sweetness, making it unnecessary to add any sugar. Dark rum or cognac both highlight the praline flavour and cut the richness. This sauce is especially delicious with the praline version of Chocolate Oblivion Truffle Torte (page 86).

STORE: 5 days refrigerated, 3 months frozen.

POINTERS FOR SUCCESS: Don't use a whisk to stir if not using an accurate thermometer because the foam makes it difficult to see when the mixture is getting close to boiling. Don't heat above 180°F/82°C or the sauce will curdle.

INGREDIENTS	WEIGHT		MEASURE
room temperature	*grams*	*pounds/ounces*	*volume*
praline paste (page 497)	77 grams	2¾ ounces	¼ cup
milk	242 grams	8½ ounces	8 fluid ounces
2 egg yolks, size 2	37 grams	1¼ ounces	2 tablespoons
salt	—	—	speck
pure vanilla extract	4 grams	—	1 teaspoon
optional: rum *or* Cognac	21 grams	¾ ounce	1½ tablespoons

If overheated and *slight* curdling does take place, pour instantly into a blender and blend until smooth.

In a food processor place the praline paste and, with the motor running, gradually add the milk. Process until smooth.

In a small, heavy, non-corrodible saucepan stir together the yolks and salt until well blended, using a wooden spoon.

In another small saucepan (or a heatproof glass measuring jug if using a microwave on high power) heat the praline mixture to boiling point. Stir a few tablespoons into the yolk mixture; then gradually add the remainder, stirring constantly.

Heat the mixture to just below boiling point (170° to 180°F/77° to 82°C). Steam will begin to appear and the mixture will be slightly thicker than double cream. It will leave a well-defined track when a finger is run across the back of a spoon. Immediately remove from the heat and pour into a bowl, scraping up the thickened cream that settles on the bottom of the pan.

Cool in an ice-water bath or the refrigerator. Stir in the vanilla and optional liqueur.

Crème Anglaise Café

Makes 340 grams/12 ounces/1⅓ cups

This classic French method of extracting coffee essence provides intense flavour. Extra sugar is used to offset the bitterness of the coffee. This sauce is lovely served with Chocolate Torture (page 89) because it deepens the subtle coffee background flavour.

STORE: 5 days refrigerated, 3 months frozen.

POINTERS FOR SUCCESS: Don't use a whisk to stir if not using an accurate thermometer because the foam makes it difficult to see when the mixture is getting close to boiling. Do not heat above 180°F/82°C or the sauce will curdle.

If overheated and *slight* curdling does take place, pour instantly into a blender and blend until smooth before straining.

Have ready near the stove a fine strainer lined with cheesecloth, suspended over a small mixing bowl.

In a small heavy non-corrodible

INGREDIENTS	WEIGHT		MEASURE
room temperature	*grams*	*pounds/ounces*	*volume*
4 egg yolks, size 2	74 grams	2½ ounces	2 fluid ounces
castor sugar*	50 grams	1¾ ounces	¼ cup
salt	—	—	pinch
milk	242 grams	8½ ounces	1 cup
finely ground coffee beans	10 grams	—	2½ tablespoons
½ vanilla pod, split lengthwise†	—	—	—
optional: Kahlúa (coffee liqueur)	25 grams	1 ounce	1½ tablespoons

* Use only 3 tablespoons sugar if adding Kahlúa.
† You may substitute 1 teaspoon pure vanilla extract for the vanilla pod, but the pod offers a fuller, more aromatic flavour. If using extract, add it after the sauce is cool.

saucepan stir together the yolks, sugar and salt until well blended, using a wooden spoon.

In another small saucepan (or a heatproof glass measuring jug if using a microwave on high power), heat the milk, coffee and vanilla pod to boiling point. Stir a few tablespoons into the yolk mixture; then gradually add the remaining milk, stirring constantly.

Heat the mixture to just below boiling point (170° to 180°F/77° to 82°C). Steam will begin to appear and the mixture will be slightly thicker than double cream. It will leave a well-defined track when a finger is run across the back of a spoon. Immediately remove from the heat and pour into the strainer, scraping up the thickened cream that settles on the bottom of the pan. Remove the vanilla pod and scrape the seeds into the sauce. Stir until the seeds separate. For maximum flavour return the pod to the sauce until serving time.

Cool in an ice-water bath or the refrigerator. Stir in the optional Kahlúa.

Vanilla Ice Cream

Makes 1 kilogram 130 grams/2½ pounds/5 cups

Crème anglaise is the base for this glorious ice cream. It is dense, rich and fragrant with the slightly flowery flavours of double cream and vanilla, yet it is not a drop too sweet. It will spoil you for even the best commercial brands. The secret ingredient for perfecting the texture is vodka – which does not impart a taste but keeps the ice cream from becoming too hard in the freezer.

Serve this ice cream alone or with Brandied Burgundy Cherries (page 397) and Hot Fudge (page 90) for a sophisticated sundae. Or use it for the summer version of Swiss Black Forest Cake (page 218).

STORE: Ice cream has the best texture within 3 days of freezing.

POINTERS FOR SUCCESS: Don't use a whisk to stir if not using an accurate thermometer because the foam makes it difficult to see when the mixture is getting close to boiling. Do not heat above 180°F/82°C or the sauce will curdle. If overheated and *slight* curdling does take place, pour instantly into a blender and blend until smooth before straining. Do not add more than the recommended amount of vodka or the ice cream will not freeze.

INGREDIENTS	WEIGHT		MEASURE
room temperature	*grams*	*pounds/ounces*	*volume*
8 egg yolks, size 2	150 grams	5¼ ounces	4½ fluid ounces
castor sugar	150 grams	5¼ ounces	¾ cup
salt	—	—	pinch
double cream	696 grams	1½ pounds	24 fluid ounces
milk	242 grams	8½ ounces	8 fluid ounces
2 vanilla pods,★ split lengthwise	—	—	—
optional: vodka	29 grams	1 ounce	2 tablespoons

★You may substitute 2 teaspoons pure vanilla extract for the vanilla pod, but the pod offers a fuller, more aromatic flavour. If using extract, add it after the sauce is cool. If using a Tahitian pod, use only 1 pod.

Have a fine strainer ready near the stove, suspended over a medium mixing bowl.

In a small heavy non-corrodible saucepan stir together the yolks, sugar and salt until well blended, using a wooden spoon.

In another small saucepan (or a heatproof glass measuring jug if using a microwave on high power) heat the cream, milk and vanilla pods to boiling point. Stir a few tablespoons into the yolk mixture; then gradually add the remainder, stirring constantly.

Heat the mixture to just below boiling point (170° to 180°F/77° to 82°C). Steam will begin to appear and the mixture will be slightly thicker than double cream. It will leave a well-defined track when a finger is run across the back of a spoon. Immediately remove from the heat and pour into the strainer, scraping up the thickened cream that settles on the bottom of the pan. Remove the vanilla pods and scrape the seeds into the sauce. Stir until the seeds separate. Return the pod to the sauce until ready to freeze.

Cool in an ice-water bath or the

refrigerator until cold. Stir in the optional vodka. Freeze in an ice- cream maker. Allow to ripen for 2 hours in the freezer before serving.

VARIATIONS

PINEAPPLE ICE CREAM:

This is a sensational flavour. Do make your own pineapple purée (page 402). It is far superior to tinned pineapple. For a generous quart of ice cream, prepare only two-thirds of the recipe, using 5 egg yolks, a 5-centimetre/2-inch long piece of vanilla pod, and 1 tablespoon plus 2 teaspoons of kirsch instead of vodka. Before freezing, stir 66 grams/2⅓ ounces/⅔ cup pineapple purée into the chilled cream mixture. This ice cream is delicious by itself but was created especially for Baked Hawaii (page 191).

FIRE AND ICE:

For a slightly nutty, slightly fiery, utterly delicious flavour, add 2 teaspoons pink peppercorns, crushed, with the vanilla extract.

Vanilla Bavarian Cream

Makes 700 grams/1½ pounds/5 cups (enough for a 1.5-litre/2½-pint/ 6-cup cake-lined mould)

This sublime cream is an ideal filling for a dome-shaped charlotte such as the Scarlet Empress (page 201). It is silken smooth, fragrant with vanilla, and very creamy. It contains just enough gelatin to hold its shape while maintaining a soft, melt-in-the-mouth texture.

STORE: Refrigerate 4 hours to 3 days before unmoulding. Remove to room temperature 1 hour before serving. The Bavarian may be frozen for 2 weeks. Defrost for 24 hours in the refrigerator.

POINTERS FOR SUCCESS: Don't use a whisk to stir when heating the custard if not using an accurate thermometer because the foam makes it difficult to see when the mixture is getting close to boiling. Do not heat above 180°F/82°C or the sauce will curdle. If overheated and *slight* curdling does take place, pour instantly into a blender and blend until smooth before straining. To prevent separation, the yolk mixture must start to thicken before adding the egg whites or whipped cream. If it starts to set prematurely, set the bowl briefly over hot water, and stir until smooth. Once the whipped cream has been added, avoid overmixing. Be sure to measure or weigh the gelatin. One envelope equals about 2¼ teaspoons.

INGREDIENTS	WEIGHT		MEASURE
room temperature	*grams*	*pounds/ounces*	*volume*
castor sugar	66 grams	2¼ ounces	⅓ cup
salt	—	—	pinch
gelatin*	9.3 grams	—	1 tablespoon
5 egg yolks, size 2	93 grams	3¼ ounces	3 fluid ounces
milk	402 grams	14 ounces	13¼ fluid ounces
1 vanilla pod, split†	—	—	—
double cream	232 grams	8 ounces	8 fluid ounces
optional: kirsch (cherry eau-de-vie)	21 grams	¾ ounce	1½ tablespoons

*This is more than one envelope.
†You may substitute 1 teaspoon vanilla extract for the vanilla pod, but the pod offers a fuller, more aromatic flavour. If using extract, add it after the sauce is cool. If using a Tahitian pod, use only half the pod.

Refrigerate the mixing bowl for whipping the cream.

Have ready a fine strainer near the stove, suspended over a small mixing bowl.

In a small, heavy, non-corrodible saucepan, stir together the sugar, salt, gelatin and yolks until well blended, using a wooden spoon.

In another small saucepan (or a heatproof glass measuring jug if using a microwave on high power) heat the milk and vanilla pod to boiling point. Stir a few tablespoons into the yolk mixture; then gradually add the remaining milk and vanilla pod, stirring constantly.

Heat the mixture to just below boiling point (170° to 180°F/77° to 82°C). Steam will begin to appear and the mixture will be slightly thicker than double cream. It will leave a well-defined track when a finger is run across the back of a spoon. Immediately remove from the heat and pour into the strainer, scraping up the thickened cream that settles on the bottom of the pan. Remove the vanilla pod and scrape the seeds into the sauce. Stir until the seeds separate.

In the chilled bowl whip the cream until it mounds softly when dropped from a spoon. Refrigerate.

Cool the sauce in an ice-water bath, stirring with a large wire whisk until whisk marks barely begin to appear. The mixture will start to set around the edges but will still be very liquid. Whisk in the optional kirsch and continuing with the whisk, fold in the whipped cream until just incorporated. The mixture will be soupy like melted ice cream. Remove at once from the water bath and pour into a 1½-litre/ 2½-pint/6-cup biscuit-lined bowl (page 425). Refrigerate for at least 4 hours before turning out.

Note: If time allows, the Bavarian cream can be chilled in the refrigerator instead of stirred over ice water. It will take about 1½ hours to thicken and should be stirred occasionally. The advantage of refrigeration over ice water is that the thickening process is more gradual so there is less danger of the mixture becoming too thick before folding in the remaining ingredients.

UNDERSTANDING

Kirsch or other liqueurs are added to Bavarian creams not only for the lovely flavours but also to mask any gelatin flavour.

VARIATIONS

ORANGE BAVARIAN:

Delicately perfumed with orange and Grand Marnier, flecked with tiny dots of orange zest, this Bavarian is delicious topped with a thin layer of Light Whipped Ganache (page 310) to create a stunning two-toned effect. If blood oranges are available, they provide a lovely pink colour and more intense flavour. Preparation is similar to basic Bavarian cream with the following changes. Use 100 grams/ 3½ ounces/½ cup sugar. Replace the kirsch with Grand Marnier. Add 2 tablespoons fresh orange concentrate and 1 tablespoon grated orange zest. To make orange concentrate, start with ½ cup freshly squeezed orange juice (about 2 oranges) and reduce it to 2 tablespoons. (Using a microwave on high power gives the purest flavour.) Add the zest to the milk before heating and do not strain the custard. Add the orange concentrate when the mixture is cool. Pour into a 20-centimetre/8-inch biscuit-lined mould (page 206) and refrigerate.

Make ¼ recipe Light Whipped Ganache (page 310) and immediately after whipping smooth over the top of the orange Bavarian. Top with Chocolate Curls (page 441) and Candied Orange Zest (page 392) or a piped disc of Daisy Biscuit (page 209). Tie a brown and an orange ribbon around the finished mould. (See Orange Chocolate Crown, page 206.)

BAVARIAN CHIFFON:

This Bavarian is also silky and creamy but has a lighter, faintly spongy texture from beaten egg whites. To make this version, beat 3 large egg whites (90 grams/3 ounces) until foamy, add ⅜ teaspoon cream of tartar, and beat until soft peaks form when the beater is raised. Gradually add 3 tablespoons sugar and beat until stiff peaks form when the beater is raised slowly. With a large whisk fold into the chilled yolk mixture. Then fold in the whipped cream. This will make enough Bavarian Chiffon Cream for a 23-centimetre/9-inch *biscuit*-lined mould (page 423).

Pear Bavarian Cream

Makes 900 grams/scant 2 pounds/6 cups (enough for one 23 × 5-centimetre/ 9 × 2-inch charlotte) (page 423)

I fell in love with charlottes and Bavarian cream fillings at the renowned Ecole LeNôtre in Plaisir, France, where I went to study seven years ago. This Bavarian cream for Ethereal Pear Charlotte (page 199) was my favourite. The flavour is purely pear and the texture incomparably creamy, billowy and light, yet, miraculously, it holds its shape for serving. The secrets are the use of pear juice instead of milk for the *crème anglaise* (LeNôtre jokingly called it *crème française*) and the addition of Italian meringue. The challenge in re-creating this recipe was to keep it from being too sweet because the meringue contains so much sugar. Instead of adding extra sugar to protect the eggs from curdling when adding the pear juice, I stole some sugar from the meringue and a little more from the poaching syrup. The result is a *succès fou*! It is one of my favourite recipes in this book.

STORE: Refrigerate 4 hours to 3 days before unmoulding. The Bavarian may be frozen for 2 weeks.

POINTERS FOR SUCCESS: *Custard:* Don't use a whisk to stir if not using an accurate thermometer because the foam makes it difficult to see when the mixture is getting close to boiling. Do not heat above 190°F/88°C or the sauce will curdle. If overheated and *slight* curdling does take place, pour instantly into a blender and blend until smooth before straining.

It is possible to heat this sauce 10 degrees higher than one made with milk because the acidity of the pear juice raises the boiling point.

INGREDIENTS	WEIGHT		MEASURE
room temperature	*grams*	*pounds/ounces*	*volume*
CUSTARD			
castor sugar	50 grams	1¾ ounces	¼ cup
salt	—	—	pinch
gelatin	9.3 grams	—	1 tablespoon
5 egg yolks, size 2	93 grams	3¼ ounces	3 fluid ounces
pear poaching liquid (page 334)	400 grams	14 ounces	12 fluid ounces
cold double cream	232 grams	8 ounces	8 fluid ounces
ITALIAN MERINGUE			
castor sugar	66 grams	2¼ ounces	⅓ cup
water	30 grams	1 ounce	2 tablespoons
2 egg whites, size 2	60 grams	2 ounces	¼ cup
cream of tartar	—	—	¼ teaspoon
poire William's *or* eau-de-vie	28 grams	1 ounce	2 tablespoons

Italian Meringue: For maximum stability, the syrup must reach 248°F/120°C and not exceed 250°F/121°C as higher temperatures will break down the whites. The whites must be free of any grease or trace of yolk. Don't overbeat.

Bavarian: To prevent separation, the yolk mixture must start to thicken before adding the Italian meringue and whipped cream. If it starts to set prematurely, set the bowl briefly over hot water and stir until smooth. Once the Italian meringue and whipped cream have been added, avoid overmixing. Be sure to measure or weigh the gelatin. One envelope equals about 2¼ teaspoons using Foley measuring spoons. It may measure 2½ teaspoons with other brands of measuring spoons. The gelatin continues to thicken under refrigeration.

First make the custard. Refrigerate the mixing bowl for whipping the cream.

Have a fine strainer ready near the stove suspended over a small mixing bowl.

In a small, heavy, non-corrodible saucepan stir together 50 grams/ 1¾ ounces/¼ cup of the sugar, the salt, gelatin and yolks until well blended, using a wooden spoon.

In another small saucepan (or a heatproof glass measuring jug if using a microwave on high power) heat the pear poaching liquid to the boiling point. Stir a few tablespoons into the yolk mixture; then gradually add the remaining liquid, stirring constantly.

Heat the mixture to just below boiling point (180° to 190°F/82° to 88°C). Steam will begin to appear and the mixture will be slightly thicker than double cream. It will leave a well-defined track when a finger is run across the back of a spoon. Immediately remove from the heat and pour into the strainer, scraping up the thickened cream that settles on the bottom of the pan.

In the chilled bowl whip the cream until it mounds softly when dropped from a spoon. Refrigerate and prepare the Italian meringue.

Have ready a ¼-litre/½-pint/ 1-cup heatproof glass measuring jug near the stove.

In a small heavy saucepan (preferably with a non-stick lining) stir together the 66 grams/ 2¼ ounces/⅓ cup sugar and water. Heat, stirring constantly, until the sugar dissolves and the syrup is bubbling. Stop stirring and turn down the heat to the lowest setting. (If using electricity, remove from the heat.)

In a mixing bowl beat the egg whites until foamy, add the cream of tartar and beat until stiff peaks form when the beater is raised slowly.

Raise the heat and boil the syrup until a thermometer registers 248° to 250°F/120° to 121°C (firm-ball stage). Immediately remove from the heat and pour the syrup into the glass measure to stop the cooking.

If using an electric hand-held mixer, beat the syrup into the whites in a steady stream, avoiding the beaters, to keep the syrup from spinning on to the sides of the bowl. If using a stand mixer, pour a small amount of syrup over the whites with the mixer off. Immediately beat at high speed for 5 seconds. Stop the mixer and add a larger amount of syrup. Beat at high speed for 5 seconds. Continue with the remaining syrup. With the last addition use a rubber scraper to remove the syrup clinging to the glass measure. Beat at medium speed until cool (about 2 minutes). Cover with clingfilm and set aside.

Cool the custard sauce in an ice-water bath, stirring with a large wire whisk just until traces of whisk marks begin to appear. The mixture will start to set around the edges but will still be very liquid. Whisk in the pear eau-de-vie and, continuing with the whisk, fold in the Italian meringue and whipped cream until just incorporated. The mixture will be very billowy and soupy like melted ice cream. Remove at once from the water bath and pour into a 23-centimetre/9-inch *biscuit*-lined mould (page 423).

Note: If time allows, the Bavarian cream can be chilled in the refrigerator instead of stirred over ice water. It will take about $1\frac{1}{2}$ hours to thicken and should be stirred occasionally. The advantage of refrigeration over ice water is that the thickening process is more gradual so there is less danger of the mixture becoming too thick before folding in the remaining ingredients.

Meringue Icings, Fillings and Decorations

Royal icing, meringue and *dacquoise* all have two major ingredients in common: egg whites and sugar. Since their texture is dependent on properly beaten egg whites, this seems like a perfect place for a brief discussion on egg whites in general. First let's deal with the great baker's controversy: which beat better, fresh egg whites or aged? It's six of one, half a dozen of the other. Fresh whites are thicker so they take longer to beat. The resulting foam has less volume but more stability and loses less volume when folded into other ingredients. Older whites are thinner so they beat more quickly and yield greater but less stable volume. When folded into other ingredients they lose the extra volume.

The flavour of fresh egg whites is slightly superior to that of older whites, so I tend to prefer them for recipes like mousses where the egg white does not get cooked.

Now for a simple demystification from my dear friend and brilliant colleague, Shirley Corriher:

Egg white is made up of water and protein. When exposed to air, heat, or acid, the proteins in the egg white change from their original form (denature). For the perfect egg white foam, the egg whites should be beaten so that the egg white proteins denature (change) just the right amount. They must remain moist and flexible and not dry out and become rigid. When the beaten egg white, filled with air bubbles, goes into a hot oven or is subjected to hot syrup, it should be soft, moist, flexible, and able to expand until it reaches the temperature that coagulates (sets) it. Overbeating produces dried out, rigid egg white foam that will not expand properly in the oven. The cook has several secret weapons to produce the perfect degree of egg white denaturisation to result in beaten egg whites with the greatest volume and stability. These are the copper bowl, cream of tartar, and sugar. The copper bowl produces stable egg whites by combining with conalbumin, the protein in the egg white that lines each air bubble, to form a totally new protein, copper conalbumin. This copper conalbumin remains moist and flexible even when slightly overbeaten and provides a more stable foam.

Cream of tartar, an acid salt (byproduct of the wine industry), provides an even more stable foam in another way. The acid serves to denature the protein just enough to produce a moist stable foam. I have performed several experiments with cream of tartar and find that when the correct amount (1 teaspoon per 240 grams/8½ ounces/cup of egg whites) is used, there is no danger at all of overbeating. Because of this, I recommend always using cream of tartar for egg whites that will be cooked. If the egg whites will remain uncooked, I prefer the copper bowl because it offers the least possibility of extraneous flavour.

Sugar is effective with either the copper bowl or cream of tartar to keep the proteins moist and flexible because sugar itself holds moisture. Castor sugar is preferable because it dissolves faster. Sugar can be added at any time while beating the egg whites; however if added early it will require much longer beating and may not reach as great a volume. If added very late in the beating process, drying may have started to occur. Most recipes specify starting to add the sugar after the soft peak stage but before stiff peaks form.

Salt not only increases beating time, it decreases the foam's stability by drawing out water from the egg whites. I prefer adding salt to the other ingredients in the recipe.

Any fat substance or egg yolk is a foam inhibitor and even one drop will keep the egg whites from becoming stiff.

For the most stable foam, start beating the egg whites slowly, gradually increasing speed. Never decrease speed as the volume will permanently decrease. When it is necessary to stop the beater to check consistency, turn it off quickly and bring up speed quickly to prevent deflation.

When making a syrup to beat into egg whites, use a pan with a non-stick lining or a lot of the syrup will stick to the pan instead of getting into the whites.

Finally, because sugar is hygroscopic (readily absorbs water), *do not make royal icing, meringue or dacquoise on humid days* as they will be soft and sticky and will not set well.

The recipes in this chapter appear as components throughout the book in many interesting and varied ways. Royal icing is used for fine decorative designs on some of the special occasion cakes. Delicious, crunchy *dacquoise* is an important part of A Taste of Heaven (page 188), while crisp French meringue is juxtaposed against soft *génoise* and buttercream in Star-Spangled Rhapsody (page 193). Italian meringue adds its billowy texture to mixtures from buttercream to Bavarian cream. And, of course, the various meringues, from chocolate to green tea, are perfect to eat by themselves.

Royal Icing

Makes 170 grams/6 ounces/³/₄ cup

The amount of sugar in royal icing is almost five times the weight of the egg white, resulting in a very stiff meringue used exclusively for cake decorating. Flowers made from royal icing and air dried will last almost indefinitely, so many bakers feel they are great to have on hand. However, it was a royal icing rose which remains in my memory as one of the great disappointments of childhood. I still remember the birthday party – holding my breath as the serving knife approached that special piece with the exquisite pink rose on it, hoping against hope that it would be mine and then, with dizzying ecstasy, there it was being lowered towards my plate. The joy of that moment ended when the rose crumbled between my baby molars like so much powdered cement.

To this day, I would never dream of putting royal icing flowers on a cake and disappointing some other unsuspecting child. Real flowers are preferable, and most people realise that they are merely there for garnish. Once, though, at a wedding, my husband nervously pointed out a certain ambassador's wife cheerfully munching on a pale lavender cymbidium from one of my wedding cakes! (See edible flowers, page 493.)

Royal icing is extremely well suited to small decorative touches: dots on Dotted Swiss Dream (page 257), lilies of the valley embroidery on White Lily Cake (page 234), monograms (page 476), string work (page 466). I tend to use it in conjunction with rolled fondant because the dead white of the royal icing stands out against the off-white of the fondant, giving the fondant an alabaster quality. An added advantage to the royal icing is that, since it contains no fat, it is easy to correct mistakes – unlike buttercream which leaves grease marks when removed.

There is no cake more elegant or breathtakingly beautiful than one covered with rolled fondant and decorated with royal icing. As they are both over 80 per cent sugar, the main taste sensation is sweet. It is the one time I put beauty over flavour as long as the cake within is absolutely delicious.

STORE: 3 days tightly covered. The icing becomes slightly spongy on standing – rebeat lightly if necessary.

POINTERS FOR SUCCESS: To avoid flecks of fabric, don't sift icing sugar and air dry all utensils. Utensils and egg whites must be absolutely grease free. Royal icing will break down if subjected to

Triple Chocolate Cake, *page 232*

Checkerboard
Cake, *page 44*

Golden Grand
Marnier Cake,
page 34

Chocolate
Lover's Angel
Food Cake
page 181

Lemon Poppy
Seed Pound
Cake,
page 12

White Spice Pound Cake, *page 16*   Orange Glow Chiffon Cake, *page 174*

Plum Cake, *page 61*

Cordon Rose Cream Cheesecake, *page 82*,   Schoggi S (Chocolate S), *page 346*
with Fresh Cherry Topping, *page 393*

Sour Cream Coffee Cake, *page 93*   Chocolate Domingo Cake, *page 52*

Holiday Hallelujah
Streusel Brioche, *page 98*,
and Sticky Buns, *page 103*

Pineapple Upside-down
Cake, *page 96*

Blueberry
Buttermilk Pancakes,
page 106

White Lilac
Nostalgia,
page 190

Ethereal Pear
Charlotte, *page 199*

Praline Brioche
Cake, *page 195*

Golden Cage *(Zauber Torte)*, *page 196*

Chocolate Chip Charlotte, *page 204*

Orange Chocolate Crown, *page 206*

Chestnut Chocolate
Embrace *(La Châtaigne)*,
page 216

Rose Trellis, *page 239*

Dotted Swiss
Dream, *page 257*
(designed for *Bon
Appétit* magazine)

White Lily Cake,
page 234

Swiss Black Forest
Cake *(Schwarzwalder
Kirschtorte)*,
page 218

INGREDIENTS	WEIGHT		MEASURE
room temperature	*grams*	*pounds/ounces*	*volume*
1 egg white, size 2	30 grams	1 ounce	2 tablespoons
icing sugar	150 grams	5¼ ounces	1⅓ cups (lightly spooned into cup)

even a trace of grease, so all equipment should be washed well and rinsed in very hot water before using.

In a large mixing bowl place the egg white and sugar and beat, preferably with the whisk beater, at low speed until the sugar is moistened. Beat at high speed until very glossy and stiff peaks form when the beater is lifted (5 to 7 minutes). The tips of the peaks should curve slightly. If necessary, more icing sugar can be added. Use at once to make decorations, keeping the bowl covered with a damp cloth.

For spider-web-fine string work piped with a 1.5 millimetre tube, Irene di Bartollo, a great cake decorating artist and teacher, presses small amounts of icing through the toe of a nylon stocking to make sure that it is absolutely lump free!

Avoid preparing on humid days. If using a hand-held mixer, don't increase the size of the recipe because the icing is very stiff and may be hard on a weak motor.

Keep the bowl and pastry tube covered with a damp cloth when not in use because the icing crusts and hardens very quickly when exposed to air.

Note: I don't know where the myth got started that royal icing made with fresh egg white cannot be rebeaten. It is true that it cannot be rebeaten as many times or for as many days as royal icing made with meringue powder, but it definitely holds for up to 3 days.

VARIATION

Royal icing made with fresh egg whites is strong and elastic, making it ideal for string work. Royal icing made with meringue powder is only slightly less elastic but can be stored and rebeaten for up to 2 weeks. Meringue powder, available at cake decorating supply stores such as Maid of Scandinavia (page 513), contains mainly dried egg whites.

To make Meringue Powder Royal Icing: Replace the egg white with 1 tablespoon meringue powder and 2 tablespoons warm water (this is approximately the amount of water contained by the white). Proceed as for basic royal icing. Extra water or corn syrup may be added to the icing to soften it slightly for borders or string work (1 tablespoon per pound of icing sugar).

The addition of water will result in a harder, more brittle icing. If the weather is very dry and the icing crusts too quickly, 1 teaspoon glycerine per 896 grams/ 2 pounds icing sugar will keep it soft longer. To store the icing, place in an airtight container (not plastic, which is petrol-based and can break down the icing) at room temperature and rebeat before using.

CHOCOLATE ROYAL ICING:

For a light chocolate royal icing which contrasts nicely with Chocolate Rolled Fondant (page 356), add 2 tablespoons cocoa to the icing sugar.

Crisp French Meringue

Makes two 23-centimetre/9-inch or three 18-centimetre/7-inch discs

The classic proportions for crisp meringue are approximately double the weight of sugar to egg white. But there is a special reason I have called this recipe French meringue. It is because of a French pastry chef named Didier who came to visit me one day when I had just baked a batch of meringue shells. He hefted one on his thumb and three fingers and muttered in a low voice *'C'est lourd.'* ('It's heavy.') I wavered between insult and curiosity and then decided that I might have something to learn. It turns out that Didier's grandfather used mostly castor sugar for the meringue in his pastry shop and always put in a *poignet* ('fistful') of icing sugar. Since Didier could not recall the size of the batches prepared in his grandfather's bakery, I spent several days in my country kitchen experimenting with quantities ranging from 100 per cent icing sugar down to about 50 per cent (which turned out to be the ideal). Didier was right. These are the lightest meringues I've ever experienced.

Crisp meringue shells provide delightful containers for ice cream and fresh fruit. Meringue discs make spectacular cake components when used to sandwich layers of *génoise* as in Star-Spangled Rhapsody (page 193).

STORE: Tightly covered at room temperature and low humidity, meringues will keep for more than 6 months.

POINTERS FOR SUCCESS: Castor sugar is as fine as sand. You can make your own by processing granulated sugar for a few minutes in a food processor. All utensils

INGREDIENTS	WEIGHT		MEASURE
room temperature	*grams*	*pounds/ounces*	*volume*
4 egg whites, size 2	120 grams	4¼ ounces	4 fluid ounces
cream of tartar	—	—	½ teaspoon
castor sugar	115 grams	4 ounces	½ cup + 1 tablespoon
icing sugar	115 grams	4 ounces	1 cup (lightly spooned into cup)

and egg whites must be free of grease. *Avoid preparing on humid days.* Do not use parchment or a greased and floured baking sheet because meringue often sticks to them. To prevent cracking, do not open the oven door during the first three-quarters of cooking time.

Line a heavy baking sheet with a non-stick liner or foil. If making discs, trace the shape on to the foil or make a template to slip under the liner as a guide.

Preheat the oven to 200°F/110°C/gas mark ¼.

In a mixing bowl beat the whites until frothy, add the cream of tartar, and beat at medium speed while gradually adding 2 tablespoons castor sugar. When soft peaks form when the beater is raised, add 1 tablespoon castor sugar and increase the speed to high. When stiff peaks form as

the beater is raised slowly, gradually beat in the remaining castor sugar and beat until very stiff and glossy.

Sift icing sugar over the meringue and fold in using a slotted skimmer or large rubber spatula. Use at once to pipe or spread on the prepared baking sheet. (See piping instructions, page 431.)

If your oven has a pilot light, the ideal way to dry the meringue is to bake it for 1 hour at 200°F/110°C and then leave it overnight in the turned-off oven. Alternatively, bake the discs for 2 to 2½ hours at 200°F/110°C or until dry but not beginning to colour. The most reliable way to test for doneness is to dig out a small amount of meringue from the centre with the tip of a sharp knife. If only slightly sticky it will continue to dry at room temperature.

VARIATIONS

FIGURE PIPING MERINGUE:

When piping figures such as swans (page 434) for Blueberry Swan Lake (page 186) or mushrooms (page 433) for Cordon Rose Chocolate Christmas Log (page 227), a less fragile meringue is preferable. Replace the 115 grams/4 ounces/½ cup + 1 tablespoon icing sugar with 4 additional ounces castor sugar (using a total of 226 grams/8 ounces/ 1 cup + 2 tablespoons). Beat all the sugar into the meringue. For piping and baking instructions, see pages 433 and 434.

PINE NEEDLE MERINGUE:

Elizabeth Andoh and I worked out this Japanese-inspired pale green meringue, ideal for piping the most fragile of pine needles (page 431). Use 2 egg whites (60 grams/ 2 ounces/¼ cup) and beat in (50 grams/ 1¾ ounces/¼ cup castor sugar which has been whisked with 2 teaspoons Japanese powdered green tea (page 495). For piping and baking instructions, see page 431.

COCOA MERINGUE:

Whisk 2 tablespoons cocoa with the icing sugar until uniformly blended. For piping and baking little puffs, round or heart-shaped discs and meringue sticks, see pages 431 and 432.

CHOCOLATE-SPANGLED MERINGUE:

For a pale tan meringue with little speckles of chocolate throughout, place the icing sugar and 56 grams/2 ounces unsweetened chocolate in a food processor and process until the chocolate is powdery. Fold into the beaten whites until uniformly blended. This meringue has a lovely chocolate flavour and dissolves in the mouth. The bitter chocolate makes it less sweet than other meringue recipes. Spangled meringue can be piped into little puffs, round or heart-shaped discs, or sticks (pages 431 and 432).

Light Italian Meringue

Makes 260 grams/9 ounces/5 cups

Classic Italian meringue has double the weight of sugar to egg whites. This recipe has only a little more than 1½ times the sugar, giving it just enough body and sweetness to support the addition of lemon curd for Lemon Cream Illusion (page 308).

STORE: 2 hours room temperature, 2 days refrigerated. Rebeat briefly before using.

POINTERS FOR SUCCESS: For maximum stability, syrup must reach 248°F/120°C and not exceed

INGREDIENTS	WEIGHT		MEASURE
room temperature	*grams*	*pounds/ounces*	*volume*
castor sugar	175 grams	6 ounces	¾ cup + 2 tablespoons
water	60 grams	2 ounces	2 fluid ounces
4 egg whites, size 2	120 grams	4¼ ounces	4 fluid ounces
cream of tartar	—	—	½ teaspoon

250°F/121°C as higher temperatures will break down the whites. The whites must be free of any grease or trace of yolk. Do not overbeat. *Avoid preparing on humid days.*

Have ready near the stove a ¼-litre/½-pint/1-cup heatproof glass measuring jug.

In a small heavy saucepan (preferably with a non-stick lining) stir together 150 grams/5¼ ounces/¾ cup sugar and the water. Heat, stirring constantly, until the sugar dissolves and the syrup is bubbling. Stop stirring and turn down the heat to the lowest setting. (If using an electric range remove from the heat.)

In a mixing bowl beat the egg whites until foamy, add the cream of tartar, and beat until soft peaks form when the beater is raised slowly. Gradually beat in the remaining 2 tablespoons sugar until stiff peaks form when the beater is raised slowly. Increase the heat and boil the syrup until a thermometer registers 248° to 250°F/120° to 121°C (firm-ball stage). Immediately pour into the glass measure to stop the cooking.

If using an electric hand-held mixer, beat the syrup into the whites in a steady stream, avoiding the beaters to keep the syrup from spinning on to the sides of the bowl. If using a stand mixer, pour a small amount of syrup over the whites with the mixer off.

Immediately beat at high speed for 5 seconds. Stop the mixer and add a larger amount of syrup. Beat at high speed for 5 seconds. Continue with the remaining syrup. With the last addition use a rubber scraper to remove the syrup clinging to the measure. Beat at medium speed until cool (about 2 minutes).

UNDERSTANDING
People have asked me if it is possible to use glucose (which has

less water than corn syrup) to replace the water and some of the sugar the way I use corn syrup for Neoclassic Buttercream (page 266).

Unfortunately, the resulting Italian meringue does not get firm enough even when the syrup is brought to 248°F/120°C.

Chocolate Italian Meringue
(Neve Nero)

Makes 18 biscuits

This fantastic recipe is a *lagniappe* (a Louisiana word defined as 'an extra gift'). It is neither a cake nor a component of a cake but rather a romantically named biscuit, crunchy on the outside, chocolaty-chewy inside. The recipe was a gift to me from a charming Swiss baker, Arthur Oberholzer. He enticed me by telling me that chocolate Italian meringue is called *neve nero* (black snow) in Italy. This mixture is used to make a famous Swiss biscuit simply known as the Schoggi S (Chocolate S) because it is piped in that shape. He said it is so tricky and delicate 'no one ever succeeds on the first try'. The challenge was on. One biscuit from my successful first batch was promptly mailed to Arthur Oberholzer, who now lives in Florida. Considering the humidity down there, I'll never know if he was adequately impressed!

Have ready a large pastry bag fitted with a large 4.5-millimetre star tube and a 43 × 36-centimetre/ 17 × 14-inch baking sheet lined with a non-stick liner or foil.

STORE: 1 week to 10 days room temperature.

POINTERS FOR SUCCESS: *Avoid preparing on humid days.* For maximum stability, the syrup must reach 248°F/120°C and not exceed 250°F/121°C as higher temperatures will break down the whites. The whites must be free of any grease or trace of yolk.

The melted chocolate should be warm (ideally 100°F/38°C) when added to the meringue. Beating must be minimal after adding the chocolate. Pipe the mixture while still hot. To prevent cracking, do not open the oven door during the

INGREDIENTS	WEIGHT		MEASURE
room temperature	grams	pounds/ounces	volume
castor sugar	285 grams	10 ounces	1¼ cups + 3 tablespoons
water	80 grams	2¾ ounces	2½ fluid ounces
4 egg whites, size 2	120 grams	4¼ ounces	4 fluid ounces
cream of tartar	—	—	½ teaspoon
unsweetened chocolate, melted and slightly cooled	57 grams	2 ounces	—
optional: 4 drops red food colour★	—	—	—

★ Four drops of red food colour give the chocolate a richer appearance.

early stage of baking. *Don't overbake*. The biscuits should be chewy, not dry, inside.

Have ready a ½-litre/1-pint/2-cup heatproof glass measuring jug near the stove.

In a small heavy saucepan (preferably with a non-stick lining) stir together 250 grams/ 8¾ ounces/1¼ cups sugar and the water. Heat, stirring constantly, until the sugar dissolves and the syrup is bubbling. Stop stirring and turn down the heat to the lowest setting. (If using electricity remove from the heat.)

In a mixing bowl beat the egg whites until foamy, add the cream of tartar, and beat until soft peaks form when the beater is raised. Gradually beat in the remaining sugar until stiff peaks form when the beater is raised slowly.

Increase the heat and boil the syrup until a thermometer registers 248° to 250°F/120° to 121°C (firm-ball stage). Immediately pour into the glass measure to stop the cooking.

If using an electric hand-held mixer, beat the syrup into the whites in a steady stream. Don't allow the syrup to fall on the beaters or they will spin the syrup on to the sides of the bowl. If using a stand mixer, pour a small amount of syrup over the whites with the mixer off. Immediately beat at high speed 5 seconds. Stop the mixer and add a larger amount of syrup. Beat at high speed for 5 seconds. Continue with remaining syrup. With the last addition use a rubber scraper to remove the syrup clinging to the measure. Beat for 1 minute.

Now comes the critical moment. Stop beating, disengage the beater, and add the melted chocolate and optional food colour. Holding the beater with your hand, immediately beat for a few seconds *only until incorporated.* Transfer at once to the pastry bag and pipe immediately while still hot. If overbeaten, the mixture will be soft and the ridges will not show.

Use a small spot of meringue at each corner of the pan to attach the liner. Pipe large, high S shapes, allowing the mixture to fall from the bag. Avoid flattening it by having the pastry tip too low. From end to end each S should measure 9 centimetres/3½ inches. They will expand 1 centimetre/ ½ inch when baked so leave at least 4 centimetres/1½ inches between the biscuits. Allow the biscuits to dry for 2 hours or until set. (When a fingertip touches the surface, the meringue stays intact.)

Preheat the oven to 350°F/180°C/gas mark 4. Place the biscuits in the preheated oven for 10 minutes. Lower the heat to 200°F/110°C/gas mark ¼ and bake without opening the oven door just until they can easily be removed (using your fingers) from the baking sheet. This will take 20 to 30 minutes. Do not overbake. The biscuits should be wet inside as they continue to dry on removal from the oven and should be soft and chewy inside even after cooling.

Put the biscuits on a rack and as soon as they are cool store in airtight containers.

VARIATION
Instead of S shapes, pipe hearts (page 479). Broken pieces of this meringue are an interesting addition when folded into Bavarian cream.

UNDERSTANDING
This recipe is based on classic Italian meringue because it needs the greatest stability to stand up to the fat in the chocolate. In fact, 57 grams/2 ounces/¼ cup extra sugar have been added for further stability. This is possible because the sweetness is tempered by the use of unsweetened chocolate.

Dacquoise

Makes two 23-centimetre/9-inch or three 18-centimetre/7-inch discs

A *dacquoise* is an exceptionally light and crisp meringue made with ground nuts. The nuts make it pale brown in colour with a delicious nutty flavour. Crunchy, flavourful nuts are best. Use almonds, hazelnuts or a combination of both. The mixture can be piped into discs or heart shapes and used to sandwich *génoise* and pink Classic Buttercream in A Taste of Heaven (page 188).

STORE: Tightly covered at room temperature and low humidity, the *dacquoise* will keep for several weeks. The nuts will eventually become rancid.

POINTERS FOR SUCCESS: Because grease breaks down meringue, it is important to grind the nuts in such a way that there is as little grease released as possible. If using a food processor, the best method is to use the shredding disc. Then add the cornflour and use the steel blade to pulse until fine. Castor sugar is as fine as sand. You can make your own by processing granulated sugar in a food processor. The *dacquoise* will not be as light and delicate if you use granulated instead of castor sugar. All utensils and egg whites must be free of

INGREDIENTS	WEIGHT		MEASURE
room temperature	*grams*	*pounds/ounces*	*volume*
toasted, peeled, and finely ground almonds or hazelnuts	113 grams	4 ounces	¾ to 1 cup
cornflour	12 grams	—	1½ tablespoons
castor sugar	113 grams	4 ounces	½ cup + 1 tablespoon
icing sugar	85 grams	3 ounces	¾ cup (lightly spooned into cup)
4 egg whites, size 2	120 grams	4¼ ounces	4 fluid ounces
cream of tartar	—	—	½ teaspoon

grease. *Avoid preparing on humid days.* Do not use parchment or a greased and floured baking sheet as *dacquoise* often sticks to them. To prevent cracking, do not open the oven door during the first three-quarters of baking time.

Line a heavy baking sheet with a non-stick liner or foil. If making discs, trace the shape on to the foil or make a template to slip under the liner as a guide.

Preheat the oven to 200°F/110°C/gas mark ¼.

In a food processor pulse the ground nuts, cornflour, half the castor sugar, and all the icing sugar a few times to thoroughly combine. Set aside in a small bowl.

In a large mixing bowl beat the whites until frothy, add the cream of tartar, and beat at medium speed while gradually adding 1 table-spoon castor sugar. When soft peaks form when the beater is raised, gradually add the remaining castor sugar and beat at high speed until stiff peaks form when the beater is raised slowly.

Fold in the reserved nut mixture with a slotted skimmer or large rubber spatula. Use at once to pipe or spread on the prepared baking sheet. (See piping instructions, page 432.) If the mixture is too soft to pipe well, pipe only an outline and fill in the centre with a spoon.

If your oven has a pilot light, the ideal way to dry the *dacquoise* is to bake it for 1 hour and then leave it overnight in the turned-off oven. Alternatively, bake the discs for 1½ to 2 hours or until dry but not beginning to colour. The most reliable way to test for doneness is to dig out a small amount of *dacquoise* from the centre with the tip of a sharp knife. If only slightly sticky it will continue to dry at room temperature.

UNDERSTANDING
Dacquoise varies in the proportion of nuts and sugar to egg white. It is possible to use as much as two-thirds the combined weight of the egg whites and sugar in nuts but the *dacquoise* will be more fragile and have less body. The above recipe uses almost equal weight nuts and egg whites and, instead of double the sugar to egg whites, it has 1¾ the sugar. This decrease in sugar and the addition of nuts makes it far less sweet than a meringue. A small amount of cornflour is used to help absorb any grease exuded by the nuts.

VARIATION

CHOCOLATE DACQUOISE:

For a delicate chocolate flavour and colour, whisk 2 tablespoons cocoa into the icing sugar.

Candy and Nut Embellishments

All the recipes in this chapter, with the minor exception of chopped nuts, are on the sweet side of the dessert spectrum. Fondants, marzipans, caramel and nougatine all have sugar as their major ingredient. Although I would not eat most of these components on their own, each can contribute something very special to the flavour and texture of a cake.

Rolled fondant is easy to prepare and fun to handle. It has a sensual, satiny texture that is lovely to smooth into place. It drapes and clings to a cake, sealing in freshness for several days and giving you time for the most painstaking and impressive piped decorations.

Chocolate rolled fondant, my newest creation, has the attributes of classic white rolled fondant with a delicious flavour and texture.

Caramel is a component that has endless possibilities: it can be spun into angel's hair, threaded into a golden cage to adorn a cake (page 361), or grated into gold dust to sprinkle on top of a cake or to add to buttercream and melted chocolate for that special burnt sugar flavour and crunchy texture.

With the addition of nuts, caramel becomes nougatine, a crunchy confection that can be moulded into forms and filled with cake and buttercream as in Barquettes Chez L'Ami Louis (page 213).

Marzipan, another confectionery component based on nuts and sugar, also adds superb flavour, texture and colour to cakes. The finest marzipan in the world is said to come from Lübeck, Germany, and there is a recipe in this chapter that rivals its silky texture and almond-imbued flavour. Pistachio marzipan can be incorporated into a cake (Pistachio and Rose Wedding Cake, see colour photograph) with its intense flavour and exquisite green colour echoing the stems of the roses garnishing the cake. Orange marzipan, flecked with bits of golden zest, is especially delicious beneath a cake encased in or drizzled with dark chocolate glaze.

The recipes in this chapter truly deserve an honoured place in this book as the most breathtaking and dramatic of all decorations. From the alabaster perfection of rolled fondant to the ethereal spun gold of angel's hair, these recipes offer joy in the making, a dramatic presentation and magical eating.

Food Processor
Poured Fondant

Makes 600 grams/1¹/₃ pounds/1³/₄ cups (enough to glaze a 23-centimetre/9-inch cake)

This shiny fondant is the traditional topping for petits fours but can be used to glaze larger cakes as well. I sometimes add it to marzipan for a more refined texture. Professional bakers rarely make poured fondant because it is available ready made and keeps for months refrigerated. Classic poured fondant has always been too slow and tedious for most people to bother with (even for me, who will spend hours embroidering a cake) until Helen Fletcher, in *The New Pastry Cook*, came up with this superb food processor method which makes it easier to prepare than to order!

STORE: 1 week at room temperature, 6 months refrigerated.

POINTERS FOR SUCCESS: See Sugar Syrups (page 500). To prevent premature crystallisation, do not stir after the syrup comes to a boil. To keep the temperature from rising too high, remove the pan from the heat slightly before the syrup reaches 238°F/114°C and pour into the processor as soon as it reaches 238°F/114°C. It is essential to use an accurate thermometer (page 520). To prevent crystallisation, the thermometer must be clean before reinsertion into syrup. When reheating fondant, do not use an aluminium pan as it causes discoloration. Fondant must not be overheated or it will lose its shine.

Avoid vigorous stirring to prevent air bubbles.

Have ready near the stove a food processor fitted with the steel blade.

In a medium-size, heavy saucepan (preferably with a non-stick lining) combine the sugar, water and corn syrup and bring to the boil, stirring constantly. Stop stirring and allow the syrup to cook to the soft-ball stage (238°F/114°C). Immediately pour into the food processor.

Wash the thermometer and reinsert into the syrup. Allow to cool, uncovered, to exactly 140°F/60°C. This will take 25 to 35 minutes. Add optional flavouring and process for 2 to 3 minutes or until the fondant becomes opaque. (The fondant

INGREDIENTS	WEIGHT		MEASURE
room temperature	*grams*	*pounds/ounces*	*volume*
castor sugar	500 grams	17½ ounces	2½ cups
water	118 grams	4 ounces	4 fluid ounces
corn syrup	82 grams	3 ounces	2 fluid ounces
optional: 1 teaspoon pure vanilla extract *or* ¼ teaspoon almond essence	—	—	—

starts as a transparent syrup. As crystallisation of the sugar starts, it becomes translucent and finally opaque or white.)

Pour the fondant into a heatproof container, such as a ½-litre/1-pint/2-cup glass measuring jug, lined with a small heavy-duty plastic freezer bag. Close the bag without sealing. When completely cool and firm, expel the air, seal the bag and lift out of the container. Store at room temperature for at least 24 hours.

TO GLAZE CAKES WITH FONDANT
Fondant must be thinned to make it pourable. Prepare a stock syrup (30 per cent syrup) by combining 1 part water to 2 parts sugar (by volume) and bring it to a full boil, stirring constantly. Cool until warm. The syrup will keep for months at room temperature.

Heat the fondant in the top of a double boiler set over hot water, stirring gently, until warm. To maintain its sheen, fondant must not exceed 105°F/40°C. Stir in enough warm syrup to make the fondant pourable.

UNDERSTANDING
This fondant is prepared by controlling crystallisation of the sugar syrup. The thermometer is washed after removing it from the boiling syrup so that, on reinsertion, the syrup clinging to the thermometer does not cause premature crystallisation. Crystallisation can also occur if sugar crystals form on the sides of the saucepan, but they usually get washed down by the steam of the boiling syrup. The syrup can be covered for 1 minute after coming to a full boil to ensure that this takes place.

Classic Rolled Fondant

*Makes 1 kilogram 40 grams/2½ pounds (enough to cover a 23 × 10-centimetre/
9 × 4-inch cake)*

A cake covered with the alabaster perfection of rolled fondant has the
most exquisite background for decorating. Rolled fondant is much less
painstaking to make than poured fondant (page 352). Instead of a shiny,
glistening surface, this fondant has a soft, matt glow.

Rolled fondant seals in the freshness of the cake for several days, giving
time for the most ethereal and elaborate of piped decorations. It also can
be cut into decorative shapes such as ribbons or *figures appliqués* (page
417).

This fondant originated in England, where it was used to cover
fruitcakes to keep them fresh. It is traditional for even a home cook to
wear only white when preparing fondant, because just tiny thread of
coloured fabric can cause an off colour.

STORE: 1 month room
temperature. Can be frozen
indefinitely.

Sprinkle the gelatin over the water
in a ½-litre/1-pint/2-cup heatproof
glass measuring jug or bowl and
allow it to sit for 5 minutes. Set in
a small pan of simmering water
and stir until the gelatin is
dissolved. (This can also be done in
a few seconds in a microwave on
high power.) Blend in the glucose
and glycerine, then add the fat and
stir until melted. Remove from the
heat.

Place the sugar in a large bowl
and make a well in the centre. Add
the gelatin mixture and stir with a
lightly greased wooden spoon until
blended. Mix with lightly greased
hands and knead vigorously in the
bowl until most of the sugar is

incorporated. Turn out on to a
smooth, lightly greased surface
such as Formica or marble and
knead until smooth and satiny. If
the fondant seems dry, add several
drops of water and knead well. If it
seems too sticky, knead in more
icing sugar. The fondant will
resemble a smooth, well-shaped
stone. When dropped, it should
spread very slightly but retain its
shape. It should be malleable like
clay, soft but not sticky.

Rolled fondant may be used at
once but seems to work more
easily when allowed to rest for
several hours. It is important to
cover the fondant to prevent it
from drying. Wrap it tightly with
clingfilm and place in an airtight
container. It will firm slightly on
standing.

When ready to roll out, spray the

INGREDIENTS	WEIGHT		MEASURE
room temperature	*grams*	*pounds/ounces*	*volume*
gelatin	10 grams	—	1 tablespoon
water*	60 grams	2 ounces	2 fluid ounces
glucose†	170 grams	6 ounces	4 fluid ounces
glycerine	18 grams	—	1 tablespoon
solid white lard	24 grams	¾ ounce	2 tablespoons
icing sugar	920 grams	2 pounds	8 cups (lightly spooned into cup)

* For a flavour variation replace 2 tablespoons water with rosewater, orange flower water or freshly squeezed lemon juice.
† 164 grams/5¾ ounces/½ cup corn syrup will give equal results if you use only 3 tablespoons water instead of 60 grams/2 ounces/2 fluid ounces.

work surface and rolling pin with non-stick vegetable spray. For covering a cake or making ribbons and *appliqués*, see pages 413 and 417.

Tips:

- If stored fondant seems very stiff, a few seconds in a microwave before kneading it makes it pliable and saves wear and tear on your hands!
- The easiest way to colour rolled fondant evenly is to add a touch of paste food colour to the finished fondant and blend it in with a food processor. At first it will separate into little pieces, but when it comes together to form a smooth ball the colour is evenly dispersed. The friction of the processor blades may heat the fondant enough to soften it slightly, but if allowed to rest for a few minutes it will firm up again. If the colour is too bright, simply knead in some uncoloured fondant.
- I use non-stick vegetable spray to grease the worktop, rolling pin, cutters – even my hands.
- For large batches: I use a 10 or 20-litre/16 or 32-pint mixer and the spade beater for the initial mixing. Kneading must always be done by hand or the texture suffers. A KitchenAid mixer can be used for smaller amounts, but stirring by hand is so quick and easy I usually don't use the mixer for small batches.
- Rolled fondant can be purchased already made, which is practical for large volume baking.

UNDERSTANDING

Rolled fondant is traditionally made with glucose. As corn syrup is merely a lower concentration of corn sugar (it contains more water) it will yield close to the same results if the water balance in the recipe is maintained. Technically, 9 tablespoons corn syrup contain the same corn sugar (glucose) as 170 grams/6 ounces/8 tablespoons glucose, but the amounts given here are more convenient to measure and work as well.

Although the outside of the fondant will form a thin hard crust, the glycerine keeps the inside soft and chewy. Glycerine is available in chemists and delicatessens.

Chocolate Rolled Fondant

Makes 1 kilogram 250 grams/2¾ pounds (enough to cover a 23 × 7.5-centimetre/9 × 3-inch cake and a 15 × 7.5-centimetre/ 6 × 3-inch cake)

This fondant is my proudest creation! When draped around a cake, at first glance it looks like 'plastic chocolate' (a traditional combination of chocolate and corn syrup), but the differences are soon apparent. Instead of a high shine, it has a soft glow that seems lit from within, strongly reminiscent of the warm sensuality of fine Italian leather. And the taste! It is intensely chocolaty and fudgy. The cocoa keeps the fondant from being too sweet. It also allows it to be more malleable than 'plastic chocolate' because there is only 3.5 per cent cocoa butter compared to the 20 per cent in the chocolate used to make plastic chocolate. This makes Chocolate Rolled Fondant a treat even for those on a low-saturated-fat diet.

STORE: 1 week room temperature, 1 month refrigerated, 6 months frozen. Although refrigerated fondant does not lose its texture, the flavour becomes unpleasant after 1 month.

Sprinkle the gelatin over the water in a ½-litre/1-pint/2-cup heatproof glass measuring jug or bowl and allow to sit for 5 minutes. Set in a small pan of simmering water and stir until the gelatin is dissolved. (This can also be done in a few seconds in a microwave on high power, stirring once or twice.) Blend in the corn syrup and glycerine, then add the fat and stir

INGREDIENTS	WEIGHT		MEASURE
room temperature	*grams*	*pounds/ounces*	*volume*
gelatin	10 grams	—	1 tablespoon
water	80 grams	2¾ ounces	2½ fluid ounces
corn syrup	215 grams	7½ ounces	5¼ fluid ounces
glycerine	18 grams	—	1 tablespoon
solid white vegetable lard	48 grams	1¾ ounces	¼ cup
pure vanilla extract	4 grams	—	1 teaspoon
icing sugar	720 grams	1 pound 9 ounces	6¼ cups (lightly spooned into cup)
unsweetened cocoa *or* 205 grams/7¼ ounces/2½ cups nonalkalised cocoa	200 grams	7 ounces	2 cups + 2 tablespoons (lightly spooned into cup)

until melted. Remove from the heat and stir in the vanilla.

Mix the sugar and cocoa in a large bowl and make a well in the centre. Add the gelatin mixture and stir with a wooden spoon until blended. Mix with your hands and knead vigorously in the bowl until it forms a ball. Turn out on to a smooth, lightly greased surface such as Formica or marble, clean your hands, and knead until smooth and satiny. If the fondant seems dry or brittle, add several drops of water and knead well. The water will make it very sticky and messy at first. When the mixture holds together, scrape the worktop clean, lightly grease it and knead the fondant until smooth.

Chocolate Rolled Fondant may be used at once but is easier to work with if made 1 day ahead to give the moisture a chance to distribute evenly. It is important to cover the fondant to prevent drying out. Wrap tightly with clingfilm and place in an airtight container.

When ready to roll out, spray the work surface and rolling pin with non-stick vegetable spray. Don't be alarmed if tiny cracks appear in the surface of the fondant; the warmth from kneading or pressure from the rolling pin will make it smooth and satiny. For covering a cake or making ribbons and *appliqués*, see pages 413 and 417.

Tips:
- If the cocoa is lumpy, process it in a food processor for a few seconds until powdery. If lumpy cocoa is used it may not incorporate evenly into the fondant. If this should happen, the chocolate fondant can also be placed in the food processor for a few seconds until completely smooth. Don't try to process the whole batch at one time.
- I use non-stick vegetable spray to grease the worktop, rolling pin, cutters – even my hands.
- If stored fondant seems very stiff, a few seconds in a microwave before kneading it will make it pliable.
- Don't be tempted to substitute butter for the solid white lard. This is one rare instance where there is no perceivable difference in flavour and the lard actually blends better (without streaking) than the butter.

UNDERSTANDING
Compared to Classic Rolled Fondant, Chocolate Rolled Fondant replaces 200 grams/7 ounces powdered sugar with cocoa. Because cocoa behaves differently, the fondant now requires double the fat, a little more glucose or corn syrup, and about double the water.

Pastillage

Makes 600 grams/1¼ pounds/1¾ cups

Pastillage is rolled fondant without any of the softening ingredients (glycerine, corn syrup or fat). It is used mainly for decorative ribbons, three-dimensional shapes and *appliqués* because it dries bone-hard and crusts more quickly than fondant.

STORE: 1 month room temperature. Can be frozen indefinitely.

Sprinkle the gelatin over the water in a small heatproof glass bowl and allow to sit for 5 minutes. Set in a small pan of simmering water and stir until the gelatin is dissolved. (This can also be done in a few seconds in a microwave on high power.) Remove from the heat.

Combine the sugar, cornflour and optional cream of tartar in a large bowl and make a well in the centre. Add the gelatin mixture and

INGREDIENTS	WEIGHT		MEASURE
room temperature	*grams*	*pounds/ounces*	*volume*
gelatin	10 grams	—	1 tablespoon
water	74 grams	2¼ ounces	2½ fluid ounces
icing sugar	454 grams	1 pound	4 cups (lightly spooned into cup)
cornflour	64 grams	2¼ ounces	½ cup (lightly spooned into cup)
optional: pinch cream of tartar	—	—	—

stir with a wooden spoon until blended. Mix with lightly greased hands and knead vigorously in the bowl until most of the sugar is incorporated. Turn out on to a smooth, lightly greased surface such as Formica or marble and knead until smooth and satiny. If the pastillage seems very dry, add several drops of water and knead well. If it seems too sticky, knead in more icing sugar. The pastillage will resemble a smooth, well-shaped stone. When dropped, it should not spread.

Pastillage is easiest to work with if it has rested for at least 1 hour. It dries very quickly so it is important to cover it to prevent drying. I wrap it in a cloth rubbed with a bit of solid white lard, then tightly in clingfilm, and place it in an airtight container.

When ready to roll out, spray the work surface and rolling pin with non-stick vegetable spray. For making ribbons and *appliqués*, see pages 413 and 417. Pastillage can be rolled out as thinly as 1.5 millimetres/¹⁄₁₆ inch. It dries and holds its shape very quickly.

Tips:
• If stored pastillage seems very stiff, a few seconds in the microwave make it pliable.
• To give pastillage the look of real marble, dab it with a bit of coffee concentrate or brown food colour and knead only until the colour streaks.

UNDERSTANDING
The acidity of cream of tartar whitens the pastillage. Because there is no corn syrup or fat, the pastillage does not have the pearly quality of rolled fondant.

Caramel

TIPS FOR WORKING WITH CARAMEL

- Do not make any form of caramel except caramel sauce in humid weather – it will be sticky.
- When making the sugar syrup, bring it to the boil stirring constantly, then stop stirring so the sugar will not crystallise.
- Oil the worktop and all utensils to prevent sticking.
- Use a pan that conducts heat well (such as unlined copper, aluminium or anodised aluminium) so that cooking stops soon after it is removed from the heat. Alternatively, have ready a larger pan or sink partly filled with cold water to immerse the bottom of the pan. Do not use a pan with a tin or non-stick lining as the melting point is below that of caramel.
- To determine the colour of the caramel, use an accurate thermometer or drop a bit of caramel on a white surface such as a porcelain plate. When making spun sugar, too light a caramel produces a ghostly effect, too dark produces a brassy colour when spun.
- To prevent breakage, never put a thermometer used for caramel into water until completely cool.
- Soaking utensils in hot water will remove all hardened caramel.
- When making a caramel cage, allow the caramel to cool until it falls in thick strands. Make extra loops at the base for strength.
- To make large amounts of spun sugar, cut the loops of a wire whisk with a wire cutter or bend the tines of a 'cake breaker' (page 531).
- *Most importantly:* When making caramel, be careful to concentrate every moment. Sugar burns are extremely painful.

DO NOT MAKE IN HUMID WEATHER – CARAMEL WILL BE STICKY

Caramel for a Cage and Gold Dust

This amber, hard-as-glass burnt sugar offers many dramatic ways to enhance cakes. Drizzled on the back of a bowl it becomes a lacy, golden cage with which to encase a cake; spun in the air it metamorphosises into golden angel's hair; ground into a powder and sprinkled on top of buttercream, it sparkles like gold dust. Combined with ground nuts and melted chocolate the caramel becomes a wonderful confection that can be rolled paper thin and draped over a cake.

STORE: The caramel cage can be returned to the outside of the well-oiled Kugelhupf tin. Stored in an airtight container at room temperature away from humidity, it will keep for 2 to 3 weeks. The caramel powder will keep several weeks at room temperature and several months frozen.

INGREDIENTS	WEIGHT		MEASURE
room temperature	*grams*	*pounds/ounces*	*volume*
castor sugar	200 grams	7 ounces	1 cup
water	80 grams	2¾ ounces	2½ fluid ounces
cream of tartar	–	–	⅛ teaspoon
optional: Crystallised Violets (page 375)	–	–	–

In a small heavy saucepan combine the ingredients and cook over medium-low heat, stirring constantly, to dissolve the sugar. Increase the heat and boil without stirring until pale amber (350° to 360°F/177° to 182°C. Remove from the heat and set the bottom of the pan in cold water to stop the cooking. Allow to cool for 7 minutes or until no more than 240°F/115°C. The caramel will not fall in thick strings when warmer. Reheat if necessary. (I like to pour caramel into a heatproof glass measuring jug. Reheating is then easily accomplished by a few seconds in a microwave on high power.)

TO MAKE CAGE

Invert a Kugelhupf tin (page 517) and cover it, preferably with a non-stick liner or foil. If using a non-stick liner, tape it to the inside of the tin to keep it in place. If using foil, mould it to the tin and trim it flush with the bottom. Do not curve the foil under the tin or the cage will crack when the foil is removed. The neck of the tin can be held or suspended from a soda bottle. Dip a spoon in the caramel and allow the caramel to fall over the tin in lacy strands. If desired, glue crystallised violets on the cage with dabs of caramel.

When the cage has hardened, remove it from the tin. With the non-stick liner it will slide right off, but with the foil it is necessary to invert on to a soft tea-towel. Carefully remove the tin and the foil by pulling it gradually away from the sides of the cage.

TO MAKE CARAMEL POWDER

Remelt any remaining caramel and pour it on to a piece of foil to harden. Break into small pieces and process in a food processor until powdery. Store in an airtight jar.

Tips: A porcelain spoon is perfect for applying caramel because it does not conduct heat.

Candied violets or dragées can be attached to the cage before it has completely hardened or can be attached later using more melted caramel or a dot of Royal Icing (page 340).

Caramel for Praline Powder and Chocolate Praline

Makes 265 grams/9¹/₂ ounces/2 cups

STORE: 3 weeks room temperature.

INGREDIENTS	WEIGHT		MEASURE
room temperature	*grams*	*pounds/ounces*	*volume*
hazelnuts, peeled	142 grams	5 ounces	1 cup
castor sugar	142 grams	5 ounces	²/₃ cup
water	60 grams	2 ounces	2 fluid ounces

Bake the hazelnuts in a 350°F/180°C/gas mark 4 oven for 20 minutes or until lightly browned. Place them on a non-stick or lightly oiled baking sheet or a 30-centimetre/12-inch square of lightly oiled heavy-duty foil.

In a small heavy saucepan combine the sugar and water and bring to the boil over medium heat, stirring constantly, until the sugar is dissolved. Increase the heat to medium-high and boil undisturbed until the sugar begins to caramelise. It will begin to look like dark corn syrup and take on the characteristic smell of burnt sugar. (The temperature should be 370°F/188°C.) *Immediately* pour the caramel over the nuts. Allow to harden completely (15 to 20 minutes). Remove from the sheet and break into a few pieces. Grind in a food processor until finely powdered.

UNDERSTANDING

This praline powder has 50 per cent hazelnuts, just like the finest quality praline paste, but it has a crunchier texture.

VARIATION

CHOCOLATE PRALINE:

Quick-temper 224 grams/8 ounces chocolate (page 439), preferably extra bittersweet or bittersweet, to 89° to 91°F/32° to 33°C. Stir in the praline powder until smooth. Pour the mixture on to six 30.5-centimetre/12-inch long sheets of greaseproof paper. Cover with more greaseproof paper and roll into thin oval sheets. Stack on a baking sheet and chill briefly or until firm enough to peel off the paper. For shaping, see decorative techniques, page 446. Store airtight. If necessary, chocolate can be retempered even with the praline in it.

Caramel for Spun Sugar (Angel's Hair)

STORE: In an airtight container at room temperature with low humidity, spun sugar nests will keep 2 to 3 weeks. Frozen they will keep for months. Spun sugar will keep for several hours at room temperature if the weather is very dry. If humid, it becomes sticky and tends to settle or mat instead of maintaining light, separate strands.

INGREDIENTS	WEIGHT		MEASURE
room temperature	*grams*	*pounds/ounces*	*volume*
castor sugar	100 grams	3½ ounces	½ cup
corn syrup	108 grams	3¾ ounces	3 fluid ounces
optional: grated beeswax	—	—	1 teaspoon

Cover the floor near the table or worktop with newspaper. Oil the handles of 2 long wooden spoons or broom sticks and tape them to the worktop 30.5 centimetres/ 12 inches apart so that the handles extend well beyond the edge of the worktop.

Have ready near the stove a ½-litre/1-pint/2-cup or larger heatproof glass measuring jug.

In a small heavy saucepan stir together the sugar and corn syrup and bring to the boil over medium heat, stirring constantly. Increase the heat and boil until amber and a thermometer registers 360°F/182°C. The caramel will continue cooking from the residual heat. If the temperature is below 360°F/182°C, the caramel will be pale and the spun sugar white instead of gold; over 370°F/188°C it will have a brassy colour. I find 370°F/188°C produces the perfect colour.

Transfer the caramel immediately to the heatproof glass measure to stop the cooking. Allow to cool for a few minutes. Add the optional beeswax and, when the smoking stops, check the caramel by lifting it with a fork to see if it will fall in strings rather than droplets. (Allow to cool a little longer if droplets form.)

Stand on a stool so that your arms are above the wooden handles. Using a cut whisk, bent cake breaker (page 531), or two forks held side by side, dip into the caramel and vigorously wave back and forth, allowing sugar to fall in long, fine threads over the handles. Waving must be continuous or small droplets will form. (It is normal to have a few of these droplets, known poetically as angel's tears.) If the caramel starts to get too thick, return it briefly to the heat but be careful not to darken or burn it.

Wrap the strands around the base and sides of a cake or an inverted oiled tin or bowl as they will not stay flexible for too long, especially if the beeswax was omitted. Any leftover strands may be shaped into little nests by pressing them into lightly oiled custard cups and freezing them in airtight containers. They can be filled with small colourful ovals of ice cream or sorbet.

UNDERSTANDING

See Sugar Syrups (page 500). The nature of sugar syrup, which is prone to recrystallisation when agitated, makes it necessary to use 'interfering agents' such as cream of tartar, lemon juice or corn syrup to inhibit recrystallisation when the caramel is to be used for dipping or agitated in any way. If, for example, when making praline you were to add the hazelnuts to caramel which does not have an interfering agent, the caramel would harden and crystallise and the texture would not be as fine as when the caramel is poured over the nuts and allowed to harden into a transparent sheet. Corn syrup is an invert sugar which inhibits crystallisation. It is added with beeswax to caramel for spun sugar because it keeps the strands flexible. Beeswax is preferable to paraffin because it has a higher smoking point.

Caramel can be made with no water by constantly stirring the sugar to prevent uneven browning. Just a few drops of lemon juice can be added to prevent crystallisation if the caramel will be used for dipping.

I find it far easier to add a little water to dissolve the sugar before allowing it to caramelise. The resulting caramel seems just as hard. Adding a large quantity of water, on the other hand, slows down caramelisation which results in a softer, stickier caramel.

Nougatine

Makes 12 barquettes (9.5 × 4.25 centimetres/3⁷/₈ × 1⁵/₈ inches)

In France nougatine, or nut brittle, is used for a number of decorative effects. When cool and hardened, it becomes strong enough to support considerable weight. It is often shaped into tiny cornucopias and filled with buttercream or into tart and barquette forms to replace conventional pastry shells. Leftover pieces can be coarsely crumbled in a food processor or with a mortar and pestle and sprinkled on ice cream or pressed into the sides of an iced cake.

The colour of finished nougatine, the shape and size of the nuts, and the proportion of nuts to sugar vary according to use. For decorative work, the nougatine is more attractive when paler in colour, with fewer nuts. Untoasted nuts make a more attractive contrast. For tiny pieces, sliced nuts are more difficult to mould, so coarsely chopped nuts are preferable. For nougatine that is prepared primarily for eating, allowing the syrup to reach a darker colour results in a stronger, richer flavour, and a higher proportion of nuts is desirable.

INGREDIENTS	WEIGHT		MEASURE
room temperature	*grams*	*pounds/ounces*	*volume*
castor sugar	132 grams	4¹/₂ ounces	²/₃ cup
corn syrup	108 grams	3³/₄ ounces	3 fluid ounces
butter	14 grams	¹/₂ ounce	1 tablespoon
toasted sliced almonds, coarsely chopped★	85 grams	3 ounces	1 cup

★ For large decorative pieces, use 64 grams/2¹/₄ ounces/³/₄ cup untoasted almond slices.

In a small heavy pan combine the sugar and corn syrup and bring to the boil, stirring constantly. Stop stirring and allow to boil undisturbed until pale amber to deep brown. Remove from the heat, add the butter and stir in the almonds.

Scrape the mixture on to a lightly oiled marble surface or baking sheet. Using oiled spatulas or triangular scrapers, turn the nougatine, folding in the corners to ensure even cooling. When cool enough to handle, cut off a small amount and keep the rest warm and flexible in a 300°F/150°C/gas mark 2 oven with the door ajar, under a hot lamp, or on a warming tray lined with lightly greased foil.

Use a lightly oiled heavy rolling pin and heavy pressure to roll the nougatine as thin as possible. In France a *laminoir* ('hollow iron rod') is used. For rolling nougatine, I prize my solid stainless-steel rod (a gift from my cabinetmaking father). The heavy weight makes rapid rolling easier, but an ordinary oiled wooden rolling pin will also work when pressure is applied.

Work quickly: if the nougatine hardens you will have to return it briefly to the heat until flexible again. When cutting shapes, be sure to oil all cutters or knives. To mould nougatine, press into or over a lightly oiled mould. Cut any uneven edges with a serrated knife while still warm. A pizza cutter or scissors work well if the nougatine is warm enough; if too cold the nougatine will shatter. For instructions on shaping barquettes, see page 422.

UNDERSTANDING

Nougatine, which is opaque, differs from transparent caramel by the controlled crystallisation of the sugar. Butter is added as the interfering agent to keep the addition of nuts from prematurely crystallising the sugar. The mixture is then turned and folded to promote the formation of fine, even sugar crystals, giving the nougatine its characteristic golden-brown opaque colour.

VARIATION

NOUGATINE HONEY CRUNCH:

I developed this honeyed version of nougatine especially for Queen Bee cake (page 211). The honey makes the nougatine delightfully sticky (as I imagine a beehive to be). For ease in application, it is best prepared the same day as the cake. For 200 grams/7 ounces/2 cups of Nougatine Crunch, make ½ recipe nougatine, replacing the corn syrup with ¼ cup honey and cooking the syrup to 360°F/182°C. Roll into a thin sheet and, when cool, chop coarsely.

Quintessential Marzipan

Makes 340 grams/¾ pound/1 cup + 2 tablespoons (enough to cover a 23 × 5-centimetre/9 × 2-inch cake)

I am really excited about this newly developed marzipan. It has the silkiest texture and most aromatic almond flavour of any marzipan I have ever tasted. Poured fondant, easily made in the food processor, is the secret for its marvellous texture. Icing sugar is added to make the marzipan stiff enough for rolling into a thin sheet.

STORE: 6 months refrigerated, 1 year frozen. Allow to come to room temperature before kneading to prevent oil separation.

INGREDIENTS	WEIGHT		MEASURE
room temperature	*grams*	*pounds/ounces*	*volume*
almond paste	200 grams	7 ounces	scant ¾ cup
Food Processor Poured Fondant (page 352), flavoured with almond essence	100 grams	3½ ounces	scant ⅓ cup
icing sugar	50 grams	1¾ ounces	½ cup − 1 tablespoon (lightly spooned into cup)

This marzipan is very easy to make in a food processor. It can also be made in a heavy-duty mixer such as a KitchenAid or kneaded by hand.

In a food processor fitted with a steel blade, combine all the ingredients and process for a few seconds until blended. The marzipan should still be in pieces. Turn on to a worktop (preferably wood to absorb excess oil) and knead until smooth.

Wrap tightly in clingfilm and place in an airtight container. Allow to rest for at least 1 hour before using.

Keep the marzipan well covered to avoid drying out while working with it. If the marzipan does become slightly dry and cracky, rub your fingers lightly with lard and knead lightly.

TO ROLL OUT MARZIPAN

Roll out 1.5 millimetres/^{1}/₁₆-inch thick between two sheets of clingfilm or on a smooth worktop lightly dusted with cornflour. See 'How to Cover a Cake with Marzipan' (page 416).

Tips: Any impurities, such as flecks of almond skin, can be removed using the tip of a sharp knife. Brushing the surface with melted cocoa butter will keep it from drying.

UNDERSTANDING

This marzipan has 62 per cent sugar and 38 per cent nuts. This is based on an almond paste which contains 33 per cent sugar (page 496). Marzipan normally has between 30 and 50 per cent nuts. The higher the percentage of sugar, the whiter the colour but the stiffer and more difficult it is to roll.

Classic marzipan is almond paste with extra sugar and glucose (or corn syrup) added to make it stiff enough for rolling. Most of the sugar/glucose is normally added in the form of a 250°F/121°C syrup. Since poured fondant is also a sugar syrup, made with the same ratio of sugar to glucose but with controlled crystallisation, it produces marzipan with a smoother texture.

Almond paste is a mixture of almonds, bitter almonds, sugar and glucose. Bitter almonds have a distinctive, aromatic flavour. As bitter almonds are very difficult, if not impossible, to obtain, it is best to use commercial almond paste.

VARIATION

ORANGE MARZIPAN:

Roland Mesnier, the White House pastry chef, shared this marvellous way of flavouring and delicately colouring marzipan. The orange zest also lends a slightly tart, refreshing quality to the marzipan. Knead 3 tablespoons very finely grated orange zest into 300 grams/ 10½ ounces/1 cup of marzipan.

GREEN TEA MARZIPAN:

Powdered Japanese green tea added to almond paste makes a speedy marzipan with a lovely, pale green colour. Although there is not really any perceivable flavour of green tea, the marzipan is far less sweet since no additional sugar is added. The marzipan is also compatible in spirit for decorating a Green Tea Biscuit filled with Green Tea Mousse Cream (page 302). Elizabeth Andoh, a food writer and specialist in Japanese cuisine, and I created this recipe as a joint effort.
To make Green Tea Marzipan: Knead 6 tablespoons almond paste with 1 teaspoon powdered green tea. Roll out between two sheets of clingfilm and cut into decorative shapes with a biscuit cutter or sharp knife.

Marzipan for Modelling

Makes 340 grams/³/4 pound/1¹/4 cups

This is a quick and easy marzipan with an ideal texture for sculpting figures or roses. Use food colour very sparingly. For the most realistic effect, vary the hues of the petals, using the lightest for the outer ones.

While the marzipan works wonderfully for shaping, it is not as delicious to eat as Quintessential Marzipan (page 368), so it is best reserved for decorations.

STORE: 6 months refrigerated, indefinitely frozen. Allow to come to room temperature before kneading to prevent oil separation.

INGREDIENTS	WEIGHT		MEASURE
room temperature	*grams*	*pounds/ounces*	*volume*
almond paste	142 grams	5 ounces	¹/2 cup
cornflour	60 grams	2 ounces	¹/2 cup (lightly spooned into cup)
icing sugar	60 grams	2 ounces	¹/2 cup (lightly spooned into cup)
corn syrup	62 grams	2 ounces	3 tablespoons
optional: paste food colour	—	—	—

This marzipan is very easy to make in a food processor. It can also be made in a heavy-duty mixer such as a KitchenAid or kneaded by hand.

Mix together the almond paste, cornflour and icing sugar until it falls in fine crumbs. Add the corn syrup mixed with a tiny speck of optional food colour and process until well incorporated. (The mixture should not look greasy. If you do overmix, the marzipan will be usable if allowed to rest until the oil is reabsorbed.) Pinch a small amount to see if it holds together. If still too dry, add a few drops of corn syrup.

Turn on to a smooth work surface and knead until very smooth and uniform in colour. Wrap tightly with clingfilm and place in an airtight container. Allow to rest for at least 1 hour before using.

Keep the marzipan well covered to avoid drying out while working with it. If the marzipan does become slightly dry and cracky, rub your fingers lightly with lard and knead lightly. Cover tightly with clingfilm and place in an airtight container.*

*For instructions on working with marzipan, see page 417.

Pistachio Marzipan

Makes 142 grams/5 ounces (enough for a 23-centimetre/9-inch disc)

People who don't like marzipan usually change their minds when they encounter this pistachio version. I created it as a surprise layer inside each tier of my brother's wedding cake (page 254). The thin line of pale green between layers of pale yellow buttercream and Crème Ivoire is an enchanting contrast, especially with the pale pink petals and green stems of the roses above. Pistachio Marzipan also makes marvellous ivy leaves to entwine around a Cordon Rose Chocolate Christmas Log (page 227).

INGREDIENTS	WEIGHT		MEASURE
room temperature	*grams*	*pounds/ounces*	*volume*
shelled unsalted pistachio nuts	38 grams	1¼ ounces	¼ cup
icing sugar	86 grams	3 ounces	¾ cup (lightly spooned into cup)
corn syrup	27 grams	1 ounce	1 tablespoon + 1 teaspoon
glycerine or unflavoured oil	3 grams	—	½ teaspoon
optional: 2 drops green food colour			

STORE: 6 months refrigerated, 1 year frozen.

Bake the nuts in a 350°F/180°C/gas mark 4 oven for 5 to 10 minutes or until the skins separate from the nuts when scratched lightly with a fingernail. Remove as much skin as possible.

Process the nuts in a food processor until a smooth paste is obtained. Add the sugar and process until well mixed. Add the corn syrup and glycerine and process until well blended, about 20 seconds. The mixture will appear dry, but a small amount pressed between your fingers should hold together. If it seems too dry, add more corn syrup, ¼ teaspoon at a time. If you wish to deepen the colour, add the optional food colouring. For ivy leaves, a dark green is desirable, so paste food colour (which is more intense) should be used. Process until the marzipan has a smooth, dough-like consistency. Knead briefly by hand until uniform in colour.

Marzipan may be used at once but is easier to work with if allowed to rest 1 hour. Wrap tightly with clingfilm and place in an airtight container.*

Note: My imaginative friend Lora Brody, of *Growing Up on the Chocolate Diet* and *Indulgences* fame, came up with a splendid idea for this marzipan. She doubled the recipe and rolled it out into a large rectangle about 42.5 × 30 centimetres/17 × 12 inches. She then prepared a Biscuit Roulade (page 157), spread it with 400 grams/ 14 ounces/2 cups of Neoclassic Buttercream (page 266), and topped it with the Pistachio Marzipan sheet before rolling it. The combination of colours, textures and flavours is exquisite.

The roll can be served unadorned or iced with Crème Ivoire (page 287) and decorated with chopped pistachios and a long-stemmed pink rose. For an even more intense pistachio flavour, make the optional syrup for the Biscuit Roulade (page 157) and flavour it with Pistasha liqueur (pistachio liqueur).

*For instructions on rolling out discs and ivy leaves see page 417.

Chopped Nuts

Nuts surrounding a cake provide an elegant decorative effect. Almonds, macademias, hazelnuts, pecans and walnuts all make wonderful coatings. Lightly toasting them brings out the flavour.

Some nut skins, such as hazelnut, are very bitter and should be removed by toasting or blanching. An easy system for skinning the recalcitrant hazelnut is to place 85 grams/3 ounces/²⁄₃ cup nuts in a saucepan containing 354 grams/ 12¹⁄₂ ounces/12 fluid ounces boiling water. Add 2 tablespoons bicarbonate of soda and boil for 3 minutes. Test a nut by running it under cold water to see if the skin slips off easily. If not, boil for a few minutes longer. Rinse the nuts well under cold running water and toast in a 350°F/180°C/gas mark 4 oven for 20 minutes or until golden brown.

Cool and coarsely chop. If using a food processor with the metal blade, pulse until uniform in size; then finish by hand using a large chef's knife for best texture.

You will need 85 grams/ 3 ounces/³⁄₄ cup chopped nuts for a 23 × 7.5-centimetre/9 × 3-inch cake; 114 grams/4 ounces/1 cup for a 30.5 × 7.5-centimetre/ 12 × 3-inch cake; and 152 grams/ 5¹⁄₄ ounces/1¹⁄₃ cups for a 46 × 30.5-centimetre/18 × 12-inch cake. I always make extra because leftover nuts keep for months in

the freezer and may be used as they are or recrisped in a 400°F/200°C/gas mark 6 oven for 5 minutes. For greater uniformity, I like to shake nuts in a fine strainer to rid them of smaller fragments and powder.

TO APPLY NUTS TO CAKE

The iced cake should be attached to a cardboard round no larger than the cake. If the cake is not too heavy, support it on the palm of your hand. Tilt the cake a bit towards the other hand, cupped to hold the nuts, and press the nuts gently into the sides. Alternatively, if the cake is heavy, place it on a large sheet of foil and use a bench scraper (page 523) or wide, flat spatula to lift the nuts on to the sides of the cake.

Chocolate Rose Modelling Paste

Makes 8 roses

This combination of corn syrup and chocolate is also known as plastic chocolate. It is not nearly as delicious to eat as Chocolate Rolled Fondant (page 356), but it has the advantage of drying to a very firm, brittle consistency, making it ideal for modelling exquisitely delicate red or dark chocolate roses. Brushing the roses with a thin layer of corn syrup creates a finish as shiny as porcelain.

STORE: The mixture will keep for several weeks if placed in airtight container or may be frozen indefinitely. Reknead just until pliable. Dried roses will keep for over 1 year if stored airtight in a cool, dry room or the refrigerator.

POINTERS FOR SUCCESS: Use the full amount of corn syrup. To ensure this, spray or grease the measuring spoon and push out all of the corn syrup with your finger. Knead the chocolate paste until completely smooth and lump-free.

Melt the coating in a double boiler set over very hot tap water (110° to 115°F/43° to 46°C) on low heat. The top must not touch the water.

INGREDIENTS	WEIGHT		MEASURE
room temperature	*grams*	*pounds/ounces*	*volume*
RED ROSES			
red summer coating★	170 grams	6 ounces	—
powdered red food colouring★	—	—	1 teaspoon
optional: powdered blue food colouring	—	—	—
corn syrup	41 grams	1½ ounces	2 tablespoons

★Summer coating, also known as compound chocolate, and powdered red food colouring are both available from specialist confectionery suppliers (see pages 513 and 531).

Remove from the heat and stir in red food colouring. Mix in a few specks of blue colouring to tone down the brightness if necessary.

Stir in the full amount of corn syrup (push it off the spoon with your finger). At this point, the chocolate will begin to harden and form a ball.

Scrape on to clingfilm and wrap tightly. Place in an airtight container and allow to rest and firm for at least 6 hours at room temperature.

Knead briefly until soft and supple before shaping. Keep well covered to avoid drying out while working.*

VARIATIONS

WHITE CHOCOLATE ROSES:

Use white summer coating or white chocolate and reduce the corn syrup to 1 tablespoon + 1 teaspoon.

DARK CHOCOLATE ROSES:

Use bittersweet chocolate and increase the corn syrup to 3 tablespoons + 1 teaspoon.

Crystallised Flowers

Commercially candied or crystallised violets are nice to have on hand but only about 1 in 20 actually resembles the flower it once was! Making your own crystallised flowers is time-consuming, but the results are dazzling. By handling each flower separately, the petals stay separate. Most flowers can be crystallised successfully (see page 493 for edible flowers). My favourites are tiny rose buds, cymbidiums (which look like miniature orchids), wild violets and lilacs. As the colours tend to fade, I add a little powdered food colouring or paste colour to the sugar. You will have to judge for yourself on the amount, as food colouring varies from brand to brand. It is best to make the colour a little more intense if not planning to use the finished flowers for several months, as it fades slightly. Most flowers will keep for years – with the exception of lilacs, which brown slightly after a few months. Crystallised flowers look spectacular caught up in strands of spun sugar (page 364). Crystallised lilacs have a firm little stub at the bottom which makes them ideal for

*For instructions on modelling roses, see page 450).

embroidering the sides and top of a cake, especially one frosted with Crème Ivoire Deluxe (page 285) such as White Lilac Nostalgia (page 190) or Classic Rolled Fondant (page 354). (Use a toothpick to make a small hole in the surface of the fondant in order to insert the lilac.)

TO CRYSTALLISE FLOWERS YOU WILL NEED

- castor sugar: 9 dozen lilac blossoms require only 2 tablespoons sugar but have to hand 66 grams/2¼ ounces/⅓ cup to have ample for spooning over the blossoms.
- lightly beaten egg white: 9 dozen lilac blossoms require ½ egg white (1 tablespoon).
- small edible flowers (page 493).

In a small bowl mix the sugar and food colour with your fingers until a uniform colour is achieved, adding more colour if necessary to deepen the shade. Pass the sugar through a fine sieve if necessary to perfectly distribute the colour. It is best not to use the food processor for this as the sugar crystals lose their glitter.

With a small paint brush, paint the egg white over the flower petals on all sides. Holding the flower above the bowl of coloured sugar, spoon the sugar lightly over it, coating all sides. Gently shake off the excess and place on a non-stick surface. Allow the flowers to dry thoroughly (about 24 hours) and then store airtight away from direct sunlight to prevent fading.

Tips: Violets will have the best shape if you allow them to dry upside down. Use a hair clip or clothespeg to suspend them by their stems until dry.

Gum arabic, available from confectionery suppliers, can be used in place of egg white for extra sparkle. Dissolve it in a tiny amount of water.

Fruit Toppings and Purées

Fruit, fresh, dried and preserved, adds much to the flavour and appearance of cakes. It can be used as a topping for cheesecakes, charlottes or even iced cakes like Star-Spangled Rhapsody (page 193).

Conserves make tart and colourful glazes which temper the sweetness of buttercreams and layer cakes.

Preserved fruits and concentrated purées make wonderfully flavoured buttercreams and whipped creams (which I call cloud creams). Making your own conserves enables you to decrease the sugar and maintain more of the integrity of the fruit. I concentrate the fruit juices so much that neither pectin nor a high proportion of sugar is necessary for gelling. My thick conserves contain whole fruit and very little sugar.

Included in this chapter are recipes for making your own chestnut and pumpkin purées. Although the tinned varieties are excellent in flavour and texture and undeniably convenient, during the autumn and winter, when these fresh ingredients are available, it's nice to be able to use them. The flavour is always a shade more delicious. This is not always true with fruit. Reconstituted dried apricots, for example, give much more flavour than the fresh fruit. Strawberries, frozen without sugar, are often more delicious than most fresh strawberries – even picked at the height of the season.

This chapter has a new and exciting technique for making fruit purées. It involves concentrating the juices without cooking the fruit itself. The resulting purées will enable you to make buttercreams and whipped creams which have the flavour of the fresh fruit at the peak of its season!

Jewel Glaze

*Makes a full 160 grams/5³/₄ ounces/¹/₂ cup (enough to glaze a
23 × 25.5-centimetre/9 to 10-inch cake)*

Fruit jellies and preserves, particularly tart ones such as raspberry, apricot
and blackcurrant, make easy and beautiful toppings for cakes. Ruby
Raspberry Jewel Glaze lends a brilliant glow to Chocolate Flame (page
89). A pale golden glisten of Apple Jewel Glaze keeps the poached pears
juicy and fresh atop Ethereal Pear Charlotte (page 199).

Jewel Glaze is also ideal for attaching chocolate bands to a cake (page
447).

A 23-centimetre/9-inch cake needs 165 grams/5³/₄ ounces/¹/₂ cup glaze,
a 30.5-centimetre/12-inch cake 290 grams/10 ounces/³/₄ cup plus
2 tablespoons. Leftover glaze keeps for months refrigerated.

STORE: 1 year refrigerated.

POINTERS FOR SUCCESS: If
glazing on top of icing, be sure that
the glaze is barely warm and the
buttercream firm to the touch or it
will melt.

INGREDIENTS	WEIGHT		MEASURE
room temperature	*grams*	*pounds/ounces*	*volume*
fruit jelly *or* jam	154 grams	5¹/₄ ounces	¹/₂ cup
fruit liqueur* *or* eau-de-vie (see suggestions following recipe)	14 grams	¹/₂ ounce	1 tablespoon

* *Complementary liqueurs*
For raspberry jelly: Chambord or eau-de-vie de framboise
For apricot jelly: Barack Palinka or apricot brandy
For blackcurrant jelly: Cassis
For apple jelly: Calvados or pear liqueur

In a small heavy saucepan melt the
jelly over a low heat. Stir in the
liqueur or hot water to thin slightly
and strain.

If you are using a glaze to seal
the surface of a porous cake prior
to glazing with chocolate, pour the
glaze on the cake while still hot and

fluid. Use a long metal spatula to spread it evenly.

To glaze a buttercream-iced cake, chill the iced cake until the buttercream is firm. Using the back of a long sharp knife, make shallow parallel diagonal slashes evenly across the cake, first in one direction and then at a 45° angle to create diamond shapes. Wipe the blade clean after each cut. When the glaze is applied it will sink deeply into these cuts, providing an intensely coloured design. The glaze should be barely warm when applied and the buttercream solid to the touch to keep it from melting.

Put any leftover glaze into a container with a tight-fitting lid and refrigerate.

To use jam or apricot lekvar: Apricot lekvar contains the skin of the apricot as well as the fruit. It is thicker and more intensely flavoured than ordinary apricot jam. It is necessary to strain apricot jam or lekvar to obtain a clear glaze. Start with 1½ times the amount you need. Use a food processor to soften the jam and then heat to melt before pressing through a fine sieve. Add the liqueur at the end or use warm water before sieving.

VARIATIONS

SHINY JEWEL GLAZE:

A small amount of gelatin will produce a thicker but transparent fluid glaze which holds up for several days. Place 7 tablespoons water in a custard cup. Sprinkle 2 teaspoons gelatin over it and allow to soften for at least 5 minutes. Heat in a microwave on high power, stirring once or twice, or in a pan surrounded by simmering water until the gelatin is dissolved. Add the gelatin to the melted and sieved jelly and liqueur. Refrigerate until thickened slightly or stir over ice water until syrupy. Use at once.

CRAN-RASPBERRY GLAZE:

This flavourful, pretty glaze is wonderful to top a creamy cheesecake (page 82) as a holiday dessert.

In a small saucepan dissolve 4 teaspoons cornflour in 6 fluid ounces cranberry-raspberry juice, preferably made from frozen concentrate. Bring to a boil, stirring constantly. Lower the heat and simmer for 1 minute. Remove from the heat and stir in 1 tablespoon Chambord (black raspberry) or cranberry liqueur. Spoon over the cake, spreading it evenly.

Cordon Rose

Raspberry Conserve

Makes 1 kg 157 gm/1 quart

It is worth every bit of the work involved to make this recipe because a conserve of this quality cannot be bought. It would take a jar of commercially made jam 2¹/₃ times the size to equal the amount of fruit used for this method. This raspberry conserve captures the magical essence of the berry. The side benefits are a kitchen permeated with the scent of raspberry and the sight of bowls filled with velvety, ruby-red berries. There also seems to be an atavistic pleasure in the act of preserving summer's bounty for the cold winter months ahead.

This unique method of preparing jam triples the concentration of the fruit so that it gels without having to add pectin or the accompanying high amount of sugar (in excess of two-thirds more). The conserve is tart and intensely flavoured, with a deep garnet hue. It is perfect for spreading on cake rolls or adding to buttercream.

STORE: I have stored this conserve for as long as 4 years. The flavour does not deteriorate, but after 2 years the colour deepens and is less bright.

In a large-diameter pan combine the sugar and water and bring to the boil, stirring constantly. Boil for 1 minute. Add 3 to 4 cups berries (so that they are in a single layer) and boil for 1 minute. Remove with a slotted spoon or skimmer to a colander suspended over a bowl to catch the syrup. Reduce the syrup in the pan to

INGREDIENTS	WEIGHT		MEASURE
room temperature	*grams*	*pounds/ounces*	*volume*
sugar	425 grams	15 ounces	2 cups + 2 tablespoons
water	266 grams	9¹/₄ ounces	9 fluid ounces
raspberries	1 kilogram 361 grams	3 pounds	3 quarts

16 fluid ounces and repeat the procedure with more berries. From time to time return the syrup that drains from the cooked berries to the pan. Skim the white foam from the surface.

When the last batch of raspberries is completed, boil the syrup down to 16 fluid ounces (the temperature will be 210°F/99°C) and reserve. Sieve the berries to remove most of the seeds. (When condensing raspberries to this degree, leaving all the seeds would be excessive; however some seeds lend a nice texture to the conserve. I use the colander and the sieve attachment on my KitchenAid, which has large enough holes to allow a few seeds to pass through. You can also use a food mill fitted with the finest disc.) You should have 16 fluid ounces raspberry pulp and discard the seeds.

Add the sieved berries to the reserved syrup and simmer for 10 minutes or until reduced to 32 fluid ounces. Fill preserving jars which have been rinsed in boiling water, leaving 9 millimetres/³/₈-inch head space. Screw on the caps and place them in a water bath, covered, for 10 minutes after the water comes to a boil. Remove and allow to cool before checking the seal.

Jars in the water bath must be sitting on a rack to allow the water to flow all around them, and the water must be high enough to cover them by 2.5 centimetres/ 1 inch. They must be upright to expel any air inside the jars, producing a vacuum which seals the jars. If this process is eliminated, be sure to store the conserve in a cool, dry area away from light as there are no preservatives in it to prevent mould from forming. (If mould does form, scrape it off and reboil the conserve.) The conserve takes 2 days in the jar to thicken.

Tip: The conserve can be prepared using raspberries frozen without sugar. Allow them to defrost in a colander, reserving the juice. Add the juice to the sugar syrup and proceed as with fresh berries. The flavour will be indistinguishable from conserve prepared with fresh berries.

UNDERSTANDING
Formula: 1 pound berries/5 ounces sugar/3 ounces water. A large unlined copper pan is traditional for jam-making because the faster the berries and syrup cook, the better the flavour and gelling. Be sure to use a pan with a large diameter to speed evaporation of the syrup.

Raspberries are very fragile and washing causes them to break down faster. Raspberry growers have assured me that any sprays are administered at a prescribed time so that their effects have entirely dissipated before harvesting. They do not recommend washing the berries. If washed, berries should be cooked as soon as possible.

Cordon Rose
Strawberry Conserve

Makes 988 grams/2 pounds 3 ounces/3¹/₂ cups

This highly concentrated conserve has very little sugar – only about one-twelfth the sugar and four times the concentration of most commercial jams made with pectin. It is designed to be added to buttercreams and whipped cream and spread on cake rolls. More sugar can be added if the conserve is to be used as a spread on toast.* Either way, it captures the quality of fresh ripe strawberries. Strawberries during the peak of the season are full of sweet sunny flavour. Out of season frozen berries make a far more delicious conserve.

STORE: I have stored this conserve for as long as 4 years. The flavour does not deteriorate, but after 2 years the colour deepens and is less bright.

If the berries are sandy, wash them before hulling and dry on paper towels.

In a large-diameter pan combine the sugar and water and bring to the boil, stirring constantly. Boil for 1 minute. Add 3 to 4 cups berries (so that they are in a single layer) and boil for 1 minute. Remove with a slotted spoon or skimmer to a colander suspended over a bowl to catch the syrup. Reduce the syrup in the pot to 14 fluid ounces and repeat the procedure with more berries. From time to time return the syrup that drains from the cooked berries to the pan. Skim the white foam from the surface.

When the last batch of berries is

INGREDIENTS	WEIGHT		MEASURE
room temperature	*grams*	*pounds/ounces*	*volume*
hulled strawberries	1 kilogram 814 grams	4 pounds	4 quarts
sugar	227 grams	8 ounces	1 cup + 2 tablespoons
water	354 grams	12 ounces	12 fluid ounces

* To make strawberry conserve for spreading on toast, add 88 grams/3 ounces/a scant ¹/₂ cup sugar.

completed, boil the syrup down to 14 fluid ounces (the temperature will be 208°F/98°C).

Return the berries to the syrup and simmer for 10 minutes or until reduced to 28 fluid ounces.

Fill preserving jars which have been rinsed in boiling water, leaving 9-millimetre/³⁄₈-inch head space. Screw on the caps and place them in a water bath, covered, for 10 minutes after the water comes to a boil. Remove and allow to cool before checking the seal.

The jars in the water bath must be sitting on a rack to allow the water to flow all around them, and the water must be high enough to cover them by 2.5 centimetres/ 1 inch. They must be upright to expel any air inside the jars, producing a vacuum which seals the jar. If this process is eliminated, be sure to store the conserve in a cool, dry area away from light as there are no preservatives in it to prevent mould from forming. (If mould does form, scrape it off and reboil the conserve.) The conserve takes 2 days in the jar to thicken.

Tips:

- Recently I discovered an extraordinary essence of wild strawberry imported from France. A few drops perform magic in this or any strawberry conserve (page 492).
- The conserve can be prepared using strawberries frozen without sugar. Allow them to defrost in a colander, reserving the juice. (This will take several hours.) Add the juice to the sugar syrup and proceed as with fresh berries. The flavour will be indistinguishable from conserve prepared with fresh berries.

UNDERSTANDING

Strawberries contain more water than raspberries so it is necessary to start with 4 pounds instead of only 3 pounds to get the same quantity of conserve.

Formula: 1 pound berries/ 2 ounces sugar/3 ounces water.

A large unlined copper pan is traditional for jam because the faster the berries and syrup cook, the better the flavour and gelling. Be sure to use a pan with a large diameter to speed evaporation of the syrup.

Apricot Purée

Makes 400–475 grams/13¾ ounces–1 pound/1½–1¾ cups (unsweetened)

Dried California apricots make a purée with greater flavour and richer hue than fresh apricots, even at the height of their season. The purée freezes well so I always have some on hand to add to buttercreams or to swirl into cheesecake batter.

STORE: 5 days refrigerated, 1 year frozen.

INGREDIENTS	WEIGHT		MEASURE
room temperature	*grams*	*pounds/ounces*	*volume*
dried California apricots	340 grams	12 ounces	2 cups, packed
water	354 grams	12½ ounces	12 fluid ounces
lemon juice, freshly squeezed	23 grams	1 ounce	1½ tablespoons
optional: castor sugar	113 grams	4 ounces	½ cup + 1 tablespoon

In a small saucepan place the apricots and water and allow to stand, covered, for 2 hours. Simmer for 20 minutes on a very low heat, tightly covered, or until the apricots are soft. Purée along with any remaining liquid in a food processor.

Press through a fine strainer (page 519). You should have 405 grams/13½ ounces/1½ cups to 473 grams/1 pound/1¾ cups.* Stir in the lemon juice. (If you have less purée, slightly decrease the lemon juice.)

To make lightly sweetened purée, add sugar to equal one-third the volume of the purée (i.e. if there is only 270 grams/9 ounces/ 1 cup purée, add 66 grams/ 2¼ ounces/⅓ cup of sugar instead of 113 grams/4 ounces/½ cup + 1 tablespoon). Store in an airtight container.

*I get 473 grams/1 pound/1¾ cups using the Cuisinart power strainer attachment. If using the power strainer, there is no need to process the apricots first.

Tip: Premium-quality California apricots, found in speciality and health-food shops, are brighter orange and have a superior flavour to most packaged varieties.

Note: It is essential to use a fine strainer to achieve the best texture.

Peach Purée

Makes 550 grams/1 pound 3¼ ounces/2¼ cups

Peaches and cream are a time-honoured combination. This purée is the base for my Peach Cloud Cream charlotte filling. When it's a good peach season I use ripe, juicy peaches and make extra to freeze for later in the year. When peaches are lacking in flavour, I buy frozen ones with no sugar added.

STORE: 2 days refrigerated, 8 months frozen.

In a food processor process the peaches briefly until broken up and liquidy. Press through a food mill fitted with a fine disc or use a fine strainer (page 519) to obtain a smooth purée. Combine the purée and lemon juice in a heavy non-corrodible saucepan and simmer until reduced to 18 fluid ounces. Cool and stir in the essences. Store in an airtight container.

INGREDIENTS	WEIGHT		MEASURE
room temperature	*grams*	*pounds/ounces*	*volume*
9 ripe peaches, peeled and stoned	907 grams	2 pounds (without peels and stones)	5 cups of slices
lemon juice, freshly squeezed	16 grams	½ ounce	1 tablespoon
almond essence	4 grams	—	1 teaspoon
pure vanilla extract	—	—	¼ teaspoon

Tip: To peel peaches, place in simmering water for 1 minute or until the skins slip off easily. Do not add this purée to cheesecake batter as it will curdle it.

UNDERSTANDING
Almond has an excellent affinity with peach. Vanilla serves as a flavour enhancer for both.

Raspberry Purée and Sauce

Makes 290 grams/10 ounces/1⅓ cups purée, 422 grams/14¾ ounces/1⅔ cups lightly sweetened sauce

Raspberries are the crown jewels of the baking world. This tart, intensely flavoured purée is ideal to temper the sweetness of buttercreams and to add flavour to whipped creams. Lightly sweetened, it also makes a velvety sauce that is the very essence of fresh raspberry.

The secret is that the juices are concentrated by four times their original volume, but the pulp is not cooked at all. Raspberry purée is wonderful with Ethereal Pear Charlotte (page 199), and 1 tablespoon poured into the hollow of a whipped cream dollop is the ideal foil for the richness of Chocolate Oblivion Truffle Torte (page 86). In fact, I wouldn't serve the cake without it. Since the purée stays fresh even after months in the freezer, I always prepare extra for storing.

STORE: 10 days refrigerated, 1 year frozen. The purée can be thawed briefly and refrozen several times with no ill effect.

POINTERS FOR SUCCESS: Be sure to use unsweetened berries. Berries in syrup cannot be reduced as much because the sugar thickens the mixture before the intense flavour can be obtained.

Raspberry seeds are very small and can pass through most food mills. This sauce used to be tedious and time-consuming to make because the seeds cling to the pulp. Pressing through a fine strainer has taken me as long as 30 minutes.

In a strainer suspended over a deep bowl thaw the raspberries completely. This will take several hours. (To speed thawing, place in an oven with a pilot light.) Press the berries to force out all the juice. There should be 8 fluid ounces.

INGREDIENTS	WEIGHT		MEASURE
room temperature	*grams*	*pounds/ounces*	*volume*
raspberries, frozen with no sugar added	680 grams	24 ounces	2 (12-ounce) bags
lemon juice, freshly squeezed	10 grams	—	2 teaspoons
optional: sugar	132 grams	4¾ ounces	⅔ cup

In a saucepan (or in a microwave* on high power) boil the juice until reduced to 2 fluid ounces. Pour it into a lightly oiled heatproof bowl.

Purée the raspberries and sieve them with a food mill fitted with the fine disc. Or use a fine strainer to remove all seeds. You should have 8 fluid ounces of purée. Stir in the raspberry syrup and lemon juice. To make a lightly sweetened sauce, measure again. There should be 10½ fluid ounces. If you have less, add less sugar. The correct amount of sugar is half the volume of the purée. (To 8 fluid ounces, add 100 grams/3½ ounces/½ cup sugar.) Stir until the sugar dissolves.

Tip: If using fresh berries, you will need 680 grams/1½ pounds/ 1⅓ litres. In order to make them exude their juices, they must be frozen and thawed to break down the cell membranes.

UNDERSTANDING
I once gave Robert Linxe of Maison du Chocolat in Paris a taste of my raspberry purée flavoured with expensive eau-de-vie de framboise. He told me without hesitation that lemon is the best possible enhancer for raspberry. And he is absolutely right (although there are times when I add both, often replacing the framboise with Chambord, a sweeter black raspberry brandy).

The microwave method of reducing the raspberry juice gives the purest flavour because it does not come into contact with direct heat, preventing any slight browning or caramel flavour.

*If using a microwave, place the juice in a 1 litre/2-pint/4-cup heatproof glass measure or bowl to allow for bubbling.

Strawberry Purée and Sauce

Makes 300 grams/10½ ounces/1¼ cups purée, 350 grams/12¼ ounces/1⅓ cups lightly sweetened sauce

It is amazing how this purée captures the flavour of sun-warmed strawberries at their peak – more so than the actual strawberries themselves when eaten out of season! This is partly because strawberries for freezing are picked at their prime and also because this method of concentrating the juices without cooking the fruit results in a purée of double the concentration and fresher flavour than conventional ones. (This is a technique I have discovered to make the berries surrender all their flavour while maintaining their brilliant colour.)

I use the strawberry purée lightly sweetened as a sauce. Unsweetened, it's great for Strawberry Cloud Cream filling for charlottes (page 307) or with Golden Butter Cream Cake as a glorious Strawberry Shortcake (page 22). It is also delicious with Génoise au Chocolat (page 141) and as a buttercream flavouring.

STORE: 10 days refrigerated, 1 year frozen. The purée can be thawed briefly and refrozen several times with no ill effect.

INGREDIENTS	WEIGHT		MEASURE
room temperature	*grams*	*pounds/ounces*	*volume*
whole strawberries, frozen without sugar	567 grams	20 ounces	20-ounce bag
lemon juice, freshly squeezed	10 grams	–	2 teaspoons
optional: sugar	50 grams	1¾ ounces	¼ cup

In a colander suspended over a deep bowl thaw the strawberries completely. This will take several hours. Press them, if necessary, to force out the juice. There should be close to 10 fluid ounces juice.

In a small saucepan (or a microwave* on high power) boil

*If using a microwave, place the juice in a 1-litre/2-pint/4-cup heatproof glass measure or bowl to allow for bubbling.

the juice until reduced to 2 fluid ounces. Pour it into a lightly oiled heatproof glass measuring jug.

In a food processor purée the strawberries. You should have 8 full fluid ounces of purée. Stir in the strawberry syrup and lemon juice. To make a lightly sweetened sauce, measure again. There should be 10 fluid ounces. If you have less, add less sugar. The correct amount of sugar is one-fifth the volume of the purée. (For 10 tablespoons purée, add 2 tablespoons sugar.) Stir until the sugar dissolves.

Tip: Fresh berries are fine to use only in season when the berries are full of flavour. If using fresh berries, you will need 567 grams/ 20 ounces/5 cups. In order to make

them exude their juices, they must be frozen and thawed to break down the cell membranes. A few drops of French essence of wild strawberry (page 492) add flavour intensity.

UNDERSTANDING
The little seeds in strawberries create a lovely textural effect and, together with the pink colour of the buttercream or whipped cream, give an unmistakable strawberry flavour.

The microwave method of reducing the strawberry juice gives the purest flavour because it does not come into contact with direct heat, preventing any slight browning or caramel flavour.

Lemon Curd

Makes 300 grams/11 ounces/1 full cup

If you love lemon (and who doesn't) the sunny lilting freshness of lemon curd will be addictive straight out of the jar. It makes an attractive topping, accentuating the lemon in Cordon Rose Cream Cheesecake (page 82). Blended with Perfect Whipped Cream (page 294) or Light Italian Meringue (page 344), it also makes a luscious filling for Biscuit Roulade (page 157) or an airy filling for charlottes (page 423). It even makes a fabulous addition to Mousseline Buttercream (page 282). Thank God for lemons. They are available year round and despite domestication are always wonderful.

The first time I tasted lemon curd I was ready to go to extremes to get the recipe. According to the *Wise Encyclopedia of Cookery* (where I found my first recipe for this English treat), the recipe was a guarded secret for years. Now many versions abound. This is my version – perhaps a little less sweet and more lemony than most. More sugar can be added to taste while the curd is still warm.

STORE: 3 weeks refrigerated. Longer storage dulls the fresh citrus flavour.

POINTERS FOR SUCCESS: If the citrus fruit is heated (about 10 seconds in a microwave oven on high power) and rolled around while pressing on it lightly, the fruit will release a significantly greater quantity of juice.

To prevent curdling, be sure to mix the sugar well with the yolks before adding the juice. Use a heavy non-corrodible pan which conducts heat evenly or a double boiler. To further prevent curdling, do not allow the mixture to boil. Remove immediately from the heat when thickened and strain at once as the residual heat in the pot will raise the temperature.

If you are working with an accurate thermometer, the temperature of the thickened curd will be 196°F/91°C.

In a heavy non-corrodible saucepan beat the yolks and sugar until well blended. Stir in the remaining ingredients except the lemon zest. Cook over medium-low heat, stirring constantly, until thickened and resembling a thin hollandaise sauce, which thickly coats a wooden spoon but is still liquid enough to pour. The mixture will change from translucent to opaque and begin to take on a yellow colour on the back of a wooden spoon. It must not be allowed to boil or it will curdle. Whenever steam appears, remove briefly from heat, stirring constantly, to keep from boiling. When the curd has thickened, pour at once into a strainer. Press with the back of a spoon until only coarse residue remains. Discard the residue. Stir in the lemon zest and cool. Pour into an airtight container. The curd will continue to thicken while resting and chilling.

TO GLAZE CHEESECAKE

Pour the lemon curd over a chilled cake while the curd is still warm and liquid. Spread quickly with a metal spatula to form a smooth film.

UNDERSTANDING

An aluminium pan should not be used because it reacts with the egg yolks, turning them a chartreuse. Sugar raises the coagulation point of the yolk. It also protects it from premature coagulation during the addition of the citric acid. If the citrus juice were added directly to the unprotected yolk, it would partially coagulate and, when

INGREDIENTS	WEIGHT		MEASURE
room temperature	*grams*	*pounds/ounces*	*volume*
4 egg yolks, size 2	74 grams	2½ ounces	2 full fluid ounces
castor sugar	125 grams	4½ ounces	½ cup + 2 tablespoons
lemon juice, freshly squeezed (about 2½ large lemons)	94 grams	3¼ ounces	3 fluid ounces
unsalted butter, softened	57 grams	2 ounces	4 tablespoons
pinch of salt	—	—	—
finely shredded lemon zest	4 grams	—	2 teaspoons

strained, a large percentage would be left behind in the strainer.

When yolks reach boiling point, they begin to curdle. Commercial establishments sometimes bring the curd to the boiling point and strain immediately. The part that has begun to curdle is discarded. This is done merely for speed (it's one way to take the guesswork out of whether the mixture is hot enough!).

Straining the lemon or lime curd (see below) after cooking produces the silkiest texture because it removes any coagulated bits of egg. The zest is therefore added after straining. If desired, it can be added with the juice and removed on straining. This way, it imparts some of its flavour without adding texture. For orange curd, it is important to add the orange zest with the juice to intensify the elusive orange flavour.

VARIATIONS

LIME CURD:

Replace the lemon juice and zest with freshly squeezed lime juice and zest. (Limes are smaller than lemons but contain much more juice. Three small limes should suffice.) Decrease the sugar to 100 grams/3½ ounces/½ cup as lime is much less tart than lemon. The Lime Curd will be yellow with green flecks from the zest. If desired, add a few drops of green liquid food colouring. Be conservative; only the palest of green hues is attractive.

PASSION CURD:

This curd has a glorious flavour and deep golden colour. Replace the lemon juice and

zest with an equal volume (100 grams/
3½ ounces) of fresh or frozen passion fruit
juice. Decrease the sugar to
100 grams/3½ ounces/½ cup.

ORANGE CURD:

Orange juice is much sweeter than lime
juice and most varieties do not have
enough acidity to thicken the curd as well
as lemon or lime does. Orange curd has a
delicious flavour and beautiful colour but
will still be slightly liquid even when
chilled. This curd makes delicious Grand

Marnier Orange Mousseline Buttercream
(page 282) or lovely orange-flavoured
whipped cream (page 306).

To make Orange Curd: Reduce 8 fluid
ounces freshly squeezed orange juice to
2 tablespoons (preferably in a microwave
on high power). Use only 100 grams/
3½ ounces/½ cup sugar and add
4 teaspoons orange zest to the yolk mixture
before heating. Do not strain. (If you can
obtain blood oranges, reduce to only
2 fluid ounces as they have higher acidity
and will thicken the curd substantially.)

Candied Zest

Makes 150 grams/5¼ ounces/1 cup

Citrus peel makes a flavourful and attractive decorative touch when cut
into fine strips and sweetened in a sugar syrup. This candied zest is
particularly suited to decorating a cake containing citrus fruit.

STORE: 1 month refrigerated.

With a small sharp knife remove
strips of peel, avoiding the bitter
white pith beneath. If any pith
remains on the zest, scrape it away.
Cut the peel into fine julienne
strips.

Place in a saucepan of boiling
water and simmer for 15 minutes
to soften and remove bitterness.
Drain and rinse under cold water.

In the same saucepan combine
the sugar, water and corn syrup
and bring to a boil, stirring
constantly. Stop stirring, add the

zest and cover tightly. Simmer
over a low heat for 15 minutes
without stirring or uncovering.
Remove from the heat and cool,
covered. To brighten the colour,
add the grenadine.

Refrigerate the candied zest in
the syrup in an airtight container
for up to 1 month. When ready to
use, drain the zest. If you wish to
use the syrup for cakes, add water
to equal 1½ times the volume of
the syrup to dilute the sweetness
and add an orange-based liqueur to
taste.

INGREDIENTS	WEIGHT		MEASURE
room temperature	grams	pounds/ounces	volume
3 large thick-skinned oranges	–	–	–
sugar	200 grams	7 ounces	1 cup
water	236 grams	8¼ ounces	8 fluid ounces
corn syrup	21 grams	–	1 tablespoon
optional: grenadine syrup	–	–	1 teaspoon

UNDERSTANDING
The corn syrup prevents crystallisation of the sugar when the zest is added.

Fresh Cherry Topping

Makes enough for a 23-centimetre/9-inch cake

For me, summer begins with cherry picking. As a New Yorker, it is always a treat to become reacquainted with how fruit grows. One of the neighbourhood farms where we have our weekend house has four sour cherry trees and a 'pick your own' policy. I love the sight of the bright green leaves against a clear blue sky and hundreds of tiny luminous red globes suspended from the branches. I'm often the only one picking (which is heaven). Last year there was a family (grandmother, mother and granddaughter) at the tree next to mine. I overheard exultations of the pie to come and the merits of different shortenings in the crust. I felt an immediate and pleasant connection with these fellow bakers. They asked me if I worked for the farm because I was using small shears to cut the stems. Actually, I've found that leaving the stem on keeps the cherries from deteriorating so quickly before processing.

I love fresh cherry pie but at least half the cherries I pick go for toppings for my cheesecakes. Tart red cherries, bursting with juice and cooked only until thickened, blend perfectly with lemon-scented cream cheese.

STORE: If stems are left on, fresh cherries will keep refrigerated 3 days. Cover lightly with a clean towel. Cherries keep their shape best when freezing if sprinkled first with 2 tablespoons sugar per 10 ounces stoned cherries. The sugar holds the juices when the cell walls break. If your freezer stays around 0°F or below, the cherries will keep 2 years without losing their bright red colour or flavour. If necessary, 1/8 teaspoon red food colouring added before cooking will perk up any colour lost during freezing.

POINTERS FOR SUCCESS: Stir constantly to prevent lumping of the cornflour. The mixture must reach a full boil for the cornflour to swell and thicken.

INGREDIENTS	WEIGHT		MEASURE
room temperature	*grams*	*pounds/ounces*	*volume*
tart stoned cherries and juice from stoning	280 grams	10 ounces	1¾ cups
sugar	100 grams	3½ ounces	½ cup
cornflour	12 grams	—	1½ tablespoons
pinch of salt	—	—	—
almond essence	—	—	⅛ teaspoon

In a 1.33-litre/2½ pint saucepan toss the cherries, juice, sugar, cornflour and salt. Allow to sit for at least 30 minutes until the sugar draws out more cherry juice.

Cook over a moderate heat, stirring constantly, until thickened and boiling. Simmer for 1 minute. The mixture should just barely drop from a spoon. Remove from the heat and stir in the almond essence. Cool slightly and spoon over cold cheesecake.

Tip: I find that commercial cherry stoners don't work very well. Either they allow a smaller stone to pass through, which can break a tooth if it makes its way into the topping, or the cherries become squashed and misshapen. I once asked the proverbial little old lady sitting on the porch selling cherries how *she* stoned them. She pointed to the grey bun perched on top of her head. When I looked mystified, she plucked out a large heavy metal hairpin. She explained that she inserts the looped end into the stem end of the cherry and uses the loop to pull out the pit.

Since that day I have tried a crochet hook, a new elaborate German cherry stoner and an antique model – and still find the hairpin the fastest and best preserver of the cherry's plump shape.

Winter Cherry Topping

Makes enough for a 23-centimetre/9-inch cake

Fresh sour-cherry season is all too short (only about 2 weeks) so if it should escape you one year, this recipe is a great way to brighten the flavour of tinned cherries. Cherry Kijafa (cherry wine from Denmark) gives the fruit a gorgeous dark red colour and luscious flavour.

INGREDIENTS	WEIGHT		MEASURE
room temperature	*grams*	*pounds/ounces*	*volume*
tart stoned water-packed cherries	454 grams	1 pound	1 pound tin
sugar	75 grams	2¾ ounces	¼ cup + tablespoons
Cherry Kijafa	96 grams	3½ ounces	3 fluid ounces
cornflour	8 grams	—	1 tablespoon
pinch of salt	—	—	—
almond essence	—	—	⅛ teaspoon

POINTERS FOR SUCCESS: Stir constantly to prevent lumping of the cornflour. The mixture must reach a full boil for the cornflour to swell and thicken.

DAY BEFORE
In a colander suspended over a deep bowl drain the cherries for 30 minutes or until they lose 6 fluid ounces juice. (Press lightly if necessary.) Reserve only 2 table-spoons juice. There will be about 200 grams/7 ounces/almost 1 cup of cherries.

In a 1.33-litre/2½-pint saucepan combine the 2 tablespoons juice, sugar and Cherry Kijafa, stirring until the sugar is dissolved. Add the cherries and bring to the boil. Cover and cool. Refrigerate until the following day.

Drain the cherries again for 30 minutes or until 7 fluid ounces (14 tablespoons) are obtained. Reduce the liquid to 4 fluid ounces. Pour into a bowl and cool completely.

In the same saucepan place the cornflour and salt and gradually stir in the cooled liquid, then the cherries. Bring to a full boil and simmer for 1 minute. The mixture should just barely drop from a spoon. Remove from the heat and stir in the almond essence. Cool slightly and spoon over cold cheesecake.

Tip: Bottled Morello sour cherries from Hungary or Poland, available in delicatessens and some supermarkets, offer exceptionally full flavour.

Brandied Burgundy Cherries

Makes 1 pint

In addition to combining with Vanilla Ice Cream (page 329) and Hot Fudge (page 90) for a deliriously good sundae, Brandied Burgundy Cherries are a traditional part of Swiss Black Forest Cake (page 218). The brandy keeps the cherries from freezing rock hard when making the ice-cream version of the Black Forest Cake.

Brandied cherries are flavourful after only 12 hours but the longer they stand, the more mellow they become.

STORE: At least 1 month in the refrigerator or a cool, dark closet. The cherries will keep almost indefinitely.

INGREDIENTS	WEIGHT		MEASURE
room temperature	*grams*	*pounds/ounces*	*volume*
stoned bing cherries in heavy syrup	454 grams	1 pound	1 pound tin
sugar	25 grams	1 ounce	2 tablespoons
kirsch or Cognac	56 grams	2 ounces	2 fluid ounces

In a colander suspended over a deep bowl drain the cherries for 30 minutes. Reserve 4 fluid ounces syrup. There will be about 234 grams/8¼ ounces/1 full cup cherries.

In a medium saucepan combine the syrup and sugar and bring to the boil, stirring constantly. Add the cherries and simmer, covered, for 1 minute. Remove from the heat. Transfer the cherries with a slotted spoon to a pint jar and add the kirsch or Cognac.

Boil the syrup until reduced to 2 fluid ounces and pour over the cherries. Cover tightly and swirl to mix. If planning to store for longer than 3 months, add enough liqueur to reach almost to the top of the jar. Cool, cover tightly and refrigerate.

VARIATIONS

MORELLO CHERRIES:

From Hungary or Poland, these are a tart and delicious alternative. They are packed in 2-pound 1-ounce jars so double the recipe, using a total of 100 grams/ 3½ ounces/½ cup sugar (tart cherries need more sugar), 8 fluid ounces cherry liquid, and 4 fluid ounces kirsch or brandy.

FROZEN CHERRIES:

Available in some supermarkets, these are more delicious than tinned and just about as good as fresh! To use frozen cherries, empty two 12-ounce bags of cherries frozen without sugar into a colander suspended over a bowl and allow to defrost. This will take several hours. Add enough water to the juice to equal 8 fluid ounces. Add 100 grams/3½ ounces/½ cup sugar and proceed as for tinned cherries.

FRESH CHERRIES:

When I have a windfall of fresh dark cherries, I use this method adapted from Helen Witty and Elizabeth Schneider Colchie's invaluable book *Better Than Store-Bought*. For 1 pint cherries, simmer 1 cup stoned cherries with 6 fluid ounces water in a covered saucepan for 10 minutes or until easily pierced with a cake tester. Remove the cherries with a slotted spoon to a pint jar and add the kirsch or brandy. Add 100 grams/3½ ounces/½ cup sugar to the liquid in the pan and bring to the boil, stirring constantly. Reduce to 2–2½ fluid ounces and pour over the cherries. Cover tightly and swirl to mix. Add enough liqueur to reach almost to the top of the jar. (The recipe can be increased if desired.)

Fresh Blueberry Topping

Makes enough for a 25.5-centimetre/10-inch cake

Quickly tossing uncooked blueberries in this hot glaze turns them a dark, bright blue without softening them. The berries remain tart and juicy with a fine sparkle. This makes a lovely topping for Star-Spangled Rhapsody (page 193) or Cordon Rose Cream Cheesecake (page 82).

INGREDIENTS	WEIGHT		MEASURE
room temperature	*grams*	*pounds/ounces*	*volume*
fresh blueberries	340 grams	12 ounces	2¾ cups
arrowroot or cornflour	8 grams	—	1 tablespoon
sugar	50 grams	1¾ ounces	¼ cup
water	118 grams	4 ounces	4 fluid ounces
lemon juice, freshly squeezed	8 grams	—	1½ teaspoons

Rinse the berries and dry well with paper towels. Place in a bowl.

Have ready a colander or strainer large enough to hold the berries.

In a small saucepan mix the arrowroot and sugar. Stir in the water and lemon juice and heat, stirring constantly, until clear and thickened. Remove from the heat and add the blueberries, tossing until coated. Remove to the colander, drain and discard any glaze not clinging to the berries. Use as soon as possible.

UNDERSTANDING

Arrowroot is preferable to cornflour because it adds sparkle and because it starts to swell and thicken the liquid before reaching boiling point, lessening the chance of overheating the berries. Cornflour must be brought to a full boil in order to thicken the liquid completely.

Note: If the liquid does not thicken, then the arrowroot is too old. Arrowroot sometimes sits on the shelf for years as not many recipes require it.

Winter Blueberry Topping

Makes enough for a 25.5-centimetre/10-inch cake

Frozen blueberries have excellent flavour but slightly lose their shape
when defrosted. This potential disadvantage turned out to be a desirable
quality in the creation of this glistening, dark blue topping. It can be used
in the same way as Fresh Blueberry Topping (page 399), but also
provides a smoother 'lake' on which to float the swans for the Blueberry
Swan Lake (page 186).

STORE: 6 hours room temperature.

INGREDIENTS	WEIGHT		MEASURE
room temperature	*grams*	*pounds/ounces*	*volume*
frozen blueberries	340 grams	12 ounces	12-ounce bag
arrowroot *or* cornflour	8 grams	–	1 tablespoon
sugar	50 grams	1¾ ounces	¼ cup
finely grated lemon zest	2 grams	–	1 teaspoon

In a colander suspended over a
bowl thaw the blueberries
completely. This will take several
hours. Reserve the juice.

In a small saucepan stir together
the arrowroot and sugar and whisk
in the reserved juice. Cook over a
medium heat, stirring constantly
until thickened. Remove from the
heat and fold in the blueberries and
lemon zest. Put in a bowl and cool
to room temperature before using
on the cake.

UNDERSTANDING
Arrowroot is preferable to
cornflour because it adds sparkle. It
starts to swell and thickens the
liquid before reaching boiling point
so it should not be allowed to boil
or it will thin. Cornflour must be
brought to a full boil in order to
thicken the liquid completely.

Note: If the liquid does not
thicken, then the arrowroot is too
old. Arrowroot sometimes sits on
the shelf for years as not many
recipes require it.

Poached Pears

Makes 4 halves

These lovely, translucent pears, enhanced by poire William liqueur or eau-de-vie, are thinly sliced and provide an elegant topping for Ethereal Pear Charlotte (page 199). Of course they are delicious alone or with a thin lacing of Chocolate Cream Glaze (page 314) for the renowned dessert Poires Belle Hélène.

STORE: 3 days refrigerated.

INGREDIENTS	WEIGHT		MEASURE
room temperature	*grams*	*pounds/ounces*	*volume*
2 large ripe but firm pears★	454 grams	1 pound	4 inches long
water	354 grams	12½ ounces	12 fluid ounces
lemon juice	10 grams	—	2 teaspoons
poire William liqueur or eau-de-vie	28 grams	1 ounce	2 tablespoons
sugar	50 grams	1¾ ounces	¼ cup
vanilla pod, split lengthwise	—	—	1 inch

★ Select pears that measure 10 centimetres/4 inches in length because they just fit when fanned inside the charlotte *biscuit*.

Peel, halve and core the pears just before poaching so that they do not darken.

In a saucepan just large enough to hold the pears in a single layer combine the water, lemon juice, eau-de-vie, sugar and vanilla pod and stir to dissolve the sugar. Add the pears and bring to the boil.

Simmer over a low heat, tightly covered, for 8 to 10 minutes or until a cake tester inserted in the thickest part of a pear enters easily. The pears should still be slightly firm.

Remove from the heat and cool, covered. Refrigerate the pears in their liquid until ready to use.

When ready to use for the charlotte, drain the pears, reserving the liquid. Remove the vanilla pod and scrape the seeds into the liquid. Reduce the liquid to 10 fluid ounces and use for preparing the Pear Bavarian Cream (page 334).

Use a sharp thin knife to slice the pears lengthwise for the top of the charlotte.

UNDERSTANDING
Sugar has been kept to a minimum so that the sweetened pear syrup, in addition to the Italian meringue, will not oversweeten the charlotte. If you are planning to eat the pears separately and will not use the poaching liquid for another dessert, it is fine to add up to 132 grams/4½ ounces/⅔ cup sugar to the poaching liquid. This liquid can be refrigerated and reused many times for poaching more pears.

Fresh Preserved Pineapple

Makes 300 grams/10½ ounces/3 cups purée

Making preserved pineapple is quite simple and well worth the effort. Ripe Hawaiian pineapple is superb but even the often underripened more local fruit comes to life when given this treatment. There is simply no comparison between fresh preserved pineapple and the tinned variety! This purée makes a sensational ice cream (page 331) and buttercream (page 270).

STORE: Syrup: 3 weeks refrigerated.
Purée: 3 days refrigerated, 6 months frozen.

In a medium non-corrodible saucepan combine the sugar and water and bring to a boil, stirring constantly. Add the pineapple and, without stirring, return to a boil.

Cover and cool overnight at room temperature.

Drain the pineapple, reserving the syrup. You will have about 300 grams/10½ ounces/24 fluid ounces.

Purée the pineapple in a food processor or a food mill fitted with a fine disc.

INGREDIENTS	WEIGHT		MEASURE
room temperature	*grams*	*pounds/ounces*	*volume*
sugar*	400 grams	14 ounces	2 cups
water	236 grams	8¼ ounces	8 fluid ounces
1 pineapple, peeled, cored, and cut into chunks	652 grams	23 ounces	4 cups

* This amount of sugar is for a purée to be added to ice cream. If planning to use for buttercream, use only 200 grams/7 ounces/1 cup of sugar.

Freshly Grated Coconut

STORE: One week refrigerated, one year frozen.

Freshly grated coconut is a fabulous topping for cakes, worlds apart from the sweetened tinned or packet varieties. A medium coconut, weighing about 1½ pounds, will yield about 300 grams/10½ ounces/3¾ cups of grated coconut.

To open the coconut, preheat the oven to 400°F/200°C/gas mark 6. With an icepick or nail and hammer, pierce three holes at one end of the coconut. Drain the liquid and reserve, if desired, for another use. Bake the coconut until the shell cracks (about 20 minutes). Wrap it in a tea-towel to keep the shell from flying about and use a hammer to crack open the shell. Separate the coconut meat from the shell and use a vegetable parer to remove the brown skin. With the fine shredding disc of a food processor or grater, grate the coconut meat.

For toasted coconut, spread grated coconut meat on a baking sheet in a single layer and bake at 350°F/180°C/gas mark 4 for about 10 minutes or until light brown.

Lagniappe: To make a delectable *Piña Colada Cake*, make Génoise Classique (page 129) and cut it into two layers. Sprinkle it on all sides with piña colada syrup. To make the syrup, stir together 4 fluid ounces reconstituted frozen unsweetened pineapple juice,

2 fluid ounces tinned cream of coconut, and 3 tablespoons light rum. Make whipped cream, using 12 fluid ounces double cream, 2½ tablespoons sugar, and ¾ teaspoon pure vanilla extract.

Use 130 grams/4½ ounces/1 cup of whipped cream to fill the cake and sprinkle it with 40 grams/ 1½ ounces/½ cup grated coconut. Spread the cake with the remaining whipped cream and sprinkle the sides and top with about 80 grams/ 3 ounces/1 cup of the grated coconut.

Chestnut Purée

Makes 510 grams/1 pound 2 ounces/2 full cups

Chestnuts are, of course, a starchy vegetable not a fruit, but when puréed and sweetened, the faintly spicy, earthy flavour is an unusual addition to buttercreams and whipped cream. The creams are wonderful for frosting chestnut butter cake, chestnut *génoise* or chocolate cake. Tinned chestnuts from France are fine to use (page 484), but the fresh chestnut purée is even more delicious.

STORE: Sweetened or unsweetened chestnut purée will keep for 1 week refrigerated, 1 year frozen.

INGREDIENTS	WEIGHT		MEASURE
room temperature	*grams*	*pounds/ounces*	*volume*
about 36 chestnuts	510 grams	1 pound 2 ounces	—
milk	242 grams	8½ ounces	8 fluid ounces

Using a chestnut cutter or a sharp paring knife, cut an X through the skin on the flat side of each chestnut.

In a medium saucepan place the chestnuts and cold water to cover and bring to the boil. Simmer for a few minutes. Turn off the heat and remove a few nuts at a time to peel. Remove both the outer shell and as much of the inner skin as possible.

In a medium saucepan combine the chestnuts and milk and simmer covered until easily pierced with a cake tester, 20 to 40 minutes, depending on how dry the chestnuts are. Add more milk if necessary to keep them covered. Cool and then drain, reserving the milk, and process in a food processor. To obtain a silky smooth purée and remove any bits of skin, pass through a food mill fitted with the fine disc, or use a fine strainer (page 519). If the purée is very stiff, stir in some of the reserved milk. Store in an airtight container.

Note: Crème de Marrons contains pieces of candied chestnut and is almost 50 per cent sugar and glucose.

Purée de Marrons has water added which makes it too soft for certain preparations.

To use tinned chestnuts, simply drain them and process in a food processor as you would fresh chestnuts.

VARIATIONS

LIGHTLY SWEETENED CHESTNUT PURÉE FOR BUTTERCREAM:

Place 244 grams/8½ ounces/1 cup chestnut purée in a food processor. Add 37 grams/1¼ ounces/⅓ cup icing sugar, lightly spooned into a bowl, and 1 tablespoon dark rum. Process briefly until smooth.

Note: The purée for adding to whipped cream has double the icing sugar (page 303).

EASY CHESTNUT BUTTERCREAM:

This buttercream is less airy but smoother and more chestnutty than either Classic or Silk Meringue Chestnut Buttercreams. It is even strong and elastic enough for piping string work! As it contains no egg it has a longer shelf-life as well. To make 600 grams/1 lb 5 ounces/3 cups buttercream, blend together 264 grams/9¼ ounces/1 cup chestnut purée, 75 grams/2½ ounces/⅔ cup icing sugar, lightly spooned into cup, 213 grams/8 ounces/1 cup softened, unsalted butter and 1 scant tablespoon dark rum.

Pumpkin Purée

STORE: Airtight: 6 months.

If the mood strikes you to make a Pumpkin–Walnut Ring (page 68) around Halloween, the chances are you may be tempted to use fresh pumpkin for the purée. It is simple to make, especially if you own an electric power strainer attachment to your food processor (page 523).

The smallest pumpkin will make a lot more purée than the 240 grams/8¼ ounces/1 cup needed for the recipe, but it's a perfect cake for holiday gift-giving as it stores well, so you can make several cakes. Alternatively, the purée can be frozen for at least 6 months.

Bake the pumpkin whole in a 375°F/190°C/gas mark 5 oven until soft, about 2 hours. If you have a microwave, cut the pumpkin in half and microwave cut side down. Start with 5 minutes per pound on high power and rotate the halves partway through to promote even cooking. In either case, cut off the stem to avoid an unpleasant odour and cook until the pumpkin feels soft when pressed.

Allow the pumpkin to cool. Scrape out the seeds.* Remove the skin and purée the pumpkin in a food processor. Press the purée through a food mill fitted with a fine disc or a fine strainer to remove any fibres.

---

*Baked pumpkin seeds are a bonus my husband adores. Place them in a single layer on a baking sheet and return to the oven until dry.

Special Effects and Decorative Techniques

Making a cake look as wonderful as it tastes can be as enjoyable as baking it. Decorations serve two important purposes: they lend a festive touch while masking imperfections in the icing.

Actually, an iced cake does not have to look perfect. In fact, it is less inviting to eat if the icing is so smooth and free of air bubbles or spatula marks that it looks almost plastic. Cake is food. Have fun with it. (When I was a food stylist for magazines, my colleagues and I would gloat about how we were brought up 'not to play with our food' but now we were having our revenge and being paid for it!) Cakes offer the opportunity to execute one's most creative fantasies. To make a cake with a simple, elegant look, however, requires a great deal more skill than it takes to cover a cake with lots of piped festoons.

Piping fine decorations takes practice but there are many 'tricks of the trade' which make it possible to produce magnificent cakes without ever picking up an icing bag.

This chapter is devoted to making the cake look terrific. Some of the decorative touches are delightfully easy, others are for the craftsperson who enjoys painstaking, detailed handiwork.

Preparing the Cake

LEVELLING

If a cake is not level before icing, it is unlikely that the iced cake will look even. Icing can be used to fill in small imperfections, but the top of the cake should be levelled with a serrated blade. If you don't have a cake leveller (page 528), an easy method is to place the cake in the tin in which it was baked and use the rim of the tin as a guide for a long serrated knife. If the cake is too low in the tin, raise it slightly by placing cardboard rounds beneath it.

If the cake is to be covered with rolled fondant, the sharp edges around the top should be bevelled slightly to keep the fondant from cracking.

LAYERING

My favourite ways of cutting a cake into layers all involve using a serrated blade at least the length of the diameter of the cake.

For one method, I also use a set of metal bars called retainer bars. They are used in the confectionery industry to mould melted sugar, retaining the flow. (They are available from confectionery suppliers such as Maid of Scandinavia, page 531.) The bars come in a set of four and each is 2 centimetres/¾-inch high. I use the bars as tracks, placing the cake between two of them and allowing the knife blade to rest on their surface while cutting through the cake. The result is two perfectly even 2-centimetre/¾-inch-high layers. (When I want to trim a cake to 4 centimetres/1½ inches high, I stack the bars so that they are that height.) This system works so well I went to a metal supply shop and found beautiful brass bars of varying heights. Wood strips also work but are much lighter, so they need to be taped to the work surface (Fig. 1).

A second method is to use an adjustable cake saw (page 528).

A third method, requiring the least equipment and the most self-

1

assurance, is known as the eyeballing method. The cake is placed on a turntable and a long serrated knife is held against the side where you estimate (by eye) the middle to be. The turntable is revolved as the knife cuts a shallow groove all around the cake. This provides a track for the knife to 'ride' in when cutting through the cake. Be sure to use a firm forward and side-to-side motion when cutting, checking occasionally to ensure that the knife is still in the groove. It is easiest to hold one hand palm downwards on top of the cake while slicing. This keeps your fingers safe when the knife slices through to the other side (Fig. 2).

2

For ease in separating the layers, slide a cardboard round or removable cake-tin bottom between them.

FILLING

A long metal spatula and turntable help to create a smooth, even layer of buttercream. A filling between two cake layers is usually 5 millimetres/¼-inch thick. Heap the filling on top of the cake layer. Use a long spatula, pressing firmly with a back-and-forth motion without lifting up the spatula; this may cause the crust to lift away from the cake. When the entire surface is covered, hold the long spatula halfway across the cake with the blade almost flat against the surface of the filling and, pressing lightly, smoothly rotate the turntable in one full circle.

Chill the cake for 5 minutes in the freezer or about 20 minutes in the refrigerator to set the filling before placing the second layer on top. This prevents the filling from becoming uneven and also enables you to move the top layer if the placement is not exact. I use the removable metal bottom of a quiche tin or loose-bottomed tin to support the second layer while placing it on top of the filling.

CUTTING DECORATIVELY SHAPED CAKES

A serrated knife is also the ideal tool to cut cakes into different shapes. To cut an octagon shape, for example, for Rose Trellis cake (page 239), make a cardboard template to place on top of the cake as a cutting guide. As the baked cake will measure 21.5 centimetres/8½ inches in diameter, first cut a circle of that size. (Plain cardboard is easier to cut than corrugated.) Then make eight 8-centimetre/3¼-inch connecting lines. Each line should begin and end at the edge of the circle. Cut exactly on the lines and the octagon template is complete. Place on top of the cake and cut eight sides, cutting straight down through the cake.

REMOVING THE CRUST

Whisked sponge cakes absorb syrup most easily if the bottom and top crusts are removed. If left on, the crusts would become pasty.

It is only necessary to remove the thinnest possible layer. To remove the bottom crust, scrape gently with a serrated knife. The top crust tends to separate easily from the cake with the help of a long serrated knife.

SYRUPING

The best technique for applying a syrup to *génoise* or *biscuit* is to sprinkle it rather than brush it because brushing picks up crumbs. The best implement is a large medical syringe. (Use your imagination; syringes are made for other, usually medical, uses and they will work well for cakes if reserved only for this use.)

SUPPORTING THE CAKE FOR DECORATING

To support the cake while icing, it should be on a rigid surface such as a serving plate or cardboard round. If using a serving plate, slide a few strips of greaseproof paper under the edges. These keep the plate clean and can be pulled out after the cake is iced.

Cardboard rounds have the advantage of providing a guide for the amount of icing used on the sides of the cake since they are cut the size of the cake tin and the cake normally shrinks 1 centimetre/ ½ inch in diameter. When smoothing the sides, keep the spatula pressed to the side of the cardboard, not allowing it to tilt towards the cake, to get a 5-millimetre/¼-inch layer of frosting (the distance between the cake and edge of the cardboard).

Whatever surface is used to support the cake, a small dab of icing or melted chocolate in the centre helps keep the cake in place.

CRUMB COATING

If the sides have a lot of loose crumbs, it is helpful to apply a crumb coating to seal them in and keep them from getting into the icing. A thin layer of warmed fruit Jewel Glaze (page 378) or piping gel (page 497) can be brushed over the cake to seal in the crumbs. It is best to allow the glaze to dry until it feels tacky before frosting. It is also possible to use a very thin coat of icing as a crumb coating.

Covering the Cake

The six basic methods of covering a cake are:
1. Dusting it with cocoa or icing sugar, placing a stencil on top before dusting, if desired, to create a pattern.
2. Glazing with or without buttercream underneath (page 314).
3. Icing and encrusting with nuts (page 373).
4. Icing and making designs in the icing with a spatula, serrated knife or other items (page 411).
5. Icing and decorating with an icing tube (page 451).
6. Covering the cake with rolled fondant (page 414).

To ice a cake using this method, place a cardboard round the exact size of the tin's diameter in the bottom. If necessary, use a few pieces of tape to hold it in place.

smooth as plaster. Actually they are as close to plaster as you can get – they are covered with royal icing (sometimes referred to as cake decorator's cement) that has been allowed to dry until very hard and is then sanded down to a smooth finish, an impossibility with buttercream.

There is a baker's trick for covering a cake smoothly and evenly which requires special equipment but little practice. The results are always picture perfect. The equipment consists of a flan ring or loose-bottomed tin and a butane torch or electric hair dryer.

The cake is moulded with the icing right in the tin, using the top of the tin to level the icing. Just enough heat is applied to the outside to melt the thinnest layer of icing so that the cake can be slid out with perfectly iced sides and top.

To ice a cake using this method, place a cardboard round the exact size of the tin's diameter in the bottom. If necessary, use a few pieces of tape to hold it in place. The sides of the tin should not be more than 5 millimetres/¼ inch higher than the cake or the icing will be too thick. Extra cardboard rounds can be used to raise the cake to the proper height.

With a metal spatula, coat the sides of the tin with 5 millimetres/ ¼ inch buttercream or icing and slide the cake into the tin. Scoop buttercream on top (repeat if using

more layers), filling the entire tin, and use a long metal spatula, ruler or knife to level it. To make a wavy line, use a serrated knife, moving it from left to right as you pull it forward (Fig. 1). Chill the cake to set the icing for at least 1 hour or freeze for 10 minutes.

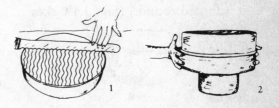

To turn out: Set a heavy canister on top of a turntable. The diameter of the canister must be smaller than the removable section of the tin. Remove any tape holding the tin to the cardboard bottom and, using a butane torch or hair dryer, rotate the turntable so the sides of the cake are heated evenly. Not much heat is required, especially if using the torch. One steady turn around is usually sufficient to release the cake.

Firmly press down the sides of the tin until it slides away from the cake. A perfectly iced cake will be perched atop the canister (Fig. 2).

To ice a cake in the traditional way, use a metal spatula to cover the sides and top with a thin icing. A stiff icing will not go on smoothly, so, if necessary, warm the icing to soften it. Heaping on large gobs will help to keep the crust from coming up and excess icing is easy to remove.

I like to start with the sides of the cake. If the cake is 23 centimetres/9 inches or smaller, I ice the sides by holding the cake in the palm of one hand, smoothing the icing with a small metal spatula. (The cake is supported by a cardboard round.) (Fig. 1.) Cakes

1

larger than 23 centimetres/9 inches are too heavy for me so I use a turntable. To smooth the icing, the spatula should be held parallel to the sides of the cake and the blade angled slightly outward so that the edge can remove excess icing. Hold the spatula steady and rotate the turntable with the other hand (Fig. 2).

2

When icing the sides, bring the icing up 5 millimetres/¼-inch higher than the top of the cake to make a foundation for the top icing. When the sides are reasonably smooth (you can go back to them after finishing the top), heap icing on top of the cake.

3

Use a long spatula, pressing firmly with a back-and-forth motion without lifting up the spatula because that might lift the crust away. When the entire surface is covered, hold the spatula halfway across the cake with the blade almost flat against the icing. Pressing lightly, rotate the turntable in one full circle (Fig. 3). Remove the excess icing from the sides by holding a small spatula parallel to the sides and rotating again. If the cake needs further smoothing, dip a spatula in hot water, shake off the water and repeat the smoothing process, pressing lightly as there will be little excess icing to remove.

EMBOSSED ICING
The iced sides of a tall cake tier sometimes look a bit plain. One solution is piping a design in icing such as a scroll border (page 466). Another solution is creating a pattern in the icing itself. Larry Rosenberg, in *Cake Decorating Simplified: The Roth Method*, came up with a most original and creative way to accomplish this. He uses the rough pattern embossed on paper towels to pattern the icing. The basic technique is to press three thicknesses of paper towels against the side of the iced layer.

Spray the paper towels liberally with water so they won't stick to the icing. Press the paper towels against the sides of the cake using a metal spatula (as if you were smoothing the icing). It is fine to do a small area at a time. Remove the towels, spraying with more water if necessary.

SWIRLED ICING

One of the most appealing decorations, especially for chocolate cake, is a luxurious series of swirls covering the sides and top. No other decoration is needed to tell the eye that this cake is going to be delicious. If making swirls, the cake should be iced with the same basic technique but great care needn't be taken to ensure evenness. Simply use a small metal spatula to make circular swirls in the icing (Fig. 1).

1

SPIKES

Perky little peaks of icing are easy to make and add a whimsical touch. They can be used only for the sides or for the top as well. To make the spikes, do not smooth the icing too thinly or evenly as there must be enough icing to pull out

2

into peaks. Use a small metal spatula to lift the icing away from the cake. The icing should be fairly stiff (Fig. 2).

RIBBON

Attractive ribbon is an easy decoration for the sides of a cake. Of course it must be removed before serving.

Choose a waterproof ribbon for soft icings; any ribbon is fine for Classic Rolled Fondant (page 354) or a firm icing such as Crème Ivoire (page 287). Gold lamé and grosgrain are two of my favourites. Most ribbon can be taped to hold it in place. Tape does not work on the lamé so I use a spot of royal icing, a paper clip hidden by a chocolate rose leaf, or a hat pin with a large head (so that it cannot accidentally be left in the cake when serving).

CUTTING AN ICED CAKE

Use a thin, sharp blade. When the blade reaches the bottom of cake, wiggle it slightly to be sure that the slice is free and slide it out. Never lift the blade straight up through the top of the cake as it will lift crumbs into the icing and mar the appearance.

HOW TO COVER A CAKE WITH ROLLED FONDANT (PAGE 354)

Working with rolled fondant is a real pleasure. It feels like silk and looks like alabaster. It's a lot easier to make a cake look wonderful with rolled fondant than with buttercream, providing that it is rolled no less than 5 millimetres/¼-inch thick. Thinner fondant will show all the imperfections of the cake it is covering.

To practise handling the fondant, try applying it to the outside of a cake tin before committing it to a cake. This way it can be gathered up, rekneaded and rerolled without being full of crumbs.

The first step before applying the fondant is to place the cake on a rigid cardboard base. If this step is omitted, the cake cannot be moved until the fondant becomes very firm, which takes about 24 hours. If the cake base is flexible and the fondant only partially dry, it will wrinkle.

The next step is to bevel the edge (page 408) and to coat the cake with a very thin layer of buttercream or melted jelly to adhere to the fondant. (A little beaten egg white will also work.)

Fondant should be rolled on a lightly greased surface until large enough to cover the entire cake layer. If a layer is 23 × 7.5 centimetres/9 × 3 inches, for example, it will require rolling the fondant to 38 centimetres/15 inches in diameter. Don't worry if it is a little small as fondant can be stretched at least 2 centimetres/¾ inch and smoothed into place. Never pull the fondant, however, because it will tear. Rotate the fondant after every two or three rolls to ensure that it is not sticking. If necessary, apply more non-stick vegetable spray or regrease the work surface. In cool, dry weather, or if rolling a large piece of fondant, I cover the fondant with clingfilm to keep the surface from drying and cracking. When covering cakes 30.5 centimetres/12 inches and larger, it helps to use a rolling pin to lift the fondant. Lightly spray the surface of the fondant with non-stick vegetable spray so it doesn't stick when rolled around the pin.

Use your hands palms down to lift the rolled fondant over the cake. Quickly smooth over the top, using a circular motion and starting from the centre to prevent air bubbles. (Bubbles can be pierced with a needle and smoothed out if necessary.) Use your palms to smooth and ease the fondant against the sides, working from the top down in a semicircular motion (Fig. 1). Oil from your hands will give the fondant a lustrous glow.

Use a pizza cutter or small sharp knife to trim the fondant at the base (Fig. 2). If necessary, it is fine to continue to smooth the fondant as it dries during the first 30

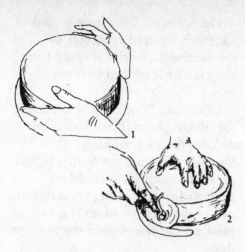

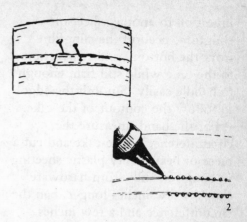

minutes or so. (Actually, it's hard to resist.)★

Small vertical slits can be made at even intervals around the sides with a knife or scalpel so short pieces of ribbon can be inserted. This gives the illusion that the ribbon is weaving in and out of the fondant.

To attach a narrow band of satin ribbon around the cake, pin one end to the cake. Wrap it around the circumference, overlap the ends and secure with a second pin (Fig. 1). Pipe tiny beads of royal icing with a number 1 or 2 round decorating tube along both edges of ribbon (Fig. 2). When the cake has been completely encircled, the pins can be removed.

For the base, use a 4.5-millimetre round decorating tube. If points form, flatten and smooth them with a damp artist's paint brush.

For a pale golden luminescence, use an artist's brush to dust on hardened fondant with edible gold petal dust (Maid of Scandinavia, page 531).

CHOCOLATE ROLLED FONDANT (PAGE 356):

Chocolate Rolled Fondant can be used to cover a cake in the same way as white fondant, but, since it is a little trickier to work with, I have developed a slightly different design for it which is easier to execute. It consists of a top disc and band.

Roll out a disc 3 millimetres/ 1/8 inch thick on top of a piece of smooth clingfilm. Transfer the clingfilm and disc to a baking sheet and cut into a circle slightly larger than the diameter of the cake, using an inverted cake tin or lid as a guide and a pizza cutter or the tip of a sharp knife to cut. Freeze for 10 minutes or until very firm.

★Confectionery suppliers such as Maid of Scandinavia carry differently shaped crimpers for decorating rolled fondant. Fondant must be crimped soon after applying, while still soft and malleable.

Invert on to another sheet of clingfilm, peel off the clingfilm from the bottom, and reinvert on to the cake while still firm enough to handle easily. Smooth the edge to follow the contour of the cake.

For the band, measure the circumference of the cake and cut a piece of heavy-duty plastic sheeting (it comes in rolls from hardware shops) a few inches longer than the circumference and a few inches wider than the desired height. A good height is 2.5 to 5 centimetres/ 1 to 2 inches higher than the sides. A 23-centimetre/9-inch cake will need a band that is 72 centimetres/ 28¼ inches long. Place the plastic on a flat surface and roll the fondant into a long rope. Lay it on the middle of the plastic and roll into a thin band 3 millimetres/ ⅛-inch thick. Using a long plastic ruler and a pizza cutter, even the edges, cutting the bottom edge flush with the bottom of the plastic. Use your finger to smooth the upper edge so that it thins slightly. Allow the band to sit for 30 minutes or until firm but still flexible. Use the plastic to lift the fondant and curve it around the sides of the cake – which have been brushed with a thin coating of melted Jewel Glaze (page 378). If the fondant is very soft and floppy, refrigerate for a few minutes to firm. Peel away the plastic and curve the top edge gently towards the top of the cake to create a graceful free-form design.

Do not store for a long period of time in a covered container as fondant will absorb moisture from the cake or icing and become sticky.

Chocolate Fondant is also perfect for making butterflies. Roll it out on clingfilm 1.5 millimetres/ ¹⁄₁₆-inch thick and cut with a lightly greased butterfly cutter. Make a V support form from heavy-duty foil or use the recesses of an egg box to prop up the wings until the fondant dries.

HOW TO COVER A CAKE WITH MARZIPAN (PAGE 368)

Marzipan is best rolled out between sheets of clingfilm to prevent sticking. Although marzipan can be used to cover a cake, because it develops a hard crust I prefer to use it only as a component inside the cake – such as the leaf-thin pistachio marzipan inside Pistachio and Rose Wedding Cake (page 254). When asked to use marzipan for the top of a cake, I am always careful to keep it covered with clingfilm until shortly before serving time or to brush it with melted cocoa butter.

As marzipan tends to be very sweet in large doses, I roll it only 1.5 millimetres/¹⁄₁₆-inch thick. A lightly greased cake tin or vol-au-vent cutter works well as a cutting guide. Because I roll marzipan so thin, discs are easiest to handle when frozen. Slip the marzipan, still on clingfilm, on to a lightly greased rimless baking sheet and freeze for a few minutes until firm. Flip the marzipan over so that the clingfilm is on top. Position over the cake and carefully slide off the sheet on to the cake. It cannot be moved once in place. Marzipan sheets can be rolled out on a surface lightly dusted with cornflour and then draped or rolled loosely over the rolling pin to transfer to the cake.

Hand-modelled and Cut-out Decorations

Both rolled fondant and marzipan lend themselve to hand-modelling and appliqués. Rolled fondant is the more flexible of the two, so it is easier to use for long cut-outs such as ribbons.

When rolling fondant for appliqués and ribbon, I use a sheet of clingfilm under it to ensure that it will release in one piece and roll it out 3 millimetres/1¹/₁₆-inch thick. Use the straight edge of a lightly greased plastic ruler to cut strips of ribbon. It is best to place the ribbons on the cake while the fondant is still flexible enough to curve the bow and drape the streamers in a natural manner. Small lightly greased biscuit cutters can be used to stamp out decorative shapes which can be dried and stored airtight at room temperature just about indefinitely. When ready to place them on a fondant-covered cake, first paint the bottoms with a little egg white.

I cut Pistachio Marzipan (page 371) in ivy-shaped leaves using a special cutter, but you could use a sharp knife. Veins can be simulated with slight pressure from the back edge of a knife blade.

To make a stem for a rose (complete with thorns), roll a piece of tinted fondant or marzipan into a long thin stem (Fig. 2). With the tip of a knife, make tiny slashes in the stem, opening them out slightly to form thorns (Fig. 3). The leaves can be cut free-hand and veined

1

2

3

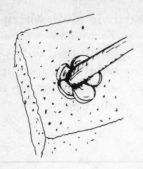

with the back of a knife. To scallop the edges, make tiny slashes in the sides.

To make curved flowers such as forget-me-nots, stamp out the shape with a flower cutter (available from special suppliers, including Maid of Scandinavia, page 531). To make it curve, place the flower in the palm of your hand (dusted with cornflour or lightly greased) or on a small piece of foam rubber and, using a little wooden stick with a rounded end (also available from the above suppliers) or a cotton swab, press into the centre of the flower, causing the petals to curve upward. Allow the flowers to dry until firm enough to hold their shape.

MARZIPAN ROSES
No icing squeezed from a tube can ever equal the exquisite delicacy and detail of a rose hand-sculpted from marzipan or chocolate paste. It is, in fact, so lifelike that it's my favourite flower to use on cakes. (I was once described by Jim Gaynor in *Cuisine* magazine as 'Marzipan Rose'!)

Marzipan is easier to work with than chocolate paste, so the technique for making roses can be slightly more elaborate and the flower can support more petals. Ceramic and cake decorating suppliers carry rose petal cutters in varying sizes, but the large end of an icing tube, almost 2.5 centimetres/1 inch in diameter, also works if you roll the marzipan slightly thicker for the larger petals. Grease the cutting edge if the marzipan sticks.

I like to tint marzipan for roses the palest possible shade of pink. To achieve this shade, use only the point of a needle's worth of paste food colour. Or tint only a small batch a stronger pink and knead bits of it into untinted marzipan. You'll be surprised at how easily the colour can turn to bubble-gum pink if too much is used.

Another realistic touch is to tint the marzipan for the inner petals a slightly deeper shade. I like to work with a real rose in front of me for inspiration.

Tip: After rolling out and cutting the petals, use a fingertip to thin the edges of the petals. If the marzipan seems slightly soft and the petals droop, allow them to dry for a few minutes before applying them.

To shape roses: Begin by forming the centre cone and base. Use the natural contours of your hand to form a pointed cone and pedestal base which will be removed after the rose is completed (Fig. 1).

Have ready a little bowl of water or lightly beaten egg white and a small artist's paint brush.

Roll out thin sheets of marzipan between two pieces of clingfilm – but not too thinly because each piece will be rolled and shaped a second time. Keep the marzipan covered at all times to prevent drying.

Cut out a free-form rounded rectangle 5 centimetres/2 inches long. Lift it from the plastic sheet and roll it a second time between clingfilm to thin it (Fig. 2). Wrap it around the cone, overlapping to form a point and then folding it back. This is the closed bud of the flower (Fig. 3).

Cut three 2.5-centimetre/1-inch rounds for petals. Remove each, one at a time, to a second set of clingfilm and roll the upper section to a thin tip and form the oval shape (Fig. 4). Place around the bud, overlapping slightly and curving one side realistically back (Fig. 5). Paint tiny dabs of water or egg white towards the base to attach the petals. A small metal cuticle pusher is ideal for moulding the petals and pushing them slightly away from the centre bud.

For the second row of three petals, the rounds must be rolled slightly more elliptically because they have a wider circumference to cover. Cut three 3-centimetre/1¼-inch rounds, again making the edges thinner than the base (Fig. 6). When the petals are in place, use a fingertip to form a centre point and curve the sides slightly back (Fig. 7).

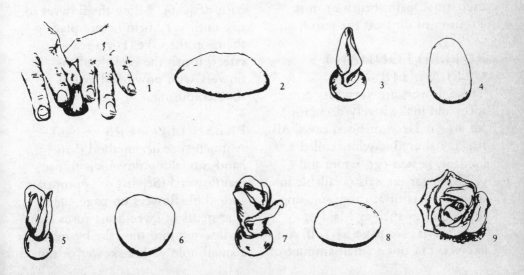

For a full-blown rose do one final row of four petals. These will be the widest – almost oval in shape as they have the greatest distance to cover (Fig. 8). Use a slightly larger cutter (4 centimetres/ 1½ inches) to cut three initial circles, because, if they are thinned too much to achieve the correct size, they will not be sturdy enough. Use fingertips to create three points on each petal, encouraging the edges in between to roll back slightly (Fig. 9). You may need to prop up this final row of petals using little balls of fondant dipped in cornflour to keep the petals in place until they dry enough to hold by themselves.

The completed rose will hold its shape well if placed in a bed of cornflour to support the petals. When the marzipan sets and is firm enough to hold its shape, cut off the base with a small sharp knife. When the rose is thoroughly dry, use a small paint brush or dust atomiser to dust off the cornflour.

ROLLED FONDANT CALLA LILIES

These flowers are very easy to form and make lovely decorations for an Art Deco-inspired cake. All that is required is white rolled fondant, beaten egg white and yellow sugar crystals (available in supermarkets or at candy-making supply stores such as Maid of Scandinavia, see page 531). If you like you can tint a small amount of fondant pale green to make sepals at the base.

Start with the centres by rolling thin 5-millimetre/¼-inch-diameter ropes of fondant. Cut off sections slightly shorter than the projected length of the finished flower. Round one end. Brush the entire piece with lightly beaten egg white and roll in the yellow sugar crystals. Allow to dry until firm enough to handle (Fig. 1).

For flowers, roll the fondant thin and cut out ovals 7.5 centimetres/ 3 inches long, with one end rounded and the other pointed (Fig. 2). Bring together the rounded ends, overlapping slightly, and use a tiny bit of egg white to hold them in place (Fig. 3). Slip the centre in place so that it comes to 2.5 centimetres/1 inch from point. Cut out a 4-centimetre/1½-inch circle of rolled green fondant for the sepal. Roll to elongate it slightly and wrap it around the base. (Fig. 6). Allow the flowers to dry until very firm before placing them on the cake. For a realistic effect, brush the centres of the flowers with powdered yellow food colouring.

FRESH FLOWERS

A much speedier method than hand-modelling flowers is to use real flowers! (See list of appropriate and edible flowers on page 493.) The stems of sweetheart roses can be inserted into the cake by making a small hole with a skewer or they

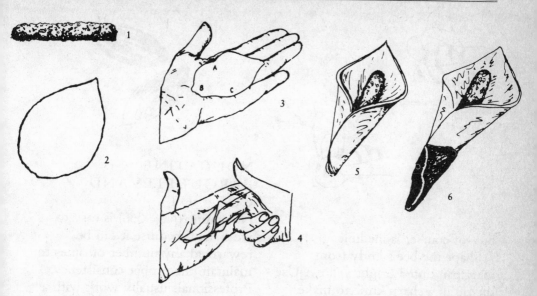

can be strewn around each tier. They will remain fresh-looking for hours. If they must be placed the day before, little flower sinkers (page 530) can be inserted into the cake to keep the flowers watered and fresh.

Real roses are sometimes too tightly closed to look their best. If time does not allow them to be placed in warm water, a florist's trick is to blow on them to force them open. Imperfect outer petals can be removed.

DRIED FLOWERS
One of my friends and former students, Jan Kish of La Petite Fleur in Columbus, Ohio, flies special-order cakes all over the country. Because shipping cakes by plane does not lend itself to the use of fresh flowers, she sometimes uses dried flowers and herbs to

decorate the cakes. The exquisite pastel shades and ethereal textures provide a slightly faded, dream-like quality. Some of the flowers and herbs she uses are: tiny pink sweetheart roses, larkspur, globe amaranth, lavender, thyme, myrtle and rosemary. Each has its own symbolic meaning: rosemary for remembrance, myrtle for virginity, lavender for love.

MARZIPAN BEES
I designed these bees for Queen Bee cake (page 211) and, quite honestly, they can be more time-consuming than the cake. But if you are a craftsperson you will love making them. The gossamer gelatin wings look almost real. Sheet gelatin and icing pens are available through Maid of Scandinavia (page 531). Thin plastic can be used in place of the gelatin

NOUGATINE BARQUETTES AND CUT-OUTS

but, of course, is inedible.

Shape the bee's body from marzipan tinted bright yellow. Use the tip of a sharp knife to make two tiny slashes at the neck to receive the wings. Use a black icing pen or pipe black-tinted royal icing to form eyes and stripes. Cut free-form oval wings with sharp pointed ends from sheet gelatin. To make the wings more visible, tint them with an artist's brush very lightly moistened with water tinted with golden food colour.

Insert the wing tips into the slashes and allow them to dry until very firm.

If you are planning to suspend the bees above the cake before drying, make a small hole in front of the neck with a sharp needle and insert a 15-centimetre/6-inch piece of dried angel hair pasta. Insert the other end of the pasta into a piece of styrofoam and allow the bee to dry for 24 hours before placing in the cake. (If there is a slight breeze, the bees will sway above the cake.)

Nougatine (page 366) is easy to work with because it can be rewarmed any number of times to maintain the proper consistency. Professionals usually work with a heat lamp to keep the nougatine soft but a hot tray or oven works well too.

Nougatine must be warm when cut or it will shatter. If it hardens while working with it, return it briefly to a 300°F/150°C/gas mark 2 oven or foil-covered hot tray.

Nougatine can be cut with a knife, heavy-duty round or oval nougatine cutters, a pizza cutter or sharp kitchen shears. The cutters should be oiled so that they don't stick to the nougatine.

To cut out ovals of nougatine for barquettes, fashion a foil template by pressing foil into the barquette mould, then flattening it and cutting out the shape. When the nougatine is cool enough to handle, cut it into four equal parts and roll one of them into a 20 × 15-centimetre/8 × 6-inch rectangle 3 millimetres/1/8 inch thick. Keep the other three pieces

1

2

warm in the oven with the door ajar. If the nougatine has cooled and hardened, warm it again until soft enough to mark easily.

Using a pizza cutter and the template as a guide, mark the oval on the nougatine. When cool enough to handle, cut out the oval with scissors (Fig. 1). Each rectangle will make three barquettes.

Press the nougatine oval into a lightly greased barquette mould (Fig. 2). The nougatine must be hot enough to remain flexible. If necessary, return briefly to the heat source just until flexible (not too long or it will lose its shape). When cool, remove the hardened nougatine barquette from the mould and proceed with the remainder. The barquettes will keep for several weeks if stored airtight at room temperature away from direct sunlight, heat and humidity.

Another interesting use for nougatine is to cut it in triangles and spread one side of each triangle with tempered dark chocolate. This can be used to make a pinwheel around the top of a cake (similar to the traditional décor for a Dobos Torte). Small triangles or irregular pieces make elegant and delicious petits fours to serve with coffee at the end of a formal dinner.

CHARLOTTE SHAPES

A charlotte consists of a cream filling encased in a thin layer of a sponge-type cake such as a *biscuit*. The filling is stabilised with gelatin to make it firm enough to hold its shape for slicing. Charlottes are formed in a mould which will support their shape until the gelatin sets.

There are many delightful cake shapes and designs for lining a mould, flan or springform. The completed charlotte often looks like a feat of wizardry, but actually the various shapes are easy to accomplish by cutting rectangles of thin cake and sandwiching them together with jam. Biscuit Roulade (page 157) is an ideal cake to use for this purpose because it is baked

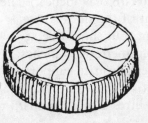

in large thin layers and is springy enough to compress and mould into complex shapes without sacrificing delicacy of texture. *Génoise* works well for cutting and overlapping long strips to form a dome shape. And, of course, Biscuit à la Cuillère (or sponge fingers) encircling the filling is the classic Charlotte Russe. Before filling the lined mould with cloud creams, Bavarian creams or whipped cream, the cake can be brushed lightly with syrup or sprinkled with liqueur. If filling the cake with a fruit cloud cream such as strawberry or raspberry, a nice addition is to brush the base of the cake with a thin coating of the fruit sauce. Piping free-form loops or swirls with the cloud cream, after smoothing the surface, and spooning some of the fruit sauce into the depressions also makes an attractive design.

A 1.5-litre/2½-pint/6-cup bowl is a good size for domed charlottes. When lined with a thin layer of cake it will hold 1.25 litres/2 pints/ 5 cups of filling. Loose-bottom 20 or 23-centimetre/8 or 9-inch tins or springforms are good sizes for other shapes. (Flan rings are fine, but will not be exactly 20 or 23 centimetres/8 or 9 inches.) The exact height of the sides is unimportant, but should be at least 5.5 centimetres/2¼ inches high to offer adequate support. A 20-centimetre/8-inch ring needs 1.25 to 1.5 litres/2 to 2½ pints/5 to

6 cups filling; a 23-centimetre/ 9-inch ring 1.5 to 1.75 litres/2½ to 3 pints/6 to 7 cups. The inner circumference of a 20-centimetre/ 8-inch ring is 63.5 centimetres/ 25 inches and a 23-centimetre/ 9-inch ring is 71 centimetres/ 28 inches. This means you will need about seventeen 4-centimetre/ 1½-inch-wide ladyfingers (or a 63-centimetre/25-inch-long cake strip) to line a 20-centimetre/8-inch ring and nineteen 4-centimetre/ 1½-inch-wide ladyfingers (or a 71-centimetre/28-inch-long cake strip) to line a 23-centimetre/9-inch ring. A 19 to 21.5-centimetre/ 7½ to 8½-inch round of cake is trimmed to fit just inside the circle of the cake to serve as the base. This can be cut from a sheet of *biscuit* or piped from Biscuit à la Cuillère batter (page 165).

CUT SHAPES

A single layer of Biscuit Roulade is easiest to cut using scissors. A serrated knife works best for layers or sandwiches of *biscuit*, which cut most precisely when frozen.

SPIRALLED DOME:

Lining the bowl with clingfilm makes it easy to unmould a dome-shaped charlotte. Lightly oil a 1.5-litre/2½-pint/6-cup bowl and line it as smoothly as possible with clingfilm, leaving a small overhang. Measure the diameter of the bowl.

You will need a round *biscuit* base slightly smaller.

When the *biscuit* has finished baking, use the lining to slip it out of the pan on to the worktop and cut off a strip from one of the short ends just large enough to serve as the base. While still hot, roll the *biscuit* as indicated in the recipe and allow it to cool. When the cut strip has cooled, cut with shears into a circle for the base. Wrap with clingfilm and set aside.

The Swiss-roll slices used to line this charlotte must be tightly rolled for the most attractive appearance. To accomplish this, unroll the cooled *biscuit*, leaving it on the non-stick liner or tea-towel, and spread with a very thin layer of Cordon Rose Raspberry Conserve (page 380) or commercial jam (about 155 grams/5½ ounces/ ½ cup). For heightened flavour, stir 2 teaspoons Chambord (black raspberry liqueur) into the conserve.

Roll up the *biscuit* tightly one-third of the way and turn so that the unrolled portion is facing you. Lap over the lining or tea-towel to cover the rolled section and a little of the flat section. Hold the edge of a straight-sided baking sheet at an angle on top of the tea-towel just at the point where the rolled section ends. Press firmly against the roll and tug the bottom of the tea-towel towards you. Lift away the overlap. Continue rolling one-third of the way and repeat the process.

Finish rolling and repeat once more, again angling the sheet just at the base of the completed roll. The roll will be 4.5 centimetres/ 1¾ inches in diameter. Wrap snugly with clingfilm, then foil, and freeze until firm enough to slice.

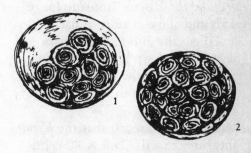

With a small serrated knife, cut into 5-millimetre/¼-inch-thick slices. To line the mould, start by placing one slice in the centre and place slices around it as tightly as possible to avoid gaps. It is sometimes necessary to cut slices in half or smaller to fit the last row. Cover the *biscuit*-lined bowl tightly to keep it from drying out until the filling is ready. Fill the mould and place the round *biscuit* base in place. Cover tightly and refrigerate until set (at least 4 hours).

To unmould: Invert on to a serving plate and lift away the bowl, tugging gently on the clingfilm to

release it. To prevent drying out,
glaze with melted jelly or Shiny
Jewel Glaze (page 379) or simply
leave the clingfilm in place until
serving time.

VERTICAL STRIPES:

For this elegant design, thin layers
of *biscuit* are sandwiched with
raspberry conserve and cut into
small rectangles to line the sides of
a loose-bottomed or springform
tin. A disc of Biscuit à la Cuillère,
cut to fit inside, serves as the base.

Bake the Biscuit Roulade (page
157) and allow it to cool flat.

To cut the *biscuit*, use a pizza
cutter or a sharp knife and a ruler
to score where the cuts should be.
Use sharp shears to do the actual
cutting.

Trim the edges so that the *biscuit*
measures exactly 25.5 × 40 centi-
metres/10 × 16 inches. Cut the
biscuit lengthwise into four equal
rectangles. Each will be 6 centi-
metres/2½ inches wide by 41
centimetres/16 inches long. Spread
three of them with a smooth layer
of Cordon Rose Raspberry
Conserve (page 380) or seedless
commercial raspberry jam. You
will need about 234 grams/8¼
ounces/¾ cup to complete the
cake. For extra flavour intensity,
thin the conserve with 1 tablespoon
Chambord (black raspberry
liqueur). If using commercial jam,
heat and sieve it and use it warm.

Stack the rectangles carefully on
top of each other, ending with the
layer without jam. The flat side of
a long metal ruler set against the
side helps to even the layers. Cut
the finished stack in half, to form
two shorter stacks (each 19 centi-
metres/7½ inches long).

You now have two four-layer
rectangles 6 centimetres/2½ inches
wide and 5 centimetres/2 inches
high (Fig. 1). (The only important
measurement is the width because
when sliced and positioned in the
tin, it will determine the height of
the striped border.) Wrap the
rectangles in greaseproof paper and
slip it into a large heavy-duty
plastic freezer bag. Place on a flat
surface such as a baking sheet to
maintain the shape and freeze until
firm.

Use a small serrated knife to cut
the rectangles into 9-millimetre/
⅜-inch-thick slices (Fig. 2). Trim
tops and bottoms so that each slice
is even and the same height.

If moulding the charlotte in a
springform tin, you may remove
the inner disc and place the outer
ring directly on a serving plate. If
using a loose-bottomed tin, leave
the inner disc in place but line with

a parchment round if planning to remove the disc before serving.

Lightly butter the inside of the ring. Place *biscuit* slices around the ring so that the stripes are straight up and down. Brush one side of each slice with a light coating of conserve before placing the next rectangle firmly against it.

Measure the inside diameter of the *biscuit*-lined ring for making the *biscuit* disc. Cover tightly with clingfilm and set aside while preparing the disc and filling.

Pipe and bake a spiral of Biscuit à la Cuillère (page 165) the desired size of the charlotte base. When cool, trim if necessary and fit snugly into the bottom of the lined ring (Fig. 3). Scoop in the filling, cover tightly and refrigerate until set (at least 4 hours).

To unmould: For a springform tin, release the sides and lift away. For a loose-bottomed tin, place on top of a sturdy canister smaller than the tin bottom opening and press firmly downwards. The sides will slip down to the worktop and the charlotte can be lifted off the canister because it is supported by the tin base.

3

STRIPED DOME:

Until it is cut into, this dramatic design defies analysis. The striped motif is achieved by cutting and overlapping thin rectangles from a square *génoise*. The chocolate-iced bottom crust determines the striping effect. No cake base is necessary for this charlotte.

Bake the Génoise Classique (page 129) using a 20-centimetre/8-inch-long by 5-centimetre/2-inch-high metal tin. Unmould on to a lightly greased rack. When cool, wrap well with clingfilm and allow it to sit overnight to firm for cutting. Prepare half the syrup recipe on page 132.

When ready to mould the cake, use a soft tape measure to measure the inside of a 1.5-litre/2½-pint/6-cup bowl. Measure from centre point to edge, making sure that the tape follows the curve of the bowl. It should measure 14 centimetres/5½ inches. Using a long serrated knife, remove the top crust and trim the *génoise* so that it is perfectly square. Cut off one edge so that one side measures exactly 15 centimetres/6 inches (2.5 centimetres/1 inch more than the curve of the bowl for safety margin).

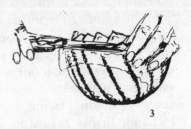

1

2

3

Make 135 grams/4¾ ounces/ ½ cup Ganache Icing (page 312). Spread 2 tablespoons of the hot ganache over the bottom of the *génoise*. Chill for 15 minutes to set the ganache before slicing. Set aside the remaining ganache at room temperature to use for piping decorations on top after unmoulding.

Invert the cake, ganache side down, on to lightly greased foil and cut into 5-millimetre/¼-inch by 15-centimetre/6-inch strips with a thin sharp knife, wiping the blade between each slice. Cut one end of the uniced side of each strip on a diagonal so it comes to a point (Fig. 1). This will prevent too much cake from building up in the center. Prepare Chocolate Chip Whipped Cream (page 298) and set aside briefly while lining the mould.

Lightly oil the 1.5-litre/2½-pint/ 6-cup glass bowl and line smoothly with buttered clingfilm, buttered side up, allowing a slight overhang. Starting at the bottom centre of the bowl, place a strip of *génoise* from centre to edge, placing the pointed edge at the centre, the cut edge

facing right, and the iced edge facing left (Fig. 2).

Brush the strip with syrup and a thin coating of whipped cream reserved from the filling. Place a second strip, starting at the centre and slightly overlapping the first strip at the rim. Brush with syrup and a thin coating of whipped cream and continue to work clockwise from right to left, always having the iced edge facing left so that it will show on the outside in a striped motif when unmoulded. When you come to the last strip, tuck the side under the first strip.

Trim the excess *biscuit* flush with the edge of the bowl using shears (Fig. 3). Cover tightly with clingfilm while preparing the filling.

Fill the cake-lined dome, chill until set (at least 2 hours if using Chocolate Chip Whipped Cream, 4 hours if Bavarian or cloud cream), and unmould on to a serving plate, tugging gently on the clingfilm overhang to release the cake. Use the reserved ganache to pipe a fluted design on top with a rose tube to cover any imperfections.

Piped Shapes for Charlotte Russe

Non-stick liner, parchment or foil can be used to line tins for piping Biscuit à la Cuillère batter (page 165). It is also possible to grease and flour the tin and create guidelines in the surface of the flour.

If using parchment, guidelines can be drawn directly on it with pen or pencil. The parchment is inverted before piping so that the lines show through, but the ink or pencil marks don't come into direct contact with the batter. Guidelines for foil can be marked with a skewer. A non-stick liner, however, is my favourite surface because the baked *biscuit* slides off it without any problem. I use a bright felt-tip marker to make guidelines on a brown paper bag and cover it with the non-stick liner.

For piping sponge fingers, make parallel lines 7.5 centimetres/ 3 inches apart. For discs, use a round cake tin to mark circles.

PIPING TECHNIQUES

Biscuit batter flows easily so it is unnecessary to squeeze the pastry bag. (If the piped designs do not hold their shape it means that the egg whites were not beaten stiffly enough.) To stop the flow of batter, tilt the tube up just before you think it will be necessary. Work steadily so that the batter can be baked soon after preparing it. This will enable it to retain as much air and lightness as possible.

PIPED SPONGE FINGERS:

Using a 5-millimetre large round tube (2-centimetre/³/₄-inch diameter), pipe sponge fingers, leaving a 5-millimetre/¹/₄-inch space in between each as the batter will spread sideways while piping the next finger. (After baking, the sponge fingers will be attached to each other in continuous strips. Each finger will be about 4 centimetres/1¹/₂ inches wide.) Start

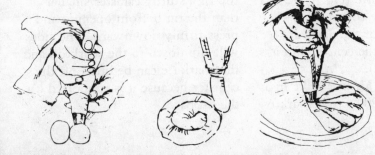
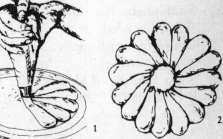

piping just inside the top guideline and stop shortly before reaching the bottom one, moving the tip slightly forward and up to control the batter flow.

PIPED SPIRAL BASE:

Using a 5-millimetre large round tube, hold the pastry bag in a vertical (straight up-and-down) position with the tube at least 4 centimetres/1½ inches above the tin. To achieve full height and a rounded shape, the batter must be allowed to fall from the tube and not be pressed against the tin. Start in the centre, moving the tip with your entire arm in smooth circles. To prevent gaps, allow spirals of batter to fall against the sides of – almost on top of – previous spirals. The weight of the batter will cause them to fall exactly in place.

PIPED DAISY TOP:

Making this fancy design to top a charlotte involves piping a teardrop shape or shell design without ridges. Review piped shell borders (page 461). Start each tear drop at the outer edge, ending with a point or 'tail' at the centre (Fig. 1). Use a 5-millimetre large round tube. When the petals of the daisy are complete, finish the centre with a round dot (Fig. 2).

To bake piped biscuit: Bake in a preheated 400°F/200°C/gas mark 6 oven for 8 to 10 minutes or until the *biscuit* is light golden brown and springy to the touch (page 213).

To assemble: If moulding the Charlotte Russe in a springform tin, you may remove the inner disc and place the outer ring directly on a serving plate. If using a loose-bottomed tin, leave the inner disc in place but line with a parchment round if planning to remove the disc before serving.

Lightly oil the inside of the ring. If the sponge fingers have not been freshly baked, sprinkle them with a little liqueur. Use the sponge finger strips to line the inside of the ring. Place the *biscuit* base in the bottom, trimming it if necessary for a snug fit. Scoop filling into the lined mould. Level with a small angled spatula. If using the daisy top, trim the tops of the sponge fingers encircling the mould so that they are flush with the filling and cover with the daisy top, sprinkled with liqueur. Refrigerate until set (at least 4 hours).

To unmould: For a springform tin, release the sides and lift away. For a loose-bottomed tin, place on top of a sturdy canister smaller than the tin bottom opening and press firmly downward. The sides will slip down to the worktop and the charlotte can be lifted off the canister because it is supported by the tin base.

Special Meringue Piping Techniques

COCOA MERINGUE STICKS:

Great for munching by themselves, these sticks are also used to create The Enchanted Forest (page 224).

Piping fine lines demands a great deal of control if you want them to be perfectly straight. Fortuitously, however, I discovered that irregularly piped sticks look even more interesting. Line three 43 × 30.5-centimetre/17 × 12-inch baking sheets with a non-stick liner or parchment. Fit an icing bag with a 7-millimetre round decorating tube and fill the bag with Cocoa Meringue (page 344). Hold the bag at a slight angle away from you with the tube several inches above the tin. Starting at the top of the tin, squeeze the meringue with steady pressure, allowing it to drop from the tube. Leave 9 millimetres/ 3/8 inch between the lines of meringue. To obtain an irregular, nubbly appearance, lower the tube while piping, allowing it to touch the surface so extra meringue will build up around edges.

Bake at 200°F/110°C/gas mark /4 for 50 minutes or until dry. If a tiny bit of stickiness remains in the centre, it will dry out after removal from the oven. Remove carefully from the baking sheet and cut or break into uneven lengths ranging from 5 to 10 centimetres/2 to 4 inches.

PINE NEEDLES:

Delicious to eat by themselves or with ice cream, they make a delightful garnish for the Cordon Rose Chocolate Christmas Log.

Line a baking sheet with a non-stick liner or parchment. Fit an icing bag with a 1.5-millimetre decorating tube and fill the bag with Pine Needle Meringue (page 344). Hold the bag at a 45-degree angle with the tube slightly above the tin. Each pine needle consists of two sticks joined at the top, but the shapes can vary. Pipe some straight in an upside-down V and others crossing one stick over the other. Bake at 200°F/110°C/gas mark 1/4 for 30 minutes or until dry but not starting to colour. Remove carefully from the baking sheet with a small angled spatula. These pine needles are quite fragile. For a realistic effect, dip the joined end into melted dark chocolate.

MERINGUE OR DACQUOISE DISCS AND HEARTS:

A non-stick liner, parchment, or foil can be used to line the baking sheets for piping meringue or *dacquoise*. They must be totally grease free. If using parchment, guidelines can be drawn directly on it with a pen or pencil. The parchment is inverted before piping so that the lines show through but the ink or pencil marks don't come into direct contact with the meringue. Guidelines for foil can be marked with a skewer. A non-stick liner, however, is my favourite surface because the baked meringue slides off without a problem. I use a bright felt-tip marker to make guidelines on a brown paper bag and cover it with the non-stick liner.

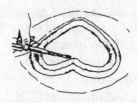

To pipe a spiral disc, fit an icing bag with a large, round pastry tube (1.25-centimetre/½-inch diameter) and fill with meringue or *dacquoise*.

Hold the bag in a vertical position (straight up-and-down) with the tube at least 4 centimetres/1½ inches above the tin. To achieve full height and a rounded shape, the batter must be allowed to fall from the tube and not be pressed against the tin. Start either in the centre or at the outer edge, moving the tip with your entire arm in smooth circles. To prevent gaps, allow the spirals of batter to fall against the sides of – almost on top of – previous spirals. The weight of the mixture will cause them to fall exactly in place.

To form hearts, use a heart-shaped tin as a guide to draw the shape. To pipe the mixture, begin by outlining the outside edge, starting and ending at the indentation. Continue piping one row at a time, ending in the centre. Use a small brush dipped in water to correct mistakes.

If time allows and the oven has a pilot light, meringue or *dacquoise* can be baked for 1 hour at 200°F/110°C/gas mark ¼ and then left to dry overnight in a turned-off oven.

Alternatively, bake meringue at 200°F/110°C/gas mark ¼ for 2 to 2½ hours or until dry but not beginning to colour. *Dacquoise* can also be baked at 200°F/110°C/gas mark ¼ for 1 to 1½ hours or until dry.

MERINGUE MUSHROOMS:

These little mushrooms look astonishingly real when dusted lightly with cocoa to simulate earth. They are perfect for decorating the Cordon Rose Chocolate Christmas Log.

Make half recipe Figure Piping Meringue (page 344). This will make about thirty 4–centimetre/1½–inch-diameter mushrooms. Line a baking sheet with a non-stick liner, parchment or foil. Fit an icing bag with a 1.5-millimetre round decorating tube and a second bag with a 1.25 centimetre/½ inch in diameter round pastry tube. Fill the bags with meringue mixture, placing about 4 tablespoons in bag

with smaller tube. Set aside. Use the larger tube to pipe the caps and stems.

To pipe the caps: Hold the bag upright with the tube slightly above the baking sheet. Squeeze with a steady, even pressure, gradually raising the tube as the meringue begins to build up but keeping the tip buried in the meringue. When you have achieved a well-rounded shape, stop the pressure as you bring the tip to the surface. Use the edge of the tip to shave off any point, moving it clockwise (Fig. 1). Points can also be removed by pressing gently with a moistened fingertip.

To pipe the stems: Hold the bag perpendicular to the baking sheet with the tube touching it. Squeeze with heavy pressure, keeping the tip buried in the meringue until you build a 2-centimetre/¾-inch-high cone wide enough at the base not to topple over (Fig. 2).

Bake at 200°F/110°C/gas mark ¼ for 45 minutes or until firm enough to lift from the baking sheet. With a sharp knife point, make a small hole in the underside of each cap. Use the smaller tube to pipe a tiny dab of meringue in the hole and attach the stem by inserting the

1

2

3

pointed end (Fig. 3). Place the mushrooms, caps down, on the baking sheet and return to the oven for 20 minutes or until thoroughly dry.

Speed Production Method: For less perfect but faster mushrooms, bake the stems until very firm, about 1 hour. To pipe the caps, wet the baking sheet and cover with parchment. Pipe the caps and bake for 10 to 15 minutes or until firm enough to lift off the sheet but still soft. Push the caps down gently on top of the stems and return the finished mushrooms to oven. Lower the temperature to 150°F/75°C and bake for 45 minutes or until completely dry.

MERINGUE SWANS:

One recipe Figure Piping Meringue (page 344) will make four swans and lots of extra parts in case of breakage.

Make templates for the head, wings and body by drawing on parchment (Figs. 1, 2 and 3). Turn over and attach to a baking sheet with a small dab of meringue.

Fit an icing bag with a 2-centimetre/¾-inch diameter round pastry tube and a second bag with a 4.5-millimetre/³/₁₆-inch diameter round decorating tube. Fill the bags with meringue.

Use the larger tube to pipe the bodies. Use a side-to-side motion as you move from the rounded front to the pointed back. Use a small wet spatula to create sharply angled, straight sides.

Use the smaller tube to pipe the wings, head and necks. For eyes, use tiny black sesame seeds or toast sesame seeds in a lightly oiled frying pan until dark. Reserve leftover meringue for attaching the parts.

Bake the meringue parts at 200°F/110°C/gas mark ¼ until they are dry but not beginning to brown, about 2 hours. Cool and gently peel off paper. Use a drinking straw to create a hole 5 millimetres/¼ inch deep near the front of the bodies. (Necks will be fitted into these holes.)

Attach the wings to the sides using some of the leftover meringue. Return the bodies to the 200°F/110°C/gas mark ¼ oven for 30 minutes. Remove carefully and cool. The swans will keep in a dry room for weeks.

At the last minute, when ready to position the swans on the finished cake, prepare stiffly beaten whipped cream (page 294). Place the whipped cream in a small icing bag fitted with a large closed star tube (6–9mm long with slashed cuts, it resembles the drop flower tube on page 452). Position the bodies on the cake. Pipe the whipped cream into the bodies to create ruffled backs. Place heads and necks in the holes in the bodies using a dab of leftover meringue or whipped cream to secure. Let rest against the whipped cream for

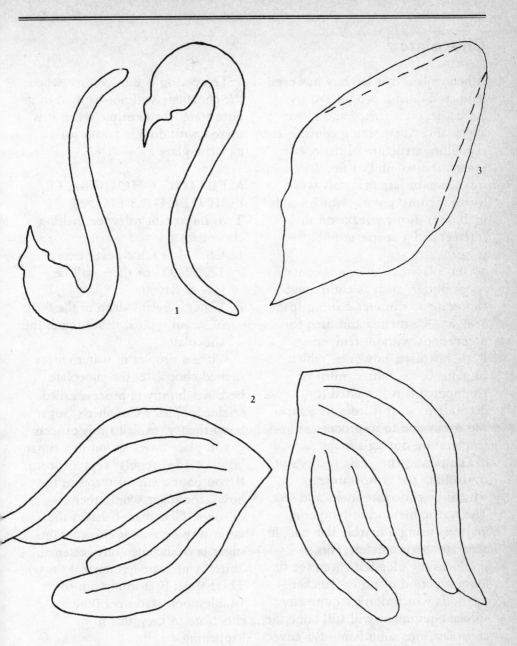

support. With a 4.5-millimetre small round tube, pipe an upside-down tear-drop shape between the front of the wings for breast.

Note: For swans the easy way, purchase plastic swans from a confectionery supplier and paint them with a thin coat of royal icing. Icing works best if not too stiff.

Chocolate

All chocolate that we buy has been tempered during production to perfect its consistency and glossy appearance. Tempering controls the crystalline structure of the cocoa butter. It also inhibits the formation of large crystals with lower melting points, which result in 'bloom' (grey streaks on the surface) and a coarse crumbly texture.

Chocolate that does not contain cocoa butter, such as compound chocolate or summer coating (page 488), can be melted and used for decorations without tempering. Real chocolate, however, which contains cocoa butter, must be retempered if it is melted for decorations or if it loses its temper and greys due to improper temperature during storage.

Tempering chocolate consists of controlling the temperature at which the chocolate melts and sets. The classic method of tempering involves using a marble slab and an accurate thermometer. This produces the glossiest sheen for the longest period of time. Quicker methods which don't require any special equipment will still tame the chocolate into submission for any of the decorative techniques offered in this chapter. If you prefer not to temper chocolate, use compound chocolate as real chocolate melted without tempering will be an unending source of frustration.

Tempering is unnecessary when the chocolate will not be used in its pure state, for example when it is mixed with double cream for a ganache glaze.

MELTING CHOCOLATE FOR DECORATIONS

Two important rules for melting chocolate:
1. Chocolate must never exceed 120°F/49°C or there will be a loss of flavour.
2. Water – even a drop in the form of steam – must never touch the chocolate.

When a droplet of water enters melted chocolate, the chocolate becomes lumpy (a process called seizing). Shirley Corriher's 'sugar bowl theory' explains this process. If you place a wet spoon in a sugar bowl, hard, irregular crystals form. If you pour a cup of water in the bowl, the sugar would merely dissolve. Chocolate behaves the same way because it also contains sugar crystals (even unsweetened, 'bitter' chocolate has natural sugar). There must be a minimum of 1 tablespoon water per ounce of chocolate to keep this from happening.

If seizing does occur, the addition of fat such as vegetable fat, clarified butter or cocoa butter will somewhat restore the chocolate to a workable condition.

For melting chocolate, unlined

copper is the traditional 'chocolate pot' because it is so responsive to changes in temperature. Aluminium, preferably lined with a non-stick surface, or heatproof glass also work well. Enamelled cast iron, however, is unsuitable because the residual heat will overheat the chocolate. Ideally, chocolate should be heated to 120°F/49°C, the point at which all the different fat fractions in the cocoa butter are melted.

When melting chocolate or cocoa butter, temperatures exceeding 120°F/49°C adversely affect the flavour. There are many acceptable methods for melting dark chocolate (or cocoa butter). If the heat source does not exceed 120°F/49°C (pilot light of oven, lowest setting on an electric griddle, or hot tray, page 526), it is fine to add the dark chocolate in large pieces and leave it to melt unmonitored. When the heat source is capable of bringing the chocolate over 120°F/49°C, however, the chocolate should be finely chopped or grated to ensure uniformity of melting. The chocolate must be carefully watched and stirred to avoid overheating. If using a microwave oven on high power, for example, the chocolate must be stirred every 15 seconds without fail. If using a double boiler, water in the lower container should not exceed 140°F/60°C and the upper container should not touch the water. The chocolate should be stirred constantly.

Milk and white chocolate must always be stirred frequently while melting because they contain milk solids which seed (lump) if left undisturbed.

Remove chocolate from the heat source when it reaches 115°F/46°C as the temperature may continue to rise and stir vigorously to prevent overheating and to distribute the cocoa butter evenly.

Always melt chocolate uncovered as moisture could condense on the lid, drop back in the chocolate and cause seizing.

GRATING CHOCOLATE

If chocolate has been stored in a cool area (not refrigerated, where it could absorb moisture), it grates more finely and evenly. The grating disc on a food processor works well for large chunks. Thin bars can be broken up and grated in the container of the food processor fitted with the stainless steel blade.

TEMPERING CHOCOLATE

The ideal situation for working with chocolate is a cool, *dry*, draught-free area at 65° to 70°F/ 18° to 21°C. At temperatures above 74°F/23°C the chocolate will not behave properly. For all methods of tempering, chocolate should be heated initially to 120°F/49°C and the final temperature of the specific kind should be:

Plain chocolate
             88° to 91°F/31° to 33°C
Milk chocolate
             84° to 87°F/29° to 30°C
White chocolate
             84° to 87°F/29° to 30°C
Compound chocolate   100° F/38°C
   (summer coating)

Compound chocolate does not contain cocoa butter so tempering is not required. Compound chocolate should be heated over hot tap water (about 115°F/46°C) only to a temperature of 100°F/38°C and used at this temperature. A dab placed just below your lower lip will feel barely warm.

To hold chocolate at its ideal temperature during use, place the container with the chocolate on a foil-covered heating pad turned to its lowest setting. Or return the container to the heat source very briefly, stirring constantly.

Because the formation of cocoa butter crystals continues as long as the chocolate is in a melted state, tempered chocolate will eventually thicken too much to produce a smooth coating. When this happens, melted untempered chocolate may be stirred in until the chocolate reaches the proper consistency without exceeding its ideal temperature. (This is known as drip feeding.)

If chocolate is allowed to exceed its ideal temperature, fat crystals will start to melt, allowing cocoa particles to drop and leaving cocoa butter crystals on the surface as unattractive streaks and spots.

If chocolate gets too cold, it will be thick and dull.

Chocolate-covered sweets are sometimes refrigerated for a few minutes after dipping in tempered chocolate. This produces a crisper coating, referred to as 'snap'. Chocolate can also be allowed to harden at cool room temperature. Any leftover chocolate can be spread thin on foil, allowed to harden, and retempered many times as long as a small percentage of new chocolate is added.

CLASSIC METHOD:

This method results in the most glossy, crisp chocolate which will set with the most reliability. Use it for the most demanding chocolate techniques such as dipping, bands and sheets.

The main difference between the classic method and other methods is that here the melted chocolate is cooled to 80°F/27°C, which is below the final dipping temperature. When heating it to the ideal temperature, all large and unstable cocoa butter crystals (which have a low melting point) dissolve, leaving only the stable crystals on which to complete crystallisation or hardening of the chocolate.

Chop or grate the chocolate and bring it to 115° to 120°F/46° to 49°C (Fig. 1). Remove from the heat, stirring vigorously for a few seconds to cool. (If using a double boiler, be careful to wipe off moisture clinging to the bottom of the upper container insert so that it won't drip on to the chocolate.)

Pour two-thirds of the melted chocolate on to a smooth, cool, dry surface (ideally marble). Spread with an angled spatula and bench scraper (Fig. 2). Move the chocolate towards the centre, clean the scraper with the spatula, and spread continuously until the chocolate begins to thicken (80° to 82°F/27° to 28°C). Scoop it immediately into the container with the remaining melted chocolate (do not allow it to harden on the worktop) and return it to the heat, stirring continuously. It will require very little heat to reach proper working temperature (page 438). (Fig. 3.)

QUICK-TEMPERING METHOD:

There are several comparable methods for quick-tempering chocolate. All involve reserving some already tempered unmelted chocolate to serve as the pattern of cocoa-butter crystal formation for the melted chocolate. (All chocolate you buy has already been tempered.) The unmelted chocolate is added to the melted chocolate and stirred until the temperature descends to the ideal temperature. This can be tested either with an accurate thermometer (page 520) or by placing a dab of chocolate just below your lower lip. At the point when it just begins to feel cool, it is about 91°F/33°C (the ideal temperature for plain chocolate). Use one of these methods for simple techniques and small decorative shapes such as pine cone petals, cigars or leaves.

1. The simplest of all methods is to remove the melting chocolate from the heat source before it has fully melted and stir until fully melted and cool.
2. It is equally simple to add

clarified butter, vegetable fat or oil to the chocolate, preferably before melting. This serves two purposes. It produces a thinner coating of chocolate and the addition of extra fat also keeps the existing cocoa butter in suspension. Because it is a different type of fat it retards formation of large cocoa butter crystals. For plain chocolate use 1 tablespoon fat for every 84 grams/3 ounces chocolate. For milk and white chocolate use only 1 teaspoon fat for 84 grams/3 ounces of chocolate. (Note: The chocolate will be softer so do not use for cigarettes or petals.)

3. When melting chocolate, reserve a large 5 to 7.5-centimetre/ 2 to 3-inch piece. Melt the chocolate to 115° to 120°F/46° to 49°C, remove from the heat, and add the reserved chocolate. Stir until the correct temperature has been reached and remove any unmelted chocolate. (Wrap this in clingfilm. It can be used for future tempering or melting.)

4. Chop or grate chocolate, reserving about one-third. Heat the larger amount to 115° to 120°F/46° to 49°C and remove from the heat. Stir in the reserved chocolate, 1 tablespoon at a time, stirring until it is cooled to proper temperature.

DECORATIVE TECHNIQUES

CHOCOLATE SNOWFLAKES:

I call these snowflakes because they should be so thin that they melt instantly on the tongue. This is an easy garnish to make as there is no need to melt or temper the chocolate. Use white chocolate for white snowflakes. Plain chocolate makes pale brown flakes.

The chocolate needs to be as hard as possible to make thin flakes, so don't leave it in a warm kitchen. A large piece of chocolate is easiest to work with, but a flat bar will also work.

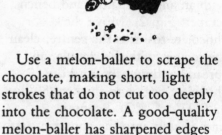

Use a melon-baller to scrape the chocolate, making short, light strokes that do not cut too deeply into the chocolate. A good-quality melon-baller has sharpened edges and works best to cut thin flurries of chocolate.

Allow the flakes to fall on to a small cool baking sheet. Place the sheet inside a large plastic bag and shake the flakes into the bag. Avoid touching them because they melt very easily. Store refrigerated or at cool room temperature. Use a large spoon to lift chocolate flakes on to the cake.

CHOCOLATE CURLS:

Another simple decorative technique that doesn't require tempering, curls are easy to make providing the correct chocolate is used and that it is at the right temperature and has not absorbed moisture from humidity. (I tried these once during a New Orleans summer, and, although the room was air-conditioned, I could not get the chocolate to curl.)

Couverture chocolate (page 487), which comes in large blocks, makes the most attractive, shiny curls. I have had the best luck with the Lindt bittersweet couverture, Courante.

If the chocolate is left in an 80°F/27°C room for several hours it is usually a good working temperature. Alternatively, a small block of chocolate can be softened to perfect consistency by placing it under a lamp (from the heat of the light bulb) or in a microwave oven using 3-second bursts of high power. It takes a few tries to get the chocolate soft enough without oversoftening it, but once this point is reached it will stay for at least 10 minutes during which time many curls can be formed.

Chocolate can be curled with a melon-baller, but my favourite utensil is a sharp potato peeler.

Hold the chocolate block in one hand, against a wad of paper towelling so that the heat of your hand doesn't melt the chocolate.

Hold the peeler against the upper edge and, digging in one edge of the cutter, bring the blade towards you. Greater pressure forms thicker, more open curls. Lighter pressure makes tighter curls. If the chocolate is not warm enough it will splinter. If too warm, it will come off in soft strips that will not curl. If not too soft, strips can be rolled into curls with cool fingertips.

CHOCOLATE CIGARETTES:

These are actually long curls. To make cigarettes, it is necessary to quick-temper the chocolate using any method on pages 437 to 440. Spread the tempered chocolate into a long band 3 millimetres/⅛ inch thick on a smooth marble or Formica worktop and allow it to

set. Don't wait too long or the chocolate will harden too much and will not curl. Test small sections at the edges to see when the consistency is perfect.

Using a knife or pizza cutter, score the chocolate to determine the desired length of the cigarette. Using a triangular scraper held at a 45-degree angle to the chocolate, push firmly against the worktop, starting at the bottom of the chocolate band and pushing away from you. The higher the angle and the thinner the chocolate, the tighter the curl.

Use a broad spatula to lift the cigarettes and store airtight, refrigerated or at cool room temperature.

CHOCOLATE PINE CONE PETALS:

Quick-temper 168 to 224 grams/ 6 to 8 ounces milk or bittersweet chocolate (page 439). This will make two 61 × 46-centimetre/ 24 × 18-inch sheet cake tins of petals – enough for Chocolate Pine Cone (page 225). Tape a sheet of parchment or foil on a flat surface. Dip the tip of a small metal spatula in the chocolate and dab it on to the parchment, pressing lightly

down to form a tapered petal shape while drawing the spatula towards you. The petals should be 1 centimetre/¾ inch wide and 2 centimetres/1 inch long. When the petals have set and are easy to remove from the parchment, store airtight refrigerated or at cool room temperature. (Use a flexible spatula to remove them from the parchment.)

Use tweezers to place the petals on the cake.

SUCCESSFUL CHOCOLATE RUFFLES:

This can be the most painstaking and frustrating of any decorative technique I know – even for a professional chocolatier – because, if working with real chocolate, the precise temperature is more critical than for any other technique. Too cold and the chocolate splinters; too warm and it melts in your fingers. This is a technique worth mastering simply because chocolate ruffles are the most spectacular of all chocolate decorations.

It has taken me years to come up with a reliable method for ruffling chocolate. Frankly, I almost gave it up as a lost cause. Especially after having traded notes from LeNôtre's professional class in France for a lesson from a French chocolatier – who gave up after claiming that he required refrigerated marble.

Only recently, through a more intimate understanding of

chocolate's varied peculiarities, I have at last worked out a method that is, perhaps, as idiosyncratic as the chocolate. It does not involve changing the chocolate's ingredients, only its texture. It is accomplished by precise control of temperature but does not involve any special equipment. With great pleasure I share the secret.

The chocolate must be melted in a special way I refer to as quick-tempering method. If tempered according to the classic method, the crisp 'snap' desirable for other uses makes the chocolate too brittle to ruffle. If fully melted and not tempered at all the chocolate will still ruffle but the surface will have a crumbly, unattractive appearance.

Room temperature should be between 70° to 75°F/21° to 24°C. Have a small bowl of ice water nearby so you can dip in the fingers of your left hand if their heat starts to melt the chocolate. (Be sure to dry your fingers before touching the chocolate.)

To quick-temper the chocolate, see page 439. While the chocolate is melting, warm a baking sheet either by placing it in the oven with a pilot light or running it under hot water and wiping it totally dry. It should feel warm not hot. You will need 140 grams/ 5 ounces bittersweet chocolate to cover a 43 × 30.5-centimetre/ 17 × 12-inch tin. 285 grams/ 10 ounces of chocolate ruffles will be enough to cover a 20 or 23-centimetre/8 or 9-inch cake.

Using a long angled spatula, spread the chocolate in a thin even layer on the back of the warm baking sheet. Place it in the refrigerator for exactly 5 minutes. Remove from the refrigerator and place on a worktop so that one edge is against the wall for stability. The top will be slightly dull which means it has set, the underneath will be soft. The chocolate will continue to firm at room temperature. Allow it to sit at room temperature for 15 to 25 minutes. Test a small area with a triangular scraper. When the chocolate is firm enough to ruffle, it will maintain this ideal texture for at least 20 minutes. If room temperature is below 70°F/21°C, however, it may harden before this time.

For ruffling, the angle of the triangular scraper has to be less than for making chocolate curls – about 20 degrees. If you are right-handed, start at the bottom left side of the baking sheet, pushing firmly against the chocolate in the direction of the wall. The right edge of the spatula should move in a straight line, but to help ruffle the chocolate it should at the same time be angled slightly to the left. About 5 centimetres/2 inches is an attractive width. As you push chocolate with the scraper in your right hand, use the thumb and forefinger of your left hand to lightly pleat the chocolate (Fig. 1).

If the chocolate is too tightly pleated, gently stretch the ruffle slightly apart.

Set the finished ruffles on the worktop where they will continue to firm. When no longer flexible, they can be transferred by hand or with a thin flexible pancake turner. Either place directly on the iced cake or on a cool baking sheet for storage. To store, keep ruffles airtight, either refrigerated or at cool room temperature.

To place on the iced cake, start at an outside edge and place a single, continuous row of ruffles. The next row should overlap the first. Use the smallest ruffles for the centre (Fig. 2). Do feel free to experiment with chocolate ruffling to your heart's content. Imperfect ruffles are still attractive or can be remelted and tempered or used for ganache.

CHOCOLATE LEAVES:

This is an impressive, easy, but somewhat tedious technique. When my assistant Hiroko Ogawa returned to Japan, she left me with a dowry of over one hundred white chocolate leaves – a much-appreciated gift. If only a few chocolate leaves are needed, summer coating is the best choice because it doesn't require tempering. When surrounding a cake with an embrace of chocolate rose leaves, I like to use the best possible real chocolate. Couverture (page 487) makes the most glossy, elegant leaves.

Rose, lemon, maple and geranium leaves are some of my favourite shapes. Select well-shaped leaves with no holes. Wash leaves and dry thoroughly. Each leaf can be used several times until it tears.

Holding a leaf by its stem and supporting it underneath with a finger or the palm of your hand, use a small metal spatula or artist's brush to smooth an even layer of chocolate on the underside of the leaf (Fig. 1). (Be sure to use the

2

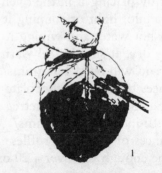

1

veiny underside as all the delicate lines will be imprinted on the chocolate.) Don't allow chocolate to get on the other side of the leaf or it may break when peeling off the leaf.

Carefully place the chocolate leaf on a baking sheet lined with foil, parchment or greaseproof paper and refrigerate or freeze for 3 minutes, until set and no longer shiny. If using large leaves, add a second coat of chocolate for stability. White chocolate and couverture also require second coats as the chocolate is thinner when melted and the light shines through in spots when placed on the cake.

2

To remove the chocolate from the leaf, peel back the stem end, touching the chocolate as little as possible (Fig. 2). If chocolate adheres to the leaf, it has not set long enough.

To apply the leaf to the cake, brush a small dab of melted chocolate (cool to the touch) on the back and gently press it against the side of the cake, angling it slightly so that the tip is at the one o'clock position.

CHOCOLATE FOSSILING:

I developed this technique quite accidentally in an amusing way. I was giving a demonstration at the Miami Hilton and time was running short, so I was forced to sprinkle a layer of icing sugar and place the prepared chocolate leaf on a still-warm chocolate cake. The effect was sensational. The chocolate melted slightly, flattening into the cake, while maintaining the shape of the leaf. It exactly resembled a fossil.

CHOCOLATE DISCS AND CUT-OUTS:

Sheets of chocolate can be cut into many shapes to decorate cakes. Quick-temper the chocolate (page 439) and with an angled spatula spread it 3 millimetres/⅛ inch thick on greaseproof paper, which will give it a high sheen. Or cover with a second sheet of greaseproof paper and spread with a rolling pin. When the chocolate is firm enough to cut but not so firm that it will break, use either a biscuit cutter or template and the sharp point of a knife to create shapes.

To make a round disc, such as the one used for Queen Bee cake, use an inverted lid or a cake ring as a guide. To cut round holes in the disc, use the back of a large icing tube or round biscuit cutter 2.5 centimetres/1-inch in diameter and the tip of a knife if necessary to lift out the chocolate rounds.

Freeze for a few minutes or allow to set at cool room temperature. When chocolate has set completely and will separate cleanly from the paper, invert on to a flat surface and peel off the paper. Use a broad spatula to lift or transfer the disc.

CHOCOLATE AND CHOCOLATE PRALINE SHEETS:

Large thin sheets of chocolate or chocolate praline look magnificent draped around a cake, transforming it into a modern soft sculpture that never turns out looking exactly the same way twice. Praline sheets adhere to the icing on the cake.

A trick I have worked out over the years is that, since chocolate is very sensitive to changing temperatures, I use this to my advantage by switching rooms for different stages. The oval sheets of chocolate are fairly rigid at cool room temperature but become perfectly flexible in a warmer (75° to 80°F/24° to 27°C) room.

Make the chocolate praline sheets on page 363. Only four large sheets are needed to encase a 23-centimetre/ 9-inch cake so the two extra are in case of breakage. Any leftovers can be remelted, retempered and cut into decorative shapes. Begin by laying each sheet on the worktop and peeling off the top layer of paper. Lift up one sheet using the bottom paper to support it and press the long side against the cake, curving it gently. Carefully peel away the greaseproof paper. Place a dab of icing near the edge and attach a second sheet, overlapping the first.

Continue with the remaining chocolate sheets until the cake is surrounded. If room temperature is warm enough, the sheets of chocolate will begin to curve towards the centre of the cake. Coax them gently into graceful, undulating shapes, allowing their natural inclination to be your guide. If the chocolate remains resolutely rigid, wave a hair dryer briefly and evenly over the chocolate sheets. Stop before they appear to have softened and wait a few moments as it is easy to overdo the heat and melt the chocolate. To this day, this process feels slightly scary, slightly risky and delightfully creative! A word of reassurance: whatever happens and however it winds up looking, the chocolate praline sheets are always delicious. A former student and good friend, Judi Elkins, once encased a cake in praline sheets that were not softened enough and shattered on top of and around the cake. She left the cake in the kitchen and served another dessert in its place. But in a moment of somewhat wacky postprandial inspiration, her husband, Paul, dubbed the abandoned cake 'The Polish Apple Torte' in deference to his Polish origins and invited the guests into the kitchen to try what Judi had thought of as a kitchen disaster. Everyone adored the cake. Not a soul questioned the fact that there were no apparent apples in it. And many ordered the cake from Judi for their own parties.

CHOCOLATE BANDS:

A dark, gleaming chocolate band, surrounding the cake and 2.5 centimetres/1 inch or more taller, provides a smooth finish for the cake's sides. The hollow at the top can be filled with whipped cream, piped into opulent swirls, brandied cherries or lots of fat chocolate curls. The top of the band can be cut straight or in graceful or even wildly irregular waves.

To make a chocolate band, measure the circumference of the cake and cut a piece of greaseproof paper a few inches longer. Fold the greaseproof paper the desired height of the band. It should be at least 2.5 centimetres/1 inch higher than the finished height of the cake. If planning to scallop the band add an extra inch or two. Brush the sides of the cake with melted Jewel Glaze (page 378) to attach the band.

For a band long enough to encircle a 23-centimetre/9-inch cake, classic-temper or quick-temper 112 to 224 grams/4 to 8 ounces plain chocolate, preferably couverture. 224 grams/8 ounces will be sufficient to make a band 13 centimetres/5 inches high. (If you don't temper the chocolate when melting it or if the room is too warm, the band will not be firm enough to wrap around the cake.)

Using an angled spatula, spread the chocolate evenly over the greaseproof paper strip, making it a little longer than the desired length. Lift the strip by the ends and transfer to a clean section of the worktop to set. When firm but still malleable, use a small sharp knife to cut a free-form scalloped design along one side if desired. Attach the strip, scalloped side up, to the side of the cake. Gently pull away the greaseproof paper and use a bit of melted chocolate or jam to attach where the ends overlap. If the chocolate sticks to the paper, allow it to set longer or refrigerate for a few minutes until firm enough to release cleanly. The scalloped edge will break away easily on slight pressure to reveal the scalloped border.

CHOCOLATE LATTICE BAND:

This is pretty much the same technique as the solid chocolate band but the chocolate is piped in a free-form filigree before wrapping it around the cake. As the sides of the cake will show through the openings of the filigree, they should be smoothly iced with chocolate icing, preferably lighter than the filigree to show off the design.

You will need 56 grams/2 ounces chocolate for a lattice band to encircle a 23–centimetre/9–inch cake, so melt 84 grams/3 ounces chocolate to have enough extra to squeeze in the parchment cone. The piping chocolate must be thickened slightly so that it will fall smoothly from the parchment cone like a spider's web. Although a drop of water will cause the chocolate to seize or lump, a fraction of a drop will thicken it in a more controlled way. Glycerine (page 495) is the ideal liquid to use because it contains a very minute proportion of liquid. Stock syrup will also work. (Bring an equal volume of water and sugar to a full rolling boil, cover and cool.) Add only 1 drop glycerine or stock syrup at a time, stirring and testing thickness by allowing the chocolate to drop from a height of 10 centimetres/ 4 inches. If it falls in a smooth string, the thickness is right.

If using real chocolate as opposed to compound chocolate, it should be quick-tempered (page 439) before adding glycerine or syrup.

Chocolate is traditionally piped from a parchment cone because a metal tube would make the chocolate too firm. To make a parchment piping cone (page 454), cut off only a tiny bit from the end and try piping a few swirls to test the thickness of the line. If too thin and the chocolate does not flow evenly, cut a tiny bit more from the tip. Allow the chocolate to fall in a thin fluid line, using the motion of your entire arm to form curves.

If the chocolate hardens in the tip, press with your fingers to soften it and squeeze out any hard lumps blocking the opening.

Pipe a free-form filigree on greaseproof paper and allow to set until dull. Wrap around the cake, peeling back one end of greaseproof paper slightly to overlap ends. Chill until very firm and carefully peel off the paper.

CHOCOLATE WRITING:

The fluid flow of melted chocolate produces a very elegant script even without perfect penmanship. Some of the most beautiful chocolate writing I have ever seen on a cake was piped by my Oriental students in exquisite Chinese calligraphy.

Chocolate writing looks most elegant on top of a chocolate glazed cake. Prepare the chocolate and parchment cone as for the above filigree lattice. If you prefer not to risk free-form writing, make a template by tracing letters (page 476) or designing your own letters. Tape a piece of non-stick liner (page 524) or parchment over the template and trace the design in chocolate. Chill the chocolate until very firm before removing from the liner. Remove with a very thin knife blade or spatula. Or set the design near the edge of a table and, pressing the back edge of the liner to the table, slowly pull the liner from the chocolate design until almost completely released. Lift the design with a small angled spatula.

If writing directly on the cake, Cocoa Piping Gel is slightly softer and much shinier than chocolate. *To make ⅓ cup:* In a small saucepan stir together 3 tablespoons piping gel, 1 tablespoon hot water, 3 tablespoons unsweetened cocoa and 6 tablespoons icing sugar. Cook over low heat, stirring constantly, until just smooth. Cool completely to obtain piping consistency.

CHOCOLATE DOILIES:

I pipe this directly on the serving plate as it is for visual effect only and does not get eaten. Summer coating (page 488) or the above cocoa piping gel are appropriate choices as they require no tempering. If using summer coating, thicken the chocolate as for filigree lattice (page 447) and fill a parchment cone.

Pipe free-form swirls or flowers directly on the serving plate, surrounding the cake. If you wish to follow a precise pattern, use a flat glass serving plate and tape a template underneath it. Remove the template after piping the design.

CHOCOLATE GLAZING WITH WEBBING:

Dark, shiny Chocolate Cream Glaze (or Chocolate Butter Glaze) is one of the most stunning adornments for a cake. The sides of a glazed cake are always, however, slightly lumpy or less perfect than the top, so I usually surround the sides with chocolate rose leaves, a chocolate band, or cut-outs.

Webbing the top of the cake with lines of contrasting white chocolate makes an interesting variation.

Glaze the cake (page 314 or 316) and prepare a white chocolate decorating glaze. Quick-temper 56 grams/2 ounces white chocolate by removing it from the heat before fully melted and stirring until melted. Stir in either 1 tablespoon flavourless oil or 1 tablespoon + 1 teaspoon Armagnac or Cognac. Fill a parchment cone or plastic squeeze bottle★ with the white chocolate, and before the glaze sets, pipe either evenly spaced straight lines across a square cake or concentric circles on a round cake.

For straight lines, start at one edge of the cake and lightly drag a small knife blade at even intervals in a straight line towards you – at right angles to the piped white lines. To reverse the direction of the lines, turn the cake around and repeat, making lines between the first set of lines.

For circles, start at the centre of the cake, dragging the knife blade to the edge at eight evenly spaced intervals. Then reverse the direction, starting at the edge and going towards the centre for eight more lines between the first eight lines.

CHOCOLATE ROSE MODELLING:

Knead Chocolate Rose Modelling Paste (page 374) until pliable and roll between sheets of clingfilm until 1.5 millimetres/^{1}/$_{16}$-inch thick. Cut small circles for petals using the back of an icing tube or lightly greased rose petal cutters (page 528) (Fig. 1). (Use a 2.5-centimetre/ 1-inch cutter for the first row, a 3-centimetre/1¼-inch cutter for the second row, and a 4–centimetre/ 1½-inch cutter for the third row.) Roll the circles to elongate them slightly, leaving the base thick for support and thinning the upper section only.

If chocolate becomes too soft, allow it to sit briefly and it will get firm.

Form the base of the rose by shaping a small ball and then pinching it to form a cone shape (Fig. 2).

Wrap chocolate petals around the base, overlapping them as you go (Fig. 3). The first set of three petals should curve inwards to hide the core. The second row of three petals should be straight up, and the third row should curve out and open up slightly. Push petals away from each other and the core with a blunt instrument such as a metal cuticle pusher (Fig. 4). For a natural look, use your fingertips to curl back softly the edges of each petal except for the first row of inner petals (Fig. 5).

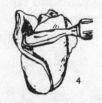

★Available in chemists' by asking for a squeeze bottle for hair colouring.

When the rose is completed, allow it to sit at room temperature away from direct sunlight for 48 hours or until firm enough to place in an airtight container on a nest of plastic wrap. Keep in a cool room, refrigerate up to 1 year, or freeze indefinitely.

PORCELAINISING CHOCOLATE ROSES:

For a glaze that dries as hard and shiny as porcelain, brush a well-dried chocolate rose* with unflavoured oil. Before the oil has a chance to be absorbed and appear dry, coat the petals with light corn syrup. Allow to dry for several hours or until the glaze is hard to the touch.

Piped Decorations

I learned both string figures and the intricate art of origami (Japanese paper folding) from books. It was not easy but it was possible. Piped cake decorations, however, were another matter. I carefully followed the printed instructions that came with the icing bag and tube set, but the blobs emerging from my icing tip bore no semblance to the fine ridged swirls in the pictures. I did not realise that the main problem was the consistency of the icing. Too soft and the shapes will not be articulated; too stiff and the icing will break sharply instead of curving into smooth designs.

It was a two-week intensive course at Wilton Enterprises in Chicago that turned me into a cake decorator. I am also indebted to Wilton for writing piping

directions that explain the angle of the icing bag in terms of both degrees of elevation and clock position. This concept, together with the *proper icing consistency*, makes it indeed possible to learn from the printed page.

Piped decorations take practice but are a lot of fun. It is a great project to do with children because they are so delighted with whatever design they manage, even if it does not resemble the 'model'. To keep icing from coming out of the top of the bag and making a mess, I use a twist-tie to secure the opening.

At Wilton the first decoration we learned was the star. It is easy to pipe and even when imperfectly executed looks attractive.

---

*A rose must dry for at least 3 days or the glaze does not take evenly.

Rose Tube: For making roses, rosebuds, sweet peas and ruffles.

Leaf Tube: For making leaves.

BASIC TUBE DESIGNS

There are six basic tubes that produce most of the popular cake decorations. Each tube is available in a variety of sizes, but the decorations they produce are the same.

Star Tube: For making stars, shells, rosettes, ropes, zigzags, puffs, fleurs-de-lis and scrolls.

Drop Flower Tube: For making two different flower varieties.

Round Tube: For writing, dots, pearls, strings, outlines and beads.

TERMS FOR PIPED DECORATIONS

Top Border: A continuous decoration piped around the top of a cake.

Bottom Border: A continuous decoration piped around the base of a cake (which has the added function of sealing in freshness).

Side Decoration: Piped decorations used around the sides of a cake.

Decorating or Icing Bag: The container that holds the decorating tube, coupler and icing or buttercream.

Coupler: A grooved insert and retainer ring that allows tube changes without changing bags.

Decorating Tubes: Open end tubes in various shapes used to form icing decorations.

Flower Nail: A round, flat nail-head used as a turntable surface for making icing flowers.

Basket Weave Tube: For making plain and ribbed stripes and basket weave design.

 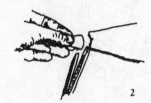 

1   2   3   4

PREPARING A POLYESTER DECORATING BAG

One of the major advantages of the polyester bag, aside from being reusable and comfortable to hold, is that it can be used with a coupler so you can change tubes without emptying or changing bags.

To cut a bag to accommodate the coupler, separate the coupler and drop the base, narrow end down, into the bag. Force down the coupler as far as it will go. With a pen or pencil, mark the spot on the outside of the bag where the bottom thread is outlined against the material (Fig. 1).

Push the base of the coupler back up into the bag and cut across where the mark was made, cutting in a slight curve rather than sharply across it. The beginning and end of the cut should be slightly higher than the middle so that when the end is open, it will be round (Fig. 2).

Push the coupler base back through the bag opening. Two threads should be showing (Fig. 3). To secure a tube in place, slip it on to the coupler base and twist the

ring over it, threading it on to the base (Fig. 4).

To fill the bag: Fold down the top to form a generous cuff and hold it beneath the cuff. Use a long spatula to fill the bag half full. Filling it more risks melting and softening the icing from the heat of your hand (Fig. 1).

To remove the icing from the spatula, hold the bag on the outside between your thumb and fingers and pull the spatula out of the bag, pinching the icing (Fig. 2, page 454). Unfold the cuff and using the side of your hand, force icing

1

towards the tip (Fig. 3). Twist the bag closed. To be sure that no air is trapped in the bag, squeeze a small amount of icing into a bowl. It is a good idea to do this when refilling the bag or the little explosion of air when old icing meets new can disrupt the piped decoration.

of the bag in the V between your thumb and forefinger. Lock your thumb over your forefinger to keep the icing in the lower part of the bag (Fig. 4). Press your remaining fingers against the side of the bag so that when you squeeze out the icing, you squeeze from the side while your thumb presses from the top.

Steady the front end of the bag with the fingers of the other hand to support the weight of the bag and to establish the direction of the tip.

PREPARING A PARCHMENT CONE

There are two major advantages to a parchment cone: it is disposable, and its stiffness keeps the heat of your hand farther from the icing.

In an emergency I have used a triangle of greaseproof paper. It works well but does not hold up quite as long.

In these illustrations, the points of the triangle have been labelled A, B and C.

Place the triangle on a flat surface with A pointing towards you (Fig. 1). Curl C up and under, bringing it towards you until points A and C meet. The curled edge from C should lie on top of the edge between A and B. The parchment will curve more easily if you extend your right elbow while doing this (Fig. 2). Hold points C and A together with your left hand while picking up B with your right (Fig. 3). Wrap B around to meet points A and C in the back, forming a cone (Fig. 4). Hold the bag with both hands, thumbs inside, and slide B and C in opposite directions to make a W formation (Fig. 5). Tugging point B slightly upwards will help to

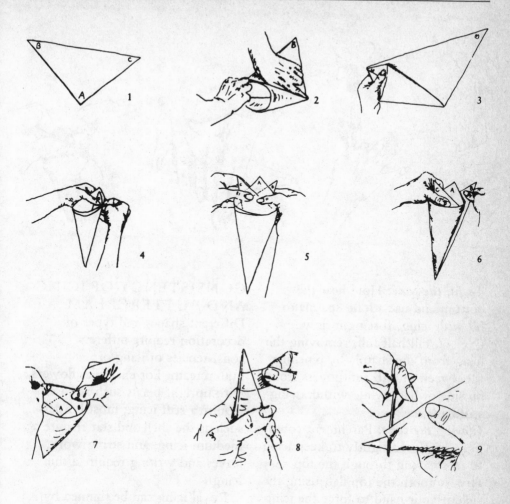

form a sharp, closed point (Fig. 6).

Turn down the top and secure with a staple. Tape the outside seam of the bag (Fig. 7). Use a small strip of tape near the pointed end. This will keep the cone from unfolding and the icing from coming out the side (Fig. 8).

If piping chocolate, cut off the tiniest amount possible from the tip. If piping icing, make an opening for the tube by clipping off 2 centimetres/¾ inch from the tip (Fig. 9). Too large a hole will allow the tube to fall through, too small and the parchment will cut off part of the icing's design. Make the cut slightly curved, as for the polyester bag, so the opening will be round and icing will not creep out around the edges.

Drop the tube into the cone, narrow end first, and push forward to make sure the tip is exposed. The weight of the icing will hold it securely in place.

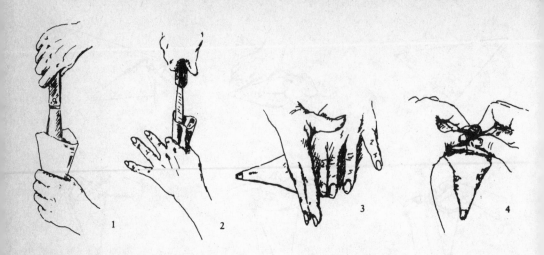

To fill the cone: Hold near the bottom and use a long spatula to fill with icing, forcing it down (Fig. 1). Fill half full, removing the icing from the spatula by pinching it between thumb and fingers from outside of bag, while withdrawing spatula (Fig. 2).

Closing the cone: Parchment cones must be closed tightly to keep icing from escaping through the top. First, smooth the top flat, using the side of your hand to force the icing towards the tip (Fig. 3). Then fold in each side and roll down the top until it is close to the icing (Fig. 4). Lock your thumb over the top with your remaining fingers curled around the side.

CONSISTENCY OF ICING AND BUTTERCREAM

Different shapes and types of decoration require different consistencies of icing or buttercream. For example, flowers with upright petals such as roses require a stiff icing; most borders such as the shell and star require a medium icing; and string work, leaves and writing require a thin icing.

Royal icing can be thinned by adding glycerine or corn syrup or stiffened by adding extra icing sugar. Buttercreams can be softened by heat or firmed up by refrigeration.

To determine the consistency of

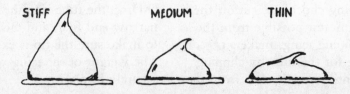

STIFF   MEDIUM   THIN

an icing or buttercream, take a small dollop and dab it on the work surface. With a small spatula, lift it to form a peak.

Stiff icing will hold a 2-centimetre/³/₄-inch peak.

Medium icing will hold a 1-centimetre/¹/₂-inch peak.

Soft icing will hold a 5-millimetre/¹/₄-inch peak.

COLOUR SHADING

This technique gives a subtle two-tone effect to each decoration piped from the tube. It is particularly suitable for piped roses.

Mix two or more batches of icing so that the colours are in the same tone but vary slightly in intensity of hue. Starting from close to the tip and continuing to the top of the bag, make a long crease. With a metal spatula place a long strip of icing against the crease. Carefully place a second shade of icing up against the first strip and continue until the bag is full. Strips should only be as long as half the bag so that it is not overfilled.

STORING PIPED DECORATIONS

Decorations made from royal icing can be air-dried and stored indefinitely at room temperature.

Buttercream decorations which are not piped directly on the cake should be chilled or frozen until firm enough to transfer to the cake. If time is short, a buttercream rose can be transferred directly to the cake with scissors: hold them slightly open to lift the rose from the flower nail; set down on the cake with the scissors still slightly open; then close the scissors and slide away from the rose.

Practice 'Buttercream'

Makes 3 cups

This buttercream is for practising piping techniques. Vegetable fat stays firmer at warm temperatures than does butter because it has a higher melting point. While this quality makes it suitable for playing with decorating techniques it makes it undesirable for eating because its slow melting point makes it feel like an oily skin against the palate.

Practice buttercream may be reused almost indefinitely. Rebeat

INGREDIENTS	WEIGHT		MEASURE
room temperature	*grams*	*pounds/ounces*	*volume*
solid vegetable fat	287 grams	10 ounces	1½ cups
icing sugar	452 grams	1 pound	4 cups (lightly spooned into cup)
water	15 grams	½ ounce	2 tablespoons*
light corn syrup	20 grams	¾ ounce	1 tablespoon†

* For *thin* consistency used for writing, stems and leaves, use 3 tablespoons water and 2 tablespoons light corn syrup. The corn syrup adds a slight shine, moistness and stretchy quality to the icing.
† For *stiff* consistency used for flowers with upright petals such as roses, omit the corn syrup.

occasionally using a flat beater at slow-medium speed to keep it smooth. It may be chilled to speed up firming if it softens during use.

STORE: 1 year room temperature, indefinitely refrigerated.

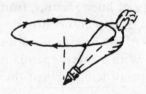

In a large mixing bowl place the fat. Gradually beat in the remaining ingredients on low speed, alternating dry and liquid. Increase speed to medium and beat until smooth and creamy. Scrape the sides occasionally. Store in an airtight container.

The two most important criteria for piping decorations with an icing tube (in addition to icing consistency) are the position of the bag and the amount and type of pressure applied.
Position of the bag: The position in which the bag is held must be precise to produce a specific design. Position refers both to the *angle* of the bag relative to the work surface and the *direction* in which it points. The two basic angles at which the bag is positioned are:
 90 degree (perpendicular)
 45 degree (halfway between vertical and horizontal)
 When decorating, one hand is used to squeeze the bag and the other to help establish and steady the angle. If drop flowers or stars come out asymmetrical, the chances are the bag is not being held at a 90-degree angle (perpendicular to the decorating surface).

Most tubes have symmetrical openings; however, there are some tubes, such as the rose tube, which are broader at the base than at the tip. When this is the case, the position of the tube must also be considered. The rose tube is almost always used with the broad end down.

Direction of the bag: This refers to the direction in which the end of the bag, farthest from the tip, is pointing. It is most easily described by using the position of numbers on a clock face. To visualise this better, try holding the bag at an angle to the surface and keeping the tip in place, make a circle with the

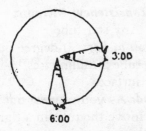

back end of the bag by rolling your wrist. Imagine that the circle is a clock face.

Direction of movement when piping: A right-handed person should always decorate from left to right; a left-handed person from right to left except when writing.

Pressure control: The size and uniformity of icing decorations are determined by the amount and type of pressure exerted on the bag. Some decorations require a steady, even pressure, others require a gradual tapering off. The more rhythmic and controlled the pressure, the more exact the decoration.

It is also particularly important to release all the pressure before lifting off the tube to prevent little 'tails' of icing from forming. Try wiggling your fingers slightly to be sure they are not inadvertently exerting pressure before lifting off the tube.

PIPED BORDERS AND SIDE DECORATIONS

STAR:

This makes a very attractive outline to border a cake or can be used to fill in sections or even the entire surface of a cake. Place the stars close enough together so that the points interlock and fill in all gaps.

Icing consistency: Medium
Tube: Any star tube (3.5 or 4 millimetre is a good size for most borders)

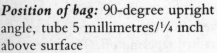

Position of bag: 90-degree upright angle, tube 5 millimetres/¼ inch above surface
Method: Squeeze bag firmly without moving it until the icing star is as wide as you desire. Push tube down slightly and stop squeezing. Slowly and precisely lift the tube straight up and away.

Note: You can change the size of the star by increasing the length of time you squeeze or by the amount of pressure. If too much icing is squeezed, the lines will start to waver.

Two of the most common problems in piping show up when piping stars:
1. continuing to squeeze while lifting off the tube.
2. not holding the tube upright for a symmetrical decoration.

ROSETTE:

Rosettes are often used as continuous borders or, when piped with a large tube and widely spaced, as a decorative demarcation for portion size.
Icing consistency: Medium
Tube: Any star tube
Position of bag: 90-degree upright angle, tube 5 millimetres/¼-inch above surface
Method: As you squeeze out the icing, move the tube in a tight arc from the nine o'clock position around to the six o'clock position (Fig. 1). Release the pressure but do not lift the tube until you have followed the circular motion all the way around to the nine o'clock position from which you started (Fig. 2). This will give the rosette a wrap-around look.

SHELL:

If there were only one border to be used in cake decorating, the graceful shell would be my first choice. In fact, the shell or one of its many variations is almost always present on some part of a decorated cake.

Icing consistency: Medium
Tube: Any star tube (3.5 or 4 millimetre are the most commonly used)
Position of bag: 45- to 90-degree angle at six o'clock, tube slightly above surface. (I prefer the flatter, wider shell you get from the higher angle.)
Method: Squeeze firmly, allowing the icing to fan out generously as you lift up the tube slightly. (Do not move the tube forward; the force of the icing will push the shell slightly forward on its own.) (Fig. 1)

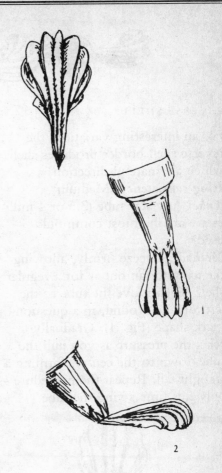

Gradually relax the pressure as you lower the tube to the surface. This gradual tapering off forms a graceful tail. Stop the pressure and pull away the tube without lifting it off the surface to draw the tail to a point (Fig. 2).

To make a second shell for a border, line up the tube at the tip of the first shell's tail. The slight forward thrust of the icing will just cover the tail of the preceding shell. When viewed from the side, the shells should be gently rounded, not humped. If humped, you are lifting the tube too high above the work surface (Fig. 3).

2

REVERSE SHELL:

For an interesting variation, the reverse shell border produces shells which alternate in direction.

Icing consistency: Medium
Tube: Any star tube (3.5 or 4 milli-metre are the most commonly used)
Method: Squeeze firmly, allowing the icing to fan out as for a regular shell. Then move the tube to the left, up and around, in a question-mark shape (Fig. 1). Gradually relax the pressure as you pull the tube down to the centre, forming a straight tail. Repeat the procedure – only this time swing the tube

1

around to the right in a backward question mark. Continue alternating shells around the border (Fig. 2).

1

2

3

FLEUR-DE-LIS:

Yet another variation of the shell, a fleur-de-lis is composed of three shells – a regular shell and two reverse shells. It is most often used for the sides of a cake

Icing consistency: Medium
Tube: Any star tube (3.5 or 4 milli-metre are the most commonly used)

Method: Pipe an elongated shell (Fig. 1). To its left, pipe a reverse shell, shaped like a regular question mark (Fig. 2). To its right, pipe another reverse shell shaped like a backward question mark. Allow the tails of the reverse shells to come up on top of the centre shell, being careful to have all tails meet to form a point (Fig. 3).

1

2

SHELL WITH FLUTE:

Combining two different piping techniques, the shell and the stand-up petal used for a sweet pea (page 468) results in an unusual and elegant decorative effect.
Icing consistency: Medium
Method: Make a shell border, allowing a little extra room between each shell to accommodate the flute (Fig. 1). To make a flute, use the 12 millimetre rose tube. Allow the wide end of the tube to rest between the two shells. Squeeze the bag while raising the tube slightly to allow the flute to rise between the two shells (Fig. 2). Stop the pressure, lower the tube, and pull away. Repeat this procedure between every shell or every other shell.

RUFFLE:

Ruffles are used on the sides of a cake.
Icing consistency: Medium
Tube: Any rose tube (12 millimetre is often used)
Position of bag: 45-degree angle at three o'clock, tube with wide end down and narrow end slightly raised from the surface
Method: Squeeze firmly using a back-and-forth motion to produce zigzag ruffles.

DOTS AND PEARLS:

One or two staggered rows of balls create a lovely, graceful border. Dots are subtle and delicate on the sides of a cake as well.

Icing consistency: Soft
Tube: Any round tube (1.5 millimetre is a nice size for the sides, 4.5 millimetre for a 30.5-centimetre/12-inch base, 3 millimetre for a 23-centimetre/9-inch base, 2 millimetre for a 15-centimetre/6-inch base)
Position of bag: 90-degree upright to surface, tube slightly above surface

Method: Squeeze with steady, even pressure. As the icing begins to build up, raise the tube with it keeping the tip buried in the icing. When a well-rounded shape is achieved, stop the pressure as you bring the tip to the surface. Use the edge of the tip to shave off any point, moving the tip in a clockwise direction. Points are more apt to form with stiffer icing. Points can also be removed by waiting until the icing crusts slightly and pressing gently with a fingertip. If the icing is still soft, dip the fingertip in water first.

ROPE:

This border consists of a chain of S shapes intertwined to create the illusion of a twisted rope. It is quite easy to accomplish.

Icing consistency: Medium
Tube: Any star tube (3.5 or 4 millimetre are usually used)
Position of bag: 45-degree angle at half past four, tube lightly touching surface

Method: Squeeze with steady, even pressure. Move the tube up, around and down to the right to create a sideways S curve. Stop squeezing and lift the bag away. Insert the tube under the left side of the S and repeat the same procedure, lifting the tube as you go up and around.

BASKET WEAVE:

When the basket weave is used to decorate the sides of a cake and flowers are used on top, it creates the illusion of a basket filled with flowers.

The basket weave is an easy but somewhat time-consuming technique. Since the entire sides of the cake will be covered with icing to form the basket weave, only the thinnest coating of icing should be used to ice the cake.

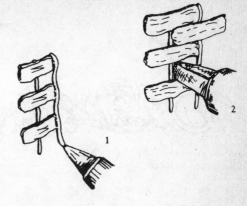

Icing consistency: Medium
Tube: 1.5, and 5-millimetre serrated flat tube
Position of bag: 45-degree angle at six o'clock for vertical lines, three o'clock for horizontal lines
Method: Basket weave goes more quickly if two bags are used. For vertical stripes, use a 1.5-millimetre tube. Starting at the top of the cake, touch the tip to the surface to attach the icing and then raise the tube slightly to allow the icing to fall freely against the side of the cake. (This will produce a more even line.) Squeeze evenly and firmly, drawing the tube down the side to the bottom and touch the tip at the bottom.

For horizontal basket weave, use a 5-millimetre serrated flat tube, with serrated side facing up. Use the round line as the centre guide for the stripes. With the tip touching the surface, start squeezing, lifting slightly to ride over the vertical line. Stop squeezing and pull very slightly to straighten the stripe. Touch down to the surface to attach. Space the second stripe one stripe width away from the first. Repeat until to the bottom of the cake.

Starting from the top, drop a second vertical line down the side of the cake to cover the right edges of stripes. (If a little stripe sticks out, don't worry, it will be covered by the next alternating row of stripes.) (Fig. 1).

For the second row of stripes, pipe between the first row, again using the vertical line as a centre guide. To create the illusion of wicker weaving in and out, be sure to tuck the tip slightly under the vertical line before you begin squeezing. Don't worry about small gaps, 'real' baskets have them too! (Fig. 2.)

Note: For a different variety of basket weave, use a 5-millimetre serrated flat tube for vertical and horizontal lines.

SCROLLWORK:

Albeit a bit baroque, scrollwork lends a charmingly antique quality to the sides of a cake.
Icing consistency: Medium
Tube: 1.5-millimetre round tube and 2-millimetre star tube
Position of bag: 45-degree angle
Method: Use the round tube, touching the surface lightly, to draw an inverted C shape with a long tail pointing to the left. Starting at the top of the C, draw a second C with a long tail upside down. Continue around the cake, reversing C shapes as you go. Add curved lines to the tails of the C (Fig. 1).

With the star tube, trace over the design, making a series of feathery reverse shells (page 462), all facing the same direction (Fig. 2).

Note: For a softer effect, use a 2.5-millimetre round tube in place of the star tube (Fig. 3).

STRING WORK:

String work is unquestionably the most refined and elegant of all borders. It does not appear often, even on wedding cakes, because it is exacting and time-consuming. All it really requires is patience and an icing of proper consistency. Royal icing made with liquid egg white is ideal because it is strong and elastic enough for the finest string work. Buttercream, however, also works if the strings are kept relatively short.

Icing which is too thick will not flow easily from the tube and will break. If too thin, it will lack elasticity and snap. To test consistency, drop a loop of icing from your finger and adjust as necessary.

Icing consistency: Thin

Tube: Any small round tube (3 is often used)

Position of bag: The height of the bag should be shoulder level and at half past four, the tube lightly touching the surface only to attach. For maximum control, keep the height of the tip constant. Do not allow the tube to follow the drop of the string. (This is a very common error in piping strings. Not allowing the tip to drop goes against all instincts!)

Method: With dots of icing, mark a row of equally spaced points around the perimeter of the cake. Touch the tip of the tube to attach the icing at first dot. While squeezing, pull the bag away from the surface towards you. Continue squeezing to allow the icing to droop naturally. Resist the temptation to follow the droop of the icing with the tip. The tip should be the same distance from the surface as the distance from point to point. Stop squeezing and touch the tip to the next dot to attach the loop. Continue around the entire cake. To form a double row of string work, complete the first row and then pipe a second row of shallow loops inside the first (Fig. 1). For an even more striking effect, overlap the string work to create an interwoven look. This is much less complicated than it appears. First make a standard-size loop, starting at the first dot and ending at the second. Starting at the centre top of that loop, attach the icing and drop another loop, attaching it between the second and third dots. The third loop starts where the first loop ended and finishes at the third dot. The fourth loop starts where the second loop ended. Believe me, this is easier done than said! (Fig. 2.)

The size of the loop and the distance between loops should be in proportion to the size of the cake. A small loop looks insignificant on a large cake; a large loop looks disproportionate on a small cake.

PIPED FLOWERS

DROP FLOWERS:

These are the simplest flowers to
make. They can be piped directly
on to a cake or on to greaseproof
paper to be air-dried or frozen and
then lifted on to the cake.
Icing consistency: Stiff
Tube: Any star tube or drop flower
tube (closed star)
Position of bag: 90-degree upright
angle, tube 5 millimetres/¼ inch
above surface
Method: For a straight flower,
squeeze the bag firmly without
moving it until the icing flower is
as wide as you desire. Push the
tube down slightly and stop
squeezing. Slowly and precisely lift
the tube up and away.

For a swirled flower, turn the
hand holding the bag as far to the
left as possible. As you squeeze,
turn your hand to the right as far
as possible and stop the pressure.
This should be a gradual motion. It
helps to use the surface as a pivot
by pressing the tip lightly to the
surface. Dot the centres if desired,
using a 1.5-millimetre round tube
and contrasting colour.

SWEET PEA:

This simple flower can be piped in
sprays directly on to a cake or
made ahead. If made from royal
icing, the sharp stem can be poked
into the side of a cake to suspend
the flower firmly in place.

Icing consistency: Stiff
Tube: Any rose tube; a 1.5-milli-
metre round tube for the stem
Position of bag: 45-degree angle at
eleven o'clock for the base and six
o'clock for the petals

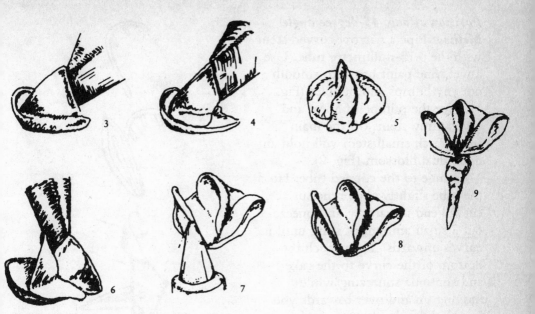

Method: To make the base, rest the wide end of the rose tube on the surface with the narrow end very slightly elevated. As you start squeezing, swing the tube gradually from eleven o'clock to one o'clock forming a flat arc (Figs. 1 and 2).

For the petals, rest the tube on the surface at the bottom centre of the base with the narrow end pointing straight up. As you squeeze, raise the tube slightly, then lower and stop the pressure.

Rock your hand slightly forward to break off the icing (Figs. 3–5). Repeat this procedure to make two side petals, angling the tube first slightly to the left, then to the right (Figs. 6–8).

For the stem, use a number 3 round tube to touch the base of the flower, and as you squeeze to build up icing, gradually draw the tube away, relaxing the pressure to form the stem (Fig. 9).

LILY OF THE VALLEY:

There is a special tube and technique that makes it possible to capture this charming bell shape.
Icing consistency: Stiff
Tube: 0.75 millimetres and 5-millimetre cupped tube

Position of bag: 45-degree angle
Method: Pipe a narrow curved stem
with the 0.75-millimetre tube. Use
a wet, fine paint brush to smooth
out any bumps and bubbles (Fig.
1). Pipe the outline of a leaf and
several tiny stems off the main
stem. Each small stem will hold an
individual blossom (Fig. 2).

Change to the cupped tube. Hold
the tube slightly above the surface,
curved end towards you. Squeeze
out a small amount of icing until it
curves upwards. Then touch the
bottom of the curve to the cake
and continue squeezing while
moving up and over towards you
in a slightly circular movement
(Fig. 3). Stop the pressure
completely and pull away the tube.
To keep the bell shape from
opening up, pull the tube away in a
slightly downward motion.

ROSEBUDS AND HALF ROSE:

These flowers are exquisitely
realistic. They can be formed
directly on the cake or made ahead.
Icing consistency: Stiff
Tube: Any rose tube; 1.5-milli-
metre round tube for the stem and
sepals
Position of bag: 45-degree angle at
three o'clock, tube with wide end
down and narrow end straight up.
Careful positioning is critical to
achieve this shape.
Method: With the wide end of the
tube touching the surface, start
squeezing, moving the tip sharply

back and forth to create a cupped base. Release the pressure and twist your hand slightly to the right to open up the right side of the cup and keep it from curving over. Slide the tip down and away from the side to release the icing and create a sharp edge (Fig. 1).

Line up the tube so that the entire opening touches the entire right edge of the base. Leaving the tube still and in place, squeeze the bag firmly. Icing will catch the edge and roll itself into an interlocking centre bud (Fig. 2).

Attach the stem or go on to create a half rose.

For a half rose, hold the tube wide end down and narrow end straight up to the left of the base. Squeeze, raising the tube slightly, then lower and stop the pressure to form a side petal (Fig. 3). This is the same basic motion as for the base only it stops midway at the centre of the flower. Follow the same procedure to make a second side petal, going from right to left and slightly overlapping the first petal (Fig. 4). To form stem and sepals, use round tube number 3. Touch the base, allowing icing to build up while gradually drawing the tube away (Fig. 5). Bury the tip in the base and gradually relax the pressure as you move the tip up the petal and slightly away to form three sepals.

PIPED ROSE:

There is something about a rose piped from an icing tube that is pure magic. People are always spellbound when watching a demonstration of piped roses – even I, after all these years of decorating cakes, find myself in awe, forgetting that I can do them too!

Piped roses make a time-honoured decoration for any cake. For a new twist, make royal icing rose candleholders by inserting a candle in the centre of each rose before the icing dries. When the icing has dried completely, lay the rose on its side and pipe a 4-centimetre/1½-inch stem from its base. When thoroughly dry, poke the stem directly into the cake by first making a small hole with a metal skewer.

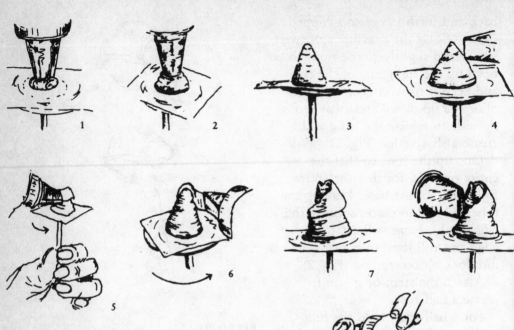

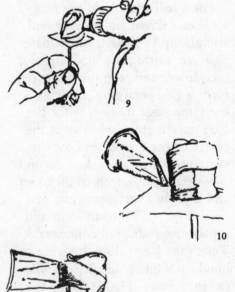

Icing consistency: As stiff as possible while still squeezable

Tube: 7-millimetre round tube for the base; any rose tube for the petals

Position of bag: For base: rose nail is held in left hand, bag at 90-degree upright angle, tube slightly above nail.

For petals: 45-degree angle at half past four, tube with wide end touching base and narrow end turned slightly inward and then gradually outward for each row of petals.

Base: Attach a greaseproof paper square to the rose nail with a dot of icing. Hold the bag perpendicular to the nail, with the round tube touching the centre. Squeeze with heavy pressure, keeping the tip buried in the icing until you build

up a good size base (Fig. 1). Ease pressure as you gradually raise the tube to form a bottom-heavy conical shape (Fig. 2). This base should be 1½ times as high as the opening of the rose tube used to make the petals (Fig. 3).

Bud: Hold the bag at a 45-degree angle to the nail, with the back over to the right so your fingertips face you. Touch the wide end of rose tube to the top of icing base, with the narrow end turned slightly inward (Fig. 4).

As you start to squeeze, pull the tube up and away from the top of the base, stretching the icing into a ribbon band (Fig. 5). At the same time, turn the nail anticlockwise and swing the band of icing around the tip and back down to where you first started, overlapping the starting point and continuing down to the bottom of the base for stability (Fig. 6).

First row of 3 petals: Touch the wide end of the rose tube to the icing bud close to the bottom, with the narrow tube end pointing straight (Fig. 7). Turn the nail anticlockwise and move the tube up, around and down towards you in a half-circle motion to form a petal (Fig. 8). Give the nail a one-third turn for each petal.

Following the same procedure, start at the base of the first petal, overlapping it slightly, and squeeze out icing as you move the tube up, around and down towards you to form a second petal (Fig. 9).

Again, following the same procedure, start at the base of the second petal and squeeze out icing as you turn the nail to form a third petal, slightly overlapping the first petal (Figs. 10 and 11).

Second row of 4 petals: Touch the wide end of the rose tip to just under the first row of petals in the centre of one of them, with the narrow end of the tube pointing slightly outward. As you squeeze, give the nail a quarter turn and move the tube up, around, and down to form a petal. Starting at the base of this petal, follow the same procedure to make three more petals. The petals should be the same height as those in the first row (Figs. 12 and 13).

12

13

Third row of 5 to 7 petals: Touch the wide end of the rose tube to the base under the second row of petals in the centre of one of them, with the narrow end of the tube pointing slightly farther out than the previous row. Again turn the nail slightly and squeeze out the

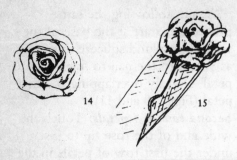

14   15

first petal. Follow the same procedure until the last row of petals has been completed (Fig. 14).

PIPED LEAVES:

Pale green tinted icing leaves, piped around and between the roses, add a nice touch.
Icing consistency: Thin
Tube: Leaf tube with 7-millimetre slashed cut on each side, or tube with 4.5-millimetre cut for leaf shape
Position of bag: 45-degree angle
Method: There are two basic types of piped leaves: the plain or flat leaf and the ruffled stand-up leaf.

For a plain leaf, touch the tip to the surface and squeeze, gradually drawing the tube away. Release the pressure gradually, drawing the leaf to a point (Fig. 1). It is practically impossible to get a sharp point using a notched leaf tube which produces the centre vein. For a leaf with a precise point but a less defined centre vein, use the tube with the 4.5-millimetre cut. One of the pointed ends should face down.

Tip: If you wish to curve the edges of the petals, dip a fingertip in cornflour and gently mould them.

Remove the rose from the nail by lifting the greaseproof paper square from the nail. If you haven't used greaseproof paper, remove the rose with scissors held in a slightly open position (Fig. 15). Do not close the scissors until the rose is positioned on the cake or other surface.

1

2

For a stand-up leaf, squeeze with heavier pressure to build up a base to support the leaf. Then pull the tube straight up and away as you relax the pressure and draw to a point (Fig. 2). If you have built up an adequate base and the leaf will not stand up, the icing is too thin or soft.

WRITING

Writing requires thin icing which flows smoothly from the tube and lots of penmanship practice. I personally do not like to see writing on a cake, but sometimes the occasion calls for it, so I try to make it as integral a part of the design as possible.

Practise on an inverted cake tin or the worktop before piping the writing directly on to the cake. Unless you have a lot of experience writing on cakes, it is easy to become rusty. Printing is a lot easier than script.

Icing consistency: Thin
Tube: Any small round tube (1.5 millimetre is the most often used)
Position of bag: 45-degree angle at six o'clock for printing, three o'clock for script
Method: For printing, touch the tip to the surface. As you start squeezing, raise the tip slightly to keep the lines even. Stop squeezing a little before the end of the line and tug ever so slightly to straighten the line before touching the tip down to attach. Release the pressure, remove the tip and start the next line.

For script, the tip should always be touching the surface lightly.

For both printing and script, be sure to move your entire arm, not just your hand. This results in a smoother design.

ROYAL ICING CALLIGRAPHY:

Because I, like most people, do not write on cakes every day of the week, it is risky business indeed to find myself with an icing bag poised above an up-to-that-point perfect cake – wondering how I'm going to fit in the letters and how they will look and what I will do if I ruin the cake.

To avoid this anxiety, I have worked out the following risk-free system for getting the letters on the cake, plus a choice of capital-letter calligraphy.

Wherever I have travelled, I have searched for attractive letters to use for cakes. My search finally ended one day on a flight between San Francisco and New York. I found the unusual type style on page 476 in a stunning in-flight magazine called *Vis à Vis*. It took months to track it down, but I finally found their headquarters and received official permission to use the letters for this book. They are courtesy of *Vis à Vis* (East–West Network) and were designed by the talented LA-based artist and logo designer Michael Manoogian.

A decorative monogram can be fun to create and makes an attractive design. Make a template by photocopying or tracing the letters, reducing or increasing the size as desired. Tape the tracing securely to rigid cardboard or a baking sheet and lay a non-stick liner on top. Use a few pieces of

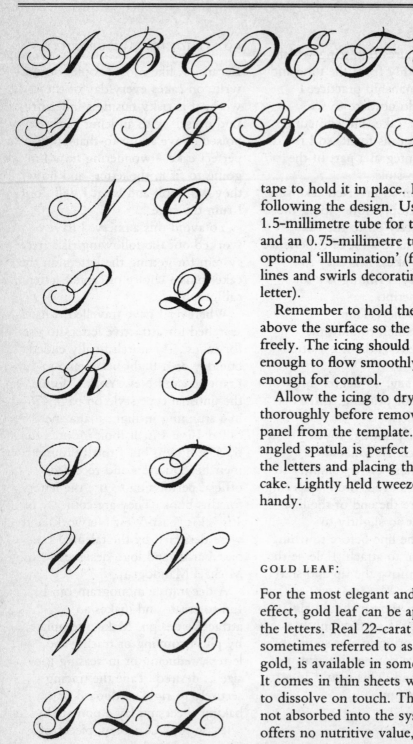

tape to hold it in place. Pipe, following the design. Use a 1.5-millimetre tube for the letters and an 0.75-millimetre tube for the optional 'illumination' (free-form lines and swirls decorating the letter).

Remember to hold the tube above the surface so the icing falls freely. The icing should be soft enough to flow smoothly but stiff enough for control.

Allow the icing to dry thoroughly before removing the panel from the template. A small angled spatula is perfect for lifting the letters and placing them on the cake. Lightly held tweezers are also handy.

GOLD LEAF:

For the most elegant and stunning effect, gold leaf can be applied to the letters. Real 22-carat gold leaf, sometimes referred to as patent gold, is available in some art shops. It comes in thin sheets which seem to dissolve on touch. The gold is not absorbed into the system so it offers no nutritive value, although some fancifully say that it is good for the heart. In India, gold leaf is used to decorate desserts or to float in a magical liquid pool on soup. Goldwasser, a German liqueur, also contains flecks of gold. My friend Bob Miller, an artist, even gilds his Thanksgiving turkey, managing partially to gild himself as well in the joyful process!

Using gold on letters is tricky but thrilling because it is so very beautiful. When I asked the salesman how to make the gold stick he suggested 'sizing' until I told him it was for eating. Egg white, however, works very well.

To apply gold, use a fine artist's brush to brush a thin coating of lightly beaten egg white on a small section of the letter. Lift a small piece of gold leaf with sharp-pointed tweezers and lay it on top. It will tend to curve around and cling to the egg white. Use the same brush to smooth it in place. If the letters are used on rolled fondant, the gold can be applied after the letters are in place as it will not stick to the fondant. Use a bit of egg white to attach letters to the fondant.

ROYAL ICING ROSE LATTICE PANELS
Icing consistency: Thin
Tube: Round 1 millimetre
Position of bag: 45-degree angle
Method: Trace or photocopy the drawing on to paper with dark ink. The ideal surface for piping these delicate panels is a non-stick liner (page 524) because it is easy to remove the delicate filigree work without risking breakage. Parchment can also be used but removal is more risky. In any event, minor breakage can be repaired even after the panels are attached to the cake, but it is always safer to make one or two extra.

Tape the tracing securely to rigid cardboard or a baking sheet and lay the non-stick liner on top. Use a few pieces of tape to hold it in place. Pipe, following the design. If desired, use pink royal icing, for contrast, to pipe roses. It is unimportant if you deviate from the design because after removing the template it will always look breathtakingly beautiful.

Remember to hold the tube above the surface so the icing falls freely. The icing should be soft enough to flow smoothly but stiff enough for control. Pipe a second line on top of the first around the outside edge for extra stability. Carefully slide out the template and use it as the guide for all the panels.

Allow the icing to dry for at least 30 minutes before removing the panels from the liner. It helps to hold the panels on a flat worktop, allowing small sections to extend over the edge. Support the panel with a broad spatula while pulling the liner down and away from the extended section. Small

breaks can be filled in and repaired even when on the cake.

PAINTED ROYAL ICING FLOWERS

Using a damp artist's brush to shape the piped icing creates subtle effects. Use only enough water to keep the brush marks from showing.

LILIES OF THE VALLEY:

Piping and then painting the tiny flowers on to a fondant-covered cake gives the illusion of fine embroidery.
Icing consistency: Thin
Tube: Round 0.75-millimetre

Position of bag: 45-degree angle
Method: Pipe a narrow curved stem, using an 0.75-millimetre tube (Fig. 1). Use a wet, fine paint brush to smooth out any bumps and bubbles. Pipe the outline of a leaf and several tiny stems off the main stem (Fig. 2). Each small stem will hold an individual blossom. For the blossoms, pipe small oval dots of icing on the ends of each stem (Fig. 3). Using the brush, pull down points from each oval to form bell-shaped blossoms (Fig. 4). Dilute green food colouring with water to produce the palest possible shade. Use the brush to highlight the flowers with touches of colour.

1   2   3   4

BLEEDING HEART FLOWERS:

Icing consistency: Thin for leaves, medium for blossoms
Tube: Round 1 millimetre and 2.5 millimetre; 1-millimetre star
Method: The heart-shaped flowers are piped entirely with a decorating tube, but the leaves are outlined and filled in with the aid of an artist's brush. For the leaves, use paste food colour to tint the royal icing a deep shade of green. Mix in a little blue if the colour is too bright. Keep in mind that the colour will darken so make it a little lighter than the colour you want. The leaves should be outlined free-form following the sketch and using a 1-millimetre tube (Fig. 1). The same tube can be used to pipe the stems. To fill in the leaves, switch to a 2.5-milli-metre tube and squeeze out the icing with a back-and-forth motion (Fig. 2). Work on one leaf at a time so that the icing does not start to crust. Smooth squiggles of icing with a wet brush (Fig. 3). Tint some of the icing bright pink for the flowers. The heart shape is piped like a shell design (page 461) but with a plain round 2.5-milli-metre tube so that it looks like a tear drop. For closed buds, pipe only one tear-drop shape. For blossoms, pipe two side-by-side tear drops, first angling the tube slightly to the left, then slightly to the right (Fig. 4). Change to an 0.75-millimetre round tube to add curved strings to the point (Fig. 5). Pipe a tiny upside-down shell with white icing and use a 1-millimetre star tube for the tip of the blossom (Fig. 6).

1   2   3

4   5   6

PART III
INGREDIENTS AND EQUIPMENT

Ingredients

My interest in the science of ingredients began when I was a freshman at the University of Vermont. I had just learned to make lemon meringue pie in a foods class and wanted to share the marvellous eating experience with some friends. We were all very poor so everyone contributed money for the ingredients. It was, therefore, especially humiliating, when, after using three-quarters of a box of cornflour, the filling still would not thicken. Determined to get to the bottom of this mystery, I analysed each ingredient and finally settled on the water as the only possible culprit. We submitted the water for a mineral test and, sure enough, it had the highest possible level. This made me aware that there was more to cooking – and especially baking – than met the eye. It was many years before I made lemon meringue pie again.

It seems like a lifetime ago that baking seemed such an utter and thrilling mystery.

It was about a decade later that I became seriously interested in cake baking and wrote my master's thesis on yellow cake. I remember making the cake one day when a neighbour called by to visit. Bob was from rural Georgia where, in those days, people raised most of what they ate. His mother had a pig killed every year, turning the entire animal into the best home-smoked sausage I have ever encountered. (Bob had endeared himself to me for life by sharing his precious supply.)

That day, as he watched me transfer the batter to the cake tin, he said: 'You must be a good cook.' 'Why?' I asked. His answer: 'Because you cook the way my mother cooks; nothing goes to waste. It's an attitude. People who cook that way seem to care about it more, so it comes out better.'

That, in a nutshell, is my philosophy about ingredients. When you love what you do, no ingredient goes to waste so only the very best need be chosen in the first place. And, of course, it is not the quality of the ingredients alone that makes the difference between the extraordinary and the mediocre – it is the reverence with which one approaches baking and the desire to offer the best of what many consider to be the best part of the meal, dessert.

BAKING POWDER:

Baking powders are mixtures of dry acid or acid salts and bicarbonate of soda with starch or flour added to standardise and help stabilise the mixtures. Double-acting means that they will react, or liberate carbon dioxide, partially from moisture during the mixing stage and partially when exposed to heat during the baking stage. It is, therefore, important to store the baking powder in an airtight container to avoid humidity. There is also a substantial loss of strength in baking powder after one year. Date the bottom of the tin when you first buy it, or write the expiry date on the lid with a felt-tip marker.

I use an all-phosphate product containing calcium acid phosphate. It lacks the bitter aftertaste associated with baking powders that also contain sodium aluminium sulphate. (The supposed advantage of these powders is that they release a little more carbon dioxide during the baking stage than during the mixing stage, but I find I can interchange equal volume and weight of either type of baking powder.)

BEESWAX:

Used for making spun sugar because of its high melting point, it helps keep the strands flexible. Beeswax is available at hardware shops, art supply stores, some drapers and, of course, through apiaries.

BICARBONATE OF SODA:

Sodium bicarbonate has an indefinite shelf-life if not exposed to humidity. In Canada I once discovered a wonderful variety called Cow Brand (goodness knows why). It contained a tiny amount of a harmless chemical ingredient which prevented it from clumping. Unless you can obtain this type of bicarbonate of soda, it is best to sift it before measuring.

CHESTNUTS:

Most of the tinned chestnuts I have seen come from France. Different types of purée vary widely in sugar content so pay close attention to the label. *Marrons entiers au naturel:* These are whole peeled chestnuts in water. *Crème de marrons:* This cream, made up of candied pieces of chestnut, has a total of 48 per cent sugar and glucose. This is not to be confused with chestnut purée, for it is far too sweet for any of the uses in this book. *Purée de marrons au naturel:* This product is virtually unsweetened. It does, however, contain water, making it too soft for some uses. *Marrons glacés:* These whole candied chestnuts are suitable for garnishing.

CHESTNUT FLOUR:

This flour, which is mainly starch, is made from milled dried chestnuts and comes from France and Italy. It is difficult to find in the UK, but if you can track some down your efforts will be rewarded by its magnificent flavour.

To retain the distinctive flavour, chestnut flour should be refrigerated. It will keep for at least one year.

Chocolate

Chocolate is a very important ingredient in cakes and buttercreams. Working with it over the past ten years, I have found there is an enormous difference in both texture and flavour among brands and have developed my own personal preferences. I highly recommend that you do a blind tasting to determine your own.

One of my favourite dark chocolates is Lindt's Courante, a couverture that can be used in place of bittersweet chocolate for the recipes in this book (see page 512 for exact sugar content equivalencies). I also love Tobler's Extra Bittersweet and Tradition and Lindt's Excellence. (Lindt also has a couverture called Excellence, so be careful not to confuse the two.) Another favourite is French Valrhôna's Extra Bittersweet, which has a delicious, winy undertone. When it comes to milk chocolate I adore Lindt for its creamy smoothness and lovely caramel flavour notes. For white chocolate, the only one I find acceptable is Tobler's Narcisse. Others are sweeter and sometimes almost chalky.

Many fine chocolates, such as Tobler, are produced under Kashruth supervision. Write to the manufacturer or distributor for a letter of certification if you want to use a chocolate in kosher cooking.

Brands of chocolate differ partly because of special formulas unique to each company, which determine the blend of the beans, the type and amount of flavourings, and the proportions of chocolate liquor and cocoa butter. Taste and texture are also greatly affected by the length of roasting, grinding, and conching. Grinding reduces particle size and conching – a wavelike motion – releases volatile oils, develops flavour, and coats the sugar and cocoa particles with cocoa butter, which reduces the feeling of gritty abrasiveness. Too much conching can result in an oily texture. European, particularly Swiss, chocolate is usually conched for up to 96 hours, which produces the characteristic velvety-smooth texture Europeans favour and which some Americans find too rich. American chocolate may be conched for only 4 to 5 hours if at all, though some brands claim as many as 74 hours of conching.

Lecithin, an emulsifier found in soya beans, is used to stabilise chocolate. Its presence reduces the amount of cocoa butter required to cover the cocoa particles. It frees the cocoa butter to act as a floating medium for the particles. It also reduces viscosity, making it less thick. Only a very small quantity is necessary, for example 1 gram lecithin per kilogram for white chocolate, slightly more for dark chocolate. Lecithin is used in even the finest quality chocolate. As it is not 'Kosher for Passover', a Swiss company, Maestrani, exports an excellent chocolate containing no lecithin. The plain chocolate contains no dairy products.

PURE CHOCOLATE:

Pure chocolate, also referred to as bitter or unsweetened chocolate, contains only chocolate liquor (cocoa solids and cocoa butter) and flavourings. Depending on the variety of the cocoa bean used, 50 to 58 per cent of the chocolate liquor is cocoa butter, averaging 53 per cent. The bulk of the remainder, the cocoa solids, contains 10.7 per cent protein and 28.9 per cent starch. (This is the same amount present in the nibs – the term for the cocoa bean after removal of the pod – before processing.) No lecithin may be added, but a great variety of flavourings is permissible, such as vanilla or vanillin (synthesised vanilla), ground nuts, coffee, salt and various extracts.

COCOA:

Cocoa is the pure chocolate liquor with three-quarters of the cocoa butter removed. The remaining cocoa is then pulverised. Most European cocoa is Dutch-processed, which means that the cocoa has been treated with a mild alkali to mellow the flavour and make it more soluble. British cocoa, however, is not Dutch-processed. There is no need to sift cocoa for a recipe when it will be dissolved in water. In recipes such as Chocolate Rolled Fondant or Chocolate Meringue, it is advisable to process or sift the cocoa if it is lumpy so that it will incorporate more evenly.

My favourite Dutch-processed cocoa is Lindt's from Switzerland, which recently has become available in this country. It comes in dark and light (I prefer the dark) and, although not generally available in British shops, it is carried by Maid of Scandinavia (page 513). Van Houten is an excellent Dutch-processed cocoa and is available in the UK.

COCOA BUTTER:

The quality of cocoa butter is related to the quality of the bean from which it came and the process of separating it from the chocolate liquor. Many chocolatiers prefer Swiss cocoa butter, which is produced by cold pressing and is lighter in colour and finer in flavour.

When working with cocoa butter, it is helpful to know that it is solid at room temperature and that it has a low melting point (just below body temperature) that is called 'sharp', meaning it changes quickly from solid to liquid, unlike butter which is more gradual. Adding cocoa butter to mixtures will make them firmer but will also offer more of a melt-in-the-mouth experience.

Store cocoa butter in an airtight container so that it doesn't pick up other flavours. Refrigerated, it will keep for several years.

Cocoa butter is a vegetable fat and contains no cholesterol. It is, unfortunately, high in saturated fat.

BITTERSWEET OR SEMISWEET AND EXTRA BITTERSWEET:

Bittersweet or semisweet and extra bittersweet are pure chocolate liquor with sugar, vanilla or vanillin, and extra cocoa butter added. Semisweet morsels have to be more viscous to maintain their chip shape during baking. Every manufacturer has his own terminology or formula for this category of chocolate. They can be used interchangeably in recipes, but their sweetness levels will vary. (For more precise sweetness equivalencies, see page 512.)

COUVERTURE:

Used for dipping and some decorative work, in Europe this is made from the highest quality real chocolate, which has a high percentage of cocoa butter, resulting in low viscosity and subsequently a thin coating and a glossy sheen when used for dipping or decorations such as chocolate bands. European couverture must have a minimum of 36 per cent cocoa butter and may have as much as 40 per cent. Japanese couverture may have as much as 42 per cent. In the United States couverture is often referred to as compound chocolate and there is no US standard.

MILK CHOCOLATE:

Milk chocolate contains pure chocolate liquor, milk solids, butter, vanilla or vanillin, and extra cocoa butter.

Milk chocolate does not have as long a shelf-life as plain chocolate because the milk solids become rancid (though not as quickly as in white chocolate due to the protective presence of cocoa solids).

WHITE CHOCOLATE:

White chocolate is sometimes not considered to be 'real chocolate' because it contains no cocoa solids. Better-quality white chocolates are, however, made with cocoa butter and have a delicious flavour. White chocolate contains about 30 per cent fat, 30 per cent milk solids and 30 per cent sugar. It also contains vanilla or vanillin and lecithin. When melted, it sets faster than dark chocolate but is softer at room temperature. Its shelf-life is much shorter than dark chocolate because of the milk solids.

In addition to making delicious buttercreams and cakes, a small amount of melted white chocolate is great in an emergency to thicken buttercream or pastry cream. This small amount of white chocolate adds firmness without significantly altering the character of the mixture.

COMPOUND CHOCOLATE:

Compound chocolate is classified as chocolate 'flavour' because, instead of cocoa butter, it contains vegetable fat such as soya, palm kernel or coconut oil. This type of fat is more stable than cocoa butter and does not require tempering (page 437) to prevent bloom (discoloration). It also affords the chocolate a higher melting point, which means it will remain unmelted at warmer temperatures.

For this reason, it is sometimes referred to as 'summer coating'. Its taste is acceptable and some people find it delicious (they can't have tasted the real thing), but it lacks the complexity and fullness of fine-quality chocolate. Still, for small decorative touches when you don't have time to temper chocolate, it is a joy to have on hand.

AVERAGE CHOCOLATE MASS AND COCOA BUTTER CONTENT:

Chocolate mass refers to the total amount of cocoa solids and cocoa butter.

cocoa (Dutch-processed): 22 to 25 per cent cocoa butter
cocoa (non-alkalised): 10 to 12 per cent cocoa butter
bitter or unsweetened chocolate (pure chocolate liquor): 50 to 58 per cent cocoa butter, averaging 53 per cent
couverture chocolate: 60 to 78 per cent chocolate mass of which 36 to 40 per cent is cocoa butter
extra bittersweet chocolate: 60 per cent chocolate mass of which 30 per cent is cocoa butter
semisweet or bittersweet chocolate: 49.5 to 53 per cent chocolate mass of which 27 per cent is cocoa butter
semisweet bits: 42.5 per cent chocolate mass of which 29 per cent is cocoa butter
sweet chocolate: 34 per cent chocolate mass of which 27 per cent is cocoa butter

milk chocolate: 34 to 38 per cent chocolate mass of which 29 to 33 per cent is cocoa butter, plus 12 per cent whole milk solids.

STORING CHOCOLATE:

The best way to store chocolate or cocoa is to keep it well wrapped in an airtight container (chocolate is quick to absorb other odours and must not be exposed to dampness) at a temperature of 60° to 75°F/18° to 24°C with less than 50 per cent relative humidity. Under these conditions plain chocolate should keep well for at least two years. I have experienced chocolate stored at ideal conditions for several years and it seems to age like a fine wine, becoming more mellow and subtle. Milk chocolate keeps, even at optimum conditions, for only a little over one year and white chocolate, about one year.

CITRON, ANGELICA AND MIXED CANDIED FRUITS:

Used primarily for fruitcake and decorative work, they are available in supermarkets and from specialist confectioners. Stored airtight at room temperature, they last for years. Do not refrigerate as they become rock hard.

CORNFLOUR AND ARROWROOT:

These two starches have twice the thickening power of flour and produce more translucent glazes. Arrowroot also adds a slight sparkle. Thickening is accomplished by absorption of liquid. As the starch granules absorb the liquid, they swell and become fragile. It is, therefore, very important not to stir vigorously after thickening has occurred because it will break down these fragile, swollen granules and the glaze will be thin.

Cornflour does not thicken until it has reached a full boil (212°F/100°C), while arrowroot requires only 158° to 176°F/70° to 80°C. Prolonged cooking past the thickening point will also break down the starch and thin the glaze.

Note: Starches have limited shelf-life. If they are stored for several years they will eventually lose their thickening power.

CREAM OF TARTAR:

Potassium acid tartrate is a by-product of the wine industry. Its shelf-life is indefinite. I have found that by adding 1 teaspoon cream of tartar per 240 grams/8½ ounces/ 1 cup egg whites, it stabilises them so that it becomes virtually impossible to dry them out by overbeating. Cream of tartar is also used as an interfering agent in sugar syrups to inhibit crystallisation and to lower the pH of certain batters, such as angel food cake, to produce a whiter crumb.

BUTTER:

Butter is one of my favourite flavours. The best fresh, unsalted butter has the flowery, grassy smell of a summer meadow. It seems downright unfair that this indispensable ingredient should not be equally wonderful for one's health. But it isn't. So the only solution is to eat smaller portions – but never to substitute any other solid fat.

Salted butter does not have the glorious flavour of fresh unsalted butter. If only salted butter is available, remove 1 teaspoon salt from the recipe per 454 grams/ 1 pound of butter used. It is also possible to make your own butter from cream, but if only UHT cream is available it may not be worth the trouble. Commercial butter is made from cream with a very high butterfat content and is churned immediately after flash pasteurisation. This ensures the best flavour and longest shelf-life. If you make your own butter, it will stay fresh for only one week. *To make butter:* Place double cream in a food processor and process until it begins to thicken. For every 8 fluid ounces of cream, add 2 tablespoons cold water. Process until the cream separates into solids. Strain out the liquid (this unsoured buttermilk is delicious to drink) and dry the resulting butter thoroughly with paper towels. 8 fluid ounces of cream yields about 85 grams/3 ounces butter.

Commercial butter contains about 81 per cent fat, 15.5 per cent water, and 6 per cent protein. Lower grades will contain more water. Two ways to determine the water content are if the refrigerated butter remains fairly soft and if, when the butter is cut, small droplets of water appear. Excess water can be removed by kneading the butter in ice water for several minutes and then drying it thoroughly with paper towels.

Store butter airtight as it absorbs odours very readily. Avoid wrapping directly in foil as the butter may absorb a metallic odour. Butter freezes well for several months. Be sure to let it defrost completely before clarifying it or it may burn instead of brown.

CLARIFIED BUTTER:

Several recipes in this book call for clarified *beurre noisette*. This refers to clarified butter which has browned to the colour of *noisettes* (French for 'hazelnuts'). *Beurre noisette* offers a richer, more delicious flavour.

When butter is clarified, the

water evaporates and the milk solids drop to the bottom. The milk solids cannot begin to brown until all the water has evaporated. When adding clarified butter to chocolate, it is important that no water remains, so milk solids in the butter should have started to turn golden brown before the liquid butter is strained.

To clarify butter: Melt butter in a heavy saucepan over medium heat, partially covered to prevent spattering. Do not stir. When the butter looks clear, cook, uncovered, watching carefully until the solids drop and begin to brown. When the bubbling noise quiets, all the water has evaporated and the butter can burn easily. To make *beurre noisette*, allow the solids to turn dark brown. Strain immediately through a fine strainer or cheesecloth-lined strainer. Clarified butter will keep for months refrigerated or just about indefinitely frozen, as it is the milk solids that cause the butter to become rancid quickly. I always make extra to have on hand. (The browned solids are excellent for adding flavour to bread dough.) Clarified butter will be only 75 per cent the volume of whole butter. For example, if you need 3 tablespoons clarified butter, start with 4 tablespoons butter.

MILK:

Milk (full-cream) contains 87.8 per cent water, 3.2 per cent protein and 3.8 per cent fat.

Nature's most perfect milk, in my opinion, is goat's milk. Goat's milk is lower in cholesterol with more finely emulsified butterfat, and the flavour is slightly sweeter and seems purer than cow's milk. If you are lucky enough to have access to goat's milk, feel free to use it in any recipe calling for milk.

CULTURED BUTTERMILK:

Buttermilk contains 90.5 per cent water, 3.6 protein, and 0.1 per cent butterfat. It is a soured product, obtained by treating skimmed or semi-skimmed milk with a culture of lactic acid bacteria.

HALF-CREAM:

Half-cream is half single cream and half milk. It contains 80.5 per cent water, 2.9 per cent protein, and 12 per cent fat. If you ever run out of milk and have half-cream, it's easy to substitute for milk required in a recipe (page 511).

SINGLE CREAM:

Single cream contains 74 per cent water, 2.6 per cent protein and 18 per cent fat.

DOUBLE CREAM:

Double cream contains 47.4 per cent water, 1.7 per cent protein and about 46 to 48 per cent fat.

Double cream can be frozen for several months, defrosted and used for making either ganache or butter cake. Freezing, however, alters the fat structure, making cream impossible to whip and unsuitable for making emulsifications such as *crème anglaise* or ice cream. (The texture will not be smooth.)

SOUR CREAM:

Sour cream contains 74 per cent water, 2.6 per cent protein, and 18 per cent fat. It is made from single cream, soured by the addition of lactic acid culture.

EGGS:

All my recipes use size 2 eggs. Values for recipes in this book are given for weight and volume so it's fine to use any size egg if you weigh or measure them. A Sainsbury's size 2 egg weighs 57 grams/2 ounces.

Egg white contains: 87.6 per cent water and 10.9 per cent protein
Egg yolk contains: 51.1 per cent water, 16 per cent protein and 30.6 per cent fat

Egg whites freeze perfectly for at least one year. It is also possible to freeze yolks. Stir in ½ teaspoon sugar per yolk to keep them from becoming sticky after they are defrosted. (Remember to subtract this amount of sugar from the recipe.)

DRAGÉES:

These little balls of silver or gold consist mainly of sugar. They are considered non-toxic and acceptable for decorative use. Of course, they are not intended to be consumed by the handful. Dragées are available from cake-decorating suppliers and some supermarkets. When asking for them, it is safer to refer to them as silver or gold balls as no two people pronounce this item the same way!

ESSENCES:

Exquisite steam-distilled French fruit essences such as wild strawberry, passion fruit and apricot are available in tiny bottles from specialist suppliers and good delicatessens. A few drops go a long way. They are quite inexpensive.

Flour

The protein content of flour is often listed on the bag and refers to the number of grams of protein per 100 grams/3½ ounces flour.

SOFTASILK CAKE FLOUR:

6 grams of protein per 100 grams/ 3½ ounces flour. Caterers have told me that when they get 100-pound sacks of cake flour of a different brand than these, they do not get as fine a texture in their cakes.

Cake flour is not generally available in the UK, but can be obtained from Maid of Scandinavia (page 513). Most of the recipes in this book have therefore been adapted, using a blend of self-raising and plain flour, to achieve the same results. (Cake flour and self-raising flour are bleached whereas plain flour is not. Bleached flour is essential for butter cakes.)

SELF-RAISING SPONGE FLOUR:

Contains about 8 to 9 grams of protein per 100 grams/3½ ounces flour, and 1½ teaspoons baking powder and ½ teaspoon salt per 100 grams/3½ ounces flour. It is fine to use this flour for recipes requiring the same proportion of baking powder if you eliminate the baking powder and salt from the recipe. The cakes preceding the Yellow Butter Cake, for example, use less baking powder, so self-raising flour will cause the cake to collapse.

PLAIN FLOUR:

About 9 grams of protein per 100 grams/3½ ounces flour. *Storage:* Flour should be stored away from the heat so that it doesn't dry out. I find that cake and plain flour can be stored for several years, but after 2 years, bread flour seems to lose some of its strength. Bread flour, which I purchase from a mill, becomes rancid after 8 months. Flour with the bran removed does not become rancid or attract bugs readily.

STRONG WHITE BREAD FLOUR:

Contains about 14 grams of protein per 100 grams/3½ ounces flour. *Storage:* Flour should be stored away from the heat so that it doesn't dry out. I find that cake and plain flour can be stored for several years, but after 2 years, bread flour seems to lose some of its strength. Bread flour, which I purchase from a mill, becomes rancid after 8 months. Flour with the bran removed does not become rancid or attract bugs readily.

FLOWERS:

Fresh flowers make beautiful and even flavourful additions to cakes but great care must be taken to ensure that they are not a poisonous variety. Some edible flowers are apple blossoms, borage flowers, cymbidium orchids, citrus blossoms (orange and lemon), day lilies (not tiger lilies, which have spots), English daisies, hibiscus, hollyhocks, honeysuckle, lilacs, pansies, petunias, nasturtiums, roses, tulips and violets. Inedible flowers such as lilies of the valley are fine to use as part of an arrangement or corsage for the top of the cake which will be lifted off before serving.

FONDANT:

Rolled fondant is available from cake-decorating suppliers and good confectioners.

FOOD COLOUR:

Liquid food colour, available in supermarkets, is fine when just a little colour is needed. For stronger colours, paste food colours are preferable because they do not alter the consistency of the icing as much. Powdered food colour is even more intense than paste but can be very messy. Both paste and powder are suitable for adding to chocolate. Liquid food colour will cause the chocolate to seize and become unworkable.

Colours are available in a great variety; there is even one that makes an offwhite icing whiter. In general, food colour intensifies as it sits so it is best to mix colours with ingredients a few hours before using them.

Use glycerine, not water, to thin

paste colour or it will become brittle. Another caveat: icings containing lemon juice will turn an off-colour if blue food colouring is added.

Paste and powder food colour are available from cake-decorating and confectionery suppliers. Cake-decorating suppliers can also supply food-colouring pens.

GELATIN:

Leaf gelatin (transparent sheets) should be soaked for 30 minutes in cold water until it becomes soft like clingfilm. Water is then squeezed out and gelatin soaked in hot liquid until dissolved. Some people prefer leaf gelatin to powdered because it imparts less flavour. I do not find the difference significant. Sheets of leaf gelatine measuring 7.3 centimetres by 21.5 centimetres ($2^7/8$ inches by $8^1/2$ inches) will set 570 millilitres (1 pint).

Powdered gelatin comes in sachets of approximately 11 grams/0.4 ounce and each will set 570 millilitres/1 pint. It should be softened in cool water for at least 5 minutes before being heated to dissolve it. According to the Lipton Research Department, 'While it is true that extensive boiling will denature unflavoured gelatin . . . normal use in recipes, including boiling, will not adversely affect the product.'

Gelatin will continue to thicken a mixture over a 24-hour period.

Once it has reached its maximum thickness, it will not thicken any further (even on freezing – another myth dispelled). Freezing also does not affect thickening power. The gelatin mixture can be frozen, thawed, remelted and refrozen several times before losing its strength.

GLYCERINE:

Glycerine is a clear, heavy liquid made from fats and oils. It is used in rolled fondant to add sheen and keep the texture soft. It is ideal to thicken chocolate to the consistency for decorative piped work. It also works to thin paste food colours. Glycerine is available from chemists, supermarkets or confectionery suppliers.

GOLD AND SILVER:

22-carat gold leaf and silver leaf are available in artists' supply stores. Gold and silver powders are available from cake–decorating suppliers.

GREEN TEA (POWDERED):

Japanese powdered green tea, which I use to flavour whipped cream, *biscuit* and marzipan, **is** available from oriental food shops.

LEKVAR:

Apricot lekvar is apricot jam which contains the skin of the apricot as well as the fruit. The flavour is more intense and delicious than ordinary apricot jam. Available from some delicatessens and Maid of Scandinavia (page 513).

NUTS:

Freshly shelled nuts have the best flavour but the shelled bottled or tinned varieties are excellent and often more convenient.

The skin on hazelnuts is very bitter and difficult to remove. An easy method taught to me by Carl Sontheimer (father of the food processor), uses bicarbonate of soda. For 71 grams/2½ ounces/ ½ cup of nuts, have 12 fluid ounces boiling water in a large saucepan and add 2 tablespoons bicarbonate of soda. Boil the nuts for 3 minutes. The water will turn black from the colour in the skins. Test a nut by running it under cold water. The skin should slip off easily. If not, boil for a few minutes longer. Rinse nuts well under cold running water and crisp or brown them in a 350°F/180°C/gas mark 4 oven for 20 minutes, watching carefully so that they don't burn.

Pistachio nuts will lose flavour if boiled. Their skin is not bitter but if added to mixtures will spoil the lovely, pale green colour. To remove this skin, toast the nuts for 10 minutes in a 350°F/180°C/gas mark 4 oven and use your fingers or fingernails to remove the skin. Salted pistachio nuts should not be used for dessert recipes.

Lightly toasting all nuts greatly enhances their flavour.

Nuts keep well for one year if stored airtight in the freezer. I use either freezer bags, expelling all the excess air, or glass preserving jars, filling the empty head space with wadded-up clingfilm.

Nuts should always be at room temperature before grinding to prevent them from exuding too much oil. When grating or grinding nuts such as almonds, starting with sliced nuts results in more even and drier ground nuts. For every 107 grams/3¾ ounces/ 1 cup of ground almonds needed, start with 106 grams/3 /4 ounces/ 1¼ cups sliced almonds.

If only whole nuts are available, start using the grating disc of the food processor. Then switch to the metal blade and pulse until the nuts are finely chopped. A tablespoon or so of cornflour, flour or icing sugar – borrowed from the rest of the recipe – will help absorb oil and prevent the ground nuts from clumping.

A small food processor seems to work best for evenly grinding nuts. A good hand-grater also does a fine job.

NUT PASTES:

Nut paste terminology is among the most confusing in the baking industry. Pure almond paste, for example, may mean that it contains no other nut substance and not that it doesn't contain any sugar! (In the industry, peach kernels are sometimes substituted for almonds to make a less expensive 'almond' paste.) Some almond pastes may contain as much as 50 per cent sugar.

Almond paste usually consists of 25 to 35 per cent sugar (some of which is invert) and sweet and bitter almonds. (The bitter almonds are much more intense in flavour than the sweet.) Almond paste is used to make marzipan by adding additional sugar.

The recipes in this book calling for almond paste require the domestic, or 25 to 35 per cent sugar, variety.

Pure 100 per cent pistachio paste with no sugar added is an excellent product made from the most flavourful pistachio nuts. The skins have not been removed, however, so a small amount of food colour will be necessary to restore the characteristic green colour.

Pure 100 per cent hazelnut paste with no sugar added is available. This is a fabulous addition to white chocolate when adding extra sugar is undesirable, as with Crème Ivoire Praliné (page 289). It is impossible to make a hazelnut paste of this smoothness without highly specialised equipment.

Praline paste consists of hazelnuts or a combination of almonds, hazelnuts and 50 per cent sugar. (Lesser qualities have a higher percentage of sugar.) I prefer the 100 per cent hazelnut and caramelised sugar variety. It is expensive but a small amount goes a long way and it is worth every penny. I have experimented endlessly only to find that homemade praline paste always has a slightly gritty consistency.

Praline paste keeps for a year refrigerated and indefinitely frozen. On storage, some of the oil separates and floats to the top. This can be stirred back into the praline paste or poured off to use in Guilt-Free Chocolate Chiffon Cake (page 178) or Crème Ivoire Deluxe and Crème Ivoire (pages 285 and 287) in place of some of the neutral oil called for in the recipe.

OIL:

Mineral oil, available from chemists and winemaking supply stores, is excellent for adding to chocolate because it never becomes rancid. Safflower or other flavourless oils are fine but become rancid quickly and cannot be stored without refrigeration for more than a few weeks. When using walnut oil, smell it first to ensure that it has not become rancid. Walnut oil is available in most supermarkets and delicatessens. When using oil to make cakes, it is important that it contains no silicates because they act to prevent the foaming necessary for aerating the cake. Most oils are made without the addition of silicates; a glance at the label will tell you if it has been added.

PAM:

I prefer Pam to other non-stick vegetable spray products because it has virtually no odour. It is composed of lecithin, a natural emulsifying agent derived from soya beans, and a tiny amount of soya-bean oil. Non-stick spray is particularly useful when working with rolled fondant. It prevents the fondant from sticking without having to add cornflour or icing sugar which could mar its surface. It is available from some supermarkets or through Maid of Scandinavia (page 513).

PIPING GEL:

Clear piping gel consists mainly of corn syrup, agar agar, and tartaric acid (cream of tartar). It is available from cake-decorating suppliers. I find it useful for attaching chocolate bands to a cake when I don't want to use a flavoured jelly. Piping gel can also be lightly tinted with food colour or mixed with cocoa, icing sugar and water to make a brilliantly glossy chocolate decorating medium (page 449).

Sugar

HOW SUGAR IS MADE:

Sucrose, the primary sugar used in cake-making, is a sugar obtained from sugar beets or sugar cane. There is absolutely no difference between these two sources in the final product if the sugar is refined to 99.9 per cent sucrose. A molecule of sucrose is composed of one fructose and one glucose molecule joined together to form a simple carbohydrate, easy to digest and full of energy. Other plants are capable of making sugar, but both cane and beet make it in quantities large enough to support refining. Sugar containing juice is extracted from the plant and the resulting syrup is boiled in large steam evaporators. The substance that remains is crystallised several times in heated vacuum pans and the remaining liquid, now called molasses, is separated from the crystals by spinning it in a centrifuge. At this stage the sugar is known as raw sugar and contains approximately 3 per cent impurities or extraneous matter.

Refined white sugar is processed from affined sugar. The affined sugar is dissolved again, clarified with lime or phosphoric acid, and then percolated through a column of ion exchange resins and/or activated carbons. This last process removes colour compounds from the sugar and removes most calcium and magnesium salts. Finally, the sugar is pumped back into vacuum pans where it is heated, seeded and crystallised. The resulting sugar is 99.9 per cent sucrose. Sugar that is less refined may be somewhat grey in colour and the protein impurities may cause foaming when the sugar is added to the liquid in a given recipe.

BROWN AND DEMERARA SUGAR:

Demerara and Muscovado sugars are varieties of raw cane sugar with a varying proportion of molasses in or around the sugar crystals. Generally speaking, the darker the colour the more molasses is present. Since these products have not been through the full refining process, they may contain some undesirable impurities such as cane trash, waxes, gums, soil, etc. These sugars have fully refined equivalents, such as light and dark soft sugars or mingled demeraras. These are prepared by mingling refined white sugar with clarified cane molasses or specially blended intermediate syrups from the cane refining process. Apart from the absence of insoluble matter, these sugars are analytically comparable and have similar flavour and cooking properties.

When a recipe calls for brown sugar, it is light brown sugar unless otherwise specified.

Equal volumes of either type of brown sugar compared to white sugar have essentially the same sweetening power, but brown sugar must be measured by weight since it is more dense than white sugar. Molasses also adds moisture to the sugar. Brown sugar contains up to about 3 per cent water while plain white sucrose only contains less than 0.5 per cent.

If you run out of brown sugar and have white sugar and molasses or black treacle on hand, it's easy to make your own (see substitutions, page 510), but make sure the white is of the correct crystal size. Soft sugars require castor.

MOLASSES AND BLACK TREACLE:

Molasses contains about 24 per cent water. Retail molasses refers only to cane molasses; beet molasses is unpalatable and not available for retail. Molasses has a very strong flavour and is variable depending on origin. More commonly available is black treacle, a blend of cane molasses and intermediate syrups from the refining process, blended to give a consistent flavour.

GOLDEN SYRUP:

Containing 17 to 22 per cent water, this is a delicious by-product of cane sugar refining. When some sugar has been extracted, intermediate syrups from the cane refining process are blended, partially inverted to increase solubility and evaporated. Lyle's Golden Syrup, the best-known brand, is generally available in supermarkets.

GLUCOSE SYRUP AND CORN SYRUP:

Containing 15 to 20 per cent water, glucose is a reducing sugar. Many plants, such as corn (maize) and potato, have high levels of starch. The separated starch is treated with acid and/or enzymes to produce a mixture of glucose and simple reducing sugars. This is evaporated to produce glucose syrup, sometimes known as 'corn syrup'. Fully hydrolised starch gives dextrose. It is manufactured in syrup form in varying concentrations. Glucose with suitable concentration for baking is thicker than corn syrup. It is subject to fermentation and will develop small bubbles and a sour taste, so once the container is opened it should be refrigerated. If kept airtight and not contaminated by a wet spoon, for example, it will last indefinitely.

GRANULATIONS AND FORMS OF SUGAR:

All fully refined sucrose (white sugar) has equal sweetening power despite the crystal size. Icing sugars may have up to 1.5 per cent anti-caking agents to prevent lumping, but aside from this small percentage 1 pound of sugar equals 1 pound of sugar. (This may seem obvious, but I have read strange things to the contrary.)

Granulated or castor: Granulated sugar is the all-purpose sugar found in most sugar bowls and available in all supermarkets. This size is suitable for making syrups, but for much other baking a finer crystal size is preferable – e.g. castor. Using a food processor it is possible to make a more finely granulated sugar, but the crystals will not be as uniform in size as in commercially produced finer grain sugars.

Cube sugar: This is merely granulated sugar that has been pressed into moulds when moist and then allowed to dry so it maintains the shape. Some recipes, particularly in the confectionery area, specify cube sugar because at one time it was considered more refined. Brown Demerara cubes are also available.

Preserving sugar: Coarser than granulated sugar and used in the preservation of fruits and often in jam-making.

Pearl sugar: The name given to irregular crystal aggregates. The large granules are sometimes used to sprinkle on biscuits and pastries.

Icing sugar: While it is possible to achieve a very fine granulation in a food processor, it is not possible to make true icing sugar. This can only be done commercially. At one time, icing sugar was stone-ground, but now it is ground in a pen and disc rotary, turbo or hammer mill, which turns against varying degrees of fine screens, each one determining a different fineness of the grind. The coarser the granulation of the initial sugar, the more even will be the final grind. As might be expected, the finer the granulation, the greater the tendency of the sugar to cake, which explains why up to 1.5 per cent anti-caking agents are added. These add what is perceived as a raw taste and make icing sugar less suitable than granulated sugar for use with ingredients that are not to be cooked. Icing sugar is also sold without any anti-caking agent for some industrial and pharmaceutical uses.

In general it is advisable to sift icing sugar to remove any partially milled crystals. Great care should be taken that all utensils and work surfaces are sparkling clean.

SUGAR SYRUPS:

When making a sugar syrup for Italian meringue or Classic

Buttercream, for example, the sugar is concentrated to produce a supersaturated solution from a saturated one. A saturated sugar solution contains the maximum amount of sugar possible at room temperature without precipitating out into crystals. A supersaturated sugar solution contains more sugar than the water can dissolve at room temperature. Heating the solution enables the sugar to dissolve. Cold water is capable of holding double its weight in sugar, but by heating it more sugar can dissolve in the same amount of water. A sugar solution begins with sugar, partially dissolved in at least one-third its weight of cold water. It is stirred continuously until boiling, at which time all the sugar is dissolved. If sugar crystals remain on the sides of the pan they should be washed down with a wet pastry brush. The solution is now considered supersaturated and, to avoid crystallisation, must no longer be stirred.

As the water evaporates, the temperature of the solution rises and the density increases. Concentration of the syrup is dependent upon the amount of water left after evaporation. The temperature of the syrup indicates the concentration. As long as there is a lot of water in the syrup, the temperature does not rise much above the boiling point of water. But when most of the water has boiled away, the temperature can now rise dramatically, passing through various stages (page 502) and eventually rising to the temperature of melted sugar (320°F/160°C) when all the water is gone.

Concentration can also be measured by density using a saccharometer or Baumé sugar weight-scale. A Baumé scale is graduated from 0 to 44° and corresponds in a direct relationship to the degrees Fahrenheit or Centigrade. The degree of evaporation can also be measured by consistency by dropping a small amount of the syrup into ice water.

Supersaturated solutions are highly unstable and recrystallisation can occur from agitation or even just by standing unless the solution was properly heated in the first place. The use of a crystallisation inhibitor such as invert sugar (a little more than one-quarter the weight of the granulated sugar), butter, cream of tartar or citric acid causes inversion and so increases the total sugar's solubility. This is useful when the solution will be used in a way that will involve repeatedly dipping into it, such as for making spun sugar.

As melted sugar reaches higher temperatures, many chemical changes begin to occur. The sugar cannot start to caramelise until nearly all the water is evaporated. As it starts to caramelise, its sweetening power decreases. At this point, stirring will not cause the sugar to crystallise. The addition of a significant amount of an ingredient, such as nuts, can lower the temperature considerably and this will cause crystallisation to occur instantly if no crystallisation inhibitor was used.

Caramel is extremely difficult to make in humid weather because sugar is highly hygroscopic (attracts water). The moisture in the air will make the caramel sticky. (Note: Caramel in this sense should not be confused with caramel colour, which requires the addition of a catalyst to increase colour.)

When sugar syrup has been prepared in advance, it is sometimes necessary to check the exact quantity of sugar and water it contains. It is important to know that the Baumé reading in a cold solution measures slightly higher than the same solution when hot.

Another variant that affects density reading is altitude. Because water boils at a lower temperature as altitude increases (there is less air pressure weighing on top of the water to prevent it from changing from liquid into vapour), there will be a different temperature for the same concentration of sugar syrup at different altitudes. For each increase of 500 feet in elevation, syrup should be cooked to a temperature 1°F lower than the temperature called for at sea level.

If readings are taken in Celsius, for each 900 feet of elevation cook the syrup to a temperature 1°C lower than called for at sea level. These adjustments should be made up to 320°F/160°C, the melting point of sugar. Altitude does not change this.

TEMPERATURES AND TESTS FOR SUGAR SYRUP

215°F/102°C	**Thread:** The liquid sugar may be pulled into brittle threads between the fingers. This is used for candy, fruit-liqueur making and some icings.
220° to 222°F/ 104° to 106°C	**Pearl:** The thread formed by pulling the liquid sugar may be stretched. When a cool metal spoon is dipped into the syrup and then raised, the syrup runs off in drops which merge to form a sheet. This is used for the above and also for jelly.
230° to 234°F/ 110° to 112°C	**Blow or Soufflé:** The bubbles in the boiling sugar resemble snowflakes. The syrup spins a 5 centimetre 2-inch thread when dropped from a spoon. This is used for making sugar candy and syrup.
234° to 240°F/ 112° to 116°C	**Soft ball:** Syrup dropped into ice water may be formed into a ball which flattens on removal from the water. This is used for fondant, fudge, peppermint creams and Classic Buttercream.

244° to 248°F/ 118° to 120°C	**Firm ball:** Syrup dropped into ice water may be formed into a firm ball which does not flatten on removal from the water. This is used for caramels, nougats and soft toffees.
250° to 266°F/ 121° to 130°C	**Hard ball:** Syrup dropped into ice water may be formed into a hard ball which holds its shape on removal but is still plastic. This is used for toffee, marshmallows and popcorn balls.
270° to 290°F/ 132° to 143°C	**Soft crack:** Syrup dropped into ice water separates into threads which are hard but not brittle. This is used for butterscotch and toffee.
300° to 310°F/ 149° to 154°C	**Hard crack:** Syrup dropped into ice water separates into hard, brittle threads. This is used for brittle and for glacéed fruits.
320°F/160°C	**Clear liquid:** The sugar liquefies. This is used for making barley sugar.
338°F/170°C	Brown liquid: The liquefied sugar turns brown. This is used for light caramel.
356°F/180°C	**Medium brown liquid:** The liquefied sugar darkens. This is used for praline, spun sugar, caramel cages and nougatine.
374°F/190°C	**Dark brown liquid:** The liquefied sugar darkens further. This is used as a colouring agent for sauces.
410°F/210°C	**Black Jack:** The liquefied sugar turns black and then decomposes.

VANILLA:

When Marcel Akselrod sent me a sample vanilla pod, I knew when it had arrived because, when I went to pick up my post, the entire letterbox was perfumed with the heavenly smell of Tahitian vanilla. The pod was fatter and more moist than any I had ever seen. Vanilla pods vary enormously in quality. The best pods come from Tahiti, Madagascar and Mexico. The Tahitian pods are larger than the others and all three are about twice the size and more highly perfumed than other pods. This makes it difficult to give equivalents for distilled vanilla (extract), which also varies enormously in concentration (referred to commercially as 'folds'). The Tahitian pods are so aromatic, I use half a pod in a recipe specifying one pod.

Sometimes you will notice a white substance coating vanilla pods. This is not mould; it is flavourful vanilla crystals.

Vanilla accentuates other flavours. The pod adds a subtle depth of flavour and unique sweet quality. The extract, though easier to use, lacks that sweet roundness and in excess will even impart a bitter edge.

My favourite vanilla extract is produced by Méro and comes from Grasse, the perfume region of France. I like to transfer it to a plastic squeeze-bottle dispenser with a pointed tip and add a Tahitian vanilla pod. (This is a great use for used vanilla pods, which still have lots of flavour even after the seeds have been removed. Be sure to rinse the pod if it has been used to flavour another liquid and dry it in a low oven or with the heat of the oven's pilot light.)

The recipes in this book which call for pure vanilla extract refer to the supermarket variety for purposes of standardisation. When I use Méro vanilla extract, I use a little less than half the amount specified in these recipes.

YEAST:

I prefer using fresh yeast to dried, just on general principle. I like its lively reaction and forthright, earthy smell. But if the yeast isn't absolutely fresh, the final baked product will have a slightly sour taste. The best way to determine freshness is by smell, as the colour may not have changed even when slightly past its prime. Fresh yeast freezes indefinitely, but certain precautions must be taken in defrosting. Yeast is a live organism and must be 'awakened' gradually from the frozen state. To defrost, place in the refrigerator for a minimum of 48 hours. Since a few yeast cells will have been destroyed in the process, use 25 per cent more than specified in the recipe.

It's fine to use dried yeast (see substitutions, page 511), but the quick-acting or easy-blend yeasts need a different procedure. For one thing, they cannot be proved. In the 10 minutes of proving time, they will have thoroughly exhausted all their energy and raising power.

ZEST:

Zest refers to the coloured portion of the citrus peel. The white portion, or pith, should be avoided as it is quite bitter. The fruit is easier to zest before squeezing.

A zester is the ideal piece of equipment to remove only the outer peel (see page 525). The fine strips should then be chopped with a knife or food processor. I like to add some of the sugar from the recipe and process it with the zest. This keeps the zest from clumping and disperses it more evenly when added to the larger mixture. A vegetable peeler will also work to remove wider strips which can then be cut or chopped fine.

Weights

The weight of all ingredients for recipes in this book is given in both the metric and avoirdupois systems. The grams have been rounded off to the nearest whole number without decimal points (except for raising agents which need to be more precise), the ounces to the nearest quarter ounce. Either system works, but do not expect the mathematics to correlate exactly.

There is no doubt about it; weighing is faster, easier and more accurate than measuring. Most bakers, including myself, prefer the metric system for its precision in small quantities. There isn't any adjustment necessary if you have a metric scale and the recipe gives metric amounts! If you do not have a scale with a digital read-out, round off the grams to the nearest convenient number. The amount will still be quite accurate as, after all, one gram is only about one twenty-eighth of an ounce.

The way I have presented the volume measures is the way in which I would measure them. Instead of writing 6 tablespoons sugar, I express it as ¼ cup + 2 tablespoons because that is the more convenient approach. Also, the fewer measures used, the less room for error.

I am offering a chart of weights for your convenience in converting other recipes. The weights were determined by innumerable trials over a three-year period at seven storeys above sea level with a Mettler scale (which is used in scientific laboratories). I spent my entire first salary cheque as a chocolate consultant on this scale, with no regrets. People ask me the point in having such accurate equipment when most people will not. My feeling is that if I am to set the standard, I want it to be as close to the absolute as possible. That way, when others deviate, it will still work because there is always a range of acceptable error.

For those who measure instead of weigh, the *dip and sweep* method of measuring refers to dipping the measuring cup into a bin containing the ingredient and sweeping off the excess with a long, flat spatula or knife.

Lightly spooned into cup refers to spooning the ingredient into the cup and then sweeping off the excess with a long, flat spatula or blade. This method yields less of the ingredient than the dip and sweep method.

Sifted means that the ingredient is sifted into a cup that is sitting on a worktop. The cup is never touched or (perish the thought) shaken. Only the handle is held when the excess is swept off with a spatula or knife.

Dry ingredients should be measured in a cup designed for solids.

Liquid ingredients, including honey and other syrups, should be measured in a liquid measure with a spout. There is a difference in volume between liquid and solid measuring cups. 1 cup of water should weigh exactly 236.35 grams/8.337 ounces, which is the dictionary definition of 8 fluid ounces of water.

FOOD SUBSTANCE	METHOD OF MEASURE	WEIGHT OF 1 CUP	
		grams	*ounces*
FATS			
butter		227	8
clarified butter (*beurre noisette*)		195	6.8
cocoa butter		256	9
vegetable fat		191	6.75
mineral oil		196	6.86
safflower oil		215	7.5
walnut oil		215	7.5
FLOURS			
self-raising sponge	sifted	89	3.5
	lightly spooned	108	4
	dip and sweep	138	4.5
plain	sifted	125	4
	lightly spooned	127	4.25
	dip and sweep	164	5
strong white	sifted	113	4
	lightly spooned	120	4.25
	dip and sweep	141	5
buckwheat	lightly spooned	115	4
	dip and sweep	125	4.5
wholewheat	sifted	125	4.5

FOOD SUBSTANCE	METHOD OF MEASURE	WEIGHT OF 1 CUP	
		grams	ounces
chestnut	sifted	109	3.8
cornflour	lightly spooned or sifted	120	4.2
Dutch-processed cocoa	sifted	75	2.6
	lightly spooned	92	3.25
	dip and sweep	95	3.33
nonalkalised cocoa such as Cadbury's: same as Dutch-processed except for	lightly spooned	82	2.9

LIQUIDS

double cream		232	8.12
milk, buttermilk, sour cream, single cream		242	8.5
black treacle		322	11.25
corn syrup		328	11.5
glucose		336	11.75
honey		336	11.75
golden syrup		340	12
apple jelly		308	10.75
water		236	8.337
lemon juice, strained		250	8.75
orange juice, strained		242	8.5
amaretto		250	8.75
apricot eau-de-vie		222	7.7
black raspberry liqueur		260	9.1

FOOD SUBSTANCE	METHOD OF MEASURE	WEIGHT OF 1 CUP	
		grams	*ounces*
cherry wine		255	8.9
Cognac		225	7.9
Cointreau		244	8.5
Kahlúa (coffee liqueur)		267	9.6
kirsch (cherry eau-de-vie)		224	7.8
light rum		224	7.8
Mandarine Napoléon		243	8.5
Myers's Rum (dark rum)		220	7.7
Pistasha (pistachio liqueur)		200	7
Vodka		230	8
Poire William *or* pear eau-de-vie		222	7.7
NUTS			
almonds	slivered	120	4.2
	sliced or coarsely chopped	85	3
	finely ground	107	3.75
	powder fine	89	3.12
walnuts, pecans and hazelnuts	coarsely chopped	114	4
	whole	142	5
pistachios	whole	152	5.32
almond paste		284	10
hazelnut praline paste		308	10.88

FOOD SUBSTANCE	METHOD OF MEASURE	WEIGHT OF 1 CUP	
		grams	*ounces*
CHESTNUT			
purée de marrons (unsweetened)		252	8.8
homemade purée de marrons (unsweetened)		244	8.5
SUGAR			
granulated and castor	dip and sweep	200	7
icing	lightly spooned	115	4
light brown	packed	217	7.66
dark brown	packed	239	8.4
EGGS			
1 egg, size 2	in shell	57	2
1 egg, size 2	without shell (3 tablespoons + ½ teaspoon)	50	1.75
1 egg white, size 2	2 tablespoons	30	1.05
1 egg yolk, size 2	3½ teaspoons	18.6	0.65
OTHER			
baking powder	1 teaspoon	4.9	–
bicarbonate of soda	1 teaspoon	5	–
cream of tartar	1 teaspoon	3.1	–
gelatin	1 teaspoon	3.1	–
glycerine	1 teaspoon	6	–
poppy seeds	¼ cup	36	1.25

FOOD SUBSTANCE	METHOD OF MEASURE	WEIGHT OF 1 CUP	
		grams	*ounces*
salt	1 teaspoon	6.7	–
vanilla *or* almond extract	1 teaspoon	4	–
grated citrus zest	1 teaspoon	2	–

Approximate Equivalents and Substitutions

Making one thing into another is never 100 per cent, but in a tight spot it's nice to know how to come close to the original.

Most substitution charts tell you how to sour milk with vinegar to replace buttermilk. While the acidity level seems the same, the sour flavour is nowhere near the rich, full tanginess of buttermilk. Of course, substituting an item such as granulated sugar and black treacle for brown sugar is another story, because adding treacle (molasses) to granulated sugar is the way brown sugar is made in the industry as well.

FOR	SUBSTITUTE
glucose	Bring 1 cup light corn syrup to a full boil and remove from the heat. Cool completely and stir in 164 grams/5¾ ounces/½ cup unheated corn syrup.
454 grams/1 pound unsalted butter	454 grams/1 pound lightly salted butter but remove 1 teaspoon salt from the recipe
242 grams/8½ ounces/ 1 cup milk	242 grams/8½ ounces/1 cup minus 1 tablespoon half cream, remove 1 tablespoon butter from the recipe, and add 2 tablespoons water
217 grams/7.66 ounces/ 1 cup light brown sugar	200 grams/7 ounces/1 cup granulated sugar plus 80 grams/3 ounces/¼ cup unsulphured light molasses
239 grams/8.4 ounces/1 cup dark brown sugar	200 grams/7 ounces/1 cup granulated sugar plus 160 grams/6 ounces/½ cup unsulphured light molasses
0.25-ounce packet (2¼ teaspoons) active dried yeast	1 packed tablespoon (0.75 ounce) compressed fresh yeast
1 packed tablespoon (0.75 ounce) compressed fresh yeast	1 packed tablespoon plus 1 packed teaspoon (1 ounce) thawed frozen compressed fresh yeast

Note: The yeast equivalency is approximate and works well. If you have a scale accurate for small amounts, you may want the more precise conversion:

1 packet active dried yeast = 2¼ teaspoons = ¼ ounce = 7 grams
1 packet compressed fresh yeast = 0.6 ounce = 17 grams
If recipe calls for dried yeast, × 2.42 is amount of fresh needed.
If recipe calls for fresh yeast, × 0.41 is amount of dried yeast needed.
Using volume, you need 1.4 times the volume of packed fresh yeast to replace dried.

CHOCOLATE
Exchanging one type of semisweet or bittersweet chocolate for another will work but will often give surprisingly different flavour results. Even if the percentages of cocoa solids, cocoa butter and sugar are the same, the type of bean and degree of roasting is responsible for significant variations. It may also result in different texture. The best way to determine which bittersweet or

semisweet chocolate to use is to taste it.

Chocolatiers are given the exact contents of the chocolate they use by the manufacturers. For the consumer to get this information is next to impossible. For me, it took two trips to Switzerland. I am greatly indebted to Dr Buser and Markus Gerber of Tobler and Rüdi Sprüngli of Lindt for entrusting me with this valuable information. (I flew home from Switzerland feeling as though I had the crown jewels tucked into my notebook.)

The main factor to consider in exchanging bittersweet or semisweet chocolate is the sugar content, so the following is a list of approximate sugar content for 28 grams/1 ounce chocolate.

Lindt Courante: 2 teaspoons sugar
Tobler extra bittersweet: 2¾ teaspoons sugar
Tobler Tradition, Lindt Excellence: 3¼ teaspoons sugar
Tobler Bittersweet and most American semisweet chocolate: 3½ teaspoons sugar

I find the quality of many bitter (unsweetened) chocolates lacking, so I always substitute a fine-quality bittersweet or semisweet. If you have a favourite chocolate recipe calling for bitter (unsweetened) chocolate and wish to improve the flavour: for every 28 grams/ 1 ounce of bitter chocolate called for, substitute 56 grams/2 ounces bittersweet or semisweet. For every 56 grams/2 ounces of bittersweet or semisweet used, remove 2 tablespoons sugar and ⅔ teaspoon butter from the recipe.

Cocoa offers a richer, stronger chocolate flavour to cakes than does chocolate. Fewer cocoa solids than contained in the chocolate are necessary to achieve the same flavour intensity (see Understanding Cakes, page 541), but it is necessary to dissolve the cocoa in liquid to unlock the full flavour.

To convert a cake recipe using bittersweet or semisweet chocolate to a more chocolaty cocoa cake: For every 28 grams/1 ounce of bittersweet or semisweet chocolate, substitute 1 tablespoon plus 1¾ teaspoons (9.5 grams/0.33 ounce) cocoa, 1 tablespoon plus ½ teaspoon sugar (14.5 grams/½ ounce), 1½ teaspoons unsalted butter (7 grams/ ¼ ounce). For full flavour, be sure to dissolve the cocoa in at least ¼ cup liquid in the recipe.

To convert a cake recipe using unsweetened chocolate to a more chocolaty cake: For every 28 grams/ 1 ounce of bitter or unsweetened chocolate, substitute 3 tablespoons cocoa plus 1 tablespoon cocoa butter or unsalted butter. For full flavour, be sure to dissolve the cocoa in at least 2 tablespoons liquid in recipe.

Other useful chocolate information: To approximate 28 grams/1 ounce couverture when you need a chocolate that will coat thinly, use

28 grams/1 ounce fine-quality
bittersweet or semisweet chocolate
plus ½ teaspoon (5.4 grams/
0.19 ounce) cocoa butter.

Ingredients Suppliers

The following supply many of the
ingredients used in this book:

Harrods Ltd, Knightsbridge,
London SW1; tel. 071–730 1234.
Mail order available.

Maid of Scandinavia,
32–44 Raleigh Avenue, Minneapolis,
Minnesota 55416, USA;
tel. 010 612 925 9256. Mail order
available.

Neal's Yard Wholefood Warehouse,
21 Shorts Gardens, London WC2;
tel. 071--836 5151.

The Grocer's Supply Ltd,
Foodstore, 50 High Street,
Milford-on-Sea, SO41 9AG;
tel. 0590 644200

Equipment

Many people assume that fine cake baking requires not only a wealth of technical knowledge but also a labyrinth of specialised equipment. In reality, apart from basics such as mixing bowls, rubber scrapers or spatulas, and non-corrodible saucepans, the equipment for successful baking can be boiled down to ten items. Of course there are many delightful gadgets designed to make work more efficient, but the following items are indispensable:

OVEN
Accurate oven temperature is extremely important for cake baking. As ovens can lose their calibration, they should be checked every few months. Most oven thermometers are quite inaccurate, so I usually use the Cordon Rose sugar syrup thermometer, wiring it to the rack to hold it in position. The thermostat in most ovens fluctuates at least 10°F above and below ideal temperature. Another test for oven temperature is to make Yellow Butter Cake (page 28). If it takes longer than the recommended time, you know that your oven is too low at the setting used.

The ideal oven for cake baking is one which has little distance from top to bottom and a rotating turntable. Home models which come closest to this ideal are worktop convection/microwave models. The turntable is actually designed for the microwave option, but it happens to be ideal for even baking as well. I do not like commercial convection ovens because the fans are too powerful for fragile items. (I'll always remember the class with White House pastry chef Roland Messnier when his *langue de chat* butterflies actually flew off the baking parchment and crashed into the gusty fan of the convection oven!)

Worktop models with fans blowing directly down on the cake are equally undesirable.

If using a convection or convector-type oven, for recipes which specify 180°C, use 165°C.

Although manufacturers say to lower the temperature 25°F when using worktop convection ovens, I find that using the same temperature as a normal oven results in the same baking time.

ELECTRIC MIXER
An electric hand-held mixer can be used for any cake or buttercream but is not powerful enough to handle a very stiff mixture such as royal icing or fondant. It also does not do quite as good a job as a large heavy-duty mixer in aerating

génoise and other whisked sponge cakes. My favourite electric hand mixer, more powerful than most, is manufactured by Krups. With an optional attachment it doubles as an immersion blender (page 523).

People who do a lot of baking sooner or later end up with a heavy-duty stand mixer. The two best mixers of this sort are the KitchenAid K5 series and the Kenwood Major. They are both excellent mixers. The Kenwood has a larger capacity (6.25 litres/ 11.25 pints compared to 5 litres/ 8 pints) but works well with small amounts. It also has a stronger motor with a device which protects it from burning out if overheated. The conical shape of the bowl and the ability to adjust the beaters to come as close as possible to the bottom make for thorough and even mixing. The K5 beater cannot be adjusted, but the whisk beater will reach the bottom of the bowl if it is not fully engaged. Push it on its holder but do not lock it into position. Lower the beater to hold it in place. It will just reach the bottom of the bowl. (Thank you, Carole Walter.)

Heavy-duty mixers offer the choice of a flat 'spade' beater and a whisk beater. The flat beater is intended for general mixing and the whisk beater to beat as much air as possible into the mixture, such as when beating egg whites, or whisked sponge cakes.

I often find pouring shields more cumbersome than helpful. When adding flour or icing sugar, which tends to fly out of the bowl, I drape a large piece of clingfilm over the top of the mixer, including the top of the bowl. Any powdery substance which leaps up does not cling to the plastic as it would to a cloth tea-towel, and the plastic enables you to see what is happening to the mixture. The Kenwood, however, has an excellent, airtight pouring shield, which also works to keep royal icing from drying.

It is useful to have a second bowl and even a second whisk beater as many cake and buttercream recipes are made in two parts.

The K5 can handle up to 16 large egg whites (size 2), a 7-egg *génoise*, an 8-egg butter cake, or any mixture that will not exceed 3.75 litres/6.5 pints. The Kenwood can handle any mixture that will not exceed 5.75 litres/10 pints.

For larger-scale baking a 19 litre/ 5-gallon mixer is an ideal size, especially if you also have a 9.5-litre/16-pint bowl. These two bowls can handle any recipe in the master cake section of this book in one batch.

CAKE TINS
The cake tins used most in this book are 23 × 4 centimetres/ 9 × 1½ inches because they are the most readily available. Aluminium tins with a dull finish are ideal and straight sides are preferable as cakes

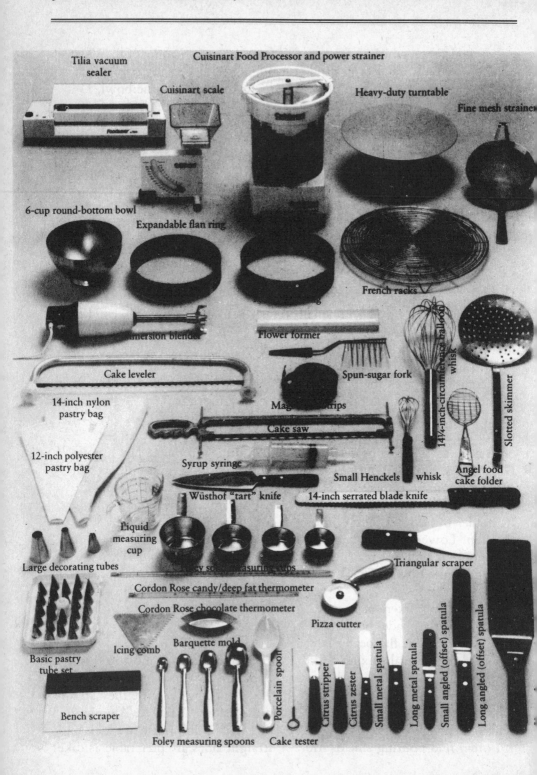

Tilia vacuum sealer

Cuisinart scale

Cuisinart Food Processor and power strainer

Heavy-duty turntable

Fine mesh strainer

6-cup round-bottom bowl

Expandable flan ring

French racks

Immersion blender

Flower former

14¼-inch-circumference balloon whisk

Slotted skimmer

Cake leveler

Spun-sugar fork

14-inch nylon pastry bag

Magnetic strips

Cake saw

12-inch polyester pastry bag

Syrup syringe

Small Henckels whisk

Angel food cake folder

Wüsthof "tart" knife

14-inch serrated blade knife

Liquid measuring cup

Large decorating tubes

Dry solid measuring cups

Triangular scraper

Cordon Rose candy/deep fat thermometer

Cordon Rose chocolate thermometer

Pizza cutter

Icing comb

Barquette mold

Basic pastry tube set

Porcelain spoon

Citrus stripper

Citrus zester

Small metal spatula

Long metal spatula

Small angled (offset) spatula

Long angled (offset) spatula

Bench scraper

Foley measuring spoons

Cake tester

inch by 12-inch sheet cake pan

Set of 2-inch-high cake pans

Magic Line 2-inch-high rectangular pans

Bundt-style muffin pans

pan

12-cup Bundt pan

Heating core

6-cup fluted tube pan

9-cup kugelhupf pan

pan

mold

Checkerboard pan set

4-cup loaf pan

9-inch heart pan

9¼-inch oval pan

9-inch by 2-inch
springform pan

3½-cup   pan

baked in straight-sided tins are easier to ice. Avoid shiny tins, black tins, or glass bakeware (see Baking and Storing Cakes, pages 4 to 7).

In addition, several other sizes and shapes of tin are required for the cakes in this book and these are specified in the recipes. Most of the tins are available from shops with a good range of bakeware; Maid of Scandinavia (page 531) carry all the tins required for these recipes, while Divertimenti (page 531) have all except the checkerboard cake tin.

Making your own tin: If you ever need a tin of a certain size and cannot order it in time, it is possible to make a tin from foil. I learned this technique when I worked at Reynolds Aluminum Company many years ago. An advantage to a foil tin is that the sides can be taken apart after baking, making it function as a springform.

To make a foil tin: Wrap a cardboard cake round with a layer of foil, securing it on the bottom with tape. Multiply the diameter by 4 (this will be the

circumference) and tear off a length of heavy-duty foil to correspond. Fold this foil in half lengthwise and in half again to make a band 11.5 centimetres/4½ inches wide. If the tin only needs to be 5 centimetres/2 inches high, fold in half

one more time. Cut short 1-centimetre/½-inch snips on a long side at 2.5-centimetre/1-inch intervals. Place the foil-covered circle on a can or other object to elevate it. Fold the foil band around it, attaching it by bending the snipped ends flat against the bottom of the circle. Attach with tape. Allow the band to overlap and secure with tape. Stand the tin upright and place it on a baking sheet for extra support.

RACKS

Any rack can be used to allow air circulation for quick cooling of a cake. The best racks I have found are from France. The wire is closer together, offering more support. To prevent cakes from sticking to the racks, I occasionally spray them with non-stick vegetable spray. I never use soap on the racks, just a spray of water or a wet brush when necessary to remove crumbs.

PALETTE KNIVES OR SPATULAS

A small metal spatula with a narrow 10-centimetre/4-inch blade and a wooden handle is the best implement for icing a cake. It is also helpful to have one with a longer blade for smoothing the top.

LIQUID MEASURES

When shopping for measuring jugs, look for ones with level markings. In addition to measuring liquids, these jugs are ideal for pouring hot sugar syrup into an egg mixture. They also help to maintain the temperature of the syrup which keeps it fluid enough to pour. The handles remain cool to the touch and the spouts control the way the liquid pours. If heated first with

boiling water, the jug will be even more effective in retaining heat.

SOLID (OR DRY) MEASURES

Solid measures must have unbroken, smooth rims, making it possible to level off any excess. Tupperware's cups are excellent.

MEASURING SPOONS

Tupperware heavy-duty plastic measuring spoons are among my favourites. I especially like them because they include unusual sizes such as $1/8$ teaspoon, 4 teaspoons and $1/2$ tablespoon. I have found other brands of measuring spoons to be somewhat smaller.

FINE STRAINER

This item can sieve fruit purées with seeds, clarify butter and sift flour. The stainless-steel extra-fine-mesh strainers from Italy are my favourite (available in gourmet kitchen shops).

LONG SERRATED KNIFE

This is the item I miss most when I teach in other places. It is difficult to take with me because planes do not allow passengers to board with knives in their hand luggage (and I never trust vital equipment to the luggage compartment). In order to level a cake or slice it horizontally, it is essential to have a serrated blade longer than the diameter of the cake – say about 35 centimetres/14 inches. The serrated blade also can be used to make wavy lines on an iced cake's surface (page 411).

NICE TO HAVE

SCALES:

Accurate scales make baking much faster and more reliable. My favourite non–electric scales weigh only up to 300 grams/10 ounces but are designed on the pendulum principle rather than spring and thus are accurate to plus or minus 2 grams. At home I use the Mettler PE 16 electronic scale, top-quality, very expensive laboratory scales from Switzerland, accurate to within 0.2 gram. They weigh up to 16,000 grams/35 pounds, which makes them convenient for large-scale baking such as wedding cakes.

VACUUM SEALER:

Vacuum sealing extends shelf–life, prevents freezer burn and is effective for keeping humidity out of ingredients like chocolate, flour and baking powder.

THERMOMETERS:

Thermometers are used in cooking when precise temperatures must be obtained, as when working with chocolate, sugar syrups and yeast. Even a few degrees of inaccuracy are enough to put chocolate out of temper so that it won't set correctly, produce Italian meringue that will never thicken or kill yeast so that brioche won't rise. For a thermometer to be reliable, it must be accurate to within 1 degree. I used to assume that a thermometer was an absolute measure of temperature. Then I discovered that the instrument, used to measure variables, could itself be a variable by as much as 20°F! And worse yet, it may vary in its inaccuracy at different degrees of its range. Driven by a personal need for reliable thermometers, I decided to have them manufactured to my own criteria.

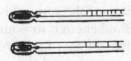

Once having made the commitment to produce highly accurate thermometers for the food industry, I approached a manufacturer specialising in laboratory thermometers, where precision is an imperative. The thermometers they produce are made to industrial specifications and are calibrated to standards traceable to the National Bureau of Standards in Washington, DC.

The Cordon Rose chocolate thermometer has a range of 40° to 130°F in widely spaced 1-degree increments. The Cordon Rose candy/deep fat thermometer has a range of 20° to 500°F in 2-degree increments. Both are available by mail order from Dean & DeLuca (page 531).

Two key points in producing an accurate thermometer: it must be glass with the calibration (scale) etched directly on it, and it must be mercury if it has a high range. Mercury exceeds the accuracy of any other material including that used for electronics. It is the only substance which will continuously repeat the identical reading of a given temperature.

Problems with other materials:
1. Thermometers with metal stems and dials are made using two different kinds of metal coils which expand and contract at different rates. When one metal expands more than the other, the dial turns. After continued use, the coils tend to wear, decreasing accuracy.
2. Thermometers with calibration or degree reading on a wooden or metal plaque attached to the glass thermometer and not directly on it may not be lined up to precisely the right point.
3. Digital thermometers are battery-operated. As the battery wears, accuracy decreases.

But no matter how accurate the thermometer, or any other instrument of measure, it is still prone to human error. It becomes necessary to understand how to use and care for a thermometer – a simple matter but one that must be learned.

How to read a thermometer: Since many people hold a thermometer with the left hand while stirring with the right, I designed the Cordon Rose thermometers with two opposing scales so that they can be read left- or right-handed.

A thermometer should be read at eye level, slanted slightly to one side. The immersion level, indicated by an etched ring towards the base, is the point at which a thermometer is calibrated to read most accurately. Thermometers should be immersed up to this level when read, although one that is well made will still read with a fair degree of accuracy despite the degree of immersion. If working with a small amount of liquid, tilt the pan slightly to increase the depth of the liquid when reading the thermometer.

The highest accuracy of a thermometer is not at either extreme of its scale.

How to care for a thermometer: It is best to hang a thermometer out of harm's way as rattling around in a drawer may cause mercury separation.

This can also occur if the thermometer was handled roughly during shipping or if it has been dropped. To reunite mercury into one solid column, the mercury must either descend to its lowest point or rise to its highest. If the highest temperature is below boiling point, this can be done by slowly immersing the bulb in boiling water and removing it as soon as the mercury is reunited. If the scale is higher but not above 450°F/232°C, it can be placed in an oven set at a temperature slightly above its highest point. Never place the bulb of the thermometer directly over an open flame.

To prevent breakage, avoid extremes in temperature. When removing the thermometer from a hot liquid, for example, do not place it on a cold draining board. Also, do not allow the thermometer to rest on a pan's bottom, because when it lies on its side the uneven heat distribution could cause it to crack. Clips to attach thermometers to the side of a pan are prone to slipping because they do not conform to a universal pan size or shape. I prefer to hold the thermometer, which is possible as the glass does not conduct the heat.

WHISKS:

I find two sizes of whisks particularly useful for baking: a small one which will reach into the corners of a saucepan or bowl and an enormous balloon whisk for folding one mixture into another in place of a spatula. My large whisk measures 36 centimetres/ 14¼ inches in circumference.

ROUND-BOTTOMED BOWL:

A perfectly round-bottomed bowl for moulded charlottes is ideal. If you can't find one, try to use a bowl with a relatively small flat area at the bottom. Stainless steel or glass is fine.

MAGI-CAKE STRIPS:

These metallic fabric strips (page 514) help to produce a level cake ideal for icing and decorating. They are available from Maid of

Scandinavia (p. 531). If Magi-Cake Strips are unavailable, heavy brown paper also helps to slow down and equalise the baking around the edges of the cake, but to a lesser degree.

SPATULAS:

Large commercial and regular rubber spatulas are very efficient for scraping and folding, but they retain odours so it is best to reserve a separate set for baking. In addition to the 10-centimetre/ 4-inch metal spatula listed on the essential list, small and large angled or offset spatulas are also convenient to spread mixtures evenly in tins or on cake rolls.

A broad inflexible spatula is useful for lifting iced cake layers.

BENCH SCRAPER:

Metal bench scrapers are excellent for cleaning worktops without scratching. Plastic scrapers (cornes in French, probably because they were originally made from horns) are also useful for other purposes because of their flexibility. At LeNôtre's school in France, the professor always had a corne tucked in his toque for levelling a cake, tasting batter or folding ingredients together. The phrase I heard the most often during my week of study was 'Où est ma corne?' ('Where is my scraper?') – like the proverbial absentminded professor looking for his glasses. Immediately following this request, twenty cornes were enthusiastically brought forth before he remembered that his was in its usual location – his hat.

BLENDER:

A powerful, portable blender that enables you to mix in any suitable container, it is particularly useful for smoothing chocolate or buttercream mixtures. (The Krups portable mixer has an immersion blender attachment.)

SAUCEPAN WITH NON-STICK COATING:

A medium-sized heavy saucepan with a non-stick lining is ideal for crème anglaise, sugar syrups and reducing liquids because very little of the liquid sticks to the pan. Do not use for caramel as very high temperatures will eventually damage the lining.

DREDGER:

The primary reason flour is sifted is to separate and aerate the flour particles, enabling them to mix more uniformly with the liquid. It does not do an adequate job of mixing dry ingredients; this is better accomplished in the mixer or even by stirring with a fork.

I am not an advocate of the triple sifter because, if I have already weighed the flour, I am never certain how much gets lost in the labyrinth of the sifter. When making *génoise*, for example, I sift the flour before mixing the batter so that it will be ready to add at the right moment. Then I sift a second time on to the batter. A sieve works well too with a tablespoon to press the flour through it.

CAKE BOARDS:

Covered corrugated cardboard rounds (also referred to as cake circles) are invaluable for supporting cake layers. Doilies can be attached to the cardboard with double-sided tape or a loop of regular tape.

GLASSINE DOILIES:

These doilies are treated with glassine to make them greaseproof so that they do not show stains or disintegrate from moisture. They are available from Maid of Scandinavia (page 531).

PARCHMENT:

Parchment is available in rounds and rolls for lining the bottoms of cake tins. I use parchment cones instead of pastry bags when working with food colouring, which usually stains the bags, and also when working with a particularly heat-sensitive icing. The stiffness of the parchment prevents your hand from coming as close to the icing as a cloth bag would allow, so the icing remains firmer for a longer time. Lining tin bottoms with parchment enables the cake to release perfectly when turning out.

REUSABLE NON-STICK LINING PAPER:

This is one of my favourite products because absolutely nothing sticks to it, making it ideal for caramel, meringues and sponge fingers. It is sometimes difficult to find, but Harrods and other kitchenware suppliers stock Pullman Black Magic lining paper.

SLOTTED SKIMMER:

A medium or large skimmer makes a much better folding instrument than does a rubber spatula, because the small holes provide just the right resistance to blend ingredients without deflating the batter. It helps to bend back the handle slightly to decrease the angle.

WIRE KITCHEN BEATER, OR ANGEL FOOD CAKE FOLDER:

This inexpensive device is almost extinct. It was designed specifically for folding flour into very stiff meringue for angel food cake and it is perfectly suited to the task.

ZESTER AND STRIPPER:

I will always remember the look on James Beard's face when he described these utensils to our class many years ago. He held a small object in either hand and said: 'This is the zester and *this* is the stripper.' He had a definite gleam in his eye.

A zester has a small metal head with tiny rough holes in it. When scraped across a citrus fruit, it penetrates just deeply enough to remove the peel without touching the bitter pith beneath. The

stripper, on the other hand, removes wider strips of the same peel.

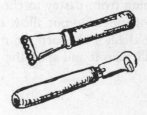

PORCELAIN SPOONS:

These spoons, made of French porcelain, are designed to be tasting spoons because they do not conduct heat or absorb odours. This also makes them perfect for stirring hot liquids, and they can be used in the microwave. I especially like porcelain spoons for making caramel cages. It's easier to see the true colour of the caramel against the white of the porcelain.

CAKE TESTER:

Cake-decorating supply stores carry thin metal wires with loops at the end which make only a small hole in a cake when testing for doneness. Wooden toothpicks are also fine to use.

MARKING PEN:

Find a marking pen which writes on plastic containers and foil and is not obliterated by moisture, and is perfect for items to be stored in the freezer.

MARBLE:

A 46-centimetre/18-inch square of marble is a good size for everything from pastry to chocolate and nougatine. Do not allow citrus juice or alcohol to touch the marble as it will stain it and spoil the finish.

HOT TRAY OR GRIDDLE:

If your oven does not have a pilot light, electric warming trays with temperature controls or electric griddles work well for melting chocolate, providing they do not exceed 120°F/49°C. To check the temperature, set the control at the lowest possible mark, place a cup of water with a thermometer in it on the tray or griddle and take a reading over a period of 2 hours or until you feel sure that the temperature will not exceed 110°F/43°C (to be on the safe side). If the heat is below 120°F/49°C, you should be able to rest the palm of your hand on its surface without discomfort for 3 seconds. Another good heat source is the area above some refrigerators. Every dwelling has different sources of natural heating or cooling areas.

HEART-SHAPED ELECTRIC WAFFLE IRON:

An electric waffle iron produces the most uniformly golden, crisp waffles with the least effort (always

a plus first thing in the morning). I prefer the non-stick version.

SPECIAL PANCAKE PANS:

Special pancake, or crêpe, pans are available – they are extremely shallow with very sloping sides. Small pans can also be obtained for making blini.

SYRUP OR ICING SYRINGE:

A large plastic syringe without the needle is more efficient for sprinkling cakes with syrup than a pastry brush. It is even calibrated to measure the amount used for each side of the cake. They are available from chemists. Although intended to be disposable, they can be reused indefinitely for syrup. I use a 70 cc syringe and shake out the liquid rather than use the plunger. After washing, do not reinsert the plunger until ready to use or it will stick. Before using, spray the inside lightly with non-stick vegetable spray. Chromed steel and aluminium icing syringes are also available from cake-decorating suppliers.

ICE-WATER BATH:

When a recipe says to 'cool to room temperature' and you want to do this quickly, an ice-water bath works well, providing the mixture can be stirred to equalise the temperature. To make an ice-water bath, place ice cubes in a large container and add enough cold water just to float them. Sprinkle a handful of salt on top to lower the temperature (as in making ice cream). If the mixture to be cooled is in a glass bowl, which holds the temperature, and it should not be chilled beyond a specific point, have ready some hot water to take the chill off the bowl when it has reached the proper temperature. Mixtures that should not be stirred, such as ganache, can be placed in a large heat-conductive pan such as copper. Setting the pan on marble will further draw out the heat.

HOT-WATER BATH (BAIN MARIE):

There are many times when you need to heat something very gently rather than over direct heat. If you do not own a double boiler, or if it is too small, use a saucepan or pot whose opening is slightly smaller than the diameter of the mixing bowl. Fill it with a few inches of hot or simmering water and place the bowl on top. In most cases you will not want the bottom of the bowl to touch the water. Stir or

fold the mixture continuously while heating.

When using a hot-water bath for custard-type cakes, it is best to place a piece of parchment in the bottom of the pan containing the water so that the pan with the batter does not come into direct contact with the metal of the larger pan.

CAKE SERVER:

My favourite server is a thin-bladed triangular 'tart' knife.

CHERRY STONER:

In the Fruit Topping section I described how to use a hairpin to stone cherries. Special stoning implements are available, but I find a large hairpin much more effective.

GLASS CAKE DOME:

This attractive and useful serving piece allows you to show off the cake while keeping it moist and fresh.

Supplies for cake decorating

Some of my best cake-decorating supplies were never manufactured with cakes in mind. Orthodontic pliers, a tiny agate spatula, a set of scalpels and a magnificent scalloped serving plate were all once used in my mother's dental office. Rose petal cutters, a tiny wooden roller I use for marzipan and a handsome stainless steel flour scoop came from a pottery and ceramic supply store. Windsor-Newton paint brushes, an 18-inch metal ruler for smoothing cake tops, a clear plastic ruler, and an assortment of flexible and unusually shaped spatulas came from an art supply shop. And small quantities of ingredients are stored in stainless-steel dressing jars from a surgical supply house.

TURNTABLE:

An inexpensive plastic turntable such as a lazy Susan works as well as a heavyweight footed variety. Either can be elevated by placing it on a large inverted cake tin. The commercial heavyweight turntable is necessary when icing and decorating large tiered cakes. Mine doubles as a sturdy but elegant cake

server by placing a large serving plate or marble round on top.

CAKE LEVELLER:

This 40-centimetre/16-inch serrated blade has three adjustable heights: 4, 4.5 and 5 centimetres/1½, 1¾ and 2 inches. As most wedding cake layers fall between these sizes, it is very practical for obtaining perfectly level layers. Available from Maid of Scandinavia (page 531).

A cake saw, with multiple adjustments using two thumb screws rather than fixed notches, is also practical.

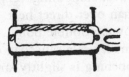

BASIC ICING TUBE SET:

The best type of tubes have welded, almost invisible seams. Less expensive tubes in which the seams are visible result in less precise piping. When tubes flatten and become deformed through much use, an inexpensive plastic tube corrector is all that is needed to put them back into shape. Plastic couplers make it possible to change tubes without emptying the pastry bag.

Bekenal tubes, the Rolls-Royce of decorating tubes, are available from cake-decorating suppliers, including B. R. Mathews (page 531). These tubes are made of shiny, sturdy cast metal. They are long and elegant, with precisely cut openings, making them ideal for the finest string and lace work. A metal coupler can be ordered for them also. They will last a lifetime.

I keep a separate set of tubes for working with royal icing as even a trace of grease will break it down. Only hot water is needed to wash tubes encrusted with royal icing. Alternatively, tubes can be well washed and soaked in a little vinegar to ensure removal of grease.

ICING OR PASTRY BAGS:

In addition to small parchment bags, I use two sizes and types of icing bags: a 30.5-centimetre/12-inch polyester bag and a 36-centimetre/14-inch nylon bag, available from most cake-decorating suppliers. The soft nylon bag is ideal for piping whipped cream mixtures. It is not as effective for fat-based mixtures because the grease seeps through the material. For this purpose, I prefer the polyester bag, which is also soft enough for comfort in the hand but firm enough to prevent too much transfer of heat from your hand to the icing. Bags larger than 30.5 centimetres/12 inches are not as suitable for buttercreams because the heat from your hand softens large quantities of buttercream. It is also more difficult to squeeze unless your hand is very large. To remove all traces of buttercream from icing bags, it helps to soak them in hot water and vinegar.

Just as I have a separate set of tubes for royal icing, I also reserve one icing bag to use only for royal icing to avoid the possibility of grease contamination. Alternatively, polyester bags can be soaked in vinegar and detergent to remove grease or odour. To dry bags, invert them over tall, narrow soda or wine bottles.

Nylon bags are so soft and floppy that the easiest way to fill them is to place them in a blender container, cuffing the top of the bag over the opening for support. (Seal off the opening first by twisting the bag directly above the tube and pushing it into the tube to keep the filling from leaking out.)

Disposable plastic bags, which can be used once and thrown out, are also available through cake-decorating suppliers.

Heavy-duty freezer bags make ideal disposable pastry bags. Simply cut off one corner and insert a coupler (page 453). The closure keeps icing from oozing out the top.

FLOWER FORMERS:

This set of long plastic tubes, cut in half lengthwise, provides concave and convex surfaces for drying icing flowers and chocolate leaves to a more natural, lifelike shape. They are available from cake-decorating suppliers.

FLOWER SINKERS:

If using real flowers a day ahead to decorate a cake, these plastic vials, equipped with tiny sponges to hold water, will keep the flowers fresh. The smallest ones are available either from a florist or flower supply shop.

RIBBON:

The most beautiful ribbon I have found comes from Ets G. Bonnet-J. Mazaud and Cie, in Paris (page 531). That is where I get my gold lamé ribbon. They also carry a ribbon line called *dégradé*, which has a rainbow of colour, each one gradually bleeding into the next. Any ribbon can be used around a cake covered with rolled fondant or white chocolate buttercream, but ribbon should be waterproof or grease resistant if the cake is iced with a softer buttercream.

CAKE BASES:

Heavy cardboard serving boards covered with decorative foil are available from cake-decorating suppliers and many supermarkets. Rolls of decorative foil are also available should you choose to cover your own base. It is also possible to use a mirror as a cake base, providing it is at least 3 millimetres/⅛ inch thick.

TRIANGULAR SCRAPER:

Cake-decorating suppliers often carry this tool for making chocolate ruffles. It is actually a hardware shop item.

PIZZA CUTTER:

The heavy-duty commercial variety offers steady, even pressure for cutting rolled fondant, marzipan and nougatine.

SPUN SUGAR FORK:

Oddly enough, this is the one item that does not have its own official design. In France pastry chefs traditionally use wire whisks, whose curved loops have been cut with snips to form straight wires. Another way to make a device for spun sugar is to use a cake breaker designed for cutting angel food cakes. Bend every other tine in opposing directions. Available from Maid of Scandinavia (see below).

Equipment Suppliers

If you have difficulty in obtaining any of the equipment required for the recipes in this book, the following suppliers should be able to help. Catalogues are available from each:

A wide range of cake tins, baking equipment and accessories and general kitchen utensils is available from:

Divertimenti, 68–72 Marylebone Lane, London W1; tel. 071–935 0689. Mail order available.

Dean & DeLuca, 560 Broadway, New York, New York 10012, USA; tel. 010 212 431–1691. Mail order available.

French Kitchen and Tableware Supply Co., 42 Westbourne Grove, London W2; tel. 071–221 2112. Mail order available.

Harrods, Knightsbridge, London SW1; tel. 081–730 1234. Mail order available.

An excellent range of cake-decorating equipment and accessories is available from:

Ets G. Bonnet–J. Mazaud and Cie., 325 rue Saint-Martin, Paris 3ième, 75003 France; tel. 010 33–1–4272–3582. Ribbons only. Mail order available.

Maid of Scandinavia, 32–44 Raleigh Avenue, Minneapolis, Minnesota 55416, USA; tel. 010 612 925 9256. Mail order available.

B. R. Mathews & Son, 12 Gipsy Hill, Upper Norwood, London SE19; tel. 081–670 0788. Mail order available.

PART IV
SPECIAL SECTION FOR PROFESSIONALS AND PASSIONATE AMATEURS

Understanding Cakes

Chefs de cuisine often boast about having worked in some of the great kitchens of France. As a baker, I am equally proud to say that I have spent time as a consultant in the research and development laboratories of one of America's largest baked goods corporations.

My taste has been honed by years of eating all over the world and my techniques by years of experience as a student and teacher. But to have had the opportunity of working with scientific experts, of tasting and seeing the results of countless experiments, is an experience that I treasure. I have, in fact, spent so much time analysing and thinking about cakes that I sometimes feel as though I've entered the microcosmic structure of the cake itself!

I am also grateful to my wonderful friend Shirley Corriher, a research biochemist and inspired cooking teacher, who over the years has unearthed many valuable articles from scientific journals and spent innumerable hours discussing and illuminating cake theory. It is this understanding which enables me to be both creative and successful.

Say, for example, that you want to convert your favourite cheesecake recipe to a white chocolate cheesecake. Adding white chocolate without taking into account that it contains 30 per cent sugar and then removing this amount from the sugar in the recipe will oversweeten the cake.

Baking without an understanding of the ingredients and how they work is like baking blindfold. Sometimes everything works. But when it doesn't you have to guess at how to change it.

Cakes made with flour fall into three basic categories:

- Butter or sponge cake, containing solid butter or other shortening.
- Whisked sponge cake containing a high proportion of eggs to flour and melted butter or oil.
- Whisked sponge cake containing a high proportion of eggs to flour but no butter, oil or other fat.

The easiest way to compare the cakes in these three categories is with a chart showing the percentage of liquid, egg, flour, sugar and fat. The chart takes into account that unclarified butter is not 100 per cent fat. Butter actually contains about 81 per cent fat and 15.5 per cent liquid. (Clarifying removes the liquid and milk solids.)

Looking at this chart, I see for the first time that, although I thought my pound cake formula had equal weights of eggs/flour/ sugar with slightly more butter, when taking into account the amount of liquid contained in the butter, the formula, in fact, has the exact same percentage of butter fat as other ingredients! The chiffon cake has almost the same proportions as the *génoise* with syrup except that the liquid and sugar are added to the chiffon cake before baking.

Analysing this chart tells you to some degree what the cake will be like. The *génoise*, when moistened with syrup, has a sugar and liquid content similar to that of butter cake. Since the *génoise* has a much higher percentage of egg, which also contributes moisture, it will seem moister than the butter cake as well as lighter in texture. The angel food cake at 34 per cent sugar and with only egg whites and no fat to weigh it down, is a lot sweeter and lighter than pound cake – which has only 22 per cent sugar, whole eggs and a lot of butter.

PERCENTAGES OF MAJOR INGREDIENTS IN BASIC CAKE TYPES

Type of cake	liquid	egg	flour	sugar	fat*
Pound Cake	12%	22%	22%	22%	22%
Pancake	52%	20%	23%	0%	5%
Basic Butter Cake	24%	10%	27%	27%	12%
Génoise Classique	0%	46%	23%	23%	8%
with Syrup	22%	31%	16%	25%	6%
Biscuit Roulade	0%	59%	14%	27%	0%
with Syrup	15%	47%	11%	27%	0%
Biscuit de Savoie	0%	51%	23%	26%	0%
with Syrup	32%	28%	13%	27%	0%
Biscuit à la Cuillière	0%	50%	25%	25%	0%
Sponge Cake	4%	45%	20%	31%	0%
Angel Food Cake	6%	47%	13%	34%	0%
Chiffon Cake	14%	35%	18%	24%	9%

* Total fat content exclusive of the milk solids and water contained in the butter.

Understanding Butter Cakes

Basic sponge or butter cake is one of the world's best. It is flavourful yet not overly sweet, soft and light in texture, and moist enough to stand on its own or to accommodate a variety of fillings and icings.

The ingredients fall into two main categories: those that form and strengthen the cake structure and those that weaken it.

In the first category are flour and eggs, both of which contain proteins that coagulate when baked to form the framework or supporting structure of the cake. The flour also contains starch which gelatinises (absorbs water) and stabilises the structure.

In the second category are fat, sugar and leavening, which in varying ways tenderise the structure by weakening it.

Liquid bridges both categories because it combines with the gluten forming proteins of flour to form gluten, one of the structural networks of the cake. But excessive liquid causes a cake to collapse. Usually a cake with weak structure resembles an M (straight sides but sinking centre). A cake containing too much liquid, however, resembles an X (level top but sides caved in towards the middle). A butter cake batter with too much liquid will be thin and the baked cake will be heavy. A batter with less liquid will be thicker and the resulting cake lighter with a more open crumb. The perfect balance of liquid offers both structural support and moistness that is also perceived as tenderness.

INGREDIENTS

CAKE FLOUR:

Cake flour contains 2 gluten-forming proteins, gliadin and glutenin. When liquid is added, they connect to form the resilient strands that provide a small part of the cake's structure. The most important structural component, however, is starch, which absorbs water and swells (gelatinises) to set the structure.

Cake flour is made from finely milled soft winter wheat which is high in starch and low in gluten-forming proteins. Because of its finer granulation, it absorbs fat and moisture more quickly than hard spring wheat which contains more protein.

The size of the gas cells in a cake determines the quality of the grain of the finished cake and is directly dependent upon how much the batter expands during baking before the cells rupture. This is influenced partly by the size of the flour particles, partly by the batter's pH, and partly by the type of shortening used. Cake flour, due to bleaching by chlorination, has a lower pH (more acid) than other flours. This produces a sweeter flavour and a finer, more velvety crumb because the greater acidity lowers the temperature at which the proteins coagulate. This also makes it possible for the cake structure to support more sugar, butter, and heavier particles such as chopped nuts or chocolate.

The chlorination process offers other advantages. It attacks the starch granules, enabling water to enter more easily. In industry, cake flour is often milled with sugar so that the sugar particles become imbedded in the flour granules, providing an avenue for the water to enter and hydrate the starch. Chlorination also serves to inhibit gluten formation. Recent research has revealed that fat adheres to the surface of chlorinated starch particles, resulting in better aeration (more even, uniform distribution of air).

It is possible to substitute equal weights of *bleached* plain flour for cake flour by adding a small percentage of cornflour. But the result will not be the same because the flour is coarser and the pH higher. Self-raising sponge flour cannot be used interchangeably with cake flour because it contains approximately 1½ teaspoons baking powder and ½ teaspoon salt per cup of flour. This will coarsen and weaken the texture of cakes requiring only 1¼ teaspoons or less baking powder per cup.

EGGS:

Eggs contribute structure and serve as a means for incorporating air into the batter. They also supply some of the cake's liquid. The yolk of an egg is a rich source of natural emulsifying agents, which help suspend the fat evenly throughout the batter. Cakes prepared with egg whites only are slightly softer than those with either whole egg or all yolk because the yolk becomes firmer after coagulating (baking) than does the white. In a layer cake recipe 1 egg can be replaced by 2 yolks or 1½ whites. If using all yolks, the structure will be slightly weaker, so the baking powder needs to be decreased by ¼ teaspoon for every 3 yolks used. (Yolks tenderise by coating some of the gluten-forming proteins in the flour, preventing excessive gluten formation.)

The advantage of using only yolks is superior flavour and a more golden colour. The crust also browns more because the yolk is higher in protein and contains fat.

BUTTER:

Butter, or solid fat, tenderises and aerates the cake. It tenderises by coating some of the gluten-forming proteins in the flour, preventing excessive gluten formation. Cells created by air beaten into the fat provide focal points for the collection of the steam formed in baking and for the carbon dioxide liberated from sodium bicarbonate by the acid in baking powder. Unsalted butter produces the best flavour, not only because of its own incomparable flavour but also because it releases the flavours of other ingredients more fully. A cake with less butter, for example, will seem less sweet. Margarine or other fats do not release flavour as well.

Butter will hold the maximum amount of air if its temperature is 65° to 75°F/18° to 24°C when beaten. During baking, the melting fat makes the batter more mobile because fat is insoluble (does not dissolve) in water. It disperses into tiny particles throughout the batter. Some people use up to 50 per cent hydrogenated fat instead of pure butter because it contains emulsifiers that disperse the fat more evenly, increasing the elasticity on the film of protein around the air bubbles for better volume and texture. I find, however, that using 100 per cent butter at the correct temperature yields perfect texture in addition to superior flavour.

incorporation of air into the fat. Castor sugar is preferable because the finer the crystals, the more numerous the air cells. Icing sugar is not suitable because it lacks the sharp crystal edges which help incorporate the air. In a batter containing a large amount of sugar, the gas cells expand more before the batter sets because the sugar elevates the temperature at which the egg protein coagulates and the starch granules gelatinise. This creates a more open texture, weakening the cake's structure and making it melt faster in the mouth. It should be noted that tenderness and softness are two different qualities. A cake high in sugar will fall apart easily (is more 'tender') but it also has a harder 'mouth feel'.

Sugar 'tenderises' cake in two significant ways. It competes with the starch to absorb the liquid by combining with the 2 gluten-forming proteins in the flour to prevent them from forming gluten, making the structure too rigid. Interestingly, even if the gluten is already formed when the sugar is added, the sugar still combines with the proteins to break up the gluten. In a baked cake sugar also serves to retain moisture.

SUGAR:

Sugar contributes flavour (sweetness) and facilitates the

SALT:

The only function of salt in a cake is to accentuate or heighten flavour.

Without salt, the cake would have a decidedly flat taste.

LEAVENING:

Baking powders are mixtures of dry acid or acid salt and bicarbonate of soda with starch or flour added to standardise and stabilise the mixtures. They are formulated so that there is no excess of either bicarbonate of soda or acid left in the product after the desired reaction is accomplished. The product of their reaction is carbon dioxide, which aerates and lightens the batter by enlarging the already existing air cells creamed into the fat. (It does not create new air cells.) Double-acting means that part of the reaction takes place when the baking powder comes into contact with liquid and the remainder is activated by heat during baking.

Too little baking powder results in a tough cake with a humped top, compact crumb and poor volume. Too much baking powder results in a coarse, open, fragile crumb and often a fallen centre.

Bicarbonate of soda may be used in a cake formula to neutralise an acid ingredient such as black treacle, sour cream or cocoa which has not been 'dutched' (treated with alkali). A half teaspoon of bicarbonate of soda is required to neutralise the acid of 8 fluid ounces of sour milk. This process (the lactic acid of the sour milk reacting with the bicarbonate of soda) provides leavening equal to that of approximately 4 times its volume of baking powder. So if a formula calls for 4 fluid ounces milk and 1½ teaspoons baking powder, it is possible to substitute 4 fluid ounces sour milk and the ¼ teaspoon bicarbonate of soda necessary for neutralisation. This equals the leavening power of 1 teaspoon baking powder so only ½ teaspoon of baking powder needs to be added. Treacle needs ½ to 1 teaspoon baking soda per cup for neutralisation.

Because the acidity of these products varies, there is the risk of adding more bicarbonate of soda than can be dissipated by the amount of acid present. This excessive alkalinity will slow down coagulation of the proteins and result in a coarse, open crumb and bitter, steely flavour. It is preferable to use too little bicarbonate of soda rather than too much.

In working with buttermilk formulas for layer cake, I find that 4 fluid ounces buttermilk + ¼ teaspoon bicarbonate of soda equals 1⅛ teaspoons baking powder. I prefer not to neutralise the flavour of buttermilk with bicarbonate of soda, as I find the taste fuller and the texture finer using baking powder alone.

COCOA:

Cocoa is superior to chocolate for cake baking because it provides more intense chocolate flavour. To get equal intensity using chocolate, it is necessary to use the equivalent of more cocoa solids, cocoa butter and dairy butter unless the chocolate is cooked with water as in Moist Chocolate Génoise (page 145). This is because the flavour components in chocolate are locked in by the cocoa butter. Cooking the chocolate in water dissolves the surrounding barrier of cocoa butter and swells the cocoa particles until they rupture, unlocking the flavour components.

Cocoa has a toughening effect on cake structure so cakes containing cocoa have a higher amount of baking powder to compensate.

Bicarbonate of soda is traditionally used for chocolate cakes because it neutralises its mild acidity. The colour of a devil's food cake is due to the pigments supplied by the cocoa or chocolate. They change colour with a change in hydrogen ion concentration. At a pH of 5.0 they are yellow. Bicarbonate of soda, which increases the alkalinity, turns the hue to mahogany red at 7.5 pH. The increase in pH also results in the coarser texture and bitter flavour usually associated with devil's food cake. If using 'dutched chocolate', it is unnecessary, in fact undesirable, to add bicarbonate of soda to neutralise acidity because the dutching process is an alkali treatment of the cocoa beans during roasting which eliminates acetic acid, giving the cocoa smoother flavour, richer colour and improved solubility. (Some people perceive undutched cocoa as stronger, others as more bitter rather than more intense in chocolate flavour.)

Sometimes a process called 'instantising' is used to roughen and fluff up the grains of cocoa and make them dissolve more easily.

LIQUID:

Milk products are the preferred liquid for yellow or white butter cakes and water is usually the preferred liquid for chocolate butter cakes. Milk products offer a richer flavour, but the proteins in milk solids cause chocolate to have a bitter taste. (Taste a chocolate cake made with milk alongside one made with water to note the remarkable difference in flavour.) Fruit juices are not recommended because they alter the acid balance of the batter, which affects the texture and causes it to become gummy.

In addition to taste, the function of liquid in a cake batter is to dissolve the salt and sugar and make possible the reaction of the soda and acid in the baking powder to form carbon dioxide. Liquid also disperses the fat and flour, hydrates the protein and starch in the flour, and provides steam to leaven the cake.

MIXING THE BATTER

I have adapted the two-stage method of mixing batter, used commercially with high-ratio fat (which makes it possible to use a higher ratio of sugar), for use with butter. (I do not consider it an advantage to have more sugar and unequivocally prefer the flavour of butter to other fats.) Fat is capable of aeration at a wider range of temperatures than butter. But if the butter is 65° to 75°F/18° to 24°C and the other ingredients are at room temperature,* this mixing method is my preferred one. It is much faster and easier than the creaming method, and the results are more consistent. The grain is finer and more velvety and the crumb more tender than with the creaming method.

The two-stage method produces a more tender cake because the butter is added to the flour with a minimum of liquid (just enough to disperse the fat) at the beginning of the mixing process. The butter coats some of the gluten-forming proteins in the flour, preventing excessive gluten formation. This protects the cake from toughening due to overmixing. A significant amount of air still gets incorporated into the batter with this method. Proof of this is that, although the tin is filled only half full instead of the usual two-thirds, the batter still rises to the top.

Another advantage of the two-stage method is that since all the dry ingredients are added together, at the beginning, it is possible to disperse them evenly with the mixer. As sifting does not uniformly disperse dry ingredients unless repeated many times, using the mixer instead is a great time and energy saver. (Flour should be sifted once to aerate and separate the particles which enable it to hydrate more evenly.)

BAKING THE CAKE

The single most critical factor to successfully baking a cake is oven temperature. No matter how carefully ingredients are weighed, measured and mixed, an oven that is too cool or too hot will ruin a cake's texture. Since most oven thermometers are less than adequate, the best test is to bake Yellow Butter Cake (page 28). This basic butter cake will give you a clue as to how your oven is calibrated.

There is a lot you can tell from the outside appearance of a baked cake. If the top crust is evenly

---

*Ideally, the butter should be 70°F/21°C, the liquid and eggs 60°F/15°C, and the finished batter 70° to 75°F/21° to 24°C.

golden brown and flat or gently rounded, the cake within will be fine-grained, soft and tender. If the cake is peaked and tests done before 20 minutes, your oven is too hot. If it sinks slightly in the middle, takes more than 30 minutes to bake and has a coarse texture, your oven is not hot enough.

When a cake bakes, expanding gas from steam and leavening enlarges the air bubbles trapped in the fat during the mixing process. The bubbles expand until the surrounding cell walls rupture, the flour and egg proteins coagulate and the flour's starch gelatinises to set the structure. At too low a temperature heat penetration is slow and the cells overexpand and collide, forming larger cells before coagulation and gelatinisation can set the structure. This explains why the grain is coarser in a cake that has been baked too slowly and why a 30.5-centimetre/12-inch cake is somewhat coarser than a 15-centimetre/6-inch cake.

WHAT CAN GO WRONG

Assuming you are working with a well-balanced formula, when a butter cake falls, peaks and cracks, or has poor texture, the first thing to consider is the oven temperature.

The next is the proportion of ingredients (how they were weighed or measured). Incorrect substitutions without adjustments are often the problem; jumbo eggs instead of large, plain flour instead of cake flour without making the necessary adjustments, or old baking powder.

The next thing to consider is the method of mixing the batter. If using the two-stage method, this is rarely a problem. It is hard to toughen the batter by overbeating because the early addition of the butter serves as protection. With the creaming method, overmixing develops the gluten, especially if plain flour has been used, and results in a tight grain with a peaked top. The leavening has to force its way through the tough cell walls, creating long tunnels and erupting and cracking the surface of the cake.

Undermixing does not form enough gluten, which results in a crumbly, coarse grain and a very flat top crust with a slightly fallen centre.

Assuming you are making one of the cake recipes in this book, and you have accurately weighed or measured the ingredients, the most common problems and their causes are:

PROBLEM	CAUSE
cracked or peaked surface and or large tunnels	oven too hot or batter overmixed
coarse grain and sunken centre	oven too cold, batter undermixed, or too much baking powder
poor volume, compact texture	old or too little baking powder or cold eggs and/or butter
dry cake, tough crust	overbaking or tin too big
burnt bottom and undercooked batter	inadequate air circulation in oven

Understanding Génoise and Whisked Sponge Cakes

Whisked sponge cakes are characteristically lighter and springier than butter cakes. When comparing the percentage of ingredients in a *génoise* to that of a basic butter cake (page 536), it's easy to see why this is the case. *Génoise* sprinkled with syrup (which is the way it is usually consumed) has about three times the amount of egg as butter cake and only about half the flour and butter.

I cut the flour for my *génoise* recipe with 50 per cent cornflour, thereby lowering the overall percentage of protein. It is possible to decrease the cake flour in this way because one of the major differences between whisked sponge cakes and butter cakes is that the whisked-sponge structure comes primarily from egg protein reinforced by starch from the flour. A *génoise* actually can be made without any flour protein by using all starch, but the texture will not be quite as light or resilient.

The main goal in making a whisked sponge cake is to achieve as much volume in the baked cake as possible. Since the eggs are the most important ingredient for volume, the way in which they are beaten, their temperature, and the manner of adding other ingredients to them are all important considerations. *Génoise*, for example, contains butter, which weighs down the egg foam, so to counteract this the eggs are warmed before beating to help them attain their greatest possible volume. The butter is also added warm to keep it from solidifying and resting too heavily on the egg foam.

Too much volume is not desirable either because if there is more volume than the structure can support the *génoise* will collapse.

Again referring to the chart (page 536), comparing Biscuit de Savoie without syrup to *génoise* without syrup shows why the *biscuit* will be lighter than the *génoise*. It has no fat to weigh it down plus it has more sugar and egg for aeration. For this reason, it is not necessary to heat the eggs for a *biscuit* in order to increase the amount of volume during beating. It is desirable, however, to bake the *biscuit* in an ungreased tin because the absence of fat (except for the small amount in the yolk) and the high proportion of egg would cause the *biscuit* to shrink away from the sides of the tin and collapse.

A *génoise* or Biscuit de Savoie would be dry and somewhat tough without a moistening syrup. The perfect amount softens the texture. If too much is added, however, the cake becomes almost mushy. Biscuit de Savoie can hold a lot more syrup than *génoise* because it has a stronger structure.

A whisked sponge cake without fat requires either a moistening syrup or a high proportion of sugar to tenderise it. American sponge cake, for example, traditionally uses no syrup but it has 31 per cent sugar and angel food cake has 34 per cent sugar. Chiffon cake, which has the moist richness of butter cake with the lightness of whisked sponge cake, uses oil to tenderise it so it can get by with only 24 per cent sugar, less than a butter cake. (It has 9 per cent oil compared to the 12 per cent butter in the butter cake but oil, which is liquid, coats the protein more effectively, so less is needed to achieve a similar degree of tenderness). A small amount of baking powder adds just enough extra volume without endangering the fragile structure. Castor sugar is preferable, as in butter cakes, because the finer the crystals, the more numerous the air cells.

Sponge, chiffon and angel food cakes are all so light and spongy they require the added support of a tube pan for maximum volume and must hang upside down to stretch and keep from collapsing until cool enough for the structure to set. Angel food is the lightest cake because it has all egg whites for the largest and most stable foam (requiring less flour for structure) and the highest proportion of sugar. Since coagulated egg whites are rubbery in the absence of fat, the extra amount of sugar is necessary to 'tenderise' the cake. There is a limit as to how much sugar can be added to a cake. Beyond a certain point, the sugar will actually prevent the batter from setting by raising the coagulation temperature of the egg and limiting starch gelatinisation.

Cake flour produces better whisked sponge cakes than does plain because of its finer granulation, lower protein content, and lower pH. Cream of tartar, which is an acidic salt, is also added to stabilise the egg whites and lower the pH, creating a finer grain, making the cake more tender and keeping it from shrinking. It is thought that the acid enables the films of protein in the air cells of the foam to last until the heat can set the structure. In a white angel food cake, the lower pH will make the crumb whiter.

As with butter cakes, a high baking temperature for whisked sponge cakes promotes a more rapid setting of the batter and absorption of less water by the starch of the flour. This results in a greater volume and a moister, more tender cake. Higher temperatures also improve texture but are not equally beneficial to the external appearance of the cake. Above 350°F/180°C/gas mark 4, the crust of whisked sponge cakes becomes overbrowned.

Foolproof Formulas and Techniques for Making Large Special Occasion Cakes

This chapter, devoted to the large special occasion cake, is for the master cake baker or dedicated home baker. It contains all the information needed to make *any* size white, yellow or chocolate sponge or butter cake from 15 to 46 centimetres/6 to 18 inches and any yellow or chocolate *génoise* from 15 to 30.5 centimetres/6 to 12 inches. It also tells you how much buttercream and syrup are required for each. There are recipes for other favourite cakes in large proportions, such as cheesecake and pound cake, and detailed instructions for assembling and storing tiered cakes.

The Showcase Cakes chapter, beginning on page 184, contains five completed examples of tiered wedding cakes. But the information in this chapter will enable you to make endless variations of just about any cake your heart desires.

While it is possible to produce large cakes without any special equipment other than large tins and a sufficient number of racks, certain pieces of equipment make the job much easier and more efficient. A 10 or 20-litre/2½ or 5-gallon mixer, for example, makes it possible to mix the batter for a 3-Tiered Wedding Cake for 150 people in one batch. With the KitchenAid K5 (5-litre/8-pint mixer), it is necessary to divide the batter into two batches for a butter cake and four batches for *génoise*. A highly motivated person could even use an electric hand-held mixer by preparing the batter in four batches (two for the 30.5-centimetre/12-inch layers, one for the 23-centimetre/9-inch layers, and one for the 15-centimetre/6-inch layers).

Another major consideration when making large cakes is oven size. I once made a four-tiered wedding cake in my apartment kitchen. The two 38-centimetre/

15-inch bottom layers and two
15-centimetre/6-inch top layers
were baking in my oven while the
two 30.5-centimetre/12-inch layers
baked in the worktop convection
oven and the two 23-centimetre/
9-inch layers in the Cuisinart Air
Surge. Since I like to turn each
layer 90 degrees halfway through
its specific baking time to promote
even baking, timers were going off
at mad intervals. I decided that,
henceforth, three tiers at a time
would be my limit.

Refrigeration space is not usually
a problem, because most cakes put
together the day before the event
can sit at cool room temperature
overnight.

A large wedding or special
occasion cake somehow manages to
require an extraordinary number of
bowls, tins and utensils and usually
takes at least 12 hours of solid
work to complete. I don't know
how the following tradition ever
got started, but somehow, when
the cake is iced and ready for the
piped decorations, that is my
moment of glory, of supreme joy
and celebration, because now the
best part can begin: the artwork. I
fill the pastry bag, pour a tiny glass
of my best Napoleon cognac
(which I find far too strong at any
other time), and am transported to
another world.

When the mess is cleared away
and the cake sitting on its pedestal,
ready to be photographed for my
album, it always amazes me how

this pristine and exquisite cake
could have created such havoc.
And I wonder idly how many non-
bakers ever realise the work that
goes into its preparation. It really
doesn't matter though; there is the
pleasure of coming into contact
with people who are at their
happiest, either about to be married
or celebrating some other joyous
event. Then there is the
unparalleled joy of creation,
making the cake.

A beginner's greatest fear when
embarking on a first wedding cake
is that it won't look even. When I
used to give week-long baking
classes, I would take the students to
visit New York bakeries. They
were surprised, when encouraged
to scrutinise the cakes and
decorations close up (as ruthlessly
as they would their own), that,
although scarcely a cake was
perfectly level or the decorations
very precise, the overall effect was
still impressive.

I'll always remember the night
my husband came into the room to
look at my latest creation before
going to bed. I had been baking
wedding cakes for about two years,
and one had even been
photographed for *Bon Appétit*
magazine. He appraised the newest
cake and then said evenly: 'You're
getting really good; they're
beginning to look level.'

Actually, it was *Bon Appétit* that
started my wedding cake business
when they asked me to make a

special occasion cake for an article featuring my cooking school. It was the first time they had ever presented a wedding cake. It was also the first time that I had ever made one. My concept was to offer a cake that the bride could bake for her own wedding and which could be prepared in advance to give her time to attend to last-minute details. The cake, covered with rolled fondant and decorated with pale pink marzipan roses and tiny dots reminiscent of pearls cascading from the top, is included in this book. It was my first experience in having an inner vision materialise with such fidelity, and it is still my favourite wedding cake.

While over the years many people have made the cake, if not for their own wedding then for a sister's or daughter's, an inordinate number of them wanted me to make the cake myself. I never considered this possibility when I wrote the article. The first person to call was planning her daughter's wedding eighteen months away. She was planning the décor to match the cake – even the bridesmaids' dresses were to be dotted Swiss! One baker from Long Island called to berate me jokingly for designing dots. She said: 'Everyone wants dots now and you know what a pain . . . they are to make!' Since that time seven years ago, I have made over 100 wedding or special occasion cakes. At first my husband and I

often attended the weddings because I had got to know the bride so well while designing her cake. Eventually, to Elliott's relief, the novelty wore off.

SPECIAL THINGS TO CONSIDER WHEN EMBARKING ON A TIERED CAKE

- *Oven space:* Assess how many layers can be baked at one time and co-ordinate this with the refrigeration space available for holding unbaked batter. Alternatively, decide how many batches of batter you will mix. Remember: cake tins *must* have air circulation all around them while baking. Do not overcrowd them.
- *Refrigeration space:* Check available space if the completed cake needs to be refrigerated. Refrigerator racks can be removed to give more height.
- *Equipment:* Beyond the basics, such as tins and spatulas, there will be special pieces of equipment necessary to complete some of the tiered cakes.

See the Equipment chapter (page 514) or the list of special equipment and structural supports needed for each recipe in the Showcase Cakes chapter (pages 184 to 260).
- *Cooling racks:* Keep in mind that you will need a rack for each cake layer.

- *Magi-Cake Strips:* Highly recommended for more even layers, an important factor in having the finished cake look attractive and professional (pages 4 and 522).
- *Mixer Capacity*
  Cake layers: Indication of mixer size and number of batches necessary is given at the top of each recipe in this chapter.
  Buttercreams: The buttercreams in this chapter can be made in one batch in a 5-litre/8-pint mixer. With a hand-held mixer you will need to make two or three batches.

SUGGESTED CAKE SIZE OPTIONS

The average-size wedding cake consists of three tiers – 30.5 centimetres/12 inches, 23 centimetres/ 9 inches and 15 centimetres/ 6 inches – and feeds about 150 people. A three-tier cake is the largest convenient size to cut and serve, so, if extra cake is desired, a sheet cake can be baked, iced and portioned in the kitchen. Since it will be behind the scenes, there is no need for time-consuming decoration.

In Canada and Japan there is another interesting approach to the problem of serving a tiered wedding cake. The Hotel Okura in Tokyo, the most fashionable location for modern Japanese weddings, devotes an entire storeroom to elaborate, artificial cake constructions. These wedding cakes are fairytale monuments of royal icing, entirely inedible save for a small hollow section into which is inserted and iced a wedge of fruitcake for the bride to cut and serve to the groom. Meanwhile, the rest of the fruitcake, baked in large rectangles, is conveniently being cut backstage in the kitchen. This way the guests don't have to wait nearly as long for their pieces of cake and all can be served more or less at the same time!

This chapter contains recipes for the standard three-tier butter cake in white, yellow and chocolate, the same size cake in classic or chocolate *génoise*, and cheesecake.

For those who prefer a towering presentation of four or more tiers, I am also offering a chart which will enable you to bake any size butter cake from 15 to 46 centimetres/6 to 18 inches and a second chart with icing amounts. These charts are the soul of this book and took years to perfect. It will save you the hours of planning, calculation and trepidation I went through each time someone requested a different amount of cake (which seemed to be every time).

Wedding cake portions are traditionally small because they are usually served after a large dinner which often includes other desserts as well. People are surprised by how little cake is actually needed in relation to the number of guests, partly because these days many people forgo dessert entirely. There are always some who leave before the cake-cutting ceremony, which comes at the very end.

When I calculate the number of servings necessary for a butter cake, I estimate that my base formula of 1 cup flour (or flour/cocoa) serves 11. This works out to be about 1½ tablespoons flour per serving. The size of the serving is either a square 5 centimetres/2 inches high by 5 centimetres/2 inches deep by 4.25 centimetres/1⅝ inches wide or a slim rectangle 10 centimetres/ 4 inches high by 5 centimetres/ 2 inches deep by 2 centimetres/ ¾ inch wide.

The only time I ran out of cake was when I made Golden Glory Wedding Cheesecake (page 252) for my niece Joan Beranbaum Stackhouse's wedding. The wedding was in Westport, Connecticut, and just prior to the event the cake was being photographed nearby for Martha Stewart's book *Weddings*. All of our relatives and Joan's friends knew about this and were eagerly saving their appetites. Some people, alas, lined up for seconds before everyone else had received a first serving. I could have used two wedding cakes that day! I encouraged Joan to serve the top tier too, as this cheesecake doesn't freeze well anyway, and promised to bake her one exactly like it for her first anniversary.

NUMBER OF SERVINGS	TIN SIZE (all tins are round and 5 centimetres/2 inches high)
40	one 30.5-centimetre/12-inch tin*
50	two 25.5-centimetre/10-inch tins
75	two 25.5-centimetre/10-inch and two 18-centimetre/ 7-inch tins
80†	one 46-centimetre/18-inch × 30.5-centimetre/12-inch sheet tin
100	one 38-centimetre/15-inch and one 30.5-centimetre/ 12-inch tin

* For butter cakes use four times the base formula, for yellow *génoise* seven times the base formula, for chocolate *génoise* eight and three-quarter times the base formula.
† Sheet cake servings are 5-centimetres/2 inches by 5-centimetres/2 inches by 4.25-centrimetres/1⅝ inches. If cut into 5-centimetre/2-inch squares, it would make 54 servings.

NUMBER OF SERVINGS	TIN SIZE (all tins are round and 5 centimetres/2 inches high)
110	two 30.5-centimetre/12-inch and two 20-centimetre/8-inch tins
150	two 30.5-centimetre/12-inch, two 23-centimetre/9-inch, and two 15-centimetre/6-inch tins
175	two 33-centimetre/13-inch, two 25.5-centimetre/10-inch, and two 18-centimetre/7-inch tins
200	two 38-centimetre/15-inch, two 25.5-centimetre/10-inch, and two 15-centimetre/6-inch tins
225	two 38-centimetre/15-inch, two 28-centimetre/11-inch, and two 18-centimetre/7-inch tins
250	two 38-centimetre/15-inch, two 30.5-centimetre/12-inch, and two 23-centimetre/9-inch tins
275	two 38-centimetre/15-inch, two 30.5-centimetre/12-inch, two 23-centimetre/9-inch, and two 15-centimetre/6-inch tins
300	two 41-centimetre/16-inch, 33-centimetre/13-inch, and two 25.5-centimetre/10-inch tins
350	two 46-centimetre/18-inch, two 36-centimetre/14-inch, and two 25.5-centimetre/10-inch tins
450	two 46-centimetre/18-inch, two 38-centimetre/15-inch, two 30.5-centimetre/12-inch, two 23-centimetre/9-inch, and two 15-centimetre/6-inch tins

Note: For aesthetics, the relationship of tiers to each other must be taken into account. If you wish to combine different sizes not on the chart, try stacking the cake tins to see the effect.

Butter Wedding Cakes

Wedding cakes are usually prepared with white, yellow or even chocolate butter cake. The firm yet tender mixture makes it ideal for constructing multitiered layers.

To keep a butter cake fresh and moist when preparing more than twenty-four hours ahead, sprinkle the layers with Syrup (page 578). Use 24 fluid ounces of syrup for every 1 kilogram 300 grams/ 2 pounds 13½ ounces/6½ cups of sugar used to prepare the cake batter.

3-Tier White or Yellow Butter Wedding Cake to Serve 150*

FINISHED HEIGHT: Each layer is about 4 centimetres/1½ inches.

STORE: Airtight: 2 days room temperature, 5 days refrigerated, 2 months frozen.

SERVE: Room temperature.

INGREDIENTS	WEIGHT		MEASURE
room temperature	grams	pounds/ounces	volume
FOR TWO 15 × 5-CENTIMETRE/6-INCH × 2-INCH LAYERS AND TWO 23 × 5-CENTIMETRE/9-INCH × 2-INCH LAYERS			
9 egg whites, size 2, or	270 grams	9½ ounces	9 fluid ounces
12 egg yolks, size 2	223 grams	7¾ ounces	7 fluid ounces
milk	484 grams	17 ounces	16 fluid ounces
pure vanilla extract	18 grams	—	1 tablespoon + 1½ teaspoons
sifted cake flour†	600 grams	1 pound 5 ounces	6 cups

*Requires a 5-litre/8-pint mixer.
†Cake flour *without* raising agent must be used for this cake (page 493).

INGREDIENTS	WEIGHT		MEASURE
room temperature	*grams*	*pounds/ounces*	*volume*
castor sugar	600 grams	1 pound 5 ounces	3 cups
baking powder	39 grams	—	2 tablespoons + 2 teaspoons
salt	10 grams	—	1½ teaspoons
unsalted butter (must be softened)	340 grams	12 ounces	1½ cups
FOR TWO 30.5 × 5-CENTIMETRE/12-INCH 2-INCH LAYERS			
10½ egg whites, size 2 *or*	315 grams	11 ounces	10½ fluid ounces
14 egg yolks, size 2	260 grams	9 ounces	8 fluid ounces
milk	564 grams	1 pound 3¾ ounces	18½ fluid ounces
pure vanilla extract	21 grams	—	1 tablespoon + 2¼ teaspoons
sifted cake flour*	700 grams	1 pound 8½ ounces	7 cups
castor sugar	700 grams	1 pound 8½ ounces	3½ cups
baking powder	38 grams	—	2 tablespoons + 1¾ teaspoons
salt	12 grams	—	1¾ teaspoons
unsalted butter (must be softened)	400 grams	14 ounces	1¾ cups

*Cake flour *without* raising agent must be used for this cake (page 493).

Grease the tins, line the bottoms with parchment or greaseproof paper, and then grease again and flour. For very even cakes use Magi–Cake Strips (pages 516 and 522).

INSTRUCTIONS FOR MIXING BATTER FOR ALL SIZES OF WHITE AND YELLOW BUTTER CAKES

Arrange two oven racks as close to the centre of the oven as possible with at least 7.5 centimetres/ 3 inches between them.

Preheat the oven to 350°F/180°C/gas mark 4.

In a medium bowl, lightly combine the whites or yolks, ¼ of the milk, and the vanilla.

In a large mixing bowl combine all the dry ingredients and mix on low speed for 1 minute to blend. Add the butter and remaining milk. Mix on low speed until the dry ingredients are moistened. Beat at medium speed (high speed if using a hand mixer) for 1½ minutes to aerate and develop the cake's structure. Scrape down the sides.

Gradually beat in the egg mixture in three batches, beating for 20 seconds after each addition to incorporate the ingredients and strengthen the structure. Scrape down the sides.

Scrape the batter into the prepared tins, filling about halfway, and smooth with a spatula. (For exact batter weight in each tin, refer to the chart on page 559.) Arrange the tins in the oven so that air can circulate around them. Do not allow them to touch each other or the oven walls. Bake for 25 to 35 minutes for 15-centimetre/6-inch layers, 35 to 45 minutes for 23-centimetre/9-inch layers, and 40 to 50 minutes for 30.5-centimetre/ 12-inch layers or until a tester inserted near the centre comes out clean and the cake springs back when pressed lightly in the centre. In the 15-centimetre/6-inch and 23-centimetre/9-inch tins, the cakes should start to shrink from the sides only after removal from the oven. The 30.5-centimetre/12-inch layers should bake until they just start to shrink from the sides. To promote more even baking, turn the 30.5-centimetre/12-inch layers 180° (halfway around) halfway through the baking time. Do this quickly so the oven temperature does not drop.

Allow the cakes to cool in the pans on racks for 10 minutes (20 minutes for 30.5-centimetre/ 12-inch layers). Loosen the sides with a spatula and invert on to greased wire racks. To prevent splitting, reinvert and cool completely before wrapping airtight with clingfilm and foil.

Note: Do not underbake the 30.5-centimetre/12-inch layers.

When preparing the cake more than 24 hours ahead of serving or if extra moistness is desired, sprinkle layers with 24 fluid ounces of syrup (page 578).

3-Tier White or Yellow Butter Wedding Cake to Serve 150*

FINISHED HEIGHT: Each layer is about 4 centimetres/1½ inches.

STORE: Airtight: 2 days room temperature, 5 days refrigerated, 2 months frozen.

SERVE: At room temperature.

INGREDIENTS	WEIGHT		MEASURE
room temperature	*grams*	*pounds/ounces*	*volume*
FOR TWO 15 × 5-CENTIMETRE/6-INCH × 2-INCH LAYERS AND TWO 23 × 5-CENTIMETRE/9-INCH × 2-INCH LAYERS			
6 eggs, size 2	300 grams (weighed without shells)	10½ ounces	10 scant fluid ounces
water (boiling)	473 grams	1 pound ¾ ounce	16 fluid ounces
pure vanilla extract	18 grams	–	1 tablespoon + 1½ teaspoons
sifted cake flour†	475 grams	1 pound ½ ounce	4¾ cups
unsweetened cocoa (preferably Dutch-processed)	125 grams	4½ ounces	1¼ cups + 2 tablespoons (lightly spooned into cup)
castor sugar	600 grams	1 pound 5 ounces	3 cups
baking powder	44 grams	1½ ounces	3 tablespoons
salt	10 grams	–	1½ teaspoons
unsalted butter	340 grams	12 ounces	1½ cups

* Requires a 5-litre/8-pint mixer.
† Cake flour *without* rising agent must be used for this cake (see page 493).

INGREDIENTS	WEIGHT		MEASURE
room temperature	*grams*	*pounds/ounces*	*volume*
FOR TWO 30.5 × 5-CENTIMETRE/12-INCH × 2-INCH LAYERS			
7 eggs, size 2	350 grams (weighed without shells)	12¼ ounces	11 fluid ounces
water (boiling)	550 grams	1 pound 3½ ounces	18½ fluid ounces
pure vanilla extract	21 grams	—	1 tablespoon + 2¼ teaspoons
sifted cake flour★	553 grams	1 pound 3½ ounces	5½ cups
unsweetened cocoa (preferably Dutch-processed)	147 grams	5 ounces	1½ cups + 2 tablespoons (lightly spooned into cup)
castor sugar	700 grams	1 pound 8½ ounces	3½ cups
baking powder	43 grams	—	2 tablespoons + 2¾ teaspoons
salt	12 grams	—	1¾ teaspoons
unsalted butter	400 grams	14 ounces	1¾ cups

† Cake flour *without* rising agent must be used for this cake (see page 493).

Grease the tins, line the bottoms with parchment or greaseproof paper, and then grease again and flour. For very even cakes use Magi-Cake Strips (pages 516 and 522).

INSTRUCTIONS FOR MIXING BATTER FOR ALL SIZES OF CHOCOLATE BUTTER CAKES

Arrange two oven racks as close to the centre of the oven as possible with at least 7.5 centimetres/ 3 inches between them.

Preheat the oven to 350°F/180°C/gas mark 4.

In a medium bowl whisk together the cocoa and boiling water until smooth and cool to room temperature.

In another medium bowl lightly combine the eggs, ¼ of the cocoa mixture, and the vanilla.

In a large mixing bowl combine all the remaining dry ingredients and mix on low speed for 1 minute to blend. Add the butter and remaining cocoa mixture. Mix on low speed until the dry ingredients are moistened. Beat at medium speed (high speed if using a hand mixer) for 1½ minutes to aerate and develop the cake's structure. Scrape down the sides.

Gradually beat in the egg mixture in three batches, beating for 20 seconds after each addition to incorporate the ingredients and strengthen the structure. Scrape down the sides.

Scrape the batter into the prepared tins, filling about halfway, and smooth with a spatula. (For exact batter weight in each tin, refer to the chart on page 559.) Arrange the tins in the oven so that air can circulate around them. Do not allow them to touch each other or the oven walls. Bake 25 to 35 minutes for 15-centimetre/6-inch layers, 35 to 45 minutes for 23-centimetre/9-inch layers, 40 to 50 minutes for 30.5-centimetre/12-inch layers or until a tester inserted near the centre comes out clean and the cake springs back when pressed lightly in the centre. In the 15 and 23-centimetre/6 and 9-inch tins, the cakes should start to shrink from the sides only after removal from the oven. The 30.5-centimetre/12-inch layers should bake until they just start to shrink from the sides. To promote more even baking, turn the 30.5-centimetre/12-inch layers 180°

(halfway around) halfway through the baking time. Do this quickly so the oven temperature does not drop.

Allow the cakes to cool in the tins on racks for 10 minutes (20 minutes for 30.5-centimetre/12-inch layers). Loosen the sides with a small metal spatula and invert on to greased wire racks. To prevent splitting, reinvert and cool completely before wrapping airtight with clingfilm and heavy-duty foil.

Note: Do not underbake the 30.5-centimetre/12-inch layers. If you cut the tops of the cake layers to make them more level, you will notice many small holes. Do not be alarmed because they do not show up when the cake is sliced. The crumb will be fine and even.

When preparing the cake more than 24 hours ahead of serving or if extra moistness is desired, sprinkle layers with 24 fluid ounces of syrup (page 578).

HOW TO MAKE ANY SIZE ROUND BUTTER CAKE FROM 15 TO 46 CENTIMETRES/ 6 TO 18 INCHES

The chart that follows will show you how to make any size cake and how many people each layer will serve. There is often confusion regarding layers and tiers. A wedding cake is made up of tiers, each tier consisting of two equal layers sandwiched with filling.

To use the chart, you will need a calculator, a piece of paper and a pencil. Refer to the size cake you want and mark down the Rose factor which applies to two layers. For example, let's say you want to make a two-tier yellow cake consisting of a 20-centimetre/8-inch tier and a 30.5-centimetre/12-inch tier. The Rose factor for two 20-centimetre/8-inch layers is 3.5; the Rose factor for two 30.5-centimetre/12-inch layers is 7.

The 20-centimetre/8-inch size falls in baking powder level 1; the 30.5-centimetre/12-inch size, in baking powder level 3. Because each size requires a different amount of baking powder in proportion to the other ingredients, two separate batters are needed.

To make the batter for the 20-centimetre/8-inch layers, multiply each ingredient in the base formula by Rose factor 3.5. For the baking powder, refer to level 1 for yellow cake. The number will be 1½ teaspoons. Multiply this by 3.5.

To make the batter for the 30.5-centimetre/12-inch layers, multiply each ingredient in the base formula by Rose factor 7. For the baking powder, refer to level 3 for yellow cake. The number will be 1⅛ teaspoons. Multiply this by Rose factor 7. That's all there is to it. Refer to page 565 if you need a review of mixing techniques. If you bake often, you will not need this because the simple technique is the same for all the butter cakes in this book.

MASTER CHART FOR BUTTER CAKES

tin size (2 layers each 5-centimetres/ 2 inches high)	number of servings (2 layers)	Rose factor (number of times to multiply base)	batter weight for each tin	baking time at 350°F/180°C/ gas mark 4
BAKING POWDER LEVELS				
Level 1 15-centimetres/ 6 inches	20	2	356 grams/ 12.5 ounces	25–35 minutes
18-centimetres/ 7 inches	25	2.5	460 grams/ 1 pound	25–35 minutes
20-centimetres/ 8 inches	35	3.5	650 grams/ 1 pound 6.75 ounces	30–40 minutes

MASTER CHART FOR BUTTER CAKES

	tin size (2 layers each 5-centimetres/ 2 inches high)	number of servings (2 layers)	Rose factor (number of times to multiply base)	batter weight for each tin	baking time at 350°F/180°C/ gas mark 4
Level 2	23-centimetres/ 9 inches	45	4	750 grams/ 26.25 ounces	30–40 minutes
	25.5-centimetres/ 10 inches	55	5	930 grams/ 2 pounds	30–40 minutes
Level 3	28-centimetres/ 11 inches	65	6	1 kilogram 140 grams/ 2.5 pounds	35–45 minutes
	30.5-centimetres/ 12 inches	75	7	1 kilogram 330 grams/ 2 pounds 13.5 ounces	40–50 minutes
	33-centimetres/ 13 inches	100	9	1 kilogram 725 grams/ 3 pounds 12.5 ounces	40–50 minutes
	36-centimetres/ 14 inches	110	10	1 kilogram 920 grams/ 4 pounds 3.5 ounces	40–50 minutes
Level 4	38-centimetres/ 15 inches	130	12	2 kilograms 280 grams/ 5 pounds	40–50 minutes
	41-centimetres/ 16 inches	150	14	2 kilograms 700 grams/ 6 pounds	45–55 minutes
	43-centimetres/ 17 inches	175	16	3 kilograms 90 grams/ 6 pounds 12.5 ounces	45–55 minutes
Level 5	46-centimetres/ 18 inches	185	17	3 kilograms 280 grams/ 7 pounds 3.5 ounces	45–55 minutes

MASTER CHART FOR BUTTER CAKES

	tin size (2 layers each 5-centimetres/ 2 inches high)	number of servings (2 layers)	Rose factor (number of times to multiply base)	batter weight for each tin	baking time at 350°F/180°C/ gas mark 4
Level 6	33 × 23-centimetre/13 × 9-inch rectangle	40	3.5–4	1 kilogram 300 grams/2 pounds 12.5 ounces	40–50 minutes
	46 × 30.5-centimetre/18 × 12-inch rectangle	80	7–8	2 kilograms 670 grams/5 pounds 15 ounces	35–45 minutes

Tips: Large layers are more prone to underbaking than overbaking. The cake should just start to shrink from the sides of the tin when done. Be sure to use Magi–Cake Strips (pages 516 and 522) for very even layers.

A 30.5 × 5-centimetre/ 12 × 2-inch tin (Rose factor 4) serves 40 to 50 people and is a good size for large parties. The single layer will be 4.5 centimetres/1¾ inches high.

Note: Batter weight takes into account the amount clinging to the bowl and beater (about the same regardless of the batter size). Larger sizes will therefore have proportionately more batter; for example, 4 times the Rose factor will yield slightly more than double 2 times the Rose factor.

Base Formula for Butter Cakes

Serves 11 Wedding Cake portions

INGREDIENTS	WEIGHT		MEASURE
room temperature	*grams*	*pounds/ounces*	*volume*
WHITE BASE CAKE			
1½ egg whites, size 2	45 grams	1½ ounces	3 tablespoons
milk	80 grams	2¾ ounces	2½ fluid ounces
pure vanilla extract	–	–	¾ teaspoon
sifted cake flour*	100 grams	3½ ounces	1 cup
castor sugar	100 grams	3½ ounces	½ cup
baking powder	–	–	see amount for each individual cake size (page 559)
salt	–	–	¼ teaspoon
unsalted butter (must be softened)	56.75 grams	2 ounces	4 tablespoons

Total Batter Weight: 387 grams/13.5 ounces (+ baking powder)

* Cake flour *without* rising agent must be used for this cake (see page 493).

Note: The weights are in more precise units than most scales are capable of registering. When making just a few tiers, I use measuring spoons. I have given these weights for large-scale baking. When they are multiplied, the amounts are more practical to weigh and more accurate.

INGREDIENTS	WEIGHT		MEASURE
room temperature	*grams*	*pounds/ounces*	*volume*
YELLOW BASE CAKE			
2 egg yolks, size 2	37 grams	1¼ ounces	2 tablespoons + 1 teaspoon
milk	80 grams	2¾ ounces	2½ fluid ounces
pure vanilla extract	3 grams	0.11 ounce	¾ teaspoon
sifted cake flour★	100 grams	3½ ounces	1 cup
castor sugar	100 grams	3½ ounces	½ cup
baking powder	—	—	see amount for each individual cake size (page 559)
salt	1.67 grams	0.05 ounce	¼ teaspoon
unsalted butter (must be softened)	56.75 grams	2 ounces	4 tablespoons
Total Batter Weight: 379 grams/13.2 ounces (+ baking powder)			

★ Cake flour *without* raising agent must be used for this cake (page 493).

BAKING POWDER AMOUNTS FOR YELLOW AND WHITE BASE CAKES				
Level 1	15 to 20-centimetre/ 6 to 8-inch cakes	1½ teaspoons per base	7.35 grams	0.26 ounce
Level 2	23 to 25.5-centimetre/ 9 to 10-inch cakes	1⅓ teaspoons per base	6.52 grams	0.23 ounce
Level 3	28 to 36-centimetre/ 11 to 14-inch cakes	1⅛ teaspoons per base	5.51 grams	0.19 ounce
Level 4	38 to 43-centimetre/ 15 to 17-inch cakes	1 teaspoon per base	4.90 grams	0.17 ounce
Level 5	46-centimetre/ 18-inch cakes	⅞ teaspoon per base	4.25 grams	0.15 ounce
Level 6	sheet cakes	1¼ teaspoons per base	6.13 grams	0.21 ounce

UNDERSTANDING

The larger the tin size, the less baking powder is used in proportion to the other ingredients. This is because of surface tension. The larger the diameter of the tin, the slower the heat penetration and the less support the rising cake receives because the sides are farther from the centre. Baking powder weakens the cake's structure by enlarging the air spaces, so decreasing the baking powder strengthens the structure and compensates for retarded gelatinisation and the decrease in support.

Serves 11 Wedding Cake portions

INGREDIENTS	WEIGHT		MEASURE
room temperature	*grams*	*ounces*	*volume*
CHOCOLATE BASE CAKE			
unsweetened cocoa (Dutch-processed)	21 grams	¾ ounce	3 tablespoons + 1½ teaspoons (dip and sweep method)
water (boiling)	78 grams	2¾ ounces	2½ fluid ounces (use glass measuring cup)
1 egg, size 2	50 grams (weighed without shells)	1¾ ounces	3 tablespoons + ½ teaspoon
pure vanilla extract	3 grams	0.11 ounce	¾ tablespoon
sifted cake flour*	79 grams	2¾ ounces	¾ cup + 2 teaspoons
castor sugar	100 grams	3½ ounces	½ cup
baking powder	–	–	see amount for each individual cake size (below)
salt	1.67 grams	0.05 ounce	¼ teaspoon
unsalted butter (must be softened)	56.75 grams	2 ounces	4 tablespoons

Total Batter Weight: 390 grams/13.65 ounces (+ baking powder)

*Cake flour *without* raising agent must be used for this cake (page 506).

BAKING POWDER AMOUNTS FOR CHOCOLATE BASE CAKES			
Level 1 15 to 20-centimetre/ 6 to 8-inch cakes	1⅝ teaspoons per base	7.96 grams	0.28 ounce
Level 2 23 to 25.5-centimetre/ 9 to 10-inch cakes	1½ teaspoons per base	7.35 grams	0.26 ounce
Level 3 28 to 36-centimetre/ 11 to 14-inch cakes	1¼ teaspoons per base	6.13 grams	0.21 ounce
Level 4 38 to 43-centimetre/ 15 to 17-inch cakes	1⅛ teaspoons per base	5.51 grams	0.19 ounce
Level 5 46-centimetre/18-inch cakes	1 teaspoon per base	4.9 grams	0.17 ounce
Level 6 sheet cakes	1⅓ teaspoons per base	6.52 grams	0.23 ounce

SPECIAL INSTRUCTIONS FOR MIXING A SINGLE BATTER FOR VARYING SIZES OF BUTTER CAKE LAYERS

Despite the different amounts of baking powder required for different size layers, there is a way to save time and mix all the batter at once. If you bake tiered cakes often, this is a very efficient and useful technique to possess. It requires a 12-litre/2½-gallon mixer and enough oven space to bake all the layers at once or a refrigerator to hold some of the layers while the others are baking. Describing this method is rather like tying a shoelace – once you learn, it's easy to do but awkward to put into words. I assure you that once you try it you will find it easier than mixing separate batches, yet each cake will come out level and with perfect texture. It's best to calculate all the amounts before starting to mix the batter. Once you have these formulas worked out for your most common size cakes, you won't need to refer to the chart. Don't be put off by the figures; it's simple mathematics. Double-check your multiplication and the system is infallible.

1. First choose the sizes of the cake layers. Refer to the Master Chart for Butter Cakes (page 559) and write down the Rose factor for each tin size. Add these numbers and the sum will be the *total Rose factor* by which to multiply everything in the base except for the baking powder.

2. To determine the baking powder, choose the level for the largest tins you are using and multiply it by the *total Rose factor* (for all the tiers).

3. Mix the batter, and scale out

(pour into tins and weigh) only the tins in the largest level, referring to the chart for the weight of the batter in each tin. (Be sure to subtract the weight of the tins!)

4. Now go back to the chart and find the Rose factors for the remaining layers. Add and the total will be the new Rose factor.
5. Multiply this new factor by the original level of baking powder. That is how much baking powder is now remaining in the batter.
6. Now choose the level of baking powder for the next largest tins and multiply it by the new Rose factor. This is how much baking powder must now be in the batter.

  To determine the amount to add, calculate the difference (subtract the amount needed in the batter from the amount already in the batter). This is how much baking powder it is necessary to add.

7. To add baking powder: dissolve it in the smallest possible amount of ice water and stir it thoroughly into the remaining batter.
8. Scale this batter into all tins in the same level and proceed with remaining batter in the same way.

Here is an example to help you double-check the system. (I am using only the metric system for the example as too many figures would be confusing, but of course the avoirdupois system or volume works in the same way.)

EXAMPLE:

Batter for a three-tier yellow cake using 15, 23 and 30.5-centimetre/6, 9 and 12-inch tins.

1. The total Rose factor for these layers is *13*.
2. *5.51 grams* (1¹⁄₈ teaspoons) baking powder (the level for the largest tin size, 30.5 centimetres/12 inches) times the total Rose factor *13 = 71.63 grams.*
3. Put *1 kilogram + 330 grams* of batter in each 30.5-centimetre/12-inch tin.
4. The Rose factor for the remaining 23 and 15-centimetre/9 and 6-inch layers is 6 (the new Rose factor).
5. Multiply the original level of baking powder (*5.51 grams*) by 6. This equals *33 grams* (the amount of baking powder now in the batter).
6. The baking powder level for the next largest tins (23 centimetres/9 inches) is *6.52 grams* (1¹⁄₃ teaspoons). Multiply by *6* to get *39 grams*. This is how much baking powder must now be in the batter. To determine the amount to add, calculate the difference between what must now be in the batter (*39 grams*) and the amount

already in the batter (*33 grams*). The difference is *6 grams* (about 1¼ teaspoons).

7. Dissolve the *6 grams* of baking powder in the smallest possible amount of ice water and stir it thoroughly into the remaining batter.

8. Put *750 grams* of batter in each 23-centimetre/9-inch tin.

9. The Rose factor for the 15-centimetre/6-inch layers is *2* (the new Rose factor).

10. Multiply 2 by the original level of baking powder used (*5.51 grams*). This equals *11 grams* (the amount of baking powder now in the batter).

11. The baking powder level for the 15-centimetre/6-inch tins is *7.35 grams* (1½ teaspoons). Multiply by *2* to get *14.7 grams*. This is how much baking powder must now be in the batter.

    To determine the amount to add, calculate the difference between what must now be in the batter (*14.7 grams*) and the amount already in the batter (*11 grams*). The difference is *3.7 grams* (¾ teaspoon).

12. Dissolve the *3.7 grams* of baking powder in the smallest possible amount of ice water and stir it thoroughly into the remaining batter.

13. Put *356 grams* of batter in each 15-centimetre/6-inch tin. All the batter will have been used.

Note: The idea of adding baking powder to the already prepared batter may seem controversial, but here's why it works: the baking powder must be double acting and it must be evenly dispersed. This is best accomplished by dissolving it. Ice water is used to dissolve the baking powder because double-acting baking powder is activated partly by liquid and partly by heat. The cold water retards this reaction.

For the same reason, cake batter, once poured into the tin, can be refrigerated for several hours before baking and will lose no discernible volume.

Génoise Wedding Cakes

It is a delightful surprise to find airy, moist *génoise* inside a large wedding cake. Despite its delicate texture it is possible to tier a *génoise* using supporting structures (page 614). The problem is that without a 12-litre/2½-gallon mixer the *génoise* has to be made in four batches. Even with a mixer of this size it should be made in two batches because there is too much loss of volume during the time it takes to divide a single batch into six tins and then place them in the oven.

If you only have a 5-litre/8-pint mixer and you want to make a three-tiered *génoise* wedding cake for 150 people, refer to the chart below for quantities. The two 15-centimetre/6-inch layers can be prepared as one batch, the two 23-centimetre/9-inch as a second batch, and each 30.5-centimetre/12-inch layer as a separate batch. (Need I add, this is a true labour of love.)

When folding the flour into the egg and sugar mixture, be sure to incorporate all the flour particles completely or they will become encapsulated in the batter and fall to the bottom of the cake. If this should happen, wait until the cake is cool and with the tip of a sharp knife pick out the particles. (Because they are heavier than the rest of the batter, they fall to the bottom.) Once, years ago, I was lazy and left them in the cake. Everyone admired the 'unusual little nuts!'

3-Tier Génoise Classique Wedding Cake to Serve 150*

FINISHED HEIGHT: After trimming the bottom and top crusts, each layer is about 4 centimetres/1½ inches.

STORE: Without syrup, 2 days room temperature, 5 days refrigerated, 2 months frozen. After completing the cake, the flavours ripen and the moisture is more evenly distributed 1 day later.

SERVE: Room temperature or lightly chilled.

INGREDIENTS	WEIGHT		MEASURE
room temperature	*grams*	*pounds/ounces*	*volume*
FOR TWO 15 × 5-CENTIMETRE/6 × 2-INCH LAYERS AND TWO 23 × 5-CENTIMETRE/9 × 2-INCH LAYERS			
clarified *beurre noisette* (clarified browned butter, page 491)	110 grams	4 ounces	4½ fluid ounces

* Requires a 9½ litre/2½ gallon mixer.

INGREDIENTS	WEIGHT		MEASURE
room temperature	*grams*	*pounds/ounces*	*volume*
pure vanilla extract	12 grams	—	1 tablespoon
12 eggs, size 2	600 grams (weighed without shells)	1 pound 5 ounces	19 fluid ounces
castor sugar	300 grams	10½ ounces	1½ cups
sifted cake flour†	150 grams	5¼ ounces	1½ cups
cornflour	150 grams	5¼ ounces	1¼ cups (lightly spooned into cup)

FOR TWO 30.5 × 5-CENTIMETRES/12 × 2-INCH LAYERS

clarified *beurre noisette* (clarified browned butter, page 491)	130 grams	4½ ounces	5½ fluid ounces
pure vanilla extract	16 grams	—	1 tablespoon + 1 teaspoon
14 eggs, size 2	700 grams (weighed without shells)	24½ ounces	22 fluid ounces
castor sugar	350 grams	12 ounces	1¾ cups
sifted cake flour	175 grams	6 ounces	1¾ cups
cornflour	175 grams	6 ounces	1⅓ cups + 2 tablespoons (lightly spooned into cup)

SYRUP: 40 fluid ounces (page 574). Refer to the chart on page 575 for how much to apply to each layer.

Grease the tins, line the bottoms with parchment or greaseproof paper, and then grease again and flour. For very even layers use Magi-Cake Strips (pages 516 and 522).

† *Or* 150 grams/5¼ ounces/1 cup + 3 tablespoons of sifted plain flour.

INSTRUCTIONS FOR MIXING BATTER FOR ALL SIZES OF GÉNOISE CLASSIQUE

Arrange two oven racks as close to the centre of the oven as possible with at least 7.5 centimetres/ 3 inches between them.

Preheat oven to 350°F/180°C/gas mark 4.

Warm the *beurre noisette* until almost hot (110° to 120°F/43° to 49°C). Add the vanilla and keep warm.

In a large mixing bowl set over a pan of simmering water place the eggs and sugar and heat until just lukewarm, stirring constantly. (The eggs may also be heated by placing them *still in their shells* in a large mixing bowl in an oven with a pilot light for 3 hours or overnight.)

Using the whisk beater, beat on high speed for 5 minutes or until triple in volume.

Meanwhile, sift together the flour and cornflour.

Transfer the egg mixture to a bowl large enough to fold in the other ingredients. Remove 3 cups of the egg mixture and thoroughly whisk it into the *beurre noisette*. (If making the batter in several batches, decrease amount of egg mixture removed accordingly. For example, if making batter for only two 23-centimetre/9-inch layers, reserve only 2 scant cups.)

Sift half the flour mixture over the remaining egg mixture, folding gently but rapidly with a large balloon whisk or slotted skimmer until the flour has almost disappeared. Repeat with remaining flour mixture until all the flour has entirely disappeared. Fold in the butter mixture only until incorporated.

Pour immediately into the tins (they will be at least two thirds full) and bake immediately 20 to 35 minutes for 15 and 23-centimetre/ 6 and 9-inch layers and 30 to 40 minutes for 30.5-centimetre/12-inch layers or until the cake is golden brown and starts to shrink slightly from the sides of the tin. Avoid opening the oven door before the minimum time is over or the cake may fall. Test towards the end of baking by opening the oven door slightly and, if at a quick glance it does not appear done, close the door at once and check again in 5 minutes.

Loosen the sides with a small metal spatula and turn out at once on to lightly greased racks. Reinvert to cool. Remove the crust when ready to complete the cake and sprinkle the syrup evenly on all layers (page 409).

Note: 30.5-centimetre/12-inches is the largest round *génoise* that can be made without loss in quality of texture. A larger tin does not offer enough support.

3-Tier Génoise au Chocolat Wedding Cake to Serve 150*

FINISHED HEIGHT: After trimming the bottom and top crusts, each layer is about 4 centimetres/1½ inches.

STORE: Without syrup, 2 days room temperature, 5 days

refrigerated, 2 months frozen. After completing the cake, the flavours ripen and the moisture is more evenly distributed 1 day later.

SERVE: Room temperature or lightly chilled.

INGREDIENTS	WEIGHT		MEASURE
room temperature	*grams*	*pounds/ounces*	*volume*
FOR TWO 15 × 5-CENTIMETRE/6 × 2-INCH LAYERS AND TWO 23 × 5-CENTIMETRE/9 × 2-INCH LAYERS			
clarified *beurre noisette* (clarified browned butter, page 491)	110 grams	4 ounces	4 fluid ounces + 1 tablespoon
unsweetened cocoa (preferably Dutch-processed)	87 grams	3 ounces	¾ cup + 3 tablespoons (lightly spooned into cup)
water (boiling)	177 grams	6¼ ounces	6 fluid ounces
pure vanilla extract	12 grams	–	1 tablespoon
15 eggs, size 2	750 grams (weighed without shells)	1 pound 10¼ ounces	24 fluid ounces
castor sugar	300 grams	10½ ounces	1½ cups
sifted cake flour†	213 grams	7½ ounces	2 cups + 2 tablespoons

* Requires a 9½ litre/2½-gallon mixer.
† Or 213 grams/7½ ounces/1¾ cups of sifted plain flour.

INGREDIENTS	WEIGHT		MEASURE
room temperature	*grams*	*pounds/ounces*	*volume*
FOR TWO 30.5 × 5-CENTIMETRE/12 ×2-INCH LAYERS			
clarified *beurre noisette* (clarified browned butter, page 419)	130 grams	4¹/₂ ounces	5¹/₄ fluid ounces
unsweetened cocoa (Dutch-processed)	100 grams	3¹/₂ ounces	1 cup + 1 tablespoon (lightly spooned into cup)
water	236 grams	8¹/₄ ounces	8 fluid ounces
pure vanilla extract	16 grams	—	1 tablespoon + 1 teaspoon
18 eggs, size 2	900 grams (weighed without shells)	2 pounds	28 fluid ounces
castor sugar	350 grams	12¹/₄ ounces	1³/₄ cups
sifted cake flour★	250 grams	8³/₄ ounces	2¹/₂ cups

SYRUP: 40 fluid ounces (page 574). Refer to the chart on page 575 for how much to brush on each layer.

★ Cake flour *without* rising agent must be used for this cake (see page 493).

Grease the tins, line the bottoms with parchment or greaseproof paper, and then grease again and flour. For very even layers use Magi-Cake Strips (pages 516 and 522).

INSTRUCTIONS FOR MIXING BATTER FOR ALL SIZES OF GÉNOISE AU CHOCOLAT

Arrange two oven racks as close to the centre of the oven as possible with at least 7.5 centimetres/ 3 inches between them.

Preheat the oven to 350°F/180°C/gas mark 4.

Warm the *beurre noisette* until almost hot (110° to 120°F/43° to 49°C). Keep warm.

In a medium bowl place the cocoa and boiling water and whisk together until the cocoa is completely dissolved. Stir in the vanilla and set aside, leaving the whisk in the bowl. Cover with clingfilm to prevent drying.

In a large mixing bowl set over a pan of simmering water place the eggs and sugar and heat until just lukewarm, stirring constantly. (The eggs may also be heated by placing them *still in their shells* in a large mixing bowl in an oven with a pilot light for 3 hours or overnight.)

Using the whisk beater, beat on high speed for 5 minutes or until triple in volume. Transfer the egg mixture to a bowl large enough to fold in the other ingredients.

Remove 3 cups of the egg mixture and whisk it into the cocoa mixture until smooth. (If making batter in several batches, decrease the amount of egg mixture removed accordingly. For example, if making batter for only two 23-centimetre/9-inch layers, reserve only 2 cups.)

Sift the flour over the remaining egg mixture, folding gently but rapidly with a slotted skimmer or spatula until all flour has entirely disappeared. Fold in the cocoa mixture until almost evenly incorporated. Add the *beurre noisette*

in two batches, folding with a large balloon whisk or rubber spatula★ just until evenly incorporated. Pour immediately into the tins (they will be at least three-quarters full) and bake 25 to 35 minutes for 15 and 23-centimetre/6 and 9-inch layers and 35 to 45 minutes for 30.5-centimetre/12-inch layers or until the cake starts to shrink from the sides of the tin. Avoid opening the oven door before the minimum time is over or the cake may fall. Test towards the end of baking by opening the oven door slightly and, if at a quick glance it does not appear done, close the door at once and check again in 5 minutes.

Loosen the sides with a spatula and turn out at once on to lightly greased racks. Reinvert to cool. Remove the crust when ready to complete the cake and sprinkle the syrup evenly on all layers (page 409).

Note: 30.5 centimetres/12 inches is the largest *génoise* that can be made without loss in quality of texture. A larger tin does not offer enough support.

★Fingers work well to feel for lumps of flour. They can be dissolved by pressing between thumb and forefinger.

Syrup for 3-Tier Génoise to Serve 150

Makes 40 fluid ounces

STORE: 1 month refrigerated in an airtight container.

INGREDIENTS	WEIGHT		MEASURE
room temperature	*grams*	*pounds/ounces*	*volume*
sugar	375 grams	13 ounces	1¾ cups + 2 tablespoons
water	787 grams	1 pound 11¾ ounces	26½ fluid ounces
liqueur	240 grams	8½ ounces	8 fluid ounces

In a 2-litre/3½-pint saucepan with a tight-fitting lid combine the sugar and water and bring to a rolling boil, stirring constantly. Cover immediately, remove from the heat and cool completely. Transfer to a liquid measuring jug and stir in the liqueur. If syrup has evaporated slightly, add enough water to equal 40 fluid ounces syrup.

HOW TO MAKE A 15 TO 30.5-CENTIMETRE/6 TO 12-INCH ROUND GÉNOISE

The chart that follows will show you how to make any size *génoise* from 15 to 30.5 centimetres/6 to 12 inches plus a 46-centimetre/18-inch sheet cake. I find that in a round *génoise* 30.5 centimetres/12 inches is the largest size possible without loss of quality in texture. Larger tins do not offer adequate support. This chart will also tell you how many people each layer will serve and how much syrup is needed for each layer.

To use the chart, you will need a calculator, a piece of paper and a pencil. Refer to the size cake you want and mark down the Rose factor which applies to 2 layers. Turn to the Classique Base or Au Chocolat Base on page 577 or 578 and multiply each ingredient by the Rose factor.* The figures on the base chart may appear awkward

*If using volume instead of weight, keep in mind that 3 teaspoons = 1 tablespoon and 16 tablespoons = 1 cup.

(such as 1.8 teaspoons) but, when multiplied by the Rose factor, will yield more reasonable amounts. If, for example, after multiplying, you end up with 4.8 teaspoons, simply round off to the nearest convenient unit of measure, 4³/₄ teaspoons. These tables are precise to enable you to have more leeway in rounding off the figures. Charts sometimes have a way of looking ominous and restricting, but there is a range of acceptable deviation and a few grams more or less will not be discernible.

MASTER CHART FOR GÉNOISE CLASSIQUE

tin size (2 layers each 5 centimetres/2 inches high)	number of servings (2 layers)	Rose factor (number of times to multiply base)	baking time at 350°F/180°C/gas mark 4	syrup needed for 2 layers
15 centimetres/ 6 inches	20	4	20–25 minutes	5¹/₄ fluid ounces
18 centimetres/ 7 inches	25	5	20–25 minutes	8 fluid ounces
20 centimetres/ 8 inches	35	7	25–35 minutes	10¹/₂ fluid ounces
23 centimetres/ 9 inches	45	8	25–35 minutes	12 fluid ounces
25.5 centimetres/ 10 inches	55	11	25–30 minutes	16 fluid ounces
28 centimetres/ 11 inches	65	13	25–30 minutes	20 fluid ounces
30.5 centimetres/ 12 inches	75	14	30–35 minutes	22 fluid ounces
33 × 23-centimetre/ 13 × 9-inch rectangle	45	8	20–30 minutes	12 fluid ounces
46 × 30.5-centimetre/18 × 12-inch rectangle	75	14–16	30–40 minutes	22 to 24 fluid ounces

Tips: Large layers are more prone to underbaking than overbaking. The cake should just start to shrink from the sides of the tin when done. Be sure to use Magi-Cake strips (pages 4 and 522) for even layers.

Tins can be filled up to 1 centimetre/½ inch from the top.

One 30.5 × 5-centimetre/ 12 × 2-inch layer (Rose factor 7) serves 40 to 50 people and is a good size for large parties. (Please check above table for two 30.5-centimetre/12-inch layers and divide in half to make one layer).

MASTER CHART FOR GÉNOISE AU CHOCOLAT

tin size (2 layers each 5 centimetres/2 inches high	number of servings (2 layers)	Rose factor (number of times to multiply base)	baking time at 350°F/180°C/gas mark 4	syrup needed for 2 layers
15 centimetres/ 6 inches	20	5	30–35 minutes	5¼ fluid ounces
18 centimetres/ 7 inches	25	7	30–35 minutes	8 fluid ounces
20 centimetres/ 8 inches	35	9	30–35 minutes	10½ fluid ounces
23 centimetres/ 9 inches	45	10	30–35 minutes	12 fluid ounces
25.5 centimetres/ 10 inches	55	14	35–40 minutes	16 fluid ounces
28 centimetres/ 11 inches	65	16	35–40 minutes	20 fluid ounces
30.5 centimetres/ 12 inches	76	18	40–45 minutes	22 fluid ounces
33 × 23-centimetre/ 13 × 9 inch rectangle	45	10	30–40 minutes	12 fluid ounces
46 × 30.5-centimetre/18 × 12-inch rectangle	75	18–20	40–50 minutes	22 to 24 fluid ounces

Tips: Chocolate *génoise* layers are more prone to underbaking than overbaking and will fall slightly if not baked long enough. The cake should start to shrink from the sides of the tin when done. Be sure to use Magi-Cake Strips for even layers (pages 516 and 522).

Tins can be filled up to ½ inch from top.

A 30.5 × 5-centimetre/ 12 × 2-inch layer (Rose factor 8.75) serves 40 to 50 people and is a good size for large parties. Multiply everything in the base by 8.75, but it's fine to use 9 large eggs.

Base Formulas for Génoise

Serves 5 Wedding Cake portions

INGREDIENTS	WEIGHT		MEASURE
room temperature	*grams*	*pounds/ounces*	*volume*
GÉNOISE CLASSIQUE BASE			
clarified *beurre noisette* (clarified browned butter, page 491)	9 grams	0.32 ounce	¾ tablespoon
pure vanilla extract	1 gram	—	¼ teaspoon
1 egg, size 2	50 grams (weighed without shell)	1¾ ounces	3 tablespoons + ½ teaspoon
castor sugar	25 grams	0.88 ounce	2 tablespoons
sifted cake flour*	12.5 grams	0.44 ounce	2 tablespoons
cornflour	12.5 grams	0.44 ounce	1 tablespoon + 2 teaspoons

* Or 12.5 grams/.44 ounce/1 tablespoon + 2 teaspoons sifted plain flour.

INGREDIENTS	WEIGHT		MEASURE
room temperature	*grams*	*pounds/ounces*	*volume*
GÉNOISE AU CHOCOLAT BASE			
clarified *beurre noisette* (clarified browned butter, page 491)	7 grams	¼ ounce	1.8 teaspoons
unsweetened cocoa (Dutch-processed)	5.8 grams	0.2 ounce	1 tablespoon (lightly spooned into cup)
water	12 grams	0.42 ounce	2.4 teaspoons
pure vanilla extract	0.8 grams	—	0.2 teaspoon
1 egg, size 2	50 grams (weighed without shells)	1¾ ounces	3 tablespoons + ½ teaspoon
castor sugar	20 grams	0.7 ounce	1.6 tablespoons
sifted cake flour	14.2 grams	½ ounce	2.3 tablespoons

† Or 14.2 grams/½ ounce/1 tablespoon + 2½ teaspoons sifted plain flour.

Base Formula for 1 Cup Syrup

Makes 8 fluid ounces

STORE: 1 month refrigerated in an airtight container.

In a saucepan with a tight-fitting lid combine the sugar and water and bring to a rolling boil, stirring constantly. Cover immediately, remove from the heat and cool completely. Transfer to a liquid measuring jug and stir in the liqueur. If the syrup has evaporated slightly, add enough water to equal

8 fluid ounces syrup. (If multiplying this base for a larger quantity, add water to equal the appropriate amount.)

INGREDIENTS	WEIGHT		MEASURE
room temperature	*grams*	*pounds/ounces*	*volume*
castor sugar	75 grams	2½ ounces	6 tablespoons
water	156 grams	5½ ounces	5½ fluid ounces
liqueur of your choice	40 grams	1½ ounces	3 tablespoons

Wedding Cheesecakes

Isn't it almost unbelievable that a creamy 30.5-centimetre/12-inch cheesecake will support two tiers of cake on top of it? Actually, I wasn't sure that it would, so the first time I tried it involved a certain amount of risk. I remember my husband saying (as he drove the cake over bumpy roads to Connecticut, trying not to hear my panicked gasps): 'What are you worried about? You've never had a cake collapse!' And my answer: 'This could be the first time! To my knowledge no one has ever tiered a cheesecake before, and it may be for a good reason.'

Completed the night before, the bottom of the 30.5-centimetre/ 12-inch tier looked like it had widened ever so slightly and tiny cracks had developed under the surrounding ribbon. None the less, the cake stayed in perfect shape throughout the 2-hour drive, and 2-hour outdoor photo session, and then an additional 2-hour wait at room temperature before serving.

Part of what supports the creamy custard filling are plastic straws and cardboard rounds between the tiers. Delicious White Chocolate Cream Cheese Icing (page 603) encases each tier and offers additional support.

If you like, you can bake two sheets of Biscuit Roulade (page 157), preferably the almond version, and cut circles to serve as bases for each tier. (The 30.5-centimetre/12-inch round needs to be patched a bit as the tin is only 46 × 28 centimetres/ 18 × 11 inches). If using the *biscuit*, you can eliminate the cornflour in the cheesecake batter because the *biscuit* will absorb any excess moisture. Attach the *biscuit* to the cardboard rounds with a little buttercream. It is also fine to turn out the cheesecake layers directly on to cardboard rounds without using any base as long as the rounds are waterproofed with a thin layer of buttercream.

The wedding cheesecake consists of a single 7.5-centimetre/3-inch-deep layer per tier. I am giving the formula for 30.5, 23 and 15-centimetre/12, 9 and 6-inch layers as well as a slightly smaller formula suitable for a 46 × 30.5 × 5-centimetre/18 × 12 × 2-inch sheet cake, which is a very convenient size for a large party. I once covered a 46-centimetre/18-inch sheet cheesecake in alabaster rolled fondant for a bar mitzvah and wrote the Ten Commandments in 14-carat gold Hebrew calligraphy on top. The border consisted of bright blue forget-me-nots with tiny silver dragées in the centres and entwined with white royal icing scrollwork (the colours of the flag of Israel). It was the most beautiful cake I ever made.

I was so happy decorating it that I started to sing long-forgotten Hebrew songs from my childhood. I had pleasant thoughts of my great-grandfather, who was a rabbi in Russia, and of his wife after whom I was named. I even found a complete miniature replica of a Torah and located the particular section appropriate for the day of the year that the bar mitzvah boy would read. I painted the plastic posts with gold paint and set the Torah between the two illuminated tabloids of the Ten Command-ments. (The owner of the paint shop refused payment because it was for a Torah, even though I told him it was going on a cake. He said he wanted to support Judaism in whatever form he found it. I was very touched.)

I still remember my surprise and bewilderment when the bar mitzvah mother told me hesitatingly that she had expected something – well – a little more elaborate. Plumes I suppose.

Note: Don't forget to arrange for refrigeration space!

3-Tier Wedding Cheesecake to Serve 150*

TINS: 30.5, 23 and 15-centimetre/ 12, 9 and 6-inch cake tins, each 7.5 centimetres/3 inches deep, plus three larger tins to serve as water baths. (The sides of the water bath tins must be 7.5 centimetres/ 3 inches or under or baking will be slowed.) Grease the baking tins and line the bottoms with parchment or greaseproof paper.

INGREDIENTS	WEIGHT		MEASURE
room temperature	*grams*	*pounds/ounces*	*volume*
cream cheese	2 kilograms 268 grams	5 pounds	10 (8-ounce) packages
castor sugar	1 kilogram	2 pounds 3 ounces	5 cups
cornflour	40 grams	1½ ounces	⅓ cup
15 eggs, size 2	750 grams (weighed without shells)	26¼ ounces	24 fluid ounces
lemon juice, freshly squeezed	188 grams	6½ ounces	6 fluid ounces
pure vanilla extract	30 grams	1 ounce	2½ tablespoons
salt	8 grams	—	1¼ teaspoon
sour cream	3 kilograms 630 grams	8 pounds	15 cups (3 quarts + 3 cups)
optional: Apricot Swirl Filling (page 584)	1 kilogram 328 grams	2 pounds 15 ounces	4 cups

* Requires a 5-litre/8-pint mixer large enough to handle the batter in two batches. It can also be prepared in several batches in a food processor (page 547).

Party Cheesecake
to Serve 100*

TINS: 46 × 30.5 × 5-centimetre/ 18 × 12 × 2-inch cake tin greased and bottom lined with parchment or greaseproof paper. If possible, have ready a larger tin, such as a full size sheet tin, to serve as water bath. (The sides of the water bath tin must be 5 centimetres/2 inches or less.)

TO UNMOULD: Have ready sturdy corrugated glassine-coated cardboards the size of the cake layers or 1 centimetre/½ inch larger if planning to ice (waterproofed with a thin layer of buttercream), to serve as a base for each layer.

Run a thin metal spatula between the sides of each cake and the tin, making sure to press well against the sides of the tin, and place the tin on heated burner for 10 to 20 seconds, moving it back and forth. Invert on to a cardboard prepared round and remove the parchment. If the cake does not release, return to the hot burner for a few more seconds.

Refrigerate until ready to frost (see White Chocolate Cream Cheese Icing, page 603).

STORE: 3 days refrigerated before icing or decorating; 24 hours refrigerated after decorating. Texture suffers on freezing.

SERVE: Lightly chilled.

INSTRUCTIONS FOR MIXING BATTER FOR ALL SIZES OF CHEESECAKE

Arrange oven racks as close to the centre of the oven as possible with at least 10 centimetres/4 inches between them.

Preheat the oven to 350°F/180°C/gas mark 4.

In a mixing bowl beat the cream cheese and sugar, preferably with flat beater, until very smooth (about 3 minutes). Beat in the cornflour. Beat in the eggs, one at a time, beating after each addition until smooth and scraping down the sides of the bowl. Add the lemon juice, vanilla and salt, and beat until incorporated. Beat in the sour cream just until blended.

Pour the filling into the prepared tin(s). (If adding apricot filling, see page 584.) It will come close to the top(s). Set the tin(s) in the larger tin(s) and fill each surrounding tin with at least 2.5 centimetres/1 inch hot water. Bake in the preheated

*Requires 5-litre/8-pint mixer large enough to handle the batter in two batches. It can also be prepared in several batches in a food processor (page 547).

INGREDIENTS	WEIGHT		MEASURE
room temperature	*grams*	*pounds/ounces*	*volume*
cream cheese	1 kilogram 814 grams	4 pounds	8 (8-ounce) packets
castor sugar	800 grams	1 pound 12 ounces	4 cups
cornflour	30 grams	1 ounce	¼ cup
12 eggs, size 2	600 grams	1 pound 5 ounces	19 fluid ounces
lemon juice, freshly squeezed	125 grams	4½ ounces	4 fluid ounces
pure vanilla extract	24 grams	—	2 tablespoons
salt	7 grams	—	1 teaspoon
sour cream	2 kilograms 904 grams	6 pounds 6 ounces	12 cups (3 quarts)
optional: Apricot Swirl Filling (page 584)	1 kilogram 79 grams	2 pounds 6 ounces	3¼ cups

oven for 50 minutes. Turn off the oven and allow the cakes to cool in the oven without opening the door for 1 hour. Remove to rack(s) and cool to room temperature (1 hour for the smaller layers, longer for the 30.5-centimetre/12-inch layer and sheet cake). Cover with clingfilm and refrigerate overnight.

Apricot Swirl Filling for Cheesecake

Makes about 1 kilogram 240 grams/2³/₄ pounds/4 cups

STORE: 5 days refrigerated, 1 year frozen.

INGREDIENTS	WEIGHT		MEASURE
room temperature	*grams*	*pounds/ounces*	*volume*
dried California apricots	794 grams	1³/₄ pounds	2¹/₂ cups, packed
water	945 grams	2 pounds	1 litre
lemon juice, freshly squeezed	47 grams	1¹/₂ ounces	3 tablespoons
castor sugar	200 grams	7 ounces	1 cup

In a small saucepan place the apricots and water and allow to stand, covered, for 2 hours. Simmer for 20 minutes over very low heat, tightly covered, or until the apricots are soft. Purée along with any remaining liquid in a food processor or blender. Press through a food mill or fine strainer (page 519). You should have 930 grams to 1 kilogram 240 grams/2 to 2³/₄ pounds/3 to 4 cups purée. Use only up to 1 kilogram/2 pounds 4 ounces/3¹/₄ cups and store the remainder. Stir in the lemon juice and sugar. Store in an airtight container until ready to make the cheesecake batter.

To use the filling, fill each of the prepared tins one-third full with batter. Drizzle the filling over the batter and swirl with a small metal spatula. Pour in more batter to a capacity of two-thirds and repeat with more filling. Top with the remaining batter and filling and swirl again. Use a total of 1 kilogram/2 pounds 4 ounces/3¹/₄ cups for sheet cake, 775 grams/1 pound 4 ounces/2¹/₂ cups filling for the 30.5-centimetre/12-inch tin, 310 grams/10 ounces/1 cup for the 23-centimetre/9-inch tin, and 155 grams/5 ounces/¹/₂ cup for the 15-centimetre/6-inch tin. (To bake, see page 583.)

Tip: Premium-quality California apricots, found in speciality and health-food stores, are brighter orange and have a superior flavour to most packaged varieties.

Party-Perfect Pound Cake

Serves 25 to 30

This is the large-scale version of Perfect Pound Cake (page 9). Baked in a large Bundt tin, it has a beautiful golden crust and impressive shape. Although firmer than the small version, it is still meltingly tender and buttery. The plain pound cake is excellent but, if you like, try one of the variations on pages 11 and 12. (You will need to multiply any variation ingredients by 3½)

TINS: One 12-cup/3-litre Bundt tin or 9-cup/2⅛-litre Kugelhupf, greased and floured.

STORE: Airtight: 3 days room temperature, 1 week refrigerated, 2 months frozen.

FINISHED HEIGHT: 7.5 centimetres/3 inches.

SERVE: Room temperature.

INGREDIENTS	WEIGHT		MEASURE
room temperature	*grams*	*pounds/ounces*	*volume*
milk	90 grams	3 ounces	3 fluid ounces
6 eggs, size 2	300 grams (weighed without shells)	10½ ounces	9½ fluid ounces
pure vanilla extract	12 grams	—	1 tablespoon
sifted cake flour★	300 grams	10½ ounces	3 cups
castor sugar	300 grams	10½ ounces	1½ cups
baking powder	5 grams	—	1 teaspoon
salt	5 grams	—	¾ teaspoon
unsalted butter (must be softened)	383 grams	13½ ounces	27 tablespoons (about 1⅔ cups)

★ Cake flour *without* raising agent must be used for this cake (page 493).

Preheat the oven to 350°F/180°C/gas mark 4.

In a medium bowl combine milk, eggs and vanilla, and beat lightly.

In a large mixing bowl combine the dry ingredients and mix on low speed for 1 minute to blend.

Add the butter and half the egg mixture. Mix on low speed until dry ingredients are moistened. Beat at medium speed (high speed if using a hand mixer) for 1 minute to aerate and develop the cake's structure.

Scrape down the sides. Gradually beat in the remaining egg mixture in two batches, beating for 20 seconds after each addition to incorporate the ingredients and strengthen the structure. Scrape down the sides.

Scrape the batter into the prepared tin and smooth with a spatula. The batter will be 4 centimetres/1½ inches from the top.

Bake for 45 to 50 minutes or until a wire cake tester inserted in the centre comes out clean and the cake springs back when pressed lightly in the centre and is just starting to shrink from the sides of the tin. Cool completely before wrapping airtight.

Note: Although a 12-cup/3-litre Bundt tin could accommodate an 8-egg formula (1⅓ times the size of the 6-egg formula), I find that the texture is not as tender.

If you are lucky enough to possess a cast-aluminium unlined Bundt tin, your pound cake will have the most beautiful crust. Avoid lighter weight Bundt tins as they do not bake as evenly and darken the crust.

As a point of interest, while developing this large-scale recipe, I discovered that contrary to a layer cake, extra baking powder makes a pound cake more chewy rather than more tender.

Large-scale Buttercreams for Wedding Cakes

The biggest dilemma when making a wedding or special occasion cake is how much icing and filling will be necessary. In a bakery this is never a problem because any excess icing from one cake can easily be used for the next. A small caterer or home baker does not usually know when the next cake will be, particularly one which will require that particular icing.

I have kept records over the years as to how much of which kind of icing I use for different size cakes. The chart on the following page reflects the results. I have given slightly generous amounts because it is better to have too much than to have to make a new batch at the last minute. And it is difficult to gauge exactly how much icing each person will use.

The amounts on the chart assume that the filling and icing will be applied no less than 3 millimetres/⅛ inch thick and no more than 5 millimetres/¼ inch thick. A layer cake usually shrinks so that it is 1 centimetre/½ inch smaller in diameter than the tin. Cardboard cake rounds are made the same size as standard cake tins. This means that there is 5 millimetres/¼ inch between the sides of the cardboard and the sides of the cake. It is easy to use the side of the board as a guide, applying 5 millimetres/¼ inch of icing all around. It isn't necessary to use this method or as much icing around the sides of a square or rectangular cake, because it is simpler to make icing level when working with a straight line instead of a curve.

The chart also suggests amounts of buttercream for decorating. I prefer piped buttercream decorations that are small and elegant for both aesthetic and gustatory reasons, but, if your preference is for a more opulent style be sure to make some extra buttercream.

The *génoise* in the master cake section are all 4 centimetres/ 1½ inches high and the layer cakes are 4.5 to 5 centimetres/1¾ to 2 inches high. This means that each tier of two layers will be about 9.5 to 12 centimetres/3¾ to 4¾ inches high when iced (the height of the layers plus the cardboard, filling and icing). This depends, of course, on the amount of icing used.

Following the chart are six buttercream recipes suitable for wedding or special occasion cakes, in quantities sufficient to fill, ice and decorate a three-tiered cake for 150 people.

Note: A 5-litre/8-pint mixer can handle up to 16 cups buttercream.

MASTER CHART FOR ICING QUANTITIES

cake size (2 layers)	amount needed between the layers	amount needed for top	amount needed for sides	total amount needed
15 centimetres/ 6 inches	⅓ cup/80 ml	⅓ cup/80 ml	1 cup/240 ml	1¾ cups/400 ml
18 centimetres/ 7 inches	⅔ cup/150 ml	⅔ cup/150 ml	1¼ cups/300 ml	2½ cups/600 ml
20 centimetres/ 8 inches	¾ cup/175 ml	¾ cup/175 ml	1½ cups/350 ml	3 cups/700 ml
23 centimetres/ 9 inches	1 cup/240 ml	1 cup/240 ml	1⅔ cups/400 ml	3⅔ cups/880 ml
25.5 centimetres/ 10 inches	1¼ cups/300 ml	1¼ cups/300 ml	1¾ cups/415 ml	4¼ cups/1 litre + 15 ml
28 centimetres/ 11 inches	1½ cups/355 ml	1½ cups/355 ml	2 cups/475 ml	5 cups/1 litre 100 ml
30.5 centimetres/ 12 inches	1¾ cups/415 ml	1¾ cups/415 ml	2 cups/475 ml	5½ cups/1 litre 220 ml
33 centimetres/ 13 inches	2 cups/475 ml	2 cups/475 ml	2⅓ cups/550 ml	6⅓ cups/1½ litres
35.5 centimetres/ 14 inches	2½ cups/600 ml	2½ cups/600 ml	2½ cups/600 ml	7½ cups/1 litre + 800 ml

MASTER CHART FOR ICING QUANTITIES

cake size (2 layers)	amount needed between the layers	amount needed for top	amount needed for sides	total amount needed
18 centimetres/ 5 inches	2¾ cups/650 ml	2¾ cups/650 ml	2⅔ cups/630 ml	8 cups/1 litre + 930 ml
20 centimetres/ 6 inches	3¼ cups/770 ml	3¼ cups/770 ml	3 cups/710 ml	9½ cups/2 litres + 250 ml
23 centimetres/ 7 inches	3⅔ cups/865 ml	3⅔ cups/865 ml	3⅓ cups/790 ml	10⅔ cups/2 litres + 520 ml
26 centimetres/ 8 inches	4 cups/950 ml	4 cups/950 ml	4 cups/950 ml	12 cups/2 litres + 840 ml
1 layer 33 × 23 × 4.5 centimetres/ 13 × 9 × 1¾ inches	1¼ cups/300 ml	2 cups/475 ml	1¼ cups/300 ml	4½ cups/1 litre + 75 ml
46 × 30.5 × 4.5 centimetres/18 × 12 × 1¾ inches	—	4 cups/950 ml	2 cups/475 ml	6 cups/1 litre + 425 ml

EXTRA BUTTERCREAM FOR DECORATING

For three graduated tiers with the bottom tier no larger than 30.5 centimetres/12 inches, add 1 to cups buttercream.

For three graduated tiers with the bottom tier larger than 37.5 centimetres/15 inches, add 3 cups buttercream.

Mousseline Buttercream for a 3-Tier Cake to Serve 150

Makes 2 kilograms 144 grams/4³/₄ pounds/11 cups (without optional additions)

This buttercream is very light, smooth and incredibly easy to use for piped decorations. It is soft enough for beautiful shell borders yet strong enough to pipe roses. Liqueur gently perfumes the buttercream, and, if it's tinted, it also enhances the colour. Mandarine, for example, lends the palest aura of apricot. If the wedding cake requires a whiter look, use a clear liqueur.

This is a thrilling buttercream to prepare because it starts off looking thin and lumpy and, about three-quarters of the way through, starts to emulsify into a luxurious cream.

A word of caution: if the butter is too soft or the room too hot, what could have been a satin-smooth cream breaks down into a grainy hopeless puddle. Once this buttercream is made, however, it holds up better than any other.

STORE: 2 days room temperature, 10 days refrigerated, 8 months frozen. Allow buttercream to come to room temperature before rebeating or it will break down irretrievably.

POINTERS FOR SUCCESS: Correct butter temperature is crucial. If you suspect that the butter was too warm (or the kitchen is very hot) and the buttercream starts thinning out and curdling, check the temperature. If the mixture does not feel cool, refrigerate it until it reaches 65° to 70°F/18° to 21°C or until cool to the touch. If by chance you have used butter straight from the refrigerator and the mixture feels ice-cold, suspend the bowl over a pan of simmering water (don't let it touch the water) and heat very briefly, stirring vigorously when the mixture starts to melt slightly at the edges. Dip the bottom of the bowl in a larger bowl of ice water for a few seconds to cool it. Remove and beat by hand until smooth.

In a mixing bowl beat the butter until smooth and creamy and set aside in a cool place.

Have ready a ¹/₂-litre/1-pint/ 2-cup heatproof glass measure near the range.

In a medium-size heavy saucepan (preferably with a non-stick lining) stir together 400 grams/14 ounces/ 2 cups sugar and the water. Heat,

INGREDIENTS	WEIGHT		MEASURE
room temperature	*grams*	*pounds/ounces*	*volume*
unsalted butter, softened but cool (65°F/18°C)	1 kilogram 134 grams	2½ pounds	5 cups
castor sugar	500 grams	17½ ounces	2½ cups
water	177 grams	6¼ ounces	6 fluid ounces
12 egg whites, size 2	360 grams	12½ ounces	12 fluid ounces
cream of tartar	12 grams	—	1½ teaspoons
liqueur such as Grand Marnier *or* an eau-de-vie	240 grams	8½ ounces	8 fluid ounces
optional additions: see below			

stirring constantly, until the sugar dissolves and the syrup is bubbling. Stop stirring and turn down the heat to the lowest setting. (If using an electric stove remove from the heat.)

In another mixing bowl beat the egg whites until foamy, add the cream of tartar, and beat until soft peaks form when the beater is raised. Gradually beat in the remaining 100 grams/3½ ounces/½ cup sugar until stiff peaks form when the beater is raised slowly.

Increase the heat and boil the syrup until a thermometer registers 248° to 250°F/120° to 121°C (firm-ball stage). Immediately pour into the glass measure to stop the cooking.

Beat the syrup into the whites in a steady stream. Do not allow the syrup to fall on the beaters or it will spin on to the sides of the bowl. Start by pouring a small amount of the syrup on to the whites with the mixer turned off. Beat at high speed for 5 seconds. Stop the mixer and add a larger amount of syrup. Beat for 5 seconds. Continue with the remaining syrup. For the last addition, use a rubber scraper to remove the syrup clinging to the glass measure. Beat at low speed for 2 minutes or until cool.

Beat in the butter at medium speed, 1 tablespoon at a time. At first the mixture will seem thin but will thicken beautifully by the time all the butter is added. If at any time it looks curdled, raise the speed slightly and beat until smooth before continuing to add more butter.

Lower the speed slightly and gradually drizzle in the liqueur.

Rebeat lightly from time to time to maintain silky texture. Buttercream becomes spongy on standing.

OPTIONAL ADDITIONS

These flavourful additions (except for the white chocolate) will also tint the buttercream. If you want the outside of the cake to be white, consider using one of these variations for the filling such as the Lemon Curd Mousseline in the Dotted Swiss Dream (page 257).

CHOCOLATE MOUSSELINE:

Beat in 336 grams/12 ounces melted and cooled extra bittersweet or bittersweet chocolate.

WHITE CHOCOLATE MOUSSELINE:

Beat in 336 grams/12 ounces melted white chocolate, preferably Tobler Narcisse.

FRUIT MOUSSELINE:

Add up to 456 grams/1 pound/2 cups of lightly sweetened Raspberry or 480 grams/1 full pound/2 cups Strawberry Purée (page 388) or 600 grams/1 pound 5 ounces/2 cups Orange, Passion, Lemon or Lime Curd (pages 389 to 392).

Neoclassic Buttercream for a 3-Tier Cake to Serve 150

Makes 1 kilogram 600 grams/3½ pounds/8 cups (without optional additions)

This pale yellow buttercream is perfect both as a creamy filling and as a silky undercoat for Crème Ivoire Deluxe in Pistachio and Rose Wedding Cake. If you would like to flavour the buttercream, see additions to buttercream (pages 595 to 598).

STORE: 6 hours room temperature, 1 week refrigerated, 8 months frozen.

POINTERS FOR SUCCESS: The syrup must come to a rolling boil or the buttercream will be too thin.

INGREDIENTS	WEIGHT		MEASURE
room temperature	*grams*	*pounds/ounces*	*volume*
12 egg yolks, size 2	223 grams	7¾ ounces	7 fluid ounces
castor sugar	300 grams	10½ ounces	1½ cups
corn syrup	328 grams	11½ ounces	8 fluid ounces
unsalted butter (must be softened)	907 grams	2 pounds	4 cups
optional: liqueur *or* eau-de-vie of your choice	60 to 120 grams	2 to 4 ounces	2 to 4 fluid ounces

Have ready near the range a lightly greased ½-litre/1-pint/2-cup heatproof glass measure.

In the bowl of an electric mixer, beat the yolks until light in colour. Meanwhile, combine the sugar and corn syrup in a medium-size saucepan (preferably with a non-stick lining) and heat, stirring constantly, until the sugar dissolves and the syrup comes to a rolling boil. (The entire surface will be covered by large bubbles.) *Immediately transfer to the glass measure to stop the cooking.*

Beat the syrup into the yolks in a steady stream. Do not allow the syrup to fall on the beaters or the syrup will spin on to the sides of the bowl. Start by pouring a small amount of syrup over the yolks with the mixer turned off. Immediately beat at high speed for 5 seconds. Stop the mixer and add a larger amount of syrup. Beat for 5 seconds. Continue with the remaining syrup. For the last addition, use a rubber scraper to remove the syrup clinging to the glass measure.

Beat until completely cool. Gradually beat in the butter, then any of the optional flavourings (pages 595 to 598). Place in an airtight bowl. Bring to room temperature before using. Rebeat if necessary to restore the texture.*

*Do not rebeat chilled buttercream until it has reached room temperature or it may curdle.

Classic Buttercream for a 3-Tier Cake to Serve 150

Makes 1 kilogram 440 grams/3 pounds 2½ ounces/8 cups (without optional additions)

This recipe produces the same buttercream as the Neoclassic version. If you would like to flavour the buttercream, see the additions to buttercream (pages 595 to 598).

STORE: 6 hours room temperature, 1 week refrigerated, 8 months frozen.

POINTERS FOR SUCCESS: See Sugar Syrups (page 500). To prevent crystallisation, do not stir after the syrup comes to a boil. To keep temperature from rising, remove the syrup from the pan as soon as it has reached 238°F/114°C.

INGREDIENTS	WEIGHT		MEASURE
room temperature	*grams*	*pounds/ounces*	*volume*
12 egg yolks, size 2	223 grams	7¾ ounces	7 fluid ounces
castor sugar	400 grams	14 ounces	2 cups
water	236 grams	8¼ ounces	8 fluid ounces
unsalted butter (must be softened)	907 grams	2 pounds	4 cups
optional: liqueur *or* eau-de-vie of your choice	60 to 120 grams	2 to 4 ounces	2 to 4 fluid ounces

Have ready near the stove a greased ½-litre/1-pint/2-cup heatproof glass measure.

In the bowl of an electric mixer, beat the yolks until light in colour. Meanwhile, combine the sugar and water in a medium saucepan (preferably with a nonstick lining) and heat, stirring constantly, until the sugar dissolves and the syrup is boiling. Stop stirring and boil to the soft-ball stage (238°F/114°C). *Immediately transfer to the glass measure to stop the cooking.*

Beat the syrup into the yolks in a steady stream. Do not allow the syrup to fall on the beaters or the syrup will spin on to the sides of the bowl. Start by pouring a small amount of syrup over the yolks with the mixer turned off. Immediately beat at high speed for 5 seconds. Stop the mixer and add a larger amount of syrup. Beat for 5 seconds. Continue with the remaining syrup. With the last addition, use a rubber scraper to remove the syrup clinging to the glass measure. Beat until completely cool.

Gradually beat in the butter, then any of the optional flavourings (pages 595 to 598). Place in an airtight bowl. Bring to room temperature before using. Rebeat if necessary to restore texture.★

Variations for One Recipe of Classic or Neoclassic Buttercream

Classic or Neoclassic Buttercream can be used plain or as a base for any number of flavours. One recipe can accommodate as much as 8 fluid ounces/1 cup liquid without becoming too soft. Spirits heighten the flavour of a buttercream but do not add them to buttercreams already containing fruit purées as they will become too liquid. Spirits are best kept in the background, so start with 2 fluid ounces/¼ cup and then add to taste.

Fresh fruit purées such as raspberry and strawberry blend beautifully with classic buttercreams and maintain their lovely hues. Apricot purée tends to curdle buttercream slightly, so heated and strained apricot jam or lekvar (page 495), cooled to room temperature, are preferable.

The sweetness level of the base buttercream is balanced so whatever is added must be neither too sweet nor too tart or adjustments to the base need to be made as indicated.

★Do not rebeat chilled buttercream until it has reached room temperature or it may curdle.

CLASSIC CHOCOLATE:

Classic buttercreams can incorporate 336 grams/12 ounces melted chocolate without becoming too stiff. This results in a light chocolate colour and flavour which does not overpower yellow or white cake layers.
To make chocolate buttercream: Beat 336 grams/12 ounces melted and cooled chocolate, preferably extra bittersweet or bittersweet, into the buttercream.

CLASSIC CHOCOLATE CARAMEL CRUNCH:

The flavours of caramel and chocolate blend beautifully and the powdered caramel adds a slightly crunchy texture. Because caramel is sweet it is best to use extra bittersweet chocolate in the base.
To make chocolate caramel crunch buttercream: Beat 95 grams/ 3¹/₄ ounces/¹/₂ cup powdered caramel (page 362) into Classic Chocolate.

CLASSIC COFFEE:

This method of making coffee extract yields a buttercream with the rich taste of good strong coffee.
To make coffee buttercream: Beat 4 tablespoons instant espresso powder dissolved in 2 teaspoons boiling water into the buttercream. For a more aromatic flavour, add 2 to 4 fluid ounces Kahlúa.

CLASSIC MOCHA ESPRESSO:

Chocolate and coffee always make a lovely combination.
To make mocha espresso buttercream: To Classic Chocolate, add 4 tablespoons instant espresso powder dissolved in 2 teaspoons boiling water. For more intense coffee flavour, add 2 to 4 fluid ounces Kahlúa.

CLASSIC PRALINE:

The best praline paste (page 497), a smooth combination of hazelnuts and caramelised sugar, makes a fabulous addition to any buttercream. Because the paste contains about 50 per cent sugar it is necessary to remove some of the sugar from the base.
To make praline buttercream: When making buttercream, decrease the sugar by 3 tablespoons. Beat 154 grams/5¹/₂ ounces/¹/₂ cup praline paste into the finished buttercream.

CLASSIC CHOCOLATE PRALINE:

Praline intensifies the delicious flavour of chocolate.
To make chocolate praline buttercream: Beat 336 grams/12 ounces melted and cooled bittersweet chocolate into Classic Praline Buttercream. Alternately, beat 154 grams/ 5¹/₂ ounces/¹/₂ cup praline paste into Classic Chocolate Buttercream if it was prepared with extra bittersweet chocolate. (Either method will be the same level of sweetness.)

CLASSIC PRALINE CRUNCH:

Praline powder (page 363) is made of ground hazelnuts and caramel but is not turned into a paste. This gives a crunchy texture to the buttercream.

To make praline crunch buttercream: When making the buttercream, decrease the sugar by 3 table-spoons. Beat 90 grams/3 ounces/ 2/3 cup praline powder (page 363) into the finished buttercream.

CLASSIC CHOCOLATE PRALINE CRUNCH:

This buttercream is like Classic Chocolate Praline except for the crunchy texture provided by the praline powder.

To make chocolate praline crunch buttercream: Beat 336 grams/ 12 ounces melted and cooled bittersweet chocolate into Classic Praline Crunch Buttercream. Alternatively, beat 90 grams/ 3 ounces/2/3 cup praline powder into Classic Chocolate Buttercream if it was prepared with extra bittersweet chocolate. (Either method will be the same level of sweetness.)

CLASSIC CHESTNUT:

This buttercream is excellent with chocolate cake.

To make chestnut buttercream: To make 1 kilogram 200 grams/ 2 pounds 10 ounces/6 cups of buttercream, start with 1/2 recipe buttercream and add twice the quantity of recipe for lightly sweetened rum-flavoured Chestnut Purée (page 404).

CLASSIC RASPBERRY:

My Raspberry Sauce is so concentrated it scarcely affects the consistency of the buttercream base. This is the purest raspberry flavour of any icing I have ever experienced.

To make raspberry buttercream: Beat 253 grams/8¾ ounces/1 cup lightly sweetened Raspberry Sauce (page 386) into the finished buttercream. If not planning to use the same day, add a few drops of red food colour to prevent fading.

CLASSIC STRAWBERRY:

The strawberry flavour is surprisingly fresh and intense. It is, of course, silky and creamy but has the added interest of the tiny strawberry seeds. I find that strawberries frozen without sugar have more flavour than most commercially available fresh-picked strawberries – even at the height of season.

To make strawberry buttercream: Beat 240 grams/8½ ounces/1 cup unsweetened Strawberry Purée (page 388) into the finished buttercream with a few optional drops of essence of wild strawberry (page 492) for further intensity. If not planning to use the same day, add a few drops of red food colour to prevent fading.

CLASSIC APRICOT:

This buttercream has a tart, honeyed flavour and a very pale golden colour.

To make apricot buttercream: Beat 310 grams/10½ ounces/1 cup heated, strained, and cooled apricot jam or lekvar (page 495) into the finished buttercream with a few optional drops of essence of apricot (page 492) for further intensity.

CLASSIC PINEAPPLE:

Home-preserved pineapple is a delicious, slightly tart addition to buttercream.

To make pineapple buttercream: Beat 16 fluid ounces/200 grams/ 7 ounces/2 cups puréed pineapple (page 402) into the finished buttercream and add 2 to 4 table-spoons kirsch or rum.

CLASSIC LEMON:

To achieve a truly lemon flavour it is necessary to use both fresh lemon juice and lemon extract (actually the pure oil of lemon). Lemon juice alone is not intense enough and the extract alone is too bitter.

To make lemon buttercream: When making the buttercream, replace 4 fluid ounces water with 4 fluid ounces freshly squeezed lemon juice. After adding the butter, beat in ½ teaspoon lemon extract.

CLASSIC ORANGE:

An intense orange flavour is difficult to achieve using orange extract because it is quite bitter. Finely grated orange zest and an aromatic French orange essence (page 492), which includes the pulp, do produce an excellent orange flavour.

To make orange buttercream: Add 4 teaspoons orange essence and 2 tablespoons orange zest to the finished buttercream.

CLASSIC ORANGE BLOSSOM:

Orange flower water gives this buttercream the perfume of orange blossoms. Be sure to add the orange essence. It consists mainly of orange oil. The small amount adds the lilting zip associated with fresh orange flavour.

To make orange blossom buttercream: Add 2 teaspoons orange essence dissolved in 5½ fluid ounces orange flower water, 2 tablespoons orange zest, and 2 fluid ounces Grand Marnier to the finished buttercream.

CLASSIC PASSION:

This buttercream captures the slightly tart, utterly distinctive taste of fresh passion fruit.

To make passion buttercream: Beat up to 450 grams/16½ ounces/1½ cups Passion Curd (page 391) into finished buttercream and add 2 teaspoons of essence of passion fruit (page 492) for further intensity.

Crème Ivoire Deluxe for a 3-Tier Cake to Serve 150

(Luxury White Chocolate Buttercream)

Makes 1 kilogram 660 grams/3 pounds 10 ounces/5¹/₄ cups

Crème Ivoire is like a bonbon or chocolate truffle. On first bite it seems firm, only to dissolve immediately in the mouth, releasing the buttery and faintly chocolaty flavours.

The colour of this glorious buttercream is pale ivory, reminiscent of an antique satin wedding gown. It is excellent as an icing for a wedding cake and ideal when someone requests a chocolate wedding cake with a traditional ivory-coloured exterior.

The contrast of the bittersweet dark chocolate cake against the silky sweet white chocolate buttercream is spectacular. Because of its richness and firm consistency, I like to fill and lightly ice the cake with Neoclassic (page 592) or Classic Buttercream (page 594). Because I then ice and pipe decorations with the Crème Ivoire, I am giving a smaller recipe than for the other buttercreams.

STORE: Mineral oil has an indefinite shelf-life, but safflower oil will become rancid in a matter of weeks. Therefore, if prepared with mineral oil, buttercream will keep at room temperature for 1 month. (The clarified butter shortens its shelf-life at room temperature.) If prepared with another oil, store at room temperature for 1 week, refrigerate for 3 months, or freeze for 1 year.

POINTERS FOR SUCCESS: Follow directions on how to clarify butter.

When melting the chocolate, stir often and be sure that not even a drop of water gets into the melted chocolate. If seeding should occur, try beating with an immersion blender (page 523) or remelt the buttercream, pass through a fine strainer and chill again, stirring constantly. Be sure to use a fine-quality white chocolate which contains cocoa butter. I find Tobler Narcisse to have the best flavour and the least sweetness.

Icing the cake first with a thin layer of Classic Buttercream offers an interesting textural contrast and gives the Crème Ivoire an ideal surface for adherence. Otherwise it will have a tendency to separate from the cake when cut. (I also use the Classic Buttercream plain or flavoured as a filling.)

Keep piped decorations simple, such as a shell border (page 461). This buttercream pipes with more exquisite detail than any other, but the heat of your hand will make piping more than a few designs at a time difficult. To counteract this problem, use several parchment bags, placing just a small amount of buttercream in each, and switch bags at first sign of softening. Cooling your hand in ice water also helps.

INGREDIENTS	WEIGHT		MEASURE
room temperature	*grams*	*pounds/ounces*	*volume*
white chocolate (preferably Tobler Narcisse)	1 kilogram 360 grams	3 pounds	16 (3-ounce) bars
cocoa butter, melted*	128 grams	4½ ounces	4 fluid ounces
clarified unsalted butter†	98 grams	3½ ounces	4 fluid ounces
flavourless oil such as mineral *or* safflower	100 grams	3½ ounces	4 fluid ounces

* Melt the cocoa butter in a double boiler, under the heat from the pilot light of an oven, or in a microwave the same way as for dark chocolate (page 437).
† If you do not have clarified butter on hand, you will need to clarify 156 grams/5½ ounces/11 tablespoons unsalted butter. In a heavy saucepan melt the butter over medium heat, partially covered to prevent splattering. When the butter looks clear, cook, uncovered, watching carefully until the solids drop and just begin to brown. Pour immediately through a fine strainer or a strainer lined with cheesecloth.

Break the chocolate into individual squares and place in a bowl set over a pot of hot water (no hotter than 160°F/71°C) on low heat. The water must not touch the bottom of the bowl. Add the cocoa butter, clarified butter and oil.

Remove from the heat and stir until the chocolate begins to melt. Return to the heat if the water cools, but be careful not to let it get too hot. Stir until smooth. (The chocolate may be melted with the oil and butters in a microwave oven *if stirred every 15 seconds*. Remove before fully melted and stir, using the residual heat to complete melting.)

Because of the milk solids in the white chocolate, the buttercream must be chilled and stirred to prevent seeding (the formation of tiny lumps). Fill a large bowl with ice cubes and water and sprinkle with 1 or 2 tablespoons salt. Fill a second bowl or the sink with very hot water. Set the bowl of buttercream in the ice water. Stir constantly with whisk until you just see whisk marks on the surface. Immediately place the bowl over the bowl of hot water to take off the chill. This will only take seconds. Feel the bottom of the bowl. It should feel cool not cold.

Allow the buttercream to sit for a few minutes, stirring occasionally with the whisk. If it does not form peaks when the whisk is raised, chill again for a short time.

Crème Ivoire for a 3-Tier Cake to Serve 150

(White Chocolate Buttercream)

Makes 3 kilograms 770 grams/8¼ pounds/14 cups

The delicious creamy flavour of this buttercream is similar to the deluxe version but is simpler and less expensive to make. It consists of pure white chocolate softened to icing consistency by a neutral oil. It has that wonderful melt-in-the-mouth quality offered by the cocoa butter in the white chocolate. (That is the only 'butter' in the buttercream.)

This buttercream has a perfect icing consistency so it does not require an undercoat of Classic Buttercream, but it is too soft to hold its shape for decorative piping. If you wish to make decorative borders on your cake, prepare 273 to 546 grams/9¾ to 19½ ounces/1 or 2 cups Crème Ivoire Deluxe (page 285).

STORE: Mineral oil has an indefinite shelf-life, but safflower oil will become rancid in a matter of weeks. Therefore, if prepared with mineral oil, buttercream will keep at room temperature for 6 months. If prepared with another oil, store at room temperature for

1 week, refrigerate for 3 months, or freeze for 1 year.

POINTERS FOR SUCCESS:
Carefully follow directions for melting chocolate. Be sure that not even a drop of water gets into the melted chocolate. If seeding should occur, try beating with an immersion blender (page 523) or remelt the buttercream, pass through a fine strainer, and chill again, stirring constantly. If the weather is 80°F/27°C or above, reduce the oil to 6 tablespoons (3 fluid ounces).

INGREDIENTS	WEIGHT		MEASURE
room temperature	*grams*	*pounds/ounces*	*volume*
white chocolate (preferably Tobler Narcisse)	3 kilograms 175 grams	7 pounds	37⅓ (3-ounce) bars
flavourless oil such as mineral *or* safflower	600 grams	1 pound 5 ounces	24 fluid ounces

Break the chocolate into individual squares and place in a bowl set over a pan of hot water (no hotter than 160°F/71°C) on low heat. The water must not touch bottom of bowl. Add the oil.

Remove the pan from the heat and stir until the chocolate begins to melt. Return to the heat if the water cools, but be careful it does not get too hot. Stir until smooth. (The chocolate may be melted with the oil in a microwave oven *if stirred every 15 seconds*. Remove before fully melted and stir, using the residual heat to complete melting.)

Because of the milk solids in the white chocolate, the buttercream must be chilled and stirred to prevent seeding (the formation of tiny lumps). Fill a large bowl with ice cubes and water and sprinkle with 1 or 2 tablespoons salt. Fill a second bowl or the sink with very hot water. Set the bowl of buttercream in the ice water and stir constantly with whisk, until you just see whisk marks on the surface. Immediately place the bowl over the bowl of hot water to take off the chill. This will only take seconds. Feel the bottom of the bowl. It should feel cool not cold.

Allow the buttercream to sit for a few minutes, stirring occasionally with whisk. If it does not form peaks when the whisk is raised, chill again for a short time.

White Chocolate Cream Cheese Icing for a 3-Tier Cake to Serve 150

Makes 2 kilograms 80 grams/4½ pounds/13 cups

This ivory-coloured buttercream is mellow and creamy – a perfect complement for cheesecake. It makes an unusual and spectacular presentation because it pipes wonderfully and is the identical colour of the cheesecake within. White chocolate adds firmness of texture, sweetness, and an indefinable flavour.

STORE: 1 day room temperature, 2 weeks refrigerated, 2 months frozen. Allow to come to room temperature before rebeating.

POINTERS FOR SUCCESS: Do not overheat the chocolate and stir constantly while melting. Be sure no moisture gets into the melted chocolate (see Melting White Chocolate, page 288). Beat constantly while adding the chocolate to prevent lumping. If lumping should occur, it can be remedied by pressing the buttercream through a fine strainer.

Buttercream may separate slightly if room temperature is very warm. This can be corrected by

INGREDIENTS	WEIGHT		MEASURE
room temperature	*grams*	*pounds/ounces*	*volume*
white chocolate (preferably Tobler Narcisse)	680 grams	1½ pounds	8 (3-ounce) bars
cream cheese (must be softened)	907 grams	2 pounds	4 (8-ounce) packet
unsalted butter (must be softened)	454 grams	1 pound	2 cups
lemon juice, freshly squeezed	62 grams	2 ounces	2 fluid ounces

setting the bowl in ice water and whisking mixture. The buttercream becomes spongy on standing. Rebeat to restore smooth creamy texture. Use ice to chill your hand during piping to maintain firm texture.

Break the chocolate into individual squares and place in a bowl set over a pan of hot water (no hotter than 160°F/71°C) on low heat. The water must not touch the bottom of the bowl.

Remove the pan from the heat and stir until the chocolate begins to melt. Return to the heat if the water cools, but be careful it does not get too hot. Stir until smooth. (The chocolate may be melted in a microwave on high power *if stirred every 15 seconds*. Remove before fully melted and stir, using the residual heat to complete melting.)

Allow the chocolate to cool to room temperature, stirring occasionally.

In a mixing bowl beat the cream cheese (preferably with a flat beater) until smooth and creamy. Gradually beat in the cooled chocolate until smoothly incorporated. Beat in the butter and lemon juice. Use at once or to ensure smoothness rebeat at room temperature before icing.★

Note: My friend Shirley Corriher reports that when using this icing for a wedding cake in the heat of an Atlanta summer, she tried decreasing the butter to 113 grams/ 4 ounces and it held up quite well.

★Do not rebeat chilled buttercream until it has reached room temperature or it may curdle.

Silk Meringue Praline Buttercream for a 3-Tier Cake

Makes about 2 kilograms 800 grams/6 pounds/13 cups

This is one of my very favourite buttercreams. It is smooth and delicious, airy yet stable. It is resistant to warm temperatures and is a dream for piping decorations. Because the buttercream takes on the pale golden colour of the praline paste it is suitable for a wedding cake only when the traditional white look is not required. It goes well with any type of butter cake or *génoise*.

STORE: 6 hours room temperature, 1 week refrigerated, 8 months frozen. If frozen or refrigerated, be sure to allow the buttercream to come to room temperature before rebeating it or it will break down. The buttercream may look almost soupy when it has reached room temperature, but rebeating will make it as firm as new!

POINTERS FOR SUCCESS: *Crème Anglaise:* The temperature must reach at least 160°F/71°C and must not exceed 180°F/82°C or it will curdle.

Italian Meringue: For maximum stability, the syrup must reach 248°F/120°C and not exceed 250°F/121°C as higher temperatures will break down the whites. The whites must be free of any grease or trace of yolk. Do not overbeat.

Buttercream: Rebeat when it becomes spongy.

TO MAKE CRÈME ANGLAISE

Have ready near the stove a sieve set over a bowl. In a medium, heavy non-corrodible saucepan combine the sugar, yolks, and vanilla pod.

In a small saucepan bring the milk to boiling point. Add 2½ fluid ounces to the yolk mixture, stirring constantly. Gradually add the remaining milk, stirring, and cook over medium-low heat, stirring constantly, until just before boiling point. The mixture will start to steam slightly and an accurate thermometer will register 170°F/77°C. (The temperature must not exceed 180°F/82°C or the mixture will curdle.)

INGREDIENTS	WEIGHT		MEASURE
room temperature	*grams*	*pounds/ounces*	*volume*
CRÈME ANGLAISE			
castor sugar	150 grams	5.25 ounces	¾ cup
15 egg yolks, size 2	279 grams	9.75 ounces	9 fluid ounces
3 large vanilla pods, split lengthwise★	—	—	—
milk	363 grams	12.75 ounces	12 fluid ounces
ITALIAN MERINGUE			
castor sugar	262 grams	9.25 ounces	1 cup + 5 tablespoons
water	80 grams	2.75 ounces	2½ fluid ounces
6 egg whites, size 2	180 grams	6.25 ounces	6 fluid ounces
cream of tartar	—	—	¾ teaspoon
unsalted butter (must be softened), beaten until creamy	1 kilogram 360 grams	3 pounds	6 cups
praline paste	454 grams	1 pound	1½ cups

★Vanilla pod offers the most delicious flavour, but, if you wish to avoid the little black specks, replace the beans with 1 tablespoon pure vanilla extract, added to the cooled *crème anglaise*. If using Tahitian pods, use only 1½ pods.

Immediately pour into the strainer, scraping up any clinging to the pan.

Scrape the small black seeds from the vanilla pod into the custard and cool to room temperature. (To speed the cooling, place the bowl in another bowl or sink partially filled with ice water.) Cover and refrigerate up to 5 days or until ready to complete buttercream.

TO MAKE ITALIAN MERINGUE
Have ready near the stove a ½-litre/1-pint/2-cup heatproof glass measure.

In a small heavy saucepan

(preferably with a non-stick lining) stir together 200 grams/7 ounces/ 1 cup sugar and the water. Heat, stirring constantly, until the sugar dissolves and the syrup is bubbling. Stop stirring and turn down the heat to the lowest setting. (If using an electric stove, remove from the heat.)

In a mixing bowl beat the egg whites on low speed until foamy, add the cream of tartar, and beat on high speed until soft peaks form when the beater is raised. Gradually beat in the remaining 5 tablespoons of sugar until stiff peaks form when the beater is raised slowly.

Increase the heat and boil the syrup until a thermometer registers 248° to 250°F/120° to 121°C (firm-ball stage). Immediately pour into the glass measure to stop the cooking.

With the mixer on high speed, beat the syrup into the whites in a steady stream. Do not allow the syrup to fall on the beaters or the syrup will spin on to the sides of the bowl. Use a rubber scraper to remove the syrup clinging to the glass measure. Beat at low speed until cool. (Italian Meringue keeps for 2 days refrigerated. Rebeat briefly before using.)

TO COMPLETE BUTTERCREAM

In a large mixing bowl (at least 5 litres/8 pints) place the butter and beat on medium speed for 30 seconds. Gradually beat in the *crème anglaise* and praline paste until smooth. Add the Italian meringue in four batches, beating briefly until just incorporated. If the mixture looks curdled instead of silken smooth, it is too cold. Allow it to sit at room temperature to warm to 70°F/21°C before continuing to beat or place the bowl in a hot water bath very briefly until the buttercream against the sides of the bowl just starts to melt. Remove at once and beat until smooth. This buttercream becomes slightly spongy on standing. Rebeat before using.

Note: To make plain Silk Meringue Buttercream, increase the sugar to 300 grams/10½ ounces/ 1½ cups and omit the praline paste. You may also make any of the variations on pages 279 to 282 by using the plain Silk Meringue Buttercream and tripling the optional additions.

Chocolate Cream Glaze for Large Cakes

Makes 960 grams/2 pounds 2 ounces/4 cups

A large single-layer round or rectangular cake looks stunning glazed with a dark, shiny Chocolate Cream Glaze. It is also the most delicious of all chocolate glazes. Cognac heightens the flavour, but if a fine-quality chocolate is used the Cognac is optional.

This recipe makes enough to glaze a 30.5 × 5 × 4.5-centimetre/ 12 × 2 × 1¾-inch cake. For a 46 × 30.5 × 5-centimetre/ 18 × 12 × 2-inch cake, double the recipe.

STORE: 3 days room temperature, 2 weeks refrigerated, 6 months frozen.

POINTERS FOR SUCCESS: Your favourite semisweet or bittersweet eating chocolate will result in the best chocolate glaze. If the chocolate is not smooth-textured in the bar it will not be smooth in the ganache either.

The butterfat content of cream varies, which will affect the consistency of the glaze. Always check for consistency at a tepid temperature. If it is the correct consistency when tepid, even if it is too cool when applied and lumps, the cake can be placed in a warm oven for a few seconds and glaze will smooth. If glaze had been tested when hot and was the right consistency, but was poured when too cool and lumped, the extra heat would not help. On the other hand, if glaze had been the correct consistency when cool, it would never firm adequately on the cake.

To reheat, use a double boiler, stirring gently, or a microwave on high power, stirring and folding every 7 seconds.

TO PREPARE CAKE FOR GLAZING

Brush all crumbs from the surface and place on a cardboard round the same size as the cake. Suspend the cake on a rack set on a baking sheet to catch excess glaze.

It is best to have enough glaze to cover the cake with one application as touch-ups don't usually produce as flawless a finish. Excess glaze can be frozen and reheated at a later date.

TO PREPARE GLAZE

In a food processor with the metal blade, break the chocolate into pieces and process until very fine (or finely grate the chocolate). Place

INGREDIENTS	WEIGHT		MEASURE
room temperature	*grams*	*pounds/ounces*	*volume*
bittersweet chocolate	510 grams	1 pound 2 ounces	6 (3-ounce) bars
heavy cream	464 grams	1 pound	16 fluid ounces
optional: Cognac	28 grams	1 ounce	2 tablespoons

in a medium-size heavy saucepan.

Heat the cream to boiling point and pour three-quarters of it over the chocolate. Cover for 5 minutes to allow the chocolate to melt. Gently mix until smooth, trying not to create air bubbles. Pass through a fine strainer, stir in the optional Cognac, and allow to cool just until tepid.

CHECK FOR CONSISTENCY
At a tepid temperature, a small amount of glaze should mound a bit when dropped from a spoon before smoothly disappearing. If the glaze is too thick and the mound remains on the surface or the glaze seems curdled, add some of the warm remaining cream by the teaspoon. If the glaze should happen to be too thin, gently stir in a small amount of melted chocolate.

When the consistency is correct, use at once or store and reheat. The glaze should be poured on to the centre of the cake, allowing the excess to flow down the sides.

Smooth quickly and evenly with a large metal spatula, moving it lightly back and forth across the top until smooth. If any spots on the sides remain unglazed, use a small metal spatula to lift up some glaze which has fallen on to the baking sheet and apply to uncovered area.

Lift the rack and tap lightly to settle glaze. Lift the cake from the rack using a broad spatula or pancake turner and set it on a serving plate or on a clean rack if planning to apply a second coat of glaze.

If you want to cover the cake more thickly and evenly, two coats can be applied by the following technique. Pour the glaze over the cake and smooth quickly with a spatula to create a thin, even coat. Refrigerate for 20 minutes or until firm. Apply a second coat of tepid glaze. (You will need about 1½ times the glaze for a double coat.)

Allow to set for at least 2 hours at room temperature. Refrigerating will dull the glaze slightly.

Pistachio Marzipan for a 3-Tier Cake

Makes 567 grams/1¼ pounds (enough for 30.5, 23 and 15-centimetre/ 12, 9 and 6-inch discs)

People who don't like marzipan usually change their minds when they encounter this pistachio version. I created it as a surprise inside each tier of my brother's wedding cake (page 254).

STORE: 6 months refrigerated,   1 year frozen.

INGREDIENTS	WEIGHT		MEASURE
room temperature	*grams*	*pounds/ounces*	*volume*
shelled unsalted pistachio nuts	152 grams	5¼ ounces	1 cup
icing sugar	340 grams	12 ounces	3 cups (lightly spooned into cup)
corn syrup	108 grams	4 ounces	2½ fluid ounces
glycerine *or* unflavoured oil	—	—	2 teaspoons
optional: 8 drops green food colour	—	—	—

Bake the nuts in a 350°F/180°C/gas mark 4 oven for 5 to 10 minutes or until the skins separate from the nuts when scratched lightly with a fingernail. Remove as much of the skin as possible.

In food processor process the nuts until a smooth paste is obtained. Add the icing sugar and process until well mixed. Add the corn syrup and glycerine and process until blended, about 20 seconds. The mixture will appear dry, but a small amount pressed between your fingers should hold together. If it seems too dry, add more corn syrup, ¼ teaspoon at a time. If you wish to deepen the colour, add the optional food colouring. Continue processing until the marzipan has a smooth, doughlike consistency. Knead briefly by hand until uniform in colour.

The marzipan may be used at once, but is easier to work with if allowed to rest 1 hour. Wrap tightly with clingfilm and place in an airtight container.

To roll discs, divide the marzipan in half. Roll half between two sheets of clingfilm into a thin circle 32.5 centimetres/13 inches in diameter. Peel off the top layer of clingfilm. Using a lightly greased 30.5-centimetre/12-inch cake tin bottom as a guide, cut out a 30.5-centimetre/12-inch circle with a sharp knife or pizza cutter. Knead the leftover marzipan into the remaining marzipan. Roll this portion between clingfilm into a thin circle 25.5 centimetres/ 10 inches in diameter. Using a lightly greased 23-centimetre/9-inch cake tin bottom as guide, cut out a 23-centimetre/9-inch circle. Knead the leftover marzipan together and again roll it out between clingfilm into a thin circle 18 centimetres/ 7 inches in diameter. Using a lightly greased 15-centimetre/6-inch cake tin, cut out a 15-centimetre/ 6-inch circle.

It is easiest to apply marzipan if it has been frozen for a few minutes to make it less flexible. Place the 30.5-centimetre/12-inch circle, still covered with clingfilm, on a baking sheet and freeze. The marzipan will adhere to the clingfilm. Position it over the 30.5-centimetre/12-inch tier of an iced cake, supporting the marzipan with your palm if necessary, and lay it on the cake. It should not be moved once it is positioned. Peel off the clingfilm. Repeat with remaining circles.

Classic Rolled Fondant for a 3-Tier Cake to Serve 150

Makes about 3 kilograms 402 grams/7¹/₂ pounds (enough to cover 30.5, 23 and 15-centimetre/12, 9 and 6-inch tiers)

The alabaster perfection of rolled fondant makes an exquisite background for decorating a wedding cake. It seals in the freshness of the cake for several days, giving time for the most ethereal and elaborate of piped decorations. It is traditional even for home cooks to wear only white when preparing it, as even a tiny thread of coloured fabric can cause an off colour in the pristine white.

These days rolled fondant is used more in Australia than in any other country – no doubt why a cake covered in rolled fondant and decorated with royal icing is often referred to as the fabled Australian method of cake decorating.

STORE: 1 month room temperature. Can be frozen indefinitely.

Sprinkle the gelatin over the water in a 1-litre/2-pint/4-cup heatproof measuring jug or bowl and allow it to sit for 5 minutes. Set the jug in a small pan of simmering water and stir until the gelatin is dissolved. (This can also be done in a few seconds in a microwave on high power.) Blend in the glucose and glycerine, then add the fat and stir until melted. Remove from the heat.

Place the sugar in a very large bowl and make a well in the centre. Add the gelatin mixture and stir with a wooden spoon until blended. Mix with lightly greased hands and vigorously knead in the bowl until most of the sugar is incorporated. Turn out on to a smooth lightly greased surface, such as Formica or marble, and knead until smooth and satiny.

If the fondant seems very dry, add several drops of water and knead well. If it seems too sticky, knead in more icing sugar. The fondant will resemble a smooth, well-shaped stone. When dropped, it should spread very slightly but retain its shape. It should be malleable like clay, soft but not sticky.

Rolled fondant may be used at once but seems to work much more easily when allowed to rest for several hours. It is important to cover the fondant to prevent drying. Wrap tightly with clingfilm

INGREDIENTS	WEIGHT		MEASURE
room temperature	*grams*	*pounds/ounces*	*volume*
gelatin	28 grams	1 ounce	3 tablespoons
water*	177 grams	6¼ ounces	6 fluid ounces
glucose†	504 grams	17½ ounces	12 fluid ounces
glycerine	54 grams	2 ounces	3 tablespoons
solid white fat	72 grams	2½ ounces	¼ cup + 2 tablespoons
icing sugar	2 kilograms 722 grams	6 pounds	24 cups (lightly spooned into cup)

* For a flavour variation, replace half the water with rosewater *or* orange flower water.
† 12 fluid ounces corn syrup will give equal results if you use only 4 fluid ounces + 1 tablespoon water instead of 6 fluid ounces.

and place in an airtight container.*
It will firm slightly on standing.

When ready to roll out, spray the work surface and rolling pin with non-stick vegetable spray. For covering a cake, see page 410.

Tips: A 19-litre/5-gallon mixer with a spade beater can be used to do the initial mixing. Kneading must be done by hand or the texture suffers. For small hands, divide the mixture into two batches. Be sure to keep each batch covered to prevent drying.

*If stored fondant seems very stiff, a few seconds in the microwave before kneading will work wonders to make it pliable.

Icing, Tiering and Storing Wedding Cakes

PREPARING THE CAKE FOR ICING

OUTSIDE CRUST:

In order to ice a cake evenly and smoothly, it must be as level as possible and have a crumb-free crust. There are two baker's tricks that make this easy to accomplish. The first is to spray a non-stick vegetable spray on to the cake tins. The second is to wrap the cake tins with Magi-Cake Strips (pages 516 and 522). Together with well-balanced formulas and varying the amount of baking powder for different cake sizes, these tips result in very level cake layers.

If a cake should come out domed, use a serrated knife with a blade longer than the diameter of the cake to level it. Or use a cake leveller or cake saw (page 528).

If the sides are uneven and there seem to be many loose crumbs, a crumb coating such as Jewel Glaze (page 378) or a very thin layer of icing keeps the crumbs from marring the surface of the frosting.

When covering a cake with rolled fondant, it is necessary to bevel the top edge to soften the angle, preventing the fondant from cracking. A small serrated knife is perfect for this.

It is also necessary to apply a thin layer of jelly or icing to all surfaces of the cake so that the fondant will adhere well. (See piping gel, page 497, or Jewel Glaze, page 378.) A pastry feather or brush works well.

CAKE SERVING BASE:

It is usually difficult to find large, perfectly flat cake plates for wedding cakes. A few possible solutions are: 5-millimetre/$\frac{1}{4}$-inch-thick plywood covered with florist foil, 5-millimetre to 1-centimetre/$\frac{1}{4}$ to $\frac{1}{2}$-inch-thick sandblasted glass, or 3-millimetre/$\frac{1}{8}$-inch Plexiglass or a mirror. All must be custom made. Wooden boards can be painted with gold leaf, but this must be done at least 2 days ahead so that the odours have disappeared before the cake is placed on the base. Cake-decorating suppliers also carry decorative silver or gold foil in rolls and large round serving boards covered with foil. Aesthetically, the serving base should be about 7.5 to 13 centimetres/3 to 5 inches larger in diameter than the bottom tier of the cake.

SUPPORTING THE CAKE

Making a tiered wedding cake is like constructing an edifice out of improbable elements. Certain supports are vital to keep one tier from sinking into another and to prevent the entire cake from collapsing. When making a wedding cake, I often feel like an architect.

BOTTOM SUPPORT:

To start with, each tier must be supported by a rigid but lightweight base. Disposable cardboard is the easiest solution.

Corrugated cardboard cake rounds the size of standard cake tins are available from cake-decorating suppliers (page 524) or can be cut from cardboard. I prefer the pre-cut rounds because their edges are smooth, making it easier to use them as a guide for smoothing the icing on the sides. Those waterproofed with a glassine surface are ideal.

To keep the cake from slipping off the cardboard, spread a few dabs of icing on the cardboard before placing the layer on it.

Ice the cake layers (see page 411 if you need to review icing techniques) and attach the bottom tier to the serving board before inserting any inner supports. To attach to serving board, use several strips of strong double-sided adhesive tape or make loops of tape on the serving board.

INTERNAL SUPPORT:

To enable the bottom layers to support the weight of additional tiers, wooden dowels are traditionally inserted into each tier to distribute the weight. Wooden dowels are difficult to cut, so one day, as my husband was watching me struggle with wire cutters and shooting stumps of dowels, he came up with the brilliant solution of using plastic rigid straws instead. My immediate response was 'Impossible', but he assured me that plastic can support a great deal of weight and the hollow centres offer more support by displacing less cake. He added that, unlike wood, the plastic would not interface with the surrounding cake, causing an off flavour. I tried a test cake, piling many brass weights on top and, after three days had elapsed, found that this technique really does work. I published the plastic straw technique as part of a wedding cake article for a national food magazine and received one indignant, bordering on outraged, letter insisting that the cake in question would certainly collapse. But since that time I have noticed the straw technique appearing in other books on cake decorating and regret that it couldn't have been patented!

To insert plastic straw supports, first mark an outline on the iced cake tier where the next tier will go. Use the tin that the layer was baked in as a guide. If the cake was iced with a soft buttercream invert the tin, centre it, and press lightly to leave an imprint (Fig. 1). If the topping is a firm one, such as the

Crème Ivoire Deluxe or Rolled Fondant, centre the tin and allow the bottom to rest on the buttercream. Use a toothpick to make little holes in the icing all around the base of the tin (Fig. 2).

Insert a plastic straw into the centre of the cake until it touches the base and mark the straw with a pencil at the cake surface (Fig. 3). Remove the straw and cut off at the pencil mark. Use this straw as a guide to cut other straw supports the same length.

Insert one straw in the centre of the cake and the other straws equidistant in a circle just inside the guide marks. A 30.5-centimetre/12-inch layer needs eight straws and one for the centre. A 23-centimetre/9-inch layer needs six straws and one for the centre. The top tier does not need supports because nothing heavy will be resting on it.

PLACING THE TIERS

An *inflexible* heavy-duty pancake turner is the best device for lifting and placing the tiers. A small angled spatula helps to support the

edge while removing the pancake turner and displaces less icing. Lift each tier with the pancake turner, using your other hand to support the other side and centre it over the tier below, using the outline as your guide. Allow the side of the cake by your hand to touch down and gently lower the other side. Leave enough space so that the pancake turner does not touch any icing. Gradually slide away the pancake turner (Fig. 1). When you

almost reach the edge, transfer the weight to the small angled spatula and carefully slide it out (Fig. 2).

Pipe a border of buttercream around the base of each tier to seal in the freshness and give the edge a finished appearance.

Note: If the cake is to be transported a great distance over rough terrain, you can stake the tiers as extra security to keep them from sliding. Sharpen one end of a wooden dowel, 2.5 centimetres/ 1 inch lower than the height of the finished cake, and using a hammer, drive it through to the bottom. Ice or place ornament on top of cake to hide the small hole.

STORING THE WEDDING CAKE

A cake iced and decorated with buttercream can be made 1 day ahead and left at cool room temperature (except for cheesecake, which requires refrigeration). If made with butter cake, it will keep refrigerated for 3 days. It is essential that a butter cake be removed from the refrigerator 6 hours before serving or the texture will not be soft and light. If the wedding cake is made with *génoise* it will keep refrigerated for 5 days. Remove from the refrigerator at least 2 hours ahead to allow the buttercream to soften. A wedding cheesecake must be refrigerated until serving day and keeps for 24 hours refrigerated.

Transporting and Serving Wedding Cakes

TRANSPORTING THE WEDDING CAKE

William Greenberg, a famous New York baker, gave me some important advice at the beginning of my cake-baking career: 'There are only two people trustworthy enough to deliver a wedding cake – the person who baked it and the person who paid for it.' As a consequence, I have never had a single disaster befall one of my cakes (except, of course, for my brother's wedding cake, which suffered the fate of a major blizzard and a hungry airline crew).

Usually I have the customer pick up the cake, but if I am going to the wedding I always deliver it personally. At first I would bring a pastry bag filled with icing in case of repair, but as I never once needed it, I abandoned the practice.

The ideal protection for a tiered cake is a corrugated cardboard box just slightly larger than the base. It is also safer for the box to be higher than the top tier so that the top flaps can be taped closed. The rigid sides of the box cannot touch the sides of the cake because the iced cake sides are smaller than the

bottom cake base on which they are resting.

If the weather is cool, the boot of a car offers the most level area for the cake. A damp bath towel under the cake box helps to keep it from sliding. Try to avoid major bumps in the road when driving.

SERVING A TIERED CAKE

Wedding cake portions are traditionally small because they usually are served after a large dinner that often includes other desserts. The size of the serving is either a square 5 centimetres/ 2 inches high by 5 centimetres/ 2 inches deep and 4.25 centimetres/ 1⅝ inches wide (the tier divided into two layers) or a slim rectangle 10 centimetres/4 inches high by 5 centimetres/2 inches deep by 2 centimetres/¾ inch wide (the full height of the tier).

The most practical way to cut 20-centimetre/8-inch or larger tiers of wedding cake is in concentric circles until the small 10 to 15-centimetre/4 to 6-inch centre round remains. That should be cut into narrow wedges. It is easiest to start with the top tier and remove each tier before cutting, but it is also possible to cut each tier while it is still resting on the tier below.

Bibliography

BOOKS

Alikonis, Justin J. *Candy Technology*. Westport, Conn.: AVI Publishing Company, Inc., 1979.

Amendola, Joseph. *The Bakers' Manual*. Rochelle Park, N.J.: Hayden Book Company, 1972.

——, Donald E. Lundberg. *Understanding Baking*. Boston: CBI Publishing Company, Inc., 1970.

Charley, Helen. *Food Science*. 2nd ed. New York: John Wiley & Sons, 1982.

Child, Julia, Louisette Bertholle, and Simone Beck. *Mastering the Art of French Cooking*. New York: Alfred A. Knopf, 1961.

Cook, Russell, L. *Chocolate Production and Use*. New York: Harcourt Brace Jovanovich, Inc., 1982.

Clifton, Claire. *Edible Flowers*. New York: McGraw-Hill Book Company, 1984.

Frohne, Dietrich, and Hans Jurgen Pfänder. *A Color Atlas of Poisonous Plants*. London: Wolfe Publishing Company, 1983.

Griswold, Ruth M. *The Experimental Study of Foods*. Boston: Houghton Mifflin Company, 1962.

Handbook of Food Preparation. Washington, D.C.: The American Home Economics Association, 1975.

Hanle, Zack, and Donald Hendricks. *Cooking with Flowers*. Los Angeles: Price/Stern/Sloan Publishers, Inc., 1971.

Healy, Bruce, and Paul Bugat. *Mastering the Art of French Pastry*. New York: Barrons, 1984.

Heatter, Maida. *Maida Heatter's Book of Great Desserts*. New York: Alfred A. Knopf, 1974.

Kraus, Barbara. *The Dictionary of Sodium, Fats, and Cholesterol*. New York: Grosset & Dunlap, 1976.

Lang, Jennifer Harvey. *Tastings*. New York: Crown Publishers, Inc., 1986.

Lees, R., and E. G. Jackson. *Sugar Confectionery and Chocolate Manufacture*. New York: Chemical Publishing Co., Inc., 1975. New York: Grosset & Dunlap, 1974.

Mattle, Von Josef. *Praline Passe-Partout*. Zürich: Schweizerischer Bäckerei-und Konditorei-Personal-Verband, 1980.

McGee, Harold. *On Food and Cooking*. London: Unwin Hyman, 1986.

Minifie, Bernard W. *Chocolate, Cocoa and Confectionery: Science and Technology Second Edition*. Westport, Conn.: AVI Publishing Company, Inc., 1980.

Montagné, Prosper. *The New Larousse Gastronomique*.

The New International Confectioner. London: Virtue & Company Limited, 1981.

Paul, Pauline C., and Helen H. Palmer. *Food Theory and Applications*. New York: John Wiley & Sons, 1972.

Peckham, Gladys C. *Foundations of Food Preparation*. 2nd ed. London: The Macmillan Company, 1969.

Sultan, William J. *Practical Baking*. Westport, Conn.: AVI Publishing Company, 1976.

Thuries, Yves. *Le Livre de Recettes d'un Compagnon du Tour de France: Pâtisserie Francaise*. Paris: Société Editar, 81170 Cordes-Sur-Ciel, 1980.

Watt, Bernice K., and Annabel L. Merrill. *Composition of Foods*. Agriculture Handbook No. 8. Agricultural Research Service, United States Department of Agriculture. Revised December 1963. Approved for reprinting October 1975.

The Wilton Way of Cake Decorating. Vol. I. Woodridge, Ill.: Wilton Enterprises, Inc., 1974.

Wirz-Fischer, Johann-Heinrich. *Manual Illustré Suisse de la Confiserie-pâtisserie*. Switzerland: Herausgeber, 1963.

Witty, Helen, and Elizabeth Schneider Colchie. *Better Than Store-Bought*. New York: Harper & Row, 1979.

ARTICLES

Ash, David J., and John C. Colney. 'The Role of pH in Cake Baking.' *The Bakers Digest*, February 1973, pp. 36–42, 68.

Carlin, George T. 'A Microscopic Study of the Behavior of Fats in Cake Batters.' *Cereal Chemistry*, Vol. 21 (May 1944), pp. 189–199.

Handleman, Avrom R., James F. Conn, and John W. Lyons. 'Bubble Mechanics in Thick Foams and Their Effects on Cake Quality.' *Cereal Chemistry*, Vol. 38 (May 1961), pp. 294–305.

Howard, N. B., D. H. Hughes, and R. G. K. Strobel. 'Function of the Starch Granule in the Formation of Layer Cake Structure.' *Cereal Chemistry*, Vol. 45 (July 1968), pp. 329–338.

Miller, Byron S., and Henry B. Trimbo. 'Gelatinization of Starch and White Layer Cake Quality.' *Food Technology*, April 1965, pp. 208–216.

Miller, L. L., and C. Setser. 'Xanthan Gum in a Reduced-Egg-White Angel Food Cake.' *Cereal Chemistry*, Vol. 60, No. 1 (1983), pp. 62–64.

Mizukoshi, M. 'Model Studies of Cake Baking. III. Effects of Silicone on Foam Stability of Cake Batter.' *Cereal Chemistry*, Vol. 60, No. 5 (1983), pp. 396–402.

Seguchi, M. 'Oil-Binding Capacity of Prime Starch from Chlorinated Wheat Flour.' *Cereal Chemistry*, Vol. 61, No. 3 (1984), pp. 241–247.

Thompson, S. W., and J. E. Gannon. 'Observations on the Influence of Texturation, Occluded Gas Content, and Emulsifier Content on Shortening Performance in Cake Making.' *Cereal Chemistry*, Vol. 33 (May 1956), pp. 181–189.

Wilson, J. T., and D. H. Donelson. 'Studies on the Dynamics of Cake-Baking.' *Cereal Chemistry*, Vol. 40 (Sept. 1963), pp. 466–481.

Wolfert, Paula. 'Brioche and Its Many Uses: A New Approach.' *The Pleasures of Cooking*, Vol. II, No. 4 (1979), pp. 2–13.

Wootton, J. C., N. B. Howard, J. B. Martin, D. E. McOsker, and J. Holme, 'The Role of Emulsifiers in the Incorporation of Air into Layer Cake Batter Systems. *Cereal Chemistry*, Vol. 44 (May 1967), pp. 333–343.

Index